From Kingdom to Commonwealth

Harvard Political Studies
Published under the direction
of the Department of Government
in Harvard University

From Kingdom to Commonwealth

The Development of Civic Consciousness
in English Political Thought
by Donald W. Hanson

Harvard University Press, Cambridge, Massachusetts
1970

To My Wife

Preface

This book deals with political ideas and practices in late medieval and early modern England. Its major preoccupation is an effort to discern and evaluate the lines of continuity and change in the relation between medieval and early modern political perspectives and styles, especially as these bear on the development of constitutionalized politics. It offers a political interpretation of a body of evidence which has been treated primarily in legalistic terms. The stress therefore is on the word "political." This springs from two convictions which the reader is entitled to know about: that legal ideas are not and cannot be radically removed from political ideas and interests, and that political behavior embodies and is affected by political and legal ideas, as well as affecting them. In short, conviction and act are much too closely related to be dealt with fruitfully in isolation. But it is a fact that the political side of medieval and early modern thought has too often been frozen and interred in the abstract and timeless categories of legal historicism. This is not to say that there is nothing to be learned from the great works of the legalist tradition, but rather that it requires a supplement, that an appropriate weight ought also to be allowed to the concrete political life of the period. One may fittingly adopt the spirit of the saying, so often repeated since the Middle Ages, that we are able to see precisely because we stand on the shoulders of giants. Preoccupations change, but the sentiment remains true. The great thing, surely, is to assess what is to be learned and preserved from the work of predecessors, and if possible to advance and refine understanding. In humanistic inquiries, this most often means not new discoveries so much as altered perspectives. It is hoped that these will shed light on some commonly shared concerns, for that is perhaps the chief function of political theory. In any case, the need is always for reassessment, for those concerns cannot remain stationary.

This study is not a survey of political thinkers in the period under discussion. Its concern is to inquire into the relation between late medieval and early modern political thinking from a particular perspective, one which necessarily excludes much that is both interesting and important. Put very briefly, it focuses on a variety of political thinking that was closely related to practice, and it deliberately neglects the more elegant and systematic but often hopelessly remote speculations of the sophisticated theorists of the age. It tries to deal sympathetically but nonetheless critically with that body of thought. The impulses in this undertaking are several. To begin with, it expresses my own effort to understand the ideas and conditions attendant upon the emergence of constitutionalized politics. This reflects the view that a rare and valuable experiment in politics is well worth our continued study from a variety of perspectives, not only for its own sake but also because in deepening our understanding we have an opportunity to accomplish a useful set of purposes. For in this way we may not only hope to understand the past and those who made it, but also to enhance our self-understanding. Moreover, the effort to improve self-understanding is by no means restricted to detailing the origins and substance of a political outlook we have inherited and to which many of us are committed, though it includes that. There is the added consideration that many of the intellectual instruments employed in the service of a hoped-for social science, however disinterestedly they are used, have an intellectual history which we do not always attend to with sufficient care.

In the context under examination, one of the critical ideas is *our* understanding of what it means to say that a society is "traditional" or "modern." This is not simply a problem of characterizing the European past in a particular way, for particular purposes. It is also a quite general conceptual problem. For in the study of traditional and developing societies by contemporary scholars, the problem of what we mean by modernity appears to have been profoundly conditioned by our intellectual inheritance. It is not contended that this observation need necessarily affect the utility of the concepts we employ in comparative and developmental studies. That is obviously a quesiton of our purposes and of the empirical evidence. All that is suggested is that we would do well to be as self-conscious of the historical content of our concepts as we can be. That, after all, is a simple matter of prudence. At any rate, the present study might be characterized from one perspective as a sustained inquiry into the political culture of a particular traditional society, though in this instance an historical rather than a contemporary one. The suggestion implied in this, of course, is that there is much potential value in the study of premodern European history for comparative political studies, particularly since these studies appear to be acquiring an increasingly developmental thrust. It would perhaps be agreed that, among the needs of contemporary social science, few are more urgent than detailed investigations of traditional societies and the course of their entry into modernity. Surely few are more deserving of such scrutiny than the English case. More generally, the availability of an abundant source of data in early European history ought not to be ignored, for in social science it is not easy to find cases suited for the purpose of broadening and refining theories generated from immediate experience.

My intention has also been to make the study of political ideas serve the more general purposes of the empirical study of politics. An effort has been made to employ and organize a body of historical data in such a way as to serve two masters: the social scientist's interest in conceptualized history, and the historian's legitimate concern with the complexity and individuality of particular men and events. This has involved trying to steer between the Scylla of unique details and sequences of events and the Charybdis of groundless concepts and generalizations which result from an excessively abstract treatment of historical data. This is necessarily a hazardous course, in which one's choices are subject to debate and quite possibly to revision, indeed fundamental alteration. But it may be doubted whether there is any alternative but to try.

The discussion ranges over a very considerable historical span which falls, in the main, between the twelfth and the seventeenth centuries, though there is included a substantial treatment of the social and political ideas and institutions of the primitive Germanic peoples, with special attention to the Anglo-Saxons. It touches upon a wide range of issues in the general history of England, for one of my chief convictions is that political thought has altogether too often been discussed in an historical and political vacuum. Not all of these issues could be dealt with in the detail which they deserve, at least not without introducing so many complexities into the argument as to risk losing the threads altogether. Not only are the issues multiple and complex, but a good many of them are just now the subject of intense debate. In effect, the student of political ideas has little choice but to take his chances, with due apologies to the host of historians from whose work he benefits and upon which he must rely if he is to discuss his own subject meaningfully. On the other hand, some matters have been dealt with in considerable detail. In particular, much of what is said about the two most discussed English writers, Henry de Bracton and Sir John Fortescue, will necessarily be repetitive for specialists, as will much of the historical material be for others. Nevertheless, the collection and discussion of these materials seemed justified in view of the general purposes of the book: to suggest that the development of premodern political ideas can be understood rather differently than has been customary, and to invite social scientists and political theorists to consider the potential value of early European history for their special concerns. In some areas, moreover, the reader will encounter extended argument on some relatively recondite matters. There are two kinds of reasons for asking the reader to bear with these complexities. In the first place, so much care and industry has been lavished by others on some of these issues that it seemed a matter of elementary justice both to present their views and to offer reasons for rejecting or amending them. Secondly, however, the general lines and methods of interpretation which I have been led to reject have in fact set the terms of discussion of one of the most important elements in our political inheritance. Whether the reinterpretation advanced here is acceptable is another question, but it is certain that no new perspective deserves reception that fails to engage what is referred to below as the received tradition. It is just this that accounts for much of the complexity and detail in the following pages.

It is a great pleasure to acknowledge here some of the many debts I owe to teachers, colleagues, and friends. I am profoundly indebted and grateful to Mrs. Judith N. Shklar, not only for instruction and supervision of the dissertation from which this book developed, but also for much encouragement and immensely valuable criticism, as well as many personal kindnesses. Owing to her also is the conception of the sorts of tasks the study of political thought ought to undertake and the kinds of questions to ask of a body of ideas which, at least implicitly, lie behind the preoccupations of this book. It is safe to say that this essay would certainly not be what it is but for this indebtedness, and probably would not exist at all. I am also greatly indebted to Professor Stanley H. Hoffmann for much of my general orientation to the study of politics, and for his unfailing help in the course of graduate study and beyond. It is my hope that I have learned to interrogate the available evidence in terms of the sorts of questions which he has suggested we ought to ask. Whether I succeed in doing so adequately or not, I am persuaded that we ought explicitly to introduce the range of problems set by the existence of international politics when undertaking the study of the ideas, institutions, and practices of domestic politics. It cannot be denied that these two levels of political life have consistently been treated in isolation, and nowhere is this more true than at the level of political ideas. I do not claim to have effected the sort of integration which he, more than any other, has argued we ought to attempt. But I have tried at least to emphasize what seems to me the absolutely crucial role of external affairs and the waging of war in the development of English ideas and institutions. I should like also to thank Professors Carl J. Friedrich and Samuel H. Beer for highly valued criticism as well as encouragement. To Professor Francis D. Wormuth I owe a huge debt both for my interest in and conception of medieval and early modern history and thought and, in particular, for my understanding of the central importance of the English civil wars in our intellectual history. To my colleagues — Professors R. Booth Fowler, Melvin Croan, and Charles Anderson — I owe a great deal learned in the course of discussing the problems dealt with here. I hope that my intellectual indebtedness to all these scholars will be more evident to those who know their work than explicit references could ever account for. I do not want to suggest that any of them are responsible for the arguments of this book, though it is probable that whatever is useful in it represents what I have carried off from them. All I should want to maintain is that I have tried to learn from them.

Donald W. Hanson

Madison, Wisconsin
August 1969

Contents

Preface   *vii*

One. Politics in Two Worlds   *1*

    The Setting of Medieval Politics 14
    The New Politics 26
    Civic Consciousness and Liberal Constitutionalism 30

Two. Double Majesty   *41*

Three. The Sanctity and Utility of Kings   *71*

Four. Counsel and Consent   *97*

    Bracton and the Tradition of Legalism 99
    Bracton Reconsidered 116

Five. King and Crown   *134*

    The Quest for Rule with Counsel 140
    King and Baronage in Uneasy Alliance 154
    Divided Allegiance and Deposition 158
    The King's Ministers and Divided Loyalty 167
    The High Court of Parliament and the Political Trial 172
    Baronial Ascendancy and the Collapse of Order 181

Six. Law, Custom, and Politics   *189*

Seven.   Political and Regal Dominion   *217*
   The Apotheosis of Double Majesty   218
   Divine and Human Law   232
   Mixed Monarchy   240

Eight.   The King's Conscience   *253*

Nine.   Law and Prerogative: Legal Deadlock   *281*

Ten.   From Kingdom to Commonwealth   *309*

Conclusion   *336*

Notes   *377*

Bibliography   *442*

Index   *461*

From Kingdom to Commonwealth

All would agree that the differences between the modern world and the medieval are many and profound, but there is little enough agreement on the content of the contrast or when it may be said to have appeared. The main argument of this book is that in the realm of politics the most meaningful line of division lies in the seventeenth century, and that the essential mark of the transition to modern political perspectives was the appearance of what may be called civic consciousness and loyalty. The essence of that alteration is simplicity itself: the development, or better, perhaps, the recovery of consciousness of a uniquely public dimension in social life — public in the sense of general or common to the social order as a whole. The idea of civic consciousness refers to the elementary perception that there is a public order, that the social order is in part a network of shared problems and purposes, and to the installation of that recognition at the center of political ideas and conduct. Like most fundamental perceptions, this awakening and channeling of public consciousness is simple, even obvious, but only if one has it. For the same reason, it is easily overlooked. Thus reference to the emergence of civic consciousness is not intended to suggest anything mysterious or even unfamiliar. On the contrary, the major difficulty is just the reverse. A civic frame of reference is so natural in modern western societies that the real problem is to appreciate its absence. For the achievement of this civic focus constituted a radical alteration in political vision. It involved not only the recognition of a novel framework, but a fundamental restructuring of assumptions concerning the nature and purpose of political authority, a wholesale redefinition of the rights and duties of citizens, and a critical shift in the primary focus of loyalties and interests. Moreover, once the centrality of civic consciousness and loyalty is appreciated, it is clear that it was the necessary precondition to the achievement of constitutional government. For constitutionalized politics rests in the last resort on self-conscious and sustained purpose at the public level.

It should be emphasized that what the expression civic or public consciousness and loyalty is intended to convey ought to be distinguished from what is often called national consciousness, national identity, or simply nationalism.[1] Both historical and analytical reasons can be offered for making the distinction. In all the usual efforts to characterize traditional societies, it is true, both of these kinds of generalized group consciousness are absent. But historically they supply convenient labels for reference to essentially different kinds of political awareness. Moreover, it is often the case that national and civic consciousness develop at different points in time. One useful way of referring to national consciousness is in terms of Rupert Emerson's "bare bones" definition of nationalism: "no more than the assertion of a particular 'we' arrayed against the 'they' of the rest of mankind, by itself giving no clue as to how the 'we' may choose to manage its own affairs." [2] Similarly, Karl Deutsch has referred simply to an indispensable precondition for the growth of national consciousness, which he characterizes as a minimal sense of "cohesion and distinctiveness" among a people.[3] The central point from the perspective suggested here is that the thrust of national consciousness is chiefly self-assertive, outward looking, and, in a sense, negative. Historically, the focus of national consciousness has been international rather than domestic politics; it expresses a self-assertive response to relatively sharp foreign rivalry and competition. Altering the angle of perspective slightly, national consciousness appears as the social counterpart to the early forms of the idea of sovereignty. In a fascinating study of the problem of modernization, Samuel P. Huntington has argued, quite rightly, that the rationalization of authority is one of the essential elements, and he equates this with the establishment of external and internal sovereignty.[4] Although it is obviously a question of what purposes a particular study has in view, what is suggested here is that it may be useful to distinguish between the achievement of external and internal sovereignty. They are historically distinct, and their relation to each other and the timing of their relation to other events can be factors of crucial importance. Thus just as there is both historical and analytical point to distinguishing between national and civic consciousness, so is there point to distinguishing between external and internal sovereignty. Indeed both distinctions are of considerable importance for the argument here, and this being so it may be worthwhile to consider them together.

Ever since the development of the modern national state in Europe, it has been the usual practice to discuss the history of political thought primarily in terms of the concepts of state and sovereignty. It is essential to notice that these concepts first obtained currency in the context of thought on international politics. Not surprisingly, this development emerged in the setting of relations among the city-states of Renaissance Italy, though it promptly migrated to the north. In this original, largely sixteenth century context of international politics, the idea of the sovereign state stood for a political order that was considered to be independent of the empire and the papacy. It was a political order whose ruler acknowledged no external superior, and it was this usage that produced the doctrine of reason of state.[5] But these ideas were not immediately applied in any systematic way to the issues of domestic politics, and this obviously makes a very great difference, for it really amounts only to a claim of independence. At the level of domestic politics, however, the idea of sovereignty was framed to posit a single agent possessing the power and authority to pronounce upon controverted questions with finality. It was this alleged concentration of power which defined the state.[6] In domestic politics, sovereignty no longer meant just independence, but rather carried with it the idea of a power that was unlimited, indivisible, subject to no higher appeal. This was no accident, for the context in which it was adapted and turned inwards was one of religiously inspired civil disorder, which raised the question of the location of final authority in a particularly sharp way. In the age of absolute monarchy, the doctrine of sovereignty made a tolerable amount of sense, despite the fact that absolute rule, strictly construed, is a chimera. As Hume observed, every system of rule in fact requires at least the tacit consent of some body of men, even if no more than a handful of "mamelukes." [7] That is, the fact that the ruler possesses the instruments of coercion is a function of the fact of consent, even if the consent is mere submission or indifference. Obviously, the range of consent and the extent of the concentration of power are matters of degree. It is probable that altogether too much attention has been lavished on these ideas. They were developed in the sixteenth and seventeenth centuries to meet the contemporary problems of religious reformation, national

4

independence, and religio-ideological warfare, and their utility did not survive the age of absolutism.[8] A failure to recognize this has meant that this collection of ideas has too often been the instrument of anachronism, too frequently employed in reading the past in terms of the present or of some other past.[9] Nevertheless, there have been and are political orders to which the concept of sovereignty may be usefully applied.

It is important to recognize, then, that the assertions of external sovereignty and distinctiveness that reflect the attainment of national consciousness in European history originated in and were directed toward issues of international politics, and that their function was essentially negative, or perhaps, neutral in this sense: neither idea involves or conveys any doctrinal substance. As Emerson makes clear, the existence of an identifiable national consciousness tells us nothing at all about the operative assumptions at work in the conduct of domestic politics. Elsewhere he points out that "nationalism," in his usage, "gives the answer to virtually none of the particular problems which the development programs pose, and, indeed, to very few of the broad array of questions which confront peoples coming to independence." [10] For that matter, the existence of national consciousness fails to convey anything of substance even at the level of international politics, as Stanley Hoffmann has observed.[11] In the case of English political development, two points are of special importance. In the first place, it is altogether reasonable to argue that a sense of national consciousness was achieved in the course of the sixteenth century, in which the major events were Henry VIII's "great affair" and establishment of the English church, and the Spanish rivalry in the age of Elizabeth. It is just this that A. L. Rowse has aptly termed and eloquently described as "the Elizabethan discovery of England." [12] But it is crucial to observe that the attainment of national consciousness did not involve alteration of the fundamental assumptions of political thinking or behavior in domestic politics. As Rowse rightly insists, the framework remained essentially medieval, that is, traditional. "The constant theme of Elizabethan thought and teaching on the subject of society is the necessity of order and degree, and the consequent insistence upon authority and obedience. The lesson was enforced through all the institutions of society . . ." [13]

Secondly in England the attempt to employ the ideas of sovereignty and reason of state in domestic political conflict did not occur until the seventeenth century. It was just such an effort by the early Stuart monarchs that was one of the principal complaints of the parliamentary opposition in the pre-civil-war period. The charge was precisely that these doctrines had been improperly translated to domestic affairs from their legitimate sphere, foreign policy.[14] It may well be that the appearance of civic consciousness and loyalty was causally linked to the prior development of national consciousness. However that may be, the argument here is that it did not appear until the constitutional crisis of the seventeenth century. For it was that which produced the prolonged political and intellectual struggle in which a substantial minority of the English people became explicitly aware of the shared and general nature of their status as citizens and the issues that were at stake. Both the argumentation and the institutional experiments and alterations of the civil war period give expression to the kind of recognition that is here being called civic consciousness. This is precisely consciousness of the existence of a uniquely public sphere, public in the sense that the issues are general to the political order and inescapably shared. It is the recognition that some matters, and these some of the most important ones, require the capacity and the willingness to focus political attention and sustained activity at the level of the central governmental institutions of the society. Moreover, while it is quite right to say, as many observers have, that the tolerance of political as well as religious diversity, which was the outcome of the civil war, was at first only a grudging concession to necessity, it nonetheless had the immensely important effect of channeling political attention to the central government, as against the traditional focus on locality. Prolonged struggle had had the effect of making it evident that some set of institutions and procedures for the management of conflicting claims was indispensable. Moreover, the very gravity of the crisis produced an awareness that political attention and policy preference could not be intermittent and casual affairs, but rather would require the deliberate articulation and prosecution of explicit political alternatives.

There remains to be mentioned, however, another important facet of this new dimension of political consciousness: the shifting of men's loyalties from decisively local and familial commitments to the governing institutions of England. For just as the existence of national consciousness tells us nothing about the content of political ideas, canalization of political attention on the central government is not enough to demonstrate the level of coherence and commitment among citizens which we associate with a modern or developed political system. As Almond and Powell have observed, "There are many cases in which centralized and penetrative bureaucracies have been created, while a homogeneous pattern of loyalty and commitment to the central political institutions has never emerged." [15] This important observation serves to underline the utility of distinguishing national from civic consciousness. In short, it is perfectly possible for a people to achieve national consciousness and yet remain so fragmented, at the level of domestic politics, that the accumulation of governmental power falls far short of anything we should recognize as a developed political system. Stanley Hoffmann has rightly emphasized, in an analogous connection, that it is quite possible, too, for political attention to become focused on a central government without the development of a level of integration high enough to warrant the conclusion that genuine political community has been achieved. For it may be the case that political attention is channeled toward the center by default, simply because there are no alternative political institutions. [16]

On the basis of European experience, it seems probable that severe political conflict conducted in terms of domestic issues is an indispensable precondition to the generation of such radically new loyalties. Civic consciousness and loyalty in English history was achieved in the course of decades of constitutional controversy, which culminated in civil war. The crucial point is that a dramatic restructuring of political vision occurred in the midst of profound crisis, and that the issues at stake came to be understood as raising all the most fundamental questions of domestic political organization. What emerged from this prolonged debate was a radically new definition of the rights and duties of citizens, which in turn involved novel conceptions of legitimate political authority. This is by itself enough to suggest that the transition would repay careful study. But this is by no means all there is to it. There is, of course, the fact that we have inherited the English achievement; but further, it ought not to be overlooked that the constitutional struggles of seventeenth century England came to have an immense demonstration effect in Europe generally.

But to return to the problem of citizen loyalty. At this level, it is important to notice that what was required was a severe domestic crisis and a successful outcome from the point of view of the opposition to the ancient kingship. For it was the very gravity of the crisis which provoked the remarkably wide-ranging intellectual exploration and institutional experimentation that eventuated in the creation of constitutional government. Prolonged crisis also had the effect of making it unmistakably clear that men were committed to a very wide range of mutually incompatible values and interests. But it was a broadly successful course of action over a number of years that created and reinforced a vital new assumption: that men were competent, that they could deliberately undertake the creation of a political system designed to satisfy their preferences and to reconcile or at least contain their differences.[17] There is surely a sense in which this assumption of competence is central to what we take to be "modern," even though it is as old as the political thought of the Sophists of fifth century Athens. In Samuel Huntington's words, "Modernity begins when men develop a sense of their own competence, when they begin to think that they can understand nature and society and can then control and change nature and society for their own purposes. Above all modernization means the rejection of external restraints on men, the Promethean liberation of man from control by gods, fate, and destiny." [18] The crisis of seventeenth century England did not have the effect of eliminating plural interests and values. But it did wrench them into a public framework, and it may be suggested that it was exhaustion with bitter ideological conflict that finally produced the grudging but widely shared acceptance of the idea of tolerance of diversity. But that very exhaustion and the consequent willingness to tolerate diversity made it clear that some set of institutions and procedures designed to manage enduring conflicts was literally indispensable. This is a species of loyalty, of commitment to an idea of at least procedural agreement. This may well be thought to be commitment at a relatively low temperature, so to speak, but it is commitment all the same. It is perhaps deflating to realize that politics is less a matter of exalted goals and divine dimensions than of prudence. But such a view has the immensely valuable asset of recognizing that when idols conflict it is best to oblige them to retreat from public to private life.

In any case, the English experience may be helpful in considering one of the most troublesome conceptual difficulties in contemporary developmental studies, which may be expressed by asking this question. What is the difference between pluralism and fragmentation?

For it was, perhaps above all else, precisely the social fragmentation characteristic of the Middle Ages that was overcome by the development of civic consciousness and loyalty. Historically, then, this facet of the problem of modernity appears to turn on a complex combination of elements. The suggestion advanced here, on the basis of English history, is that it involves profound but successfully managed crisis. This seems to account for the attainment of civic consciousness and loyalty, together with the novel assumptions that diversity is to be expected and can be accepted, rather than being seen as a regrettable lapse from the one true standard of rectitude, and that men are capable of contriving institutions which make politics a complex affair of articulating, managing, and negotiating human preferences rather than a matter of destiny. At this point, obviously, the crucial questions center on the effort to identify those elements of analogous and contrasting courses of development that seem to account for the successful management of crisis or the lack of it. It seems clear that few undertakings could be more profitable, in this regard, than systematic efforts to compare the developmental histories of the European nation states. It is, after all, fascinating to reflect on the fact that the diverse outcomes of European development took their point of departure in the Middle Ages from amazingly similiar sets of social, political, and technological conditions. No doubt the lessons of such inquiry would be limited, but that is scarcely novel.

The attainment of civic consciousness was the central achievement of seventeenth century English politics, and the working out of its implications the principal task of political thought. For what modern men recognize as the distinctively or preeminently political — matters of general concern and consequence — was precisely the area in which medieval men, prince and people alike, were least sensitive. Thanks to the efforts of a generation of pluralists — Gierke, Maitland, Figgis, Barker — students of political thought have long been familiar with the rich and varied character of medieval social organization. Primary loyalties and interests were tied to kin, dependents, and neighborhood, and political activity was expressed, not in terms of a citizen's relationship to his government, but in complex and shifting patterns of personal allegiance. It is this essentially personal and localistic mentality and the political assumptions to which it gives rise that are to be contrasted with the politics of civic consciousness and loyalty. It is natural enough that civic consciousness should appear to be the normal case to modern western man. But that is only because he has had time to grow habituated to his public political system. We have become domesticated in the integrated national community. But this is not at all a common occurrence.[19] In fact, comparatively few societies have been organized in terms of civic consciousness and loyalty. The political frailty of many of the new states of the contemporary world is eloquent testimony to this fact, for they have made the sentiments and patterns of behavior characteristic of societies still organized in part in terms of kin, tribe, and locality increasingly familiar as one of the crucial obstacles to the achievement of political stability. As one acute observer has said, in "most of the more complex societies of Asia, the Middle East, Latin America, and even parts of Africa . . . traditional social forces, interests, customs, and institutions are strongly entrenched." [20] The European Middle Ages correspond rather closely to that range of problems in western history.

In English history, civic consciousness was the child of the spiritual and material turmoil of decades of constitutional controversy. Precisely because we have inherited the achievements of seventeenth century England and internalized them, it is a task of some difficulty to recover the flavor of premodern political ideas and practices, for even though it is our own it is nonetheless an alien past. One purpose of this study is to suggest that an effort to do so is rewarding, for an appreciation of the lines of continuity and change between these political worlds possesses much more than a solely historical interest. In broad outline, three considerations lead to this suggestion. To begin with, the argument here is that the emergence of civic consciousness was the indispensable prelude to constitutionalized politics, which was, in turn, the precondition of the era of political stability which followed.[21] It was just this new self-consciousness that underlay and motivated the dazzling outburst of political speculation and institutional experiment which confronts the observer of seventeenth century England. There is little enough in the political climate of the preceding centuries to prepare one for this first great avalanche of modern political thought, and the reason is that it turns on the achievement of a consciousness that there are alternatives to tradition. But despite the profundity of the change, it is important to recognize also that England's medieval past supplied the setting in which it occurred, and that is reason enough to examine it. Constitutional government, after all, is a very rare method of conducting politics. It is a political triumph first achieved in England and one quite obviously difficult to duplicate, as the political history of western Europe demonstrates, to say nothing of the experience of the non-European world.

In the second place, the contrast between modern political ideas and practices and those of our own traditional past will serve as a useful reminder. It underlines the fact that the stresses produced in the process of bridging the gap between fundamentally different political styles is a feature, not only of the contemporary world, but also of European history. It is painfully evident that a significant element in the disjointed character of the contemporary world derives from the radically different political styles appropriate to diverse levels of development and paths of change. The social and political systems of the Middle Ages supply an abundance of instructive parallels with much of the underdeveloped world. Medieval history reveals a good number of distinct patterns of transition from traditional social structures to differing kinds and degrees of modernity. The great merit of these medieval systems for comparative purposes is that they have completed the process. The parallels are by no means exact. The most important single difference, of course, is the contemporary international system, representing rival states with advanced technology. Moreover, the paths of change in European history were marked by quite different obstacles, cast up by particular traditions and the varying impact of the international system, as well as by substantial differences in the time in which critical phases of change occurred. What is perfectly clear, however, is that the record of our own past contains a very rich source of comparative material. This study is concerned with but one of these courses of change — by all odds the most successful — and it concentrates on the realm of political ideas. A major point here, in Harry Eckstein's words, is simply "that political behavior in the past is an indispensable datum for the analysis of political behavior as such; hence we must make the best we can of the sources we have on past political behavior, and the history of political thought is one of these sources." [22] This need not mean, nor, indeed, ought it to mean, that ideas should be treated exclusively or in isolation from behavior, both individual and institutional. For as Almond and Powell have argued, while a wide variety of writings and speeches, indeed, even myths and legends, can provide useful clues to the nature of a political culture, it is also true that behavior is an indispensable indication of political orientation.[23] The author is convinced that study of both ideas and behavior is needed, and together, for the sake of the light they shed on each other. This is, of course, an extremely simple idea, but it is too frequently ignored.[24] Moreover, it may be suggested that there are additional advantages to be gained through inquiry into our own traditional past in this way: not only is the history of English politics our own history in important ways, but the transition to modernity in England was the first to occur in European history. This has meant, in the first place, that we have inherited a particular achievement in politics which surely justifies our continued preoccupation with it, not only because it is an inheritance but also because it has had so much to do with our self-perception. Further, this appears to involve even the intellectual apparatus that we are inclined to bring to the general study of political development. These are matters that will be referred to in the conclusion of this study. The general point is that a number of important intellectual assumptions in contemporary social science derive much of their content from the ideology of classical liberalism, which emerged in triumph from the English civil wars. This problem need not be pursued further at present, however, since it will be more profitable to examine it after the record under investigation has been explored.

The third broad consideration is this. Inquiry into the development of civic consciousness throws into relief an interesting paradox in the dominant strains of constitutional theory since the late seventeenth century. The crux of that paradox is that constitutionalism took its origin from a climate of opinion in which concern with politics and the general political order was intense. But the principal beneficiaries of this achievement came to adopt the ideology of liberalism, which tends to neglect precisely that public orientation which made it possible.[25] This narrower vision has had important and not altogether fortunate consequences upon reflection on the problems of constitutional politics. Thus, inquiry into the development of civic consciousness will afford an opportunity to examine a range of problems that remain relevant to the ideal of constitutional government. Since the emphasis here is directed to a basic contrast in political styles, it will be helpful to consider first the general setting of medieval politics and then the character of the transformation which overtook it. This will set the stage for a discussion of the relation of this change to modern constitutionalism.

Before proceeding, however, one broad qualification to the treatment of the medieval period offered here requires mention.

A primary aim of this essay is to suggest that the secular political orders of the Middle Ages lacked a constituency with a civic point of view. In the last resort, it will be argued, it is this which imparts to medieval political life its distinctive content and style. As with any distinction of this kind, it is largely a matter of emphasis rather than a contrast of absolutes. In particular, it is an observation which cannot fairly be applied to the medieval Church. The comparatively sophisticated writers sheltered and fostered by the Church took over much from the political thought of classical antiquity. One finds in their writings the language of civic concern and devotion, appropriately transferred from the ancient city to the Church.[26] It is true that in the early Middle Ages even the Church suffered from the strains of inadequate organization and, viewed spiritually, from a very imperfect relationship with secular power.[27] But in the later Middle Ages it is clear that the Church had achieved comparative independence, and a level of integration and governmental efficiency substantially in advance of the secular kingdoms.[28] In brief, the Church was partly the vehicle and partly the creator of the high culture of the Middle Ages, and for much the greatest part of the period sophisticated theory of all kinds was almost exclusively the product of men of the Church. The discussion in this book does not deal with this side of medieval political thought at all. Rather, it turns on a distinction between systematic political theory — grand theory if you will — and what may be called operative political thought — the ideas and assumptions which accompany and inform the actual political life of the age.

Understandably enough, historians of ideas have been inclined to deal almost exclusively with grand political theory, because it represents the highest level of intellectual achievement in the Middle Ages. It is systematic, detailed, and subtle, and it exhibits a certain continuity in form and content. It is, in other words, a recognizable and coherent universe of discourse. It is also one which has been often and skillfully analyzed. But most of this literature was developed on so lofty a plane of abstraction that it is extremely difficult to see any connection between it and the political life of the kingdoms and provinces. Many of the ablest students of medieval thought have acknowledged this, as, indeed, one must. Walter Ullmann, for example, has said in one of his discerning studies that "the canonists merrily, and sometimes irresponsibly, put forward their claims unhampered by considerations of expediency, practical wisdom or diplomacy, working in the serene atmosphere of an august theory." [29] Similarly, in a fine essay on the publicist literature, Michael Wilks observes that "to the papalist what is factually realised is of much less significance than what ought to be according to the divine pattern of society. True reality . . . is what is known to be right, not the inadequacy of the existing situation." [30] In general, the great systematic theorists have relatively little to say about the practices and institutions of the societies in which they lived.[31] Thus the systematic political theory of the Middle Ages rests on a paradox. Deriving its vocabulary and organizing ideas from classical antiquity, as it did, it expressed institutional ideas and ideals generated in a period of civic loyalty and integrated rule, and this corresponded not at all to the conditions of governance in medieval Europe. Hence it is difficult to disagree with the observation that "medieval political theory is only rarely related to actual conditions." [32]

Let it be said immediately that the distinction between operative thought and grand theory is not meant to suggest any denigratory judgment on the great systematic works. It would be a mistake to dismiss them on the ground that they fail to make substantial contact with politics, for this lack of connection is only a matter of degree. In all periods, grand political theory has been an essentially esoteric undertaking restricted to the few. That does not mean that it lacks value, for the test of high cultural achievement has never been popularity or utility. In any case, the argument is not that inquiry into operative ideas is in any sense a substitute for studying grand theory. On the contrary, in part it is intended to be only a supplement. In part it is a suggestion that certain important features of late medieval and early modern politics can be approached from another avenue.

Thus the subject explored in this book is a good deal humbler than the great political theories of the Middle Ages. It deals with an altogether less illustrious and sophisticated but perhaps not less important breed of men. However, since a principal aim here is to explore in detail the operating assumptions and ideologies of the principal actors in a traditional political order, it is important to recognize, as Samuel H. Beer has pointed out, that "political philosophers are often not entirely accurate guides to the really

14

operative ideal or ideals of authority in a political system." [33] The various strands which went into operative political thought in England were not the products of any great systematic theorist, or even a collection of these. Rather, it was an accumulation of ideas and practices, necessarily the work of a great number of men: politicians, judges, lawyers, propagandists, parliamentarians, and even rebels. On this subject, Harry Eckstein pointed out some years ago that in failing to launch inquiry in such a direction, we were depriving ourselves of "a vast territory of politically significant information . . ." For in addition to those enduring intellectual achievements we refer to as the great tradition of political theory, we have available to us, as Eckstein quite rightly said, "legal documents, novels, letters, memoirs, pamphlets, [and] handbills . . ." [34] It is precisely these kinds of source materials that have been employed here, and a major contention of this study is that a fascinating system of ideas, though largely implicit, emerges from them. The authors of some of these ideas are nameless; most would not find a place in a catalogue of the great in the history of political theory. Yet the accumulation is an achievement of immense significance and value, for it underlies and supports the remarkable stability and continuity of English political life. Certainly the history of that achievement includes some very remarkable men. Anyone familiar with English thought in the Middle Ages will think immediately of Henry de Bracton and Sir John Fortescue. But it remains true that the title to authorship cannot be restricted to those few upon whom posterity inclines to fasten and bestow its special praise.

The Setting of Medieval Politics

With the proviso relating to the life of the Church, then, it can be justly said that the political horizon of medieval men was normally bounded by the attractions of manor, hundred, and shire and but rarely rose to the level of explicit and sustained involvement in and commitment to matters of public or general concern.[35] But it is important to appreciate that this was a perfectly understandable state of affairs. One need only recall the dislocation and violence produced, not only by the disintegration of the Roman Empire and the initial settling of the Germanic tribes, but by the repeated incursions of barbarian peoples, as well as the pressures exerted upon western Europe by Islam and Byzantium. The chronicles of the period leave us in no doubt on the question. They reveal a society plagued by recurrent violence and devastation. It was this atmosphere which conditioned the practical vision and social organization of the Middle Ages and set so high a value on local fortification and subsistence. The society could not help cultivating a generous estimation of the virtues of the warrior, and one need hardly be surprised to find these values knit through the whole fabric of society.[36] If one bears in mind the awful uncertainty and brevity of life, the medieval attachment "to things tangible and local" [37] is very far from inexplicable, nor is it to be denigrated. But the work of consolidation and expansion required centuries.

The central fact, therefore, is that medieval political life was set in a framework of radically fragmented and locally oriented social organization. This entailed two immensely significant effects. The uncentralized structure of society produced the characteristic medieval assimilation of property right and the right to govern. Moreover, it reflected and accelerated the dissolution of the bonds of civic loyalty which had sustained antique society and replaced them with the ties of personal allegiance centering on local residence. This is obviously a radically different principle of social organization, a fact the importance of which cannot easily be overestimated. The interests, ideas, and emotions which collected around these personal loyalties impeded the development of a coherent, self-conscious citizenry for centuries, and it was precisely these phenomena which formed the peculiar style, as well as the major share of the stuff, of medieval politics. These conditions also produced a persistent tension in the political order, for the needs and demands of late medieval monarchs tended in a centralizing and rationalizing direction. Inevitably kings were met again and again by narrow, specialized, and centrifugal interests. This is not to say that medieval politics may be summarized as the incessant collision of baronial and kingly interests. On the contrary, the facts will not support such a view. An eminent student of the early Middle Ages, J. M. Wallace-Hadrill, is surely right in insisting that "no untruth is blacker than that which represents early medieval kingship and aristocracy as two fundamentally opposed forces." [38] The same observation may be applied to the later period as well.[39] Moreover, this view is not only empirically inadequate; it will not do conceptually, bceause it makes the obvious facts of cohesion incomprehensible. Throughout the greater part of the Middle Ages, kings

puzzles in the later Middle Ages and early modern times is immense. Profound and substantial differences of view have collected, for example, around the problem whether feudalism — whatever it was — was introduced into England at the hands of the Conqueror or was already there in substance,[49] or indeed whether there was ever a feudal system in England at all.[50] Another celebrated and similarly unconcluded debate has revolved around the interpretation of the Tudor monarchy and its social environment: "New Monarchy" or simply tightened and refurbished medievalism? absolutism or the dawn of genuine parliamentarism? rise of the "middle class" or no? [51] There are a great many such issues, and the discussion here cannot help touching on most of them.

In brief, any attempt to periodize is both difficult and risky, for human affairs are too multifarious to fit neatly into the pigeon holes contrived by hindsight. Still the operation may be useful, and in any case it is necessary if any order is to be introduced into the discussion.[52] Moreover, though it may satisfy a scholarly urge to attain certainty and a nice sense of tidiness, it is unnecessary to contend that a scheme of periodization is hard and fast, or that it applies no matter what problem is being discussed. On the contrary, the nature of the problem is the heart of the matter. To periodize and classify is not automatically to indulge in the fallacy of essentialism. It is only to mark shifts of emphasis — sometimes subtle, sometimes radical — and all of it is unavoidably purposive. Thus the Middle Ages might be said to have ended as early as the fourteenth century, with the passing of the heyday of feudalism or with the writings of Petrarch; or perhaps with the end of the Thirty Years' War in 1648; or with the Renaissance (whatever it was, and whenever it began), or the Reformation; or, yet again, with the overthrow of the ancien régime in 1789, or the destruction of the Holy Roman Empire at the hands of Napoleon.[53] There is something to be said for all these suggestions. The answer is — it all depends.

The argument advanced here is that, on the whole, political thinking was not decisively severed from medieval assumptions until the seventeenth century. Though there is much to be said in favor of the Tudor period, there is also much against it.[54] The background of Tudor political thought as well as its mode of expression was still the hierarchical world view.[55] Again, despite the Tudor monarchs' inclination to employ parliament in their political designs, the monarchy remained the indisputable center of politics.[56] Moreover, regal ambitions and programs never really overcame the dynastic ethos characteristic of late medieval monarchies.[57] The day of national consciousness and national interest had not yet appeared.[58] In all these respects it would perhaps be fair to say that changes were under way in the sixteenth century; but the critical shifts of emphasis did not appear until the seventeenth century. In politics the crucial institutional alteration was the achievement of the independence and centrality of parliament.[59]

Having suggested the seventeenth century as the terminus ad quem, there remains the rather more difficult task of considering an appropriate terminus a quo. Perhaps the most satisfactory point is the twelfth century. The complex currents which impelled the feudal kingdoms of western Europe toward the development of the nation state were then well under way. This movement was general, and many of the causes appear to have been common to western Europe. The following summary derives from Marc Bloch: "The cessation of the invasions had relieved the royal and princely powers of a task which exhausted their strength. At the same time it made possible [an] enormous growth of population . . . The increased density of population not only facilitated the maintenance of order, but also favoured the revival of towns, of the artisan class, and of trade. As a result of a more active and abundant circulation of money, taxation reappeared, and with it salaried officials; and the payment of troops began to be substituted for the inefficient system of hereditary contractual services." [60] Bloch goes on to point out that this broad change induced alterations in outlook as well. Cultural advance exposed men to Roman governmental and legal ideas and planted the first seeds that in time would mature as civic loyalty. Education began to penetrate outside clerical circles to the laity, and "the practice of writing and the growing interest in its potentialities enabled states to form those archives without which there could be no real continuity to government." The emergence of a vast variety of written records in the twelfth and thirteenth centuries "was the premonitory sign that there was arising a new power, or at least one that had hitherto been confined to the great churches and the papal court, namely the bureaucracy." [61]

These momentous changes were felt first by the monarchs, so that it was through kings that the impulses of change were transmitted. It was the king who first learned to intone the language of public interest and public emergency.[62] He was confronted, especially, with problems of increasing complexity in the conduct of foreign affairs. It was often the exigencies of international relations which supplied the occasions for departures from tradition. In the main, innovation occurred in administrative techniques and in novel uses of ideas, in terms of both organization and justification.[63] Both had important but largely unintended consequences, as will be seen. Feudal kings found themselves in need of increased revenues and a much more elaborate and efficient military arm. The arrangements of the past were altogether insufficient, and kings often discovered that their enterprises were acutely underfinanced and undermanned. They certainly could not conduct the affairs of government from the revenues and military obligations owed to them by feudal vassals. It is unnecessary to indulge in an examination of the variety of techniques employed to satisfy these needs. The essential point is that they resulted in a proliferation of governmental machinery, a royal bureaucracy, which impinged on the lives and pockets of the king's subjects in a much more systematic and sustained way than had been the case in the early Middle Ages.

In English history, more particularly, the twelfth century has rightly been called "the last century of the old order," yet also the century that "carries with it the elements of change." [64] Above all, it was the period in which the essential lines of late medieval government were worked out. The heart of this accomplishment was the administrative reforms of Henry I and Henry II, for they provided the basis of a governmental system which, in its main lines, survived for the rest of the medieval period. For present purposes, it is enough to notice that the king's courts and justices, whether stationary or itinerant, largely replaced local administration in the course of the twelfth century. The development of centrally organized governmental routines both produced and began to satisfy the need for a critically important kind of man: the educated, indeed trained, but secular royal servant.[65] The entire subsequent course of English politics and law owes an immense debt to successive generations of such royal servants. It would be difficult to overestimate the importance of this precocious centralization. It was surely this, for example, which ensured that there would be no large-scale reception of Roman law in England, for the fundamental elements of the common law system of writs and courts provided a functioning alternative.[66] In the practices and ideas generated by the royal administration of justice, it is possible to detect the first signs of the development of a public political order, fashioned from above and imposed upon an ill-organized patchwork of communities and predominantly personal relationships.

In sum, the Angevin monarchy endowed England with a tradition of strong government. By modern standards, certainly, it was inefficient and rudimentary enough. But in terms of medieval experience it set an enviable standard, one not excelled perhaps until the reign of the Tudors. It was this embryonic but vigorous Angevin bureaucracy which undertook the task of satisfying the monarch's need for systematic administration and collection of revenue. Both were accomplished with unaccustomed efficiency, and it seems clear that the reactions of the king's subjects were understandably mixed. Increased governmental efficiency meant easier access to justice, and this could be and was welcomed, but there was a failure equally to rejoice in more systematic collection of revenue.

Even so, the more adroit rulers of medieval England were able on the whole to pursue their needs and interests without large-scale resistance. The social order over which they presided was so diffuse and preoccupied with private concerns that kingly intrusions and exactions most often went unchallenged. Yet as rulers pressed in upon their subjects, the result was sporadic local resistance. But as long as the organization of resistance remained fragmented, matching the structure and primary interests of the social order, the monarch's will was likely to prevail. The fact of local resistance, however, meant that violence or the threat of violence, on a piecemeal basis, was very nearly the normal mode of resolving critical differences of view, so that there was a kind of unpredictable oscillation between force and acquiescence. The temptation of the ruler in distress, usually financial, was very great. Vigorous rulers were inclined to press their subjects for money or services right up to the point at which these demands would be met with resistance. This is surely a risky way to conduct important political business, for the king and his advisers may miscalculate or fall foul of unfortunate circumstances. This kind of miscalculation was far from rare. But no settled pattern had emerged as to precisely how such matters were to be conducted. To be sure, there was an old tradition that the king could and should obtain advice and consent concerning the affairs of the kingdom. In England, as it turned out, this proved to be a very important idea. But it was also a conception fraught with ambiguities which supplied both monarch and barons with a source of justification.

In the normal course of affairs, however, the monarch had a marked advantage: his subjects largely failed to act in conjunction. On the occasions when the English baronage did unite temporarily in their disaffection, they could outmatch the king's military strength, but they were not often able to present a common front. The fundamental defect in baronial opposition was that it lacked a civic focus. This is not to say that the barons had no ideas or no program. On the contrary, some of the baronial claims show considerable continuity over time. It is true that these claims were based on a loosely articulated collection of ideas, themselves comparatively narrow and unrefined. But this is not by itself a fatal shortcoming. The decisive flaw was that the barons failed to recognize that the effort to effectuate their own interests could not be set on a lasting basis without involving them, as a continuous matter of course, in the conduct of routine public business. They understood the routine of government to be the king's affair, thus failing to appreciate the importance and cumulative weight and strength of administrative routine. From a later vantage point one can see that this amounts to a misunderstanding of rationalized government. As a general rule, it may be said that the barons began to feel the impact of governmental policy only after the royal bureaucracy was well toward bringing a program to completion. Thus, time and again, they found themselves confronted with some governmental fait accompli and, therefore, in a poor bargaining position. That was the essential political mechanics of an opposition lacking sustained, self-consciously shared purposes. The barons responded to pressure, to be sure, but the limit of their achievement was an ideology of crisis, sporadically resurrected to meet situations often too far advanced to be reversed.

As a political opposition, then, the medieval baronage suffered from a crippling form of blindness. But to make such an observation is not to condemn them for their delinquency. The judgment is harsh but it is not a reproach, for there is little to be gained from retrospective chastisement. The point is that medieval political ideas and practices cannot be grasped without recognizing the shortcomings as well as the achievements of the principal opposition to government. It is well to remember that the medieval aristocracy was not only an opposition, but the most important source of support of monarchical government as well. Moreover, it does not follow, nor is it even true, that medieval barons were incapable men. On the contrary, the evidence shows that some were quite expert estate managers and soldiers. Nor were their talents limited to these merely economic and military matters. Within the context of the counties in which their holdings lay, and in their dealings both with subordinates and peers, some were able governors and shrewd politicians. A few even appreciated the necessity of alliances in their negotiations with the monarch. It would be wrong, therefore, to conclude that baronial failures ought to be attributed to perversity or stupidity. It is simply not a question either of incapacity or wickedness, but of how the most important men of the day construed their interests, and how they understood themselves and their relation to the royal government.

The lack of a civic perspective and sustained political purpose at the public level is mirrored in the poverty of political ideas in the twelfth century. By and large, the facts of political life fail even of conceptual expression, much less sustained theoretical treatment. This is true of the monarchy itself, for despite its vigor and efficiency it found "few comprehending critics and no apologist with imagination to give it a mind and a soul." [67] It is true that the vital connecting tissue in the complex mass of organizational life was the king. But he too lacked a genuinely public point of view. Essentially he was the head of a ruling dynasty and the preeminent landlord of the realm. Yet there are perceptible indications of change as well. It has to be admitted that twelfth century England was theoretically inarticulate, but it was not quite mute, for one begins to hear a good deal about the king's duty to do justice as the vicar of God, of the king's need for counsel and consent, and assertions concerning the community of the realm made by and on behalf of the great landed magnates. English kings were learning to speak in important new accents. Much is said about the demands of public utility and necessity, about the imperatives of the *status regis* and *status regni* (the state or condition of the king and the kingdom), the inalienability of the rights of the king, the crown, and the royal demesne, the immunity of the king to the processes of law, and the king's prerogative power. From all sides, a great deal is said concerning the laws and customs of England, of the king's council, and, in the thirteenth century, of parliaments.

Altogether these preoccupations involve a bewildering assortment of ideas. At first they were quite innocent of any precise or technical significance. The work of generalization and theoretical refinement was the labor of centuries. Even the greatest legal treatise of medieval England, that of Henry de Bracton, employed current ideas without managing to achieve their reconciliation or even to organize them systematically. But they were not thereby deprived of their force or their value. Indeed, quite a good case could be made for the view that it was precisely their ambiguity which was responsible for their vitality and viability. In any case, these ideas underwent a gradual process of transformation during the later Middle Ages and survived to pass into the modern age, though in many cases only at the cost of fundamental alteration.

In sum, the primary habits of thought and practice, as well as many of the chief points of controversy of late medieval and early modern England, began their course in the twelfth century. Certainly the succeeding centuries were full of change, yet these early ideas and habits supply the observer with a very fair clue in the labyrinth of political development in the subsequent five centuries. For even though the late medieval period does not quite present the picture of placidity which is sometimes imagined, the fundamental conceptions of operative political thought exhibit a very substantial degree of continuity. For at the heart of these operative ideas there lay a persistent conception of the nature of political authority. It will be argued that this outlook rested on a fundamental dualism which was not overcome clearly and decisively until the period of the civil wars. In essence, the idea was that legitimate authority was vested in both the king and the great magnates independently. This view is referred to in the following pages as the idea of double majesty. The greatest part of the discussion here is focused on the articulation of that notion through the later medieval period. Less space is devoted to the sixteenth and seventeenth centuries, because the real burden of the case rests on the interpretation of the medieval period proper, and only a few of the many strands of development in later centuries are central to the main contention. The idea of double majesty reached a kind of apogee in the work of Sir John Fortescue in the latter part of the fifteenth century. His writings represent the only sustained discussion of medieval government produced in England and, therefore, supply a welcome subject for detailed investigation, as well as a fitting climax to the Middle Ages. From the perspective adopted here, the Tudor period forms a bridge between the clearly medieval and the clearly modern. A large number of themes might be dwelt on to illustrate this. Here only one has been explored, and it was selected deliberately to underline the nature of the dualism in medieval thought. But the Tudor expression of the idea was different. The essential point about the idea of double majesty was that it coupled prince and "people," understood during most of the period as the great magnates of the realm. Tudor authors, however, began an important shift of emphasis which became the reigning orthodoxy in the early Stuart period. For the coupling of prince and people, Tudor writers began to substitute that of prince and law, but they did not escape the basic ambiguity inherent in a dualistic conception of authority. It will be contended that the constitutional debates of the first four decades of the seventeenth century could not be resolved in the framework of the medieval inheritance, essentially because the partners of double majesty had parted company and yet each still had an independently grounded source of authority.

But most of the great political issues in which the assumptions of operative thought had been employed for centuries were resolved, or given a fundamentally new framework, in the constitutional struggles of the seventeenth century. That is why it stands as a watershed in the history of political thought. By midcentury political writers were preoccupied with a new range of issues or had come to deal with perennial problems from a profoundly different angle of vision. It is in this period that the ideas of sovereignty, the modern state, constitutionalism, and liberalism receive clear, though by no means final, theoretical statement. Above all, it is from the turbulent and fruitful age of the civil wars that civic consciousness and loyalty in English politics dates. This meant that the politically articulate had come to recognize that their interests were necessarily involved in a public setting and, therefore, that they must be deeply and continuously concerned with matters of public policy. Vital interests and values were cut loose from their traditional moorings in family connections and provincial holdings and were secured in a civic frame of reference. But it must be added at once that this transformation did not involve or require the adoption of superhuman virtue. The achievement of a public consciousness did not mean that henceforth men miraculously forbore private interest in order selflessly to embrace the public good. If this had been true, Rousseau's utopia would have leapt instantly into being. Civic consciousness and loyalty does not demand that men abandon their interests. Rather it requires that they weigh and pursue them from a civic perspective. It does require an appreciation of the fact that individual and collective interests are often inextricably tied to issues which concern not only other individuals and groups, but the political order as a whole. Once again, let it be said that there is little enough of altruism in all this. The very possibility, however, that particular values can be consistently advocated as general guides in the consideration of public policy is most significant, for it means that the public dimension has become a part of the stock of primary political responses. It means that men have come to recognize that they have important and enduring interests and loyalties relating to a civic order, as distinguished from the sorts of interests which center on one's self, one's family, property, or livelihood.

The New Politics

It is suggested, then, that the birth of civic consciousness was the necessary prelude to the great wave of political thought and constitutional experiment which, especially in the interregnum, swept away the assumptions which had supported the medieval political scheme. The traditional political arrangements of the English monarchy reached a stage of crisis in the first decades of the seventeenth century. In seeking a solution, the English people, or rather those who acted in their name, found it necessary to destroy the independent authority of the monarchy, and in doing so they fashioned the modern English state in practice and in theory. This process required the expenditure of prodigious physical and intellectual energies. Indeed, about a century elapsed before the contours of the settlement were firmly established.

The critical assault on the monarchy was mounted by those untitled gentlemen whose vehicle was parliament. It was their withdrawal of allegiance from Charles I which produced the fatal breach in the traditional scheme. But in the process of galvanizing sufficient power and support to unseat the monarchy, they produced a situation which, for a time, they could not control. To achieve

their own aims, they were constrained to seek the support of substantial numbers of common men. Their political and military
necessities afforded the opportunity for all sorts and conditions of
men not only to play a part, at least temporarily, at the highest
political levels, but to ventilate novel ideas and proposals for a
constitutional settlement. Thus, the years of the interregnum mark
the entrance of the common man into politics. Moreover, he entered not only politics but the hallowed precincts of political
thought as well. Despite the long-run political weakness of the
more democratic elements, the radical literature was composed and
the constitutional experiments of the interregnum were put on
record. As Christopher Hill has said, "although the Puritan revolution was defeated, the revolution in thought could not be unmade . . ." [68]

In the seventeenth century the medieval subject became a citizen.
His relationship to political authority was no longer that of an
individual occupying a rank somewhere in the universal hierarchy
and a role preordained by his parentage. This hierarchical idea of
an ordered, graded universe, in which the really vital levels of
authority are personal and immediate, while the government of
the kingdom is the remote apex of an ascending scale, was overturned by the widespread adoption of alternative approaches to
the problems raised by reflection on politics. New political theories
were informed by the powerful solvent of equalitarian and libertarian assumptions and values. These were to be the leading criteria by which the value of institutions would be measured. It is
doubtful if prolonged search would reveal any more profound
breach from medieval assumptions than the often quoted words of
Colonel Rainborough, uttered in the course of the Putney Debates
in October 1647. Surely few are more deserving of repetition. "For
really I think that the poorest he that is in England hath a life
to live, as the greatest he; and therefore truly, sir, I think it's clear,
that every man that is to live under a government ought first by
his own consent to put himself under that government; and I do
think that the poorest man in England is not at all bound in a
strict sense to that government that he hath not had a voice to
put himself under." [69] In medieval England not only the "poorest
he," of course, but the vast majority had no place in the scheme of
governance. But in the period of the civil wars, the subject of discussion was the people considered as a whole. The institutional re-

flection of the birth of the citizen was the creation of parliamentarism — the subordination of kingship to the ancient assembly
— while at the level of political thought it gave rise to social contract theory and the idea of government as a trust, bestowed by
the whole body of citizens and revocable at their pleasure. In 1647
a certain Captain Clarke felt able to presume "that all people, and
all nations whatsoever, have a liberty and power to alter and change
their constitutions if they find them to be weak and infirm. Now if
the people of England shall find this weakness in their constitution,
they may change it if they please." [70] They could, and they did.

Thus the struggle to reach a constitutional settlement involved
introducing appeals to and claims for the nation as a single, politically homogeneous whole. This time the political settlement was
not a matter of arranging a more or less temporary modus vivendi
between the king and some assortment of the great landed magnates.
In the writings and debates of the interregnum there is a flavor of
generality, of universality, which is altogether alien to the past. The
problem of a new settlement was no longer being discussed in terms
of conflicting claims to this or that barony or custody of one of his
majesty's castles, nor in terms of the grant of some specific franchise,
nor yet in terms of ancient liberties.[71] It was not even a more general and vigorous prosecution of the old baronial claim to a rightful place in the councils of the king, perhaps even a determining
role. These were the sorts of claims prosecuted in the great political crises of the Middle Ages. On the contrary, what was mooted
now was the relationship of the whole body of the governed to their
rulers, monarchical or otherwise. It was at once a matter of political
theory and national politics, and what it meant was the abandonment of traditional medieval perspectives. By making the terms
of the discussion general in scope, political thinkers introduced an
unmistakable novelty. To be sure, the generality of the views
advanced in the several quarters of the opposition was in practice
more or less limited. It has been stressed recently, for example, that
even the Levellers would have excluded servants and alms-takers
from the franchise.[72] But this does not affect the point which is
being urged here, for the problem of effective enfranchisement is
always a matter of degree. The crucial point is not that the civil
war did not introduce democracy. Clearly it did not. However
narrow or wide the practical extension of the "people," the important point is that, by embracing the notion of a civic order,

the politically interested had incorporated a novel and vital dimension into political thinking.

By no means all the remnants of the Middle Ages disappeared, but the ancient polity had been turned on its axis and set upon a new course. Again, neither did all the old ideas vanish, but they were profoundly altered. Thus, despite the civil wars, the transition to modernity presents a problem in continuity as well as change, for the revolution did not shatter the political order beyond recovery. As Samuel H. Beer has pointed out, no settled constitutional pattern emerged until the eighteenth century. The preceding period was, as he says, an interlude between relatively stable views of the constitution.[73] But it is an interlude of vital significance, for the eighteenth century constitution was a subtle blend of the new elements, fashioned in the age of revolution, and the medieval legacy. In the barest terms, England had inherited from the medieval past a tradition of strong central government, and this was restored, albeit on an entirely different footing. The restoration of the monarchy represents that legacy, but only symbolically. To it were attached the warmth of sentiment, popular devotion, and familiarity. Even so, the revolution had struck the monarchy a fatal blow. It is vital to recognize that the great difference between the seventeenth century and the opposition movements of preceding centuries is not that the king was defeated. That had happened often enough. The kingship had been subdued before; it had been put into commission; kings had been deposed and murdered. What matters is that the monarchy was deprived of its claim to a source of legitimacy independent of the kingdom, and that this reduction of the king to the status of a mere officer of the realm was made to stick. This was never true of medieval kingship, however debased it might be in fact. Before the seventeenth century the king was unquestionably the center of government and the only conceivable representative of the kingdom as a whole.[74] For kingship, the seventeenth century substituted parliamentarism. It would be difficult to imagine a more significant change, even though the restoration and the theory of mixed monarchy served to mask the depth of the alteration quite skillfully for another two centuries. It was not until the mid-nineteenth century that Walter Bagehot exposed the theory of mixed monarchy for the hollow husk that it was.[75]

Civic Consciousness and Liberal Constitutionalism

The preceding discussion has suggested that the emergence of a distinctly public perspective in seventeenth century England constituted a transformation in political outlook of the most fundamental kind, one which decisively demarcates modern and medieval political perspectives. This reorientation gave rise to a whole constellation of novel ideas and practices, ordinarily summed up as liberalism and constitutional government. The close historical connections between civic consciousness and liberal constitutionalism raise a number of important questions. The main point is that liberalism, as the chief ideological offspring of the revolutionary era, contributes to two kinds of political myopia. On the one hand, its marked individualism, however beneficent and valuable, neglects the critical importance of the civic frame of reference which is the essential condition of its successful operation. On the other hand, it puts inordinate weight on the techniques of constitutional government and, more particularly, on legal processes. Each of these lines of emphasis merits further exploration.

Historically, modern constitutionalism emerged as an attempt to effect an accommodation between the new demands for personal liberty and the perennial problems of political order. It may be only an accident of history that liberalism and the practices of constitutional government made their appearance in politics together. If so, it was an accident of first-rate importance, because it has meant that the substantive content of constitutionalism has been supplied primarily by the emphasis on individual liberty which is the chief mark of liberalism. But it is just this which obscures the fact that the constitutionalist answer to the problems of political order assumes the solution of the most difficult of all political problems. It assumes the existence of a politically conscious community on a national scale — a public aware of its common citizenship. It has often been pointed out that the principal theoretical weakness of liberalism is the assumption that interests may be prosecuted in strictly individualistic terms and yet achieve desirable public results. However true this may be, what really requires notice is that liberalism is but one possible set of values in a constitutional system. What is indispensable, liberalism or no, is that men have internalized a civic point of view.

In short, neither the existence nor, for that matter, the maintenance of a public consciousness and loyalty capable of vitalizing
a constitutional political order ought to be assumed as a matter of
course. To be sure, the essence of modern constitutionalism is that
public governmental power must be subjected to effective and regu-
larized restraints,[76] and the point of it all is to ensure that the
sphere of private concerns possesses real content. This point of
view is expressed in a complicated set of ideas and practices. It
involves all the manifold difficulties associated with the ideas of
representation and consent and with the nature and status of a
binding rule of law, as well as the institutional devices designed to
avert excessive concentration of power. Historically this side of
our political heritage has been complicated by association with
democratic thought, though there is no logical necessity in this conjunction. But it was their confluence that produced the political
ideals most of us cherish. Underlying them all is the idea that there
is a meaningful and immensely valuable contrast between what is
understood to be public and what is supposed to be set apart as
private, removed from the reach of public authority.

But it ought to be borne in mind that what makes possible our
jealousy of private rights and their constitutional guarantees is the
general political tradition, energized, as it were, by public appreciation of its worth. Americans are inclined to emphasize the institutional devices built into the Constitution, but important as they
may be, the practice of constitutional rule in England ought to be
reminder enough that it does not necessarily involve precisely those
arrangements. Whatever the particular institutional techniques, the
maintenance of constitutional government cannot be reduced to
the preservation of these forms, though it may involve this. The
main point is really simple enough, though perhaps for that very
reason it is terribly easy to overlook. It is not enough to rely on
techniques alone for the vitality of a system which is essentially a
matter of civic loyalty. Moreover, mere reiteration of demands for
personal liberty will not by itself infuse life into the system. In
short, constitutional theory ought not to be reduced to the idea
of checks and balances and the liberties that are supposed somehow
to flow from them. This is to mistake a purely mechanical description, popularized in the eighteenth century, for what is necessarily
the practice of a politics of moderation, restraint, and tolerance. In
turn, this is a matter of substantial numbers of men having internal-

ized these restraints, having converted what was once, perhaps, a matter of necessity into a prized political virtue. Its external forms are negotiation and compromise. However loathsome these may be to the exponents of the several forms of modern political fanaticism, they are nonetheless necessary to the practice of politics in a plural society if it is to achieve both stability and the political values of the constitutional tradition.

Modern industrial society is inevitably productive of multiple interests and aims, and the impulse to criticize modern society, while refusing to recognize this, is pathetic and futile. Yearning for a past allegedly less fractured by divergent interests, the passionate quest for universal principles, nowadays conducted in the forms of social science, the frantic anxiety about cohesion, with its thinly disguised appeal to the standard of less advanced societies — all these kinds of nostalgia are fundamentally misdirected.[77] There is very little point in engaging in the contemplation of an idyllic but imaginary past, for the one thing we cannot do is capture an historical ghost. Universal principles, alas, turn out to be vacant, because the process of generalization consists in eliminating all the particular features which make standards relevant to the affairs of a society. The notion, finally, that premodern societies are models of cohesiveness is a myth.[78] Medieval society has been one of the most intensely mined quarries in all these varieties of search for the pure ore of social rectitude, but it is certainly not a good place to look. Indeed, as Friedrich Heer has written, it "was volcanic territory, with the threat of eruption always just below the surface; not a year passed, not a day, without outbreaks of war, feud and civil conflict." [79]

Neither nostalgia nor affirmation of the forms of restraint will supply an ethos adequate to constitutional politics. This is nothing unfamiliar, after all. Pious repetition of verbal formulas, conformity to all the legal niceties, elaborate paper provisions — all these may be attended to scrupulously and yet produce only a counterfeit of the genuine coin. The observance of proper legal form in ridding themselves of troublesome political and dynastic rivals was a favorite technique of the Tudors, and they were neither the first nor the last to bend legality to base purposes.[80] In practice, again, we commonly distinguish between constitutions whose restraints are nullified in fact and genuine constitutional government. For genuine constitutionalism is at bottom an intangible but recognizable pattern of political activity, channeled through particular constitutional forms yet neither created nor sustained but, at most, reinforced by them. The habits of constitutional politics are, to be sure, the vital reflexes of the day-to-day operation of the system, but they are not themselves creative. This is not to say that forms make no difference. But they ought not to be taken for the substance, which is essentially restraint in both method and content in everyday politics. The substance of constitutional government, then, is neither mechanical devices nor particular liberties — though the former are its techniques and the latter its fruits — but rather the tradition of political moderation, which, in turn, depends upon civic consciousness and loyalty.

Thus the surface features of the constitutional tradition are neither self-generating nor self-sustaining. The priority and necessity of public consciousness has eminently authoritative credentials in our own tradition. *The Federalist* puts the problem of constitutionalism this way: "you must first enable the government to control the governed; and in the next place oblige it to control itself. A dependence on the people is, no doubt, the primary control on government; but experience has taught mankind the necessity of auxiliary precautions." [81] The first order of reliance is upon the people. The separation of powers, federalism, and judicial review, to the extent that it was expressed by Hamilton,[82] are all auxiliary precautions. First there must be a people. This was a problem at the founding of the republic, for, as is well known, the principal loyalties of many were directed not to the United States but to the several states. Yet if there was to be a national political order at all, those concerns and loyalties had, in part at least, to be redirected. There had to be a public outlook focused on the new national government, and *The Federalist* itself stands as an enduring expression of civic consciousness. The quality and quantity of the debates in Philadelphia and in the states bear abundant testimony to the existence of a conscious and well-developed civic point of view. The doctrines and arguments of those debates were largely an inheritance, one which, as it happens, is principally English. The public points of view adopted by the English people in establishing their modern political order in the seventeenth century were bequeathed to us, and behind this legacy there lie centuries of political experience. When the English people hammered out the contours of

34

a modern state in the civil wars, they brought to maturity a long line of development. A major purpose of the present inquiry is to emphasize the complexity and difficulty of that achievement.

Both the liberal emphasis on individualism and the faith in constitutional techniques, then, should be considered in terms of what must be presupposed if either is to be workable. Both drive in the direction of setting the general political order and the necessity of civic consciousness in a condition of permanent eclipse. But it is the legalistic spirit of liberalism which is the best single indicator of its triumph. The insistence on an allegedly neutral law, a law somehow pitched above the political process, is a function not just of predominance but of overwhelming power, as E. H. Carr has observed.[83] In English and American discussions, this outlook draws its inspiration from the seventeenth century. In view of the profound changes in the English social and political order, it is understandable that the impact of the civil wars on the discussion of political thought has been deep and persistent. This is as it should be. It is possible, nevertheless, that it has been too much affected by the Whig interpretation. The classical Whig view consisted in a reduction of those complex events to a single issue. It had been a struggle between Stuart absolutism and the forces of popular right and liberty. This particular image has grown tarnished, because it is easy to show that the aims of parliament were not democratic and that parliament was constituted on a radically undemocratic basis. Hence a second image has been projected, in which the struggle is depicted as one between the defenders of the ancient law of the land and Stuart absolutism.[84] It is true that English opinion did harden into just such a frame of reference. The Whig interpretation is an ideological reading of the past sponsored by the legatees of the victorious party. It is precisely for that reason, of course, that it possesses a truth value on the level of ideology. But as an account of the complex religious, economic, social, and political ambitions involved it is woefully inadequate.

Nevertheless, the Whig outlook was inherited by the Liberals and survived to give birth to an impressive progeny. Its effects have not been uniformly beneficial. One of these is the inclination to discuss politics as if it were a bipolar affair, on the model of law pitted against the royal prerogative. It yields the simplistic construction of political theory in terms of the individual locked in perpetual combat with illegal governmental acts. At the level of constitutional theory, it has led to the view that the essence of constitutionalism is the rule of law. Law is discussed as if it were quite unmarked by the impact of the political process, as if it were, in Justice Holmes's famous phrase, a "brooding omnipresence in the sky." [85] It is an ideal in which law adjudicates impartially on the tawdry affairs of *homo politicus*, while remaining uncontaminated itself. Judith Shklar has recently directed our attention to the legalistic outlook, and to the fact that it is but one aspect of our complex intellectual heritage. Most importantly, it is itself an act of choice in politics. This, as she says, is no reason to despise or reject it. On the contrary, it is an invitation to examine it. [86]

Just such an examination is particularly pertinent for the subjects under discussion here, for, among its other accomplishments, the outlook of legalism has supplied an approach to the history of political thought which has dutifully reflected its principal preoccupations. This has involved expounding the past in terms of a contemporary ideal. It has meant that the textual remains of the political past have been refracted through a legalistic prism, and the result is a severely attenuated account. The prism is simply too opaque. It filters out too much of the historical process. Even though such an enterprise is necessarily historical, it has largely excluded the principal driving force of history, those acts of conflict and cooperation we call politics. History, even intellectual history, written in this way runs a grave risk. It risks treating an idea employed in a given historical context as though it were the same idea when it, or an analogue, is used in an entirely different historical context. It exposes itself to the charge that only texts have been compared to texts in a political vacuum. In short, this outlook has riveted attention on but one element in the historical development of what we now call constitutionalism.

The primary analytical instrument in this line of argument is a sharp distinction between the processes of adjudication and legislation. This is thought to be the really crucial difference between the Middle Ages and modernity. In the Middle Ages, both ordinary litigation and more obviously political disagreements are represented as having been resolved by acts of judgment, which were merely applications or elucidations of a pre-existing body of law. Arbitrary command, on the other hand, is specifically modern and finds its most important expression in the idea of a sovereign legislature. The root idea seems to be a contrast, then, between reasoned judgment and mere legislative fiat.[87]

Certain more detailed aspects of this outlook will be considered below. Here it is enough to indicate its most general frailty. It rests, like modern liberalism generally, on a separation between law and politics which does not accord well with the facts. This general subject has been given penetrating treatment in the work of Judith Shklar already referred to and need not, therefore, be explored at any length. In brief, since the outlook of legalism is itself a political ideology, in fact subject to all the strains of political struggle, the form of adjudication may reflect legalistic ideals more or less well. At one extreme is the political trial, in which the form of judgment according to general and prospective rules is sacrificed to political expediency. At the other is the trial that nearly everyone, except perhaps the losing party, would admit has been conducted fairly, and that therefore is an embodiment of justice. Thus adjudication can be the name of a more or less openly political process. Simply because legislation proceeds from deliberate choice does not make the process one of arbitrary fiat. Normally legislation results from the same kinds of considerations of principle and expediency as any other judgment. Human judgment may be described as moral, legal, and political, but these distinctions are only analytical, and the boundaries between them are difficult to locate and impossible to freeze. They constitute, rather, a fluid communicating continuum, each having subtle connections with the others, which allows the substance of beliefs, values, and interests to be expressed in a variety of forms. In this respect the Middle Ages did not differ from our own times.

The outlook of legalism has taken a peculiarly tenacious hold on the treatment of late medieval and early modern political thought. It is widely held that lawmaking was unknown and unconceived of, that the medieval period may be summed up by the idea that the good old law of immemorial custom was supreme. Indeed, the recitation of these phrases has assumed the character of a ritual incantation. So beguiling has this legalistic outlook been that students have often mistaken mere litigiousness as evidence of law-abidingness in society, when in fact it is often just the reverse. The effect is to set aside the concrete political processes which supply whatever law there is with its content and efficacy. But an operating legal system cannot reflect no one's interests. It must necessarily embody some kind of political consensus, some pattern of conflicting and overlapping interests and values. I believe, in brief, that the character and place of law in medieval and early modern political thought requires reassessment. The subject needs many more distinctions and much more attention to historical and political context than it normally receives. Beneath the legal blanket, if one looks, may be found some very active bedfellows, king and community, whose acts of contention and cooperation supply the contours of the blanket. To put the matter bluntly, the law was neither the immemorial custom of the folk nor was it fundamental. Rather, to the extent that it was common law it was primarily the king's law. This does not exclude traditional usage as a source of law, nor appeals to it in support of political proposals and interests. Further, as one might expect of a social instrument, the law was in a fairly continuous process of change, both deliberate and unconscious.

Certainly there were political ideals, and these cannot be ignored. Much on the level of ideals, of standards, derived from the general outlook of Christianity, though the traditional usages of the Germanic peoples have a place also, as do ideas extracted from Aristotle and Roman law. These ideals were often cast in the language of law, both natural and customary. But this is very far from establishing the proposition that the political thought of the Middle Ages may be summed up in the idea of the sovereignty of the good old law, thought of as the immutable custom of the folk. Medieval politics and the thought which accompanies it are considerably more lively and involved than that. It is perfectly true that medieval authors wrote a very great deal about law, and that they discussed many of their problems in terms of law. There is a vast legal literature of varying provenance: the writings of canonists and civilians, of papal and imperial publicists, and a little later, of those who espoused the claims of the secular kingdoms to independence of both papacy and empire. However, as has been remarked already, much of this theoretical work occupied ground which was excessively remote from the working conditions of the period. Moreover, it was a variety of grand theory which was almost exclusively continental in origin. The fact that there was no English parallel raises some very interesting questions.

It is surely curious that medieval England did not generate any extensive body of grand theory, and it is clearly important to confront the problem as squarely as possible. At bottom, it raises all the most basic questions concerning the essential nature of the English political order and the larger European setting of which it was a part. But to borrow a reflection from Marc Bloch, it is difficult enough to account for the presence of something, and next to impossible to explain the absence of something one finds elsewhere.[88] In such a situation one can only suggest a set of considerations. In the case in hand, the crucial factors appear to be these. Above all, medieval England was comparatively isolated from most of the complex jurisdictional and territorial disputes which proximity bred on the Continent. These quarrels account for the efforts of a great many political and legal theorists. In effect England was insulated from the international system by the English Channel, poor technology, and a Continent occupied with its own problems. To be sure, England was by no means free of entanglement in international affairs, but their impact was certainly dampened in crossing the Channel. This meant that the domestic political process was not submerged in the irresistible demands of military preparedness. In addition to this favorably permissive international framework, medieval England had the good fortune of being small and rich enough to be conquered and lastingly unified much earlier than the countries of continental Europe. Lamentable as it may be, the plain fact is that "many of mankind's achievements have been obtained through violence." [89] Of nothing is this more true than the generally effective government of medieval England. The Danish and Norman conquerors did their work well.

Together these factors provided the setting for a fruitful, if somewhat parochial, history from the twelfth to the sixteenth and seventeenth centuries. The able monarchs of the house of Anjou followed hard on the heels of the Norman Conquest and provided England with a comparatively effective general government in the twelfth century. From the middle of the thirteenth century, the governing classes of England abandoned even the common language of educated Europe and settled into the use of French. The effect of the peculiar growth of law French was to reinforce the relative isolation of England and, more particularly, to cut off any extensive influences from continental political and legal theory.[90] Just as in the case of American political thinking, and for some of the same reasons, much English thought is to be found not in formal treatises but in the all-too-brief remarks embedded in the working records of judges, lawyers, and administrators, eked out only occasionally by sustained reflection. Whatever the causes, what is not open to dispute is the fact that England largely stood to one side of all the great literary debates of the later Middle Ages, from the investiture controversy to the conciliar movement.[91]

The argument, then, is that while the emergence of civic consciousness was the critical fulcrum with which the personal monarchy of the Middle Ages was dislodged and parliamentary monarchy installed in its stead, the political thought of liberal constitutionalism, thus made possible, tends to ignore the fact and thereby to cut itself away from crucial presuppositions and a source of strength it can ill afford to lose. The advent of modern politics and the consequent possibility of constitutional government resulted from a fundamental restructuring of the polity in response to the emergence of public consciousness. Its concrete content was a set of new ideas on the nature and purpose of political authority. The aim of this study in the contrast between the medieval and the modern political worlds is to offer an evaluation of both the element of change and the element of continuity, both the medieval legacy and the novel angle of vision introduced in the seventeenth century. It is hoped in this way to accomplish two broad purposes. In the first place, to advance an assessment of the place of medieval ideas in the achievement of constitutional government, and secondly, to frame a useful interpretation of the perspectives which not only contributed to the emergence of constitutional government, but which are also central to its continued vitality. The general argument on the first of these purposes will be that the medieval contribution was very slight, certainly a great deal more modest than is often suggested. In essence it was restricted almost entirely to the realm of general conditions of stability in government. This was no mean accomplishment and its importance ought not to be underestimated, but it has nothing to do with the positive promotion of constitutional ideals. The main contention with respect to the second purpose has been advanced already. I believe that the birth of public consciousness was plainly central to the accomplishments of the seventeenth century, and that it is just as vital today as then.

The linchpin of any body of political ideas is its conception of legitimate authority, and the operative thought of the Middle Ages was no exception. What makes it difficult to deal with is not that there were no such assumptions, but the fragmentary character of their expression and a complete absence of self-consciousness. In this, medieval thought resembled that of any traditional society. But it was not just a matter of the sanctity of tradition — Roman political thought had rested explicitly on tradition — but rather that it was unexposed to any alternative angle of vision, at least any that was perceived as an alternative. For this reason it lacked what is perhaps the chief driving force behind explicit, self-conscious political theory — an antagonistic impulse. Instead there was just the massive weight of one's own society, the most impressive and elementary imperative of all: what has always been done, the practices of one's ancestors from time immemorial. At first sight one might suppose that such a standard would imply both simplicity and coherence; in fact it did not. We will have occasion to notice time and again that operative thought suffered from radical incoherence and imprecision. So much is this the case, that the test of logic, of internal consistency, is seldom an appropriate instrument of analysis. For operative political thought was neither systematic nor sustained, much less a conscious intellectual construction. On the contrary, it was more nearly a style of argument, cast in terms of a common store of evocative symbols. It was a ramshackle structure at best, whose only intellectual mortar was a loosely assembled set of catch phrases, all of which were easily employed at cross-purposes. Argument was a matter of marshaling tag lines and multiplying examples of praiseworthy or reprehensible conduct and its just desserts, rather than orderly progress from premises to conclusions. As for simplicity, it is best to recall Maitland's judgment:

"As we go backward, the familiar outlines become blurred; the ideas become fluid, and instead of the simple we find the indefinite." [1]

We have to do with a body of thought, then, that was vague in conception, structurally incoherent, complex yet unrefined, and, above all, merely assumed rather than argued out. It is necessary to underline these features, since the primary effort of the following pages is to present as orderly an account as the evidence will permit, to make the implicit more nearly explicit. Perhaps the best avenue of approach, as was suggested, is inquiry into the notions of authority and political legitimacy. At this level the central characteristic of operative thought was that it rested on the foundation I am calling double majesty.[2] The heart of this outlook was that both the predominant elements of the social order, the king and his leading men, were thought to possess an independently grounded title to authority. Neither order derived its standing in society from the other. A particular man might be king because he had been chosen by the great men of the realm. But that is a very different thing from saying that kingship itself derived from such selection. For no one regarded the institution of kingship as the work of another order of society. No one believed that there was anything contingent about kingship. The same observation holds for the greater nobility, though the numerous and shifting membership of that order necessarily made it a less distinct idea. A given title or estate may have been the gift or grant of the king. But again the order as a whole was not the king's creation. Did not the greater nobility select the king himself? It is not easy to see how such an institution can have been wholly dependent on the king's grace, whatever may be said about its particular members, and medieval man certainly did not think so. There is no doubt that this conception is ambiguous and that the balance involved in it was often uneasy. Certainly it is an idea which raises the possibility, perhaps even the inevitability, of stress. Collision between kings and barons is, of course, the most familiar of all medieval political phenomena. Yet while this was the most spectacular form of political behavior, it was neither constant nor the most important facet of medieval politics. If this had been true, the medieval political order would have collapsed into anarchy. It would be wrong to deny that the threat of anarchy was often very real. The fact remains, however, that these political orders did survive, and they did so on the basis of the idea of government as a cooperative enterprise. Double majesty was reflected in the actual practice of government in terms of a partnership between the king and his great men.

The nonregal partner in double majesty presents a considerable difficulty, for it appeared under a variety of names. It was sometimes referred to quite unhelpfully as the "people," though the term carried no genuinely popular content. On the contrary, the vast majority of the people, if they are referred to at all, are not the *populus;* they are the *vulgus,* who normally fall outside the range of vision or concern of the educated or wellborn. It should occasion no surprise, therefore, to find that alternative terms were plainly aristocratic. Thus one hears of the great men or great magnates of the realm, of the earls and barons, and, in time. the three estates and parliament. In all cases, however, the essential point is that the political order may be characterized as the conjunction of two native and independent sources of legitimacy and, therefore, of sporadic but nonetheless authentic political initiative. To be sure, no one doubted that all authority was from God. But this was an ultimate source, articulated in any number of ways and capable of supplying ultimate justification for virtually any established order. The proximate source of authority was both king and people. By itself neither element was considered competent to conclude any and all disputed questions of politics and law. This central assumption was the foundation of a variety of subsidiary ideas.

The main suggestion of this chapter, then, is that the notion of a double location of authority — double majesty — is the appropriate ground for the examination of operative political thought. To begin with, it provides a frame of reference which accounts for the striking ambivalence of a large number of texts. Second, it supplies a general formulation of premodern attempts to conceptualize the elements of political life which is a tolerably accurate reflection of medieval society. Finally, it offers a politically oriented perspective, rather than the predominantly legalistic one which has characterized so much of the secondary literature on medieval and early modern times. The discussion which follows examines some of the most fundamental and persistent attitudes and ideas of the period. It begins with an examination of the dominant cast of mind of the early Middle Ages, which may be summed up as veneration of the past, and with the ethical content of that outlook, the martial values of the aristocratic warrior. There follows a brief

44

inquiry into some of the leading ideas of the Germanic peoples in the early stages of their history. Here there are several points of considerable importance. It is essential, first, to notice the primitive character of their political organization and ideas. More particularly, however, special attention is directed to the institution of the comitatus, that relationship of personal allegiance between the Germanic war leader and his companions, because it was from the conquests of these bands of warriors that the successor kingdoms emerged. Most importantly for present purposes, the aristocratic and military outlook of the barbarian war band persisted for centuries after its appearance, and so it supplies us with the best introduction to the dominant assumptions and values of the medieval nobility. Indeed, the remarkable tenacity of ideas generated very early in the Christian era is perhaps the most outstanding single feature of the medieval outlook. Finally, these ideas and practices are examined in the particular context of Anglo-Saxon England.

The very persistence of some of the basic ideas of medieval political thinking is a most important element of the whole. By itself it reveals a great deal about the character of the society we are dealing with. The most fundamental point is that all the standards were regarded as having been established in the past. For the medieval lay aristocrat this meant the practices and achievements of his ancestors, his family, his blood.[3] To be sure, he was capable of admiration of Roman civilization, though it is certain that he could neither attain nor understand it, but at best could only attempt to imitate it. As J. M. Wallace-Hadrill has aptly put it, "Early medieval men could live like barbarians; but they could think that they were Romans." [4] There can be no doubt that the Germanic warrior was awed by Roman achievement. Compared with his rude wooden shelter, even Roman ruins he saw as the "cunning work of giants . . ." [5] simply because they had been made of stone. Nor was the impact of Roman civilization by any means restricted to architecture. Above all there were the imperial religion and its devoted servants. With the exception of the Anglo-Saxons, the barbarian peoples settled among and were to a great extent absorbed by the remains of the Roman Church and its administration. The Church was later to prove itself a most important ally of Germanic kingship. Moreover, it was through the needs and training of churchmen that barbarian law came to be set down in writing, and imitation of the Romans was part of the motivation. Thus Bede tells us that the laws were written down on what he supposed to be the Roman model. Actually, it was not much more than the idea of composing a written statement of the law that was adopted, for with few exceptions the substance of the barbarian law codes was Germanic.

Nevertheless, this admiration did not eliminate the barbarian's veneration of his familial and tribal past, a prepossession which is evidenced in any number of ways. One of the best is the idea of the personality of the laws. In the successor kingdoms, the law applicable to a man, wherever he lived, was not local law, not territorial law, but the law of his people.[6] The Anglo-Saxon king, Edgar, says, "It is my will that there should be in force among the Danes such good laws as they best decide on, and I have ever allowed them this and will allow it as long as my life lasts, because of your loyalty, which you have always shown me."[7] Another preoccupation which well illustrates this frame of mind was the immense energy lavished on the recitation of genealogies. In the case of Anglo-Saxon kingly families, ancestry was invariably traced back to the Germanic gods.[8] Former usage as a standard appears clearly in the Anglo-Saxon laws. Thus King Edgar decreed that "that is to be in force which I and my councillors have added to the decrees of my ancestors . . ."[9] King Ethelred and his councillors made breach of the peace declared by the king personally an offense which could not be compounded for, so that it might "remain as firm as it best was in the days of his ancestors . . ."[10] According to this king, since Edgar's days "Christ's laws have waned and the king's laws dwindled."[11] Accordingly he exhorts his people to "do as is necessary for us; let us take as our example what former rulers wisely decreed, Athelstan and Edmund, and Edgar who came last . . ."[12] This conception of ancestry provided even the hero with his sense of what was fitting conduct. We are told, for example, that the sons of King Edward at the battle of Brunanburh fought well "as befitted their descent from noble kinsmen."[13]

There was, thus, a studied preoccupation with the past which it is right to call reverence for one's ancestors, and which was presumed to be the necessary and sufficient mode of validation. This is, of course, indicative of a simple society, where political conceptions were similarly unsophisticated and durable. It should not be inferred from this, however, that early medieval society was unusually stable, abiding in a kind of timeless equilibrium supported by this backward-looking cast of mind. Indeed it was not a question of stability at all, but rather the reverse. For not only were the barbarian peoples unable to understand alternative standards and quite lacking in self-consciousness, but they were constantly harassed by instability, violence, deprivation, and insecurity. For settled people, especially the clergy, the answer was not to seek a causal account, not to investigate and perhaps to innovate, but to freeze, to iterate endlessly that things were not wont to be this way. Thought was transfixed by a myth of stability which led straight away from any conception of change as such. Explanation therefore stuck at the level of the notion of interruption. Thus Abbot Aelfric tells us, "When there is too much evil in mankind, councillors should investigate with wise deliberation, which of the supports of the throne has been broken, and repair it at once." He goes on to explain that the "throne stands on these three supports: *laboratores, bellatores, oratores.*" There are, that is, those who work, those who fight, and those whose task is to intercede with God. If one of these supports breaks down, the throne "falls at once." [14] This is surely a narrow basis on which to found understanding, but it is typical. But for peoples on the move, war and the quest for food, land, and booty was a way of life, something to be sought and exulted in, and this outlook was never far below the surface in the upper levels of lay society, for medieval aristocrats were above all warriors. The sixth century historian, Jordanes, reports a speech of the Hun leader Attila at the time of the great battle of the Catalaunian Plain (451 A.D.), in which Attila met defeat. It breathes the fierce spirit of the Heroic Age. Attila is said to have exhorted his warriors thus. "For what is war but your usual custom? Or what is sweeter for a brave man than to seek revenge with his own hand? It is a right of nature to glut the soul with vengeance. Let us then attack the foe eagerly . . . Let your own fury burst forth! Now show your cunning, Huns, now your deeds of arms! Let the wounded exact in return the death of his foe; let the unwounded revel in slaughter of the enemy . . . I shall hurl the first spear at the foe. If any can stand at rest while Attila fights, he is a dead man." [15] The views Jordanes attributed to Attila were not unusual. Beowulf vows that he will either do great deeds or die.[16] His advice to others is, "Let him who can win glory before death; that will be best for warriors after life is over." A man "must gain a lasting

praise in war; he will have no care for life." [17] These were the
ideals of what Chadwick called the Heroic Age. The term is exalted;
the behavior was not. "Heroic leaders were those who stole their
neighbours' property and used it to reward their followers and buy
favours . . ." [18] This is true and sobering enough. What is especially
interesting is that this heroic ethic proved to have a very long lease
on the sentiments and behavior of the medieval aristocrat. The
Anglo-Saxon Chronicle contains a panegyric on King Edgar which
stresses his martial prowess, for

> No host however strong,
> Was able to win booty for itself
> In England, while that noble king
> Occupied the royal throne. [19]

It is thus an intrinsically important point that early modes of
thought were oriented to the past and displayed the durability
natural to such an outlook. This may be seen best by turning to
the reports on the Germanic peoples which have come down to
us from Caesar and Tacitus. [20] For some of the most important
political assumptions of the Middle Ages appear among the Germanic barbarians as early as these Roman writings, which are our
first substantial sources of information. [21] Both the forms of political
organization and the expression of ideas underwent great changes
in the course of medieval history. But it is still true that one of
the most striking aspects of operative thought was the persistence
of its first principles. [22]

The setting of the ideas and political behavior associated with
the notion of double majesty was initially a technologically primitive
society. [23] Certainly the testimony of Caesar suggests that the peoples
encountered by the Romans in the first century B.C. were primitive
folk by any standard. [24] It may be gathered from his account that
Germanic social life was organized at three levels. Most of life
centered on the kindred. [25] Except for some limited purposes, clans
were grouped as tribes. Those few occasions were important, for
according to Caesar the leading men of the tribe had the task of
arranging the annual allocation of lands to be worked by the kin
groups. These men, whom Caesar called magistrates, also mediated
disputes, but apparently they possessed no coercive authority. [26]
Finally, the great men of the several tribes which composed a whole

people constituted a general council. This intertribal council was responsible for putting the people on a war footing, for it was at this level that war leaders were selected. There may have been an element of genuine coercive authority here, for Caesar says these war leaders had the power of life and death.[27] Even if this is true, however, it is important to notice that their authority was temporary.

Clearly, the society had an extremely simple political structure. Most of life was not even organized politically, and even where it was it did not operate at the same levels in all matters. For some purposes the tribe was the relevant political unit, while for others this would have been the whole people. All in all, the arrangements described by Caesar are strikingly similar to the type Lucy Mair has called "minimal government" among several peoples of East Africa,[28] and this surely enhances the general plausibility of Caesar's description. Mair found, just as did Caesar, that people with a bare minimum of authority above the clan are likely to act as different political units for different purposes. Thus, among the Nuer most of life is not organized politically; some affairs are conducted at the tribal level, and really concerted behavior is provoked only by warfare. In no case can coercive authority be identified.[29]

For present purposes, another institution described by Caesar is the most interesting: the habit of forming groups of warriors under a self-declared leader for purposes of adventure and booty.[30] This is the kernel of the institution made famous in the account of it by Tacitus: the comitatus, or retinue. In Caesar's book the comitatus is a casual affair, but matters were very different by Tacitus' day, at the end of the first century A.D. It had become the expression and the vehicle of changes in Germanic society and politics which were of the utmost importance. For it had taken on a well-defined and stable existence outside blood relationships and had produced, if nothing so clear as a nobility, at least groups of distinctly privileged people.[31] The leader (*princeps* or *dux*) of a war band represented a principle of lordship independent not only of lineage relationships but even of the more extensive tribe and people, for followers (*comites*) were often drawn from all corners of the Germanic world by the reputation of a great warrior.[32] Yet such a man was also involved in a reciprocal relationship with his men, for the relation of princeps and *comes* turned on the idea of mutual advantage, support, and loyalty. The leader supplied his men with the implements of war, with adventure, booty, and general support.[33] His followers were committed to him to the death by the terms of a solemn oath.[34] It is important to notice two things at the level of ideas about this relationship. It depended in the first place on a radically personal bond; all other ties were strictly extraneous and subordinate to this. Secondly, however, it was a contingent relationship, dependent upon the ability of the leader to reward his men and, hence, upon constant renewal of successful raiding enterprise. So early, then, do we find the cult of martial prowess and the notion of contingent allegiance. Largesse, liberality, and therefore success were essential for the maintenance of the leader's position.

Thus the comitatus was both the expression of change and the agency for carrying it out. It is most likely that the Romans themselves were primarily responsible for this development. For the sine qua non of the comitatus was wealth, as Tacitus pointed out.[35] More than a simple subsistence economy was required if an enterprising warrior was to be in a position to accumulate wealth with which to reward his followers. In the early stages of development, this took the form of merchandise supplied by Roman commerce.[36] After the barbarians settled in the Empire, the system could operate without this support, since the collapse of Roman provincial administration meant that a lord's faithful followers could be rewarded with land.[37] Moreover, many an ambitious warrior sought service in the imperial armies, a career which could easily earn him not only prestige but the wherewithal to command his own comitatus. Indeed, in addition to the magnetic power of "the enchanting mirage of Roman civilization," [38] the audacious barbarian war leader was a useful soldier, if he could be disciplined and trained. The result of this utility was a concerted diplomatic effort by Rome to lend her support and prestige to these Germanic *duces*.[39] Finally, the contraction of Roman military power opened up endless opportunities not simply for plunder but for large-scale settlement on the lands of the Empire. This last development was crucial, because it meant that the most fortunate of the Germanic duces developed into kings.[40] For it was the institution of the comitatus which appears to have become standard in the age of the migrations of the barbarians into the western provinces of the empire.

From the beginning of the history of the successor kingdoms, then, we are confronted with a society structured in terms of personal allegiance; one which was markedly aristocratic and severely hierarchical, designed for and governed — to the extent that it was governed — by a warrior caste seated on the lands of a decrepit empire. It is fair to say that this amounted to the institutionalization of the forms and values of the comitatus; it was government by princeps and comites. Settlement and the demands of even elementary territorial administration in such a context naturally sharpened the hierarchical structure of society. Not even the original form of the comitatus could be described in equalitarian terms.[41] But it made comparatively little difference politically if one warrior were given a brighter sword or a stronger horse than another. It did make a difference when one man held a richer or more extensive or more governable district. From such differences, steep discrepancy of rank and power emerged. But the most significant point is to notice how focus and, therefore, the possibility of public policy dissolved in such a context. There was no "public," but only a partly overlapping series of personal and familial dependencies. Interest and attention were quite naturally centered on the security and extent of one's land, and the personal dependencies spun out on it, for it was these which enabled a great man to discharge his own duties to his lord and to maintain power. But under stress even the ties of personal allegiance, and the unquestioning obedience which it was supposed to involve, often dissolved in the pursuit of local security. When the Anglo-Saxons were under attack by the Danes, the king appealed to his great men for warriors. But "there was no leader who was willing to raise levies, but each fled as quickly as he could, nor even in the end would one shire help another." [42] A great man, like Ealdorman Eadric, went over to the Danes, taking forty ships with him. Indeed, for Eadric changing sides was a habit. The Danes were no different: "forty-five ships transferred their allegiance to the king, and promised him to guard this land, on condition that he fed and clothed them." [43]

At its upper levels, and these were the only relevant ones politically, society was not so much a system as a web, with the king at its center. Political relationships amounted to an immensely complicated, crisscrossing series of discrete threads running from the center to the periphery, where it was weakest, for there the king's relationship to his lesser subjects was indirect, mediated by other threads. Considered from this perspective, all loyalties stood on the same plane. The warrior swore a solemn oath of unconditional loyalty to his lord.[44] He promised to "be loyal and true to N, and love all that he loves, and hate all that he hates . . ." [45] To be sure, any man would have recognized that he had duties to God and to his king. But in practice, loyalty to his lord led many a man into war against his king at the behest of his lord. That was the real difficulty at the edge of the social web. The king was remote, and direct loyalties, unmediated loyalties, were local and demanding. This led to the assertion by kings that all men owed personal and direct allegiance to them. Thus King Edmund required that "all shall swear in the name of the Lord . . . that they will be faithful to King Edmund, *even* as it behoves a man to be faithful to his lord, without any dispute or dissension, openly or in secret, favouring what he favours and discountenancing what he discountenances." [46] The *Anglo-Saxon Chronicle* reports that William the Conqueror required all his men to assemble on Salisbury Plain and swear an oath of allegiance directly to him, "no matter whose vassals they might be." [47] The Conqueror's sons required a similar oath of allegiance at the time of coronation. Thus a knight might owe a duty to a viscount, but he owed a separate and distinct duty to the king. At bottom these loyalties represent entirely different lines of obligation, and throughout the Middle Ages clarity was never really achieved.

There is, moreover, another and subtler reason for the nonexistence of a public outlook or anything that looks like public policy. Men's political energies were absorbed in the continuous and difficult business of maintaining a competitive position.[48] If a lord, whether a king or lesser man, failed for long to satisfy his followers' appetite for reward — for war and for land — he would find himself deserted. Warriors almost naturally gravitated to the successful chief. But the incessant shifting of allegiances, jockeying for position and followers, was capable of solving only local or small-scale problems. It was an outlook and a political prepossession incapable of perceiving or solving problems larger than personal allegiance, despite the fact that these larger problems were the context of the former. This incomprehension was yet another long-lived element of medieval political behavior and ideas. This is exemplified well in the problem of alienation of the king's lands. To be rewarded from these holdings was the normal expectation of the warrior.[49] Baronial ideology slipped easily into the assumption that land was a reward for service and ought, therefore, to be exempt from taxation. The result was a contradictory demand: warriors ought to be rewarded, but the king should live on the revenues of his own lands. In retrospect it is easy to see that the alienation of royal lands would eventuate in the impoverishment and collapse of the monarchy. But few men saw it this way, even in the late Middle Ages, and least of all the landed warriors. Worse still, most kings do not seem to have appreciated the problem fully either.[50]

How was order maintained at all? The short answer to this — and it is a perfectly good one — is that the king and his men cooperated on the basis of a shared outlook. They were all cut from the same cloth, all entertained the same set of values, those of the comitatus. It is true that the bonds between men were tenuous and fissiparous; they tended to dissolve and reform. That was part of the baronial point of view. But not all the bonds dissolved at the same time. Nor should it be forgotten that the governing elements of medieval society amounted to a very small number of men, most of whom knew one another and many of whom were related to one another. Thus even so significant an event in the later history of feudalism as the signing of the Magna Carta involved only a handful of men. Moreover, a skillful ruler knew how to divide whatever opposition there was by handling one baron at a time: threatening, bribing, cajoling, perhaps making him an ally through marriage.[51] It is also true that what strikes the observer as the most obvious feature of the period was violence and dissolution, but this is partly deceptive. The reason is that much of the political business of a kingdom simply went unrecorded or was merely noted by chroniclers. It is not at all atypical to meet laconic reports such as this: "In this year there was a great council in London at mid Lent, and nine ships of [King Edward's] household troops were paid off, and five remained behind." [52] That is all! Like most men, most of the time, medieval chroniclers were struck by the bizarre, the spectacular and violent, not by normality, and it was the bizarre on which they were inclined to linger.[53] Moreover, cooperation as such was not an article of the barons' political creed. What these men admired was valor, loyalty, and liberality. Cooperate they did, and that most of the time, but it was largely unconscious and went unrecorded. Furthermore, during a great part of the Middle Ages the peace was kept on a local basis; the fief, as Rushton Coulborn has said, was for many purposes the vital unit of government.[54] But not many fiefs found their activities celebrated in the written word.

The main point is that politics in the successor kingdoms consisted of the relations between the king and his, ideally, faithful men. It has been suggested that the style of this relationship appears already in the comitatus, and that it takes on so much importance historically because the spirit which informed it proved to be immensely durable. Thus it may be said with much justification that the origin of the outlook we are calling double majesty was the comitatus. This does not mean that it did not change nor that its setting remained static. But the values men embrace often lag far behind alteration of structure, and medieval men kept a steady eye on the past. However much weight one thinks should be attached to origins — and the subject is overweighted more often than not — there was the same critical ambiguity at the root of medieval political ideas. It took its origin from the primitive comitatus, but that is not really the point. What matters is that these ideas continued to rest on the assumptions found in that institution. It comes down to this. An adventurer, a bold and enterprising warrior, steps outside the traditional kin structure, offering himself as leader to those who are interested in following. Those who are interested accept him and swear allegiance to him. But that allegiance is a bond between two men, dependent upon mutual satisfaction. The leader's men are his companions; they have chosen him; and these are ideas that hang on through the settlement and establishment of the successor kingdoms, finding expression in the notion that the king is chosen for rule by his chief men. It is easy to understand that in conditions of relative stability these ideas of contingent allegiance, choice, and mutual satisfaction could be pressed in opposing directions. This is precisely what happened. Through all the changes the notion of mutuality persisted, and what it implied was that rule involved "counsel" between leader and followers. It is proper to describe this notion as a shared outlook, despite the fact that it lent itself to contrary interpretations.

It is important to recognize that this idea had nothing to do with subjects, much less citizens, participating in government. For both of these kinds of participation depend on an appreciation of men's relations to each other and a general sense of the identity of the whole. But the relation of king to baron was direct, personal, and individual; it was a relation not of one with many but of one with one. What tied the medieval barons together was a shared outlook on the nature of baronial status and the behavior befitting a man of that standing, a class notion, not a corporate one. That is why it was so easy to alter allegiances, even to shift sides in time of war. The discrete character of the tie of allegiance is strikingly illustrated in

54

the idea of treason. As Eric John has well said, "The Old English sources know of only two kinds of disloyalty, betrayal of one's lord or betrayal of one's kin. Of the crime of treason of subjects against a 'polity' or any kind of state or nation they know nothing." [55] The idea of an order, a class — in Bradley's famous phrase, a "station and its duties" — was there, but that is a very different thing from an idea of citizenship. At most one can say that the idea of rule with counsel was an idea of consent, though there were no stable rules as to who was to give it, or when and how it was to be given. When a baron gave his assent, he did it as himself; he represented no one but himself. Moreover, the king might summon whom he liked for this purpose or fail to summon anyone at all, though this was a risky practice. From this perspective, double majesty denotes a society lacking overall integration and self-consciousness. The web of personal dependencies did not add up to an integrated society. The shared sense of status of the warrior caste was the limit, and the point of reference here was not the community but ancient propriety. Politics did not involve the relationship of all men, one to another, and their relation in turn to government, but the relations of one or another status to what came to be called the king's majesty.

Having surveyed thus briefly some of the general contours of medieval society and politics, in all their crudity and violence, it is only just to observe that this was but one side of the coin. Equally important for a balanced understanding of operative thought is an appreciation of the positive motives which supplied the springs of action and the binding power of obligation. We have been concerned with the form of an intensely personal conception of authority and obligation. That these ideas were crude simply admits of no doubt. But that is not to say that the motives involved were base, nor that they were invariably self-seeking. Personal allegiance was entirely appropriate under the circumstances: a technologically backward, volatile, and violent society. By itself, however, this implies nothing about the dignity or indignity of motives. On one level, it is evident that these relationships sprang from a desperate need for security in a thoroughly disjointed environment. They were, in fact, the sole remaining refuge for some shred of personal security, tenuous perhaps, but for that very reason carrying an intense emotional charge. Consider this striking expression from eighth century England.

He who experiences it knows how dire a comrade is grief to the man who has few beloved confidants. The track of exile holds him, not twisted gold, a frozen heart, not the riches of the earth. He recalls the retainers and the receiving of treasure, how in his youth his generous lord entertained him with feasting; joy has all passed away. For this he knows who must long forgo the counsel of his dear lord, when sorrow and sleep together lay hold on the wretched solitary man, that it seems in his mind that he is embracing and kissing his liege lord, and laying hands and head on his knee, as sometimes in days of yore he enjoyed the bounty from the throne. Then the friendless man awakens; he sees before him the dark waves, the seabirds dipping, and spreading their wings, frost and snow falling, mingled with hail. Then the wounds of his heart are the heavier, in grief for his loved one. Sorrow is renewed . . .[56]

So the root of obligation was personal affection, nor should this side of the matter be underrated simply because it appears in a period not only given to much violence but exulting in it, characterized by a ferocity which jars modern sensibilities. All that is true, but it does not alter the fact that men felt themselves bound by affection. This love was powerful enough to overcome not only mere expediency but life itself, for themes very frequently encountered are those of death met out of loyalty and of the unhappy man voluntarily submitting to exile to follow his lord. "Quickly was Offa hewn down in the battle; yet he had accomplished what he promised his prince, as erstwhile he boasted with his giver of rings, that they should both ride to the stronghold, unscathed to their home, or fall amid the host, perish of wounds on the field of battle. Near the prince he lay low, as befits a thane." [57] Thus was a battle of tenth century England celebrated. It gives expression to an ideal which Tacitus clearly admired in the first century. "On the field of battle it is a disgrace to the chief to be surpassed in valour by his companions, to the companions not to come up to the valour of their chief. As for leaving a battle alive after your chief has fallen, *that* means lifelong infamy and shame. To defend and protect him, to put down one's own acts of heroism to his credit — that is what they really mean by 'allegiance.' " Similarly, Beowulf says, " 'Death for each earl is better than a life of shame.' " [58]

To be sure, there is a more sober side to all this. The very multiplication of injunctions and exhortations to honor one's lord suggests that all was not well. Indeed, much of the evidence is negative as well, for while extolling the merit of personal loyalty the moral is pointed with examples of cowardice and betrayal.[59] Yet, in the last analysis, these facts do not invalidate the ideal any more nor any less than they ever do. Politically the essential point is to recognize the sharpness of the alternative introduced by the idea of obligation grounded in personal affection. To the Roman, with his, ideally, acute sense of civic loyalty, the Germanic view of obligation seemed utterly perfidious.[60] For personal loyalty may easily mean following one's lord into treason, or rather what the sophisticated Roman saw as treason and the barbarian saw as his highest duty. It was precisely this incomprehension of public loyalty which was to be the striking feature of operative political thought in the Middle Ages.

The establishment of the successor kingdoms was essentially a process in which the Germanic war band became institutionalized and settled on the land. These societies were compounds of Roman and Germanic ideas and institutions from the start and were thus something different from either. That is why it is futile in the last resort to ask whether they were essentially Roman or essentially Germanic. What is not in doubt is that they were structured in terms of both lordship and kinship; that they were societies necessarily geared for violence and war, sharply aristocratic and hierarchical, and still relatively primitive. At this stage it will be helpful to turn to a specific case, that of the Anglo-Saxons, to examine these features and some of the important changes which occurred in Anglo-Saxon ideas.

It seems probable that the Anglo-Saxon settlement, like other continental successor kingdoms, was primarily an adventure carried off by war leaders and their followers.[61] In any case, whatever the condition and number of "free peasants," about whom we know virtually nothing, the main point is that Anglo-Saxon politics amounted to the relations between kings and aristocratic warriors, the internal relations, as it were, of a cluster of expanded retinues. Apparently the rewards in land, together with political superiority over the base persons who worked it, which were given by a king to his companions were at first held by precarious tenure: contingent upon service and not available to pass hereditarily to a man's heirs.[62]

The barbarians, in other words, had no native idea of permanent tenure or inheritance of land.[63] But the understandable inclination, so ably portrayed by Marc Bloch, to convert precarious into hereditary title set in swiftly.[64] The ideas employed for this purpose were derived from a debased form of Roman law, the Vulgar law, and the vehicle was the Roman Church. The conversion of the English peoples to Christianity thus came to have important side effects on the available store of political ideas. The Church obviously required an enduring form of tenure if it was to establish permanent institutions. The result was the introduction of what was called in England bookland. The term referred to land awarded by the king in perpetuity, with full right of the owner to dispose of it freely. Initially, booked estates were held only by the Church, but laymen quickly realized the desirability of holding land by the book rather than merely on "loan" from the king or other lord. The extension of book right to the warrior class was thus instrumental in the creation of a landed aristocracy, a fact whose importance it would be difficult to overestimate.[65]

It is essential to recognize too that this was not only a question of the evolution of proprietary ideas.[66] For it involved the ground of the political power of the nobility and an implicit collision of principles. Hereditary tenure runs directly counter to the idea that the bestowal of reward is the prerogative of the king. Moreover, both perspectives could be and were defended from the same point of departure: the ideal of the comitatus. This development was the sociological basis of double majesty throughout the Middle Ages. For kings continued to assert their prerogative of reward, while barons insisted on holding those rewards as of right. The terms in which such arguments were carried on changed a good deal, but the issue itself, as well as the heart of techniques of justification, remained remarkably stable. A wonderful example of this occurred several centuries later. In the last decades of the thirteenth century, King Edward I undertook a systematic inquiry into the legitimacy of landholders' titles to estates and franchises. When one of the great magnates of the kingdom, Earl Warenne, was summoned to court to show by what warrant he held his estates, he appeared, holding a rusty sword aloft, and made this speech: "Here my lords, here is my warrant! My ancestors came with William the Bastard and conquered their lands with the sword, and I shall defend them with the sword against anyone who tries to usurp them. The king did not conquer and subject the land by himself, but our forefathers were partners and co-workers with him." [67] Context and personnel had been profoundly altered by the Norman Conquest, but the assumptions and rationale remained.

The development of a stable landed aristocracy was the setting for the politics of the Anglo-Saxon king and his folk, his noble warrior companions.[68] On this subject we have a considerable body of evidence suggesting that the central political idea of the Anglo-Saxon period was kingly rule in conjunction with the counsel of his witan, literally one who knows, in fact his principal warriors and, after the conversion, leading members of the ecclesiastical hierarchy. That this was regarded as the appropriate method for considering politically important matters hardly admits of doubt. King Aethelbert of Kent, we are told, "introduced, with the consent of his counsellors, a code of law framed on the Roman pattern, which was written in English, and remains in force to this day." In 627 the pagan King Edwin faced the question whether to accept Christianity. Accordingly he "summoned a council of the wise men, and asked each in turn his opinion of this new faith . . ." [69] Among these early statements, perhaps the most interesting occurs as a prefatory remark to the laws of Alfred. It says in part: "Now I, King Alfred, have collected these laws, and have given orders for copies to be made of many of those which our predecessors observed and which I myself approved of. But many of those I did not approve of I have annulled, by the advice of my councillors, while [in other cases] I have ordered changes to be introduced." It continues, "I, then, Alfred, King of the West Saxons, have shown these to all my councillors, and they have declared that it met with the approval of all, that they should be observed." [70] In short, we may readily agree with P. H. Blair that the "close concern of the king's council with the promulgation of laws can be observed throughout the Anglo-Saxon period." [71] On the other hand, however, this consultative ideal and practice ought not to be unduly inflated. For, in the first place, such meetings were casual in the extreme. Indeed, of the period before the tenth century, it has been rightly observed that they were "scarcely distinguishable from the *comitatus* of Tacitus." [72] It is true that in the later period the original multiplicity of kingdoms had been welded into a single kingdom, and that the increased complexity of government had produced systematic administration on a territorial basis.[73] Yet even in the reign of Edward the Confessor (1042–1066), the frequency of meeting, the issues considered, and the persons consulted remained uncertain and highly fluid.[74]

From this perspective, double majesty refers to the idea and practice of government in terms of cooperation between the king and his folk, as long as the word folk is understood in the aristocratic and military sense appropriate to the period.[75] Viewed from another angle, however, double majesty refers to the fact that very extensive areas of political and legal life were simply not organized on a general or public basis. This side of the matter is best seen in the operation of the legal system. The Anglo-Saxon legal outlook turned on two main principles: blood and status. The notion of blood achieved its most vivid expression in the feud, and that of status in the varying grades of worth associated with individual men. In approaching these topics, it is essential to bear in mind that the categories and assumptions of modern legal systems do not correspond to those of the Middle Ages.[76] Just as was the case with the political structure, the legal system was a primitive one. It was largely procedural in character, highly ritualized, and driven primarily by self-help rather than public prosecution. The "courts" kept no records, heard no lawyers, and weighed no evidence, nor was there any police force to execute orders. Indeed, in the earliest laws there is no mention of courts at all. It is also important to notice that the seemingly obvious division of offenses into criminal and civil causes was not a part of Anglo-Saxon legal equipment.

Then what are the rules set out in the law codes? In great part they are more or less detailed price lists, establishing the amounts of compensation to be paid for various offenses. The basis of this scheme was the notion of wergeld, that is, "man-price," which was certainly one of the most fundamental ideas among the barbarian peoples. A man's wergeld was the amount of compensation due to his kindred or his lord if he was killed, and these amounts were graded according to rank. Thus a man might be referred to as a 1200-shilling man, or 600, 200, and so on. This rating was the key index in Anglo-Saxon society, since all sorts of liabilities and privileges were expressed as multiples or fractions of a person's wergeld. Much of the space in the law codes is taken up with amazingly detailed tariffs for personal injury. Thus, for example, the code of Aethelbert says: "If an eye is knocked out, 50 shillings shall be paid as compensation." [77] Each finger was evaluated separately: 20 shillings for striking off a thumb, and 3 for the nail; but 9 for the forefinger,

4 for the middle finger, 6 for the ring finger, and 11 for the little finger.[78] Each fingernail was assessed at one shilling.[79] The problem of theft was central, and it was dealt with in the same way, though a thief was more likely to lose his life. At the level of compensation, however, the principle was to assess multiples of the value of the stolen property. Thus, theft of "God's property and the Church's shall be compensated twelve fold; a bishop's property eleven fold; a priest's property nine fold; a deacon's property six fold; a clerk's property three fold." [80] But not everything could be compounded for. Treachery to one's lord involved the death penalty. "And we have declared with regard to one who is accused of plotting against his lord, that he shall forfeit his life if he cannot deny it, or [if he does deny it and] is afterwards found guilty in the three fold ordeal." [81] Like severity was the penalty for a thief caught in the act, for arson, housebreaking, slaying by witchcraft, or manifest murder.[82] Similarly the repeating offender might be executed, or, according to the laws of Cnut, "his eyes are to be put out and his nose and ears and upper lip cut off, or his scalp removed, whichever of these is then decreed by those with whom the decision rests; thus one can punish and at the same time preserve the soul." [83] The author of Cnut's laws was Archbishop Wulfstan,[84] and in this ghastly mutilation as an alternative we find the attempt of the Church to mitigate punishment. It is certainly true that the men of the Middle Ages were liberal with the death penalty. Wulfstan's efforts are to be detected elsewhere. Thus Ethelred's code says that "it is the decree of our lord and his councillors that Christian men are not to be condemned to death for all too small offences. But otherwise life-sparing punishments are to be devised for the benefit of the people, and God's handiwork and his own purchase which he paid for so dearly is not to be destroyed for small offences." [85] Apparently, however, these efforts came to very little.

Procedures of determining guilt were at once simple and complex: simple in conception, but complex in variation and ritual. A number of points illustrated by these techniques are especially interesting from the perspective of political ideas. The first thing to be noticed, as was mentioned earlier, is the extent to which the preservation of order was removed from the public level and made dependent upon those great men who were the king's companions. This is reflected in the sharply hierarchical cast of trial processes, with their evident bias for the aristocrat. Again, one sees the mutual penetration and assimilation of the organizing principles of loyalty to kin and lord. Trial procedure and execution of the findings turned on three ideas: the oath, the ordeal or judgment of God (*judicium dei*), and blood vengeance. If a man stood accused but failed to appear in court, he would lose. It then became his responsibility and that of his kindred to pay the appropriate compensation, on pain of his being declared an outlaw, which would mean that he could be killed by anyone and recourse to vengeance would be illegal. On the other hand, if he chose to go to court, the method of replying to an accusation was to deny it and produce compurgators, oath helpers, whose role was to swear that the oath of the accused was true. If the defendant satisfied the law in regard to the number of oath-helpers required to answer to the charge, he was free. The number required varied according to the gravity of the charge. But that is not all. For the value of a man's oath varied with his rank, computed in terms of the wergeld. Thus in Wihtred's laws a king or a bishop need give no oath, for his word alone was enough.[86] A priest, on the other hand, must swear, while an ordinary clerk or commoner needed three compurgators of his class.[87]

A man could not always produce the required number of compurgators to satisfy the law, however, and there were also circumstances in which the right to produce an oath was denied. That right was foreclosed, for example, to a frequently accused man or one regarded as suspicious, to a convicted thief or perjurer, or a thief caught in the act.[88] In these cases, the defendant had either to pay the penalty or go to ordeal, and among the Anglo-Saxons the popular forms of ordeal were hot iron and water, either cold or hot.[89] This aspect of the proceedings was administered by the Church. Prior to the ordeal itself, according to the laws of Aethelstan, anyone who is to undergo it "shall come three days before to the mass-priest who is to consecrate it, and he shall feed himself on bread and water and salt and herbs before he proceeds thither, and he shall attend mass on each of the three days. And on the day he has to go to the ordeal, he shall make an offering and attend communion; and then before he goes to the ordeal, he shall swear an oath that according to the public law he is innocent of the accusation." [90] At this point, the accused was ready to be formally adjured by the priest, as follows: "I charge you by the Father and the Son and by the Holy Ghost, and by your Christianity which you have received, and by the holy cross on which God suffered, and by the holy gospel and the relics which are in this church, that you should not dare to partake of this sacrament nor to go to the altar if you did this of which you are accused, or know who did it." [91] It was the privilege of the accuser to specify which ordeal the accused should undergo.[92] In the ordeal of hot iron, he had to carry a pound of hot iron nine feet. His hand was then bandaged, and if after three days it had not festered he was declared innocent. In the ordeal of hot water, the accused thrust his hand to the wrist in water heated "so hot as to boil" and brought out a stone; the result was determined as in the ordeal of hot iron. These two forms were conducted in the Church itself, under the watchful eyes of supporters of each party.[93] The ordeal of cold water had to be held outside, since it involved throwing the accused into a body of water, God having been asked to reject the guilty. This meant that if the accused party floated he was guilty.[94]

So in the area which might roughly be called criminal justice Anglo-Saxon law was certainly crude and marked by ferocity. But it is more important to underline the wholly procedural role of the court and trial technique. The court merely provided a framework in which men might undertake to settle their quarrels by mechanical means. Compurgators were not asked to testify as to the facts at issue, but to swear to the validity of another's oath. Trial by ordeal, of course, meant that the responsibility of a finding was left to the Deity. Even more interesting, however, is the fact that dependence upon oath helping as a means of clearing an accused man threw the door open to the man of standing and power, for he was unlikely to have any difficulty producing the oath. The case would obviously be far different for a humbler man or one regarded with suspicion by his neighbors, however poor the pretext.[95] In this latter connection, we have an account of an extremely interesting civil suit.[96] A man named Helmstan held a booked estate, a place called Fonthill, but was subjected to challenge because he was debarred from producing the oath. He was a known thief, and this meant he was not oath worthy. The fascinating thing about this case is not that Helmstan retained possession of his estate in the end, but how the issue was settled. To save his estate, he managed to persuade a prominent man, Ealdorman Ordlaf, to intervene. Through Ordlaf's influence with the king, arbitration was arranged, and the finding was that Helmstan's title was good. But this did not end the matter. It meant only that now Helmstan could try to find enough oath helpers to make his case. In order to do this he had to appeal to Ordlaf again. When Helmstan promised that after his death he would turn over Fonthill to Ordlaf, Ordlaf supplied the compurgators and Helmstan succeeded. As Eric John points out, it is clear "that a man only got his rights if a fair number of the local thegns . . . would stand by him." [97]

Anglo-Saxon legal ideas thus exemplify in a most striking way the immense importance of lordship and the steeply vertical design of the social setting. As was remarked earlier, however, medieval politics was not organized exclusively in terms of the idea of lordship. The other great principle was that of kinship, and despite the prominence of lordship, it did not entirely supplant kinship as a political force. In fact, there is abundant evidence of the persistence of kinship throughout the Middle Ages.[98] There is good reason, indeed, to attribute to it a significant place in politics, for as Dorothy Whitelock has insisted, "fear of the kindred was originally the main force for the maintenance of order, and to the end Anglo-Saxon law regarded homicide as the affair of the kindred . . ." [99] What men feared was the blood feud, and it was this threat that supplied the sanction lying behind the idea of compensation.[100] On the other hand, however, there can be little doubt that kinship came to be subordinated to lordly allegiance. Before turning to the blood feud, then, it is necessary to consider its setting in a society organized primarily in terms of personal loyalty and characterized by more complex patterns of rule than the minimal arrangements described by Caesar and Tacitus. For despite the longevity of some of the principles of blood vengeance, it also underwent changes which are important clues to the character of the larger alterations of social structure.

It was suggested earlier that a fruitful approach to the political life of the successor kingdoms is afforded by the history of the comitatus in the Heroic Age, and the persistence well beyond it of the outlook generated in that period. Anthropological theory suggests that the blood feud is also a characteristic element of contemporary primitive societies with governmental and legal conceptions broadly similar to those of the period before the establishment of the successor kingdoms.[101] But the successor kingdoms were more complex, in the sense that the social order had a settled agrarian basis. One might expect to find the role of the feud sharply attenuated. In fact, however, we have it from as great an authority as Marc Bloch that the "Middle Ages, from beginning to end, and particularly the feudal era, lived under the sign of private vengeance." [102] What must be noticed is that private vengeance may refer to prosecuting a feud in the name of one's lord as well as a kinsman, and in fact the coexistence of the two and the tendency to assimilate them is evident throughout the early Middle Ages. This does not mean, however, that the various forms of private warfare should all be lumped into a single category. Certainly this would not be a useful approach at the level of empirical analysis of social systems, for the result would be to equate vital elements of quite different social orders. Taken in the general sense, private warfare still existed in the sixteenth century, for the early Tudors were obliged to campaign against livery and maintenance. It is surely worthwhile to acknowledge similarities, as in the present case, for they are symptomatic of premodern societies in various stages of change and development. Equally, however, there seems abundant reason to distinguish a society like that of the early Germans, so simple that its primary foundation is kinship, from others in which kinship has a competitor or in which it represents the solidarity of a great landed family. The chief task therefore is to draw distinctions.

There are both important differences and important similarities in Germanic societies if one compares the account of Tacitus with what can be learned of the successor kingdoms. In the simplest societies kinship is the chief if not the sole bond between men, and feud represents the only reliable method of securing redress. Among the early Germans, Tacitus tells us, a "man is bound to take up the feuds as well as the friendships of father or kinsman. But feuds do not continue unreconciled. Even homicide can be atoned for by a fixed number of cattle or sheep, and the satisfaction is received by the whole family." [103] Unquestionably, however, the triumph of the comitatus resulted in a sharp reduction of the political importance of the kindred. For it involved a form of leadership and coercion extraneous to blood relationships. This is certainly enough to warrant a distinction between a stage organized primarily in terms of kinship and one based on the heroic ethic of the comitatus. In Tacitus the two stand side by side, and only hindsight enables us to focus attention on the comitatus. Similarly, these stages ought to be distinguished from the settled agricultural foundation of the early successor kingdoms, with their tendency to convert precarious to hereditary tenure of land. The social significance of the transformation to hereditary tenure was enormous. Preoccupation with family lands and family loyalty reasserted itself vigorously in these circumstances. But in such comparatively stable conditions, the patterns and aims of conflict and cooperation turned on different principles. It was the possession of a landed estate that made the difference, together with the valuable object lesson in political power which the great men of the Church supplied to the landed warrior. The Germanic peoples had no notion of perpetual tenure, and even when they had been taught its value, they had still to learn the disastrous effects of partible inheritance. Their inclination was to divide the inheritance among the survivors, and obviously an estate, or for that matter a kingdom, would not last long this way. The answer to the problem was the idea of primogeniture, though it did not appear until the later Middle Ages. For practical purposes, however, the idea of book right was enough to secure the endurance of landed wealth. This was the foundation of political power, and eventually the personal military prowess of the holder was no longer decisive. Landed wealth also called for a difference in technique, for shrewd marriage alliances led not only to obvious political reinforcement, but also to the linking and amalgamation of lands. Thus marriage policy became a political instrument of the first importance. But consolidated and durable power in land meant that the forms of the feud were profoundly altered: blood feud became private vengeance, which shaded off imperceptibly into organized private warfare. The motive of personal revenge in this context is certainly not to be excluded, but the central aim was the acquisition of more land.

It cannot be denied that competition for land was the chief domestic expression of political instability. But it would be just as shortsighted not to recognize the increased solidity of later medieval monarchies by comparison with the earlier period. Following the suggestions advanced by a number of anthropologists,[104] it may be argued that intermarriage among the great had a positive as well as a negative effect. That is, while the obvious surface tendency of a society dominated by a landed aristocracy is bitter and dangerous competition, it has also the less obvious advantage of providing both a motive for and an avenue to reconciliation. Thus conflict would be dampened because family members belonged to other great families. Moreover, in England the idea of primogeniture came to be followed more systematically than on the Continent.[105] This meant that the younger sons of great families were often compensated for exclusion from title and estate by a start in another career, perhaps the Church, the law, or commercial enterprise. Here again the effect would be to reinforce overlapping interests and the channels to amicable, or at least peaceful, reconciliation of divergent interests.

However this may be, it is clear that the strength of kinship ties was very much a variable quality throughout the period, and that it was never able to achieve superiority over lordship. From the early Middle Ages on, young warriors had learned to look to great men and especially to their king for rewards in land. An account of the remarkable popularity of kingship will be offered in a later chapter. Here the point is to notice the extremely elementary character of the bond of lordship. It made its first successful appearance in European history when the Germanic tribes began to break up under the pressure of deprivation and attack by other barbarians, as well as by the Romans with their immensely advanced standards. Willing, indeed eager, submission to lordship recurred on a grand scale as a response to the several new waves of barbarian invasions in the ninth and tenth centuries. In these circumstances, the "very ties of kinship . . . yielded place to the obligations of personal dependence." [106] All this certainly suggests that lordship is a fundamental tie between men, and one peculiarly appropriate to periods of intense insecurity and profound social disturbance. Recurrent episodes of this kind dominated medieval history until the eleventh century, so that the principles of kinship and lordship coexisted. But there was a great difference between the two at the level of political values, for the ties of kinship involved an element of equality in an otherwise radically hierarchical setting. The killing of any kinsman involved the duty of seeking compensation, if necessary by blood vengeance, and here distinctions of rank were not paramount. But coexistence involved the possibility of stress or outright collision, though there is little doubt in the long run about the superiority of the obligation to one's lord. Thus the laws of Alfred in ninth century England declare that "a man may fight on behalf of one who is related to him by blood, if he is attacked unjustly, except it be against his lord. This we do not permit." [107] Not even the conversion of the Germanic peoples to Christianity undermined this conception of loyalty. On the contrary, the bond of the oath was sanctified by the Church. No less a man than Archbishop Wulfstan could say: ". . . all that ever we do out of just loyalty to our lord, we do it all to our own great benefit, for assuredly God will be gracious to him who is duly loyal to his lord." [108] A classic case of the relation between kinship and lordship is reported in the *Anglo-Saxon Chronicle.* It is well worth close examination because it exemplifies several of the most important features of the medieval outlook extremely well.

The chronicler says that Cynewulf, and in one version his councillors, "deprived" Sigeberht of his kingdom, confining him to Hampshire. Sigeberht remained there until he killed a faithful ealdorman of his. This provoked an act of revenge and Sigeberht was killed. Later in his career, Cynewulf wanted to expel a prince, called Cyneheard, from his kingdom. Now this Cyneheard was the brother of the former king, Sigeberht. Cyneheard learned that king Cynewulf, with an understandably small retinue, was visiting a mistress, surprised him in his dalliance, and killed him. Cyneheard then offered the king's men their lives and money as well if they would join him, but they all fought to the death, "except one Welsh hostage, and he was badly wounded." The next day, a group of the dead king's warriors arrived on the scene. According to the beautifully compressed account of the chronicler, Cyneheard "offered them their own choice of money and land if they would grant him the kingdom, and they told them that kinsmen of theirs were with them who would not desert them; and then they replied that no kinsman was dearer to them than their lord, and they never would follow his slayer; and then they offered to let their kinsmen depart unharmed. And they replied that the same had been offered to their comrades who had been with the king; then they said that they themselves did not care for this 'any more than your comrades who were slain with the king.' And they went on fighting around the gates until they forced their way in and slew the prince and the men who were with him . . ." [109] The preeminence of the bond of lordship is clear in this remarkable story: kinsman fought kinsman in the name of loyalty to lordship. But this is not all. The element of blood vengeance is a part of it. Moreover, the evident importance of the support of such warriors in succession to the kingship deserves emphasis.

Nevertheless, kinship and vendetta remained very prominent features of Anglo-Saxon society, and they serve as a sharp reminder of the limitations of early medieval government. The prosecution of vengeance was regarded both as a duty and a right, and there is nothing to suggest that anyone thought of it as anything less. It is true that both kings and the Church sought to regularize the feud and to mitigate its effects by encouraging the payment of compensation. Thus King Alfred (871–899) decreed that a man might not seek vengeance until he exhausted certain procedures designed to enhance the possibility of composition.[110] King Edmund (939–946), who was himself stabbed to death, laid down a special body of laws on the blood feud, the principle of which was the attempt to restrict vengeance to the slayer alone, rather than to one or more of his kin. The rest of his code sets out a system of procedures to be followed when composition is being arranged, and these show what a touchy affair it could be. Contact with the slain man's kindred was to be made through some third party whose task was to arrange a safe-conduct. Then the slayer was to meet the kindred and make his pledge to pay the appropriate wergeld.[111] But none of this makes feud as such illegal, and indeed that style of thought not only persisted but was even employed as a model for artificial associations. When men bound themselves together in fraternal associations, they made their brotherhoods similar to blood relationships. Thus the guild of thegns established in tenth century Cambridge rested on an agreement by which "each was to give to the others an oath of true loyalty." Among other things, this meant that "if anyone kill a guild-brother, nothing other than eight pounds is to be accepted as compensation. If the slayer scorn to pay the compensation, all the guildship is to avenge the guild-brother and all bear the feud." [112]

Certainly the blood feud survived throughout the Anglo-Saxon period, and even beyond. Sometimes feuds lasted over extraordinary lengths of time, such as the one launched between Earl Uhtred of Northumbria and a great man of Yorkshire, called Thurbrand, who killed the earl. This feud dragged on for no less than three generations.[113] Despite the persistence of the feud and the proliferation of its forms, however, the very fact of artificial groups to prosecute revenge suggests the inadequacy of kinship in achieving personal security, and there is much to reinforce this impression. After the murder of King Edward, the *Anglo-Saxon Chronicle* relates, his "earthly kinsmen would not avenge him," but it adds that God had amply done so.[114] Archbishop Wulfstan expressed the point more generally. "Now too often a kinsman does not protect a kinsman any more than a stranger, neither a father his son, nor sometimes a son his own father, nor one brother another . . ." [115] This may be, of course, only the reflection of a moralist on a failure of familial duty,

garnished by a dose of the medieval tendency to believe that the past
was better. It is more likely that the question was one of power, of
inability to cope with the established position of the great on any
other basis than joining them. Moreover, it seems clear that the
conditions of territorial settlement and the diversity of opportunity,
location, and occupation it involved would be enough to damage
clan organization severely.

In sum, it is clear that the principle of loyalty to one's lord survived as the central organizing principle of medieval society, for
even the idea of loyalty to one's kindred tended to be subordinated
to and modeled upon it. Thus what might be called an elaborate,
domesticated version of the comitatus and its heroic ethic proved
to be the central ingredient of medieval politics. In the several
phases of Anglo-Saxon politics, which culminated in a single kingdom organized on a systematic territorial basis, the standards of personal allegiance and government with the counsel of the leading
men remained at the heart of English political assumptions. The
political system succeeded in achieving order, but it was certainly
volatile and susceptible to recurrent episodes of profound instability. The political ideas involved, which I have summed up in the
term double majesty, had their root in the fact that king and folk
lacked any sense of political loyalty beyond the cardinal bond of
personal attachment. This precluded the separate and distinctly
political focus I have been calling civic consciousness.

The Middle Ages certainly do not represent the only time and
place in which civic allegiance has been absent. It was precisely this,
for example, that Aristotle pointed out in contrasting the earlier
stages of Greek politics, which had been organized in terms of kinship and lordship, with the polis. People associated chiefly in terms
of trade and war, he says, cannot be considered to have reached a
genuinely political stage. This is not to be ascribed, he goes on to
say, "to any lack of contiguity in such an association. The members
of a group so constituted might come together on a single site; but
if that were all — if each still treated his private house as if it were
a state, and all of them still confined their mutual assistance to action
against aggressors (as if it were only a question of a defensive alliance) — if, in a word, the spirit of their intercourse were still the
same after their coming together as it had been when they were
living apart — their association . . . could not be deemed by any
accurate thinker to be a polis." [116] Aristotle's aim, of course, was to

contrast this with the peculiar essence of the polis and the political virtues through which it could achieve not simply organization but what he called the good life. But the antique conception of final fidelity to the city died with pagan Rome, and medieval Europe replaced it with two entirely different ideas: devotion to the city of God, and the idea that has been explored here, the personal allegiance of the medieval warrior to his lord. It is important, for comparative purposes, to distinguish these quasi-political loyalties not only from the ancient ideal but also from bureaucratic loyalty, a kind of institutional and impersonal attachment that is generated by the civil servant. For the outlook of the lay magnate centered on personal loyalty, his own status, and the standards and practices of a social order grounded, so he was inclined to think, in the immemorial past of his kind. He conceived of his own status and its privileges as validated by the only standard he could comprehend, the myth of antiquity. The shared outlook of the great magnates gave rise to consultative ideas and practices which constituted at least an intermittently effective counterpoise to kingly power, and it was this shifting, uneasy balance that was at the heart of the politics of double majesty.

three The Sanctity and Utility of Kings

It has been well said that in the Middle Ages "thought on the structure of government revolved, from the beginning, around the king." [1] Indeed, medieval kings were indispensable men, and for that reason they were truly more than men. At all levels of political thought, the principle of monarchical rule was fastened upon from the beginning of the Middle Ages and faithfully upheld for a thousand years and more. In fact, it is impossible to speak of the medieval monarch without appealing to the language of religion, to the language of devotion and faith. Certainly it would be a mistake to take this as proof of Christian piety or of political tranquility, for often enough the reverse would be more nearly accurate. The Middle Ages were frequently troubled times, beset by barbarian ferocity, disease, ignorance, and poverty, and all these meant a life too often filled with violence. Yet it remains true that kingship survived and flourished, despite long periods of weakness and the deeply divisive ambitions of lordly men who were more than a match for kingly power. Kings were overpowered, deposed, and murdered, but this never involved rejection of the principle of kingship. The Middle Ages knew no republicans. James Harrington put the point beautifully in the seventeenth century: "A nobility strikes not at the throne without which they cannot subsist, but at some king they do not like . . ." [2] The same observation has been made of kingship among contemporary primitives.[3] It is as if all the social imponderables, all the perturbation and anxiety involved in simple societies hovering constantly, as they do, on the edge of hunger, violence, and war, were compensated for by the idea of stable kingship. The only visible alternative in the European Middle Ages would have been collapse into baronial anarchy, and not even the barons wanted that. At bottom, it seems likely that an unconscious anxiety about the endurance of the social order, as well as a largely unexpressed sense of its enormous value, is the psychological truth lying behind the adulation of kings.

However this may be, the fact of sacred kingship is not in doubt. The problem is to try to account for the resiliency of kingly rule. During the Middle Ages there were two main reasons for it, and though they were quite different in character they reinforced each other most effectively. On the one hand, nearly all men firmly believed that a king was an extraordinary person. He was a man, to be sure, but medieval men would not have added, "even as you and I." For a king was quite literally taken to be a presentment of God on earth. When men said that the king ruled by the grace of God, that he was the vicar of God on earth, it was not just court rhetoric, not mere politesse, as it often had been in the later Roman Empire.[4] They meant it, and they acted upon those views. But there was more than these formal views, which were linked more or less systematically to Christian theology. There were also powerful sentiments attached to kingship which did not enjoy so august a standing. But this lack did not deprive them of their force or their political value. Reigning dynasties were surrounded with a rich and complex aura of the miraculous.[5] These attitudes were expressed in traditional legends and in the belief that kings possessed the power to heal certain diseases by a mere touch of the royal hand.

Moreover, these attitudes concerning the sanctity of kings did not exist in a social vacuum. Kings were also eminently useful. Their utility consisted in two major sorts of services. To begin with, the king was the capstone of the social order. His exalted position supplied at once a principle of cohesion in a diffuse society and a mode of justification for its hierarchical ordering. The rationale for the privileged position of the baronage was that it derived from the needs of society and the grace of the lord king. Those needs were military, governmental, economic, and social. Further, insofar as there was a single focus of interest and loyalty, however desultory and tenuous, that focus was the king. Secondly, the king was in his own person the apex of the legal order. It was to the royal justices in the first instance, but perhaps also to the king himself, that quarreling magnates turned to seek resolutions of their conflicting claims to land, jurisdiction, and other privileges. Normally this resort to the acknowledged fountain of justice was preferable to violence between great men, since violence had the disadvantage of provoking retaliation and, hence, was only a temporary solution.

It is suggested, then, that these are the cardinal elements to be considered in accounting for the remarkable staying power of medieval monarchy, and the rest of the chapter will be devoted to following out these threads. Needless to say, setting them out analytically does them considerable violence. In fact they were interpenetrating and mutually interdependent. Because of the centrality of the kingly figure, much depended on the personal prowess and ability, at first purely physical or military, of the reigning monarch. Few events even in the early history of the English monarchy present so vivid a demonstration of this as the contrast between, for example, the fruitful reign of Edward I and the commotions under his hapless successor, or the similar contrast between the reigns of Elizabeth Tudor and the Stuarts who followed her. What is most important for present purposes is that the relationship of prince and people was not merely, or even primarily, one of conflict. Rather it was essentially one of mutual support and reinforcement. The complex lines of interdependence within the hierarchy supplied the crucial social cement, sometimes insufficiently adhesive to be sure, which held the medieval political order together. In the early fourteenth century the Bishop of Exeter put the matter very neatly when he observed that the "substance of the nature of the Crown is principally in the person of the king as head, and in the peers of the land as members . . . and in this way the Crown is so conditioned that it cannot be severed without division of the realm." [6]

It would be wrong to suppose that the profound addiction of medieval men to the institution of kingship was unusual. Whether their attachment to monarchy is a fit subject for reproach or applause, it was nothing if not persistent, nothing if not conformable to human experience. For of all the political institutions fashioned by men, the most common and durable is surely kingship. The earliest written records of the civilizations of the ancient Near East reveal kingship already full grown, already hedged by divinity. Indeed, the social ideas of pre-Greek antiquity revolved around one or another kind of divinized king.[7] Plato and even Aristotle extolled the merits of rule by the best man, if only one could find such a man. The extravagances of Hellenistic and Roman ruler worship are well known.[8] In short, there is no novelty in the idea of the Christian Middle Ages that a king is the representative of God on earth. To be sure, Christianity introduced a flavor and refinement of its own.

In particular, it overcame the outright divinization of the ruler himself. But to assume that the ideas centering on sacred kingship were
novel or specifically Christian would be a mistake.

The history of European kingship began as a pagan institution
when the leaders of Germanic war bands attained kingly status in
what had been the provinces of the Empire. Once again the barbarian foundations are well worth examination, for even when European kingship had developed much beyond this early form and
had been embellished and legitimized with a rich accretion of belief
and ritual, the tendency to cast it all in an ancestral Germanic
frame persisted. Indeed the endorsement and support of the Church
itself was assimilated to this customary mode of thought. Even late
medieval dynasties insisted upon their descent from Germanic ruling families. Thus the Capetian kings of France represented themselves as the genuine descendants of the Carolingians, and the latter,
in their turn, of the Merovingians. Nor was this the end of the impulse to indulge in the mythology of the continuity of royal blood.
The sixth century history of the Franks by Gregory of Tours links
the Merovingians with even earlier kingly stock, and Gregory's work
became the foundation of royal genealogical enthusiasm in medieval France. Again, the Anglo-Saxon kings of England boasted of
genealogies which ran back to a divine origin in the god Woden, and
the Norman dynasty of the Conqueror held itself to be the legitimate
successor to the Anglo-Saxon monarchy.[9] The evidence suggests,
then, a belief in the efficacy of blood which might be characterized
as spiritual Lamarckism. This is but one form of the very general
habit of mind encountered already; it is an important one, however, for all forms of argument addressed to problems of legitimacy
centered on the appeal to the traditions of the ancestors. For medieval men it was most important to have had the right ancestors,
especially in the case of a man aspiring to kingship. Throughout the
medieval period a king had two chief tasks, and both required the
possession of extraordinary personal gifts. The king was both a warrior and the giver of justice, understood not in a thin and merely
legal way but in the very full sense of assuring peace. Given the
turbulent circumstances of the age and the meager administrative
techniques of medieval government, these two roles tended to
amount to the same thing. For the administration of justice required
not so much judges and courts as a strong arm. Indeed, as late as the
latter half of the fifteenth century Sir John Fortescue argued that a

kingdom could not afford a female ruler because a woman would not be able to indulge in the bloodletting required in giving justice.[10] Now, the best way to raise the presumption that one possessed the requisite gifts was to establish the correct genealogy. This is surely why men took so much trouble with genealogies and, in fact, simply invented them if necessary, as Philip Augustus did when he insisted on his descent from Charlemagne.[11] So important was it to be able to identify bearers of the royal blood that the need gave rise to legends relating how this was to be accomplished. There was, for example, the popular belief very widespread in medieval Europe that a lost child, predestined for the throne, could be identified by the mark of a cross on his right shoulder. This was the sign of his lineage, but more, it was a promise of kingship.[12]

But to return to the barbarian war leader. It has been persuasively argued that these military chieftains, what continental scholars refer to as *Heerkönige,* represent a blend of the two distinct forms of leadership found among the early Germans.[13] What makes this suggestion attractive is that it supplies a link between the early rulers of the successor kingdoms and what little information we have on the idea of kingship among the Germans before that time. Apparently each of the Germanic peoples had one of the two kinds of chieftainship. Tacitus drew a distinction between the king and the war leader (*rex* and *dux*), but he does not tell us a great deal more than that. He says only that the Germans chose "their kings for their noble birth, their leaders for their valour." [14] The chief difference, it would seem, was that a king was chosen from a royal clan or royal stock (*stirps regia*), any member being eligible to succeed, and once chosen he held office for life. The dux, on the other hand, was chosen from among the "nobility," that is, the leading men (*principes*), but probably held his position only for the duration of a war. Both types were elective in some sense, though we have no details. E. A. Thompson has suggested, plausibly enough, that a candidate would be selected by the leading men and endorsed by the warriors in general.[15]

Unfortunately, little information is available to us concerning the two and a half centuries between Tacitus' writings and what remains of the historical works of Ammianus Marcellinus. Two things may be observed, however, with comparative safety. The first concerns the proliferation of the comitatus, a disintegrative tendency in the tribal structure that was noted in discussing Tacitus. In the period of the migrations and settlement the war bands apparently became the decisive social grouping among the barbarians. But, secondly, apart from the predominance of the comitatus and its leader, little else had altered.[16] The collapse of Roman government supplied the opportunity for these retinues to settle on the land and their duces to become kings. Whatever may have been the character of Germanic kingship before the successor kingdoms, there the king is an exalted dux. The question whether he or his predecessors possessed any divine or sacral powers has been much discussed, but the available evidence does not offer any support for such a view.[17] What is perfectly clear is that these were men of outstanding audacity and military prowess, men possessing *virtus*, and, as J. M. Wallace-Hadrill has observed, "it is surprising how quickly *virtus* will lead to *nobilitas*." [18] Many such leaders founded "royal" families, thus harking back to the primitive king, though it is true that most of these families turned out to be ephemeral. What matters, however, is that some, like that of the Merovingians, lasted. Here a further appeal to comparative work done in anthropology is illuminating. It has been suggested that the transition from a type of minimal government lacking coercive authority to a monarchically organized political system depends on two critical factors: a group of followers whose primary loyalty lies with their leader rather than with their kindred, and a belief in some hereditary sacred power in the leader.[19] The Germanic successor kingdoms illustrate this very well indeed, for they were founded on the king's retinue and the creation of a *stirps regia*.[20] Among the Germanic peoples, the element of hereditary sanctity is best summed up as the possession of royal blood.[21]

More particularly, the multiple kingdoms of the early centuries of Anglo-Saxon history seem to have rested on just such a combination of secular and sacred elements. For hereditary kingship was certainly the exclusive political form from the outset, though the line of succession was quite irregular. It is fair, nevertheless, to say that the one mandatory element was royal birth.[22] The basic historical document in Old English, the *Anglo-Saxon Chronicle*, begins with an extended genealogical recitation, which assumes the character of a kind of foundation myth. The author was clearly taking special care to assure the reader that the Anglo-Saxon settlement in Britain was linked by blood to the homeland, to its kings and the gods from whom they were descended. This lineage is adverted to again and again.[23] There can be little doubt that it was a kind of verbal ritual. Even so comparatively sophisticated a man as the Venerable Bede informs us that the leaders of the Anglo-Saxons, Hengist and Horsa, were descended from Woden, and from them derive the royal stock of many provinces.[24] Despite the establishment and obviously sacred character of the royal races of the Anglo-Saxons, however, it is necessary also to take account of the limitations of such a conception of kingship. For the Anglo-Saxons did not treat any particular king as irreproachable. On the contrary, what the evidence suggests is that it was the blood that mattered, not the individual king. They were quite willing to replace one with another, but always from the royal family. Or rather, nearly always, for one entry in the *Anglo-Saxon Chronicle* says that the Northumbrians "had repudiated their king Osberht and accepted Aella, a king not of royal birth (*ungecynde cyning*)." [25] But this choice of a king not of the royal family is just exceptional enough to prove the validity of the rule. Within the royal blood, however, all the evidence indicates that there was little else that can be regarded as normative. Succession was casual in the extreme. Thus it appears sometimes to have resulted from appointment by the preceding king.[26] But often the mode of succession is simply omitted from the account, and we are told only that someone has succeeded, often a son, but also brothers, nephews, and so on.[27] Deposition certainly occurred, though what it involved and how it was done we do not know. King Oswulf of Northumbria was killed by members of his household, and in 774 King Ahlred was expelled from the kingdom. Similarly, King Ethelred was killed by members of his court, and the West Saxon king, Sigeberht, was "deprived" of his kingdom on account of "unlawful actions," but we are told no more than that.[28] Thus what little can be learned does not suggest that particular kings were sacrosanct, but rather the royal stock as a whole.

Matters stood very differently in later centuries when, as Bloch has pointed out, there was little enough violence visited on kings, considering its prevalence in the period as a whole.[29] It seems clear that the role of the Church was a most important factor in this.[30] The Church was by no means responsible for the idea that kingship was a sacred institution. That notion the Germanic peoples had arrived at without assistance. What was added by the Church was a great heightening of the sanctity and dignity of the reigning king as such. The motives of churchmen are easily understood. What was required for the practice of the Christian life was political stability. What better method than the conversion and sanctification of kings? The greater part of Bede's history is devoted to this. He relates the conversion of barbarian kings, of their followers, and the great benefits that stemmed from this: victory and increase of territory.[31] To be sure, lasting conversion was not easily come by. Bede's work is studded with anguished accounts of relapse into paganism.[32] But he made it a point to underline the disastrous consequences of such defection.[33] Still, overcoming the bellicosity of the barbarian comitatus was far from easy. Thus the uncomprehending Bede tells us that King Sigeberht, who had been converted, "was murdered by his own kinsmen. This horrid crime was committed by two brothers, who on being asked their motive, had no answer to make except that they hated the king because he was too lenient towards his enemies, and too readily forgave injuries when offenders asked pardon." [34] Bede ought not to have been amazed, for his Christian king was setting aside the fundamental mores of his people. There can be little doubt, however, that the position of individual kings was greatly enhanced by the Church in the long run. This is reflected in the dictum in Ethelred's laws that "a Christian king is Christ's deputy in a Christian people . . ." [35] The relation of the original practice of choosing the king from the royal blood to Christian conceptions of stability is best expressed in these words of Abbot Aelfric. "No man can make himself king, but the people has the choice to choose as king whom they please; but after he is consecrated as king, he then has dominion over the people, and they cannot shake his yoke from their necks." [36] This is certainly a very far cry from the apparently dispassionate acceptance of deposition in the earlier period. It cannot be maintained that conversion to Christianity immediately accomplished the elevation of kingship above that level, for kings continued to be disposed of very rudely for some time to come. Just as surely, however, a trend had been initiated which culminated in really remarkable veneration of the king's person.

It should be noted, too, that this represented an important alteration in the original structure of double majesty. The fiction of "election" remained. Indeed it persisted until the idea of primogeniture, the automatic succession of the king's oldest son, was borrowed by the monarchy from baronial practice in the late thirteenth century.[37] This development occurred almost simultaneously in England and in France. Thus in 1272 Edward I succeeded Henry III without any of the customary fictions or delays, for at the time he was away from England on crusade. It was assumed that he had succeeded by the law of primogeniture. A similar succession took place in France in 1270. But even before this development, the increased sanctity of kingship had put double majesty on a new footing. Clearly such a king was a more formidable partner.

The key idea of medieval kingship is contained in Aelfric's observation on the importance of consecration. Much the fullest source of our information derives from the collection of ritual practices involved in accession to the throne: the oath, unction, coronation, and acclamation. The political significance of these ceremonies and the myth on which they rest is immense.[38] Indeed, sheer ceremonial is by no means politically negligible, for it is clearly important to emphasize the ruler's dignity and to underline the vast distance between a king and other men. But this was not the only function of the accession ritual. In the first place, these rituals reflected and validated the social order. They may be interpreted best, in other words, as affirmations of the validity and permanency of the social structure. Secondly, these ceremonies bestowed special powers on the king, which served the double function of removing him from the rest of the people, especially those of his own blood, and reinforcing his inherited powers. It is understandable enough, after all, that a ritual designation and transformation of the man selected should be performed in a political order in which the rule of succession is unsettled, except for the rule that it belonged to a dynasty. The entire performance rests on these two things: the appropriate ancestry, and the ritual individuation of the royal species.

If the accession rites are considered in this way, the emphasis on ancestry not only is understandable but its political significance is clear. The central point is that the whole matter turns on a political myth, the myth that links the social order to a supernatural order through the reigning king's descent from the gods. This line of descent validated the king's claim to rule, for it was his ancestors who had led the people to victory; it was Hengist and Horsa who had brought them from the Continent to their new home and established the social order. Thus it is no accident that a chronicler's account of a new accession becomes the occasion for the recitation of a genealogical myth. It will be worthwhile to quote one rather long passage, because it contains all the elements mentioned. According to the tradition of the Anglo-Saxons, the king of the Britons,

Vortigern, had invited the Angles to Britain to help him subdue the ferocious Picts. They came and "fought against the Picts and had victory wherever they came. Then they sent to Angel; ordered (them) to send more aid and to be told of the worthlessness of the Britons and of the excellence of the land. They then at once sent hither a larger force to help the others. These men came from three nations of Germany: from the Old Saxons, from the Angles, from the Jutes . . . Their leaders were two brothers, Hengest and Horsa; they were the sons of Wihtgils. Wihtgils was the son of Witta, the son of Wecta, the son of Woden; from this Woden sprang all our royal family and that of the peoples dwelling south of the Humber." [39] Here are the vital hereditary link with supernatural beings, the conquest of a new home, and inauguration of the royal clans. Moreover, the chroniclers never tire of making this point. The repetition is indeed monotonous, but to the people concerned it was vital. Each new recitation was, so to say, a reaffirmation of the whole.

It is not until after the conversion of the Anglo-Saxons to Christianity that we learn anything of full-blown accession ritual. No doubt the increased power of the kingship, together with more elaborate ceremonial, would have developed even had there been no conversion. For such developments have occurred too often to attribute a decisive role to Christianity. Nevertheless, there is good reason to think that churchmen were very helpful in the consolidation of kingship. Certainly they were intimately involved, and in due course they became the official custodians of the ritual aspects of political life, which were important and many. Their role in the administration of justice, as guardians of the ordeal, was mentioned earlier. Similarly, they were the administrators of the coronation service. The Christian kings of Europe came to be consecrated by bishops in a ceremony in which they were anointed with holy oil on the Biblical model of the anointing of Saul by Samuel.[40] This was the most important element of the service, for the unction signified that the king was God's chosen vessel. It was this that bestowed upon him his character as a compound or "mixed" person (*persona mixta*). It endowed him with a spiritual character, akin if not identical to that of the clerical gift of sacramental power, superadded to his temporal one. It "exalted the king above other men and bestowed upon him the divine gifts of glory, knowledge and fortitude . . ." [41] This could only reinforce popular belief in the sanctity of the king's blood.

The consecration of the king thus represents a true, if extraordinary, service of the kind van Gennep called *rites de passage,* for it accomplished the ritual transformation of the man chosen as king, removing him from one status to another.[42] Through it were accomplished his elevation, sanctification, and removal, as it were, from the merely profane sphere. But this was not the only aspect of the accession rites. From the tenth century on, at least, English kings were obliged to give an oath before they were crowned, and it is well worth examination. The new king was required to swear as follows.

> In the name of the Holy Trinity! I promise three things to the Christian people who are under my authority. Firstly, that true peace shall be assured to the church of God and to all Christian people in my dominions. Secondly, I forbid robbery and all unrighteous deeds by all classes of society. Thirdly, I promise and enjoin justice and mercy in the decision of all cases, in order that God, who liveth and reigneth, may in his grace and mercy be brought thereby to grant us all his eternal compassion.[43]

The oath was an integral part of the ritual whole, and its political importance lies in the fact that it represents as complete a normative statement on kingship as we have from the early Middle Ages. It is not a constitutional statement at all, as has sometimes been thought, but a standard, an indication of what kingship ought ideally to mean. Like the notion of ancestry, it was a political myth: an assertion of stability and tranquillity in a factual setting which defied them. Its function, so to speak, was to close the gap between the ideal and the real. It was not so much a promise, then, as an affirmation, or better, a wish, a dream.

The ceremony was capped with festivities, including the singing of special hymns, the *laudes regiae,* celebrating the king's exalted, Christlike status as vicar of God on earth.[44] A twelfth century chronicler preserved a remarkable account of the jubilation at the coronation of Aethelstan in 994. From this we learn that a " 'royal son prolonged a noble line, when a splendid gem illumined our darkness, the great Athelstan, glory of the country, way of rectitude, noble integrity, unable to be turned from the truth.' " Here hoped-for virtues are strung out almost like elements of the royal title. Then we are told that the young man had been properly schooled, and when he reached manhood "he practised the pursuit of arms at his father's order. Nor in this did the duties of war prove him remiss . . . then the young man's name was acclaimed in omen of the kingdom, that he might hold auspiciously the hereditary reins." Now comes the most interesting description of the coronation. "The nobles assemble and place the crown, pontiffs pronounce a curse on faithless men; fire glows among the people with more than wonted festivity, and by various signs they disclose their deepest feelings. Each burns to show his affection to the king; one fears, one hopes, high hope dispels fear; the palace seethes and overflows with royal splendour. Wine foams everywhere, the great hall resounds with tumult, pages scurry to and fro, servers speed on their tasks; stomachs are filled with delicacies, minds with song. One makes the harp resound, another contends with praises; there sounds in unison: 'To thee the praise, to thee the glory, O Christ.' The king drinks in this honour with eager gaze, graciously bestowing due courtesy on all." [45]

The political importance of this series of rituals and the emotional intensity tied up with them ought not to be underestimated. For the king's person was a living symbol of the whole social order. His person represented a kind of concentrated essence of the people. His exaltation and the myths supporting and surrounding it were acts of affirmation in defiance of the actual world. That is the true function of political myth. It is no accident that such myths are to be found in poorly integrated and therefore poorly controlled and governed traditional societies. So much significance attaches to the king because he is the only visible hope for stability. A good example of the immense importance attributed to kingship is the social anxiety bound up with the inevitable occurrence of the king's death. In the absence of the idea of automatic succession, which did not develop until 1272, an interregnum was bound to occur. In theory the king's peace, that is, his protection, died with him, and this meant that a good part of the law was in abeyance. On this topic Sir Frederick Pollock observed that in "England we now say that the Crown is a corporation: it was certainly not so when the king's peace died with him, and 'every man that could forthwith robbed another.' " [46] On this, as on so many other points, we may hope for illumination from anthropological studies of other primitive king-doms. Lucy Mair writes that among the African peoples she studied there is a common belief "that a time when there is no ruler is a time of lawlessness and anarchy, though this may only be a meta-phorical way of expressing their conception of the king as the ulti-mate source of order and justice." [47] No more in medieval kingdoms than in African did the king's death actually reduce society to chaos.[48] But there can be no doubt that it was a time of intrigue and, sometimes, of actual fighting to determine upon whom the king-ship should devolve. This was certain to be the case when, as in Anglo-Saxon England, any man with royal blood could consider himself a suitable and rightful claimant to the throne. The one ob-vious remedy for this short of murder, which was not uncommon, was to exile potential competitors, and the Anglo-Saxons certainly employed it.[49] Thus Bede tells us that the future king Sigeberht had been in exile in Gaul because of the enmity of the reigning king.[50] Similarly the exiled Cadwalla returned to kill the reigning king and seize the throne for himself.[51] But besides inviting revenge this tech-nique had other drawbacks, and they provide useful insight into medieval political life. A young man of royal blood might recruit a body of followers and proceed to loot and terrorize some unhappy district. Such was the course of the early life of St. Guthlac.[52] Again, the reception of a royal exile in another court could lead to strained foreign relations, even, indeed, to war.[53]

It is clear, then, that the elements of intrigue and instability in-volved in Anglo-Saxon kingship cannot be ignored. It remains true, however, that the accession rites were an important source of stabi-lization. They provided an ideal occasion for reconciliation and endorsement of the social order. Indeed, the assignment of specific tasks to the great men assembled for the occasion, it may be argued, represents nothing so much as a kind of tableau of the right social order. At the time of coronation the king was surrounded by the great in all their ranks, with roles to perform in the ceremony in accordance with rank. Vigorous competition developed over these places, though in time many of them became settled hereditarily in certain aristocratic families.[54] Thus the rituals and festivities sur-rounding the crowning of a king were very much more than merely ceremonial. Altogether they present a most impressive political self-portrait, idealized to be sure, but nonetheless valuable.

84

All the ideas and hopes expressed in the accession rituals were powerfully reinforced by popular adulation of kings. Indeed, what can only be called a belief in the magical efficacy of the king's person was reflected in popular legend and behavior.[55] The most striking of all the popular superstitions was the belief, persisting over some seven centuries in France and England, that kings possessed the power to cure disease by touch. It was believed, more particularly, that scrofula could be cured in this way; hence its designation as the king's evil.[56] The historian of this belief, Marc Bloch, has demonstrated its importance so conclusively that it will be worthwhile to follow his argument on the course of its development. The belief did not take its decisive form, as the hereditary gift of the English and French monarchies, until the eleventh century. Bloch's suggestion is that its appearance at that time is best explained in terms of the crisis in the relations between the Church and secular rulers which began in the eleventh century. Though this was the immediate cause, the vital background to it, Bloch argues, was the ancient tradition of sacred kingship, which centered on the idea of a sacred kingly race.[57] But even if the range of inquiry is narrowed to instances of miraculous healing by kings, there are a few cases of interest before the eleventh century, as Bloch notes. Bede relates at some length how the remains of the saintly King Oswald healed persons afflicted with ague and restored the faculties of the "possessed." [58] Gregory of Tours tells us of the similar powers of the Merovingian king, Guntram. Gregory reports that it "was commonly told by the faithful that a certain woman, whose son was sick of a quartan ague . . . came up through the crowd immediately behind the king, and tore off by stealth some particles of the fringe upon his royal mantle. These she steeped in water, which she gave her son to drink; and immediately the fever was quenched, and he was made whole. I cannot doubt the story, since I myself have often heard evil spirits in the hour of their possession invoking the king's name, and confessing their crimes, compelled by his miraculous power." [59]

Despite some evidence of this kind from the early successor kingdoms, however, it was not until after the reception of Christianity was assured that the traditional conception of kingship underwent any very considerable change, the most important feature of which was the coronation ritual. From the eighth century, at least, the prestige of the Church was systematically employed in the effort to enhance and stabilize the rule of kings. This fruitful alliance of the secular and the spiritual continued until the eleventh century, when the great wave of reforming piety named after one of its principal figures, Pope Gregory VII, reversed the traditional position. It seems fair to say that the major impulse in the reform movement was a concerted effort to distinguish the spiritual realm from the temporal. So it was that many of the most prominent men of the Church came to regret the old alliance.[60] For one of the main effects produced by the Christian veneer laid over pagan belief in the successor kingdoms was a persistent tendency, especially among lay persons of all ranks, to assimilate kingship to the priestly order. When kings came to be anointed with holy oil, just as the priest was when he was ordained, it was difficult to refrain from the inference that the king too had received that infusion of divine grace which made an indelible mark on the soul, transforming a mere man into a sacred vessel.[61]

In sophisticated Christian circles, to be sure, the distinction was clearly recognized. For on Christian principles it was impossible for any man to be both priest and king. That dual character was reserved for Christ alone. Even in the Carolingian period, when these practices emerged and were expressed in very exalted language borrowed from Roman antiquity, trained Christians insisted on the difference. Archbishop Hincmar, for example, held that "the dignity of bishops is superior to that of kings, because kings are consecrated to the kingly height by bishops, whereas bishops cannot be consecrated by kings." [62] For simple folk, however, and, one may add, for the politically astute, the matter was never entirely cleared up, for the coronation services were visible testimony that kings were anointed with the same holy oil as that with which priests and prophets were consecrated, so endowing them with the gifts of the Holy Spirit. So from the time of the Gregorian reformers onwards most of the arguments tended to focus on the unction, for, despite the best efforts of other churchmen, this continued to be popularly considered the critical moment in the life history of the king's person. The official position of the Church took its point of departure from the view established by the Gregorians. Thus in 1204 Pope Innocent III insisted upon a sharp differentiation between episcopal unction and the anointing of kings, signified by the fact that the bishop was anointed on the head, while a prince ought to receive his anointing on his arm. In fact, however, the kings of England and of France continued to be anointed like bishops and with the special oil ap-

86

propriate to episcopal consecration, as distinguished from that used for priests.[63]

All in all, it is fair to say that the high theory of the Church failed to have the desired effect on secular practice or on popular belief. The insistence of the Church that kingly consecration conferred no sacramental powers did not prevent Philip Augustus from blessing his troops at the battle of Bouvines.[64] Nor were the kings of England by any means slow to appreciate the importance of unction with oil from a divine source. On this subject, Bloch relates the following delightful tale. In 1318 Edward II sent an emissary, a Dominican friar by the name of Nicholas de Stratton, to the Pope at Avignon. His mission was to persuade the Pope that Edward ought to be permitted a second consecration, for Edward was then in serious political difficulty and badly in need of reinforcement. Nicholas told the Pope that while St. Thomas Becket was in exile he had been visited by Christ's mother. He was told, so the story goes, that the fifth king after Becket's great adversary Henry II — who would be Edward II — would be a great champion of the Church, indeed, would reconquer the Holy Land. Accordingly he would need to be anointed with an especially holy oil, which Mary duly gave to Becket. From his hands it passed to a variety of other people, finally coming into the possession of John II of Brabant, who married King Edward's sister Margaret. So King Edward came into possession of the holy oil. The Pope, however, insisted that Edward recognize the Church's position on the unction and that it be performed secretly, which certainly would not have suited Edward's needs. The result was that the king's efforts came to nothing. But Henry IV (1399–1413) had better luck, for he was actually anointed with what purported to be Becket's oil. Now the story was that it had been found in Poitou by the king's father, the Duke of Lancaster. The blessings to be derived from the oil were altered also, in order to fit the circumstances of the Hundred Years' War. For the king anointed with Becket's oil was destined to reconquer Normandy and Aquitaine. Despite England's loss of all the French territories, the legend has it that the oil was used until the coronation of James I in the seventeenth century, for, true to his Calvinist upbringing, James refused to countenance a practice so closely associated with the cults of the Virgin and the saints.[65]

Thus the pagan veneration of ruling families was supplied with an elaborate Christian framework. The king's new and quasi-priestly attributes, however, were not a substitute for the earlier notion of the sacred stock but were added to it. Indeed, they were even assimilated to it by that impulse to ground legitimacy in ancestral usages, for the Hebrew kings and even the priests and prophets were treated as if they were the king's ancestors. Even Pope Stephen referred to the Carolingian dynasty as a sacred race, both royal and sacerdotal.[66] Whether rightly or wrongly, the Church had thus set its own seal on the exaltation of royalty in the eighth and ninth centuries, and from a Christian perspective the result had been a lamentable confusion of the temporal and sacerdotal orders. So it seemed, at any rate, to the reformers. It was through their enthusiasm that a new level of clarity was introduced into the discussion of all political topics. They insisted not only on drawing a sharp distinction between the secular and clerical spheres, but they came also to argue that even the most exalted secular ruler was radically subordinate to the clerical order. Pope Gregory VII formulated a famous expression of this view in a letter to Bishop Hermann of Metz in 1081.

> Who does not know that kings and princes derive their origin from men ignorant of God who raised themselves above their fellows by pride, plunder, treachery, murder — in short, by every kind of crime — at the instigation of the Devil, the prince of this world, men blind with greed and intolerable in their audacity? . . .
>
> Does anyone doubt that the priests of Christ are to be considered as fathers and masters of kings and princes and of all believers? [67]

As if this were not enough, Gregory went on to subordinate any layman not only to any ordained cleric but even to a mere exorcist, who was not even ordained.[68]

The point of discussing the thaumaturgical powers of kings in this context is that this miraculous power made its appearance at the same time as the Gregorian reform movement. Bloch's suggestion is this: kings became workers of curative miracles from the eleventh century on as a kind of compensation. For henceforward their religion forbade the attribution to them of any direct relation to the supernatural order, or any personal influence on cosmic phenomena.[69] Certainly there can be no doubt about either the popularity or the persistence of the belief. Thus the author of a life of Edward the Confessor informs us that Edward was glorified by God, and he offers as evidence the story of a young woman afflicted with scrofula and barrenness who came to the king on advice received in a dream. At "the king's anointing the diseased part softens, the scab is loosened, and as he draws back his hand, worms come out from several openings along with much bloody matter." The king succeeded in curing the disease, and also "she who for this or some other infirmity was barren, in the same year became fertile by her husband, and thenceforth lived a pleasant sight for all that shared her home to see." Moreover, "the French say that he [the king] often did the same thing in his young days, when he was in . . . Normandy." [70] Again, Peter of Blois writes concerning Henry II that the lord king "is holy and the Lord's Anointed: nor has he received the sacrament of regal unction in vain, for if its efficacy be not known or be in doubt, the disappearance of plague and the cure of scrofula will beget the fullest belief." [71]

It is true, as Bloch is at pains to show, that the history of thaumaturgical power had its vicissitudes. Thus from the Gregorian reform until the mid-thirteenth century, literary sources say very little about it. But in the context of the political struggles between the kingdoms and the papacy, the tradition was exalted and embellished, reaching real audacity by the fourteenth and fifteenth centuries.[72] In the English case we are especially fortunate, because there have survived public records from the reigns of the first three Edwards listing the numbers of persons ministered to, and they run in the thousands.[73] Moreover, it should not be supposed that this belief in the king's power was restricted merely to crude and unlettered folk. In the reign of Edward III (1327–1377), Thomas Bradwardine, Archbishop of Canterbury and sometime Chancellor of the University of Oxford, assured doubters that if they would bring any people afflicted with the king's evil into the royal presence they would be cured, just as had happened before in England, Germany, and France. Bradwardine was generous too, for he explicitly recognized that French kings possessed this power as well as English.[74] From the fifteenth century, we have a statement from no less a figure than Sir John Fortescue, Chief Justice of the King's Bench, and the principal political writer of the century. The king, he tells us, is a *persona mixta*: he possesses both temporal and spiritual aspects.

The Kings of England in their very anointing receive from heaven such infusion of grace that by touch of their anointed hands they cleanse and cure those who are infected with a certain disease, commonly called the King's evil, who are said to be otherwise incurable. Epileptics also, and persons subject to the falling sickness, are cured by means of gold and silver devoutly touched and offered by the sacred anointed hands of the Kings of England upon Easter day, during divine service (according to the annual custom of the kings of England); even as by means of rings made of the said gold or silver, and placed upon the fingers of such sick persons, the same hath been in many parts of the world by frequent trial experienced . . .[75]

Fortescue's opinions have another interesting facet, especially relevant to the political aspect of thaumaturgy. In his day the houses of York and Lancaster were contesting for the throne. Fortescue was a partisan of the Lancastrian cause and so undertook to deny the healing power to the rival princes of the house of York. Indeed, the political rivalry produced a debate on the location of genuine thaumaturgical power. "Each camp," as Bloch says, "sought to discredit the rite practiced in the adverse camp. Why was not a little of this discredit reflected on the rite in general? The legitimate king, it was thought, knew how to cure; but which was the legitimate king?" [76] The ability to cure, then, was one of the tests of true royalty, and so it was to remain for at least two centuries longer. By the seventeenth century, touching was numbered among the king's exclusive prerogatives. Pre-empting that gift was one of the charges of treason levelled against the rebellious Duke of Monmouth in the reign of James II. It is reported that Monmouth "caused himself to be proclaimed king, and did take upon him to be king, and was saluted by the people as king, and they kissed his hands and cryed God blisse the king, and he was called sir, and his majestie, and was prayed for as king, and commandit as king, and payed the armie, and touched children of the king's evill, and did exercise the other functions of royall dignitie . . ." [77]

The new wave of enthusiasm concerning the king's powers in the later centuries of the Middle Ages is attributed by Bloch to the decline of the Church: the Great Schism, and criticism of Church discipline and even of the religious life itself. These conditions amounted, he thinks, to a sufficient set of permissive circumstances.[78] It would seem perfectly reasonable to infer, also, that the emotional and religious needs of medieval men had begun to find a new focus in the king, in place of a Church whose popularity was badly weakened. Thus in the sixteenth and seventeenth centuries the whole procedure of touching was institutionalized. Some order had to be introduced, it would appear, because the sheer numbers of those who sought to supplicate the king produced a considerable physical and administrative problem. In any event, the ceremony of healing by the king's touch was reduced to the form of a quasi-religious service in the reign of Henry VIII, at the latest.[79] Polydore Vergil testifies to the practice in early Tudor times and gives expression to the view that it descended from Edward the Confessor, who "by his touch alone used to cure strumous patients . . . This imperishable gift has descended by right of inheritance, as it were, to the kings since his time. For even now the kings of England cure strumous persons by touch, after the singing of a service and the recital of certain ceremonies." [80] Similarly, the Elizabethan historian, Holinshed, writes of the Confessor that it "hath beene thought he was inspired with the gift to prophesie, and also to have had the gift of healing infirmities and diseases. He used to helpe those that were vexed with the disease, commonlie called the king's evill, and left that virtue as it were a portion of inheritance unto his successors the King's of this realm." [81] These remarkable powers attracted the attention of Shakespeare in *Macbeth*, which rests on the account of Holinshed. A doctor tells Malcolm that the king is coming, but

> . . . there are a crew of wretched souls
> That stay his cure: their malady convinces
> The great assay of art; but at his touch,
> Such sanctity hath heaven given his hand,
> They presently amend.

Macduff asks what disease he means, and Malcolm answers that it is called the evil.

> A most miraculous work in this good king;
> Which often, since my here-remain in England,
> I have seen him do. How he solicits heaven,
> Himself best knows: but strangely-visited people,

All swoln and ulcerous, pitiful to the eye,
The mere despair of surgery, he cures,
Hanging a golden stamp about their necks,
Put on with holy prayers: and 'tis spoken,
To the succeeding royalty he leaves
The healing benediction. With this strange virtue
He hath a heavenly gift of prophecy,
And sundry blessings hang about his throne
That speak him full of grace.[82]

The first Stuart king, James I, did not believe in the healing service himself but was constrained to administer it under considerable pressure.[83] A seventeenth century newspaper reports that Charles II cured no less than six hundred persons in a single gathering.[84] The diarist John Evelyn informs us, from the year 1684, that "there was so great a concourse of people with their children to be touched for the Evil, that 6 or 7 were crushed to death by pressing at the chirurgeon's doore for tickets." [85] Indeed, science notwithstanding, touching for the cure did not fall into disuse until well into the eighteenth century. Boswell reports, for example, that in 1712 the young Samuel Johnson was brought before Queen Anne to be cured.[86] The cure, alas, did not take.

Altogether, then, there is a very impressive body of evidence that kings could rely for support upon a mass of unrefined superstition and adulation. The political effectiveness of this sort of support must not be underestimated merely because it now seems difficult to understand. Even when the barons went so far as to exercise compulsion on a reigning monarch, they normally denied that it was compulsion. The leading idea was that kingly error could be rectified only by divine agency. "That human hands should rashly execute divine vengeance upon God's vicar was a thing too horrifying to be thought: men shrank even from the charge that they had put constraint upon the king." [87]

It is a great deal easier to grasp the flavor and significance of the king's position in the social and legal order. It will be possible, therefore, to deal with this side of kingly popularity much more briefly. Moreover, the king's role in lawmaking and the administration of justice will be explored at length in a subsequent chapter. For the moment it is necessary only to see that the king's sanctity was not his sole claim on the loyalty of his subjects. As was suggested earlier, there is the fact that a hierarchical ordering of society requires an apex. How better to legitimize graded privileges? If challenged, a lord's rights and privileges could be defended, short of brute force, only by relying upon royal justice. A man might submit in evidence a claim that his lands and privileges derived from a royal grant. Not infrequently, however, there would be a counterclaim. The other party might also claim a royal grant, or he might allege that his opponent's grant was not good. The way to solve the difficulty was to resort to royal justice. But here a more general point requires notice: the king's indispensability in the working of the political order. The king's utility is abundantly demonstrated in two major areas: the administration of justice, and lawmaking.

Unfortunately our knowledge of the working of royal justice in the Anglo-Saxon period is very thin. The major achievements are clear in outline: unification, and territorial administration on the basis of the shires and their subdivisions, the hundreds. But in the present context the most notable achievement was the invention of the writ system. Essentially this was a very simple idea. The writ was just an authenticated royal note of instruction or information to the local administrator, thus linking the locality with the king's government. In a word, writs were the instrument in solving the problem of government at a distance. Simple as the writ was, it should not be forgotten how rudimentary medieval government was in its early stages, and that in fashioning this tool the Anglo-Saxon monarchy was well ahead of the continental kingdoms. The Norman-Angevin kings adopted this idea and based the most efficient central government of medieval Europe on it. But in the Anglo-Saxon period most justice had been done on the local basis. The king's council was utilized only in important questions, such as the outlawing of a powerful man. It was the Norman administrative reforms of the twelfth century, essentially the articulation of the writ system, that was the great turning point in the history of the English judicial system.

Following on the centralizing reforms of Henry I and Henry II, the position in matters of litigation is quite clear. The plea rolls of the later twelfth century demonstrate that the English people were appreciative of centralized justice.[88] Indeed, the evidence suggests that even the magnates wanted not less but more royal justice.[89] This point is well illustrated by some of the baronial demands in

Magna Carta, particularly by chapters 17 and 18. The first of these registers a demand for a stationary court for common pleas, as against the court's practice of following the king in his travels. Chapter 18 arranges for itinerant royal justices to visit each county four times a year. Neither of these arrangements was new. Both represent, in fact, a routinization of Angevin justice.[90] Most impressive evidence of dependency on his majesty is supplied by the legislation of Edward I (1272–1307). It affords eloquent testimony to the needs of his subjects. In particular it demonstrates, as Plucknett has said, that in the thirteenth century the feudal landlord could no longer obtain by his own devices the income expected from feudal relationships.[91] What was required was the vigorous hand of the king.

One of the best examples of this is to be found in the great statute Quia Emptores (1290). The general purport of the statute is that it abolishes the practice of subinfeudation. Its significance, for the purposes in hand here, is that it was framed upon the request of the magnates. Feudal lords were in serious difficulty and they sought a remedy in the king's lawmaking power. Their problem was raised by loopholes in the law which opened the door to severe economic loss. Essentially the difficulty was that subtenants could employ the radically porous nature of the common law in such a way as to deprive the lord of his expected income from escheats, marriages, and wardships. If Plucknett's explanation is adopted, the situation may be characterized in the following way. A tenant could subinfeudate his entire holding from his lord to another man, a subtenant. Under strictly feudal principles this would not necessarily produce any hardship, but the system took no account of the possibilities raised by a more complicated economy than the one in which it had grown up. If some service was due to the lord for the land in question, he was entitled to seize chattels in order to compel performance of the service. It would make no difference to him whether those chattels belonged to his tenant or to the subtenant. But suppose now that the tenant has conveyed the land for a set sum of money. Having struck an essentially nonfeudal bargain and received his payment, the tenant may require from the subtenant only a purely nominal service for the land, "perhaps a rose at midsummer," as Plucknett suggests, in no way equal to the services owed to the original lord. Disaster would overtake the lord if his tenant died and left a minor heir. On feudal principles the lord would become the guardian of the land for the period of the minority, and as guardian he was entitled to whatever profits the land would yield. All he would receive in the imagined case, however, would be a rose at midsummer. Similarly, should the tenant die without heirs, the estate would no longer escheat to the lord. Again all he would receive would be the rose. Now, the solution supplied by Quia Emptores is radical in its simplicity and effects. It forbids subinfeudation. In the event that a tenant should desire to convey his holding, the statute provides that he is to be replaced by the purchaser, who takes on all the responsibilities of the original tenant. Thus a royal statute circumvented an important segment of the common law and came to the rescue of large numbers of distressed landlords by rendering the appurtenances of their holdings invulnerable to one of the principal pieces of tenant craft.[92]

Another example of reliance upon statute law and the king's justice is supplied by considering the problem of feudal aids. Feudal law recognized three compulsory aids: those due when the lord's oldest son was knighted, when his oldest daughter was married, and when it was necessary to ransom the lord himself. In the past, the exaction of these aids had been enforced by the lords in their own honorial courts. But in the thirteenth century feudal lords were constrained to seek the king's assistance in securing payment. One of the provisions of the Statute of Westminster I (1275) deals with the problem. It sets a price on these aids and makes the use of royal writs in securing them available to a lord. This shows not only that feudal lords required the king's assistance but also that the underlying rationale of the feudal relationship was badly eroded. The original significance of the aids was that they expressed a relation of mutual dependence within the military class. The fact that a money price was willingly placed upon them is a measure of the decay of the social bond which these ties had formerly represented.[93]

A last example may be drawn from the complications surrounding the law of wardship. Here again the loose structure of the common law exposed men to deceit and fraud. Considerable cunning was employed by both lords and tenants. From the side of the tenant, the idea was to deprive the lord of his right of wardship should the tenant die leaving a minor heir. There were two principal methods of doing this. One was extremely simple but had the drawback of obviousness; the tenant enfeoffed his oldest son in his own lifetime, thereby circumventing the problem of inheritance. The other method was to subinfeudate the land in question, with effects broadly similar to those of the subinfeudation case mentioned above. Obviously Quia Emptores made all such resorts impossible. But the particular problem here had been dealt with earlier, by the Statute of Marlborough (1267). The technique in question was this. The land would be conveyed in exchange for an outrageous rent, together with a deed stating that the rent had been paid up to the time when the minor heir would reach legal maturity. Actually no rent would have been paid because it had intentionally been set too high. The idea was that once the heir reached maturity, the subtenants could be counted on to return the land to him because the rent was too high to be paid. This provision would obviously prevent a kind of secondhand fraud in the proceedings. Suppose, then, that the tenant should die leaving a minor heir. His lord would come into wardship only to discover that no rent was due to him until the year in which he had to return the land to the heir. He would thus be deprived of his expected income. But the Statute of Marlborough enacted that neither enfeoffment nor such collusive subinfeudation could deprive the lord of his wardship. Once again, then, statute law had come to the aid of the feudal lord.

The lord, however, had ample opportunity to practice fraud on his own account. If he came into a wardship he could, wrongfully, enfeoff his ward's lands to someone else. To be sure, the law afforded a remedy to the deprived heir, but it had two radical defects. It could not be pursued until the heir reached legal age, and the procedure was an involved one. Moreover, if it should happen that the guardian died in the meantime, the whole matter could be complicated to the point where the litigation might go on for years. The Statute of Westminster I, chapter 48, cuts off this sort of chicanery. It provides that the infant heir, through his "next friend," may employ the swiftest remedy of the law, the assize of novel disseizin.[94]

The illustrations just given indicate the extent and importance of the monarch's statutory intrusions into the working of the common law. Certainly they reveal the subject's dependence upon him and his courts. This reliance, together with the intangible but immensely effective reserves of power resting on the belief that kings were sacred persons, goes far toward accounting for the vitality of medieval kingship. In the early Middle Ages, then, the king and his great men provided the double foundation for legitimacy and authority. This idea — double majesty — was an essential and durable part of the central political assumptions and attitudes of the age. This much is clear, but the evidence upon which those attitudes rest is so patchy that it is impossible to develop an explicit statement, much less a theoretical position, regarding early medieval political views.

In the twelfth and thirteenth centuries this situation began to improve. With the appearance of the professional lawyer, an immensely important figure in European history, there became available a much more sophisticated body of evidence, the statements of the judges and lawyers. The professional lawyer was no deus ex machina. On the contrary, he was the product of the king's bureaucracy. By the middle of the thirteenth century, one of the greatest of the king's justices, Henry de Bracton, had written a monumental treatise on English law. Bracton's work, which presents the first full statement of the central idea of double majesty, merits an extended description and analysis.

four Counsel and Consent

Bracton's imposing treatise on the laws and customs of England contains the most important single treatment available to us on kingship and law in medieval England before the works of Sir John Fortescue, some two centuries later. The burden of his lengthy work is an exposition and commentary on the system of royal writs, which by his day had largely supplanted the older systems of local law. Most of his book, therefore, is primarily of interest to the historian of law. But, scattered here and there in his work, Bracton inserted a number of passages of a more general kind. These contain his views on the nature of kingship, law, and governance in medieval England. A problem is raised by them because they appear to fall far short of presenting a coherent point of view. For one set of passages seems to say that the English king is supreme within his kingdom, that he is emancipated from legal restraint. But other passages appear to maintain that the king is limited in some way. Thus one encounters such statements as these. "Neither the judges nor private persons can or ought to dispute about royal charters and the deeds of kings . . . Likewise, no one can judge the deed or charter of the king so that the king's act is made void." [1] Indeed, "let no one presume to dispute his deeds, much less to oppose his acts." [2] But Bracton also says that "the king, since he is minister and vicar of God, can do nothing on earth save only that which is according to law . . ." [3] Again, "the king ought not to be under man, but under God and under the law, because the law makes the king." [4] He says, further, that English laws and customs, "when they have been approved by the consent of the users and confirmed by the oath of kings, cannot be changed nor destroyed without the common consent of all those by whose counsel and consent they were promulgated." [5] Now whatever else may be said about them, these passages certainly suggest, at least at first sight, that their author entertained incompatible views on the relation among the king, the law, and those who gave counsel and consent. Similar passages can be multiplied easily, but they appear to compound the difficulty rather than to resolve it.

In view of the ambiguity which statements of this kind involve, it is certainly understandable that the task of interpreting Bracton's views has prompted much debate. The first part of this chapter is devoted to an examination of some of the most skillful contributions to that debate, since they have set the terms of the discussion of English political ideas, not only in Bracton but in relation to the later Middle Ages and early modern times as well. The chief purpose of this chapter, however, is to advance an interpretation of Bracton and his milieu in the light of the tradition of operative thought explored in the preceding pages. It will be argued that Bracton was not a theorist of constitutionalism, nor was he an absolutist; neither was he an exponent of the sovereignty of the law. His book contains, instead, a cluster of ideas on kingship, law, and politics, many of which are wanting in theoretical precision and even in generality. There is no unified and coherent system to be found in Bracton. But it will be suggested that there is, nevertheless, a central political idea in Bracton's book. This is his characterization of the English political order in terms of the idea that I have been referring to as double majesty. His doctrine is that English government is a joint enterprise, a partnership of king and great men. One point in emphasizing this, it will be recalled, is that it serves as a reminder of the political element which is a necessary feature of any legal order. It is possible to imagine a political order which lacks law, but it is impossible to imagine a legal order without politics. It is also intended to underline the peculiar dualism of the conception of authority in operative political thought. Finally, following the examination of Bracton's ideas, it will be suggested that his version of double majesty is primarily a native inheritance, though he gave it a more complicated and explicit formulation than his predecessors. Bracton's expression of the idea is a quite apt attempt to characterize the political order of his day, and it is best illuminated by earlier and roughly contemporary statements of the same idea.

Bracton's definition of what is held for law in England is eminently political. Suitably enough in a legal treatise, the principle of double majesty is expressed in those places where the discussion seems to require ultimate justification. Time and again, he asserts that the formulation, alteration, or repeal of a law requires both regal authority and the counsel and consent of the magnates. This principle does not solve all the problems raised by his book, nor does it tell us exactly what he meant. Bracton nowhere elaborates the idea, nor did he undertake to justify it. On the contrary, as Ewart Lewis has rightly insisted, he accepts it as a fact.[6] His silence, although regrettable, does not detract from the importance of the idea. While it is impossible to escape the observation that Bracton repeatedly employs the idea of double majesty, the literature on Bracton has displayed relatively little interest in it. What is nearly always emphasized is the role of law. It is as if the law somehow constituted a body of principle quite apart from the concrete interests of the king and the great magnates, as if it did not require any external impulse, but, like the Constitution of Mr. Justice Sutherland, "speaks itself." [7]

Bracton and the Tradition of Legalism

Bracton's importance is attested by the wealth of secondary literature dealing with his political thought. All the sustained examinations have one element in common. They have all been cast in terms of the relation between the king and the law. This approach is at once too broad and too narrow. It is too narrow because it tends to overlook the political element in the text as well as the historical context, which affords us the only means of suggesting an interpretation faithful to the times. It is too broad because it tends to impress a timeless set of ideals on a line of development in history which can be made out only by hindsight. Broadly, these are the ideals of constitutionalism, understood as the rule of law. The result has often been excessive ingenuity and subtlety. Despite this emphasis on a single relationship, there have been three variations on the common theme. Some commentators have argued that there is simply no doubt that Bracton's king was subordinate to law.[8] Others have thought that the important point is that Bracton found no way to implement legal control of the king, even if that was his aim.[9] Finally, the number of logical alternatives available within the common framework is exhausted by a compromise interpretation. Here there are several species of a mixed genus. Ernst Kantorowicz contends that Bracton's king is simultaneously above and below the law.[10] Professor McIlwain has argued that Bracton's work contains a neat division between law and government.[11] Walter Ullmann maintains that Bracton's king is simultaneously feudal, that is, bound by contractual relationships with his vassals, and "theocratic," which involves illimitability, at least in principle.[12]

It has been suggested already that a good prima facie case can be made to the effect that Bracton's text contains a substantial number of statements which do not seem compatible with one another. The variety of scholarly opinion just outlined provides as striking a confirmation of this as one could desire. But this is not the most important point. The contention here is that existing interpretations present us with an abbreviated Bracton. The excision of or studied inattention to troublesome language allows Bracton's thought to be reported rather too neatly, and with a suspiciously happy modernity. But it is possible to pay too high a price for the values of consistency and unity. In this case, the price is an historically implausible Bracton. Indeed, the price is even higher than that, because Bracton occupies an undeniably important place in the history of the most highly valued political and legal ideas in Anglo-American culture. But this is not a warrant for reading contemporary ideas into those scattered utterances of his which seem most congenial to us. The effect of this kind of reading is to cut investigation off just at the point where it ought to be getting under way. Indeed, it ensures the result of the inquiry in advance. Bracton is cast in the role of a primitive but well-intentioned theorist of constitutionalism and the rule of law. The effort to trace cherished ideas and institutions to their source is an honorable and estimable enterprise, but there is an especially seductive temptation inherent in it. For what begins as a kind of unconscious working method becomes an answer. The method rests on the idea that locating the origins of a contemporary ideal or institution will somehow reveal its essence. Having done this it is easy to slip insensibly into an identification of that genetic essence with the present, and thus to close the gap between past and present. But to disclose an origin is not the same thing as to identify the essential principles of a working institution, nor is this genetic fascination likely to result in a just assessment.[13]

My first aim, then, is to suggest that the legalistic approach presents only a purified Bracton and, as a result, fails to resolve the problems which are raised by his text. This will require the exploration of some of the most important interpretations of Bracton offered in recent years. The burden of this discussion is admittedly but unavoidably critical. It aims at a single suggestion: that the legalistic framework by itself has not resolved and cannot resolve the problems raised by the text. This is well illustrated comparatively, for the major varieties of legalistic interpretation are themselves mutually exclusive and contain powerful criticisms of one another, either explicitly or implicitly. Following out the issues raised in these arguments will, therefore, provide a valuable critical introduction to the study of Bracton and his time.

In the attempts to cope with the problem of alleged inconsistency in Bracton, a great deal of attention has been directed to a particularly puzzling passage. It contains not only the standard elements of Bracton's political thought, but also a reference to a famous maxim of the Roman law which seems peculiarly inappropriate to the context. The passage in question occurs in the course of a discussion of the king's jurisdiction. Bracton tells us that the king is the vicar of God and, as such, his raison d'être is to supply and enforce justice. In order to accomplish these tasks, the king ought to possess more power than any of his subjects. Bracton continues as follows:

Moreover, he ought to have no peer, still less a superior, especially in the administration of justice . . . Although in the receiving of justice he may be compared to the least person of his kingdom, although he excels all in power, yet since the heart of a king ought to be in the hand of God, lest his power be unbridled let him put on the bridle of temperance and the reins of moderation, lest if it be unbridled he be drawn towards injustice. For the king, since he is minister and vicar of God, can do nothing on earth save that alone which he can do of right, nor is this contrary to the saying that "what pleases the prince has the force of law," for there follows after "law," "since by the *lex regia* which was made concerning his rule" [etc.]: that is, not what is rashly presumed to be the king's will but what has been duly defined with the counsel of his magnates, the king warranting its authority after deliberation and discussion upon it. Therefore his power is of right and not of unright, and since he is the author of right there ought not to be born occasion of unrights thence whence rights are born; and he who by virtue of his office must prohibit unright to others ought not to commit it himself in his own person. Therefore the king ought to exercise the power of right as God's vicar and minister on earth because that power is from God above; but the power of unright is from the Devil and not from God, and the king will be the minister of him whose works he does. Therefore, when he does justice he is the vicar of the Eternal King, but he is the Devil's minister when he falls into injustice. For a king is so called from ruling well and not from reigning, because when he rules well he is a king, but he is a tyrant when he oppresses with violent domination the people entrusted to him. Therefore, let him temper his power by law, which is the bridle of power, that he may live according to the laws, since a human law has stated that laws bind the law-giver himself, and elsewhere in the same source, "It is a saying worthy of the majesty of rulers that the prince profess himself bound by the laws." Again, nothing is so proper to empire as to live by the laws, and "it is greater than empire to submit the principate to the laws," and deservedly he ought to give back to the law what the law has given to him, for the law makes him king.[14]

It is clear that the king is the apex of the legal order. Yet there is the suggestion of an unspecified standard apart from the king's will. The price of falling away from what he may do of right is loss of the name of king. He ought, therefore, to adopt the bridle of temperance and the reins of moderation, that is, conduct according to the laws. What is held for law in England are the judgments arrived at through the counsel supplied to the king by the magnates of the realm. All these ideas of Bracton's are repeated with variations in other contexts.

This passage raises two important questions.[15] The first is Bracton's reference to the *lex regia*, which has disturbed commentators more than any other Bractonian phrase. The problem is this: how are we to account for the fact that Bracton failed to cite the whole text? In full the passage reads, "What pleases the prince has the force of law, since by the *lex regia* which was enacted concerning his rule (*imperium*), the people confers on him all its authority and power (*imperium* and *potestas*)." [16] Now, if the purport of this Roman text was understood to be absolutist, why should Bracton use this language? He has just said that the king may do only that which he can do of right (de jure). Then he informs us that law is the result of the joint deliberations of the king and his magnates. But, even supposing that a satisfying answer can be given for his reference to the prince's pleasure, the passage as a whole is not quite clear. Is the king legally bound, or is restraint only a matter of his voluntary acceptance of the bridle of law? This passage does not supply the answer. Before turning to the various scholarly interpretations, however, it will be convenient to deal with the narrower question of the prince's pleasure, which has provided the platform for the most detailed discussions and interpretations of Bracton's political thought as a whole. An examination of the three quite different arguments that have been advanced will supply examples of each of the major lines of interpretation of Bracton mentioned above.

Perhaps the most influential treatment is that of McIlwain, whose interpretation takes its departure from this passage. His view is that Bracton distinguished two spheres in politics, those of *jurisdictio* (jurisdiction, law) and *gubernaculum* (government, administration). In the realm of gubernaculum, the king is said to be absolute. In the realm of jurisdictio, however, the king is bound to the rule of law, which protects a number of private rights, chiefly property. It is the ancient customary law which is supposed to provide the distinction between jurisdictio and gubernaculum and to supply the content of each. The proper place of each of the principal social elements of the medieval polity, the king and the magnates, is assigned by a law which is ultimately sovereign. This is what McIlwain means by medieval constitutionalism.[17]

In connection with the passage just quoted, McIlwain's interpretation rests on two points. The first of these depends on the translation of the lex regia itself, as it was used by Bracton. The argument is that the relevant words are to be translated one way in Justinian's text and another way in Bracton's. McIlwain's reading of Bracton is this: " 'Nor is that to the contrary where it is said *quod principi placet legis habet vigorem,* for there follows at the end of the law *cum lege regia quae de imperio eius lata est* (together with the *lex regia* which has been laid down concerning his authority).' " [18] In the Roman law, the phrase means that what pleases the prince has the force of law because the lex regia has been enacted. But in Bracton, "the prince's will is law together with, or if in accordance with the *lex regia* . . ." [19] Bracton suppressed the remaining words of the maxim precisely because of their absolutist tone; this would not have suited his purpose.[20] This brings us to McIlwain's second point: that Bracton intended to compare the lex regia to the coronation oath of the English king. He draws attention to the fact that Bracton reports a version of that oath in the same section of his book, just before the passage which includes the troublesome maxim. But the coronation oath bestowed no such *imperium* and *potestas* on the English king as the lex regia did on Roman emperors. On the contrary, it was supposed to limit them through the promises they made in it. One of these, McIlwain says, was the promise "to give effect to the laws 'which the common people have chosen' . . ." So the coronation oath should be construed as the English equivalent of the Roman lex regia. Like the lex regia, it is the law which makes the king.[21] But there is a crucial difference. Justinian's text contains an account of how the emperor came to be absolute. But Bracton's "*lex regia* admits of nothing beyond a true definition of what the law already is, promulgated by the king's authority only after discussion with the magnates and on their advice. Justinian's is a doctrine of practical absolutism; Bracton's seems to be a clear assertion of constitutionalism. In the one the prince's will actually is law, in the other it is only an authoritative promulgation by the king of what the magnates declare to be the ancient custom." [22]

This is surely an ingenious and attractive line of argument, but it encounters a number of serious difficulties. To begin with, the warrant for translating the Bractonian lex regia depends on the assumption that Bracton meant to suppress the balance of the maxim. But this is very doubtful for two reasons, as Ewart Lewis has pointed out. For "how could Bracton have hoped to refute the dangerous thesis of a well-known text by blatantly misquoting it? And how could he have expected his readers to follow an argument based on an (inherently implausible) assimilation of the *lex regia* with the coronation oath, without explaining what his reasoning was?" [23] Actually, there appears to be a very simple reason for Bracton's omission: to abbreviate citations of familiar texts was a common practice in the Middle Ages.[24] Secondly, the Bractonian version of the coronation oath fails to support the argument. It is reported by Bracton thus:

And it should be known that the king himself and none other can and ought to judge, if alone he is adequate to this, since he is considered bound to this by virtue of his oath. For in his corona-

tion, the oath having been presented, he ought in the name of
Jesus Christ to promise these three things to the people subjected to him. First, that he will command and, so far as he can,
see to it that for the church of God and all the Christian people
a true peace may be preserved throughout his time. Secondly,
that he will forbid plunderings and all iniquities in all ranks.
Thirdly, that in all his judgments he will prescribe equity and
mercy, that the clement and merciful God may impart His mercy
to him, and that through his justice all men may enjoy a firm
peace.[25]

The Bractonian version of the oath thus presents the same three
promises as did that sworn in the tenth century.[26] But whatever
else may be said about it, it contains nothing concerning "an
engagement to govern according to the laws which the people have
chosen (*quas vulgus elegerit*)." [27] It is true that McIlwain noted the
fact that this phrase did not occur as part of the coronation oath
until after Bracton's time. He nevertheless felt free to use it in making a crucial point about Bracton's text. In addition to this difficulty, it is very hard to say what the phrase meant when it emerged
into prominence in the reign of Edward II.[28] The important point
at present is that using it to elucidate a technical feature of Bracton's
text is inadmissible.

It is interesting to note, however, that both the translation and
the problematical assimilation of the lex regia to the coronation oath
fit nicely with and, indeed, support McIlwain's interpretation of
Bracton's thought as a whole. These comparatively minor matters,
therefore, come to assume considerable importance. For Bracton
supplies McIlwain with a model with which he believes he can
characterize the most important features of the political thought
of the Middle Ages. Having explained to his own satisfaction the
odd conjunction of what he took to be absolutist and constitutionalist sentiments, he proceeds to the exposition of his main argument.
He believes he has established the point that for Bracton English
political life is ultimately governed by law. However, a number of
statements to be found in Bracton require a refinement of the general theory. There are several passages which suggest that the king
is supreme in his kingdom, that he is not subject to legal restraint.
It is at this point that the distinction between gubernaculum and
jurisdictio is employed. According to Professor McIlwain, this im-

portant distinction is to be found in a section of Bracton's book devoted to the subject of franchises. Now, not only does this discussion offer a solution to the seemingly contradictory passages in Bracton, it also supplies us with "nothing less than the solution of the great problem of our medieval constitutionalism . . ." [29] Bracton raises the question of whose right it is to grant liberties. His answer is, the "lord king himself," for it is he who

> has ordinary jurisdiction and dignity and power over all men who are in his kingdom. For he has in his hand all the rights which belong to the crown, and the secular power, and the material sword which pertains to the governance of the realm. He has also justice and judgment, which belong to jurisdiction, that by his jurisdiction he may as minister and vicar of God assign to each what is his. He has also those things that belong to peace, that the people entrusted to him may be quiet and tranquil in peace and that no one may strike or wound or maltreat another, that no one may take away or carry off the goods of another by violence and robbery, and that no one may maim or slay any man. He also has the coercive power, that he may punish and coerce wrongdoers. He also has it in his power that he may himself in his own person observe and make his subjects observe the laws and statutes and assizes which have been provided and approved and sworn in his kingdom. For it is of no avail to establish rights unless there be someone to protect the rights. Therefore the king has rights and jurisdictions of this sort in his hand . . . the administration of justice and peace, and those things which are annexed to justice and peace, belong to no one save only the crown and the royal dignity, nor can they be separated from the crown, for they make the crown what it is.[30]

With special reference to this passage, McIlwain wished to make two points. First, he draws attention to the fact that, in the passage about the king obliging his subjects to observe the laws, decrees, and assizes, the word *consuetudo,* custom, does not occur; therefore, it must be excluded from the reach of regal authority.[31] The second point is that if this passage were combined with others, which he thinks express constitutionalist sentiments, it would be possible to develop a clear-cut distinction between *gubernaculum,* government, and *jurisdictio,* law.[32] This argument allows him to characterize medieval political society as a general regime of custom. Custom is law in the only true sense of law, and it can only be found, not made. The king's council, in effect, is a group of experts, lacking authority, which convenes to instruct the king as to the content of the ancient customary law. It is the law which supplies limits to medieval kingship. The king, like everyone else, is under the law.[33]

However, just as in the case of the first stage of McIlwain's argument, serious criticism may be brought against this interpretation. His first point is that custom is not included in the sentence concerning the king's coercive power. In view of the language in the passage as a whole, however, McIlwain himself recognizes that this is not enough. Later in his discussion he says that Bracton used the word *leges* sometimes in a wide sense, sometimes in a narrow sense. For Bracton, he says, "*leges* (in the narrow sense of the word), *constitutiones,* and *assisae* are nothing more than administrative orders and therefore a part of 'government' — something which 'pertains to the administration of the realm (*pertinet ad regni gubernaculum*)' — and as such are properly within the king's exclusive control." [34] But Bracton nowhere indicates that the word lex has such a specialized meaning. As Brian Tierney has observed, "the really important thing here was the inclusion of *leges.* Bracton himself defined quite clearly his understanding of these terms at the beginning of his treatise. *Leges* constituted the body of laws common to the whole kingdom; *consuetudines* were local customs." Now this is exactly right and it is an especially significant point, in view of the immense importance which is so often attached to the idea of custom in discussing late medieval and early modern political thought. Tierney goes on to say, quite rightly, that there "is no reason at all to suppose that Bracton was using the word *leges* in some quite different sense in this passage . . ." [35] Here is what Bracton actually says in the introduction to his book.

> Moreover, although in nearly all regions the written law is used, England alone uses within her bounds unwritten law and custom. Here indeed right is based upon unwritten law, which use has proven. But it will not be absurd to speak of the English laws, although unwritten, as laws, since whatsoever has been justly defined and approved, with the advice and consent of the magnates and the common engagement of the commonwealth, with the authority of the king or prince presiding, has the force

of law. Also, there are in England many and diverse customs, according to the diversity of places. For the English hold many things by custom which they do not hold by law, as in various counties, cities, towns, and vills, where it must always be inquired what the custom of the place is and in what way those who allege custom use custom.[36]

Thus, what Bracton does is to assimilate the general body of English custom to law, and then he draws a distinction between such general laws and local customs. He does not say, here or anywhere else, that custom is supreme, lying beyond the reach of king and people.

There is another point which reinforces the observation that Bracton employed the Roman concept of lex to embrace all the laws of national scope. Incidentally, it will also go some way toward explaining the vexed problem of Bracton's use of the maxim *quod principi placuit*. The important point is that Bracton uses the word lex to assimilate the validity of the English legal system to that of the Roman law, the very model of a legal system. Like his twelfth century predecessor, Glanvill, Bracton had been exposed to the imposing intellectual challenge of the "written reason," the *ratio scripta* of the Roman law. Apparently both writers felt obliged to undertake a defense of English law. What they seem to be doing is offering an apology for their legal system. What they say is that some persons might be led to think that unwritten law and custom do not constitute a genuine legal system. Their reply to this is that it simply is not true: unwritten law, use, custom are also law. They are apologizing for English law as compared to Roman law and, of course, it was perfectly natural for them to do so; their legal system was very much more primitive. They cite Roman texts which say that custom also is law: custom may compose part of a legitimate legal system. The very apology they offer is derived from Roman law. With reference to the point discussed above, then, Bracton is engaged in an assimilation of the English legal system with the Roman, and the principal device for accomplishing this is the prestigious word lex. If this is correct, then it seems very doubtful indeed that he would exclude the most important part of the law of England from the reach of the concept lex. Moreover, if he had wanted to convey this point, surely his text would contain some slight hint to that effect. But, in fact, he nowhere suggests that lex has two specialized meanings. So much, then, for the first point.

The crucial distinction between gubernaculum and jurisdictio really rests on a single phrase. Bracton says the king "has in his hand all rights touching the crown, and the secular power, and the material sword which pertains to the governance of the realm (*qui pertinent ad regni gubernaculum*)." McIlwain claimed that this constituted "a separation far sharper than we make in our modern times between government and law, between *gubernaculum* and *jurisdictio*." [37] The truth of the matter, however, is exactly the reverse of this. It is only since the advent of genuine constitutional government in the seventeenth century that men have been inclined to draw such a distinction. For constitutionalism turns on the idea that there is a higher law which is not subject to alteration by any ordinary legislative or judicial processes. It can be contended that natural law was regarded as an unchangeable higher law, but operative thought made no important use of it until the later fifteenth century. Fortescue did make systematic use of the idea of natural law, but even then it was not employed in any juristic sense. Bracton's text simply makes no such distinction. On the contrary, there are a number of passages, including the one in question here, which tell us that jurisdiction is an essential ingredient of regal authority. Bracton writes, for example, that "those things which belong to jurisdiction and the peace, pertain to no one except to the crown alone and to the royal dignity; nor can they be separated from the crown, since they constitute the crown itself." The contrast that appears in this discussion of regal power is not that between gubernaculum and jurisdictio but, as Tierney has argued, that between temporal and spiritual power.[38] Bracton says that the rights of the king are those that "regard the crown, and the lay power and the material sword."

Thus it must be concluded that the alleged distinction between government and law does not supply a method for dealing with the puzzlement raised by Bracton's book. This means, of course, a return to the initial difficulty: attempting to account for apparently contradictory views on the nature of English government. Two important discussions of the problem have appeared recently. Both of them are suggestive and illuminating, and both reach broadly similar conclusions. But what is particularly interesting is that these authors reach similar conclusions by quite different and, indeed, mutually incompatible exegeses of Bracton's thought. One of these studies, by Brian Tierney, contends that the crucial point is that

Bracton's king is *legibus solutus* after all, but that this does not mean he is conceived of as absolute, as free to disregard lawful procedures. On the contrary, Bracton's point is that while the king is beyond legal restraint, he has an obligation to behave according to law. The key to a correct understanding of Bracton is to recognize that neither he nor his contemporaries drew a sharp distinction between legal and moral obligation. In short, "the ruler had a duty to obey the law, but . . . the fulfilment of the duty could be ensured only by his will to adhere to its provisions, not by legal coercion." [39] The principal difficulty in Tierney's interesting discussion is that it leads him to unify Bracton's system and at the same time to admit that this is a solution unobtainable in Bracton's day. This problem will be discussed again below. The second of these studies is a penetrating discussion by Ewart Lewis. She accepts the view that Bracton's king cannot be legally coerced but insists, nevertheless, that the essence of Bracton's political thought is that the king is under the law, that he can do nothing which is not according to law.[40] It will be argued here, however, that it is surely an oddity to contend that the essence of a theory is that the king is clearly subordinate to law but cannot be reached by any legal process.

Both of these discussions turn on the passage set out above, in which Bracton says that since the king is the minister and vicar of God he can only do that which he can do de jure, and then goes on to say that the maxim, "What pleases the prince has the force of law," is not contrary to this.[41] Tierney argues that the point Bracton wished to make by his reference to the lex regia was that even in this text, which underlines the vast personal authority of the Roman emperor so sharply, the ruler's legislative authority was conferred by law. The case is the same in England: Bracton "plainly attributed a legislative function to the king, but held that that function itself was to be exercised in accordance with the law of the land (which, in England, required counsel and consent)." [42] Tierney supports this view by pointing out that the sources from which Bracton appears to have drawn his knowledge of Roman law contain a resolution of the difficulty presented by the lex regia. The crux of this resolution is the series of glosses in civilian writings which link the doctrine of the lex regia with another famous passage, known as the *Digna vox*. This text of the Roman law reads: "It is a saying worthy of the majesty of the ruler that the prince profess himself bound by the laws, since our authority depends on the authority of the law.

And it is indeed a thing greater than empire that a prince submit his government to the laws." [43] It will be recalled that Bracton employs this language toward the end of the passage which contains his reference to the seemingly contradictory doctrine of the lex regia. Tierney's point is that civilian legists used the Digna vox to explain the obligation of the supreme magistrate to obey the law himself because his authority depended on it.[44]

Lewis has rejected this line of argument. Her objection is that it obliges us to believe that Bracton thought it necessary to argue for the doctrine that counsel and consent was required, and yet not necessary to show how he did this.[45] She insists, rightly, that Bracton's words suggests that, whatever his doctrine was, it was supposed to be evident from an inspection of the words following "What pleases the prince has the force of law." [46] Bracton does say, quite simply, that this doctrine is not contrary to the one he is expounding, because "there follows at the end of 'law,' since by the lex regia which has been laid down concerning his rule." Here the citation ends, and Bracton presents his version of what is held for law in England. It is true that Tierney puts his problem in this way: "how did Bracton come to imagine that a lex regia which conferred 'all imperium and power' on the ruler could be cited to support an argument that the king's personal authority was limited by the counsel of the magnates?" [47] But Tierney's reconciliation of quod principi placuit with Bracton's doctrine does not depend on the assumption that Bracton is developing an argument for it. What matters is whether or not the two doctrines can be made out to be compatible and their conjunction to be a sensible, or at least plausible, attempt to deal with a famous and potentially troublesome doctrine. All that we are required to believe is that Bracton does not appear to have thought that they were incompatible ideas and, apparently, that he saw a parallel of some sort between English ideas and these Roman maxims.

Lewis argues that Bracton's doctrine in this passage is intelligible only if we are prepared to recognize two points. First, that Bracton is drawing attention to the technical sense of the term *placere*. This means that it refers "only to the prince's legislative decision that something is, or is to be, the law." It is a meaning that excludes the notion that the prince possesses absolute freedom. It might refer either to an authoritative law-interpreting decision, or to an authoritative law-enacting decision. In the case of legislation "it says nothing about its appropriate content and is as non-committal in regard to motives and wishes as, e.g., 'signed' or 'enacted.' " The second point is that in this passage Bracton is not discussing lawmaking at all. The argument is strictly confined to the king's role as judge. In this connection, Bracton is credited with the perception that the maxim quod principi placuit "may be cited to authorize judgments based on the mere will of the king, in disregard of established legal rules and procedures, on the erroneous assumption that it means that whatever pleases the prince can be used as a juridical alternative to law . . . But . . . a quick reference to the context reminds the reader that the maxim specifically concerns the legislative authority conveyed by the *lex regia*. Thus it attributes the force of law only to what the prince authorizes in establishing law: which is, specifically, what will have been justly defined by the *consilium* of the king's magnates, which the king warrants as law after it has been considered and discussed." Bracton's only concern in this passage is that regal judgments "must be made *legum auctoritate,* not *proprio arbitrio.* It is as a norm for concrete judgments, not as a norm for legislation, that he rejects the misinterpretation" of the maxim. Then we are told that Bracton did not see that the maxim "could be construed as eliminating the need of *consilium et consensus* in lawmaking — still less, as asserting the prince's right 'to legislate . . . *as he pleases.*' " [48]

A number of objections may be brought against this view. Lewis criticizes McIlwain for supposing that Bracton could avoid the dangers of this maxim by suppressing part of it. She rightly notes that it was too well known for that.[49] But if it was that well known, and its technical meaning for Bracton and his contemporaries was so clear that all he had to do was mention it to convey its specialized meaning, it is hard to see why he bothered to mention it at all. Would not any reader who could be counted upon to recognize this point immediately, without further explanation, also be one who would not need to be reminded of the meaning of the maxim? Again, just as Lewis objects to Tierney's argument that it is difficult to believe that so much is conveyed by the "bare citation" of the maxim,[50] it is difficult to believe that there is this much subtlety in Bracton's discussion. It is true that the context is the king's role as supreme judge. But Lewis' argument here appears to depend on a sharp distinction between the legislative and adjudicative functions of the king and his curia. Yet later in her article she draws attention to the fact that Bracton sees no significant difference between case law and enacted law.[51] Does this not suggest that one ought not to put too much weight on a distinction between adjudication and legislation? It seems to require a great deal of sophistication, not only on Bracton's part but on the part of his readers, to perceive (with a bare citation of the maxim) the point that Lewis believes he had in mind. Moreover, while Lewis is prepared to credit Bracton with the perception of one possible danger in quod principi placuit, she denies that he was aware of others. But what is not supposed to have occurred to Bracton's acute intelligence did occur to his contemporaries. In fact, the author of a baronial propaganda tract dating from the baronial wars of the period 1258–1265 explicitly charges King Henry III with the attempt to do away with baronial counsel and consent on the ground that "what pleases the prince has the force of law." [52] The barons, in other words, were saying exactly what Lewis says cannot have been in Bracton's mind. Moreover, the composition of his treatise appears to fall in just this period. While it is scarcely possible to be certain of Bracton's views, Lewis' interpretation relies on a point which seems far too subtle.

At any rate, having offered an explanation of one difficult passage, Lewis proceeds to an examination of two others, which have sometimes been thought to express the doctrine that the king is above the law. Her concern here is to show that neither of them contains such a doctrine. Once this is done she proceeds to her primary contention, that the key to Bracton's thought is the idea that the king ought not to be under man, but under God and the law. One of these passages has been quoted already. It is the one dealing with franchises, in which McIlwain believed he found the distinction between gubernaculum and jurisdictio.[53] It will be recalled that one of the statements made there is that "the king has it in his power that he may himself in his own person observe and make his subjects observe the laws and statutes and assizes . . ." Now, Lewis says, "the main point in regard to the king's observance is that he himself controls it . . ." But, she says, "I find no suggestion that the king can rightfully choose whether or not to use these powers . . ." [54] The statement is not perhaps quite clear. It appears to maintain that the king's observance of law is an act of self-control, except that he is not really free. If this is the argument, it seems too paradoxical to be useful, since the second statement drains all the meaning out of the first one.

The other passage is from Bracton's discussion of the law of persons. He tells us that there are various sorts of persons under the king, ranging from barons down to serfs, while the king himself is under no one but God.

> Moreover, the king has no peer in his kingdom, because thus the precept would be lost, since an equal has no authority over his equal. Again, much less ought he to have a superior or anyone more powerful, since he would thus be subjected to his inferiors, and inferiors cannot be the equals of superiors. Moreover the king ought not to be under man, but under God and under the law, because the law makes the king. Therefore let the king attribute to the law what the law attributes to him, namely, domination and power. For there is no king where will rules and not law. [And that he ought to be under the law, since he is the vicar of God, appears evidently through his likeness to Jesus Christ, whose place he occupies on earth. Because the true mercy of God, when many ways were available to Him for the recovery of the human race, ineffably chose the most preferable way, by which He would use not the force of power but the reason of justice for the destruction of the devil's work. And thus He wished to be under the law, that He might redeem those who were under the law. For He did not wish to use force, but judgment. Likewise also the blessed bearer of God, the Virgin Mary, Mother of the Lord, who by a singular privilege was above the law, yet to show an example of humility did not refuse to be subject to legal institutes.] Thus, therefore, the king, that his power may not remain unbridled. Therefore, there ought not to be anyone greater than he in his own kingdom in the administration of law; but, he ought to be the least, or as if he were the least, if he seeks to obtain judgment. But if judgment is sought from him, since no writ runs against him himself there will be place for a supplication that he may correct and amend his act, and if he does not do so it suffices for his punishment that he await the vengeance of God. Let no one, indeed, presume to dispute his deeds, much less to oppose his acts.[55]

This passage is especially interesting for the purposes in hand here, because the exponents of the several types of legalistic interpretation have construed it so differently. Thus Ernst Kantorowicz thinks this passage contains a striking confirmation of his thesis that Bracton's king is both above and below the law. Schulz, on the other hand, thought the section enclosed in brackets might be an interpolation. The Latin, he explains, is not Bractonian. Lewis thinks it "incredible that Bracton would himself have composed these loosely-conceived and flaccid sentences . . ." However, the "ambiguities of the parallel with Christ and the utter irrelevance of the parallel with the Virgin do not, I think, exclude Bracton's responsibility for inserting these sentences; they do, however, exclude the possibility of drawing from them any inference about Bracton's conception of the king except, as stated, "quod sub lege esse debeat." ["that he ought to be under the law."] Thus I see no reason to infer a supralegal status of the king from this theological excursion . . . Its role in his text is, at most, to adorn, to confuse . . ." [56]

But Tierney believes that Bracton's point here is to show that the king's obedience to law is a matter of his own good will. "This view was expressed quite clearly . . . where Bracton compared the role of the king to that of Christ and of Mary, in that they had conformed to the law because of their regard for justice and humility, not because they were subject to coercive sanctions." [57] Surely this is a more reasonable view. Why should we not expect a thirteenth century writer to make his point by the use of a sacred analogy? For most men in that day, the appeal to more or less dubious examples and to strained analogies was the nature of argument. To be sure, after the recovery of the logical writings of Aristotle, there were some men who could compose a disciplined argument. But as always they were comparatively few. Moreover, it is obvious on the face of it that Bracton's statements on government and law were no refined scholastic exercise. On the contrary, they reflect widely received views. Other men thought it appropriate to argue in precisely the same way. The technique was simply to state the ancestral tradition — kingly rule in association with the great men — and then undertake to reinforce it with a liberal sprinkling of tag lines from Scripture and Roman law. There is no reason why we should expect twentieth century intellectual rigor, nor for supposing that these phrases were included to confuse the reader. They are confusing only if one insists on ignoring the main thrust of the argument and concentrates, instead, on problems of logical coherence within the general context of legalistic interpretation. The result of this is that we are presented with a wide range of choices resting on a variety of considerations. In all cases, however, what strikes one is the immense ingenuity and subtlety involved. But a reading of these disputed passages does not inspire confidence in the use of these extremely refined tools of analysis. For the texts certainly do not present sophisticated arguments, and this suggests that the test of logical incompatibility is not a fruitful way of interpreting them. Again, it is to take a great deal for granted to suppose that Bracton knew the technical meanings of Roman legal concepts, for the beginning of precision on these topics did not appear until the Renaissance. Finally, it is very difficult to accept the notion that troublesome texts can be disregarded on the ground that they reflect an inappropriate literary style. What really matters is that someone, whether Bracton or his scribe or an interpolator, wrote this way at that time. Bracton's views were far from singular; indeed, the case is quite the reverse, for they appear to represent a normal outlook. Therefore the attempt ought to be made to interpret the words as they stand, rather than to refine and delete them until they express the modern idea that government is founded on a body of constitutional law.

Bracton Reconsidered

It seems clear that the legalistic approach to Bracton is not entirely satisfying. It will be convenient now to set Bracton's thought in a somewhat broader frame, which will include an appeal to the political side of the text as a possible key to his thought. A useful way of working into this is supplied by another much debated text, called the *addicio de cartis*.

> Neither judges nor private persons ought or may dispute concerning royal charters and the acts of kings; nor, if some doubt arise in regard to them, can they interpret it. Also, in doubtful or obscure matters, or if any expression may contain two meanings, the interpretation and wish of the lord king ought to be awaited, since interpretation belongs to him whose it is to establish. And even if it is altogether false because of an erasure or because the seal affixed is forged, it is better and safer that the judgment proceed in the presence of the king himself. [Likewise, no one can judge the deed or charter of the king so as to make the king's act void. But someone will be able to say

that the king might have done justly and well, and if, by the
same reasoning, he has done this, that it is ill done; and will be
able to impose upon him the obligation of amending the injustice, lest the king and his justiciars fall into the judgment of the
living God on account of the injustice. The king has a superior,
namely, God. Likewise the law, by which he was made king.
Likewise his court, namely, the earls and barons, because the
earls are so called as being the companions of the king, and he
who has a companion has a master. And therefore, if the king
be without a bridle, that is, without law, they ought to put a
bridle on him, unless they themselves are without a bridle with
the king. Then the subjects will cry out and say, "Lord Jesus,
fetter their jaws with rein and bridle." To whom the Lord,
"I will call upon them from afar a nation mighty and unknown,
whose tongue they will not understand, who shall destroy them
and tear up their roots from the earth, and by such they shall
be judged for they would not justly judge their subjects," and
in the end He will send them bound hand and foot into the
fiery furnace and outer darkness where there shall be wailing and
gnashing of teeth.] [58]

Numerous commentators have argued that the portion of this text
enclosed in brackets must be corrupt.[59] Others have thought it genuinely Bractonian despite the difficulties it presents.[60] The majority
opinion, at least, is that it must be an interpolation. Essentially, the
reason is the one pointed out long ago by Maitland. The idea that
the king has a superior in his council is contradicted in at least five
other places in the book.[61] However, what seems most reasonable
in view of the condition and variety of the surviving manuscripts
is that the problem of the addicio is not susceptible of an entirely
satisfying solution. The important point is that such a view could
have been entertained by Bracton; there were those who surely
would have endorsed it, both then and later. Hence the question
of authorship is not the most interesting aspect of the matter. Here,
at any rate, the effort will be made to understand the doctrine, whoever was responsible for it.

Tierney has advanced an interesting treatment of the addicio.
While he admits that any view of the matter seems incapable of
demonstration, he draws attention to a parallel from the canonist
literature. Canonist authors developed "the principle that one could

appeal from a prelate to the same prelate with counsel as to a higher authority." Translating this to the temporal sphere, he suggests that the "view that the *curia* was superior to the king did not necessarily contradict the view that the king had no superior judge set over him precisely because the judgments of the *curia* were the judgments of the king and derived their authority from the fact." However, this view of the difficulty really only drives the problem back a step; it does not solve it. Tierney recognizes that the question raised by the addicio is that the "king's own acts were to be considered and judged in his *curia*. Whose judgment then would prevail in the last resort," he asks, "that of the king or that of the magnates?" Having raised the crucial question, Tierney recurs to the canonists, who had raised the question with reference to the pope. The canonists had given both of the possible alternatives. But Tierney's opinion is that Bracton appears to have settled on the view that "if the king persisted in upholding a royal act that was unjust, his judgment had legal validity." This is carrying the point too far. Tierney's solution gives us a unified legal system, a system with a sovereign in the strict sense. In fact, the problem raised by the addicio is not primarily legal, it is political. In Bracton's day, as Tierney himself explicitly recognizes, there was no clear answer. Tierney says that "it was indeed impossible to extract a theory of the constitutional state from the English materials because they lacked the idea of a state in the classical or modern sense." [62] Precisely. And that is why Bracton could not have entertained the view which Tierney suggests.

Once again, it can be argued that the rather restricted framework generally employed in elucidating Bracton's text fails to provide a satisfying resolution of what seem to be obvious logical failings. Most of these discussions proceed on the tacit assumption that only one kind of factor external to Bracton's text is relevant. This factor is prevailing doctrine among canonists and civil lawyers. More particularly, it constitutes an appeal to the received meaning of certain much-used maxims of the law of Rome.[63] But even within the confines of this approach there have been serious disagreements on what Bracton must have understood by a given maxim.[64] This method has led to a lengthy debate as to Bracton's skill, or, as the case may be, shortcomings, as a Romanist. Both kinds of disputes are very far from settled.[65] Indeed, they sometimes leave the impression that the inquiry into Bracton's thought has been short-circuited, so to speak, and that the major inquiry has been transferred to another level.

It was suggested that the problem raised in the addicio is not exclusively a legal one, indeed not even primarily legal, but political.[66] To be sure, the emphasis on the conciliar principle in this particular passage appears to have been carried too far, carried so far as to introduce a contradiction. But the problem is not logical either. This would only be the case if Bracton were consciously attempting to present the kinds of general propositions that are expected in modern legal treatises. However, there is no good reason for supposing that he had any such thing in mind. Now, without suggesting that any evidence that might be adduced as to the meaning of the doctrine of the addicio is in any way proof that Bracton himself wrote it, there are reasons for suggesting that as a thirteenth century Englishman he could have entertained such views. In particular, he could have and did entertain views which exalted the king, indeed, views at times so extravagant as to suggest that the king was formally *legibus solutus*. At the same time, he could express views that suggest, rather imprecisely, the idea of a traditional or customary manner of conducting some part of the business of the realm. What must not be assumed is that either of these views expresses a general constitutional theory.

What is most interesting about many of the important passages in Bracton is that they contain a common element. That common element is his repeated emphasis on the principle of baronial counsel and consent. This, in turn, constitutes an inherited tradition. Moreover, it is quite unnecessary to appeal to sources in the civil or canon laws in this connection. There are good grounds, in fact, for remaining quite insular. H. G. Richardson has rightly stressed, for example, the striking doctrinal similarity between Bracton and the collection known as the Laws of Edward the Confessor (*Leges Edwardi Confessoris*).[67] His point is that both contain the idea that there is an important distinction to be drawn between judgment and mere will, and that both rely on the idea of a council of the great men of the realm.[68] Here are the chief passages relating to kingship in the Laws of Edward.

The king, who is the vicar of the highest king, was constituted

for this: that he should rule the earthly kingdom and the people
of God and above all things should reverence the holy church
of God; and he should defend them from injuries and drive evil
doers from them, so that these be entirely dispersed and destroyed . . .

The king ought to do right in all things in the kingdom and
by the judgment of the magnates of the kingdom. For right and
justice rather than evil desire ought to rule in the kingdom.
Law is always what right does; but will and violence and force
are not right . . . He ought to erect good laws and approved
customs and to abolish evil ones and entirely remove them from
the kingdom. He ought to give right judgment in the kingdom
and maintain justice by the counsel of the magnates of his kingdom.

You are the vicar of God in the kingdom, according to the
king of the psalms: "Of the Lord is the land and the fullness of
the earth . . ." The Christian folk and the people of the kingdom are the sons of the king, who exist and endure in the
kingdom under your protection and peace . . . You ought to
sustain them, maintain and protect them, to rule them and
always to defend them from injuries and malicious and hostile
men . . . The king is so called from ruling, not from the kingdom. You will be king while you rule well; if you do not, the
name of king will not remain in you; you will lose the name
of king . . .[69]

The important point about these passages is that they contain
a cluster of ideas broadly similar to some expressed by Bracton.
What is most apparent is the obvious centrality of the king. But
the author gives us no theoretical expression of kingship *legibus
solutus* or, for that matter, of kingship restrained by law. The
exalted position of the king does not prevent the author from
expressing the principle of baronial counsel. There is here no
attempt to produce a sustained, orderly treatise on kingship. Instead,
we are presented with an obviously ill-digested assortment of ideas.
Could it be that the case is essentially similar in Bracton? To be
sure, Bracton had learned to quote passages from Roman law which
referred to the legal position of the emperor. But it is perfectly
clear that he does not then engage in any constitutional discussion
of English kingship. Substantively the doctrine remains the same:

government by king and magnates. There is nothing in Bracton's text to suggest that one ought to seize on the idea that the king is beyond legal reproach, nor on the idea that he is bound by the law.

The same general principle of counsel by the magnates Bracton also quite clearly derived from the twelfth century legal treatise attributed to Glanvill. When he came to present his own version of the doctrine of Glanvill's prologue he incorporated two ideas. There is, on the one hand, the notion that English laws may legitimately be called laws and, on the other, that the reason for this is that in England the decisions of king and council are by definition what is held for law.[70] Glanvill says that each decision taken in the king's court is governed by the laws of the kingdom and by customs, whose basis is reason and long observance. Moreover, the king avails himself of the advice of outstanding subjects, those whom he knows to be experienced in the laws and customs of the realm. Glanvill goes on to announce other themes echoed by Bracton. "Although the laws of England are not written, it does not seem absurd to call them laws — those, that is, which are known to have been promulgated about problems settled in council on the advice of the magnates and with the supporting authority of the prince — for this also is a law that 'what pleases the prince has the force of law.' For if, merely for lack of writing, they were not deemed to be laws, then surely writing would seem to supply to written laws a force of greater authority than either the justice of him who decrees them or the reason of him who establishes them." [71] No more than the author of the Laws of Edward or even Bracton in the next century did Glanvill expand on his views or undertake to justify them, and that in one way is exactly the point. All that is supplied is a statement of the prevailing political outlook. But that is enough in an intellectual atmosphere which rests on an assumption of changelessness, or rather, one in which no idea of change or development had yet occurred to anyone, let alone been worked out. The unexpressed presumption was that a static condition was normal; change meant that someone had interfered or, to put it another way, had lapsed from his accustomed duty and place. But that is as far as it goes.

In the twelfth and early thirteenth centuries, then, were expressed virtually all the ideas relating to kingship later expounded by Bracton. There were the ideas that the king is the vicar of God and therefore responsible for the protection of his subjects through the administration of justice, but that the affairs of the kingdom ought to be conducted in conjunction with the magnates of the realm. Now, this idea of double majesty suggests the possibility of stress, and the politics of the later Middle Ages affords a wealth of examples of fairly wide oscillation within that framework, as the next chapter will show. Bracton expresses the conjunction repeatedly. But he also oscillates. Perhaps the doctrine of the addicio may be best understood in this way. Thus Bracton expresses in another place an idea which approximates that of the addicio, though it is true that his language suggests that he may not have been sponsoring it himself. It occurs in his discussion of the assize of novel disseisin. In determining whether the assize is applicable, one of the principal matters to be settled is who did the dispossessing in question. For "if it be a prince or a king, or another who has no superior save the Lord, there will be no remedy against him by an assize. On the contrary, there will only be place for a supplication that he will correct and amend, and if he will not do so, one must be content to await the Lord the Avenger, who says, 'Vengeance is mine, I will repay.' Unless there be someone who will say that the community of the realm and its baronage [*universitas regni et baronagium*] may and ought to do this, in the court of the king himself." [72]

Further illumination on the possibilities implicit in this idea may be derived from other interesting sources roughly contemporary with Bracton. What they show is that Bracton was not alone in his difficulties, if it is assumed for the sake of argument that they were his. Shortly after the composition of Bracton's book a gloss was written on the passage which says the king has no peer. It is attributed to John de Longueville, who was a justice of assize in Edward II's reign (1307–1327).

> The king therefore associates earls, barons, knights and other ministers with him, that they may share the honor and burden [of his office], for he does not himself suffice to rule the people. Thus he is called king from ruling, and he who ought to rule should give and not receive orders, because otherwise it would follow that he was not ruler and governor, but rather subject and governed; which, indeed, is not right, and this is sufficiently established by the word [*rex* from *regere*]. For he has no peer or superior. But this seems to involve the objection that the earls are called the colleagues of the king. And I argue thus: he who

has a colleague has a master; the king has a colleague, therefore the king has a master. And further: he who has a master has a superior; the king has a master, therefore the king has a superior.[73]

Clearly, this is no more than a heightened expression of the doctrine of the addicio.[74] The writer has learned to clothe a simple thought in an overly elegant syllogistic form but still seems unable to make logic serve its true purpose, the achievement of clarity. For the argument is left on a cleft stick logically.

The primarily decorative quality of logical exercises and learned quotation emerges very sharply in the next writer to be considered. Whoever he was, his book is one of the most persuasive literary indications of the ability of writers in this period to entertain what seem to be incompatible doctrines. This is the discussion of kingship in the anonymous legal treatise known as Fleta. Here all the major features of Bracton's treatment of kingship, widely scattered in his work, are collected in one place. Fleta's discussion occurs in a chapter devoted to the subject of delegation of the king's authority in the administration of justice. Here long passages are lifted wholesale from Bracton and from Glanvill. The knitting together of all these themes is so instructive that it is worth setting down a very long excerpt from this chapter. No one, he says, can

give judgment in matters temporal except the king, either personally or by a delegate. For by virtue of his oath, he is in especial bound to do this, and therefore the crown is a symbol that he will rule the people subject to him by the process of law. Nor is he called *rex* because he reigns, but his title is derived from *bene regendo,* ruling well. He is, in truth, a king if he rules well and a tyrant if he governs by force to the oppression of the people. And verily, he is elected to this end, that he shall cause equal justice to be done to every one of his subjects without acception of persons, so that the Lord may dwell in him and that through him He, whose concern it is to defend and sustain what has been rightly adjudged, may declare his judgments, for if it should not be that the king does justice, peace might easily be driven away. The king has in his hand all rights that belong to the crown and to the lay power, and the material sword that belongs to the governance of his realm. He has also the judgment seat and justice that belong to jurisdiction, wherefore, as the vicar and servant of God, he is bound to award to every man that which is his own. He has, moreover, those things that belong to peace, so that the people entrusted to him may rest and repose in peace . . . He has, too, the right of coercion, that he may punish and restrain offenders, and it lies in his power to ensure that the laws, customs and assizes, enacted, approved and sworn in his realm, are steadfastly observed, both by himself and by all his subjects. For it would be useless to establish laws and to employ courts of justice unless there was one who could safeguard the laws, and this jurisdiction the king has in his hand. Therefore he must exceed in power all others in his realm, for he may have no peer, much less a superior, in administering justice, so that it may be said of him "Great is our lord and mighty in power," but so that if he is plaintiff, he will receive justice on the same level as the lowliest in his kingdom. And although he exceed all others in power, yet his heart should be in the hand of God. And lest his power should remain unbridled, let him put on the bridle of temperance and the rein of moderation, that he be not drawn into wrongdoing, for he can do nothing on earth except that which he can do lawfully. Nor is it inconsistent with this to say that "the prince's pleasure has the force of law," for it is a consequence of the law of kings, enacted to invest the prince with sovereignty, that his pleasure is not whatsoever is rashly supposed to be the king's wish, but what has been properly determined by the counsel of his magnates, with the king's authority, after due deliberation and discussion thereon. His power, therefore, is the power of right, for he is the origin of right, and the source from which rights arise cannot produce the occasion of wrongs. And further, what by reason of his office he must forbid to others, he may not in his own person commit. The power of right is from God alone; the power of evil from the Devil; and he will be in the service of Him whose work he performs.

Since therefore it has been enacted that any man who is pursuing what is his right should resort to a court of justice rather than to force, it behooves those who have been wronged to go to the king, so that, when the wrongs they suffer are shown to him, he may cause justice to be administered to the plaintiffs. And if the king will not do this, by himself or by another, then let those who complain await the vengeance of God, for none may presume to debate the act of a king nor dispute his deed. Nevertheless in the governance of the people he has superiors, namely the law, by which he is constituted king, and his court, that is to say the earls and barons. Earls indeed are called *comites* from *comitiva,* companionship, and when they perceive the king to be unbridled, they are bound to bridle him, lest the people cry "O Lord, Jesus Christ, with bit and bridle bind fast their jaws." To them the Lord [shall answer] "I will call down upon them a fierce nation, strangers from afar, whose tongue they shall know not, and I will destroy them and root them out of the land, and they shall be judged by these because they would not judge the people justly" . . . Let kings therefore temper their power with law, which is the bridle of power, so that they may live according to the laws, for the law of mankind has decreed that laws bind their author, and there is elsewhere a worthy saying "It is a consequence of his sovereignty that a prince profess himself bound by the laws." Moreover, nothing is so distinctive of authority as living by the law, and for the sovereign to submit to the law is a greater thing than to command. And since a king should not always be armed with weapons but with laws, let him learn wisdom so that he may maintain justice, and, when he has found it, blessed will he be if he swerve not from it . . .[75]

In the next paragraph, Fleta repeats the coronation oath as it was reported by Bracton, and the rest of the chapter discusses the delegation of the powers of administering justice. Thus, in his own way, the author of Fleta is even more convincing than Bracton on the crucial point that medieval men were quite likely to entertain views, one after the other, which leave us wondering which one they preferred. We feel compelled to choose; apparently they did not.

Finally, the views expressed in one more law book of the late thirteenth century may be usefully sampled. They derive from the prologue to the law book called Britton. The entire text is represented as a record of the commands of Edward I. The relevant passage reads as follows: "Desiring peace among the people who by God's permission are under our protection, which peace cannot well be without law, we have caused such laws as have heretofore been used in our realm to be reduced into writing according to that which is here ordained. And we will and command, that throughout England and Ireland they be used and observed in all points, saving to us the power of repealing, extending, restricting and amending them, whenever we shall see good, by the assent of our earls and barons and others of our Council; saving also to all persons such customs as by prescription of time have been differently used, so far as such customs are not contrary to law." [76]

Thirteenth century writings, then, contain a variety of expressions of the idea of double majesty, and, more particularly, of the doctrine of the addicio — the idea, that is, that the great men are the king's companions and, therefore, a bridle on the king's power. As the passage from Fleta shows, it was perfectly possible for a writer of that day to take over the doctrine of the addicio and lay it side by side with the ideas that the king has no equal, much less a superior, and that no one can dispute his deeds. Moreover, if the problem of the addicio is examined from a broader viewpoint, as a variation on the idea of double majesty, its importance in Bracton's text is diminished. Whether Bracton wrote the addicio or not, the more general idea of double majesty is the leading political idea in his book, and it is within this framework that variations occur. These variations form a wide spectrum of expression. Some writers may stress the principle of baronial consent, others may emphasize the regal principle. But the dualism persists.

It has been said that the doctrine of the addicio "touched the most vital point in politics in Bracton's time." [77] If this is true, and there is abundant reason to think so, is it not premature, to say the least, to expect a resolution of it in Bracton's work? What is suggested is that Bracton was in touch with the political realities of his day, and that he allowed them a central position in his discussion of English law. There is no reason to suppose that Bracton was immune to the political currents of his day. Indeed, living when he did and pursuing his career in the king's courts, he cannot have been unaware of periodic disagreements between the king and some of his leading men.[78] Bracton assumed, quite rightly, that disputes should ordinarily be settled according to the forms of the law, but he also recognized that not all disputes could be resolved in this way. Some of them required a political settlement. In fact, serious disagreements often concerned what may be called the explication of the idea of double majesty. Even when the barons were engaged in resistance to their ruler, they did not challenge the necessity of kingship. However, they sometimes did dispute the king's reading of what it meant to conduct affairs of the kingdom in the traditional way. This lifted the question outside the normal processes of law and converted it into a political matter. This difficulty is reflected in Bracton's text.

Certainly much of the argumentation took place within the realm of discourse called law, but it is important to be clear about what this meant in the Middle Ages. In the first place, the customary law of England was almost entirely procedural and, secondly, it quite lacked the quality of generality which the modern mind associates with legal rules. Finally, the idea of "custom" was not so much an idea of a body of law as it was a mode of argument. Thus Bracton says that while the king ought to be under no man, he ought to be under God and the law since it is the law that makes the king. What did he mean by this? The first thing to be noticed is that he did not give these expressions any explicit content. It follows that they have no substantive or operational import and, hence, no constitutional meaning. The statement that all men are under God required no justification nor any extended explanation in a Christian context. It conveyed the notion that the king, like any other Christian man, ought to live according to Christian ethics. It enjoined upon the king, that is, the private virtues of the Christian tradition: he ought to worship God, he ought not to steal or covet his neighbor's wife and possessions, and so on. But the political bearing of all such injunctions was small indeed. If a king should be a tyrant, he would lose the name of king, but nothing would follow in this world. On this point medieval authors were perfectly clear: tyranny must await the vengeance of God. That is all that Bracton or any other medieval author until the sixteenth and seventeenth centuries meant. Bracton says the king should adopt the bridle of the law, and what he meant was that the king should act like a Christian.

On the other hand, Bracton says that the laws may not be changed or repealed without the consent of the magnates. He was referring to a procedural ideal. The political disputes that centered on the ideal did not concern the relationship of the king to "the law," thought of as a body of substantive rules containing proscriptions and prescriptions relating to regal powers, to be set over against the arbitrary will of the king. On the contrary, as the Laws of Edward suggest, the contrast was drawn between judgment and will. It is the idea that, in those legal and political processes which modern writers distinguish as adjudication and legislation, the king ought to proceed by the method of judgment, that is, decision with and through the counsel and consent of the barons. It is obvious that the king was not bound to do so by any law. Bracton was referring to a working arrangement which had its roots deep in the past: the conception of the great men as the king's companions. Not all the major business of the realm was in fact settled this way. It had long been an ideal, however vague, but as J. E. A. Jolliffe has said, the royal will, without benefit of baronial judgment was, "perhaps, the most characteristic and effective administrative weapon of the twelfth century." [79] In the thirteenth century, this became a recurrent and abrasive political issue. But it is crucial to recognize the procedural character of the idea. It says nothing, that is, about the content of any specific rules of law. The defense of the principle was cast in terms of traditional usage, and this is the kernel of truth in the otherwise extravagant claim that the medieval polity was governed by a body of ancient customary law. Customs there were, but many were merely local in their provenance, as Bracton testifies.[80] Moreover, even those whose range was general were primarily procedural: that is, they provided not general rules of law but methods for resolving disputes.[81] The baronial claim to give counsel and consent rested on the simple fact that that was the ancient way. But this does not mean that these usages were thought of as the product of the folk, as has been claimed so often. On the contrary, they were conceived of as the grants of former kings. The idea of "custom" derived its importance not from the fact, or claim rather, that it was a disembodied set of legal rules which limited kingship, but from the fact that it was the fundamental ingredient of the idiom of baronial ideology. Thus in his incisive study of the baronial movement that eventuated in the signing of the Magna Carta in 1215, J. C. Holt concludes that to "penetrate beyond the Charter in search of substantive law is to discover not so much a body of established custom, still less of statutes, as an argument." [82] Not unnaturally, the meaning of traditional usages was often what was at stake in the great political struggles of the later Middle Ages. Although the struggle over Magna Carta marked a new stage in the relations between king and barons, it was not yet the case that the issues had been generalized, much less erected as substantive principles of law governing the political process. For neither kings nor barons had raised their political sights to a genuinely public level. This point brings me to a final set of observations on the general setting of baronial disputes with their kings.

I have contended that much argumentation proceeded in terms of what was and was not custom, but that this is not a warrant for reading everything in terms of legal doctrine. For what was involved often enough was a political struggle over the place of traditional procedures in new and changing circumstances. It is true that baronial action sometimes went very far. But the fact that the barons engaged in rebellion and deposition does not mean that they possessed any general theory of the constitution. What the evidence always suggests is a comparatively narrow range of vision. But from the thirteenth century on, baronial ideology became increasingly articulate. This was due primarily to the increasing pressure exerted on them by the growth and increased range and efficiency of the royal administration. The impetus behind this was the quickening tempo of commercial life, both foreign and domestic, and above all the impact of the expanding art of war. These broad developments quite naturally impinged on the king first and foremost, giving rise to increased military demands, the need for a much expanded revenue, and the gradual development of a specialized central bureaucracy. Thus late medieval kings represented a drive in the direction of unity, of bureaucratic rationalization of governmental business. But over against this centralizing impulse was set the fragmented organization and stubbornly regional outlook of ancestral England. The observer must beware of reading modern political ideas and impulses into the intermittent collisions of monarch and magnates. For no one then appreciated the general currents that were driving medieval England willy-nilly into the modern world. Her kings were not engaged in the conscious enterprise of creating the nation state. They are best thought of as pursuing the welfare of the royal demesne, in much the same way as their great men pursued their own interests in land, and for the same reasons.

Increased governmental pressure, then, provoked baronial response. But the barons' resistance was largely an unreflective adherence to traditional procedures. What they did not do was to frame any general theory. More sophisticated ideas and arguments emerged in time, but only as the kingdom itself took on a coherent, organized character. Nevertheless, the old notion of a king limited by the need for judgment, for the counsel and consent of the barons, did good service, for it was a functional principle which intermittently rose to the surface of political life, particularly in opposition to a weakened or an overambitious king. The grievances of the barons were specific and so were their remedies. Thus, about the same time that Bracton was composing his treatise the rebellious baronage were insisting that Henry III had wrongfully and dangerously taken to himself counsellors who were not members of their own class. They charged that the king's position was "what pleases the prince has the force of law." [83] They had learned, like Bracton and Glanvill, to use the language of Roman law. But its generality is misleading, for neither the ideas behind it nor the issues at stake were general. The barons insisted merely that the king dismiss his advisers and accept certain of their own number as his rightful counsellors. In short, the barons had no general ideas or notions of public policy because the issues themselves had not been generalized.

This is the context in which Bracton's ideas and those of his contemporaries have to be assessed. It is certainly true that a legal and political thinker may pursue his inquiries with almost no reference to the realities of his society and the political issues of his day. The political and legal literature of the Middle Ages supplies numerous examples of authors who appear never to have considered matters of ordinary politics or concrete jurisdictional disputes. It is all too easy to find treatises which nowhere consider the nature and workings of what has come to be called feudalism, of concrete disputes over titles to land, liberties, privileges, franchises, and the like. They operate instead at a much more exalted level. But the price of that elevation is irrelevance to the political process. Bracton's work is not of that kind. He was much more closely related to the realities of his day. Certainly his main effort was a legal one — the attempt to introduce a measure of organization into the principles of English law — and he did not often venture into generalization. When he did, he left many important questions not just unanswered but unaddressed. The various solutions offered to the political problems raised by Bracton's book all rely, implicitly or explicitly, on the assumption that it contains a general theory and that the whole is integrated in some way. But this is exactly what it is not. The problem of the alleged or seeming contradictions can be neatly resolved only by imposing an order upon it which it does not possess. In order to arrive at an interpretation which unites his ideas it is necessary to jettison portions of the text on various grounds ranging from dubious assertions about literary style to logical incompatibility. These operations make it possible to count as genuine or significant only those passages which say that the king is under God and the law — QED. It has been argued here that this result is unsatisfactory, not because it is manifestly wrong — these passages do appear in the text — but for two different reasons. On the one hand, such interpretations do not represent the whole Bracton, understood in terms of the political climate of his day. On the other hand, they portray a Bracton who is too advanced theoretically. Thus, insisting on the principle of unity and excessive fixation on the modern idea of law not only involves implausible subtleties but multiplies disagreement. More importantly, such interpretations have the effect of cutting Bracton away from his time and environment.

The argument here, then, is that Bracton's ideas have been generalized in a way that is inappropriate to their context. What he meant by the idea of a king under God and the law was, in the first place, that the king ought to proceed by the judgment of the barons and, secondly, that a king ought to practice the Christian virtues. But neither notion carries with it any connotation of a body of substantive, much less constitutional, law that the king ought not to contravene. Certainly it ought to be recognized that emphasis on a sharp distinction between the king's moral and his legal duty will fail to do justice to Bracton's thought, as both Lewis and Tierney have rightly insisted.[84] Legal and moral ideas form a continuum which cannot be demarcated easily. But it has been persistently overlooked that political ideas are a part of the same continuum. Bracton and his contemporaries did not overlook this fact. It is only their modern interpreters who have been so singleminded. For the outstanding feature of Bracton's political thought is an idea which expresses the view that politics and law should be conducted through the cooperation of king and barons. Certainly this is itself a moral idea, for it sets a standard. But if there is any sense in which moral, legal, and political ideas can be at least analytically distinguished, then the idea of counsel and consent is a political idea. Bracton's king, then, was limited not so much by law as by the existence of a tradition. But the ideas of absolutism, constitutionalism, and the rule of law are anachronistic when applied to Bracton. His most general statements say nothing of this kind, for his cardinal doctrine is that law is the product of regal and baronial cooperation. The problem of disagreement is present, but he did not confront it squarely, much less solve it. Nor, for that matter, did any other medieval author. To insist that something very like Dicey's rule of law emerges from Bracton's pages is a distortion. It is radically unhistorical and apolitical. Instead of tracing the vicissitudes and development of what is now seen to have been the growth of the idea and practices expressed in the phrase, the rule of law, it is to assert that the whole matter was virtually solved at the beginning of its course. It is to assert that the oak was not only contained in the acorn but that it was already full grown. Somehow, the ideals of constitutional rule were there all the time. This is to substitute timeless forms for historical inquiry, and to deprive several centuries of their interest and importance.

In thirteenth century England, then, the idea of kingly rule in conjunction with baronial counsel and consent was the center of operative political thought. The legal treatise of Henry de Bracton is much the best known expression of the idea, but he was by no means the only writer to operate on the assumption of its normality. It is reasonable to conclude, moreover, that the principle of baronial counsel and consent was an outgrowth of the very old notion that governance was properly the business of the king and his companions. To be sure, that relationship had changed a good deal, for the king's men were no longer rude barbarian warriors. Long before Bracton's day they had become Christian knights and landed aristocrats. Even so their outlook and their raison d'être were still very much those of a warrior class and were to remain so for several centuries. But the root assumption of rule by kings and great men had not changed, nor had its hierarchical and aristocratic social foundation. By the twelfth and thirteenth centuries, however, men had learned at least to express their conception of government in normative terms: government and law ought to proceed as a joint undertaking. They had not yet begun to supply this outlook with any precise meaning, or with any very elaborate argumentation or justification, though what they did say was a considerable advance on the merely reportorial style of the earlier period. But the great defect in the baronial outlook was that it lacked any conscious appreciation of the general situation and, therefore, any focus. The barons knew that the royal bureaucracy impinged on them, and they reacted to its costly intrusions, only to lapse again into the assumption that some irregularity had been repaired or forestalled. This is what gives the surface history of baronial relations with the king its spasmodic and turbulent look. The disorder was there, to be sure, but it was not the result of any deliberate baronial plan or any persistent antimonarchical impulse. It is true that the barons shared the assumptions of double majesty, but these turned on direct and personal ties with the king. Moreover, the major interests of a great landed magnate were focused locally, for his own land was the seat of his power. The personal nature of political ties and the fragmented structure of interests meant that concerted action by the barons was only occasional. Unusually heavy and broad demands by the king's government provoked group reaction, but the barons had no sense of the circumstances which induced such demands. On the contrary, they were likely to regard any royal policy as an improper disturbance. It was this which made their outlook an ideology of crisis: the natural course of affairs had suffered an interruption which required correction, that is to say, restoration. As yet they had failed to formulate any methods or settled institutional patterns through which their views or their conception of their role in government could be articulated. But despite the episodic and often narrow scope of their resistance, the whole complex of reciprocal needs of kings and barons did give rise to the institutionalized avenue of adjudication, advice, and counsel which began, in the thirteenth century, to be called parliament. The institutional devices and political methods of the nonregal partner in double majesty were hammered out in the concrete politics of the late Middle Ages.

The political ideas of Bracton and his contemporaries in the thirteenth century were a classical expression of the idea of double majesty, which, it was suggested, was a quite accurate conceptualization of medieval political and social reality. It is inaccurate, however, to picture the ambiguity involved in this idea as conscious and incessant animosity between kings and barons. On the contrary, the political order rested on their cooperation in rule, thanks to the fact that the king and his men shared a common outlook. But like any bipolar balance, this one suffered from a serious tendency to instability. In part, this feature was built into medieval politics. For the absence of a civic frame of reference meant that even the most important political issues were reduced to a merely personal or at best a regional level. Instead of assessing matters in terms of their general implications and thus offering genuine alternatives in the realm of public policy, the barons interpreted them in the framework of personal, familial, and dynastic welfare. The consequence of rule by an extremely small and locally oriented aristocracy was a natural disposition to regard any policy initiative of the monarch as a dangerous innovation. There was, therefore, not merely an absence of sustained public policy but a positive antipathy to it among the most influential men of the realm.[1] However, political instability was not entirely a matter of the outlook of the medieval aristocracy, for both they and their king, like most men most of the time, were caught up in broad historical currents they could neither control nor recognize fully. But the combination of these two things — the objective factors of increasing complexity and expense in politics and war, and the absence of any appreciation of the public dimensions of these complications — resulted in recurrent and sometimes serious strain between the king and the great magnates.

Thus the political life of late medieval England was punctuated

by a series of collisions between the king's government and its chief
constituency. It cannot be repeated too often that these contests do
not exhaust the record; had they not been embedded in a framework of cooperation, there would remain only the story of a very
long civil war. But it is true that political life was volatile at best,
and on occasion the English political order was reduced to head-on
collision between rival majesties. In terms of sheer power, the magnates could and sometimes did overpower their monarchs. Political
crises were a recurrent phenomenon throughout the later Middle
Ages, and it cannot be said that any lasting solution was ever
achieved, for the fundamental dualism persisted, reflecting the
absence of civic consciousness among those who held effective power.
But the repeated encounters between the king and what came to be
called the community of the realm resulted in a gradual alteration
in the overall relationship between king and "people" — in changes,
in other words, in the content of double majesty. The aim of this
chapter is to trace the path of change in the period from the
thirteenth through the fifteenth centuries. This will involve rather
an extensive excursion into history, which in a treatment of political
ideas, perhaps, requires a word of explanation. The justification for
such an enterprise is simple enough: the development and meaning
of operative political thought cannot be altogether disengaged from
the particular collisions of king and barons and the attempts to
solve them. The following discussion is by no means an essay in
narrative history, even in summary form, for it is neither detailed
nor continuous enough for that. At the same time, it is not an inquiry into ideas alone, for operative ideas simply did not move on
the sort of rarefied level which alone justifies treatment in total
abstraction from politics. The aim, then, is to straddle the worlds of
events and ideas in an effort to knit the two together.

The vital impulse behind the political controversies of the period
was a gradually expanding claim by the baronage to a role, largely
undefined, in the consideration of the great political business of
the kingdom. The assertion of this claim was not only ambiguous
but sporadic. It was made only in times of crisis, when the intensely
individualistic members of the baronial class were provoked, driven
to a temporary state of cooperation over particular grievances. The
outlook of the magnates was thus an ideology of crisis. But this does
not mean that it did not undergo change. In the early Middle Ages
there was merely an assumption that rule was the affair of the king

and his companions. The views expressed in the twelfth and thirteenth centuries were a modest but distinct improvement, for they were at least explicit statements of the central political norm: rule with counsel and consent. The assertion of a standard, however, solves no problems by itself. The barons' main difficulty was an inability to define the nature and source of political and economic irritants and to devise some method for relieving them. For twelfth century administration was not exact, consistent, or systematic, but rather a complex of processes and techniques.[2] The result was a shifting, undefined target. Moreover, the king's government itself was often confused by the events which produced its own need to press hard for revenue. Yet it was precisely those needs which led to the emergence and growth of the royal bureaucracy, and as it grew more systematic it provided an identifiable though not always culpable agent on which baronial dissatisfaction could be focused. At just this point there appear two of the most important factors in the development of government and politics in medieval England. In the first place, it was the royal bureaucracy which made England the best governed of late medieval kingdoms, and yet ironically enough, this very institutionalization of monarchy had the effect of teaching the baronage that the government could be run with any king, indeed, with no king at all if necessary. Thus in the long run it was the very vigor of English government that sapped its ancient sources of personal kingly dynamism. In effect, the discovery that a king is only a state officer and so not indispensable, not personally essential to government, was a royal gift. Secondly, the ideas with which vigorous royal rule was justified proved to be double-edged. For policies and ideas promoted by the monarchy in its own interest were later taken up by the baronage and turned against the king's government. In short, the baronage learned its vital political lessons from its monarch and his bureaucracy.

The king's bureaucracy, then, was perhaps the principal element in the maturation of operative political ideas and behavior in the later Middle Ages. The royal bureaucracy emerged primarily as a response to two sorts of problems. In the twelfth century, English kings found it necessary to visit their dominions overseas repeatedly and for extended periods. The royal absence was necessitated sometimes by war and sometimes by administrative demands, but in either case the result was the same: the creation of offices which could discharge the royal business without the king's personal attendance. Also, within England itself the king was confronted with the management of a vast estate in land. This too required administrative innovation. The great trouble was that the administrative machinery could work too efficiently for baronial tastes, especially in the collection and expenditure of revenue.[3] The result was that the king's council, the central governing institution, became the chief focus of politics and remained at the center of the political stage right through the fifteenth century.[4] For it was in the king's council that most major matters were discussed, and thus it was there that the regal and baronial outlooks collided. By following the controversies which centered on the king's council in the period of the thirteenth through the fifteenth century, certain major trends can be made out. Broadly speaking, the principal question at issue in the thirteenth century was the composition of the king's council. Intense baronial concern over this question is reflected in several political crises in the reign of Henry III (1216–1272). The heart of the barons' claim was that they not only should have a voice in the selection of the king's counsellors, but also that some among their number had a rightful place in the council. These claims were quite consistently rejected by Henry when he was sufficiently strong to do so or when his baronial adversaries were too divided to make good their claims. The king's view was that the business of naming counsellors was his own. But even when the principle of joint rule through king and council — a council with a baronial complement — was an accepted formula, the terms had to be worked out. It was this difficulty that provided the characteristic flavor of contention from the end of the thirteenth century through the fourteenth century. It was an intensely turbulent period, opening and closing with the deposition of a king. The vital question from a legal perspective was this: what sorts of matters require the consent of the great men? From a political point of view, the problem is better expressed by asking: which policy matters did the baronage perceive as their proper concern?

The most important feature of the fifteenth century, from this point of view, is that effective power came to be lodged in the hands of the great magnates. To be sure, there was nothing new about the fact of baronial power. The difference was that a dangerous imbalance had emerged, for the weakness of the monarchy in this century is well known. But from the perspective of the problem of civic consciousness this is not the decisive point. Regal rule was not replaced by an oligarchy, which after all means another form of political order. It was subverted by contending baronial and royal families. The price was all too often a near absence of central political control. The chaos of civil strife finally led to the jubilant reception of the strongest monarchy since Norman-Angevin times.

At the level of political ideas the principal point about the process of institutionalization is that it opened up important new possibilities. For it supplied the context in which a meaningful distinction could be drawn between the king and the kingdom. This development crystallized in the concept of the impersonal crown. Somehow the crown was a compound of the king and the great men of the realm. But the fact that the crown was endowed with this dual character meant that it symbolized the instability inherent in double majesty as well as the advancing rationalization in government. Most importantly it involved the possibility of a transference of loyalties from the king to the crown. This was an immensely significant development, because it meant that the realm could be conceived of as something other than the king's personal estate. Opposition to royal policy, therefore, could rise to the level of issues, if not quite of principle, rather than focusing on merely personal loyalty or disloyalty to the king as feudal suzerain. Politics could be something more than a personal contest for the king's ear or control of the king's person. Civic consciousness, it has been suggested, did not appear until the seventeenth century. The same point may be expressed by observing that it was not until then that there emerged a politics of principle on a national scale. Nevertheless, important stages in the process were worked out during the later Middle Ages, rather slowly, erratically, and not without violence. What might be called the politics of issues, as contrasted with purely personal politics, was the vital intermediate step.

There are two closely related aspects to the distinction between the person of the ruler and the realm. On one side, there were the actual institutions of a government rapidly becoming more centralized and coming to find embodiment in a vigorous bureaucracy. As the personal monarch receded from view and was more and more replaced by his servants, it became possible for men to understand a contrast between the royal person and an institutional structure. Parallel to this proliferation of institutions, there ran an effort to conceptualize, to come to an understanding of these institutions, their workings, and their relationship to those who were touched by them.

From one point of view, therefore, the history of the later Middle Ages was very largely the course of the transition from personal to institutional monarchy. But this did not mean that men achieved intellectual clarity about the contrast. Their outlook remained ambiguous because it was a compound of both. It has been pointed out that the roots of personal rule were the long-lived principles of leadership of the war band, and that in the late Anglo-Saxon and Norman periods this personal dynamism was transformed into the royal practice of demanding a direct oath of loyalty to the reigning king himself. The English monarchy never relinquished the claim to personal loyalty, including the view that kingly dignity and royal rights inhere, so to say, in the blood and bone of the man who is king. But institutionalized monarchy is profoundly different from this, for it turns on the idea that the king is merely a man who occupies the office of kingship. From that view, loyalty could find a focus not in the man but in the office. Today, of course, an act of imagination is required to avoid assuming this critical distinction, for it is so much a part of thinking about politics that it fails even to rank as a commonplace. But in the Middle Ages this was not so. This fundamental ambiguity persisted until the middle of the seventeenth century. Once again, however, there existed a running confusion which underwent significant changes of content. For the vital addition of an institutional framework afforded the means to shift political loyalty from king to kingship. Moreover, once the standard of governance through counsel and consent achieved institutional expression through the presence of leading magnates in the king's council, other ideas came to occupy the center of the stage. The king and his advisers relied primarily on the idea of the royal prerogative, on the notion that there were certain inalienable regal rights and claims concerning the necessities of the common good or public welfare (*utilitas publica*). But baronial claims also grew more sophisticated. In times of crisis the barons registered claims, more and more consistently in the name of the community of the realm (*communitas* or *universitas regni*), and embraced the idea of guardianship of the common good for themselves. But the most important feature of the barons' opposition was the fact that their claims to participation in decision making were gradually extended, so that they encroached more and more on areas formerly dealt with by the king alone. All these general lines of institutional and intellectual development were hammered out in the concrete political life of these centuries and, therefore, an adequate understanding of operative political thought is inseparable from that political context. It will be useful now to turn directly to an examination of some of the leading episodes in the developing relationship between king and community.

The Quest for Rule with Counsel

There is an abundance of information to be gathered from the long reign of Henry III (1216–1272). It was in this period that the baronage first embarked upon serious efforts to temper the exercise of royal power by the principle of counsel and consent. Henry's answer was to cling fast to the notion that the naming of his counsellors was exclusively the king's concern. Thus the contrast between the outlook of personal monarchy and the principle of counsel and consent was virtually complete. The period exemplifies the difficulty of achieving even a modest amount of actual cooperative rule, as contrasted with the mere assumption that this was the proper method. It also illustrates the theoretical poverty of the baronial party as well as its ephemeral character. In 1216 Henry III fell heir not only to the throne but also to the baronial discontent which had produced the Magna Carta. His reign was marked by considerable unrest, culminating in the great Barons' War (1258–1265). It will be helpful to begin by considering briefly certain aspects of the Great Charter.

Personal monarchy in England suffered its first great shock when the barons forced King John to consent to Magna Carta. Paradoxically, this famous statement is less important for what it says in detail than for the fact that it was accomplished. Hence it will not be necessary to inquire into all its provisions. The chief point is to recognize its two-sided character, for it was at once retrospective and prospective. Its specific measures are in the main backward-looking, for what they do is sum up and, in part, define more exactly the indefinite usages of the twelfth century. Considered from this perspective, the Great Charter takes on the character of a rather long list of specific grievances, and the character of the complaints reveals the essentially feudal concerns of the great barons.[5] Even on the

retrospective side, however, two matters of special interest here
emerge from the consideration of what the barons wanted. First and
more important, the sum of the magnates' efforts to define their
relations with the king shows that their movement may be reasonably interpreted as a protest against arbitrary rule, that is to say,
against the imprecision of feudal exactions and obligations.[6] The
effort to achieve increased stability of expectations through a detailed legal instrument, in other words, was a great improvement
on baronial protests in the twelfth century. For earlier expression of
baronial discontent had been very largely a matter of aimless dis-
orderliness. But it is important to notice here, as in so many other
ways, that this taste for legal regularity had been cultivated through
the barons' exposure to the king's courts. Secondly, the struggle over
the Great Charter shows that the chief political preoccupations of
the baronage were local or regional rather than national. For they
had expended great energy and money on purchasing exemptions
from the operation of the king's taxes and laws in their own lands or
regions. This appetite for "liberties," too, as J. C. Holt has shown,
men had acquired from the monarch's desire to sell them.[7]

The rather limited outlook of the retrospective side of the Great
Charter and the vital role of political instruction from above are
clear enough. But the barons' document has a prospective side too.
Here the main point is that some of the language of the charter
was extraordinarily general. Later generations were able to seize
on this and, in effect, to extend some of the principles of the charter
well beyond the meaning of the original. Among these, three lines of
thought are of special interest here: the version of counsel and consent in the Great Charter; the notion of judgment by peers and the
law of the land; and a cluster of ideas centering on the demesne
lands of the king. None of these was new in 1215, but each had an
extraordinary future.

The principle of baronial counsel and consent was far from novel
in 1215, but the expression of the idea in Magna Carta represents a
distinct improvement. Its great virtue is that it is specific and involves a definite claim by the barons to a place in the king's council.
Thus, after excepting the recognized, ordinary feudal aids, chapter
12 states: "No scutage nor aid shall be imposed on our kingdom,
unless by common counsel of our kingdom . . . ." Chapter 14 supplies the content for the expression "common counsel." It says that
the king "will cause to be summoned the archbishops, bishops,

abbots, earls, and greater barons . . . and . . . all others who hold of us in chief . . ." [8] The principle was framed very narrowly: all those summoned were the king's chief military tenants—subjects, that is, whose lands were held directly from the king. Moreover, each one was to be summoned as an individual. Thus no great breadth was involved, nor was there expressed here any idea of representation, since the great magnates came for themselves.[9] Yet despite its restricted scope and the further fact that this chapter was actually omitted from subsequent reissues of the Charter, the idea persisted and was gradually refined and generalized.[10] Its omission, therefore, was far from decisive. The fact that it had been part of the original charter, hallowed by baronial victory, was enough to make it a standard, as, indeed, was the Charter as a whole, even though many of its provisions had no real utility in altered circumstances. Its value was chiefly symbolic.[11]

The best known passage in Magna Carta, however, is chapter 39, which gives expression to the idea that free men must be tried by their peers, and this in accordance with the law of the land. "No freeman shall be taken or [and] imprisoned or disseised or exiled or in any way destroyed, nor will we go upon him nor send upon him, except by the lawful judgment of his peers or [and] by the law of the land." [12] It has been suggested, quite plausibly, that these ideas were essentially an effort to impose upon the monarchy a model derived from the practice of baronial courts, where issues between tenants or retainers of a lord were tried by the other tenants.[13] However this may be, the main thing to notice is that chapter 39 did not impose any substantive limits on kingship. But it did supply a powerful statement of an important procedural ideal that has been noticed before: that the king could proceed in certain sorts of business, at least, only after his counsellors had given their judgment in the matter. Together with the presence of barons in the king's council, then, came the beginning of the search for methods whereby baronial interests might affect regal policy.

Thus as early as 1215 the English baronage had learned to value definition and the security of expectations which is the great merit of legal rules. They had embarked on the long quest for techniques to obtain the effectuation of their interests. These were distinctly narrow, and the immediate results were not particularly auspicious. To begin with, a good many of the more extreme provisions of the original charter were struck out in the definitive issue. Moreover, too many of the barons of 1215 failed to rise above immediate interests. The result was that the coalition dissolved almost immediately.[14] As Jolliffe has observed, they took their victory in terms of private gain. They saw it, not as a constitutional landmark, but "as a pledge of material gains immediate and to come. The *jura* and *libertates* which it promised, or that had been promised during the negotiations, were not, and in that age of short views could not be, abstractions of law. They were a revival of feudal glories . . . If any of the secular rebels was able to forget his family ambitions his words and actions have gone unrecorded." [15] The barons, therefore, were not even an especially good pressure group, much less a body of civic-minded subjects. Having achieved the immediate object, they returned to their local concerns. Nevertheless, the combination of their victory at Runnymede and the general language they used concerning some issues of critical political importance served to make the Great Charter the greatest single standard of governmental rectitude in the history of English politics. The barons had wrought far better than they knew.

Now it will be useful to consider the set of ideas and issues surrounding the royal demesne. This term signifies the king's personal landed estates, and Magna Carta marks the appearance of this subject in politics. The provisions of the Charter on this matter do not have the immediate impact and obvious importance of those just discussed. But during the course of the thirteenth century they came into their own as most important elements of baronial ideology. They proved to be an important aid in the development of the distinction between the king and the crown, and they were also linked to the idea of consent to taxation and the notion that the king should live of his own. Finally, it is important to recognize that these lines of development emanated from above, from royal policy.[16] They are especially intriguing because they came to be prominent among those ideas which were originally fashioned and promoted by the monarchy but were later taken up by the baronage and turned against their author.

It has already been noted that the king's primary concerns attached to the working of his own landed estates. This was not unnatural because, as Hoyt has said, the royal demesne "was the immediate basis of royal power, not only as the source of the bulk of his revenues, but also because it was closely associated with the whole administrative system." Administrative innovation, that is, was a part of royal policy because it was required in the management of the royal demesne. With respect to the demesne lands, the king was in the same position as any feudal lord, deriving from them the profits of agriculture and the administration of justice. "Beyond that fact there was no fundamental distinction between the royal demesne and the rest of the realm." [17] Moreover, there was no distinction between the lands which the king held as king and those which he held as a private person.[18] Here, therefore, even at the apex of the legal order, appears the characteristic feudal assimilation of public jurisdiction and administration with private proprietary right.

Reacting to the pressures of rising costs in government and war, the monarchs of the last half of the twelfth century employed a variety of techniques to increase royal revenue. The details of these techniques need not be spelled out. The point here is that it was possible to prosecute the attempt to increase revenue more freely and efficiently on the royal demesne. In general, the monarchs resorted to systematic increases in the price demanded from those who purchased the right to collect the revenues at the local level. It was a system which invited abuse and oppression, because the "farmer," as he was called, paid a settled sum to the government and was entitled to keep whatever surplus he could squeeze from his "farm." King John appears to have pursued the effort to increase revenues with special vigor. The negotiations which led to Magna Carta mark the appearance of the royal demesne in politics, as was said, and this was especially dangerous to royal interests. For there was an important difference between royal demesne and the rest of the realm. The king was entitled to levy the tax called tallage on his demesne and, at least in theory, this could be done at will. Just as with other levies, John had exacted tallage with increasing frequency and at a higher rate.[19]

Complaint about such financial exactions was one of the chief concerns of the baronial movement of 1214–1215, and King John did acquiesce in some of the barons' demands. But royal resistance to interference with the demesne lands was marked, and the result was that John's charter did not prohibit tallage and that it expressly excluded the royal demesne from a provision forbidding the increase of rents.[20] This meant that the demesne lands were "left exposed to arbitrary increases of their annual rents." [21] Thus, the distinction between royal rights over demesne and other lands was a deliberate royal policy. Insistence on this distinction and royal concentration on exploiting demesne lands are easy to understand. In these ways the necessity of obtaining counsel and consent could be avoided, and so, too, the danger of baronial demands in exchange for consent to any extraordinary aid. In short, the distinction worked to the advantage of royal interests. Yet by the middle of the thirteenth century the baronage had seized on the idea that the king should seek his revenues exclusively from the royal demesne. The king, it was argued, should live of his own. They had thus taken up a royal policy and employed it in resisting royal efforts at national taxation.[22]

The king and his advisers reinforced their position with another line of argument: that the royal lands were inalienable. This idea was a solution to the problem of rising prices, for the government argued that royal lands could always be taken back into the king's hand. The point of doing so was that they could then be re-awarded, but only in exchange for a fine or, perhaps, a higher price for the farm.[23] The idea of inalienability was the principle of justification here, and by 1257 Henry III required his counsellors to swear that they would "consent to the alienation of none of those things which belong to the ancient demesne of the crown." [24] But precisely as in the case of the idea of a royal demesne distinct from the rest of the realm, the baronage took up the principle of inalienability. Indeed, they became zealous advocates, demanding that the royal lands not be frivolously alienated. Their motives are perfectly plain. If the king alienated his lands, the eventual result would be the impoverishment of the crown. On the other hand, if his income could be maintained, there would be no need to require revenue from the barons.

In addition to these rather obvious extensions of regal ideas prompted by cupidity, the ideas associated with the royal demesne also promoted the development of the vital distinction between king and kingdom. For in the attempt to retain a free hand in the taxation of the royal estates, the king and his ministers had drawn a sharp distinction between the lands that belonged to the king as a man and those that did not. This certainly invited the inference that the king was, in effect, two people: a landlord like any other, and a monarch whose proprietary rights over the rest of the realm were indirect and impersonal. To be sure, to him belonged the business of government, but it was also clear that he had a merely private capacity, and the king's subjects had been invited to distinguish between the rights which attached to each of these two capacities. Though these ideas were indefinite enough to produce profound disagreement, they all became part of the baronial ideology of crisis.

The baronial concerns which were only shadowed out at the time of Magna Carta emerged more clearly in the outstanding conflicts of the reign of Henry III.[25] The king had ascended the throne as a boy, and the fact that rule was in the hands of a regent, William Marshall, and his baronial advisers served to sharpen consciousness of the isue of baronial rights in relation to the council. But in the 1220's Henry assumed personal command and pursued a policy of ruling with counsellors of his own choice. Resentment over this was repeatedly expressed by the barons. In 1233–1234 they mounted sufficient force to require the king to replace certain of his advisers with men congenial to themselves. Their complaint was that the king had removed all his "natural" ministers and replaced them with foreigners. He had given to these unnatural advisers custody of wardships, castles, earldoms, and baronies. "And he gave to them the custody of his treasury and the laws and justice of the country . . . Judgments were given into the hands of outlaws; peace to those who are full of discord; justice to the unlawful. And when the magnates of the kingdom stated their case before the king, on behalf of the kingdom, regarding the oppressions which these men had inflicted, there was nobody to give them justice." [26] In connection with this report, the baronial claim to have been acting for the kingdom deserves special notice, for despite the presumptuousness involved, it did become a standard claim and one of very considerable value as propaganda. Certainly it is a very simple idea, almost natural to any group involved in the prosecution of its interests. But that is exactly the point, for it is an indication of some degree of group consciousness. The quite different point that the barons complained that there was no one to give them justice is equally significant. This too was a recurrent item of contention, for the justices were all the king's appointees, removable by him. Later this became an important factor in the appearance of political trials in parliament, a device which circumvented the ordinary courts.

In the case of baronial opposition in 1233–1234 the king bowed to force, but only temporarily. For by the year 1248 the chronicler Matthew Paris reports another collision of baronial desires with those of personal monarchy. He says that in that year the nobility gathered in London with the expectation that the king was about to mend his ways. But they were to be rebuffed, Matthew reports, for the king gave the assembled magnates "an unmannerly reply" in these words.

> You have wanted, all you leading men of England, and not particularly politely either, to bend your lord the king to your own will, and to impose on him a much too servile condition whenever he refuses any of your requests. Furthermore any man may make use of whatever counsel he likes and from whomsoever he likes, and every head of a household may place in office or defer or even depose anyone he chooses of his household; but yet you have boldly presumed to deny this to your lord king, though least of all ought servants to judge their masters and vassals their prince. Nor ought they to rope him in with conditions. Nay, rather are they bound to be directed by their lord's will and be set in order according to his wish, since they are accounted inferior to him . . . Therefore he will neither remove nor find substitutes for chancellor, justiciar, or treasurer, as you have proposed to arrange.[27]

This is an excellent statement of the ethos of personal monarchy, though its interest extends farther than that. In addition to a vigorous assertion of the view that selecting counsellors was solely the king's affair, it also illustrates the ambiguity of the traditions involved. Henry's appeal was to an idea that the barons knew very well, indeed, could not help agreeing with, for the king based his reply on an analogy with lordship in general. This entailed the view that the kingdom was assimilable to a barony and hence indistinguishable in principle from any private estate. In short, the familial and political were still badly blurred, and the baronage had not yet learned the value of a sharp distinction between them, nor the application of a different set of principles to the political sphere.

Politically the reign of Henry III reached its high point in the great baronial wars of the middle of the century (1258–1265). Here all the issues discussed above became subjects of active political contention. The surface issue was the same: the barons' demand for influence in the appointment and management of the king's counsellors. But by 1258 the baronial party had advanced beyond mere complaint: they had developed a program, and they proceeded to impose it upon the king. It was expressed in the famous Provisions of Oxford. The impasse reached is nicely symbolized in the very mode of composition of the Provisions, for they were drafted by a group of twenty-four magnates, half of whom had been appointed by the king and half by the barons. In 1258 they were presented to Henry, who had already sworn to uphold their findings. But the following years were occupied by conflict over their interpretation. The immediate outcome of this struggle was the collapse of the baronial party, led by Simon de Montfort, and the triumph of the king. Wilkinson has rightly suggested that the fundamental reason was that "the magnates could devise no satisfactory method of maintaining a permanent . . . control over the ruler . . . The medieval tradition of government was indissolubly connected with the personal authority of the monarch." [28]

Among other things, the Provisions contained language concerning the management of the affairs of the kingdom which could be and was interpreted in diametrically opposed ways by the contending parties. Four magnates were named and were said to have the power to elect the king's council, which was to be composed of fifteen barons. Further, it was ordained that there should be three parliaments each year. It should be noted, however, that the composition of these parliaments was entirely aristocratic, for in addition to the fifteen members of the council, only the attendance of twelve other "good men" was made obligatory.[29] Simon's precedent in calling for regular parliaments was probably not decisive in that particular connection, though it is significant that a regular pattern was being called for, at least. What is most important here is to notice the depth of the political collision. In the last resort it represented a struggle for supremacy between the monarch and the baronage.[30] The baronial effort was abortive, however, and Simon fell at Evesham. The collapse of his movement was followed by the Dictum of Kenilworth in 1266. The Dictum did not sweep away the complaints of the baronial party. On the contrary, it gave expression to them, but the interesting thing is that now they are expressed as supplications. The king is asked to employ as advisers men who will settle matters according to the laws and customs of the realm; he is urged to observe the liberties of the Church and the charters of liberties and of the forest, to which he is bound by oath. Further, "the lord king shall provide that grants which up to the present he has made of his free will, and not under compulsion, shall be observed; and that he will firmly establish other necessary [measures] determined by his men and at his own pleasure." But the most general language of the Dictum is contained in the opening paragraph. "We declare and provide that the most serene lord prince Henry, illustrious king of England, shall have, fully receive, and freely exercise his dominion, authority, and royal power without impediment or contradiction of any one, whereby, contrary to the approved rights and laws and the long established customs of the kingdom, the regal dignity might be offended; and that to the same lord king and to his lawful mandates and precepts full obedience and humble attention shall be given by all and singular the men of the same kingdom, both greater and lesser." [31] It may perhaps be said that the Dictum represents a compromise, but it seems clear that the monarch has had the best of it. It is more interesting to notice the deep ambiguity in the language of the Dictum, for it is an excellent example of an element inherent in double majesty. Both sides appeal to the same standards: the ancient customs of the realm. This makes it quite clear that what is involved is not so much a legal question as a persistent style of argument.

Now in the present case there is a fine propaganda piece from the baronial side, from which a great deal can be learned. Called the Song of Lewes after the great battle of the war, it is a propaganda tract composed by some ardent follower of Simon de Montfort. The general purpose of the song is to characterize the king's position and to supply a rebuttal. In the course of doing so, it makes the aims and attitudes of the baronial party quite clear. The king, it is said, thinks he is released from law.

See! we touch the root of the disturbance of the kingdom about which we are writing, and of the dissension of the parties who fought the said battle; to different objects did they turn their aim. The king with his party wished to be thus free, and urged that he ought to be so, and was of necessity, or that deprived of a king's right, he would cease to be king, unless he should do whatever he might wish; that the magnates of the realm had not to heed, whom he set over his own counties, or on whom he conferred the wardenship of castles, or whom he would have to show justice to his people; and he would have as chancellor and treasurer of his realm anyone soever at his own will, and counsellors of whatever nation, and various ministers at his own discretion, without the barons of England interfering in the King's acts, as "the command of the prince has the force of law"; and that which he might command of his own will would bind each.

According to the songwriter, this is the king's pleading. Then he turns to an exposition of the baronial point of view.

Which party in the first place openly makes protestation, that it devises naught against the royal honour, or seeks anything contrary to it; nay, is zealous to reform and magnify the kingly state; just as, if the kingdom were devastated by enemies, it would not then be reformed without the barons, to whom this would be proper and suitable . . . He who can contribute aught of aid to the king's honour, owes it to his lord when he is in peril, when the kingdom is deformed as it were in extremity.[32]

Here is the development of a kind of doctrine of emergency: it is as if the kingdom had been invaded and is in extreme danger. Under these admittedly unusual circumstances, the barons have a duty to the kingdom. There is here, one might observe, just the germ of a distinction between the king and the kingdom. But at this date the barons had not really formulated that useful doctrine. Without it, there is little alternative but to resort to unadorned coercion. If the king is misguided or deceived, or if he endangers the kingdom out of willful malice, "then ought the magnates of the kingdom to take care, that the land be purged of all errors. And if to them belongs the purging of error, and to them belongs foresight, governess of [good] conduct, how would it not be lawful for them to take foresight lest any evil happen which might be harmful?" [33] This is the baronial position, and the writer next turns to the task of framing a reply to the view he has attributed to the king and his party. The rebuttal takes this form. There is only one king who needs no assistance whatever in his rule, and that is God. Other rulers require assistance and counsel, which "keeps them right." Now, the king admits this but claims that the naming of such counsellors is his own choice, for otherwise he would be wrongly constrained. The songwriter's reply is that "all constraint does not deprive of liberty, nor does all restriction take away power . . . To what purpose does free law wish kings to be bound? That they may not be able to be stained by an adulterine law. And this constraining is not of slavery, but is the enlarging of kingly virtue." [34] Consider, says the author, that God himself is unable to err, and this "is not impotence but the highest power." Thus, they "who guard the king, that he sin not when tempted, are themselves the servants of the king, to whom let him be truly grateful, because they free him from being made a slave, because they do not surpass him, by whom he is led. But whoever is truly king is truly free, if he rule himself and his kingdom rightly; let him know that all things are lawful for him which are fitted for ruling the kingdom, but not for destroying it." The king must render his duty to God; otherwise obedience is not due to him, for he holds his place from God. Moreover, the people are God's people, not his.[35]

What is the alternative to the king's position? At this point the songwriter develops a rhetorical eulogy to the law. For

> law rules the dignity of the king; for we believe that law is a light, without which we infer that the guide goes astray. Law, whereby is ruled the world and the kingdoms of the world, is described as fiery, because it contains a mystery of deep meaning; it shines, burns, glows; fire by shining prevents wandering, it avails against cold, purifies, and reduces to ashes, some hard things it softens, and cooks what was raw, takes away numbness, and does many other good things. Sacred law supplies like gifts to the king . . . If the king be without this law, he will go astray; if he hold it not, he will err shamefully. Its presence gives right reigning, and its absence the disturbance of the realm. That law speaks thus: "By me kings reign, by me is justice shewn to those who make laws." That stable law shall no king alter . . . It is commonly said, "As the king wills, the law goes"; truth wills otherwise, for the law stands, the king falls.[36]

One is reminded immediately of the Bractonian maxims that the king ought to be under God and the law, and that it is the law which makes the king. In the discussion of Bracton it was argued that these statements had only the kind of ethical content that the songwriter clearly intends. It should be remembered that Bracton's treatise was contemporary with the events in question here. In both cases it is fair to say that distaste for arbitrary rule is being expressed. But, just as clearly, no rules of law emerge from this rhetoric. Fortunately, the songwriter tells us more exactly what he has in mind. If the king undertakes to solve the problems of rule by himself, he says, it will be easy for him to be deceived. Such matters concern the whole realm; therefore, it is a matter of concern to the whole community that the wrong people not be the king's counsellors. The present king has taken to himself foreign advisers, and this cannot help proving abortive. Instead, the community of the realm is to engage in counsel, and their opinion should supply the matter of what is to be decreed.[37] The king's counsellors ought to be those who "have the will and knowledge and power to be of profit . . . men to whom the various customs of their country are known; who may feel that they themselves are injured if the kingdom is injured . . ." Indeed, the issue is made plainer still. Thus, "if the king loves the magnates of the kingdom, although he alone, like a great seer, knows what may be needful for ruling the kingdom, what may become him, what must be done, he will not conceal that, which he has prudently decreed, *from those without whom he will be unable to bring to effect that which he shall ordain;* therefore he will discuss with his own men those things which he will not think to do by himself. *Why will he not communicate his plans to those from whom he will as a suppliant ask for aids?*" The important point, then, is that the king must have consent to effectuate his rule and to obtain the necessary funds to do so. The writer concludes on an even stronger note. "From all that has been said above, it will be clear that it is the duty of the magnates of the kingdom to see what things are convenient for the governance of the kingdom, and expedient for the preservation of the peace; and that the king have natives at his side, whether as councillors or as the greater men of the realm, not strangers nor favourites who supplant others and the good customs . . . But if he have sought to degrade his own men, have overturned their rank, it is in vain that he will ask why, when so deranged, they do not obey him; nay, they would be mad if they were to do so." [38]

At the level of anything that might conceivably be called a reference to "higher" law, the author never contrives to rise above rhetoric. The concrete argument of the Song is political. It is the demand that kingly rule be joined to the advice and consent of the magnates of the realm. The magnates have a right and a duty to see to the governance of the realm, at least in cases of extreme danger, as they construe it. This right and duty are quite independent; they are not derived from kingly authority. That general point of view is linked to practical matters of political life: the ruler simply cannot rule if he lacks consent, tacit or otherwise. Power, however exalted, requires as a practical matter of fact a social base on which to stand. It is true that the rebellion of Simon and his followers and the political thought of the Song involve baronial supremacy. Had the barons been able to make good this claim, it would have meant the end of double majesty: the monarch would have been a mere instrument. But their movement collapsed and with it the temporary ascendancy of the magnates. Even so, it seems just to say that Montfort's rebellion marked a turning point, for it established the general principle of baronial counsel. To be sure, even the bare principle did not go entirely unchallenged subsequently. But it was the accepted criterion of cooperation. Much of the rest of the high politics of medieval England revolved around boundary disputes concerning the details of appropriate coordination between the claims of prince and community. These disputes involved the development of a more refined conceptual apparatus.

Two other aspects of the ideology of Montfort's rebellion require attention. First, there is the immensely significant fact that when Simon's baronial support began to dissolve, he turned to the lesser men, the knights. His resort to this alternative political base proved to be a harbinger of repeated attempts by both king and magnates to broaden their support in subsequent disagreements.[39] Secondly, it is important to notice that Simon's baronial support did collapse. This was nothing new; it was a pattern which was to be repeated again and again. The baronial movement of 1214–1215 had dissolved at the moment of victory. Similarly, in connection with Montfort's movement, Treharne writes that it failed "from internal division and betrayal. The baronage of 1258 was a small body of men, perhaps a hundred and fifty all told, who knew each other well, and whose co-operation was a matter of personal and individual feeling for a cause shared with friends and acquaintances." [40] Those who abandoned the movement did so because the proposed reforms involved a loss of power and prestige in administering their feudal estates. The result was the triumph of the king.[41]

King and Baronage in Uneasy Alliance

From the time of Magna Carta to the end of the reign of Henry III, then, both the claims and the ideological position of the baronage had matured rather considerably. For the barons had learned to make institutional claims as contrasted with merely personal ones, to focus on the composition of the king's council rather than their individual relationships to the king. They had learned, further, to couch their demands in the language of ancestral piety and the claim that they were speaking on behalf of the whole community of the realm and its welfare. But crucial ambiguities remained and so did the baronial propensity to abandon serious political enterprises after what seemed to be victories. The conflicts that marked Henry's reign form an interesting contrast with that of his popular and successful son, Edward I (1272–1307). For, on the whole, relations between Edward and his barons were good.[42] In the earlier years of the reign, a great number of statutes of first-rate importance were produced. Some of these have been discussed already and others will be examined in the next chapter. But toward the end of the reign the alliance between Edward and his magnates dissolved, and the king found himself confronted with a powerful opposition resting on an alliance between the magnates and the smaller land-holders, the knights of the shire. Both Edward and his subjects were enmeshed in the pressing demands of a rapidly maturing political system, particularly the incessant increase of scale in warfare. Edward's financial and military needs prompted marked increases in his demands on the realm, and it seems fair to say that the origins of a genuinely representative parliament are traceable to these governmental needs. However that may be, it is certain that in the last quarter of the thirteenth century the king sometimes issued writs summoning to parliament not only the great magnates but also knights representing the shires and burgesses representing the towns. The contrast between the individual summons of the great men and the representative character of the lesser men must be emphasized. The knights and burgesses were really representatives, for they were commanded to come to parliament with full power delegated to them to bind their constituencies to the decisions of the parliament. In this way Edward at once reached a much broader source of revenue and soldiers and developed an effective method for carrying the decisions of government to the local level. This practice remained intermittent in the reign of Edward I and in that of Edward II (1302–1327), for "commons" were not always summoned to parliament. But from 1327 on the commons were always summoned.[43] None of this meant any remarkable breakthrough of ordinary men into the world of politics, for these knights and burgesses were themselves men of substance. But the obvious increase in their role in politics, modest though it was, was closely tied to the fact that both king and barons were in need of allies, and both sought them in the same place. In addition to this, the reign of Edward I illustrates very well the potential volatility in the relations between the king and his great men even under an able and generally successful monarch. For Edward was very much what a medieval monarch was supposed to be: a great soldier and giver of justice. Baronial opposition certainly did not go so far as it had under Henry III, nor as it would under Edward II. There was no attempt to alter the administration or to control the king's person. Even so, the last years of the reign show that the issues had been submerged rather than solved. For the conflict between personal kingship and baronial expectations emerged anew in the years following 1297. The immediate questions involved the king's military needs, but they were soon cast in the traditional framework.

In the spring of 1297 Edward was about to embark on a military campaign in support of the Count of Flanders against the French king, Philip the Fair. Accordingly, he issued a writ summoning to his aid all the smaller landowners whose property was of a given value, as well as a writ summoning his great tenants-in-chief. Resistance was immediate; it appears to have issued from the magnates' perception of the gravity of the challenge to their place in the social order. From one point of view, Edward's summons to the small landowners was a concrete application of one of the principal ideas in the outlook of personal kingship. It was an assertion of the idea of the allegiance owed by all directly to the king, bypassing the mediation of the great feudal lords. If the king could succeed in this, the result would be to shatter the military predominance of the magnates. That predominance was, at once, the source of baronial power and the expression of the ethos which supplied the rather limited measure of class cohesion exhibited by the barons. The magnates appear to have been conscious, in some degree, of the threat to their status. The small landowners found themselves in an enviable position, for both Edward and his barons needed their support. The magnates took up the cause of the small land-owners and gave expression to the general reluctance to respond to the king's summons. Now, there is no doubt that the king's tenants-in-chief were under a recognized obligation to perform the services asked. On the other hand, it is just as clear that the summons to the small landowners was unusual.[44] At any rate, the earls presented a petition, the Monstraunces, to Edward. It says that the "community of the land" considers that it does not owe service in Flanders, "for neither they nor their predecessors nor forefathers ever did service in that land." Moreover, even if they did owe such service they could not perform it, because they have been taxed too much to afford it. "Also, all the community of the land feel themselves much grieved because they are not treated in accordance with the laws and customs of the land, in accordance with which their ancestors used to be treated; nor do they enjoy the liberties which they were wont to have, but these are arbitrarily put aside." The Monstraunces go on to complain about departures from Magna Carta and the Charters of the Forest and the tax on wool. The petition ends with a bit of advice: The community thinks it would not "be to the king's advantage to cross into Flanders . . ."[45]

Clearly, Edward would have to conciliate one or another of the groups opposed to him or the Flanders campaign would be impossible. He elected to pacify the small landowners by granting a renewal of the Charters (the Great Charter and the Charters of the Forest), for which he received an aid. Apparently the aid was granted by the knights alone, or so at any rate the magnates complained to the king's council after Edward had departed for France. Following Edward's effort to split the alliance, the magnates launched their own campaign to broaden the base of their support. This is what seems to account for the royal document called De Tallagio non Concedendo, which lays stress on taxation. It looks as if it were designed to appeal to the knights and, incidentally, to the burgesses as well. Two passages from this document are especially interesting. One of these states that "no tallage or aid shall be laid or levied by us or our heirs in our realm, without the good will and assent of the archbishops, bishops, earls, barons, knights, burgesses, and other freemen of our realm." The other reads thus: "We will and grant for us and our heirs, that all clerks and laymen of our land shall have all their laws, liberties, and free customs, as largely and wholly as they have used to have the same at any time when they had them best and most fully; and if any statutes have been made by us or our ancestors, or any customs brought in contrary to them, or any manner of article contained in this present charter, we will and grant, that such manner of statutes and customs shall be void and frustrate for evermore." [46]

The immediate upshot of the crisis of 1297 was a concession by Edward which goes under the name of the Confirmatio Cartarum: that is, its principal import is to confirm the charters which, it says, "were drawn up by the common assent of the whole kingdom in the time of King Henry, our father . . ." They are to be observed, and any judgments contrary to them "shall be null and void." Taxes that have been granted "for the sake of our wars and other needs . . . we will not make into a precedent for the future . . ." Such exactions, it is affirmed, will not be taken "except by the common assent of the whole kingdom and for the common benefit of the same kingdom, saving the ancient aids and prises due and accustomed." [47]

Once again, then, a monarch had given ground in the face of formidable opposition. But the Confirmatio was not Edward's last word, nor did it put an end to baronial discontent. In the years following, Edward expressed views which reveal that the cleavage of 1297 ran deep. Once more under pressure, in 1299, Edward promised to confirm the Charters, and it was recorded that, "the king did indeed confirm the articles which they [the earls] had demanded from him, but added at the end 'saving the right of our Crown.'" In view of this, the earls "went to their homes unappeased," and the people "exchanged their blessings for curses." [48] In 1300, at the end of certain articles on the charters, it was said that "both the king and his council, and all they that were present in the making of this ordinance, will and intend that the right and prerogative of his crown shall be saved in all things." [49] This reservation appears in a document of the same year dealing with the forests. [50] The full bearing of the breach between Edward and his barons emerges in the events of 1305. In that year the king obtained a bull from Pope Clement V which absolved him from the promises he had made, since they had been extorted under compulsion. This applies, according to the bull, even if the king has given his oath, for "when you performed the ceremony of your coronation, you took an oath, as it is claimed on your behalf to preserve the honour and rights of the crown." [51]

Clearly, then, the range of cooperation between kings and barons was narrow and the relationship volatile at best. The documents which emerged from their quarrels are valuable illustrations of several important themes. It is clear that appeals to the Great Charter had become a typical device. Moreover, the language of consent had been supplied with some substantial clothing in the form of a representative parliament. Yet the king insisted upon reserving the rights of the crown in these concessions, and this reservation was to become the leading device for royal insistence on the personal character of kingship. Finally, the generally backward-looking aspect of all these documents deserves notice, for it serves as a reminder that men were still very far from imagining that the future might contain a goal; rather, the sanctity of the past continued to be the standard in politics.

Divided Allegiance and Deposition

Whereas the reign of Edward I exemplified generally good relations between king and barons, that of his son Edward II (1307–1327) illustrates the reverse. For the reign as a whole was a disaster, occupied by a running collision and ending in Edward's deposition. The issues separating the partners in double majesty were greatly sharpened, and this was reflected in a considerable refinement of ideology. The principal point is that the idea of a distinction between the king's person and the crown was spelled out clearly. This meant that a group in opposition could claim that it was acting on a respectable impulse, allegiance to the crown rather than to its wearer. Moreover, Edward's dissident barons undertook to supply a specific content for the general principle of counsel and consent. The king's reply to the challenge was a similar sharpening and broadening of the claims of prerogative power.

It has been suggested that the remarkable growth of administrative machinery in the twelfth and thirteenth centuries made possible the politically vital distinction between the king and the crown. This distinction emerged clearly in 1308. The immediate occasion of the enunciation of the idea was the banishment of the king's favorite, Peter Gaveston. Apparently Gaveston had an extraordinarily powerful influence on the king. Immediately upon his accession

Edward had bestowed an earldom on his confidant and had show-
ered him with other profitable gifts. For the magnates, however, the
important point was that Gaveston was the prevailing power in the
king's court. He was their political enemy because he had succeeded
in insinuating himself between the king and the magnates, his rightful counsellors.[52] Finally it is reported that Gaveston was indicted
at the Easter parliament of 1308. The indictment charges him with
treason, but it recognizes that he cannot be judged in any legal
action because of the king's protection. The people, therefore, "had
awarded him to be a robber of the people and a traitor to his lord
and the realm, as though he were a man attainted and judged.
Therefore, the king was begged to execute the award." [53] But it is
the general language of the opening paragraph of the indictment
that is of primary interest here.

> Homage and the oath of allegiance are more in respect of
> the Crown than in respect of the king's person and they are
> more allied to the Crown than to the person. This appears from
> the fact that, before the estate of the Crown has passed by de-
> scent, no allegiance is due to the person. Wherefore, if it happen
> that the king is not ruled by reason in regard to the estate of
> the Crown, his lieges are bound by the oath sworn to the Crown
> to lead the king back by reason into the estate of the Crown, or
> else their oath would not be kept. It must next be asked, how
> should the king be led, whether by an action at law or by coer-
> cion? By an action at law may no man obtain remedy, for he
> would have no judges, except those of the king's, and in this
> case, if the king's will were not accordant with reason, he would
> obtain nothing except the maintenance and confirmation of
> error. Wherefore, when the king will not remedy the matter and
> remove that which is evil for the people at large and hurtful
> for the Crown, it is necessary, in order that the oath may be
> saved, that it be adjudged by the people that the matter be
> removed by coercion, for the king is bound by his oath to
> govern his people, and his lieges are bound to govern with him
> and in aid of him.[54]

Here baronial defiance of the king is based explicitly on the principle of allegiance to the crown: disobedience is thus made to look
like a higher loyalty. This is surely a much more sophisticated idea

than any encountered before. Moreover, it proved to be the central assumption of resistance to the king until the entire question of the king's place in the political order was set on a new foundation in the seventeenth century. This does not mean that nothing was added to the idea in the intervening centuries. On the contrary, it underwent a good deal of refinement. The essential thing, however, was the achievement of the basic distinction.

In 1321 this same line of thought was employed, though it is true that the circumstances are puzzling. In 1308 it had provided a rationale for the barons in obliging Edward II to banish his favorite. In 1321, however, the doctrine was used by the barons to accuse Hugh Despenser the younger. Despenser was the king's servant and had been engaged in efforts to consolidate the king's position in Wales. Once again, the barons were provoked to unified action in defense of their interests. As in the case of Gaveston, Despenser was accused of treason and his banishment was demanded. What was Despenser's treason? The magnates accused him of entertaining the views which had supplied the rationale of baronial action in 1308. The bill for the banishment of the Despensers alleged that they believed, treasonously, that "homage and oath of allegiance is more by reason of the crown than by reason of the king's person and is more bound to the crown than to the person . . . Wherefore if the king by chance be not guided by reason, in the right of the crown, his lieges are bound by oath made to the crown to guide the king and the estate of the crown back again by reason, and otherwise the oath would not be kept." [55] What had been a rationale in 1308 was apparently declared by the barons themselves in 1321 to be treason. There is no doubt that this is puzzling, and what happened to bring about this change of front, if that is what it was, is not clear. It has been suggested that the Marcher lords had initially adopted the declaration of 1308 as a platform for the rising of 1321, and that they were later persuaded to condemn it under royal pressure. In effect, the outcome was a compromise: Edward banished his ministers, but in return the offensive doctrine was condemned.[56] This interpretation is supported by two other important developments. First, the resistance of the Marcher lords crumbled away, and the reason seems to be that they were unable to obtain the support of the northern lords in their enterprise. Secondly, the result of this failure was the Statute of York of 1322, which may be regarded as a repudiation of the baronial point of view of the preceding years.[57]

Whatever the truth may be concerning the apparent reversal of view in 1321, the important point is that an explicit and reasoned distinction between the king and the crown had been achieved. Moreover, the doctrine, as expressed in 1308, had received wide publicity. It is true that there is no parallel during the rest of the Middle Ages to the clarity of these two declarations. But this does not mean that the political idea or the outlook involved was lost, nor that politics could not be practiced from such a perspective. In any case, these explicit declarations are but a single thread in the tangled political skein of Edward's reign. It will be useful now to cast back to the beginning of the reign to take account of two other subjects: the Ordinances of 1311 and the Statute of York, and the king's deposition.

As early as 1310 the barons grew sufficiently restive to petition the king, whose dilatory treatment of their earlier concerns now provoked a rather dark threat. They had asked that twelve men should be elected by the joint consent of king and barons to consider reforms. Now they declared "that unless the king granted their demands they would not have him for king, nor keep the fealty that they had sworn to him, especially since he himself had not kept the oath which he had taken at his coronation; since in law and common sense there is this reservation, that with the breaker of faith faith may be broken." The result was that Edward "expressly granted . . . the elections, ordinances, and whatever (saving the royal honour) they thought should be decreed for the common good of the realm." [58] The reservation of the royal honor supplied the loophole through which Edward later escaped to the famous Statute of York. The report just given comes from a chronicler conventionally called the Monk of Malmesbury. Others also reported the specific grievances of the barons. The Bridlington writer tells us, for example, that the king's advisers were seizing goods and chattels without sufficient payment.[59] Another writer, reporting the petition for reforming ordinances and baronial ordainers, says the petitioners warned the king of "the great perils and damages which appear every day, which, if they are not quickly redressed, will bring destruction of the liberties of holy church, and disinheritance and dishonour to you and to your royal power, and disinheritance of your crown and loss to all in your realm, rich and poor." This cannot be avoided "unless speedy remedy is provided by the counsel of the prelates earls and barons, and of the wiser men of your realm." This account goes on to complain that Edward has been misled by bad counsel. The result is royal poverty, preventing suitable maintenance of the king's household and the realm's defense except through extortion, which violates Magna Carta. Taxes paid have been dissipated and still the king's war goes badly. Hence, your "good people pray you humbly, for your own salvation and that of them *and of the crown, which they are bound to maintain by their allegiance,* that you will assent to their request, so that these dangers and others can be removed and redressed by ordinance of your baronage." [60] Here is a clear echo of the declaration of 1308, the essence of which was the crucial shift of the bond of allegiance from the king's person to the crown. It should be noted that, in this account of the crisis, the king is described as consenting to the framing of ordinances, providing that they are "according to right and reason and the oath which we took at our coronation." The barons are reported as agreeing to this, and to the proviso that the king's concessions "shall not be regarded as a custom or precedent . . ." [61]

These complaints of the barons were summed up in the Ordinances of 1311. They need not be repeated, but certain of the ordinances deserve consideration.[62] The fourth clause, for example, ordains "that the customs of the kingdom shall be received and kept by men of the kingdom itself and not by aliens . . ." All revenues are to be paid into the exchequer, to be paid out by the treasurer and chamberlains for maintaining the king's household and other matters, "so that the king may live of his own, without taking prises other than those anciently due and accustomed. And all others shall cease . . ." To fortify the king's solvency, the seventh clause ordains that royal grants which have impoverished the king and crown shall be annulled and not given back without the common assent of the baronage in parliament. Elsewhere it is provided that Magna Carta be kept and that any doubtful points concerning it be interpreted by the Ordainers and those whom they choose to consult. In another article this is again stipulated, though here doubtful points "shall be explained in the next parliament after this, by the advice of the baronage, the justices, and other persons learned in the laws." The ninth article contains what appears to be an important new baronial view. It states that "henceforth the king shall neither go out of the kingdom nor undertake an act of war against any one, without the common assent of his baronage, and that in parliament . . ." The Ordainers also removed the king's advisers, exiled Gaveston, and made a number of the principal offices of the realm removable only "by the counsel and assent of the baronage, and that in parliament." Further, there was to be a parliament once a year, and twice if need be, and "in each parliament, one bishop, two earls, and two barons shall be assigned, to hear and determine all plaints of those wishing to complain of the king's ministers" who contravene these ordinances.

It is clear from the baronial Ordinances that a number of ideas had matured considerably. The crown had been detached from the natural man who was king, and final allegiance, at least in those recurring moments of discontent, might be focused on that abstraction. This idea was now secure as the leading justificatory device in the barons' ideology of crisis. It emerged into prominence only spasmodically, as did baronial opposition, yet the advances on the outlook of the thirteenth century are clear. Opposition to what the earls and barons, and sometimes elements of the less exalted ranks, chose to construe as misrule no longer needed to be a naked attack on the vicar of God on earth. Misrule in all its forms might be condemned in the name, not of rebellion, but of a higher loyalty, to which both king and people were subordinate. Yet there lingered that aura of sanctity about the king's person which raises a general presumption that his construction of the interest of the crown was the interest of the crown. Nevertheless, though political thought had not yet achieved more than the first elements of an ideology of opposition, a parliament dominated by the great magnates had emerged as an intermittent institutional contrivance for the attempt to compose diverging interests. In the years immediately after Edward's deposition, the petitions of the commons became a recognized method for making the needs of the king's subjects known. The barons had made the idea of counsel and consent considerably more specific, as the Ordinances make clear, for it was no longer just a general sentiment about baronial advice. Certain elements of the business of king and kingdom had been explicitly tied to baronial consent. Again, the barons had learned to turn a variety of regal ideas to their own purposes. The inalienable demesne and royal rights had, so to say, begun their migration from king to crown.

It was no longer entirely safe for monarchs to appeal to these ideas. Certainly the panoply of prerogative had been rent. The barons had learned to appeal to something much more powerful, much more evocative, than expediency or convenience. They had invoked as always the ancient laws, the laws of their ancestors, but now had begun the process of attaching a modest degree of specificity to them. Although English political thought was still rather far removed from the notion of a fundamental law, some of its components were beginning to emerge.

Before considering Edward's dramatic repudiation of the ordinances and, finally, his deposition, something should be said about a political and legal treatise belonging to the period of Edward I or Edward II. The date of the Mirror of Justices is still under debate, but it derives from about this time. A few passages will serve as a further illustration of the ideas under investigation here. According to the writer, the "first and sovereign abuse is that the king is beyond the law, whereas he ought to be subject to it, as is contained in his oath." Further, "it is an abuse that whereas parliaments ought to be held for the salvation of the souls of the trespassers, twice a year and at London, they are now held but rarely and at the king's will for the purpose of obtaining aids and collection of treasure. And whereas ordinances ought to be made by the common assent of the king and his earls, they are now made by the king and his clerks and by aliens and others who dare not oppose the king but desire to please him and to counsel him for his profit, albeit their counsel is not for the good of the community of the people, and this without any summons of the earls or any observance of the rules of right, so that divers ordinances are now founded upon will rather than upon right . . ." [63] Although the writer appeals to the relatively new idea of parliament as the proper method of levying taxes, he assumes the sharply aristocratic nature of that institution. For he mentions only the earls, the king's companions par excellence, who were a mere handful of the greatest men of the kingdom. Even so, it is the contrast between lawmaking by the king and his bureaucrats and lawmaking by the king and his greater barons that is most significant, resting as it does on the already old distinction between judgment and will.

One other passage from the Mirror is of special interest, for in it the writer agrees with the doctrine of the *addicio,* as it was expressed in Bracton and Fleta. Thus he holds that although it is true that "the king should have no peer in his land, nevertheless in order that if the king should by his fault sin against any of his people, in which case [neither he] nor any of his commissioners could be judge, he being also party, *it was agreed as law* that the king should have companions to hear and determine in the parliaments all the writs and plaints concerning wrongs done by the king, the queen, their children, and their special ministers, for which wrongs one could not otherwise have obtained common right." [64] Parliament was never mentioned by Bracton, but this concern of the author of the *Mirror* is at least that old. The problem of reaching the misdeeds of the king or his natural or official family had caused Bracton no little difficulty, and he had also confronted the legal principle that the king ought not to be both party to litigation and judge. Bracton had no solution. When dealing with the subject of treason, for example, he observes that the king would be both judge and party to the cause. The difficulty is not overcome by the fact that the case may be dealt with by the king's justices, since they are merely his delegates. Bracton admits that such a problem may involve working an injustice, but if the king refused to prosecute offenders the result might be damaging to the community. Bracton concludes, therefore, that "without prejudice to a better opinion, it seems that the court and the peers should judge lest crimes should remain unpunished." [65]

In another place Bracton raises the problem of an illegal act committed by a man who claims to have been in the king's service. It is possible, of course, that the king has been deceived by his servant, but if the king chooses to support him, no one can oblige him to do justice, for he has no superior save God. Bracton also discusses here the problem of the king imposing a judgment on the court. His answer, as one might expect, is thoroughly ambiguous. The king's act cannot be set aside nor disputed, and no doubt it will be just. Should it be unjust, however, it is not the king's act and may be disputed. Nevertheless, it cannot be amended without his leave.[66] By the time the Mirror was written, there had developed at least the idea that there ought to be a law, agreed to by the king and magnates, which would provide an avenue to correction of the misdeeds of the king and his family.

The barons had tried to accomplish just that in the Ordinances of 1311. But the ambiguities inherent in the outlook of double majesty persisted, and this is sharply underlined by Edward's repudiation of the Ordinances in the Statute of York.[67] It is thus an excellent example of the oscillation between the regal insistence on a personal interpretation of kingship and the baronial inclination to temper that dynamism by embedding it in institutional procedures. The startling aspect of the Statute of York is that Edward obtained it from parliament itself. It has already been noticed, in connection with the baronial attack on the Despensers in 1321, that the opposition to Edward failed to hang together. The upshot of that demonstration of the weakness of the baronial front was a vigorous assertion of the regal point of view. The Statute of York declares that the Ordinances have been examined, after a lapse of eleven years, and parliament has found

> that, by the ordinances thus decreed, the royal power of our said lord the king was wrongfully limited in many respects, to the injury of his royal lordship and contrary to the estate of the crown . . . [therefore] it is agreed, and established at the said parliament by our lord the king, by the said prelates and earls and barons, and by the whole community of the realm assembled in this parliament, that everything ordained by the said Ordainers . . . shall henceforth and forever cease [to be valid], losing for the future all title, force, virtue, and effect; and that the statutes and establishment duly made by our lord the king and his ancestors prior to the said ordinances shall remain in force. And [it is decreed] that, henceforth and forever at all times, every kind of ordinance or provision made under any authority or commission whatsoever, by subjects of our lord the king or of his heirs, relative to the royal power of our lord the king or of his heirs, or contrary to the estate of the lord king or of his heirs or contrary to the estate of the crown, shall be null and shall have no validity or force whatever . . .

The statute concludes with the declaration that whatever is to be determined concerning the estate of the king or kingdom shall be established in parliament "by our lord the king and with the consent of the prelates, earls, and barons, and of the commonalty of the kingdom, as has been accustomed in times past." [68] Thus, the statute presents a remarkable coupling of the principle of consent and the king's repudiation of substantive reform.

In 1327 the magnates were at last driven to the desperate expedient of deposition. Even so, it should be remarked that the driving force behind it was not an antimonarchical principle. Edward was not even accused of tyranny, nor, apparently, did the magnates feel they were too much governed. The complaint against him was incorrigible incompetence. He had consistently ignored wise counsel, and the result was the loss of Scotland and territories in Gascony and Ireland. He had ignored his coronation oath, and the result was injustice.[69] So it was that Edward was forced to abdicate in favor of his son, "of his free will and by the common counsel and assent of the prelates, earls, barons, and other nobles, and of the whole community of the realm . . ."[70]

It is evident, in sum, that the fundamental political difficulty remained, for the framework of dual authority was still the setting of both conflict and cooperation. But by the time of Edward's deposition the vital establishment of a parliamentary platform for such matters had been accomplished. Moreover, from this time forward the commons were an integral part of the institution, rather than a merely occasional addition to it. However, it should not be inferred from this that henceforth parliament was the center of English government. On the contrary, that stage of its history did not come until the seventeenth century. Throughout the Middle Ages the heart of the king's government was his council. On the other hand, however, the availability of the new institution did make a great difference in the style and technique of opposition. For the presence of the commons meant that parliament became not only a forum but a stake in the struggles between the king and his great men, since both could attempt to enlist the commons' support. In fact, it was just such an alliance — between lords and commons — that had carried out the king's deposition.

The King's Ministers and Divided Loyalty

Clearly, the combination of lords and commons was a very dangerous matter from the king's point of view. Edward III (1327–1377) appears to have taken the lesson to heart, for his reign was long and relatively stable. It rested on a solid foundation of agreement between king and baronage until the last years of the reign, with but one exception, the crisis of 1341. This quarrel is illuminating for two reasons. First, it produced a profound, if short-lived, challenge to royal control of the administration. The form of the challenge was more important than its result, for it adumbrated the joint claim of commons and lords to judge ministerial misbehavior in parliament. Secondly, in this reign not only did the commons achieve continuous membership in parliament, as has been noted, but also an alliance solidified between lords and commons. It will be convenient to begin by considering the latter development first.

Shortly after his accession Edward III announced that he desired "all men to know that in future we will govern our people according to right and reason, as is fitting our royal dignity; and that the matters which touch us and the estate of our realm are to be disposed of by the common counsel of the magnates of our realm, and not in any other manner." [71] No mention of the commons occurs in this expression of Edward's intent. Yet it was in this reign that important new emphases emerged with respect to the commons' role in parliament.[72] Perhaps these developments were the result of the kind of broad support that had been required to effectuate the deposition of Edward II. It is true to say that the commons were excluded from the settlement of matters of high politics. But from 1327 onwards they were always summoned to parliament. Further, a significant development took place in the form of the legislative process. Beginning in this reign, much legislation explicitly declares that it derives from commons' petitions. These petitions are then granted by the king and magnates.[73] However, the fact that this usage grew more frequent, and in the fifteenth century achieved the standing of a formula, does not exclude important reservations concerning the role of the commons in medieval parliaments. It should be noticed, first, that an announcement that a statute results from a petition of the commons granted by king and magnates is compatible with actual origination from the barons or king and council. Again, the commons were as yet very far from the time when their petitions would no longer be amended by the lords or his majesty. Moreover, there is a body of evidence which suggests that the commons were quite reluctant to accept responsibility for matters of high politics. In these early years of consistent participation in parliament, there is even some question whether the summons to parliament was not regarded as a burden.[74] In all this, it should be borne in mind that, from 1337 on, England was involved in the Hundred Years' War. The increasing demands of warfare supplied a constant rationale for governmental growth. But it also made imperative at least the acquiescence of the commons in financial and military matters.

The knights and burgesses were far from anxious to take on such responsibilities, even though some attempt seems to have been made by the king's ministers to lead them in this direction. In 1347 Edward sought the counsel of the commons, and their reply is very instructive. "As for *your* war, and the arraying of the same we are so lacking in understanding and so simple that we know not how to, and cannot, give counsel about it . . . if it please you, ordain on this matter, with the advice of the great men and wise of your council, that which seems best to you for the honour and profit of you and of your realm." [75] The same outlook was reiterated in 1354; and in 1383, with reference to the king's proposed campaign in Flanders, the commons' speaker reported that this pertained not to them but to the king and the lords.[76] High politics was still preeminently the business of the king and his council. Nor had kings as yet abandoned the view that the selection of their advisers was the king's affair. Yet the role of the magnates was growing clearer and more nearly continuous. In the fifteenth century their preeminence in the king's council would be continuous and undoubted. The membership of the magnates found its expression in the development of the idea of "peers" of the realm.[77] Perhaps the most striking statement of this fourteenth century outlook was coined in 1337 by John de Grandisson, Bishop of Exeter. "The substance of the nature of the Crown," said the bishop, "is principally in the person of the king as head, and in the peers of the land as members, and in this way the Crown is so conditioned that it cannot be severed without division of the realm . . ." [78] The collision of barons and kings had often ruptured the unity now symbolized by the crown, and it would do so again.

It was remarked above that, on the whole, relations between Edward III and the baronage were good. The reign began with an explicit alliance between them, and the effects of this were double: the reign was comparatively tranquil, and the commons were effectively excluded from the summit of political power. This remained true until Edward's declining years, with the one exception of the crisis of 1341.[79] The financial pressures of the war in France led the king to an intemperate outburst in 1340. In that year he returned from France and proceeded to dismiss large numbers of his officials. This action precipitated a quarrel which turned on more important issues than the dismissals themselves. For during the course of the struggle the lords and commons advanced claims to control over the administration which entailed a sharp reduction in regal power.

Once again we encounter the familiar complaint of the magnates. Earl Warenne, a chronicler reports, "began expostulating as follows: 'Lord king, how goes this parliament? Things were not wont to be like this. They are now all turned upside down, for those who should be the chief men are shut out, and other unworthy persons are here in parliament who ought not to be at such a council, but only the peers of the land, who can aid and maintain you . . .'" This complaint centered on Edward's dismissal of John Stratford, Archbishop of Canterbury, upon whom the king had fixed the burden of blame for his financial distress. The earls, however, proposed that he be heard in parliament: " 'if he can defend himself,' said the earl of Arundel, 'against certain accusations made against him, that is good; if not, *we will ordain what it is best to do.*' " [80]

The opposition to Edward which the archbishop had begun ignited an explosion of far-reaching ideas. The most advanced claims were expressed in a document preserved in the chartulary of Winchester Cathedral, which purports to have been presented in parliament. However, the account of grievances and remedies recorded in the rolls of parliament is by comparison rather moderate. Even so, the ideas recorded in the rolls supplied the basis for a reforming statute passed in 1341, which contains a sharp derogation of regal power. It was short-lived, however, for in 1343 it was repealed. Nevertheless, the general shape of the complaint in the chartulary is very instructive. Whether the radical petition of the "community of the kingdom" was presented in parliament or not, its content is extremely interesting. It begins by complaining about departures from Magna Carta and other statutes and then passes to a general condemnation of dissipated revenues. It says that the "community cannot in future support such charges. *All the great business of the land* shall be ordained, tried, judged and dispatched by the . . . *peers, and by no one else* . . . No part of the aids granted to our lord the king shall be given, assigned or in any way granted if not by ordinance of the Peers, *as they will reply in full parliament.*" Even if this language was intended to refer only to fiscal matters, rather than to literally all the great business, it is nevertheless remarkably general. A little farther on, it is requested that such peers be elected in the present and successive parliaments, so that they "can continually supervise the business of the king and of the realm . . ." These peers will have power to hear cases delayed in ordinary courts, and "full power whenever they are in session . . . to call to account all the ministers of the king . . ." The petition also requests that all lands of the royal demesne wrongfully alienated be "reseized into the king's hand, and thus the king will be able to live without laying charges on his people." [81]

The requests recorded in the rolls of parliament are considerably more moderate and less general. What does appear, however, is a concern for tightening the application of legal rules and trial by peers. "And whereas, among other matters contained in the petition of the lords, it was provided that peers of the land, whether officials or others, should not be held to answer concerning trespasses with which they had been charged by the king, except in parliament, it was the king's opinion that such provision would be improper and opposed to his rightful estate. Wherefore the said lords prayed the king to agree that four bishops, four earls, and four barons, together with certain men skilled in the law, should be chosen, to consider *in what cases* the said peers should be held to answer in parliament and nowhere else, and in what cases they should not be, and to report their advice to him." [82] The rolls go on to mention other petitions, and the final form appears in the statute of 1341. Here the language is again modified, though the concerns expressed in the preceding documents are still apparent. The king concedes the keeping of Magna Carta and all other statutes "made by our sovereign lord and king and his predecessors, by the peers and by the commons of the land, for the common profit of the realm . . ." The statute provides also that peers shall not be judged except by peers in parliament. The king's principal officers are to swear in parliament to keep the charters and statutes, and ministerial vacancies, for whatever cause, shall be filled "with the agreement of the great men . . ." Moreover, at each parliament numerous offices are to be in abeyance until their holders answer whatever complaints there may be against them. If required, judgment is to be done upon them by the peers in parliament.[83]

Clearly, this is a marked attenuation of the various demands provoked by the crisis, but it is nonetheless very damaging to the regal position. Edward III certainly thought so, for he said that certain of these articles were "expressly contrary to the Laws and Customs of our realm and to our Prerogatives and the Rights Royal . . ." These offensive articles, said the king, "were *pretended* to be granted by us . . ." [84] A statute of 1343 reasserted the royal command of affairs, repealing the statute of 1341 "as being prejudicial and contrary to the laws and usages of the realm and to the rights and prerogatives of our lord the king." [85]

Yet again, then, there has occurred an episode centering on the characteristic clash and oscillation between alternative principles of political organization. But in the crisis of 1341 there was shadowed out a shift in the relationship between king and community. To be sure, much is familiar. The lords and commons renewed efforts to secure reform, and there was a striking assertion of the principle of baronial oversight of certain aspects of the administrative process. Both of these were significant impulses. But perhaps the most striking feature of this particular exchange was the assertion of the claim to judge the king's charges against Stratford in parliament. In order to appreciate the impact of this claim, it will be necessary to consider the elaboration of the idea and procedure of political trials in the last quarter of the fourteenth century.

The High Court of Parliament and the Political Trial

Many of the issues thus far surveyed, and the halting development of a cluster of ideas and practices hammered out in the repeated attempts to solve them, reached a dramatic crisis in the deposition of Richard II in 1399, at the hands of the "estates of the realm." [86] The issues, however, were transformed in the last quarter of the fourteenth century. The crux of the matter was this. The hitherto occasional alliance of lords and commons became a standard occurrence. Moreover, that alliance jelled in a new political and legal form. During this period the opposition honed to a fine edge the menacing instrument of political trial in parliament. In part, at least, this procedure rested on the outlook expressed in the crisis of 1341, when the answer to the king's dismissal of Stratford was that the matter should be tried in parliament. The technique of political trial by no means exhausts the course of development in this period, but it may be approached conveniently in those terms. The king's ministers were repeatedly attacked, impeached, and judged in parliament. There are several important points to be extracted from this. The whole matter came to center on an intrinsically unattractive and dangerous process, the political trial. This suggests an extremely important point: that there was no law to appeal to. From a political perspective, a political trial may involve the laudable aim of securing ministerial responsibility to someone other than the king. But the cure may be worse than the disease, because it is a procedure which operates without benefit of general rules of law. It introduces a distinct possibility of governmental paralysis in the politics of faction, which is bound to appear when those who achieve a substantial measure of control over the monarchy possess no sustained civic purposes. The triumphant magnates in fourteenth century England operated without any firm notion or tradition of civic responsibility. The crown's weakness in such a context was the signal for promoting their designs at the expense of public order and welfare. The clear mastery of the great magnates in the fifteenth century produced a crisis threatening central governmental control of the political order.

The upshot of this line of development was the idea of impeachment and its corollary, the notion that the king's ministers were, in some sense, responsible to parliament. This entailed the notion that lords and commons in parliament *were* parliament, somehow separable from the king. It was the alliance of lords and commons in the procedure of impeachment which, in 1388, produced an explicit statement referring to parliament as the high court. The commons undertook to denounce ministers, and the lords proceeded to pass judgment on them. In effect, the lords and commons together were set over against the monarch. Unlike the critical junctures of the reign of Edward II, there were no clear statements on the distinction between king and crown. This period, however, produced the operational equivalent of the distinction.

The process was set in motion late in the reign of Edward III. In 1376 the king summoned a parliament and requested a subsidy from the commons, who replied that they would not proceed without the counsel of the magnates. It was decided that they "were going to treat with the king notwithstanding that he would find it hard to accept what was intended for the safety of his body and mind and for the advantage and profit of his kingdom." It was agreed that the royal requests would not be met until certain abuses were corrected, and "until certain persons who seemed to have impoverished the king and the kingdom, to have vilely tarnished his fame and greatly to have diminished his power, should have been eliminated, and their excesses properly punished according to their kind." [87] The principle implicit in this statement is clear: the king had a political capacity which required defense against what he as a man was actually doing.

The commons' particular target was Lord Latimer, the king's chamberlain. The commons and lords joined in resistance and obtained his impeachment. Moreover, the commons had achieved a sufficiently advanced sense of corporateness to act in the attack on Latimer through their speaker, Sir Peter de la Mare. The commons' complaint was that despite burdensome taxes the military affairs of the kingdom were going badly. Their assumption was that this was simply incredible: the explanation must be ministerial disloyalty. They proceeded to depose against Latimer, and he was judged in parliament by the lords.[88]

The periodic but persistent alternation between assertions by the magnates — and now by the commons — to some measure of control over the king's council and the monarchical repudiation of the substantive implications of this principle has been noticed repeatedly. This framework for the conduct of politics reached its apogee in the reign of Richard II. But it was also in this period that a significant transformation took place. The gulf between the king and the opposition widened, and the two positions hardened into extremes. Opposition to the king was sometimes so formidable that "nothing was really left to Richard except his legal rights." [89] These proved to be a fragile buttress. Yet at other times the opposition was so vulnerable that the king was able to reassert his position, even to advance the regal view with unaccustomed vigor and clarity. In the end he was deposed, and a new reconciliation was forged between Henry Bolingbroke and his "people."

A measure of the distance between Richard and his successor may be found by contrasting two statements, which appear to describe the situation accurately. It is reported that Richard "expressly said . . . that his laws were in his own mouth, or occasionally, in his own breast; and that he alone could establish and change the laws of his realm." [90] Henry IV, however, gave expression to the following view, which is even more conciliatory than that by which Edward III had mended the realm after the deposition of 1327. "It is the king's wish to be advised and governed by the honourable, wise and discreet people of his realm, and to do what is best for the government of himself and of his realm by their common counsel and assent. He does not desire to be governed by his own will, nor by his arbitrary purpose or singular opinion, but by common advice counsel and assent." [91] Between these two regal postures lay the institutionalization of the idea and practice of impeachment of the king's ministers. This technique rested upon a practical severance of parliament from the king, upon the exercise of a governmental will which was distinguished from the monarch's personal will. The estates of the realm had translated a long line of development into something approaching an institutionalized procedure. Opposition had moved from baronial petition, sometimes backed by the threat of force, to commons' petitions and occasional alliances between lords and commons, to a much more radical idea. Opposition now involved deposition, in the form of action by the estates of the realm. In effect, opposition had moved from a strictly defensive position, resting on the idea of petitioning for a royal concession, an act of royal grace, to an offensive posture. As yet, however, the use of force was only thinly disguised by justificatory appeals to the rights and privileges of parliament. The theoretical relationship of king and community, at least in general terms, remained substantially unaltered. Richard's absolutist pretensions provoked a vigorous challenge in the years 1386–1388. But the very radicalism of the challenge to the king involved its collapse, for it drove many moderates into the king's camp. Indeed, the opposition found itself so weakened that Richard was able to extract from parliament a full endorsement of his position. Yet this acquiescence lasted only until 1399, when Richard was deposed for tyranny.

The result of the crisis of 1386 was, once again, the impeachment of certain of the king's ministers. Temporarily, the king lacked support and gave in. Even so, the extent to which the law and courts were the king's instruments emerges very clearly. For even in the face of practical retreat the king was able to elicit from his justices a full repudiation of the actions of the parliament of 1386. The parliamentary complaint of 1386 exhibited the usual features. An attack was mounted against the king's chancellor, Michael de la Pole, Earl of Suffolk; and a committee was appointed to undertake reforms. But the discussion was coupled with an unusual breadth and depth of expression. The exchange of argument warmed rapidly. Parliamentary complaints concerning the king's evil ministers were carried to the king by two men selected by common assent. The king's reply was that if necessary he would appeal for help to the King of France. It seemed to Richard, says one chronicler, that it would be "better to submit to him [the French king] rather than to succumb to our . . . subjects." The parliament's reply was equally drastic. They alleged, in accordance with an old statute, that "if the king from any malignant design or foolish contumacy or contempt, or through wanton wilfulness or in any irregular way, should alienate himself from his people and should not be willing to be governed and regulated by the laws, statutes and laudable ordinances of the realm, with the wholesome advice of the lords and peers of the realm, but should headily and wantonly, by his own mad designs, work out his own private purpose, then it should be lawful for them, with the common assent and consent of the people of the realm, to depose the king himself from the royal throne, and to elevate . . . some near kinsman of the royal line." [92] Already, then, the opposition had threatened deposition. Richard, lacking significant support, eventually acquiesced in Pole's trial and impeachment. The same lack of support accounts for the sweeping powers conferred on the reforming committee, for it was empowered to investigate all phases of government and to frame adequate remedies for all deficiencies.[93]

It was shortly after this that Richard obtained from his justices an equally sweeping condemnation of the opposition. The judges were asked a long series of questions which ran to the heart of both the regal and opposition views. To all the questions the judges' answer was the same: the actions of the opposition were treasonous and derogated wrongfully from the king's prerogative and regality. This condemnation embraced the statute establishing the committee of reform, the presumptuousness of proceeding in parliament upon topics not set by the king, the exercise of compulsion on the king, and the procedure of impeachment. According to the judges the king could dissolve parliament at his pleasure and dismiss ministers at will. The judgment against the Earl of Suffolk was, they held, erroneous and revocable.[94]

Perhaps the attack of the lords upon the king's party in the Merciless Parliament of 1388 may be viewed as their reply to Richard and the judges.[95] It is true that their intended victims were not impeached. Instead the lords indicted them by an "appeal." Nevertheless, the lords acted as judges with the king's assent, though under constraint, to be sure. The theoretical gap which the procedure opened up was merely papered over rather than closed, for the lords had no new formula for the relation of king and dissident parliament. Their position is recorded in the rolls of parliament. The lords of parliament, "in common agreement, with the assent of the king . . . declared: That in so high a crime as is alleged in this appeal, which touches the person of the king . . . and the state of his realm, perpetrated by persons who are peers of the realm and by others, the process will not be taken anywhere except to parliament, nor judged by any other law except the law and court of parliament . . ." [96] This procedure was natural enough. Richard and the judges had made it perfectly clear that the courts and the law of the land were foreclosed as an avenue to change. For the time being, the lords appellant, as they were called, were in a commanding position, however, and their resort was the claim that parliament was the high court of the realm.

Despite the obvious frailty of the king's position in 1388, he recovered quickly. As always, a radical departure from the prevailing arrangement splintered the magnates' group, allowing the crown to reassert its position. The climax to the widening oscillation which characterized Richard's reign came with stunning rapidity in the years 1397–1399. A measure of Richard's strength as late as 1397 may be found in the illuminating case of Thomas Haxey. Haxey had presented a petition which complained about the monarch's extravagance. At this, "the king was greatly aggrieved and offended at the fact that the Commons, his lieges, should take unto themselves or presume [to make] any ordinance or governance relating to the king's person, or to his household, or to any person of 'estate' whom he pleased to have in his company. And it seemed to the king that the Commons herein committed a great offence against his regality and his royal majesty and the liberty both of himself and of his honourable progenitors." The king, then, would entertain no interference in the choice of his household or ministers. By itself this is no surprise, since it was the normal posture struck by the monarchy on this question. What is surprising was the commons' reply. For, "by the king's order, the Commons came before the king in parliament; and there, with all the humility and obedience of which they were capable, they expressed deep grief . . . that the king had formed such an opinion of them. And they humbly besought the king to hear and accept their apology: that it had never been their intention or will to express, present, or do anything which would offend or displease the king's royal majesty, or would contravene his royal estate and liberty, either in this matter concerning his own person and the government of his household . . . or concerning any other matter touching [the king] himself; for they well knew and understood that such matters did not pertain to them at all, but solely to the king himself and to his ordinance." [97] This capitulation was followed by an even more striking utterance on the matter by the lords. They declared with the king that, if "any one, of whatever estate or condition, shall move or excite the Commons of Parliament, or any other person, to make remedy or reformation of any matter which touches our person or our government or our regality, he might be, and should be, held as a traitor." [98] The king's answer, then, to the advancing procedures and idea of impeachment, as well as to unwonted interference in the king's business, was a drastic extension of the idea of treason, the crime of lèse-majesté. That was the instrument which the judges and the king had elaborated in 1387 and here reiterated.

The actual deposition of Richard II and the elevation of Henry Bolingbroke to the throne as Henry IV produced less political theory than one might expect. But there is a considerable difference between Richard's deposition and that of Edward II in 1327. Edward had been deposed on the ground of incompetence, quite without institutionalized process. The charges levelled at Richard were much more elaborate and raised fundamental constitutional questions. Moreover, the deposition of 1399 was conducted as though it were a trial by and before the estates of the realm and the people. It seems hardly too much to suggest that the political trials of the preceding years supplied a ready source of analogy. The charges brought against Richard appear to represent an accumulation of grievances, but, as was seen, the king still occupied a position of strength in 1397. This is confirmed by the turn of events in the Shrewsbury Parliament of 1398. Richard contrived to extract remarkable financial grants from that parliament. Indeed, they were so lavish that they would have allowed him to dispense with further resort to that source of revenue. Nor was this all. The Shrewsbury Parliament also established a committee of parliament empowered to deal with a wide variety of matters after the parliament was adjourned. The king's intentions relative to this committee and its powers have been much debated. It has been held that Richard made a deliberate attempt to free himself of parliament altogether. On the other hand, it has been argued that his intention was only to avoid any attempt by a baronial commission, such as that appointed in 1387, to control his government.[99] Whatever the truth may be, however, the important point is that Richard was charged with an attempt to eliminate parliament, and this may be taken as the last straw that broke the camel's back.

The deposition purported to be broadly based. Students of the period agree that the accounts of the crisis suffer from a marked Lancastrian bias. Still, it is the outlook expressed that is of principal value for present purposes. According to the rolls of parliament, "the estates and commons unanimously and in accord publicly constituted and deputed certain commissioners . . . to bear [the] sentence of deposition, and to depose king Richard from all the king's dignity, majesty and honour, in lieu of, by name of, and by authority of all the foresaid estates . . ." [100] This declaration was accompanied by a lengthy recital of the king's crimes. Unlike those lodged against Edward II, they centered on the king's alleged attempt to rule despotically. Richard was condemned as a tyrant and subverter of the law: "he expressly said . . . that his laws were in his mouth, or occasionally, in his own breast; and that he alone could establish and change the laws of his realm." The king "desired to enjoy such a large freedom that no statutes should bind him to the extent that he could not act and do according to his free will." [101] He had acted in derogation of the status of parliament and to the detriment of the crown of the realm.[102]

Thus, by the end of the fourteenth century, the peculiar dynamics of the political order of double majesty, interacting with a maturing commercial and military environment, had propelled the English kingdom along a curiously ambiguous path. It was suggested earlier that the fundamental framework persisted through change. But those changes supplied the content of the framework at any given moment. At the beginning of the period surveyed here, the outstanding feature of the political order was the unquestioned dominance of personal monarchy. Referring to the Angevin kings of the last half of the twelfth century, J. E. A. Jolliffe has observed that each of these kings "exercised unchallenged power to act *sine judicio* [that is, without judgment] in what was in effect a void of political thinking." [103] The great significance of the baronial movement which produced Magna Carta was that it launched a new era, one in which kingly action "without judgment" no longer passed unchallenged. The king's great subjects learned their political lessons primarily from their liege lord, but they also learned to turn those ideas to their own needs and purposes. For the most part, the evolving relationship between king and community could not be embraced by legal principles. At the beginning of the thirteenth century there was so little substantive law that the question of legality at the level of high politics hardly arose. The answer of the great twelfth and thirteenth century law books to fundamental political questions was that such matters lay with the king and the magnates of the realm. Richard II and the kings who reigned before him were very often on perfectly solid ground in resisting baronial intrusions into the king's great business. This was not so much because theirs was infallibly the correct legal position, but because their wide-ranging powers were the accustomed thing and had long resisted definition. But as is always the case, change could not be prevented by showing that conditions were not wont to be this way or even that they were illegal. Neither kings nor magnates, knights, and burgesses could suppress or resolve the massive difficulties confronting them.

Fortunately for the long-run stability of the English polity, the king and his greater subjects shared a common outlook. When quarreling, both parties appear not to have comprehended the nature of the difficulties which had driven them to collision. The standard recourse of both sides was to couch their defense in the language and rhetoric of tradition, casting back to the usages of their fathers and the ancient kings. In this sense, both kingly ideology and baronial ideology were reactionary. This is a startling enough commentary on the narrowness of vision exhibited by both parties. If the observer resists the impulse to put on the spectacles of constitutionalism in reading the events and ideas of those distant centuries, the precedents for the rule of law in politics are meager indeed. Surely the threat of force, actual coercion, political trial, and deposition by declaration of notorious incompetence or tyranny do not supply such precedents. This does not mean, however, that nothing was accomplished in this period. The contribution of the magnates to the principles of constitutional rule was slight. What they did accomplish was the fastening of the conciliar principle on the monarchy. In the long run this assured the survival of the parliament, though the latter remained a subsidiary institution throughout the Middle Ages. The deposition of Richard II brought the leading ideas and practices evolved in the preceding years to a head and gave them an institutional standing. By the close of the fourteenth century the opposition had contrived a process, together with a measure of rationalization for it, by which they might go so far as to assert a right to depose a notoriously deficient or wicked king.

Baronial Ascendancy and the Collapse of Order

On the whole, the fifteenth century was not so fertile as the thirteenth and fourteenth. Indeed, the most striking thing about it was the near breakdown of effective central government. This fact itself is of great significance, of course. But it does not require detailed investigation for the purposes in hand here. For the truth is that the political turmoil which dominated the period appears to have precluded the sort of development in ideas and practices which occurred in the preceding two centuries. For this reason it will be possible to treat the fifteenth century much more briefly. Moreover, a separate chapter is devoted to the most outstanding political thinker of the period, Sir John Fortescue. In the present context, it is most important to notice the result of a serious imbalance in the relationship of king and great men; for the combination of a weak, sometimes imbecile and destitute, crown with the intense rivalries of the great baronial families produced a marked impairment of orderly government.[104] As one observer has put it, "the country came to be parcelled out into spheres of influence, where no will prevailed but that of the great man and his affinity." [105] There is little doubt that it was the support of the great Percy family that secured the throne for Henry IV. By the same token, the combination of the houses of York and Warwick was enough to unseat the Lancastrian dynasty.[106] To be sure, the central institutions built up in the preceding three centuries did not disappear, nor did political ideas cease completely to undergo change and development. It is true, however, that there was relatively little innovation in ideas.[107] It is possible to exaggerate the turmoil of the fifteenth century, as an earlier historical tradition was inclined to do. It should be remembered that it concerned not the whole body of ordinary people but the upper levels of English society. Moreover, it is a fact that violence, disorder, lawlessness, and baronial rivalry were far from being unique to the fifteenth century. All the same, many of the problems inherent in medieval government were sorely exacerbated by the last stages of the Hundred Years' War with France. For, in the end, England suffered severe reversals in this most important area of foreign relations, eventually losing all the territories formerly held in France. As always, defeat had serious consequences. In addition to the financial strain and the inevitable loss of prestige by a king unable to achieve victory, many soldiers and their leaders returned to England to live a life of brigandage or hire for private warfare.

The coupling of frequently ineffective rule with the existence of armed bands and the incessant pursuit of land normal to an agrarian society certainly meant an increase of lawlessness. Perhaps Holdsworth exaggerated when he said of the fifteenth century that the "forms of law and physical violence had come to be merely alternative instruments to be used as seemed most expedient," [108] but it is clear that many great men entertained no scruples and few qualms in turning the processes of law to their own purposes. In the Paston correspondence we have a rich body of evidence illustrating the acquisitive ambitions of the great and near-great and their unabashed manipulation of the law in satisfying those ambitions. Indeed, perhaps the most pervasive themes running through this monumental collection of letters and documents are those of lawlessness and land-grabbing in one form or another. Needless to say, the effects of disorder tended to be communicable. Thus it has been said that the Paston family "found, as did most of their neighbors, that if they wished to hold, or still more to increase what possessions they had, it was necessary to fight vigorously with every weapon law, use, experience or cunning could devise." [109] For the countryside was continually afflicted with the depredations of roving armed bands. Some of these bands were simply collections of brigands, ruffians, and poor folk driven from their land. Others, however, were the armed retainers of those who could afford them. Slightly more systematic but no less predatory were the private wars between great families.[110] The result was that the forcible seizure of property was a common experience. Men learned to garrison their homes to resist siege by a covetous neighbor.[111] This was necessary because legal avenues were often foreclosed by influence, bribery, and force. To be sure, if the result of a trial could be established in advance, one might well repair to the courts, for, as one of the Pastons' correspondents said, anything could be had for a price.[112] But if one's opponent was supported by a great man, there was no point in appealing to law. Hence William Paston would seem to have been offering sound advice when he informed a correspondent that he would be ill advised to press his suit, because the other party had been taken under the wing of the Duke of Norfolk.[113] The techniques employed to obtain guarantees were bribery and force. The Paston letters are studded with reports of bribed justices, sheriffs, and juries.[114] Sometimes these subtle techniques would fail, but in that case a litigant could still resort to force, and the intimidation of juries or witnesses or the forcible disruption of the proceedings were standard devices.[115]

In view of all this it is not altogether surprising that the men of the fifteenth century added little to the received stock of political ideas. But there did occur some noticeable trends toward a settling of some of the ideas into patterns that survived. These may be briefly summarized as the solidification of certain conceptions of parliament. The most important aspect of this was a growing consciousness of the representative character of parliament, though it cannot be said that the idea was unambiguous; indeed, it was partly a mere legal fiction.[116] But some indication of increasing precision may be gathered from the fact that in this period parliament came to be conceived of as consisting of three estates: lords spiritual, lords temporal, and commons.[117] This was a considerable improvement over the fourteenth century, for which we have a document dividing members of parliament into some six grades.[118] There was another refinement associated with this which serves to reinforce it. For at the same time the usage of referring to the commons and lords as separate houses also appeared.[119]

The somewhat confused, indeed casual, use of these ideas is easily illustrated. It has been noticed that parliament, acting as the three estates of the realm, had constituted itself a high court for the deposition of Richard II. But this by no means excluded the view that it was a representative institution. Thus as early as 1365 Chief Justice Thorpe had held that, even if a statute had not been proclaimed in the country, "everyone is held to know a statute from the time it was made in parliament, for as soon as parliament has decided anything, the law holds that everyone has knowledge of it, for parliament represents the body of all the realm . . ." [120] This is clearly a fiction; but the idea as it was expressed in the Modus Tenendi Parliamentum is direct if not precise, for the commons were equated with the community of the realm.[121] This direct tie, as well as the blending of the judicial and representative aspects of parliament, is nicely illustrated by the drafts of Bishop Russell's proposed sermons to parliament in 1483, in his new capacity as chancellor. At one point he says, "I speke not to yowe that nowe represent the hele [whole], but to them that ye come fro, whome for ther gret and confuse nombre and multitude nature can not wele

suffre to assemble in oo [one] place apt to the makynge of a lawe." [122]
He also refers to parliament as "the kynges most hyghe and sowrayne
courte." [123] Indeed, by the time of Edward IV (1461–1483) this outlook could be expressed by the king himself, for he addresses himself to "ye that be commyn for the Common of this my Lond
. . ." [124] As Chrimes has said, "representation was passing in idea
from local to national implications." [125]

The idea of the estates of the realm in parliament was equally
imprecise. Once again, Bishop Russell's sermons provide a good
index to the confusion. Thus, in one draft the bishop says that the
public body "is compowned of iij notable partes, of the prince, the
nobles, and the peuple." But in another he tells us that in "thys
politike body of Englonde there be iij estates as principalle membres
under oone hede — thestate of the lordys spiritualle, thestate of the
lordes temperalle, and thestate of the cominallete. The hede is owre
souverayne lord the kynge here presente." [126] Despite some ambiguity, however, the notion that parliament is a meeting of the
estates is surely an advance on the idea that it is a collection of the
king's principal subjects, for the later notion suggests a growing
sense that parliament possesses a corporate character.

It is fair to say, then, that at least a degree of modification and
refinement had been achieved with respect to the prevailing conception of what "parliament" meant. But having noticed that much,
one must be careful not to infer that parliament had arrived at the
center of the political stage. It is true that the petitions of the commons occupied an increasingly important place in parliamentary
business, especially in the first half of the century. But, as was mentioned earlier, the commons' petitions were still rather freely
amended by their betters. Moreover, toward the end of the century,
parliamentary legislation came more and more to emanate from the
council. Even so, neither council nor parliament, for the better part
of the fifteenth century, was the seat of power. Although the king's
council remained the central political institution, for the time being
effective power lay with the great landed magnates.

Parliament could not help suffering in the long run from the
contentions of the great families. It came more and more to be a
stage on which the politics of faction and family were played out,
and a kind of registry where the results of the most recent coup
d'etat were inscribed and validated. Then there would follow a

judgment of treason on the losing side, together with the confiscation of property.[127] Time and again, parliament complained of and legislated against the leading evils of the day, but to little or no effect. A politically minded rhymester observed that there were "many lawys, and lytelle right," for few were truly kept.[128] In the year 1461, when Edward IV replaced the Lancastrian "usurper," Henry VI, the commons dilated at length on the desperate condition of the realm. In Henry VI's time, it was said, "not plentie, pees, justice, good governaunce, pollicie, and vertuouse conversation, but unrest, inward were [war] and trouble, unrightwisnes, shedying and effusion of innocent blode, abusion of the Lawes, partialite, riotte, extorcion, murdre, rape and vicious lyvying, have been the gyders and leders of the noble Reame of England, in auncien tyme among all Cristen Reames laudably reputed of grete honoure, worship and nobley, drad of all outeward Landes, then beyng the Laurier of honoure, prowesse and worthynes of all other Reames; in the tyme of the seid usurpacion, fallen from that renomee unto miserie, wrechednesse, desolation, shamefull and soroufull declyne . . ." [129] To be sure, this was a statement directed against a deposed monarch and his dynasty, but it does not follow that there was no foundation for the ills complained of. Indeed, the radical expedient of deposition is itself good evidence of the breakdown of government. The great landed magnates helped to contrive the collapse and then rushed into the vacuum to consolidate and expand their control of local affairs.

But the power of the magnates was not restricted to local affairs, for they now sought to rule directly through the king's council; or rather, they contended among themselves for that role.[130] It is important and interesting to notice, however, that even when the medieval monarchy was most debased the magnates clung to the idea of its independent authority. In 1427 the chancellor, John Kemp, observed in the name of the council that even though "the Kyng as nowe be of tendre age, neverthelesse the same auctorite resteth and is atte this day in his persone that shall be in hym at eny time hereafter when he shall come, with Goddes Grace, to Yeres of discretion." In the meantime, however, the "execution of the Kynges said auctorite, as toward that that belongeth unto the Politique Reule and Governaille of his Lande and to th' observaunce and kepyng of his Lawes, belongeth unto the Lords Spirituall and Temporall of his Lande, at such tyme as thei be assembled in Parlement or in grete Counsaille, and ellus hem not being so assembled, unto the Lords chosen and named to be of his continuel Counsell . . ." [131] Similar events occurred in 1435 and 1455.[132] But there is little doubt that the greater men of the kingdom had achieved a commanding position, and this was, for present purposes, the most striking development of the fifteenth century. They could certify the truth of the statement that "nowadays . . . the king is intrinsicate within his council and may not do without them . . ." [133] The really important point is that conciliar rule demonstrated the necessity of able kings, for the magnates did not succeed in the experiment of substituting their own rule for that of the peculiar blend of personal kingship and counsel and consent. This was not simply the result of wicked designs, however, but of the weakness inherent in an outlook in which political behavior is primarily an extension of local activity and interests. For it means that problems actually affecting the political order as a whole are not perceived as public problems, which have somehow to be solved for the general good, but as more or less serious disruptions of one's own region. To be sure, this is a perfectly natural response in a diffuse society resting on an agrarian basis, for the land is necessarily localized and there is little enough in such an economy to prompt a man to look beyond it. But the thrust of political activity is only toward restoration through removal of the seeming source of disturbance, not toward analysis with a view to a general solution. The line of vision runs, so to say, along a narrow track between this or that locality and the king and back again, thus failing to see the spatial extension of political problems. The outcome at the level of policy is at best only a series of palliative measures. Throughout the Middle Ages, the dominant political focus remained at this local and familial level rather than at the public level.

The evolution of the conception of double majesty has now been followed over a long and involved course. In retrospect one is struck by both the durability of the basic assumption and the gradual development of more elaborate formulations, including a much refined rationale. For the idea had moved from the level of a simple assumption of joint rule, quite without pattern or ideological adornment, to the rather involved notion that it provided the justification of kingship limited by parliamentary consent. There were two crucial stages between these poles, and most of the political life of late medieval England centered on working them out. The first was the establishment of a baronial complement in the king's council, and the second was the achievement of a somewhat loosely conceived distinction between the king and the kingdom. Both were involved in a very patchy career at the center of the magnates' crisis ideology, and both remained profoundly ambiguous. For no one really thought through the alternative principles involved to anything approaching a logical conclusion. In the last resort the idea of personal kingship was incompatible with that of restraint. To combine the two would have required the use of a monstrous fiction: that the natural man who occupied the kingship could be corrected and coerced in the name of the king, understood as a political role superimposed on the natural man. In that case, however, kingship would be an office, not an infusion of divine grace, and the king would not be sacrosanct but merely an agent of the kingdom. But in the operative thought of the Middle Ages, men did not arrive at either logical terminal. Rather they embraced both ideas at the same time, without ever recognizing the heart of the problem.

Nevertheless, medieval Englishmen had worked their way to a notion of kingship balanced by a complex institution which was assumed to have a representative relationship with the people, or with some of them, at any rate. Neither the idea of parliament nor that of representation could be fully worked out, for that would have required a clarity concerning their relationship to the king's majesty which was not achieved until the seventeenth century. By the end of the fifteenth century parliament was still overshadowed as a political institution by the king's council, for it met on too irregular and contingent a basis to be the center of government. Indeed, this indefinite balance was really the limit of the medieval achievement. The chief political writer of fifteenth century England, Sir John Fortescue, retained all the assumptions and ambiguities that have been associated with double majesty. During the period of the vigorous Tudor monarchy, which intervened between the end of the fifteenth century and the constitutional debates of the early seventeenth century, important new emphases were added to the ancient tradition, but its foundation remained undisturbed.

It is now abundantly clear that the operative thought of the later Middle Ages was related intimately to political values, interests, and behavior. This fact has been emphasized because historians of political ideas and constitutional government have been inclined to interpret this period in extremely abstract and legalistic terms. But neither moral nor political ideas and practices are radically removed from those called legal. A complete analysis of later medieval thought must give attention to the legalistic line of interpretation and to legal ideas, particularly the idea of custom.

six Law, Custom, and Politics

The relationship of law and politics in the Middle Ages raises a cluster of closely related problems, and they are of capital importance in attempting to frame a general interpretation of the political thought of the period. The task of the present chapter is to direct sustained attention to this crucial topic. It will be argued, first, that there was substantial lawmaking in the later Middle Ages and that it was recognized as such. Lawmaking was, in fact, a purposive and sometimes effective instrument of social and political change. Secondly, the common law was above all else the king's law, and, in principle, he lay beyond its reach. This involves a third point which, for present purposes, is the most important. The common law did not constitute the chief reliance of movements of opposition to royal governance. On the contrary, there emerged a distinct set of ideas centering on claims to certain privileges and rights of parliament. These three propositions involve a thesis that is contrary to the widely received view that the central political idea of the Middle Ages was that of fundamental law. The contention here, however, is that operative political thought in medieval England produced no such conception as is conveyed by the idea of fundamental law.

As against the view that law was always "found," never made, in the Middle Ages, it has been observed that in fact "the student of medieval English government is confronted with assizes, establishments, provisions, ordinances, proclamations, and statutes that men observed or infringed and that judges enforced. They existed, and they mattered; they are both a monument to human activity and an indication of human intentions and opinions." [1] Indeed, the evidence for conscious lawmaking is so abundant that Plucknett appears to have been staggered by the contention that it did not or could not occur. He expressed the view that this perspective is "a paradox brilliantly sustained." [2] It is indeed; but it is also something more than this. It is an attempt to order a vast body of inhospitable material with the aid of modern ideas and preoccupations, chiefly the ideas and practices associated with the rule of law and judicial review. It is a sustained effort to read back into history the reverence for a supposedly depoliticized law which, in fact, is a product of postmedieval speculation. In effect, it appears to be an effort to replace cosmology with history. Since the pursuit of external validation for ideals in cosmological and metaphysical speculation has lost favor in most quarters, it has been replaced with the characteristic nineteenth century technique of mining history for this purpose.

The second point mentioned above was that the common law was the king's law. It grew primarily from the lawmaking activities of England's medieval kings, their justices and courts.[3] The law that came to be uniformly applicable to the whole realm was, in short, the child of the royal prerogative, and this too was acknowledged by contemporaries. The baronial opposition certainly recognized it, and they also recognized that the king and his family, both personal and governmental, were immune to ordinary legal processes.

It is precisely this recognition that leads to the third point. Gradually, certain aspects of the vast, undefined powers of the king and his servants were given expression in ascertainable principles, both legal and political. To the extent that this development touched matters of vital political significance, it came as the result of political agreement, often following hard on the heels of baronial coercion. The chief ingredient in the baronial program, the repeated attempt to establish a secure place for the baronage in the king's council, was expressed only vaguely at first, though as time passed the baronage asserted that certain kinds of governmental business were to be determined only with the counsel and consent of the community. The development of an institutional expression of this method of joint governance was slow and fitful, for long was resolutely resisted by the monarch, and was repudiated time and again. The most important development from a legal perspective, however, is that in their role of political opposition the baronage did not resort to the principles of the common law. On the contrary, they worked their way to the establishment of an entirely different approach, which eventuated in the political alliance between lords and commons in parliament. That is why the solution to the problem of double majesty, which was finally aired and solved in the seventeenth century, required a resort to the doctrine of parliamentary sovereignty, not the sovereignty of the law. Legal sovereignty, indeed, was the doctrine of the conservative common lawyers, whose aim, in effect, was to preserve double majesty by embalming it in the law of the land. But this was a position they were driven to by the political controversies of the early Stuart period and not a medieval inheritance, though they argued that it was. Baronial opposition had been quite different. It had moved through several fairly clear stages. At first it had been simple coercion, provoked by more or less momentary disaffection with royal policy. But such resistance was gradually institutionalized: it passed through a stage of ad hoc political trials, prosecuted in moments of triumph, to become consolidated in the idea of parliamentary impeachment and trial of ministers for treason. At the close of the fourteenth century, this practice produced the idea of the high court of Parliament. Later the parliamentary estates were to divorce this idea explicitly from the common law. As an instrument of the politics of faction, political trials reached their apogee in the fifteenth century, only to be snatched up and elaborated by the Tudor monarchs, though their institutional instruments were prerogative courts rather than parliament. Once more, in the seventeenth century, the triumphant commons employed impeachment and trial lavishly against the monarch and his servants.

Before considering some of the evidence for the three lines of argument just outlined, it will be useful to explore the notion of fundamental law as a tool of interpretation. The idea of fundamental law is complex, embracing a variety of different ideas. Its elements may be set out in a series of propositions. The root idea is that medieval political life was governed by a body of substantive legal principles. This general contention is supplemented by several subsidiary points: that any laws contravening the fundamental law were void and were actually set aside in courts of law on that ground; that the fundamental law was ancient custom exclusively; that it was immutable; that it was always found or declared and never made; and, finally, that fundamental law was the only true law.[4] Stated categorically and generally, as they have been, all these propositions are false.

Proponents of the thesis that custom reigned as fundamental law in medieval England rely on two complementary techniques in prosecuting their argument. First, they consistently refrain from giving the concept "custom" any content. Second, they contend that anything which constitutes change is not really law, not true law, which is custom by definition. This argument survives, in spite of abundant evidence of legal and political change, precisely because there is no way of contrasting such evidence with a vacuous concept. Like a well-argued metaphysical system, "custom" is immune to evidential criticism. The complementary character of these techniques allows the argument to proceed without specifying what rules are supposed to have bound the king, making him a limited or a constitutional monarch. Nor is consideration given to the changes that medieval political and legal ideas underwent in a centuries-long course of development, for the notion of unalterable custom invites a timeless approach to a thousand years of European history. Recently, Frederic Cheyette has demonstrated other major flaws in the fundamental-law approach to the political thought of the later Middle Ages. Cheyette's primary concern is to show the prevalence and importance of judicial lawmaking in the later medieval period. In establishing this, he has shown that the fundamentalist argument rests on a reading of the earlier Middle Ages in the light of the later period. Then the argument has been inverted, and it has been claimed that late medieval ideas were an outgrowth of the usages of the folk in the earlier period. It is, as he says, "a constant source of amazement" to see Bracton treated as though he represented the legal thought of the early Middle Ages.[5]

Moreover, the law of the earlier Middle Ages was almost wholly procedural in character, the settlement of substantive issues being left to the judgment of God in the form of battle and ordeal. "Law," Cheyette rightly observes, "entered into the settlement of disputes mainly by prescribing procedural rules and by setting penalties. The judge or judges did not themselves determine the issue on the basis of facts ascertained; they only decided the way in which the parties would settle their own dispute."[6] In this sort of context — a legal system virtually exhausted by procedure — the notion of a fundamental law simply makes no sense. This is not to say that procedural rules make no difference. But the real difference comes only when they are accompanied by substantive principles. Lacking such principles, law provides no barriers against governmental intrusion, nor does it provide any safeguards for expectations. The most elaborate procedural devices are, in fact, perfectly compatible with tyranny.[7]

Indeed, procedure by itself cannot even exclude the element of the arbitrary and unpredictable, as a legal system is supposed to do. It can guarantee nothing except that a certain form will be followed. Certainly this is better than no regularity at all. But it is rather slender comfort to know that if someone challenges one's title to land the issue of right will be determined by relative proficiency in the use of a weapon. In any case, it hardly answers to the notion of an irrefragable code forbidding interference with or deprivation of specified rights.

In the twelfth and thirteenth centuries the introduction of substantive rules began, and this worked a gradual but nonetheless immense revolution in law. It meant that law began to offer something more than a complicated mass of rituals; it meant that the issue of right would be determined by the application of legal norms to states of fact. But this momentous development derived not from immemorial usage, which had little substantive content and virtually no ideas or organizing principles to offer, but from the monarchy, and from the study of law in the great universities. Substantive law, in the felicitous phrase which Cheyette has borrowed from Sir Henry Maine, was gradually " 'secreted in the interstices of procedure.' " [8] All this was a "deviation from custom, a deviation introduced . . . by the kings and not by the people." [9] So, in the case of generally applicable rules of substantive law, matters stood just as they did in politics generally: both derived from regal initiative.

While the important idea of custom performed many services in the late medieval period, it is possible to distinguish four major uses of the concept. Custom was a general term synonymous with law; it might refer to local usage; it sometimes meant the fact of seizin of lands, services, revenues, franchises, and the like; and, finally, it was an element in ideology, an argumentative appeal, very like some American invocations of the founding fathers. Needless to say, it is not always clear which meaning, or meanings, a particular reference involves.

The most general use of the word custom was as a synonym for law. The view, as in Glanville and Bracton, was not that there was some sort of contrast between custom and law, but rather that English law, even though unwritten, was nonetheless law.[10] The impact of Roman law provided both the inspiration and the justification for this assimilation.[11] Roman law holds that unwritten law is custom and may also be called *lex*. Glanville and Bracton knew the *Institutes* and cited the relevant passage in evidence: "unwritten law is that which usage has approved: for ancient customs, when approved by consent of those who follow them, are like statutes." [12]

The same sources indicate that custom also referred to the innumerable usages of local communities. By the time of Bracton, however, these local usages were explicitly contrasted with the law which applied throughout the kingdom. Bracton tells us that "the English hold many things by custom which they do not hold by law, as in various counties, cities, towns, and villages, where it must always be inquired what the custom of that place is and in what way those who allege custom use the custom." [13] Perhaps the clearest statement in this connection comes from Britton, another thirteenth century legal writer. The author says that King Edward I had "caused such laws as have heretofore been used in our realm to be reduced into writing according to that which is here ordained. And we will and command, that throughout England and Ireland they be used and observed in all points, saving to us the power of repealing, extending, restricting and amending them, whenever we shall see good, by the assent of our earls and barons and others of our Council; saving also to all persons such customs as by prescription of time have been differently used, so far as such customs are not contrary to law." [14] Already by the end of the thirteenth century, then, the principle of regal grace had advanced so far as to hold in reserve the claim to determine the legal standing of local usage. In this way, of course, local custom might be a source of law. But it must be remembered, too, that by the time men, especially lawyers and judges, became sufficiently self-conscious and professional to reflect on law at all, the principal force in the creation of common law was the writ system introduced by the king and his administration. English lawyers did not draw a distinction between custom and law, they assimilated them for apologetic purposes. But they did distinguish between custom as law obtaining throughout the kingdom and local custom.

The third kind of use is rather more complicated, for it unquestionably referred to "rights." But here one must be careful not to vault into the seventeenth century and equate this use with the idea that men possess certain specific rights, civil or natural, for such an idea was alien to the Middle Ages. The modern idea of rights includes generality and universality, features which put it at a great remove from medieval ideas. In the modern view, rights are general in two quite different senses. On the one hand, they enjoin or permit all actions or claims of a particular class. In the United States, certain constitutional provisions forbid abridgement of religious freedom or double jeopardy, and others permit the citizen to ventilate his views, petition his government, and so on. On the other hand, rights are general in the sense that they are claims which survive automatically, claims which are presumed to be valid. The modern idea is also distinguished by its universality, its tendency to hold that rights apply to all men in the same way. To be sure, exceptions and qualifications to these characteristics can be adduced readily enough, but this does not affect the theoretical point.

These features of the modern conception of rights involve a difference of kind from the medieval view, not merely a difference of degree. Rights in the Middle Ages were thoroughly pluralistic and highly particular. Moreover, they did not refer to legal rules describing general sorts of claims to which men were entitled. Broadly, medieval "rights" were of two kinds. On the one hand, there were a great variety of liberties and franchises conferred upon particular persons, groups, municipalities, or entire counties. These were either certain exemptions from the operation of law or specified privileges. A particular guild might have received a franchise to produce gold cloth, or a manor might be exempt from a certain tax ordinarily levied on manors. These exemptions or privileges normally rested on a royal charter or grant and as such were matters of kingly grace. But it is easy to understand how men would be inclined to regard them as rightfully theirs. The second sort of rights also referred to singular states of fact. In this usage, custom might refer to "an acquired right to have the regular use of something or to collect money from someone on given occasions." [15] At this level the principal idea was that of "seizin." [16] It denoted a species of right in property which rested on a state of fact, namely, that one's ancestors, perhaps, or one's self had entered on a parcel of land and managed to stay on it. This normally meant that someone else had to be expelled. A contested claim turned on a question of fact: had the person who alleged seizin in fact been seized of the land for a certain period of time? Proof rested on the production of witnesses to this alleged state of fact. There was no question of ultimate title to the land, no question of a substantive rule of law which distinguished a right of ownership by one man as against another. All that was testified to and all that was litigated in such a proceeding was the fact of seizin.

These three uses of the term custom are all more or less technical. The words "custom" or "law" were applied to rules if they were proven, that is, upheld in court, or if they were agreed upon by king and magnates. The "existence of one judgment concerning a custom was sufficient to prove that custom's existence and lawfulness." [17] On this subject, Cheyette has pointed to a striking passage from Azo, who was one of Bracton's chief intellectual sources. Azo asks how one can know that a custom "has been introduced." His answer is, "mainly by one of these three signs. First, that it was so decided without anyone denying it. Second, that complaints regarding the custom in question have not been received by the court. Third, that someone claimed in court that the custom did not exist, and a judgment declared on the contrary that the custom did indeed exist." [18] So, custom constituted a legitimate source of law. But medieval men also knew that novel situations could arise. In that case, the court might undertake to proceed by analogy, but the case might be difficult enough to warrant referring it to the king's court. If "new and unaccustomed things emerge which were not previously used in the kingdom," says Bracton, "they may be judged by similar things, if similar things have occurred, and when there is a good opportunity to proceed from like to like. But if such things never happened before, and judgment of them is obscure and difficult, then the judgments are to be brought all the way to the great court, and they are to be settled there through the counsel of the court." [19] There is surely nothing in this to suggest that custom was regarded as fundamental or immutable. To be sure, interested parties resisted change which threatened to affect their liberties or lands. But other interested parties encouraged such alterations. Cheyette concludes his remarkable study of medieval case law by observing, quite rightly, that "when the sources speak of the unchangeableness of custom, they are speaking of acquired rights, those that have already been used and proved. As such, the idea of 'custom' places no limits on princely or judicial power to make new law for new problems." [20] In short, it is hardly surprising to encounter resistance to change which appears to run against a man's interests. Needless to say, it is frequently very difficult to disentangle this kind of legal usage from ideological appeals.

Distinct from the technical uses of the idea of custom was the ideological use. In times of crisis both king and magnates consistently appealed to the laws and customs to justify contradictory political postures. But the arguments couched in these terms were not charges that the other party had violated a body of substantive law, much less a constitutional law; they were invocations of the past. In England the peculiar circumstances of the Conquest produced a fixation on the time of the sainted king, Edward the Confessor, who was the last Anglo-Saxon ruler before the imposition of what would later be called the Norman yoke.[21] Englishmen naturally began very early to periodize their history in terms of the year 1066. As Maitland said, Edward quickly became "a myth — a saint and hero of a golden age, of a good old time . . ." [22] But apart from the specificity occasioned by the Conquest, such a style of argument should cause no surprise. English law was fundamentally procedural, which meant, in part, that decisions had to be reached through judgment. But in political argument, references to the laws and customs had a retrospective character. Their major use in the political arena was to invoke the emotions and aura of prestige and sanctity which attached to the time of the fathers. The vagueness and ambiguity of the appeal is not difficult to understand, for surely elasticity is a leading requirement for a useful ideological tool. If the idea of the laws and customs of the fathers had been specific, it could not have been used to support both the baronial claim to a rightful place in the king's council and the royal view that the choice of counsellors rested exclusively with the king.

The idea of custom, then, was an exceedingly complex and characteristically ambiguous one. Although it is not possible to separate easily in the documents the several threads just discussed, it is helpful to bear the several senses in mind. All the evidence — and there are many interesting statements — shows that the idea of custom was extremely vague but that it very often meant simply "law." There is no suggestion of any kind of distinction between law and custom, though there is an explicit association of both with the laws of preceding kings, especially Edward the Confessor. In the earliest sources after the Conquest, these ideas were frequently expressed in regal documents, but from the beginning they were associated with the notion of some sort of agreement between king and magnates. Thus a document of the early twelfth century, which purports to represent the legal enactments of the Conqueror, is prefaced with the statement that it sets "down what William, king of the English, established in consultation with his magnates after the conquest of England." These Laws of William the Conqueror contain very little that is general, but one clause says: "This also I command and will, that all shall have and hold the law of King Edward in respect of their lands and all their possessions, with the addition of those decrees I have ordained for the welfare of the English people." 23

The Coronation Charter of Henry I (1100) reads in part as follows: "Know that by the mercy of God and by the common counsel of the barons of the whole kingdom of England I have been crowned king of this realm . . . I abolish all the evil customs by which the kingdom of England has been unjustly oppressed." Further on, Henry's charter says, "I restore to you the law of King Edward together with such emendations to it as my father made with the counsel of his barons." 24 The same outlook is expressed in the Charter of Stephen, the date of which is probably 1135. "Know that I have granted, and by this present charter confirmed, to all my barons and vassals of England all the liberties and good laws which Henry, king of the English, my uncle, granted and conceded to them. I also grant them all the good laws and good customs which they enjoyed in the time of King Edward. Wherefore I will and firmly command that both they and their heirs shall have and hold all these good laws and liberties from me and from my heirs freely, fully and in peace." 25 In 1154 King Henry II issued a Coronation Charter of much the same purport and diction.26 It grants the good and abolishes evil customs.

The dispute between Henry II and Thomas Becket, from the time of the Constitutions of Clarendon (1164) to Becket's murder (1170), affords interesting material on the meaning and place of custom. The Constitutions arose from a dispute over criminous clerics between the king and some of his clergy, especially Thomas Becket, Archbishop of Canterbury. The general language of the preamble has been cited as an illustration of the proposition that written law was regarded merely as a recognition of the fundamental law of ancient custom.27 To be sure, it says that "in the presence of the said king was made this record and declaration of a certain part of the customs, liberties and privileges of his ancestors, that is, of King Henry, his grandfather, and of other things which ought to be observed and maintained in the realm." Observe, however, that the subject is the king's privileges and that the whole matter resulted from "dissensions and discords . . . concerning the customs and privileges of the realm . . ." [28] If the context is taken into account, one learns that the customs and privileges it refers to are far from being a finding of some law that hedges the king and protects the people, as the fundamental law is supposed to do. On the contrary, its purpose was to register an expansion of royal authority. In particular, the king demanded jurisdiction over criminous clerics. Moreover, the appeal to the idea that the Constitutions were a declaration of custom was an interested use of an ideological idiom. Henry was engaged in a struggle with the clergy, and he did his best to make out that what he claimed was nothing new. Becket recognized this and explicitly rejected it.

Becket objected to the concessions extracted from the clergy and declared in the Constitutions, and some of the language employed in the subsequent quarrel is most illuminating. The king was determined to have a judgment in council against the archbishop for his refusal to obey the royal commands, but a dispute quickly developed as to whether judgment upon Becket should be rendered solely by the bishops, or by the barons. Neither group wanted the responsibility. Finally, according to William Fitz Stephen, who was present at the debate, "the king, having listened to this argument concerning the pronouncement of sentence, was moved to anger, and soon put an end to the dispute. At his command the Bishop of Winchester, though very unwillingly, finally pronounced the sentence." [29] The vigorous assertion of the king's will is worth remarking, but it is Becket's reaction that is most interesting. "When the archbishop heard that judgment had been passed upon him, he said 'Even if I were to remain silent at such a sentence, future ages will not do so. For this is a new form of judgment, perhaps in accordance with the new canons recently promulgated at Clarendon. From time immemorial such a thing has never been known as this, that an archbishop of Canterbury should be tried in the court of the king of the English . . . It is contrary to custom on account of the dignity of the Church and of the authority of his person, and also because the archbishop is the spiritual father of the king and of all men in the kingdom.' " [30]

Becket accused the clergy of deserting the cause, threatened them, and altogether put them in an extremely delicate position. Through the Bishop of Chichester, they addressed Becket thus: "My lord archbishop . . . we have much to complain of against you. You have gravely injured us, your bishops . . . you have placed us, as it were, between the hammer and the anvil; for if we disobey, we are ensnared in the bonds of disobedience, if we obey, we infringe the constitution and trespass against the king. For recently, when we were assembled together with you at Clarendon, *we were required by our lord the king to observe his royal dignities and, lest perchance we should be in any doubt, he showed us in writing the royal customs of which he spoke.* At length we pledged our assent and promised to observe them, you in the first place and we . . . afterwards at your command." [31] Becket's own point of view was expressed in a letter to the king (May 1166). For the issue being explored here, the interesting point is that Becket regarded the Constitutions of Clarendon as but imagined ancient customs; he attributes them to kingly innovation. He tells the king, "you have not the power to give orders to bishops, nor to absolve or excommunicate anyone, nor to drag clerks before secular tribunals, nor to judge concerning churches or tithes, to forbid bishops to adjudge causes concerning breach of faith or oath, and many other things of this kind which are written among those *customs of yours which you call ancient* . . ." [32]

Finally, notice may be taken of a most interesting letter from the Bishop of London, Gilbert Foliot, to Becket, which undertakes to defend the bishops against Becket's reproaches. It begins by recalling the events at Clarendon, maintaining that the bishops had not collapsed before the king and the barons, even in the face of threats. "We were all shut up in one chamber, and on the third day the princes and nobles of the realm, waxing hot in their wrath, burst into the chamber where we sat, muttering and clamouring, threw off their cloaks and shook their fists at us, exclaiming, 'Attend all ye who set at naught the statutes of the realm and heed not the king's commands. These hands, these arms, yea, even our bodies are not our own, but belong to our lord the king, and they are ready at his nod to avenge every wrong done to him and to work his will, whatever it may be. *No matter what he may command, it will be most just in our eyes since it proceeds from his will alone.* Take fresh counsel then, and bend your minds to his commands . . .'" [33]

From all this it seems clear that the idea of custom was much more dynamic than has been supposed. It played a variety of roles. In general, it seems merely to have been another word for law, and this was sometimes a royal command — nothing more, nothing less. It is also clear, however, that "custom" was embedded in the idea of ancestral laws, the laws of the fathers. This is a standard ingredient in the idiom of argumentation and justification. But the central element in legal and political dispute was the vague but persistent appeal to the idea of counsel. From a legal point of view it is important that in those relations which constituted high politics there was little but this procedural ideal. The partners in double majesty could agree in general terms on the advisability, indeed the necessity, of counsel. But the operational range of this agreement was indefinite in the extreme. Even on the procedural level kings and magnates were frequently at odds, for the king could claim to have satisfied the demand for counsel by having asked the advice of those whom he chose to ask. Clearly, not even the principle of counsel and consent can usefully be called fundamental law. Rather it was the focus of political dispute. The very model of the alleged fundamental law, the Magna Carta, was nothing of the kind. On the contrary, it was "a stage in an argument and bore all the characteristic features of the argument — the erection of interests into law, the selection and interpretation of convenient precedent, the readiness to assert agreed custom where none existed." [34] To be sure, it took on the quality of an ideal, like the principle of counsel and consent and the appeal to the good laws of Edward the Confessor, but this is very different from being fundamental law. Some of its provisions became a part of the common law, others were omitted from the reissues, and still others lost their relevance. Thus individual chapters of the charter could be employed in courts of law. But politically none of this touches the main point. What the charter came to signify in moments of crisis was the triumph of 1215, and the general idea that it represented an expression and promise of royal good faith with the baronage. In this context, what mattered was not so much this or that clause but general endorsement of the spirit of the agreement. Time and again in the thirteenth and fourteenth centuries, the magnates insisted on confirmation. Yet the fact that this was a matter of casting back to a general idea rather than mere legalism is perfectly clear. Thus the original chapter 14, for example, had been deleted from the genuinely legal documents of the reign of Henry III, but this did not prevent the magnates from supposing that the principle of baronial counsel and consent it contained was still a standard. Indeed, they gradually extended its range far beyond that of chapter 14, which had been concerned only with consent to aids. It was that principle that occupied the center of the political stage.[35]

It is clear, then, that law and custom were very much a part of the political process. But were medieval men unaware that they were sometimes engaged in lawmaking? What they said as well as what they did demonstrates that this contention cannot be sustained. They habitually thought and argued in a retrospective frame: the good days were those of their ancestors, and they were good because the king's ancestors had kept the peace and refrained from interfering with local routines. This was not true, but there was very good reason for wishing it had been. In a violent age in which men have little hope and less chance of mastering their environment, standards are habitually projected backwards, for a political theory of aspiration and expectation of future good requires a buoyant atmosphere, one in which large numbers of men are in fact and in potentiality bettering their lot. In the Middle Ages men sought only to repair and restore what they imagined had once been, and then they tried to freeze it once and for all. But this did not mean that they could not imagine fashioning a new rule. Its purpose would most likely be seen as restorative, and its justification almost certainly would be cast in terms of ancient standards.

The subject of lawmaking is well illustrated by some of the events connected with the meeting of the king's council at Merton in 1236. King Henry III and his great men had gathered to discuss a variety of legal issues. There was considerable diversity of opinion on the questions involved; on some of them change was refused, while other matters were agreed upon.[36] But one issue in particular provided the occasion for some very revealing remarks. Bishop Robert Grosseteste, the eminent scholar, and others urged that English law should be changed on an important point. What they wanted was a provision that children born out of wedlock should be regarded as legitimate if the parents married subsequently. This would have meant that such children could inherit without regard to their bastardy. On this issue "all the earls and barons replied with one voice that they were not willing to change the laws of England which have been used and approved." [37] But as Helen Cam has observed, the implication of this is "that they could have changed them if they liked . . ." [38]

Grosseteste had argued in favor of the change on the ground that it was needed to bring the common law into agreement with divine and natural law and with canon and civil law. He had worked hard at marshaling support for the change, so hard, indeed, that he had provoked a rebuke from William Raleigh, one of the king's justices. He wrote an interesting letter to Raleigh in reply. "You insinuate," he says, "that I have tried to change the laws of the realm by the witness of the Old Testament. But you will not find in the course of the letter which I have sent you a claim to do this, if you will read it through without prejudice. I try to persuade you by my letter to attempt to change the laws and customs which are contrary to the divine law and the church's decree — to persuade you, and also those with whom lies the power of changing and establishing laws who are won over by your effective persuasion. Nor have I suggested anywhere in the letter I have sent that you alone should be the maker of laws, or that you could do anything you wished at court; nor am I so simple as to believe any suggestion that laws can be made or changed by you or anyone else without the counsel of the ruler and of the magnates." [39]

A clearer statement of the idea and, indeed, the politics of lawmaking could hardly be desired. Nor was the good bishop alone in his views. Later in his reign, Henry III attempted to introduce a new measure which would have involved his subjects in financial liabilities. He wanted to make it possible for a man who had suffered a loss through robbery to recover from those responsible for pursuing the thief if they had failed in their duty. Apparently the king thought a royal command to this effect would be enough, but there was so much resistance to it that he had to abandon the plan. [40] In connection with this episode the chronicler Matthew Paris opined that "a great change has negligible force without the common assent of the baronage." [41] According to Bracton, writing at midcentury, English laws and customs, "since they have been approved by the consent of those using them and confirmed by the oath of kings, can neither be changed nor destroyed without the common consent of all those with whose counsel and consent they have been promulgated. But they can be changed for the sake of improvement without such consent." [42]

The most striking evidence of conscious lawmaking derives from the reign of Edward I. Some of the many statutes enacted in that reign which effected significant changes in the law of the land have been discussed already. In addition, Edward and his judges acted on two extremely important matters which reached the heart of the law on questions of property — matters on which T. F. T. Plucknett has done penetrating research. One of these areas relates to the feudal lord's claim to proprietary and jurisdictional rights deriving from seizin of land. The other represents a regal innovation on the subject of claims by the king's tenants to regally endowed liberties and franchises.

The general nature of the law of seizin and distress, upon which the land law rested, deserves special consideration. This subject is particularly instructive because land law was the principal matter of the common law, and it was altered in important respects by the lawmaking activities of Edward and his justices. As stated above, the idea of seizin referred to claims resting only on a state of fact. Obviously, in times of civil commotion this arrangement made possible, indeed encouraged, the forcible seizure of lands by those who had the armed might to suppress resistance. Seizin of land, however it had been acquired, also could and often did involve the victimization of the tenants resident on the land. The idea was to extort from them the customs and services which were commonly associated with the possession of land. The exaction of these services reinforced the presumption that the lord demanding them was seized of the land. Each successful usurpation or extortion was just so much more evidence of seizin. Proceedings of this sort had been all too common during the Barons' War (1258–1265), when a disseizing lord, a mere usurper, could set about extorting profitable customs and services from his tenants. Moreover, the common law provided such a lord with a powerful legal instrument. The core of the matter lay in the lord's right of distress within his fee. This was the method of compelling performance of customs and services allegedly due from his tenants. From the point of view of the thirteenth century lord, the great merit of the right of distress was that he needed no judgment of his own or any other court to proceed. He had at hand, therefore, a swift and effective legal instrument. But the tenant was not entirely without recourse.

The system worked in the following way. Suppose that a lord demanded a service, such as the tenant's duty to do suit in the lord's court, and claimed that his tenant had failed to discharge this obligation. The lord could then distrain his tenant's chattels, that is, seize his beasts, for example. The tenant could then choose to acquiesce and perform the service demanded, or he could sue out a writ of replevin. The effect of this writ was that the king's agent, the sheriff, would undertake to return the tenant's chattels to him, pending the outcome of trial. In court the lord could reply with an avowry, by which he admitted distress but justified it by contending that the services demanded were due to him. The issue to be tried, then, was what services, if any, were due. If the decision was favorable to the tenant, he received damages; if favorable to the lord, his tenant's chattels would be returned to him (the lord), thus leaving both parties just where they had been before the litigation began, except that a judgment had been made on the question.[43] Clearly, such a state of affairs in the law could easily lend itself to systematic abuse, and it was well recognized that it could and did provoke profound discontent. Simon de Montfort remarked that distress without judgment was "the beginning of all wars." [44] Edward I undertook to deal with the problem by statute. In order to appreciate the significance of the alterations which were worked in the law by his effort and that of his judges, it is necessary to recognize the contrast between the legal actions just described and those which were, in contemporary usage, higher up in the right. The procedures of distress, replevin, and avowry were legal forms at a merely possessory level. Such actions did not even raise, let alone settle, the question whether the land was rightfully the lord's fee. To conclude this question of higher right, altogether different writs were required, and the issue would be tried by combat or grand assize.[45]

At the level of right, the crucial question was this: In order for a lord to prove his right to distrain for customs and services allegedly due him, how long a seizin must he show? This question had been dealt with in chapter 9 of the Statute of Marlborough (1267). It established as law that a particular service, suit of court, might be enforced by distraint if seizin before the year 1230 could be established. It is important to notice two points about this provision. First, it deals only with suit of court; second, it is not merely possessory, for it raises the question of right. The statute also provided forms of action. For present purposes, it is necessary to comment only on the action afforded the tenant. It was called *contra formam feoffamenti*, and judgment favorable to the tenant pursuant to this action forbade further distresses by the lord. But this provision of the Statute of Marlborough did not affect the action of replevin, and it was much more popular. Despite the fact that replevin did not reach the subject of right, it was preferred for an eminently practical reason. To pursue the action provided by the Statute of Marlborough, the tenant had to suffer the considerable inconvenience and expense of resort to the central courts. The action of replevin, on the other hand, could be pursued in the local courts. Since the tenant's chief concern, quite naturally, was the recovery of his chattels, the action of contra formam feoffamenti was largely ignored. But in 1285 Edward treated the problem of distress in the Statute of Westminster II. The provision enacted, however, produced the occasion for a striking display of judicial lawmaking. The Statute of Marlborough had dealt with the question of right and had required that at that level seizin must be shown to have obtained before 1230. The Statute of Westminster II, however, raised only the possessory question, and it laid down that seizin be later than the year 1242. The important point socially and politically is that the action provided by the Statute of Marlborough, if employed, would have invalidated many claims to suit of court at the level of right which were nevertheless enforceable if the parties allowed them to remain at the merely possessory level.

The great change which took place was that tenants continued to use the more convenient action of replevin, but their counsel began to plead the action as if it were contra formam feoffamenti. That is, they wanted the best of both worlds — convenience, and settlement of the issue of right — and the king's justices eventually gave it to them. The tenants preferred the swifter local procedure of replevin, but they wanted also to cut off repeated distresses by concluding the issue of right. This was accomplished by a judicial transformation of the rule concerning suit of court in the Statute of Marlborough into a general rule of law, reaching the whole area of customs and services.[46] Plucknett has illustrated what happened by a case of 1305. Relying on the provision of the Statute of Westminster II, a lord avowed upon a seizin dating since 1242. The tenant's reply was that the lord had not been seized before 1230. The lord's answer, of course, was that if this was to be claimed, then the tenant would have to "bring *contra formam feoffamenti* which was made for the purpose." At this point, Chief Justice Hengham accomplished a minor legal revolution. He held that chapter 9 of the Statute of Marlborough "says that none be distrained for suit unless he or his ancestors have been accustomed to do it before 1230; now you have distrained him." The lord's answer, Plucknett remarks, "was inevitable: 'that statute will not help him, for Westminster II is more recent, and it gives power to distrain on a seizin since 1242.' " The chief justice had brought the two statutes into collision by generalizing the Marlborough rule and assimilating right and possession. But in reply to a query, Hengham snapped: "do not gloss the statute; we know it better than you, for we made it, and one often sees one statute undo another." [47] This makes good sense, but the startling thing about this case is that Hengham was making a statute of 1267 undo a statute of 1285. The result of this judicial law-making was that distraining lords now had to make out seizin before 1230 even for possessory title. As Plucknett says, it was "a denial of one of the central doctrines of the common law." But it did become the settled view. Plucknett concludes that this is "judicial legislation of the most drastic sort, and the well-known words of Bereford in another of this series of cases become all the more significant — 'by [a decision on] this avowry we shall make a law throughout all the land.' " [48]

It is obvious, then, that the king, his servants, and his men were aware that laws might be made and unmade, both by statute and by judges. But even more revealing evidence is at hand. This relates to the second area mentioned above: the problem of claims to liberties and franchises. Indeed, inquiry into what are called Edward's quo warranto proceedings will serve to illustrate several important points.[49] In the first place, the arguments on both sides of these cases are excellent examples of the idea of double majesty. The king's attorneys and the franchise holders being sued by them in the name of the king advanced arguments which rested on incompatible premises, but, as always, they failed to drive them beyond an illogical but working muddle of first principles. Moreover, the quo warranto suits illustrate very well the close link between operative political thought and the actual pleadings in court, as well as the compromise solution worked out after 1290. Finally, these proceedings make two valuable points concerning the royal bureaucracy. They show clearly that the king was served by a large and able body of men, some of whom, indeed, were more royalist than the king. But the multiple confusions, delays, and stalling of the bureaucratic machinery also underline the shortcomings of medieval government even when led by an able ruler. Nevertheless, Edward and his advisers accomplished a considerable alteration in a vital area of the common law. The essence of this change was that title to franchises was shifted from the basis of mere use and usurpation to explicit royal charter. This is remarkable enough, but it claims attention for other reasons as well. First, the legal ideas employed by the royal lawyers were new to England and reflect distinct advances in precision and generality. Secondly, the disputes which arose from the king's demand that his tenants show their warrant illustrate quite well the politics of lawmaking.

The new outlook that emerged from the campaign was eventually set forth in the statute Quo Warranto (1290), but in order to appreciate its impact it will be necessary to cast back to the parliament of 1278. The king confronted that parliament with the announcement that the holders of royal franchises would be required to register formal claims for their liberties, and show their warrants for them to the king's justices. The principal question at stake was what would be considered a legally sound warrant. Broadly, there were two sorts of cases. Some of the king's tenants, especially churchmen, possessed charters which had theretofore been perfectly valid legal instruments. In many cases, however, these charters were very old and suffered from vagueness as to just what liberties had been granted. Other tenants were much worse off; they had no charters at all. Previously, even this loose arrangement would have raised no insuperable problems, since seizin and use were valid claims at common law.

The quo warranto inquiries mounted by the king and his lawyers turned on two legal ideas, both of which ran contrary to the assumptions of the common law.[50] On the one hand, the king's attorneys relied on a concession theory of franchises; that is, a franchise attained legal validity only by a grant from the crown. This general view was buttressed by a demand for verbal clarity in charters. Legally it represented a considerable advance in sophistication, but it meant that many charters lost their validity. But it was not just a legal question; on the contrary, the king's challenge ran to the foundations of baronial power, at least in theory. The second legal idea involved in the quo warranto proceedings was an explicit answer to traditional claims resting on some form of prescription, namely, the answer that time does not run against the king.

Resistance to the quo warranto proceedings was widespread. From 1278 onwards, litigation and complaint multiplied. The courts were understandably confused, for there were available to them first principles driving in opposite directions. Many of the king's tenants went on pleading long use, but from the point of view of the king and his lawyers this was an invalid plea. The result was that many of these hard cases, like "political questions" in American constitutional law, were evaded by the courts. In novel cases, it will be recalled, the justices had the option of reference to the great court. Thus undecided cases multiplied until 1290, when the statute Quo Warranto provided an answer to claims resting on long tenure.[51] What the statute shows is that the great magnates had been able to organize enough resistance to compel the government to reverse decisions and validate the claim of long tenure. On the other hand, however, it was only the retrospective aspect of the matter that the crown abandoned. For the statute also established the principle that any claim to a franchise must be proved by a legally acceptable charter from the crown. In order to do both of these things at the same time, the statute provides that those who have old claims may follow a merely formal procedure which will result in the issuance of a charter. Indeed, the evidence suggests that the government's retreat was rather more decisive than the statute itself implies. In fact, a summary of the statute which circulated at the time makes it unnecessary for a man even to follow that formal procedure. It says that proof of seizin since 1189 is itself a sufficient answer to the challenge of quo warranto.[52]

The combination of the alternative principles of royal grant and prescriptive claim is a striking enough illustration of double majesty. But certain claims of long tenure are even more interesting. There were two ways in which prescriptive claims were justified in the quo warranto proceedings. One line of argument did not deny that any franchise was ultimately a grant of the king but asserted only that immemorial tenure was either a sufficient answer to a writ "by what warrant" or was acceptable proof of a royal grant in the past. But a second line of argument denied that liberties were royal grants at all. This was a view presented by the great earls of the kingdom, who had long been regarded as the king's companions par excellence. The theory was that "the men who first conquered England under King William had an equal right with the king to possess its land and liberties, a right founded not in grant but in conquest." [53] This was the background to the striking reply of Earl Warenne when he was summoned to supply the warrant by which he held his lands. He appeared in court brandishing a sword and arguing thus.

> Here my lords, here is my warrant! My ancestors came with
> William the Bastard and conquered their lands with the sword,
> and I shall defend them with the sword against anyone who tries
> to usurp them. The king did not conquer and subject the land by
> himself, but our forefathers were partners and co-workers with
> him.[54]

On this view, then, at least the earls of the realm had a status which
did not derive its legitimacy from the king. It will be recalled that in
the political thinking of Bracton and his contemporaries it was also
the earls who figured in the doctrine that the king was restrained by
his *comites,* his companions. That was the core of the dualistic conception of authority around which more complicated conceptions
had collected, eventuating in the assumption that the estates of the
realm in parliament were a legitimate counterpoise to regal authority.

On the whole, then, it is clear that medieval men of affairs knew
perfectly well that laws could be and were made, and that such law
often set aside the common law. On the other hand, it would be a
mistake to equate medieval lawmaking with modern legislation. The
medieval form resembled the efforts of a carpenter to shore up a
sagging beam more than the general plans of an architect. But
medieval men did consciously introduce new rules. It is true that
neither lawyers nor other persons in the later Middle Ages were
given to sustained theoretical treatment of their work. For the most
part they simply went about the performance of their duties. The
result is that explicit statements of theoretical interest are relatively
infrequent. Even so, a few of these scattered and rather isolated statements are worth quoting. For the year 1310, this statement appears
in the Year Books: "as one canon defeats many laws, so the statute
defeats many things that were at common law." [55] In a case argued in
1348 it was said that the "king makes the laws with the assent of the
peers and of the commons, not through the peers and the commons."
Moreover, the king "has no peer in his land; and . . . ought not to
be judged by them." [56] The parliament rolls for 1388 state that "the
law of the land is made in parliament by the king, and the lords
spiritual and temporal and all the commonalty of the realm." [57]
Addressing parliament in 1442, the Bishop of Bath affirmed that the
business of parliament was to make new laws and, where necessary,
to renovate old ones.[58] In 1454, the rolls report that the Chief Jus-

tice of the King's Bench, presumably Sir John Fortescue, in answering a query for the whole bench, said that parliament was "so high and so mighty in his nature, that it may make lawe, and that that is lawe it may make noo lawe . . ." [59]

There remain for explicit consideration only two of the points mentioned at the beginning of this chapter: the relation of the king to the law, and the magnates' view of the role of the common law in opposition to the king. It will be seen that while the king's relation to law was certainly not one of subordination, it was never perfectly clear. The baronial opposition recognized that the king was not subject to legal reproach and, therefore, that something other than the common law would have to be appealed to.

Considering the general paucity of systematic theory, statements indicative of the king's relation to law are fairly abundant. In the twelfth century, Richard of Ely, the author of The Dialogue of the Exchequer, which he dedicated to his royal master, Henry II, used some remarkably candid language. In stressing the importance of "portable wealth" to kingship, Richard held that "although this wealth is not invariably theirs by strict process of law, but proceeds sometimes from the laws of their countries, sometimes from the secret devices of their own hearts and sometimes even from their mere arbitrary purpose, their subjects have no right to question or condemn their actions." [60] In a case before the King's Bench concerning a charter granted in 1242, one Hawise asserted that her charter was good because the king had given it to her "and the king himself is above all law . . ." [61] In 1279 "John le Fauconcer, who sues for the king, put forward many arguments . . . One is that the lord king is not bound by the laws and has no necessity to use ordinary writs . . ." [62] To be sure, since the last two passages occur in the context of a pleading, they obviously need not be taken as descriptive of the law. But this does not detract from the point that the king's relation to law was not clear, for it was not absurd to argue that he was above the law or that he was not bound by it. In the course of a quo warranto suit, counsel asserted that the king was above all his subjects and the law in his kingdom.[63] In 1291, in a suit between the earls of Gloucester and Hereford, the litigants were told that for "the common welfare the lord King, by his prerogative, is in many cases above the law and customs used in his kingdom." [64] William de Bereford, Chief Justice of the Common Bench in the time of Edward

II, observed in the course of an argument with his colleague, Herle, that "if you could appeal to legal principle what you say would be well enough, but against the King, who is above the law, you cannot rely on legal principles." [65]

The case of Scoland v. Grandison, which Plucknett has discussed in detail, indicates another side of the general ambiguity surrounding the king's relation to law. The setting of this case was that the king's justices, in accordance with a statute, had declared a closing date for pleas resting on original writs. But they received a royal command to entertain such a writ after the closing date, and they did so. The argument which developed supplies evidence on two important issues: the king's relation to statute, and the distinction between the king acting alone and the king acting with counsel. There are two manuscript reports of the argument. After one Stonore had objected to the court's entertaining the writ because it was too late, one of the manuscripts reports that Justice Ormesby replied, "You are only challenging and disputing the king's authority, and that neither we nor you can do." Reference to the statute was then made, with the claim that it rendered the proceedings void. To this, Justice Staunton replied: "We have the king's warrant, and so we must go on; if you think it is wrong, then sue error afterwards." [66] The second manuscript reports the following exchange:

> Staunton, J. "We have a later warrant from the king, and that is as high as the statute."
>
> Stonore. "The answer we put forward is fully warranted by the statute and no one can go against the statute."
>
> Spignurel, J. "You would be correct if the sheriff had taken the writ after the proclamation, but we have received it by the king's command, and by a new authority that is as high as a statute."
>
> Passeley. "Sir, the statute is given by common counsel of the realm and that cannot be defeated by the king's simple command; wherefore it seems that such a command ought not to exceed the bounds of the statute."
>
> Ormesby, J. "When the king commands, one must suppose that it is by common counsel, and besides, no one may counterplead the king's deed." [67]

On the question of the king's relation to statute, then, two quite different lines of argument were advanced by the court, without any indication as to which was preferred. Did the question turn on the presumption that the king had acted with counsel, or on the principle that the king's deed could not be disputed? The answer is that there was no answer. These matters were not settled, and they remained unsettled far beyond this time. As for Passeley's interesting effort to distinguish between the king's simple command and a command given with counsel, it should be enough to recall that it was in this same period that the barons drew a distinction between the king and the crown. The best assessment would seem to be that ideas of this sort were in the air, ready to be seized upon if the occasion required it.

The question of the relation of the king to the law may be concluded by citing an interesting case from 1460. In that year the Duke of York had asserted his claim to the throne as against the House of Lancaster. The lords appealed to the judges for counsel in the matter, but the judges replied that they could give no counsel on it, especially because it "was so high, and touched the Kyngs high estate and regalie, which is above the lawe and passed ther lernyning, wherefore they durst not enter into eny communication therof, for it perteyned to the Lords of the Kyngs blode, and the apparage [the peerage] of this his land, to have communication and medle in such maters; and therfore they humble bysought all the Lordes, to have theym utterly excused of eny avyce or Counseill . . ." [68] It would be unwise to conclude that the English king was *legibus solutus*. Certainly there was no formal theory on the question. Indeed, even statements that rise to the level of a generalization are few. But such views as those just cited show that the king's relationship to law was certainly not one of clear and continuous subordination. At the very least, it is obvious that the king was not subject to the law himself, and that for some purposes he was clearly regarded as above it.

Turning now to the relation between the opposition and the common law, it is apparent that neither the magnates nor the commons relied upon the law in resisting their monarch. On the contrary, opposition movements explicitly recognized that the common law and the ordinary courts were the king's. The barons of 1233–1234 complained that they had no avenue of appeal against the king's use of unnatural counsellors: "there was nobody to give them justice." [69] The barons who composed the declaration of 1308 asked, "how should the king be led . . . by an action at law or by coercion? By an action at law may no man obtain remedy, for he would have no judges, except those of the king's . . ." [70]

It has already been shown that the political struggles of the reign of Richard II, culminating in his deposition, brought a number of ideas and practices to a head. These collisions produced an explicit elaboration of the idea of parliament as a high court, resting on the liberties and privileges of parliament. For present purposes, the most interesting and important point is that the parliamentary claims were explicitly divorced from the common law. It is easy to see why this should have been so. The king's justices, in 1387, had supported Richard to the full, and their reward for this was impeachment. It does not take an advanced political theory to show that, in order to impeach the justices, parliament needed a principle of a higher order than the common law and the ordinary courts. The view adopted is set out clearly in the Rolls of Parliament. The occasion was the discussion of the parliamentary proceedings of 1388 against the Archbishop of York, the Duke of York, and others accused of treason. It is reported that justices, sergeants at law, and others wise in the law were consulted concerning the appropriate procedure. They "reported that the appeal was not made nor affirmed according to the order which either the one or the other of these laws [Common or Civil] requires." The lords then conferred and arrived at this conclusion: "That in so high a crime as is alleged in this appeal, which touches the person of the king . . . and the state of his realm, perpetrated by persons who are peers of the realm and by others, the process will not be taken anywhere except to parliament, nor judged by any other law except the law and court of parliament, and that it pertains to the lords of parliament and to their franchise and liberty, from ancient custom of parliament, to be judges in such a case, and to judge such a case, with the assent of the king." The report goes on to say that the ordinary courts "are only there to execute the ancient laws and customs of the realm and the ordinances and establishments of parliament." [71] Farther on the position is summed up thus: "In this parliament all the lords, both spiritual and temporal, then present, claimed as their liberty and franchise, that the great matters moved in this parliament and to be moved in parliaments in the future, touching peers of the land, should be introduced, judged and discussed by the course of parliament and not by civil law nor by the common law of the land, used in other and lower courts of the land." [72] Obviously, the estates of the realm in parliament were quite clear that these matters of high politics were not governed by the common law. In short, the men of the Middle Ages were unwilling to attribute to the common law the constitutional bearing which modern enthusiasts have been so ready to see there.

As Plucknett says, English law in the Middle Ages was "alive and vigorous, growing and changing. Both king and people desired amendments from time to time, and achieved them." [73] Moreover, their testimony indicates that they knew full well what they were about. Conscious legal change, often touching the most important affairs of the realm and its people, is revealed in legal and political writings, year books, rolls of parliament, and chronicles. In framing a theory which accounts for the thought and practices of this period, the thesis that political life was governed by an ancient and immutable body of custom must be abandoned.[74] To insist that these ideas were central to the period produces a paradox of colossal proportions. It introduces a disjunction between the theoretical account and the available facts which is too wide to be serviceable. Everything that the observer can learn of the operative beliefs and practices of this period runs contrary to the fundamental law thesis. To be sure, the celebration of that thesis has been nothing short of astonishing. But the confidence with which it has been reiterated is inversely proportional to its evidential basis. Yet its reception is not surprising, for it finds in the usages of our forebears the elements of an outlook to which many of us are attached. Nevertheless, it is a mistake to suppose that any historical evidence which suggests that our ancestors believed as we do somehow validates what we believe. Historical corroboration of contemporary values, as it happens, has been purchased at the price of misunderstanding how and when those ideas emerged. Certainly the existence of stress between what men profess and what they practice — between theoretical and justificatory accounts of what is done and the motives which dispassionate investigation and hindsight can supply — is familiar enough to social theorists. But a gap is one thing and a yawning gulf is quite another. The former is native to the requirements of political life; the latter, one suspects, is the product of misplaced attachment to an ideal which ought to stand on its merits, rather than on the wobbly legs which the record of medieval social fragmentation and endemic disorder and lawlessness supplies. Acceptance of the ideas and practices associated with the rule of law or a fundamental law depends on the achievement of a much more unified, coherent, and self-conscious political community than was ever achieved in the medieval period.

All the essential elements of the evolving outlook which has been traced in the preceding chapters, together with its fundamental incoherence and the ambiguities entailed by the maintenance of a dual conception of authority, received their fullest statement toward the end of the fifteenth century. The next chapter is devoted to a study of that statement, which is presented in the political writings of Sir John Fortescue. These form the literary pinnacle of the medieval political outlook in England. The assumptions of double majesty were not abandoned after Fortescue's day, but the prevailing focus of thought in the Tudor period was altered in such a way as to presuppose the traditional medieval outlook and yet to produce an important modification in the terms of the recurrent debate over its specific content and operation.

seven Political and Regal Dominion

It will be recalled that the outlook of double majesty turns on the notion that government is organized in terms of two principles rather than one: both kings and some manifestation of the "people" were considered to possess legitimate political authority. It is essential that this outlook be distinguished from the theory of mixed monarchy — the idea that the best form of government is some combination of the virtues of monarchy, aristocracy, and democracy. Each of these is supposed to be separately institutionalized and to have different governmental functions annexed to it. The result, so the theory goes, is a salutary system of checks and balances. A number of commentators have described Fortescue's writings in this frame of reference, but there is no such theory in his work. It will be argued here that a satisfactory interpretation of Fortescue and of the working assumptions of the English political order depends on distinguishing double majesty from mixed monarchy and attributing only the first to Fortescue. Double majesty describes a distinctly medieval perspective, while the idea of mixed monarchy has enjoyed great popularity only in antiquity and in modern times. Hence the distinction is also crucial, though by no means exhaustive, in formulating an adequate account of the differences between medieval and modern political thought. While establishing this distinction is the primary aim of this chapter, an extended discussion is best postponed until Fortescue's ideas have been explored in some detail.

Fortescue's writings supply valuable commentary on the relation of law, morality, and politics.[1] Here the idea of natural law is basic. Fortescue employs it in three rather different ways, though none of these is specifically jurisprudential. It is used as a cosmological idea, to affirm the order and coherence of the universe and to supply a link between heaven and earth. Secondly, natural law is used as a standard of moral excellence. This is not far removed from the first usage, since moral excellence within the Christian frame of reference consists in congruity with the cosmic order. Finally, Fortescue uses the idiom of natural law as a rhetorical instrument, and again, obviously, this is not unrelated to the other uses. Fortescue's text, however, does not warrant the view that he regarded natural law as either a constitutional or a legal restraint upon kingship, nor does it offer any support for the argument that the alleged legal restraints upon the king consisted of a body of immutable fundamental law, common law, or any other human law. There can be no question at all that Fortescue thought the English king was limited. But the restraint upon him was political: it was the consent of parliament. These are the major points to be considered within the general framework of Fortescue's theory.

The idea of double majesty found ample expression in English law and politics from very early times, but it was Sir John Fortescue who, in the fifteenth century, fashioned a name for the scheme, and a very apt one it was. He described the government of England as a *dominium politicum et regale* — regal and political dominion. The term is surely ingenious. It suggests precisely the root principle of double majesty: that English government falls into two parts. England was not a simple or absolute monarchy; this Fortescue calls *dominium regale*. Nor was its principle of organization nonregal, which he calls *dominium politicum*. Rather, English government incorporates both of these principles at the same time. Moreover, Fortescue's exposition of regal and political dominion reveals that he also embraced the subsidiary ideas of the working system. Somehow king and people have independent standing in English politics. It is true that there is considerable ambiguity in his writings as to the exact form which the nonregal partner takes. In this connection he refers to the people, the great men of the realm, the three estates, and to parliament. But the essential point is perfectly clear: the restraint upon kingship is political and derives its legitimacy from the independently based authority of the "people."

The Apotheosis of Double Majesty

Fortescue set out his political ideas in three major works, all of which require attention. The earliest of these was *De Natura Legis Naturae* — Concerning the Nature of the Law of Nature. The announced purpose of this book is to employ the law of nature to settle a question of disputed succession to the crown. Fortescue's aim was to demonstrate the legitimacy of the Lancastrian title against the claim of the House of York. In the process, however, he engages in a much more general discussion. Only the second part of *De Natura* deals directly with the succession question. The first part is devoted to a broad exploration of law and kingship, which supplies the background for the narrow question Fortescue wishes to settle in the second part. This discussion of underlying principles is Fortescue's most sustained treatment of those ideas of his which have since interested historians of political thought and the English constitution.

Fortescue tells us that the law of nature was introduced into human concerns at the time of the creation. Among the other works, God created also man and his office; that is, he made the first man the prelate over the rest of the creation. But since this was before the fall, Adam's rule must have been perfect, and to be perfect he must have had justice, which Fortescue defines as rectitude of will.[2] The next stage of his argument is that justice and natural law are identical in nature, quality, and substance. Justice begets law, and from justice and law proceeds equity: law and natural equity are one with justice.[3] All that Fortescue offers by way of argumentation is an analogy. The only thing that is perfect, he says, is trinity. The trinity of justice, natural law, and natural equity is likened to the Holy Trinity: God the Father begets the Son, and from the same substance proceeds the Holy Spirit. Fortescue concludes that natural law and man are coeval, that man's office of prelacy and the natural law are innate in him, contemporary with him, and eternal. Together they rule the whole creation.[4]

This order of things is the result of Providence, which is the eternal reason of God. Through its operation everything in the universe acquires an appropriate mode of conduct. Man has a special place. Following St. Thomas Aquinas, Fortescue says that man partakes of eternal reason, from which he derives a natural propensity to seek his rightful end by right action. This participation of man in God's eternal reason is the law of nature. It follows that this law is itself a divine law. The difference between eternal reason, which is divine law, and the natural law is that eternal reason is concerned with spiritual ends, while the natural law rules the dark night of this life. The function of natural law is to dispose man to virtue, and this is also the chief task of government.[5]

Fortescue's reflections on the origin of government begin with a scheme for the periodization of human history. First there was the state of innocence. From the fall of man until Moses delivered law to the Israelites, the race was governed solely by the law of nature. Then, "although the succeeding period to the coming of Christ is named the time of the Law, and the whole period from then until now the time of Grace, nevertheless the law of nature itself was not in those succeeding times abolished, but continued through them all, and still continues in its own force and effect." The stage is now set for some of Fortescue's most elevated language concerning the natural law and, more particularly, for his use of it as a link between heaven and earth. He says that "whatever other laws there are, called human, they are either by this law established, or by its authority, as supplementary to it, they subsist. For laws put forth by man are all either Customs or Statutes . . . concerning the excellence of which, and the dignity of this law, the sacred Canons instruct us in these words: 'Now in dignity, the law of nature is superior to custom and statute; for what things soever are either recorded in customs or comprehended in writings, if they be adverse to natural law, are to be held null and void.' " Fortescue goes on to cite other passages of the canon law which he says teach us that natural law obtained from the creation of man, that it never varies, and that it is immutable.[6] In another place, he says that the law of nature "is the mother of all human laws, and if they degenerate from her deserve not to be called laws. What she adjudges is just, and what she condemns is condemned by every human law." And again: "This Law of Nature sprang from God alone, is subject to His Law alone, and under Him, and with Him, governs the whole world; whence it comes that all other laws are its servants, so that there is not a law on earth put forth by man which obeys not the commands of nature's law . . . the order of nature requires that all laws that are called human do pay her deference." [7]

Perhaps this is enough to demonstrate Fortescue's conception of the dignity of the law of nature. It is clear that he conceived of it as excellent far beyond human law. Such utterances as these have led one observer to say that "according to Fortescue, an unjust statute could be disregarded," [8] and have led another to contend that the rules of the natural law and custom guarantee the limitation of both king and people in Fortescue's system, and that any statutes would only be a translation of a rule of natural law or custom into writing.[9] In fact, this line of interpretation fails to do justice to Fortescue's text. In the first place, it does not account for the sense of a substantial number of passages which say that laws may be made and reformed. Secondly, Fortescue does not say that a statute cannot be anything except a custom committed to writing or a translation of natural law. Indeed, he says nothing that even suggests that this is the case. It is true that in his classification of laws Fortescue asserted that the category of human laws was exhausted by the natural law, statutes, and customs. But the only way the interpretation in question can be arrived at is by the use of a suppressed premise to the effect that no law, no statute, can be a new law. But this is what the evidence must be made to show, and all that Fortescue has done is to offer a classification of types of law.

Again, the view that medieval monarchs were thought to be restrained by the law of custom is easily disposed of in Fortescue's case. In his theory, in fact, custom appears to be subordinated to statute. He says that "if custom is committed to writing by the prince's order, thenceforward it transforms the name of custom into the name of statute, and then punishes offenders more sharply than before, because then there is contempt of the command of the prince."[10] In a later book, Fortescue extends this idea so that it embraces even natural law. "I want you, then, to know that all human laws are either law of nature, customs, or statutes, which are also called constitutions. But customs and the rules of the law of nature, after they have been reduced to writing, and promulgated by the sufficient authority of the prince, and commanded to be kept, are changed into a constitution or something of the nature of statutes; and thereupon oblige the prince's subjects to keep them under greater penalty than before, by reason of the strictness of that command."[11] Fortescue does not say, then, that custom is in any way superior. What these passages suggest is that both customary rules and ideas derived from natural law may be promulgated as statutes. Further, there is nothing here to suggest that statutes are never anything but written customs and rules of natural law. On the contrary, what is suggested is that statute law is an independent type of law, one whose sanction is considerably more rigorous than that which attaches to custom or natural law. This is reinforced by what

Fortescue says farther on in the passage just quoted. He makes the observation that statutes, customs, and the law of nature are the three fountains of all law. Surely this does not suggest that statute law is merely a form whose content is supplied by other law. If anything, statute emerges as a more definite legal form than any other.

As it develops, Fortescue's argument reveals the more political side of his thought and reinforces the points just discussed. He explains that kingly power had its beginning from the law of nature, and that just kings have always reigned under its authority.[12] But it is true, he says, that from a merely human perspective the history of kingship shows that it was instituted by wicked men. To illustrate his point, Fortescue relates the biblical story of Nimrod, who was in the eyes of God only a hunter of men. But he seemed to men to be the king of Babylon. Nimrod is the model of the tyrant. Just as in the case of a law which contravenes the natural law, a king who takes on the manner of Nimrod departs from the standards supplied by natural law and thereby deserves to lose the name of king. The important question at this point is whether the tyrannical departure from the standards of natural law has legal effect in this world. Fortescue's answer is clearly negative. He gives examples of tyrants slain by their subjects and then says, "Nevertheless, although the death of these and such like men came opportunely for the world, it was not lawful for any one to do this thing, least of all for their subjects, to whom many times, as required by their own deserts, the Lord appointed wicked kings . . . for though like Nembroth [a tyrant] he be not worthy of the name of king, yet the kingdom is his . . ."[13] This finding leads Fortescue to a celebration of the great goodness of Providence, which gives an insight into the author's point of view: "Oh! how great is the weight of Divine power, and how great is the goodness of His Providence, which is Eternal Law, that not only the good things of the good man, but also the good and bad things of the bad man all work for the advantage of the good, and that no impious man hath ever perpetrated anything which is not turned to the glory of the universe."[14] Fortescue concludes that kingly power is good, even though it was initiated by evil men pursuing their own ambition. This must be the case, for, as he has already said, it was the natural law which really instituted kingship. For "although the unjust began the kingly dignity for ambition, the law of nature began it for man's good by means of those unjust — they by sin, the law by a most righteous working, so that in one and the same act not only the virtue of justice but the maliciousness of sin contended in the works of nature's law." [15] He then proceeds to argue his case in more detail. Kingship must have begun under the natural law because before the time of Moses there was no other law. There were some customs among men, but these cannot have created kingship, "since custom only grows from repeated acts and length of time . . ." Moreover, "the constitutions of princes, which only bind subjects, were not capable of constituting the kingly height, which knows no superior . . ." [16]

Thus far Fortescue has presented a picture of a coherent universe, but not one in which politics is subordinated to law, whether natural or customary. At this point he begins an extended digression in which he introduces his most famous idea, the dominium politicum et regale. If this theoretical account of English government is interpreted as a refined version of the idea of double majesty, as is argued here, it meshes very nicely with the general outlook just sketched. Referring to St. Thomas Aquinas' *De Regimine Principum* — Concerning the Rule of Princes — he says that Aquinas commends to us two kinds of dominion, regal and political. But, says Fortescue, we learn from history and experience that there is a third kind; we find it also, he remarks, in St. Thomas himself. This third form is regal and political dominion, and it is found in England.

> For in the kingdom of England the kings neither make laws nor impose subsidies on their subjects, without the consent of the Three Estates of the Realm [Trium Statuum Regni]. Nay, even the judges of that kingdom are all bound by their oaths not to render judgment against the laws of the land, although they should have the commands of the prince to the contrary. May not, then, this form of government be called political, that is to say, regulated by the administration of many, and may it not also deserve to be named a royal government, seeing that the subjects themselves cannot make laws without regal authority, and the kingdom, being subject to the king's dignity, is possessed by kings and their heirs successively in hereditary right, in such manner as no dominions are possessed which are ruled only politically.[17]

Fortescue does not always describe this form in precisely the same way, but the principal point is always there. Clearly, there is no sovereign. Fortescue's theory does not touch this problem. Instead, English government rests on the idea of double majesty: on one side there is kingship, and the other side is described variously as the people, the three estates, parliament, and the chief men of the realm (*proceres*). Together they make laws. This is not a description of a political order in which law is the decisive factor; it is a political description. It tells how the law is made.

In describing this form of government in *De Laudibus Legum Anglie,* Fortescue says that a king who rules his people politically "is not able himself to change the laws without the assent of his subjects nor to burden an unwilling people with strange imposts, so that, ruled by laws that they themselves desire, they freely enjoy their properties, and are despoiled neither by their own king nor any other." [18] There is also the famous passage from *The Governance of England* in Fortescue's own English. Here he says that the difference between dominium regale and dominium politicum et regale is that in the first the "kynge mey rule his peple bi such lawes as he makyth hym self. And therfore he mey sett uppon thaim tayles and other imposicions, such as he wol hym self, withowt thair assent. The secounde kynge may not rule his peple bi other lawes than such as thai assenten unto." [19]

Having given his description of rule in England, Fortescue proceeds to develop an elaborate defense for it. His primary interest at this stage is to show that a king who rules both regally and politically is in no way less powerful or inferior in dignity to the monarch who rules only regally. It is clear that all dominions are in some sense established under natural law, for the function of both natural law and government is to promote virtue among men. In both cases, departure from the rules of the law of nature comes at the expense of falling away from excellence and into corruption.[20] But unjust governmental acts do not justify resistance. Is a human law which contravenes natural law literally null and void? Is such a law juristically no law at all? Once again, Fortescue's answer is no. A prince ruling merely regally (*tantum regaliter*) derives his power from God equally with other monarchs. The law of the king (*jus regis*) is his rightful power, but for his subjects it is law. It is sometimes good, sometimes bad. Now, asks Fortescue, how can an unjust rule be called law? His answer is that "to say, Tell this people the law of the king, was the same as saying, Tell them the power which the king, when set over them will be able to assume. And although an unjust king may unjustly use that power, the power itself is always good . . ." Even the monstrous decree of Herod condemning children to death was nonetheless a law.[21]

Royal law, however, is not the law of all kings. What differentiates the king who rules both regally and politically is that he always subjects himself to natural law. But such subjection is a matter of individual human will; it is perfectly possible for a king, or any other man, to disobey the law of nature. Just as the king ruling regally and politically submits, as a matter of fact, to the law of nature, it becomes the king ruling tantum regaliter so to submit. What happens if he does not? The lowest place in hell is reserved for such kings.[22] It is even possible for a king ruling politically to depart from the natural law: "no edict or action of a king, even if it has arisen politically, has ever escaped the vengeance of Divine punishment, if it has proceeded from him against the rule of nature's law." It does not depreciate the restraining value such beliefs may sometimes have had to observe that, nevertheless, this is an ethical and religious idea, not a juristic one. True, Fortescue says that "all the decrees of the royal law, when they are in error, ought to be corrected by the rules of the law of nature. Thus also we have proved that the rules of the political law, and the sanctions of customs and constitutions ought to be made null and void, so often as they depart from the institutes of nature's law, which we have above defined as the mother and mistress of all human laws." [23] But, as Hinton has observed in a penetrating discussion, Fortescue "said nothing to suggest that in England the proper place . . . [for correcting and repealing laws] was not the place where the laws were made, the parliament. On the contrary he remarked that if statutes turned out to be ineffectual they could be quickly reformed in parliament, and the same would apply, for all we can tell from the text, if they turned out to be unjust." [24] Fortescue also contends that most of the time merely regal rule has another consequence: the impoverishment and resulting weakness of a country ruled tyrannically. It is to establish this point that he draws his well-known contrast between England and France, much to the disadvantage of France.[25]

To return to the main line of Fortescue's argument: his effort to show that kings ruling regally and politically are not inferior in power to those ruling regally. For this purpose he marshals three lines of argument. First, he says that the Israelites were ruled politically by God, yet no one who deserved it went unpunished, nor was anyone free to transgress the principal injunction of the natural law: do unto others as you would have them do unto you. The second line of argument appears, superficially at least, to be incompatible with the first. It is part of Fortescue's express doctrine that the king ruling regally is most nearly akin to the rule of God in the universe. He refers to Aristotle and Aquinas as authorities for the view that the rule of the best man is the best form of government, but he observes with them that it often degenerates into tyranny.[26] He has, therefore, to admit that dominium regale can be most like God's rule. But, he says, it does not follow that regal dominion is exalted above regal and political rule. He offers two reasons why this is not the case. First, regal and political dominion is like the governance of the blessed who reign with Christ, "where there shall not be wanting the consent of all the citizens in every judgment of the king." [27] As Chrimes has remarked, how this is to be reconciled with the assimilation of regal rule to divine rule is "a delicate point." [28] Secondly, both kinds of kings are equally endowed in their creation in God's likeness. This, says Fortescue, makes them equal, and therefore their laws must be equal as well.[29]

It was the third argument, however, upon which Fortescue chiefly relied. As Plummer observed, he must have been proud of it, because it appears prominently in his later works.[30] The king ruling regally ought not to pride himself on the lack of any restraint upon him, because the possibility of committing sin is not power at all; it is impotence and slavery. A sinner is a slave to his vices. "Wherefore to be able to sin is not power or liberty, no more than to be able to grow old or rotten . . ." Action, says Fortescue, is accomplished through will and power. If a man has wished to do a thing and has not done it, he lacks power. But God has so created humankind that they always desire good. Thus, "it follows that, if a man forsake the doing of good, it comes of impotence, since it cannot have proceeded from will." The king who rules politically rules as he wishes and is therefore powerful. He is "not hindered by any more powerful than himself." [31] Clearly, the flavor of the argument is very old. It passes from Plato through St. Augustine and is far from invulnerable. Nevertheless, Fortescue was very fond of it.[32]

In *De Laudibus*, Fortescue makes the Prince, who is being instructed by Fortescue in the role of the Chancellor of England, ask why kings have unequal power. Consistent with his discussion in *De Natura*, Fortescue's reply is that they are not unequal in power. But, he says, he has "by no means denied . . . that their authority over their subjects is different." The Chancellor explains that kingdoms ruled merely regally originated in conquest.[33] The origin of the kingdom ruled politically, however, is altogether different. Fortescue, still speaking as the Chancellor, takes this up in the thirteenth chapter. He quotes St. Augustine as saying that " 'a people is a body of men united by consent of law and by community of interest.' " But, he says, a body politic does not deserve the name unless, like a natural body, it has a head. Hence, a people wishing to constitute itself a body politic must set one man over itself. Usually he is a king. "So the kingdom," Fortescue goes on, "issues from the people, and exists as a body mystical (*corpus misticum*), governed by one man as head." But "the will of the people is the source of life." This kind of political order "is bound together and united into one by the law . . ." The king, he says, "is unable to change the laws of that body, or to deprive that same people of their own substance uninvited or against their wills. You have here, prince, the form of the institution of the political kingdom, whence you can estimate the power that the king can exercise in respect of the law and the subjects of such a realm; for a king of this sort is obliged to protect the law, the subjects, and their bodies and goods, and he has power to this end issuing from the people, so that it is not permissible for him to rule his people with any other power." [34] Such was the origin of regal and political dominion in England.[35]

This portion of Fortescue's work raises a number of questions more sharply than the argument of *De Natura*. Most importantly, does it mean that the doctrine of *De Laudibus* should be interpreted as expressing the view that English kings are limited by law? If so, is that limiting law the natural law or the common law? It is certain that Fortescue's principal aim in this book is to persuade the prince and the reader that English law is as good as, indeed better than, any other legal system.[36] On the other hand, in *De Laudibus* the law of nature receives very short shrift indeed. "The Laws of England, in those points which they sanction by reason of the law of nature, are neither better nor worse in their judgments than are all laws of other nations in like cases. For, as Aris-

totle said, in the fifth book of the *Ethics,* Natural law is that which
has the same force among all men. Wherefore there is no need
to discuss it further. But from now on we must first examine what
are the customs, and also the statutes, of England . . ." [37] The
natural law supplies only that which obtains everywhere. Clearly,
then, it cannot be the case that human law is nothing but a translation of natural law. It follows, also, that it cannot be the natural
law which limits kingship, for otherwise it would limit the King
of France just as much, or as little, as the King of England, and
Fortescue makes it perfectly clear that he regards the King of France
as ruling regally only.[38]

It has already been suggested that for Fortescue one function of
the law of nature is to supply an ethical standard, rather than a
jurisprudence. It has been shown that he thought men could choose
to follow it or not. There are other words of Fortescue's which
reinforce this interpretation. In *De Natura* he discusses the nature
of the law of nations, the jus gentium. There he tells us that the
jus gentium is those portions of the law of nature which all nations
have chosen to observe. This by no means exhausts the content of
natural law, for there are other laws of nature which all nations
have not adopted.[39] On the one hand, this view seems contradictory,
or at least confusing, when compared with statements which say
that the rules of nature are those rules which apply everywhere, to
which all human laws owe deference, and so on. But if the law of
nature is regarded as an ethical rather than a legal idea, this stress
in the system is avoided. Obviously, stresses in a system of thought
need not be reconcilable. Indeed, there are features of Fortescue's
system which appear to be incompatible. On the other hand, however, incompatibilities ought not to be supposed needlessly. The
interpenetration of moral and legal ideas is, after all, precisely what
one might expect in a medieval author. There is sometimes an
intimate relationship between standards of value and an operative
rule of law. Needless to say, Fortescue lacked the benefit of Hume's
discussion of the relation of normative to factual statements. But
it does not follow that he saw no difference between them. The
question of logical confusion is quite separate from the question
whether an author makes no operating distinction between "ought"
and "is."

In any event, the solution of this problem does not need to be
sought in such abstract terms. Fortescue actually made himself

reasonably clear. He says that human laws ought to be corrected in order to conform to natural law. Kings ruling merely regally ought to consider the benefits of regal and political dominion. In part, then — as is often the case in medieval writing — it is a question of what seems to the author profitable and expedient. Fortescue thought that the regal and political dominion was the best form of government. He paid his respects to the idea that the best form would be the rule of the best man regaliter; but, like Aristotle and St. Thomas before him, he doubted whether it was a practical proposition in this world. Dominions ruled regally and politically, he was sure, enjoyed the benefits of prosperity, tranquillity, and the best laws. Here he employed the idea of natural law as an endorsement for his own value: the kingdom of England. Because it was ruled regally and politically it conformed to the natural law; or at least it did most of the time, for here appears what seems to be another gap in the system.

In some places Fortescue asserts that a dominium politicum et regale is to be distinguished from a dominium regale because the former is always subject to the law of nature. In other places, Fortescue tells us that the laws of England are already excellent indeed, but in case of need they can easily be corrected. If, for example, English laws should cause improper delays in litigation, "they can be cut down in every parliament." But he has also said that the natural law is immutable. If this is so, it cannot very well be a part of the actual legal system of England. Is there, then, a contradiction between the idea of the immutability of the natural law and the fact of alterations in parliament? This assumption is unnecessary: the natural law is an ethical standard. The quotation just given goes on to say that "it can be rightly concluded that all the laws of this realm are the best in fact or potentiality, since they can easily be brought to it in fact and actual reality." [40]

The important question, of course, is how this assimilation of man-made law with the natural law is to be accomplished. It is not done by consulting a supra-empirical body of law and then translating it into statute or a judgment. Fortescue has an answer. In regal dominions laws sometimes benefit their makers only.

> Sometimes, also, by the negligence of such princes and the inertia of their counsellors, those statutes are made so ill-advisedly that they deserve the name of corruptions rather than of

laws. But the statutes of England cannot so arise, since they are made not only by the prince's will, but also by the assent of the whole realm, so they cannot be injurious to the people nor fail to secure their advantage. Furthermore, it must be supposed that they are necessarily replete with prudence and wisdom, since they are promulgated by the prudence not of one counsellor nor of a hundred only, but of more than three hundred chosen men . . . as those who know the form of the summons, the order, and the procedure of parliament can more clearly describe. And if the statutes ordained with such solemnity and care happen not to give full effect to the intention of the makers, they can speedily be revised, and yet not without the assent of the commons and nobles of the realm.[41]

Here, then, is the cement of the system. The prince, together with the parliament, enacts statutes which "cannot be injurious to the people nor fail to secure their advantage." Such enactments are "necessarily replete with prudence and wisdom." Surely this is the way in which ethical ideals find expression, if they are to find legal embodiment at all. Indeed, the argument is stronger than that: what is enacted by the conjunction of regal will and parliamentary advice and consent is, ipso facto, an embodiment of justice. There are other expressions of Fortescue's which suggest that he considered this to be the normal state of affairs. The Chancellor tells the Prince that human laws are the embodiment of perfect justice; that is why the Prince should study, not the natural law, but the customs and statutes of England.[42] Fortescue's doctrine is not far removed in this respect from those of Christopher St. Germain and Richard Hooker in the Tudor period.

A final aspect of Fortescue's theory of regal and political rule should be considered. Having made the point, to his own satisfaction at least, that kings ruling politically are not inferior in power or dignity to kings ruling regally only, Fortescue passes to another question.[43] He advises kings who rule regally to rule politically as well: that is, to admit more than one man's will to be involved in the governing process. He also says that kings ruling politically ought sometimes to rule *regaliter*. This observation leads him to some extremely treacherous theoretical ground, the extraordinary powers of the king, and he rushes over it swiftly. Thus he merely notes, without extended discussion, that the king may act *regaliter* in instances of domestic rebellion or foreign invasion.[44] Again, all kinds of cases cannot possibly be embraced by statute and custom, so the king may here employ his discretion. The king may also act regaliter in dealing with matters of criminal law and in dispensing pardons and mitigation of punishment. Finally, equity is left to the king regaliter, "lest the strictness of the words of the law, confounding its intent, should hurt the common good." [45] It was around just such exercises of royal prerogative that the constitutional debates of the early Stuart period centered. As found in Fortescue, this point of view suggests that the restraints upon the ruler even in a dominium politicum et regale were personal and political, not legal. This suggestion is reinforced by other statements. In concluding his discussion of the occasions for regal action in a political and regal dominion, he says that what really raises one ruler above another is his goodness and justice. "Therefore, clap your hands, ye subjects of a king ruling royally, under a good sovereign, when such a one there is, because ye must needs mourn when an insolent or grasping king rules over you. And you, ye subjects of a king presiding royally and politically over his kingdom, console yourselves in this respect, that, if your king be equally arrogant, he hath not a loose rein for it, like the other." And again: "the Philosopher says, not without cause, that a kingdom is better governed by the best king than the best law. But let a king ruling politically ever beware lest, repudiating such laws of his own kingdom as are pregnant with justice, he enact new laws without consulting the chief men of his kingdom, or bring in foreign laws, so that, refusing for the future to live politically, he oppress his people with his *jus regale*." [46] Thus Fortescue makes it clear that any king may depart from the standard of rectitude and that there is no fundamental law designed to restrain him.

It is possible to conclude now that the chief aim of Fortescue's writings was to set out a particular characterization of the English political order. His only intellectual instrument was the notion that English government was a conflation of the principles of regal and political dominion. He set out expressly to combine the features of the dominium regale with the dominium politicum. Regal dominion is easily defined: kings may make laws and impose taxes at their own pleasure, and the title to the crown descends hereditarily. Political dominion is variously characterized. Sometimes Fortescue appears to be saying that such a political order must not only be administered by "many," a notion which is nowhere given specific content, but also that it must be governed by laws made at the pleasure of the "people" themselves. But he allows that Rome, even under some of the emperors, was a political dominion, "not because they always consulted the Senators, for many of the Emperors to their own damage despised their advice, but because they governed the commonwealth for the advantage of the many, namely the Romans, and because the Roman empire did not descend to their own heirs, as kingdoms are wont to do." Similarly, the Israelites were governed regally, by God himself, but also politically, because the Judges "administered everything for their common advantage, and nothing for the individual advantage of them, the Judges." [47] The criterion here suggested is certainly much looser than the former, but when Fortescue discusses the political element in the English case, he always includes the notion that laws may not be made or changed nor taxes levied without consent.

Fortescue nowhere considers the problem which today seems the crucial one: how is a decision to be made if the two majesties, prince and people, fail to agree? But there is no reason why our concerns should have been his. Chrimes has well said that "in the last resort conflict between king and parliament is unthinkable." [48] The theoretical question of sovereignty did not come up even in the Tudor period, though sovereignty was often exercised on the level of fact. During the Tudor period the question did not arise, broadly speaking, because prince and people were at one on the major political questions until near the end of Elizabeth's reign. It was the conflicts of the Stuart period, many of them long suppressed, which broke the medieval scheme in practice and in theory.

Divine and Human Law

Fortescue's principal theoretical statements are set out in the works just examined: the first part of *De Natura,* and portions of *De Laudibus.* One matter remains to be considered — the argument of the second part of *De Natura* — before turning to the question of the overall interpretation of Fortescue's thought. The argument of the earlier part of *De Natura* carries the reader over an extensive general terrain; but, according to the author, these observations were intended to supply a platform upon which the disputed succession to the throne could be settled. The second part of his discussion suffers from a variety of frailties. The argument is not well disciplined, and, even worse, it fails of its object. It is also extremely repetitive, which may account for the uneven character of scholarly judgment on the book.[49] Certainly the particular point at issue is not one likely to arouse excitement today, but this is not the only question it raises. In fact, the second part supplies interesting information on a number of important topics.

To begin with, it illustrates that on such a vital question as the mode of succession there was no settled public law. A statute ratifying the "usurpation" of Henry Bolingbroke had been framed in 1406, but Fortescue ignored it. His interest was to contrive a more elevated rationale, presumably because the Duke of York had repudiated the statute of 1406 on the ground of indefeasible hereditary right.[50] In any case, this is enough to show that men were still unable to conceive of the kingdom as organized on a single principle. It shows that Fortescue was not willing to attribute finality, that is to say, sovereignty, even to the king in parliament, let alone to either of them separately. In short, there persists the idea of a right in kingship apart from the kingdom. Secondly, however, there is an explicit argument here that kingship is a public office, definitely distinct from ordinary possession. But even though this important principle is recognized and employed in the argument, it is not disentangled from private proprietary right. The kingdom is treated as a piece of real property capable of descent by the law of inheritance, and the crucial arguments are drawn by analogy from the English law of real property, supplemented by Roman law. Finally, Fortescue's argument reveals a great deal concerning the state of legal and political theory in England in the fifteenth century. Most of the discussion proceeds on the level of analogy rather than law or logic. Arguments are drawn from anywhere and everywhere, without any serious effort to explain their relationship to each other or the relative value to be put upon them. To be sure, Fortescue says time and again that the question can be settled only by the natural law. Nevertheless, this reconciliation is only verbal and is not to be accepted as concluding all the questions raised in his book. On the contrary, it is a proposition to be tested against what his argument actually does.

Before proceeding, it should be noted that in this work Fortescue is a conscious advocate. He was a staunch partisan of the Lancastrian claim to the crown, although at a later date he found it convenient to repudiate his advocacy and attachment to the Lancastrians.[51]

Still, it has to be admitted that Fortescue made a concerted effort to solve his problem by appealing to natural law, though he did not succeed in making out a very orderly line of argument. The facts just noted — his conscious advocacy and the repudiation of his writings dedicated to furthering the Lancastrian cause — do not settle the primary theoretical question. The question is this: what is Fortescue able to accomplish with his chosen instrument, the natural law, and how is it related in this concrete instance to human law? The answer has already been suggested. He purports to settle the title in the light of natural law. Actually, he ekes out a case which rests on the English law of real property.

Fortescue presents his problem in a thinly masked hypothetical setting. The King of Assyria has died, leaving a brother, a daughter, and her son. Who shall succeed? [52] The parties come before Justice, as judge, to advance their claims. Their arguments are involved and move through lengthy replications and duplications by each of the parties against the others. It is not necessary to recount the details of these somewhat tedious representations. The important point is to observe how Fortescue solves the difficulty. To achieve the desired result he has to do three things. He has first to show that the daughter of the late king cannot succeed; next, that this incapacity on her part deprives her son as well; and finally, that the king's brother is the rightful heir. The first two stages of the problem are handled reasonably well, but at the third stage the argument falters badly.

All three litigants contend that they succeed by hereditary right. The daughter's plea rests on an ordinary claim to inheritance of her father's estate.[53] Her son claims that he inherits through his mother, who is herself ineligible.[54] Finally, the late king's brother asserts that the throne is his because women cannot succeed, and since no right vests in the female claimant she can transmit none to her son. The grandson and the brother are agreed as against the daughter's claim.[55] In common they advance two lines of argument. The first one is that there is a difference between a public office, especially the regal office in a kingdom which acknowledges no superior, and the inheritance of an ordinary estate.[56] A surviving daughter may inherit her patrimony, her father's private movable possessions.[57] But the royal dignity is altogether different. It is a public office, and it is real property.[58] The rules applicable to immovable property show that it does not descend automatically but may go instead to executors or trustees.⁵⁹ Already the law of real property is introduced to establish the vital distinction. Next the two male parties undertake to show that women are ineligible to inherit any public office. It is in this connection that arguments from divine law and natural law are utilized. The principal source is the biblical account of the fall of man from innocence. The idea is to show that from the time of the creation women have been subject to men. Practically all of the second part of *De Natura* is taken up with variations on this theme. It all comes down to this: God first made Adam and then made Eve from his rib to be his helpmate. She is clearly subordinate to him because, while man was made after the image of God, woman was fashioned after man. At first, however, Adam's superiority was only directive; he had no power to threaten or punish her. But because of her origin she was naturally obedient. Then she ate the forbidden fruit, and divine sentence was passed upon her. Henceforth woman would bear children in pain and be subject to her husband coercively.⁶⁰ So much is divine law. Its meaning is learned from natural law, and here the principal reliance is on Aristotle.⁶¹ Because woman has strayed from her natural condition, she suffers a wide variety of physical and moral deficiencies which render her incapable of discharging the essential duties of supreme rule: the ability to do battle and prosecute judgment against subjects, which may well involve violence and bloodshed.⁶²

In the brother's plea, which is the most interesting one, Fortescue develops three lines of argument. One is from the civil law, which settles inheritance according to agnate relationship.⁶³ If the premises of Fortescue's discussion are taken seriously, this introduces a considerable difficulty, since he is concerned to emphasize the proposition that the case can be settled only by natural law. But he has to allow the introduction of "evidence" from concrete legal systems, or his argument will contain some enormous gaps. So at this point the king's brother opines that while Roman law will not settle the case, it is good evidence, because the several systems of municipal law proceed from the same reason which is obtained in its purity in the natural law. It is true, he admits, that human laws sometimes decide differently from the law of nature, but they do not decide contrary to it; the civil law decides nothing "against the equity of the Law of Nature." ⁶⁴

At any rate, according to the hypothesis that the case cannot be settled by any law but the law of nature, the brother must turn elsewhere. The argument which he develops at this point is not so prominently displayed as that which purports to show the natural subjection of women to men. But it is the most elaborate and careful argument in the second part of *De Natura*. It is also strikingly specious. And it turns out rather badly, since it falls short of proving the brother's case. Indeed, if it proves anything, it proves that the brother cannot succeed by inheritance. He begins by observing, quite rightly, that the whole case turns on elucidating the idea of inheritance. He points out that it is an accident that there is anything called property. It resulted from original sin, for when Adam fell under divine sentence for disobedience, he was told that henceforth man would have to make his way by the sweat of his brow. Then Fortescue advances a notion of property akin to Locke's. Property in a thing results from the fact that a man has bestowed his labor on it. A son may inherit the fruits of his father's labor because he carries his father's blood and so is a portion of his father. This is the root of the idea of inheritance.[65]

Then the brother undertakes to set this doctrine in a cosmic framework. The whole order of the universe is a kind of ladder which runs between heaven and earth. The ladder is at once a chain of degrees of being, causation, and truth. The steps of the ladder are interlocking efficient and final causes, in the Aristotelian sense. Nature never proceeds by leaps; that is God's prerogative alone. Hence to follow nature is to follow each step, up or down as the case may be. How is this related to the natural law of inheritance? A father is an efficient cause of his son, while the son is the final cause of his procreation. Inheritance passes according to this sequence of efficient and final causes. So, at last, the brother comes to the grandson's claim. He cannot succeed because the chain was broken by a defective female link. This interrupted the steady succession of efficient and final causes, which is ipso facto a breach of the natural order.[66] From all this the brother draws an appropriate conclusion, but it is very damaging to his own case. If the mother interrupts the chain, then the king has left no heir, and the people of the kingdom should proceed to choose (*eligere*) a new king according to the usage of their country.[67]

However, this alarming observation is abandoned in the sequel, and so is the majestic continuity of the chain of being. Fortescue now asserts that the kingdom should descend to the nearest male blood.[68] Evidently a minor premise is missing, for what the argument establishes is that inheritance is defined in terms of the unbroken transmission of blood from father to son. The brother clearly is not a link in this chain: he stands off to the side, waiting, so to say, for the failure of male issue. If one concedes that the daughter and her son have been excluded, there is still no demonstration of the brother's title. In fact, however, Fortescue has supplied the necessary minor premise. It is the crucial point in the whole argument and was introduced very early on. If accepted, as it finally is, it concludes the matter in the tenth out of seventy-one chapters. It is not an argument from divine or natural law, nor even Roman law. It is a rule drawn from the English law of real property. Fortescue sets this case. Suppose a grant of land is conveyed to a man and his male heirs. If the man dies without male heirs, the land reverts to the donor. If he has a daughter who later has a son, that son may not claim the land. There are lots of cases like this, he says, in English and French law. Suppose, further, the holder has two sons, the older of whom has only a daughter, who, in turn, has a son. Does the grandson inherit on his grandfather's death? On the contrary, the inheritance goes to the younger brother. The author then asks, rhetorically, how this case differs from the one in hand.[69] As it turns out, it does not differ at all. The reader may be left to wonder whether the whole matter turns on an analogy from private land law or on a tautology. In any case, this is the only argument that conveys any title to the brother.

Altogether, Fortescue's argument betrays some serious defects. There are failures in the structure of the argument, but, more importantly, this sort of frailty reveals and rests upon a major conceptual confusion. Fortescue oscillates between two assertions. He insists that the case can be settled only by natural law and that this is sufficient by itself. On the other hand, his argument requires a particular assertion, which he cannot find in the traditional sources on natural law. He has to show that the brother of the late king is the rightful heir. In order to do this he is led to develop a collateral line of argument. In its most general form, this argument is that rules other than those of the natural law are not superfluous to the case. At this point the argument forks in two directions. In both directions, Fortescue shows too little and too much.

One line of argument is that appeal may be lodged appropriately to divine law. Here the rationale is that man's reason is capable of error. This means that some views which purport to be derived from natural law would only be man's opinion. The proper thing to do is to consult the divine law. The truths of divine law are known by faith, and this is not subject to the frailties of reason.[70] This admission entails more than Fortescue's argument can compass, because it raises a general presumption that runs counter to the argument which will be considered next. It also shows too little, since all that he purports to establish from divine law is that women are subject to men. This will not help in deciding which rules on the subject of inheritance are natural and which merely human.

The second argument produces a startling anomaly in his system, as well as a fatal lesion in the argument on the succession. He argues that human laws are infused by and reflect the same reason as that which constitutes the natural law.[71] But he must show, in arguing against the grandson, that the analogy from the Roman law of guardianship is not good. The reason Fortescue offers is that laws concerning guardianship vary in different legal systems. He is thus able to conclude that the Roman law of guardianship is not a decree of nature but only of the emperor.[72] The criterion, then, for distinguishing human law from natural law is the uniformity of natural law. He has to have some criterion, since the brother's case rests on rules derived from English and Roman law. Once again, however, his argument shows both too little and too much, and the effect is to destroy his case for the king's brother. His argument from the uniformity of the rules of natural law means that he has no way to show that the particular rules he needs are natural ones. Further, since rules governing succession vary, this principle excludes his whole argument from the sphere of natural law. But the effects are even more serious than that. The more general propositions of the first part of *De Natura* would also be excluded from the realm of natural law, because Fortescue admits, indeed stresses, the fact that the features of the dominium politicum et regale are not uniformly embraced. In the earlier portion he had seen that he was obliged to hold that the rules of natural law were not universal, and that he could not argue from uniformity either.

It is impossible to say whether Fortescue knew what he was doing when he solved the case by an appeal to the law of real property, or whether he was laboring under an unconscious self-deception.

It is interesting, at any rate, to notice that immediately after setting forth the crucial analogy the brother asserts that he has shown that the daughter cannot succeed nor transmit title to her son, so "his kingdom will by every right belong to me, the King's Brother, just as we shewed that an estate entailed in the above-described form on heirs male devolves in a similar manner." [73] This announcement comes before the elaborate arguments from nature and law are developed, and in truth the principles of the English law of real property do settle the question. The trouble is that this is the only avenue to a successful conclusion which Fortescue offers. He appears to realize the delicacy of his position. When the judge comes to sum up and deliver his sentence, he spends all his time reviewing the arguments developed to show the naturalness of female subjection. As for the grandson's claim, against which the brother's most elaborate arguments are directed, the judge does not summarize. He is content to observe that the claim has been exploded, and he does not dignify it with any discussion at all. The form of the judgment itself reinforces the suspicion that Fortescue was uneasy about it. The judge claims that it has been shown that "a woman is not capable of holding a kingdom which is subject to no superior, and that her son, therefore cannot by any Law of Nature, succeed in right of his mother . . ." [74] The brother succeeds as rightful heir. One gets a feeling here not unlike that which a Platonic dialogue provokes. Just as Thrasymachus, for example, gives in to Socrates too easily, so the grandson's case is quietly put aside. The point about the judgment is that the grandson was careful to point out that he was not claiming the title by his mother's right, which indeed he denied. Rather, he claims it as a male descendant of the deceased king.[75]

Thus it is clear that Fortescue's great effort to deal with a concrete political problem by means of natural law was unsuccessful. At the level of fact, too, his solution in terms of English law was refuted first by the facts and then by himself. In both lines of argument he was unfaithful to his own theory of English government. Certainly this ill-framed argument ought not to be taken as his theory of government. It is inconsistent, in the first place, with his repeated reliance on the political idea of double majesty and is, anyway, an exceptional, a singular case. To the extent that a dualistic principle can be coherent, Fortescue made it so, and it underrates him seriously to ignore the political cast of his thought in order to insist that what he really maintained was either a political platitude or a contradiction.

Mixed Monarchy

Finally, there is the problem of the general interpretation of Fortescue's work. There is a marked tendency in the secondary literature to characterize it as a theory of the mixed polity.[76] It will be argued here, however, that there are good reasons for distinguishing the theory of mixed monarchy from double majesty. The primary reason is that the theory of mixed monarchy has a specific content of its own, considerably more detailed and a great deal sharper than anything to be found in Fortescue. The use of this theory in relation to Fortescue produces an anachronism, the result of which is to assimilate the late fifteenth century to the mid-seventeenth century.

It is possible that Fortescue's repeated references to St. Thomas Aquinas have provided the inspiration for characterizing his dominium politicum et regale as a theory of mixed monarchy. It is true that in every sustained discussion of regal and political dominion Fortescue refers to St. Thomas. This has been much discussed and much puzzled over.[77] Considered merely as a case of misuse of authority it would not be an intrinsically important question. Such misuse was a common enough phenomenon in medieval writings. In fact, however, inquiry into the relation of Fortescue's idea to the political writings of Aquinas, more particularly to the treatise *De Regimine Principum* (Concerning the Rule of Princes), serves two purposes. Not only does it throw some light on Fortescue's purposes; it also provides an opportunity to draw a distinction between the theory of the mixed polity and the idea of double majesty. The main objective is to achieve an appropriate distinction between the operative political thought of the Middle Ages and the antique idea of mixed monarchy, which met with a spectacular reception in the seventeenth century.

There is a distinct oddity about the concern with Aquinas' mention of the mixed polity in connection with Fortescue. Though Fortescue refers to passages from the *Summa Theologica*, which does contain a discussion of the mixed polity, this does not occur when he is discussing political and regal rule. In this context he always refers to the *De Regimine Principum*. Despite the availability to him of a version of the doctrine of the mixed polity in Aquinas, Fortescue made no use of it. Could it not be the case that Fortescue meant it when he so perversely insisted upon claiming *De Regimine Principum* as an authority? [78] It may be useful to re-examine certain aspects of Aquinas' political thought with this in mind.

St. Thomas did not write a great deal about politics, and what he did write has produced a variety of interpretations.[79] It is no part of the purpose of this discussion to engage in the debate on the question of which form of government Aquinas preferred.[80] All that needs to be said is that his text is far from unambiguous. Certainly it contains expressions which can only be described as emphasizing the principle of regal rule.[81] The difficulty is that these passages do not stand alone. There are others whose tone is distinctly nonregal. The nonregal passages are of two kinds. On the one hand, there are statements which appear to hold that all the events of the universe are ultimately governed by natural law, and this includes the political life of humankind. Here the view is advanced that the merely positive law of the prince must conform to the natural law.[82] On the other hand, there are passages that adopt the view that royal power is derived from the grant of the people.

In the *Summa Theologica* Aquinas deploys a theory of mixed monarchy. He tells us that "with respect to the right ordering of power in a city or nation, two points must be considered: the first is that all should in some respect participate in the government. It is this, in fact, that ensures peace within the community, and . . . all peoples prize and guard such a state of affairs." [83] Drawing upon the *Politics* of Aristotle, he goes on to say that the best form of polity is a blend of the principles of monarchy, aristocracy, and democracy. In this mixed form, one man governs because of his virtue, but he is assisted by a group of virtuous men. The democratic element is accounted for in the sense that all are eligible to govern and the rulers are chosen by all. This, says Aquinas, is the form of government established by divine law, for it was the form practiced by Moses and his successors. Nevertheless, "monarchy is the best form of government for a people, provided it does not become corrupt. But because of the wide powers conferred upon a king, it is easy for a monarchy to degenerate into tyranny, unless there is perfect virtue in the one into whose hands such power is given . . . But perfect virtue is found in few persons . . ." [84] These statements hedge the monarchical principle, and the context is a consideration of the problem of tyranny. The antidote recommended would seem to be mixed monarchy.

In the treatise *De Regimine Principum,* the troublesome question of tyranny arises again, but here Aquinas' answer differs from the one just considered. To be sure, there is a pronounced emphasis upon regal rule, and an extended analogy between God and kings is developed. In order that there be cities and kingdoms to rule, someone must create them. It is the role of kings to found them as well as to govern them.[85] This is no light parallel; it is a part of the structure of the universe.

> Now in nature there is to be found both a universal and a particular form of government. The universal is that by which all things find their place under the direction of God . . . The particular is very similar to this divine control . . . Just as the divine control is exercised over all created bodies and over all spiritual powers, so does the control of reason extend over the members of the body and the other faculties of the soul: so, in a certain sense, reason is to man what God is to the universe. But because man . . . is by nature a social animal living in a community, this similarity with divine rule is found among men, not only in the sense that a man is directed by his reason, but also in the fact that a community is ruled by one man's intelligence; for this is essentially the king's duty.[86]

The whole of the second chapter of Book I is given over to a variety of arguments which purport to prove that "it follows of necessity that the best form of government in human society is that which is exercised by one person." In another place, Aquinas says the prince is above the law. He is formally *legibus solutus,* because it is he who makes law and invests it with coercive power. "A ruler is said to be above the law with respect to its constraining force: for nobody can be constrained by himself; and law derives its power of constraint only from the power of the ruler. So it is said that the prince is above the law, because if he should act against the law nobody can bring a condemnatory judgement against him." [87] But when Aquinas comes to discuss the problem of tyranny, he argues that in the case where a king has been appointed by a free people, at least, he may legitimately be deposed should he become a tyrant. What makes such a deposition legitimate is that the tyrant no longer has any claim to allegiance; his subjects would no longer be bound by the *pactum*. If this argument were pressed, the result would be an individual right of rebellion. Aquinas takes up this question and rejects the strictly individualist solution. The remedy for tyranny lies "rather in the hands of public authority than in the private judgment of individuals." [88]

Aquinas refers elsewhere to the case of a community of free men. In this sort of community the ruler's "power to enact laws derives from the fact that he represents the community." The question being discussed is whether the customs of a people can attain the status of law, and in the case of a free community Aquinas holds that its customs will have "more value than the authority of the ruler . . ." [89] The same sort of view is expressed in the discussion of law in general. "A law, properly speaking, regards first and foremost the order to the common good. Now to order anything to the common good belongs either to the whole people or to someone who is the vicegerent of the whole people. And therefore the making of a law belongs either to the whole people or to a public personage who has care of the whole people . . ." [90]

Among other things, then, one finds in Aquinas the recitation of a theory of mixed monarchy out of Aristotle. But an altogether different theory is advanced in the discussion of tyranny in *De Regimine Principum*. Aquinas has said that the prince is freed from the coercive power of law. But a prince who is legibus solutus, though he has an obligation to abide by his laws, is not the servant of the body politic. It cannot be the case that he derives his authority from the people in any meaningful sense. It is true that a text such as the *lex regia* could be employed to establish just such a relationship, but if the prince is above legal restraint the point is lost. The important thing here is that a regal element is set apart from the people: somehow kingship is independently organized. On the other hand, if the prince derives his authority from a pactum and is strictly bound by it, he would lose his regal character. He would be the mere servant of the body politic. But Aquinas does not choose between these alternatives, he combines them. This is the point of view that has been called double majesty. The *populus* is not the final authority. Neither is the prince. He may not be overthrown simply because he is a tyrant. Something called the "public authority" is required for an act of deposition. In a community of free men, the prince is not absolute even in terms of positive law.[91]

Aquinas considers the problem of monarchy collapsing into tyranny, and the power of the public authority to restrain a tyrant, in *De Regimine Principum*. When Fortescue refers to that book in discussing political and regal dominion, he is also quite often discussing precisely that problem. The great difference between his treatment of a dually organized political order and that of Aquinas is that Fortescue lived two centuries later. By the last half of the fifteenth century in England, it was easy to put a solid content into the notion of a restraining "public authority," because parliament was by then just such an authority. Aquinas says that this political arrangement exists in communities of free men, and Fortescue says substantially the same thing. In short, Fortescue did not refer to the discussion of the mixed polity in Aquinas, if he knew it at all, because he had found what he needed elsewhere.

In addition to this general point about forms of government, there is a more restricted but more illuminating one. The suggestion that Fortescue turned *De Regimine Principum* to good use is powerfully reinforced by the observation that Fortescue's famous phrase, dominium politicum et regale, is found in almost the same words in that portion of the book which is normally attributed to Ptolemy of Lucca.[92] It occurs in a discussion of the government of the empire, in which Aquinas-Ptolemy observes that because of the absence of the principle of heredity in rulership the empire cannot be considered a regal dominion pure and simple. But it is not a political dominion either, because the prince, once elected, has kingly jurisdiction and a right to taxes. So it falls between regal and political lordship. Moreover, when Fortescue discusses his version of these combined principles, he employs the same examples as the author of *De Regimine Principum*. But this point about an apparently clear literary link is not the really important one. What is most fascinating is that Fortescue fastens on the idea of a combination of principles and ignores the substance of the discussion. He insists on putting his own content into the frame provided by his authority; otherwise it would not accomplish the task of describing English government. In short, Fortescue was not engaged in a slavish literary enterprise. He found the notion of dual legitimacy in *De Regimine Principum*, but he filled it with what seemed to him an accurate theoretical account of English government. Moreover, it was not an account of mixed monarchy. If Fortescue had undertaken to persuade us that English government answered to that kind of formula he would have been wrong, and he would have had a much slighter claim to our attention. He had the good sense, however, to ignore a theory which bore no resemblance to any European kingdom.

Thus the first, and admittedly minor, point is that Fortescue was not indulging in mere literary fabrication, that there was some justification for his appeal to the *De Regimine Principum*. It is more important to observe that what he found there were hints on the nature of a polity organized in terms of a dual principle of legitimacy. Now it will be appropriate to examine more fully several interpretations of Fortescue's ideas, still paying special attention to the view that they are to be understood as a version of mixed monarchy.

Charles Plummer, the editor of Fortescue's *The Governance of England,* thought Fortescue's theory was appropriately interpreted as a constitutional monarchy.[93] This view was attacked by McIlwain, who went on to describe Fortescue's theory as one in which the king was absolute in certain spheres but in others was restrained by law.[94] This is followed by the contention that Fortescue's regal and political dominion may be likened to the elements of Bracton's thought which McIlwain calls *jurisdictio* and *gubernaculum*. Gubernaculum is replaced by the regal element in Fortescue, and jurisdictio by the political. Thus Fortescue is supposed to have envisioned a monarch whose rule, while absolute in some areas, was nevertheless limited by a body of immutable fundamental law.[95] As in the case of Bracton, the textual support for this line of argument is problematical. In the case of Bracton it has been shown that this interpretation is misleading at best; it neglects the political element in his text, which does supply a limitation upon kingship. The case is exactly the same with Fortescue. It is true that Fortescue sometimes appears to be making statements which support the view that English government was limited by law. His work does contain passages which exalt natural law. But this is true only in a special sense, and even that is not a juristic sense.

Chrimes has also contributed to the discussion. He believes that it is imperative to maintain a sharp distinction between "limited monarchy" and "constitutional monarchy," and that both Plummer and McIlwain did not maintain the distinction, which, he says, has been misleading. "A limited monarch is one whose power is absolute except in certain spheres delimited by law and custom. A constitutional monarch is limited but not absolute, for his power is controlled by some other co-existent power whose authority he cannot lawfully override." [96] Fortescue, he argues, had a theory of limited monarchy, because in some spheres the king was uncontrolled. More recently, however, Chrimes has said in discussing certain passages of *De Laudibus* that it "is quite clear . . . that Fortescue has in mind the limitation of the king by the assent of parliament." He maintains, therefore, that Fortescue is advancing a theory of parliamentary monarchy. But he has also reaffirmed the view that Fortescue had in mind a "monarchy limited but absolute in certain spheres." [97]

It has already been shown that it is an error in perspective to interpret Fortescue's theory as one in which the monarch is absolute in certain spheres but limited by law in others. On the contrary, it is not a question of spheres at all. There simply are no clear limits to the competence of king and people acting jointly. Recently, however, Plummer's constitutional-monarchy interpretation has found an able defender in R. W. K. Hinton. He has but one reservation: Plummer would have been less anachronistic if he had said that Fortescue was discussing the theory of mixed government,[98] the theory "that acts of government require the prior agreement of the people whom they will affect. In this theory there is no need to set any limit to the power of government, since the people share in it." "Fortescue," he says, "was thinking of England as governed by a king in co-operation with the estates by means of laws made in parliament by the king and the estates together." [99] While Hinton's description of the theory advanced by Fortescue is certainly correct, may it not be useful to distinguish double majesty from the doctrine of mixed monarchy? Although theories of mixed government come down to us from classical political theory, the use of the concept in the interpretation of fifteenth century thought is an anachronism.

Classical antiquity, in fact, originated two quite different theories of the mixed state. The first theory is found in both Plato and Aristotle. In the *Laws*, Plato discusses a form of government he elected to call the polity. He says that there are two basic forms of government, monarchy and democracy, and "almost all the rest . . . are variations of these. Now, if you are to have liberty and the combination of friendship with wisdom, you must have both these forms of government in a measure . . . no city can be well governed which is not made up of both." Plato later makes clear what sort of mixture he intended. The mode of election is to be contrived in such a way that magistrates will derive from each of four classes, divided according to the principles of wealth and number.[100]

The idea of the polity was taken up by Aristotle. "There are, indeed, some thinkers who hold that the ideal constitution itself should be a mixture of all constitutions; and they commend, for this reason, the constitution of Sparta. These thinkers are all agreed that the Spartan constitution is composed of all the three elements — monarchy, oligarchy, and democracy . . . According to some of them, monarchy is represented by the two kings: oligarchy by the Council of Elders; and democracy by the Ephors, who are drawn from the ranks of the people." [101] Aristotle later recommends the polity as the best form of government for most states.[102] For Aristotle, as for Plato, the mixed state is an institutional arrangement for reconciling collisions between rich and poor. This is to be done by introducing a blend of all the classes into institutions, by combining the oligarchical and democratic methods for choosing magistrates and for carrying on public affairs.[103]

The second form of the theory of the mixed state was given its classical statement by Polybius in the second century B.C. He believed that this form offered a solution to the problem of revolutionary changes in constitutional structure. It had been contrived by the great Spartan legislator Lycurgus and had been developed in Rome as well. "For if one fixed one's eyes on the power of the consuls, the constitution seemed completely monarchical and royal; if on that of the senate it seemed again to be aristocratic; and when one looked at the power of the masses, it seemed clearly a democracy." [104] Polybius' theory is quite different from the idea of the polity in Plato and Aristotle, where a balance was achieved by infusing into institutions and procedures both oligarchical and democratic principles. In Polybius' theory the balance resulted from assigning different functions to different organs of government. Each had distinct powers, any one of which would serve to offset the others.[105] It was Polybius' view which reappeared in triumph during the English civil wars in the seventeenth century.

It is true that an examination of the literature of English political thought before the 1640's reveals occasional use of the classical notion of mixed rule. As early as 1538, Thomas Starkey, in *A Dialogue between Cardinal Pole and Thomas Lupset,* had observed that "the most wise men, considering the nature of princes . . . and the nature of man as it is indeed, affirm a mixed state to be of all others the best and most convenient to conserve the whole out of tyranny. For when any one part has full authority, if that part chance to be corrupt . . . the rest shall suffer the tyranny thereof, and be put in great misery." [106] In 1559, the year after Queen Elizabeth's accession to the throne, John Aylmer set himself the task of explaining to Englishmen that it was not a dangerous matter to have a feminine monarch because English rulers were not absolute. "The regimen of England is not a mere monarchy, as some for lack of consideration think, nor a mere oligarchy nor democracy, but a rule mixed of all these, wherein each of these have or should have like authority. The image whereof, and not the image, but the thing indeed, is to be seen in the parliament house, wherein you shall find these three estates; the king or queen which represents the monarchy, the noblemen which be the aristocracy, and the burgesses and knights the democracy . . . If the parliament use their privileges, the king can ordain nothing without them: If he do it, it is his fault in usurping it, and their fault in permitting it." [107] Other references to the idea of a mixed polity in Tudor times have been collected,[108] but it was still very far from being a clear and coherent doctrine, nor was it as yet a prominent intellectual instrument in the efforts of Englishmen to characterize their political order. This was to come with the development of the peculiar historical circumstances of the 1640's.[109] If a comparison is made between the substance of the Tudor use and the seventeenth century usage, it will be seen that the sixteenth century formula more nearly resembles the traditional doctrine dressed up in a little humanist learning. For all it does is set up a vague counterweight to kingship; there is no specification of separate functions to the three estates.

The theory of a mixed polity came to assume a different character during the seventeenth century. "What chiefly gave currency to the idea of the mixed state was the reply of Charles to the Nineteen Propositions of Parliament in 1642. The mixed state now represented the King's highest ambition; he wished only to be recognized as one of three equal estates, in order to prevent hostile action by the other two." [110] Charles's answer outlined English government as follows.

There being three kinds of government amongst men, absolute monarchy, aristocracy, and democracy, and all these having their particular conveniences and inconveniences, the experience and wisdom of your ancestors hath so molded this out of a mixture of these, as to give to this kingdom (as far as human prudence can provide) the conveniences of all three, without the inconveniences of any one, as long as the balance hangs even between the three estates, and they run jointly on in their proper channel (begetting verdure and fertility in the meadows on both sides) and the overflowing of either on either side raise no deluge or inundation. The ill of absolute monarchy is tyranny, the ill of aristocracy is faction and division, the ills of democracy are tumults, violence, and licentiousness. The good of monarchy is the uniting of a nation under one head to resist invasion from abroad, and insurrection at home: the good of aristocracy is the conjunction of counsel in the ablest persons of a state for the public benefit: the good of democracy is liberty, and the courage and industry which liberty begets.[111]

This interpretation of the English constitution held the field from the middle of the seventeenth century until it was at last exploded by Walter Bagehot in his classic work of the nineteenth century, *The English Constitution*. Charles's view was quickly taken up and widely discussed by authors representing both sides in the civil wars.[112] It has been justly said that "whatever the theoretical soundness of the conception of mixed monarchy, it took an extraordinarily firm grip on the public mind." [113] The theory survived the onslaughts of Filmer and Hobbes[114] to be memorialized by Blackstone, who states that "herein indeed consists the true excellence of the English government, that all parts of it form a mutual check upon each other. In the legislature, the people are a check upon the nobility, and the nobility a check upon the people, by the mutual privilege of rejecting what the other has resolved: while the king is a check upon both, which preserves the executive power from encroachments. And this very executive power is again checked and kept within bounds by the two houses, through the privilege they have of inquiring into, impeaching, and punishing the conduct (not indeed of the king, which would destroy his constitutional independence; but, which is more beneficial to the public) of his evil and pernicious counsellors." [115] Blackstone's treatment, in turn, survived the savage criticism of Jeremy Bentham, who argued that Blackstone's effort to prove that the English constitution was wise, perfect, and honest because it possessed all the merits and none of the defects of monarchy, aristocracy, and democracy could just as well have proved instead that it was *"all-weak, all-foolish,* and *all-knavish."* [116]

King Charles's own version, or rather that of his literary ghosts,[117] in addition to the idea of balancing institutions and classes, contained also the idea of "the assignment of appropriate functions to each of the three singly. The king was charged with the conduct of foreign relations, the power of appointment, the pardoning power, and other functions; the Commons possessed the sole right to propose taxes and to impeach; the Lords possessed power of judicature." [118] Such was the theory of mixed monarchy. Clearly it was not the theory developed by Sir John Fortescue. His theory contains no discussion of the differentiation of lords from commons, or, needless to say, of the attachment of specific tasks to each house; it contains no notion that the three estates represent three different principles, each with separate institutional expression; it contains, as Chrimes has pointed out, no system of checks and balances.[119] To attribute the theory of mixed monarchy to Fortescue imposes upon his views far more clarity and precision than they contain. Moreover, the theory of mixed monarchy arose in an atmosphere which produced theories and arguments about sovereignty. According to the theory of mixed monarchy, "there was a single sovereign authority, the exercise of which required the co-operation of the three powers." [120] In Fortescue's work this question does not even arise.

There is abundant reason, then, for distinguishing the theory of mixed monarchy from double majesty, and for attributing to Fortescue only the second, looser view. The element that is really crucial in his system is the presumption that prince and people are happily harnessed together. The facts, of course, might belie such an assumption, and they quite often did; but, though the system exhibited signs of stress, it did not explode until the seventeenth century. This assumption of Fortescue's gives the really important tension to his system and makes his political theory an expression of double majesty. At bottom the stress cannot be resolved without abandoning double majesty as a political scheme. It is true that Fortescue often indicates that it is the parliament which stands for the *populus,* and this marks an advance over the expression of double majesty in Bracton. But representation of the people in parliament is perhaps too clear an idea to be fairly applied. Fortescue nowhere seriously discusses who it is that has the title to be the "people." The concept of citizenship is still, so to say, imprisoned in the limbo of double majesty. There is the idea of allegiance to the prince and the idea of feudal obligation, but neither of these is an idea of citizenship. The confusion is reflected in Fortescue's language. When he discusses regal and political dominion, he refers not just to parliament but to the people, to the chief men of the realm, and to the three estates quite indifferently.

Fortescue states that regal rights derive from the authority of natural law. This is the common element in all powers. Nevertheless, not all dominions are the same. When he comes to explain why this is so, he relies on historical origins. In doing so, however, he argues that in a regal and political dominion the king's power derives from institution by the people. The important question here is whether Fortescue is involved in a flat contradiction. In a sense, of course, he is. It cannot be the case that royal right derives its authority from natural law — in such a way as to possess certain prerogatives free from human interference — and from the people at the same time. It might be argued that the people derive their authority from the natural law, and that this composes the difficulty. But either there is a *judex ordinarius,* capable of resolving all disputes, such as the popes claimed to be, or the vox populi itself determines what the content of natural law shall be. In short, in the end a political question cannot be resolved with a legal instrument. But this kind of precision is not to be found in Fortescue. Indeed, his arguments do not even have this flavor. Rather he argues, like his contemporaries, in terms of analogies, similitudes, and conflicting authorities. He did not undertake to solve the problems of the seventeenth century.

In another sense, Fortescue supplies material with which a kind of reconciliation between the authority of kings and the authority of the people can be patched together. At least this can be done in the absence of fundamental conflicts. Some kinds of regal rights and duties may be added to those derived from natural law. They are expressed in customs and statutes.[121] But every native regal right must be discussed in terms of natural law, while any customs that are repugnant to the nature of kingship are corruptions.[122] It is these arrangements deriving from the populus that are intended to forestall kingship from degenerating into tyranny. If a king deserts political rule, however, he cannot be lawfully restrained. Nevertheless, double majesty persists, for as Chrimes has said, the "king may be deposed, if not by parliament, at least by the 'people' or 'estates' of the realm, but only if he fail to discharge the duties of his office . . . Otherwise he cannot be coerced, except by force. He alone can authorise reform; all resistance to him is rebellion and unlawful . . . Parliament to be sure, has an authority of its own as the assembly of the estates, as the agent of the public weal, and perhaps of the public will, if there be any; it is entitled to speak and act for the people." [123] Here again is the assertion of a native authority possessed by the populus. There is always the possibility, perhaps the inevitability, of conflict in double majesty. Several instances of severe stress have been referred to, when the baronial party attempted to coerce the king. These conflicts helped to produce an idea of kingship from which the king could be separated and coerced as a mere man. Still, most such attempts failed until the whole arrangement reached a point of crisis in the 1640's. English society polarized around the old partners in double majesty and, as Wilkinson has said, "both king and parliament . . . had right on their side, but in their contentions the medieval political scheme was finally destroyed." [124]

Whatever its merits and defects, Fortescue's work is the fullest statement of operative political thought in late medieval England. He was perfectly clear that English politics rested on the idea of legitimacy that has been called double majesty; it is equally clear that he made no use of the theory of mixed monarchy. The idea of the sanctity of natural law is there, but it was not employed for any constitutionalizing purpose. Nor does the idea of restraint rest on immutable custom. On the contrary, Fortescue plainly acknowledges the possibility of receiving new law at the hands of prince and people, whose joint competence has no clear limits. The painful question of an irreparable breach between the two majesties was never confronted. Immediately following Fortescue's day, however, the notion of double majesty entered upon a period of eclipse and eventual transformation. These were the major developments in the period of royal vigor rightly associated with the Tudor monarchs. Yet even though the fundamental ambiguity was neither resolved nor even squarely confronted in the sixteenth century, the shift of emphasis from prince and people to prince and law was to play a most important role in the future.

eight The King's Conscience

From the point of view of the history of political thought, the most striking feature of the Tudor era was its exaltation of kingship. There were two principal lines of emphasis in the Tudor celebration of the prince. One theme was insistence on the subject's duty of obedience. The idea of resistance to the ruler was almost universally despised and condemned. Indeed, admonitions on the sin of rebellion were often marked by a shrill tone of urgency, and when they were not shrill, they were solemn. The idea of obedience was stressed so much that it exhausts the reader and threatens to drive all other ideas into eclipse. Nevertheless, for present purposes the most interesting theoretical idea developed in the Tudor age was that of equity. The principle that it was the king's duty to insure that justice was done was so elaborated and refined as to amount to what has rightly been called a surrogate for the idea of sovereignty.[1] For its function was nothing less than to unify the legal order, to supply an apex for the legal system under the name of the king's conscience and in the person of the king's chancellor, who came to be called the keeper of the royal conscience.[2]

The present chapter focuses on the idea of equity for several reasons. To begin with, the theme of obedience has been well recognized and plentifully discussed by historians of political thought, while equity has been unduly neglected except by legal historians.[3] More important, reliance on equity in the sixteenth century furnishes a theoretical link with two extremely significant developments. On the one hand, it is difficult to avoid the observation that the Tudor polity behaved like a sovereign state. If there were ever any acts of sovereign power, the reformation and the seizure of church lands belong in that class. The second development did not get under way until the end of the sixteenth century. There emerged then the first signs of serious cleavage between the monarchy and its constituency. The theoretical form of their disagreement was a contrast between attachment to and disaffection with equitable jurisdiction. Common lawyers and their allies began to argue that the common law alone furnished legal certainty, and they set this notion over against what seemed to them the vagaries of the jurisprudence of conscience. As matters developed, this meant that the content of the developing struggle between king and parliament took on a peculiarly legalistic flavor. Regal claims in the sixteenth century had turned on legal ideas, and when the great rupture began to appear it was only natural that counterclaims should be mounted on legal principle. It was this legal emphasis that transformed the ancient heritage of double majesty, but without solving the dualism at its center. For until the Tudor age the assumption had always been that government was the affair of king and people jointly. The new legalism, however, produced a new partnership: prince and law, rather than prince and people. Nor was this an accident, for the chief architects of the change were common lawyers. Under the impact of worsening relations with the early Stuart monarchs, they came eventually to assert that the common law was sovereign. This is most plausibly explained as the result of the sharp legal rivalries produced by Tudor and Stuart reliance on their prerogative courts, to the disparagement of the common law and its courts, or so common lawyers came to feel. The scope of the conflict gradually widened until it took the form of a fundamental collision between the claims of an exalted and inalienable royal prerogative and the common law. It was at this point that the idea emerged that there were certain fundamental laws, embedded in the law of the land, which lay beyond the reach even of the royal prerogative.

Despite the practice of sovereignty by Tudor governments, however, there were no explicit discussions of the idea of sovereignty akin to those produced in the seventeenth century. The momentous changes of the sixteenth century were launched during the reign of Henry VIII, and the central preoccupation of the kingly party was, as Franklin le van Baumer has said, the creation of a "monarchy supreme above feudal and ecclesiastical jurisdictions . . ." [4] But Tudor theorists did not undertake to deal with two other problems, or rather, what seem now to be problems: the relation of the king to parliament, and of the royal prerogative to the common law. These were the central problems of the seventeenth century, and the fact that these matters did not rise to the surface of political life in the Tudor period meant that, despite the profound changes effected, the characteristic ambiguity of medieval political thought survived. While it is true that there were important strains in Tudor society, some of which adumbrated the collisions of the Stuart period, it is nevertheless the case that, for the most part, Tudor rule rested securely on broad agreement on most of the important matters of state. The great theoretical enterprise was the vindication of regal and, more broadly, governmental jurisdiction, as against that of the Bishop of Rome and the internal disorder which had been the most obvious feature of the fifteenth century. The intellectual and administrative instrument of the Tudor restoration of stability was the king's prerogative jurisdiction. Toward the end of the century, it was turned against the proponents of religious change.

The assertion that the king was the supreme head of the Church on earth involved a wholesale transfer of papal jurisdiction to the English ruler. Courts Christian, with their appellate summit in the papal curia, had long claimed jurisdiction in matters of faith and morals, and this embraced important secular concerns, such as marriage, legitimacy, and the oaths upon which contractual arrangements were based. Still more, the papacy claimed a broad appellate competence in case of defect of justice in secular courts. In effect, the exercise of equitable jurisdiction by the king's chancellor was the regal assumption of that sweeping papal prerogative. This was accomplished by the Act in Restraint of Appeals, which forbade the carrying of appeals to Rome and thus made the king the court of last resort.[5] Again, royal jurisdiction operating outside the system of common law courts was turned on the problems of internal order. On this level, the prerogative courts were frequently employed to curb the overmighty subject.[6]

The tendency in the Tudor period to stress theoretical principles which, had they been driven home, would have unified the political order, is evident in the works of Christopher St. Germain and Richard Hooker. Neither of these authors confronted the problem of sovereignty head-on, and for good reason. They were both concerned with particular issues, which is only to say that the problem of political order had not reached such general proportions that an answer to the question of the location of final authority could no longer be avoided. St. Germain's problem was to explain the regal assumption of papal jurisdiction, and his method was to frame a legal theory with the king's equity at its apex. Hooker's problem was to explain why the Calvinists' challenge to the established order was groundless and therefore illegitimate. In doing so he contrived an imposing general theory which very nearly strikes off a full-blown theory of royal sovereignty. But he tried to embrace in his system not only Tudor practice but the medieval heritage of a dually organized political order, and the idea of a controlling body of law as well.

Today, St. Germain is remembered principally as a lawyer and, more particularly, as perhaps the chief theorist of the early history of equity in English law.[7] But considered in the context in which he lived and wrote, the period of the Henrician Reformation, he was much more than a lawyer. He was also a political pamphleteer, and he engaged actively in the great controversies of the day.[8] Certainly he was one of the leading opponents of the old order in church and state, as his lengthy debate with Sir Thomas More demonstrates. His works are especially pertinent, because, as J. W. Allen correctly observed, "of all the writers of Henry VIII's time the lawyer, Christopher St. Germain, expressed most clearly the nature and implications of the change that the Tudor government was bringing about." [9] Baumer regards him as the leading writer in the controversy with Rome, and as one of the principal theorists of Tudor kingship.[10]

St. Germain's best-known work is the important legal treatise, *The Doctor and Student or Dialogues Between a Doctor of Divinity and a Student in the Laws of England.*[11] What emerges from his writings is a national monarch, possessing legal instruments sufficient to conclude any and all legal questions. This enterprise was accomplished in two stages. The first and most prominent aim was the transfer of papal jurisdiction to the king. The second was the development of a legal theory which, in the last resort, subordinated all law to regal authority. St. Germain began by absorbing the natural law into the common law; then he completed the task by subordinating the common law to the king's equitable jurisdiction.[12]

Most of the difficulty in construing St. Germain's work springs from the fact that in *The Doctor and Student* he embarks on his discussion from a distinctly medieval platform. Indeed, much Tudor political theory has a medieval ring.[13] Because this can be seriously misleading, it will be best to begin with St. Germain's treatment of the traditional framework. The argument of *The Doctor and Student* may be examined conveniently under two broad headings.

The first of these is the discussion of types and sources of law, and the second is the discussion of equity, which occupies much the larger part of the book. The dialogue begins with the doctor of divinity asking his friend, who is a student of the laws of England, to explain the grounds of English law. The student modestly says that this is a task beyond his cunning but that he will try. First, however, he asks the doctor to inform him concerning the other laws.[14] There follows a fourfold classification of law, which is quite normal medieval doctrine. First there is the law eternal, which is the reason of God. This law is unknowable in itself, but, to the extent that it is necessary, it is made accessible to man through the three other kinds of law: the law of God, the law of nature or reason, and the law of man.[15] The law of God is revelation, the sole purpose of which is to direct man to eternal felicity. It is true, St. Germain notes, that some provisions of this law have been incorporated in the law of man, such as laws designed to suppress heresy. On the other hand, however, no part of revelation which has reference to political rule is to be construed as the law of God. This observation is directed, in particular, against the canon law. Canon laws framed for the political ordering of the Church are excluded. Moreover, church property is itself merely temporal.[16]

The law of nature is to be considered in two ways. First there is the law of nature general. Like the natural law of Ulpian, this is not really a legal idea, for what it refers to is animal behavior. According to St. Germain it may be disregarded. Secondly, however, there is the law of nature special, and it refers exclusively to reasonable creatures, that is, man. Now this law ought to be kept by all men, whether Jews, gentiles, or Christians, for it "is written in the heart of every man, teaching him what is to be done and what is to be fled; and because it is written in the heart, therefore it may not be put away, ne it is never changeable by no diversity of place, ne time: and therefore against this law, prescription, statute nor custom may not prevail: and if any be brought in against it, they be not prescriptions, statutes, nor customs, but things void and against justice. And all other laws, as well the laws of God as to the acts of men, as other, be grounded thereupon." [17] Thus, St. Germain presents the reader with a familiar theme. But as was true in connection with Fortescue, the recitation of this formula is very far from conclusive in the matter of arriving at a just estimate of an author's perspective. St. Germain has a great deal more to say.

Finally, there is the law of man, or positive law. This, he says, is arrived at through reason and consists partly in the law of God and partly in the law of reason or nature. Hence, in every well-made positive law there is "somewhat of the law of reason, and of the law of God; and to discern the law of God and the law of reason from the law positive is very hard." Here is the first hint of St. Germain's reduction of the traditional hierarchy of laws to the positive law of England. The law of man results from a coupling of wisdom and authority, and it promulgates what is expedient for the commonwealth. All the laws of men which do not conflict with the laws of God or reason are binding in conscience.[18]

Having developed this framework, St. Germain turns to the topic of the grounds of English law. There are six of these: the law of reason, the law of God, custom, maxims, particular local customs, and statutes "made in Parliaments by the king, and by the common council of the realm." [19] In considering the first ground, the law of reason, St. Germain develops a closer treatment of the law of nature. He begins with the often-quoted passage which states that in England the law of nature is called the law of reason.[20] This law has two departments. By the law of reason primary, various crimes are prohibited in English law. The law of reason secondary is divided into two parts. What St. Germain calls the law of reason secondary general supplies the concept of property, and this operates through a great number of specific provisions of English law. The provisions under this heading are a kind of jus gentium, for, says St. Germain, they are "generally kept in all countries." The law of reason secondary particular consists of general and local customs, maxims, and statutes. These are peculiar to England.[21]

The second ground of English law is the law of God, and it follows that some, at least, of the rules of this law are administered in English courts. According to the particular case, as provided for in the law of England, the king's courts may sometimes proceed according to the law of the church, while in others the spiritual courts are obliged to proceed according to the king's law. At this point, St. Germain offers no general doctrine[22] but passes on to the third ground of English law, which is custom. Customs that do not contravene God's law or the law of reason, and that have been accepted by kings and people, have the force of law. This is the common law. By this law the several courts of the realm and their jurisdictions have been established, and these may not be altered without the assent of parliament. After presenting a number of examples, St. Germain proceeds to an extremely important point. There is nothing in these customary arrangements which makes them necessary, for they cannot be shown to be any more reasonable than others might have been. Moreover, we are now informed that the law of property is "not the law of reason, but the law of custom . . ." [23] St. Germain then embraces the doctrine that statutes may override any of these customary arrangements.[24]

The fourth ground of the law of England is maxims of the law. Like the common law as a whole, these rest on customs, but they are not generally known. Rather, they are the province of those who "take great study in the law of the realm . . ." What these maxims include is to be decided by judges, and they have the same force as statutes. Yet, like all custom they may be altered by statute.[25] The fifth ground is "particular customs, used in divers counties, towns, cities, and lordships in this realm." Should a question arise as to whether there is a custom, as someone alleges, it is decided by twelve men and not the judges.[26] The sixth and last ground is statute law. Statutes, St. Germain says, are made "by our sovereign lord the king and his progenitors, and by the lords spiritual and temporal, and the commons in divers parliaments, in such cases where the law of reason, the law of God, customs, maxims, ne other grounds of the law seemed not to be sufficient to punish evil men and to reward good men." [27]

It is clear already that St. Germain has employed traditional categories for a novel purpose. All the types and grounds of law have been absorbed into the law of England and thereby made subject to ordinary courts of law. This means that the law of God and the law of nature are not set apart as superior alternative standards to English law but are, rather, embraced by it. Moreover, English law is ultimately subject to alteration by statute, and this includes even the law of property. But this is only the first stage of St. Germain's enterprise. He proceeds next to the introduction of the idea of equity, and through it he achieves the subordination of all law to the king's conscience. But it should be noted that the idea of double majesty has survived, for he says quite clearly that both custom and statute are made by king and parliament jointly and may not be altered except by them. Despite St. Germain's stress on the concept of equity, he does not work out the problem of its relation to the traditional doctrine. On the contrary, both ideas stand side by side.

He introduces his argument on equity in the following way. It is possible that the customs, maxims, and statutes of English law will offend in conscience, and the doctor asks how English law deals with such matters. St. Germain's general position is that in many cases there will be a remedy in equity. The instrument for resolving equitable questions is conscience, which is institutionalized in the person of the king's chancellor. The upshot of this line of argument is that equity is a facet of the positive law of the realm, for it is administered in the Court of Chancery. St. Germain's program of absorbing all law into the positive law of England emerges quite clearly in his treatment of equity. For equity, while it is the result of exceptions to the normal operation of the law — exceptions which are supposed to be based on the law of God and the law of reason — is the exclusive right of the king's chancellor. Should a man find himself "without remedy at the common law, yet he may be holpen [helped] by a *subpoena;* and so he may in many other cases where conscience serveth for him, that were too long to rehearse now." [28] St. Germain is here raising a problem of critical importance, and it is understandable that he should hesitate to generalize.

Problems giving rise to offenses against conscience occur because general rules of law will not always be adequate to the circumstances of particular cases. This is an observation as old as Greek antiquity. St. Germain puts it this way.

And for the plainer declaration what equity is, thou shalt understand that since the deeds and acts of men, for which laws have been ordained, happen in divers manners infinitely, it is not possible to make any general rule of the law, but that it shall fail in some case: and therefore makers of laws take heed to such things as may often come, and not to every particular case, for they could not though they would. And therefore to follow the words of the law were in some case both against justice and the commonwealth. Wherefore in some cases it is necessary to [leave] the words of the law, and to follow that [which] reason and justice requireth, and to that intent equity is ordained; that is to say, to temper and mitigate the rigor of the law. And it is called also by some men *epieikeia;* the which is no other thing but an exception of the law of God, or of the law of reason, from the general rules of the law of man, when they by reason of their

generality would in any particular case judge against the law of
God or the law of reason . . .[29]

Deciding when a problem of equity has arisen is an exceedingly difficult question. But St. Germain has an answer for it, and it is this
that really assures the monarch's place at the summit of the legal
system. St. Germain begins by allowing that equity or conscience
ought generally to be ordered according to the law of the land.
Indeed, he says that the common law itself provides exceptions to
its general rules.[30] According to those who are learned in English
law, the question "where the law is to be left for conscience, and
where not, is to be understood in divers manners, and after divers
rules . . ." [31] It is true that St. Germain supplies no general rule,
but despite his unwillingness to generalize in a perfectly straightforward way, he does say that the decision as to whether a man may
appeal to conscience is made in Chancery. The effect of a subpoena
is to enjoin further proceedings at common law "till it be determined in the king's chancery, whether the plaintiff had title in
conscience to recover, or not . . ." [32] The door is obviously open to
royal discretion. But once having set forth the general framework
of his argument on the types and grounds of law, and the theory of
equitable jurisdiction, St. Germain refrains from general language.
The rest of *The Doctor and Student* is given over to the examination of a very large number of particular cases. These are discussed
in two broad sorts of ways. One sort of discussion centers on cases in
English law, and the point is to consider in which cases a party has
an equitable remedy. The other type includes cases in which English
law or equity departs from the opinions set forth in certain summae,
composed for use in civil-law countries.

Despite the specialized and disjointed character of St. Germain's
examination of equity, it is possible to see in it the formulation of
an immensely useful instrument of regal interference and general
supervision of the legal system. To be sure, it is only a system of cor-
rective justice. For the ordinary run of governmental and legal
affairs the common law and statute law will suffice. Under normal
circumstances, St. Germain assumes the effective operation of double
majesty. As it happened, the assumption that king and parliament
would function cooperatively was justified. Moreover, St. Germain
agrees with Fortescue in assuming that there can be no gap between
parliamentary enactment and higher law. His view is that "it can not

be thought that a statute that is made by authority of the whole realm, as well of the king, and of the lords spiritual and temporal, as of all the commons, will recite a thing against the truth." [33] Thus the idea of equity is injected into the traditional scheme without any serious effort to explain precisely how it is related to the generally controlling role of parliamentary statute. Whatever St. Germain's view might have been in another context, the fact remains that his work introduced that discretionary jurisprudence which so angered common lawyers from Tudor times until the revolutionary Long Parliament destroyed prerogative jurisdiction. Common lawyers insisted that the effect of the chancellor's jurisdiction was to set the common law aside. St. Germain appears to have discussed this problem in his own day. In a tract on suits in Chancery, which may have been written by St. Germain, a common lawyer maintains that reliance on the principle of conscience produces an undesirable uncertainty in the law. The author of *The Doctor and Student*, it is said, speaks too "much of conscience," but it is a "thing of great uncertainty." [34] "You make my lord chancellor judge in every matter and bring the laws of the realm in such uncertainty, that no man can be sure of any lands be it inheritance or purchase, but every man's title shall be by this means brought in question into the chancery; and therefore it shall be tried whether it be conscience or no conscience, and the law of the realm, by which we ought to be justified, nothing regarded." [35] St. Germain had no very satisfactory answer. Indeed, the one he gives is not compatible with the doctrine of *The Doctor and Student*. He replies that writs of subpoena are perfectly legal because they are issued by the king and his council. Moreover, no subpoena would be issued which departed from a statute or maxim of the law.[36] This last proviso, of course, runs directly contrary to his earlier discussion, in which the idea is that equity remedies the deficiencies of all the grounds of law, including maxims and statutes. Thus St. Germain does not solve the difficulty, but for this he can hardly be blamed, for the relation of equity and law is a perennial problem of legal theory.

The Doctor and Student appeared before the decisive acts of the Reformation Parliament, but it supplies a useful framework for St. Germain's works which appeared during the final break with Rome. Some of the views only implied or expressed piecemeal in this first work — particularly the idea of royal supremacy — were turned to direct use in the period 1532–1534. These later works are controversial pieces and do not contain the kinds of theoretical points developed in his discussion of legal theory. Their value lies in the fact that they represent not St. Germain the legal theorist but St. Germain the royal apologist. Generally speaking, these writings fall into two classes. One consists of those produced in his debate with Sir Thomas More on the causes of friction between the laity and clergy.[37] The second class is a group of writings which appeared after the Act of Supremacy and which are directed specifically to the problem of royal supremacy.[38] The general drift of the first group is that St. Germain blames the clergy for the disorder in the land. He assembles long lists of types of misconduct by the clergy and complains at length about the procedure of church courts in heresy proceedings. His general recommendation entails a severe limitation of the spiritual sphere, which is closely akin to the view set forth much earlier by Marsilius of Padua. Spiritual jurisdiction ought to be limited to things of the spirit. The proper office of the clergy is the performance of the sacraments and teaching.[39]

The second group of writings is more explicitly addressed to the general problem of jurisdiction. Papal authority was a wrongful usurpation. The Act of Supremacy, therefore, restores what had always been the rightful prerogatives of the king. The true doctrine is that the king has no superior save God.[40] The papal contention that temporal jurisdiction compasses only matters of land and goods is "a right great error." [41] On the contrary, even the cure of men's souls is the king's responsibility.[42] To be sure, the clergy have an important function, namely, to administer the sacraments and to teach. But it is the king's duty to see that they perform these tasks.[43] Should conflicts arise between the common law and the canon law, the latter should be repealed.[44] The General Council of the English Church should renounce any usurped authority which the council "should think expedient to be renounced: *then* it would appear that they intend the honor of God and wealth of the people." [45]

In sum, then, St. Germain's work represents an effort to knit traditional legal materials into a novel fabric in which the dominant thread is royal supremacy. The spiritual problems of the Tudor polity are solved by the adoption of a markedly Erastian position. More importantly, *The Doctor and Student* marks the beginning of the great legal and political struggle between the prerogative of the prince and the courts of the common law. The intriguing thing about St. Germain's discussion is that he tried to knit together precisely those two elements — English law and regal equity — that were eventually to be sharply separated, indeed, to become the central ideological ingredients of the opposition between the monarchy and the common lawyers. He equipped the monarchy with a powerful new idea of equity, which could be used by a willful monarch in such a way as to disrupt the traditional balance, and that is exactly what happened in the early Stuart period. On the other hand, he outlined the peculiarly English conception of the law of reason, a conception which had the effect of making all genuine law a part of ordinary English law. He worked his way into this doctrine backwards, so to say. For he began on a traditional platform, such as the one expressed by Fortescue, in which the ultimate validity of human law derives from its participation in natural law. At first glance, St. Germain does not appear to be maintaining anything very different. Actually, he has shifted the emphasis in such a way as to constitute a sharp departure from tradition. To be sure, he does not set it out in a straightforward way. Taken together, however, the several stages of his argument amount to a near reversal of the relationship between human and divine law. For those parts of divine law that have political relevance are simply incorporated into English law, a law subject to alteration by ordinary political and legislative processes. Fortescue assumed coincidence between parliamentary enactments and the values of natural law, and St. Germain made the same assumption. But he took an important step beyond Fortescue when he incorporated all other law into English law outright. Thus not only was the traditional idea of double majesty set in a legalistic framework, but the center of gravity was shifted so as to make all the most important questions matters of national rather than natural law. This quiet but nonetheless dramatic alteration in the terms of discussion was obviously required by Henry VIII's assumption of papal prerogatives. But St. Germain left untouched the question of final authority and, in this sense, only reproduced the stress implicit in the medieval outlook. It is perfectly clear that statute law emerges as superior to custom and that it will be controlling under normal circumstances. But the assumption of cooperation between prince and people survived automatically, quite without discussion. The main thing to notice, however, is the shift toward a legalistic setting for double majesty, for its gradual translation into a legal idea was to be the next stage of development.

It is in this connection that Richard Hooker's work takes on its great interest.

The imposing system developed in Hooker's principal work, *Of the Laws of Ecclesiastical Polity,* is unique, for he undertakes to set the major lines of the medieval heritage and much of contemporary English thought on government and law in a broad philosophical framework. Hooker's work illustrates two important points. First, since English political thought in the Middle Ages was closer to a patchwork than a theory, Hooker's attempt to systematize it underlines its theoretical incoherence rather sharply. There is in Hooker a marked tendency to settle on the doctrine of royal supremacy, but the principle of double majesty survives despite his efforts. He wished to emphasize the need for a unified legal system, and this led him to make a number of statements which suggest that royal power is, at bottom, unrestrained. On the other hand, he wanted also to assert that power rested with the people. Secondly, Hooker's work reflects a growing tendency in English thought to convert the original partnership of prince and people into a coupling of prince and law. Still other statements appear to contain a doctrine which amounts to the outright supremacy of law. In the early Stuart period, this last tendency emerged as the dominant strain of thought among the partisans of parliament.

Henry VIII and his parliament had made the king the supreme head of the Church in England, and Christopher St. Germain had supplied a new set of emphases in English thought to account for it. But the king's theology had been that of the Catholic Church. During the minority of his son, Edward VI, Calvinists came into the ascendancy and gave the Church a Calvinist bias. Mary, however, drove them into exile on the Continent. With her death, the so-called Marian exiles returned to England determined to impress Calvinist church organization and doctrine on the Church of England. Elizabeth, however, was markedly hostile to Calvinism. Indeed, she might have preferred Catholicism had it not been for the fact that to recognize it would have made her illegitimate. To be sure, the changes made in the Church after Mary's death were in the direction of Calvinism, but they by no means satisfied the Calvinists, and a considerable literature grew up in the last half of the sixteenth century attacking the Church of England. Hooker's immense book is a detailed reply to this literature.

In general terms, his system of thought places power in king and parliament. He believed that this settled all the questions then being controverted: the king in parliament had concluded the question of the form of the Church. This had been rightfully done, and therefore the question ought not to be debated any further. The whole matter is no longer open to discussion. What this amounts to is the doctrine that intellectual problems may be finally concluded by the appropriate political authority. Hooker sets out the general conclusion of his book in the *Preface,* which is a sweeping rejection of the Calvinist position. This statement also introduces his principal argumentative device, a distinction between logically necessary arguments and merely probable arguments. This device is absolutely crucial in all the vital turns of the argument, and he resorts to it time and again. It enables him to draw the conclusion that the critics of the established form of the Church of England have failed to produce any demonstrable arguments against the prevailing system, and this failure means that no changes are justified.[46]

The general purpose of Book I of the *Ecclesiastical Polity* is to supply a cosmic framework for this broad conclusion, and Hooker's vehicle is an exposition of the types of law. His intellectual tools are recognizably medieval. The account he gives of law is strikingly similar to the views set forth by St. Thomas Aquinas.[47] The general definition of law is an Aristotelian notion. It is the idea of *telos,* the notion that there is purposive behavior built into the very nature of things. Everything has "some fore-conceived end for which it worketh." [48] But there is an even more striking resemblance to Stoicism. Hooker begins with the eternal law, and it is here that the Stoic analogy emerges. Actually, he has two eternal laws, and it is the first one which affirms the coherence of the universe. The first eternal law is God's method, the method of operation which he has set for himself: "that order which God before all ages hath set down with himself, for himself to do all things by." [49] It is God's plan, then, and the ancients, he says, called it destiny. With the Stoics, destiny was a kind of divine providence which guided the whole universe, and Hooker's eternal law is very similar.[50] In addition, however, there are more specialized laws which God has appointed to the several segments of the universe. All of these together add up to the second eternal law. "All things therefore, which are as they ought to be, are conformed unto this second law eternal . . ." [51]

Besides the two eternal laws, Hooker discusses the celestial law or the law of the angels, revealed or scriptural law, the law of nations, natural law, and human law. There are several varieties of natural law, but they all fall into two classes. On one side there are natural laws for physical objects and animals, and on the other the natural law for reasonable creatures. The distinction between these is that objects and animals obey natural law unwittingly, while reasonable creatures have free will.[52] The natural law of reasonable creatures is a kind of principle of discovery of what is built into the fabric of the universe. All save innocents, madmen, and children are possessed of reason, "whereby good may be known from evil." [53] "Goodness is seen with the eye of the understanding. And the light of that eye is reason." [54] More particularly, there are two ways in which the good may be discerned. One of these is to acquire a knowledge of causes, but men universally shun this avenue because of its extreme difficulty. At this point, Hooker indulges in one of his not infrequent condemnations of his times: "this present age," he laments, is "full of tongue and weak of brain." So it is that men resort to the second method, which is to observe signs and tokens.[55] At this point occur some of Hooker's best-known words: "The most certain token of evident goodness is, if the general persuasion of all men do so account it . . . The general and perpetual voice of men is as the sentence of God himself. For that which all men have at all times learned, Nature herself must needs have taught; and God being the author of Nature, her voice is but his instrument." [56]

In passing, Hooker confronts the problem of epistemology: how does the mind discover what is reasonable? Reason is the constituted structure of the universe; the principles of the law of nature or reason, he says, are "drawn from out of the very bowels of heaven and earth." But how does man come to grips with it? Hooker recognizes that one cannot establish reason by reason, that one must have a given point of departure. "The main principles of Reason are in themselves apparent. For to make nothing evident of itself unto man's understanding were to take away all possibility of knowing anything." [57] It is necessary, then, to have a certain number of postulates. At this point, Hooker anticipates the heart of Cartesianism. The appropriate method for arriving at postulates, it would seem, is to reduce propositions to the utmost simplicity, and then they are somehow true. In this way he concludes that there are certain fundamental axioms of nature which are recognized by obtaining the most general kinds of statement. From these one derives more specialized axioms and then particular rules.[58] Hooker gives no examples of this process, nor does he give any very large number of illustrations of laws of nature. It is clear, however, that they are ethical propositions, with their most characteristic representatives in some of the Ten Commandments.[59]

It would appear, then, that every man has cognizance of the law of nature in his own mind in the form of guiding axioms. For "the law of Reason or human Nature is that which men by discourse of natural Reason have rightly found out themselves to be all for ever bound unto in their actions." [60] At this point, Hooker encounters a difficulty in his exposition of natural law. On the one hand, he wants to insist that knowledge of its rules is general and easily come by. Indeed, it is so easy that once its general principles are proposed no man can reject them as unreasonable or unjust. Knowledge of these principles is difficult to avoid, for any man may find them out.[61] But he also contends that "general blindness hath prevailed against the manifest Laws of Reason." [62] It is the same difficulty that Cicero had confronted, and Hooker offers the same solution: deviation is to be accounted for by the introduction of wicked customs.[63] Despite this strain of contrary sentiments, however, it seems clear that Hooker's inclination was to settle on the view that the "first principles of the Law of Nature are easy; hard it were to find men ignorant of them." [64]

Man, however, is a creature of free will and is therefore capable of evil. He possesses conscience, and this is the sanction of the law of nature. But man is capable of violating his conscience.[65] It is this which necessitates some sort of government. The frailty of man's conscience is the result of original sin. For "there being no impossibility in nature considered by itself, but that men might have lived without any public regiment. Howbeit, the corruption of our nature being presupposed, we may not deny but that the Law of Nature doth now require of necessity some kind of regiment; so that to bring things unto the first course they were in, and utterly to take away all kind of public government in the world, were apparently to overturn the whole world." [66] It is Hooker's contention that the Puritan position entails just such a reduction to anarchy, and it is at this point that he makes his greatest error, for he assumes that dissent is equivalent to the subversion of the commonwealth. He contends that the greatest danger in the current controversy is that by accepting the Calvinist argument the whole world would "be clean turned upside down . . ." [67]

At any rate, the law of nature now dictates that men live in organized society, for "wickedness and malice have taken deep root." It could not well be otherwise, he says, and here Hooker anticipates the insights of Hobbes and Rousseau on the inescapable consequences of competition, for "when families were multiplied and increased upon earth, after separation each providing for itself, envy, strife, contention and violence must grow amongst them." [68] Government is the remedy. "To take away all such mutual grievances, injuries, and wrongs, there was no way but only by growing unto composition and agreement amongst themselves, by ordaining some kind of government public, and by yielding themselves subject thereunto; that unto whom they granted authority to rule and govern, by them the peace, tranquility, and happy estate of the rest might be procured." [69] The fellowship of society, according to Hooker, has twin roots, and both are Aristotelian ideas. On the one hand, men have a natural inclination to seek life in a body politic. On the other hand, Hooker says that men obtain order and peace through the institution of government by mutual consent or, more precisely, by express or implicit agreement. Such agreement yields "the law of a Commonweal, the very soul of a politic body, the parts whereof are by law animated, held together, and set on work in such actions, as the common good requireth." [70] At this point considerable caution is necessary, because Hooker is not adumbrating the kind of contract theory which revolutionized political thought in the seventeenth century. In that century the content of the social contract was supplied by the principle of individual will. For Hooker the idea of agreement is altogether different. Its content is the notion of a teleological purpose in society. Hooker does not give the idea of consent any operational meaning; moreover, his system is at the opposite pole from the individualist assumptions which lie at the heart of social contract theory.

So men come to live in a society which is the fruit of consent. All government, Hooker says, seems to have emerged from "deliberate advice, consultation, and composition between men . . ." [71] The choice of form, however, is an arbitrary matter. Monarchy appears to have been the primitive form, but men "saw that to live by one man's will became the cause of men's misery. This constrained them to come unto laws . . ." [72] Laws are the appropriate instruments of organization. Men are prone to promote their private good exclusively: hence the need for systematic rewards and punishments.[73] "Laws politic, ordained for external order and regiment amongst men, are never framed as they should be, unless presuming the will of man to be inwardly obstinate, rebellious, and averse from all obedience unto the sacred laws of his nature; in a word, unless presuming man to be in regard of his depraved mind little better than a wild beast, they do accordingly provide notwithstanding so to frame his outward actions, that they be no hinderance unto the common good for which societies are instituted: unless they do this, they are not perfect." [74] Two things are necessary for a properly framed law: wisdom and power. The positive laws of the commonwealth ought to be formulated by the wise.[75] Here Hooker's argument takes an interesting and crucial turn, for he goes on to say that human, positive laws do not, like the natural law, merely teach. They have coercive power, and their validity is not dependent on their substantive content. On the contrary, the validity of a law depends entirely upon the authority which made it. It is this which gives it the strength of law. Laws, then, derive their force from the authority promulgating them and not from their inner merit: "Howbeit laws do not take their constraining force from the quality of such as devise them, but from that power which doth give them the strength of laws." [76]

This qualification introduces a serious strain into Hooker's system, for it appears to cut the whole system of human law away from natural law. He does have a device for avoiding this, namely, the distinction between necessary and probable proofs, by which he assimilates human and natural law. But the price which he has to pay for the reconciliation is very high. In the last resort it amounts to the doctrine that men should always obey human laws unless they are necessarily contrary to the law of God or the law of reason. The crucial notion, of course, is that of necessary contrariety. Hooker does not provide an explanation, and this is unfortunate because so much is made to depend on it. However, it can be said with considerable confidence that Hooker regards almost all the truths accessible to man as merely probable truths. Certainly the number of matters susceptible of demonstration is very few, and the test of necessity is rigorous. It is clear, for example, that Hooker regards all questions relating to the outward forms of life as falling in the area of probable truth. All that is necessary for the attainment of salvation is already available to man, because nothing is needed beyond what is plainly prescribed in Scripture, or what all may learn by the light of nature. All the other arrangements brought in by man are merely "probable collections." It follows that any group, like the Calvinists he was combating, who allege that what they demand is necessary are quite mistaken.[77]

The most revealing discussion of the distinction between necessary and probable truths occurs in the *Preface*, where it is made perfectly clear that in the area of probable truth men have no right to private judgment. The difficulty is that this area embraces nearly all human concerns. In short, the community has given up will and conscience to public authority. Hooker assumes that if individuals follow their consciences in the sphere of probable truth the result will be total disorder. Once such a problem has been resolved by public authority, it is every man's duty to respect the solution. It is clear, Hooker believes, that what the Calvinists are contending for has not been established by demonstrated arguments because there are a good many people who do not accept their views. A necessary proof has an infallible appeal to conscience and may therefore be followed. The Calvinists could rightfully overthrow the Church of England if they could produce necessary truths, but their alleged necessities are drawn from Scripture "only by poor and marvellous slight conjectures." [78]

Hooker's demand is that the dissenters submit to the definitive judgment of competent authority. What constituted competent authority, however, was an important part of the dispute. But this is Hooker's position, and he is prepared to go to great lengths to accommodate it. Indeed, he assures us that God would prefer "that sometime an erroneous sentence definitive should prevail . . . than that strifes should have respite to grow . . ." In effect, conscience is given up and institutionalized, for it is God's will that men accept judgment even if it appears to depart from what is right. At this point, Hooker has only an expediential argument to offer: this is the only way to avoid confusion and attain peace. His counsel is that men should dispute no longer, but obey.[79] Here is one of the most illuminating passages.

Be it that there are some reasons inducing you to think hardly of our laws. Are those reasons demonstrative, are they necessary, or but mere probabilities only? An argument necessary and demonstrative is such, as being proposed unto any man and understood, the mind cannot choose but inwardly assent. Any one such reason dischargeth, I grant, the conscience, and setteth it at full liberty. For the public approbation given by the body of this whole church unto those things which are established, doth make it but probable that they are good. And therefore unto a necessary proof that they are not good it must give place. But if the skilfullest amongst you can shew that all the books ye have hitherto written be able to afford any one argument of this nature, let the instance be given. As for probabilities, what thing was there ever set down so agreeable with sound reason, but some probable show against it might be made? . . . of peace and quietness there is not any way possible, unless the probable voice of every entire society or body politic overrule all private of like nature in the same body.[80]

So, the whole corpus of Calvinist literature does not contain so much as a single necessary proof.[81] In the absence of such arguments, the established order must stand. Further dissent is mere perversity. At this stage, Hooker's ideological use of the legal apparatus of his book comes out clearly. He simply appropriates it all for the established order. For "equity and reason, the law of nature, God and man, do all favour that which is in being, till orderly judgment of decision be given against it; it is but justice to exact of you, and perverseness in you it should be to deny, thereunto your willing obedience." [82] The fact that judgment has been delivered on an opinion is, for Hooker, enough to discharge an individual conscience. Judgment is "ground sufficient for any reasonable man's conscience to build the duty of obedience upon . . ." [83]

To return to Hooker's views on the establishment of government, his doctrine is that the proper authority for deciding questions of probable truth is the king and parliament. It is in this way that Hooker employs the distinction between the necessary and the probable to assimilate human and natural law. In effect, human law can never be contrary to natural law except in the area of necessary proofs. This means that virtually all human laws are valid at natural law and divine law because they are merely probable truths, and public authority may rightfully determine these. In substance, it is impossible for the king and parliament to be wrong about probable truths. To be sure, Hooker argues that the true source of power in the community is neither king nor parliament but the whole body politic. This doctrine is extremely useful to his argument, since it can be turned against the Calvinist minority much more effectively than a simple appeal to king and parliament. Thus Hooker is led to argue that "a law is the deed of the whole body politic, whereof if ye judge yourselves to be any part, then is the law even your deed also. And were it reason in things of this quality to give men audience, pleading for the overthrow of that which their own very deed hath ratified? Laws that have been approved may be (no man doubteth) again repealed, and to that end also disputed against, by the authors thereof themselves. But this is when the whole doth deliberate what laws each part shall observe, and not when a part refuseth the laws which the whole hath orderly agreed upon." [84] Hooker is thus able to promote a doctrine which suppresses a part of the people in the name of the whole. At the same time, however, he weakens the force of his position radically by depriving the doctrine of a societal source of power of any operational significance.

Hooker works into the problem of governance through his prepossession with the need for order, without which "there is no living in public society, because the want thereof is the mother of confusion, whereupon division of necessity followeth, and out of division, inevitable destruction." Once again, he is floundering on the ancient misconception that dissent entails ruin, and like Plato he embraces the idea that society should be a unity. It was in the name of plural organization that Aristotle had criticized his master, and Hooker has failed to learn the lesson. "Yea, the very Deity itself both keepeth and requireth for ever this to be kept as a law, that wheresoever there is a coagmentation of many, the lowest be knit to the highest by that which being interjacent may cause each to cleave unto other, and so all to continue one." [85]

In his more detailed discussion of government in Book VIII, Hooker repeats the view, presented earlier, that the form of government is an arbitrary matter. He says that rulers are appointed either by agreement or by divine intervention. A ruler whose place derives from conquest falls into the latter category, for "it is God who giveth victory in the day of war." [86] It would even seem that Hooker thought English rule rested on the right of conquest, which involves absolute power.[87] "Kings by conquest make their own charter: so that how large their power, either civil or spiritual, is, we cannot with any certainty define, further than only to set them in general the law of God and nature for bounds." However, Hooker does have an explanation for the limited character of English rule. Kings whose powers derive from agreement have their lawful authority circumscribed by the articles of the original compact. Moreover, any subsequent agreements between ruler and subjects arrived at freely and voluntarily are also binding upon the parties. There is no reason to doubt that he has England in mind when he says that by such "after-agreement it cometh many times to pass in kingdoms, that they whose ancient predecessors were by violence and force made subject, do grow little and little into that most sweet form of kingly government which philosophers define to be 'regency willingly sustained and endured, with chiefty of power in the greatest things.' " [88] At any rate, Hooker expressly gives it as his opinion that not the most-limited but the best-limited kingly rule is to be preferred. By this he means kingly rule "tied unto the soundest, perfectest, and most indifferent rule; which rule is the law; I mean not only the law of nature and of God, but very national or municipal law consonant thereunto." This is followed by a passage which is notable not only for its exalted view of law, but also for its repudiation of the antique-medieval view that the best king would be better than the best laws. "Happier that people whose law is their king in the greatest things, than that whose king is himself their law. Where the king doth guide the state, and the law the king, that commonwealth is like an harp or melodious instrument, the strings whereof are tuned and handled all by one, following as laws the rules and canons of musical science." [89] Hooker continues his celebration of English rule by noting that even though all persons and causes are subject to the king's power, "yet so is the power of the king over all and in all limited, that unto all his proceedings the law itself is a rule." [90] Elsewhere he says that it "is neither permitted unto prelate nor prince to judge and determine at their own discretion, but law hath prescribed what both shall do. What power the king hath he hath it by law, the bounds and limits of it are known; the entire community giveth general order by law how all things publicly are to be done, and the king as head thereof, the highest in authority over all, causeth according to the same law every particular to be framed and ordered thereby. The whole body politic maketh laws, which laws give power unto the king, and the king having bound himself to use according unto law that power, it so falleth out, that the execution of the one is accomplished by the other in most religious and peaceable sort." [91]

But this is only one side of Hooker's argument. Closer inspection of the ideas which appear to entail limitation upon government reveals that Hooker has qualified them so severely as to deprive them of their value as restraining principles. He employs the idea of consent again and again, but it is an excessively loose notion. At best it is little more than a convenient peg on which to hang points directed against the Calvinists, and at worst it contains no trace of the modern idea at all. At one point, for example, we learn that in such polities the command of an absolute monarch may be taken to represent the assent of the people.[92] Again, in a passage in which Hooker deploys the idea that power rests fundamentally with the people, he goes on to ask the crucial question. "May then a body politic at all times withdraw in whole or in part that influence of dominion which passeth from it, if inconvenience doth grow thereby? It must be presumed, that supreme governors will not in such case oppose themselves, and be stiff in detaining that, the use whereof is with public detriment: but surely without their consent I see not how the body should be able by any just means to help itself . . . Such things therefore must be thought upon beforehand, that power may be limited ere it be granted." [93] Men should have had the foresight, then, to impose suitable limitations upon the king at the time of the original agreement. This is surely rather cold comfort, and it is worsened by the fact that Hooker does not seem to have taken it seriously. Suppose that the progenitors of the English had done this. It would have been of little avail to Hooker's contemporaries, for he maintains that the terms of the original compact "for the most part are either clean worn out of knowledge, or else known unto very few . . ." [94]

It is this sort of difficulty which leads Hooker to formulate an interesting expression of the doctrine of double majesty. He wishes to maintain that power derives from the people as a whole, but also that it rests with the king. Thus, if one compares "the body with the head, as touching power, it seemeth always to reside in both, fundamentally or radically in the one, in the other derivatively; in the one the habit, in the other the act of power." [95] Again, "whereas it is not altogether without reason, that kings are judged to have by virtue of their dominion, although greater power than any, yet not than all the states of those societies conjoined . . ." [96]

The strain of these contrary tendencies runs throughout Hooker's discussion, though he has clearly begun the shift of emphasis from *populus* to law. But even Hooker's resounding declarations on the limitations supplied by law are seriously attenuated by his perception of the problem that soon came to have a label all its own — the problem of sovereignty. It is on this more general level, too, that one encounters a cluster of statements which deprive the idea of limitation of its force. Supreme authority in the commonwealth devolves on a single source, for men recognize the inconveniences which beset a state with multiple authorities: "surely two supreme masters would make any one man's service somewhat uneasy in such cases as might fall out." [97] Elsewhere Hooker sets out the problem quite pointedly, locating supreme jurisdiction in a single source and denying that that source, the king, may itself be subject to lawful coercion. Jurisdiction, he says, "must have necessarily a fountain that deriveth it to all others, and receiveth it not from any; because otherwise the course of justice should go infinitely in a circle, every superior having his superior without end, which cannot be: therefore a well-spring it followeth there is, and a supreme head of justice, whereunto all are subject, but itself in subjection to none. Which kind of preeminence if some ought to have in a kingdom, who but the king should have it? Kings therefore no man can have lawfully power and authority to judge." [98] It is the king, then, who possesses supreme authority or dominion, and this embraces both civil and spiritual affairs. Everyone concedes this supremacy in secular affairs, says Hooker, but the great question is what power the king may exercise lawfully in God's causes. The answer is, the same fullness of power.[99] So, he concludes, "there is not any restraint or limitation of matter for regal authority and power to be conversant in, but of religion whole, and of whatsoever cause thereto appertaineth, kings may lawfully have charge, they lawfully may therein exercise dominion . . ." [100] The reason for this coalescence of powers in England is, according to Hooker, that in England all men are members of both the commonwealth and the Church of England. English society, therefore, is one.[101] Civil and spiritual organization are merely two aspects of the same society. It was just this, of course, which was being disputed. Hooker's insistence that there was no gap between the secular and spiritual aspects of English society led him, as one observer has commented, into a great and increasing fallacy.[102]

To be sure, Hooker argues that in England the laws provide that the king may do only some things alone, while others require the joint action of king and parliament. "The parliament of England together with the convocation annexed thereunto, is that whereupon the very essence of all government within this kingdom doth depend; it is even the body of the whole realm; it consisteth of the king, and of all that within the land are subject unto him: for they all are there present, either in person or by such as they voluntarily have derived their very personal right unto. The parliament is a court not so merely temporal as if it might meddle with nothing but only leather and wool." [103] Moreover, despite his exalted position the king does not possess priestly powers. He cannot perform ordination, administer the word or the sacraments, excommunicate, bind and loose, nor judge as an ordinary.[104] Thus the effective administration of powers in the state is fragmented. But, once again, Hooker's impulse to drive in the direction of a full-blown doctrine of sovereignty pulls his argument away from effective limitation and fragmentation of power. As before, he appeals to the principle that there must be a final authority, a court of ultimate appeal: "there is required an universal power which reacheth over all, importing supreme authority of government over all courts, all judges, all causes . . ." Thus, unlike the common lawyers of the early Stuart period, Hooker holds that the courts themselves cannot exercise this function. Nor can they oversee jurisdictional disputes, as Lord Coke was to claim. For that same universal power has as its function "to strengthen, maintain and uphold particular jurisdictions, which haply might else be of small effect . . ." [105] This same drift toward royal supremacy appears in Hooker's consideration of legislative matters. His doctrine is that whether "in states of regiment popular, aristocratical, or regal, principality resteth in that person, or those persons, unto whom is given the right of excluding any kind of law whatsoever it be, before establishment. This doth belong unto kings as kings . . ." [106] It is true that in "devising and discussing laws, wisdom is specially required: but that which establisheth and maketh them, is power, even power of dominion; the chiefty whereof, amongst us, resteth in the person of the king." [107] Any alteration in this arrangement would require a demonstration of necessary contrariety to the laws of God or nature.[108]

Hooker also raises the problem of equity, like St. Germain before him, and locates it in the king. It is the king's duty "to remedy that which they [the courts] are not able to help and to redress that wherein they at any time do otherwise than they ought to do. This power being sometime in the bishop of Rome, who by sinister practices had drawn it into his hands, was for just considerations by public consent annexed unto the king's royal seat and crown." [109] Thus the papal claim to ultimate jurisdiction in case of defect of justice is placed in the hands of the English monarch. Hooker employs the idea of equity, then, in the way St. Germain had, and for the same purpose: to unify the legal system. To be sure, the ordinary course of affairs ought to proceed according to the general rules contained in English law, but the king's equitable jurisdiction supplies him with a potentially powerful instrument of interference, should the need arise. As the following years demonstrated, it was an effective device. In the argument just cited, Hooker does not actually use the language of equity, but he deals with the problem in another place and there refers to this discretionary jurisprudence as "public equity." He raises the perennial problem of general rules as against the uniqueness of particular cases and says that general rules are "cloudy mists." [110] That is why there is a "special equity" from which proceed privileges, immunities, exceptions, and dispensations. "Not that the law is unjust, but unperfect; nor equity against, but above, the law, binding men's consciences in things which law cannot reach unto. Will any man say, that the virtue of private equity is opposite and repugnant to that law the silence whereof it supplieth in all such private dealing? No more is public equity against the law of public affairs, albeit the one permit unto some in special considerations, that which the other agreeably with general rules of justice doth in general sort forbid . . . principles and rules of justice, be they never so generally uttered, do no less effectively intend than if they did plainly express an exception of all particulars, wherein their literal practice might any way prejudice equity." [111] Since men pursue their own particular benefit, they cannot be left "to judge what equity doth require" in their own cases. The remedy is to locate that power in a single authority. Once again, Hooker identifies this discretion as having formerly rested with the pope.[112]

Despite all the difficulties of the argument, however, Hooker did succeed in solving his primary problem. It is perfectly clear that all questions concerning the form, rites and ceremonies, and even a statement of the articles of faith to be held by the Church of England — that is to say, what men are to believe — are matters of probable truth and are, therefore, determinable by king and parliament as expressed in human law. In the name of public unity, the law may "require men's professed assent, or prohibit contradiction to special articles, wherein, as there haply hath been controversy what is true, so the same were like to continue still, not without grievous detriment to a number of souls, except law to remedy that evil should set down a certainty which no man is to gainsay." Hooker is clearly sensitive to the bearing of his argument, for he admits that it may well be unclear why "human laws should appoint men what to believe." [113] But while he is aware of the difficulty involved in his claim, it is the doctrine he wishes to espouse; yet his effort to make it palatable is unclear and unpersuasive. He says that "the law doth not make that to be truth which before was not . . . but it manifesteth only and giveth men notice of that to be truth, the contrary whereunto they ought not before to have believed." [114] The presumption, then, is that king and parliament will declare the truth infallibly and so cannot depart from the truth. The truth, therefore, is not in any danger. All the same, it is bound to appear to men that change has been effected, for it is impossible to solve empirical problems with definitions. Hooker does not solve any problems with this verbal trick, any more than does the legal theory which holds that what the court says is law currently must always have been the law. The past is error, then, but change there is, however one looks at it. Injured consciences notwithstanding, Hooker concludes that "to define of our church's regiment, the parliament of England hath competent authority." [115]

It is clear, then, that Hooker's work is shot through with ambiguities. Indeed, these are puzzling enough to make it impossible to say whether they amount to formal contradiction or not. It does seem clear that he did not settle resolutely on any of the principles which might have been employed to unify the system. Because this is so, his argument really drives in four directions: towards royal sovereignty, the ultimate supremacy of the national law of England, the sovereignty of the body politic, and the traditional doctrine of the joint supremacy of king and parliament. He ought not to be condemned overmuch for this, however, for it was typical of the times. Indeed, his very confusion is what makes us most indebted to him, for it serves at once as a codification of past and present ambiguities and as a superb introduction to the immediate future. For the several threads which were so intricately interwoven in

Hooker's work could be unravelled and emphasized singly, and that is substantially what happened in the pre-civil-war period. St. Germain had supplied the double emphasis on royal equity and English law, and Hooker broadened and embellished both in his effort to fashion a philosophically grounded general theory. The traditional doctrine of double majesty survived in St. Germain's work without being subjected to any examination; it is simply there, lying alongside the new set of emphases. But in Hooker's work, matters are quite different. For despite the multiplicity of doctrine, all the elements are cast in legal terms, which involves an element of rigidity that had not been a characteristic of the traditional outlook. This is, necessarily, the case when a political process is converted into a legal principle. It remained for the common lawyers, above all Sir Edward Coke, to attempt the task of piecing together a body of concrete rules to fit the legal scaffolding. But Hooker obviously anticipated future developments in quite another direction. For royalists could as easily take up the arguments which drove in the direction of royal supremacy.

It was in this way that the issues at stake were both sharpened and broadened in the first half of the seventeenth century. The most remarkable feature of the debate, however, was its indecisiveness. For despite an undeniable increase of clarity, none of the parties succeeded in cutting to the heart of the ambiguity in the received tradition. Still, double majesty had come to be expressed in terms of legal principle instead of a loose working notion about the appropriate terms of political cooperation, and the result was theoretical deadlock. That was to be the outstanding feature of political thinking before the outbreak of civil war. The next chapter is devoted to an exploration of the theoretical and political perplexity produced by the new combination of legalism and double majesty.

nine Law and Prerogative: Legal Deadlock

English political thought in the first four decades of the seventeenth century centered on a single great issue: the relation between the royal prerogative and the common law. This was a broadened form of the contrast between law and equity which had been launched on its course under Tudor auspices. During the first two decades of the century, the seriousness of the collision between these principles was masked by the particularity of concrete disputes. At bottom, these principles represented entirely different, indeed, incompatible ideas of legitimacy and organization. In this sense, the coexistence of law and prerogative was the seventeenth century form of double majesty. As the arguments progressed, however, the issues gradually came to be generalized. As Thorne has said, the contrast between law and equity widened until "they were mutually exclusive, equity gradually becoming synonymous with and confined to the justice, independent of the common law, administered by the Privy Council, Chancery, the Star Chamber, and the Court of Requests." [1] The opposition to the jurisdictional claims of the prerogative courts argued that the common law governed all matters of jurisdiction. The result was a series of jurisdictional disputes and, in the end, legal deadlock.

This condition of stalemate was reflected in the political and legal thinking of the period. It produced resentment, bafflement, and inconclusiveness. This chapter undertakes to describe the theoretical reaction by focusing on the work of three authors. The first of these is Edward Hake, an Elizabethan common lawyer, whose work straddles the moods of the Elizabethan and Stuart periods. He operates on the assumption that the political order rests securely on the foundation of cooperation between prince and parliament. But he also expresses the common lawyers' anxiety and resentment of equitable jurisdiction, thus foreshadowing the fundamental disagreement which emerged under James I. The other two writers to be discussed are Sir John Eliot and Sir Edward Coke, both of whom were outstanding leaders of the opposition to the crown. But their intellectual reactions to the developing crisis were entirely different. The disjunction between the aims of parliament and king involved Eliot in bafflement. On the level of practical politics he was one of the Stuarts' principal parliamentary opponents. Yet when he came to set down his views in writing, he managed to deprive himself of any theoretical justification for his own behavior, for he embraced a doctrine of royal supremacy. It was the great common lawyer, Sir Edward Coke, who framed the legalistic ideology which gave tone to the opposition. It was he, above all, who sponsored the claim that the common law was a controlling body of pre-existent law, whose main principles, at least, were fundamental. It was the common law which prescribed and guaranteed the place and function of the various organs of English government. But Coke failed to achieve a solution to the legal deadlock, for he did not regard even the common law as sovereign. The king retained important, independent prerogative powers.

The crucial point is that the jurisprudence of regal conscience was institutionalized in the Chancery, and it came to be realized that it "depended solely upon the prerogative and was a prerogative court — the court of the king's absolute power." [2] Before the period of the civil wars, the reply of the opposition proved to be too narrow and too traditional to constitute a viable alternative. True to their inheritance, Englishmen were content to frame distinctions in regal capacities rather than confront the possibility that king and parliament might be involved in an unresolvable dilemma. "It was assumed that a proper understanding of monarchy would supply the solution of the problems of constitutional law." Attempts to reach such an understanding were cast in terms of the prerogative itself. It was argued that the prerogative power was of two sorts: ordinary and absolute, disputable and indisputable, or separable and inseparable. The great difficulty was that whichever distinction one preferred, the independent power of the monarch survived. The opposition made the mistake of trying to meet the claims of prerogative power on its own terms. The result was that crucial issues remained unresolved to the last, for the king still possessed "the powers of appointment, of arrest, of issuing commissions and patents, of staying execution and of pardoning offenders, of convoking and dissolving Parliament . . . in short, most of the governmental machinery of the country, and the right of dealing with it within the precedents to be found in the common law." [3]

The essentially conservative appeal of the opposition to what were coming to be called the fundamental laws was inadequate because enshrined there were not only what men were now referring to as the safeguards of their lives, liberties, and property, but also the independent and indefeasible prerogatives of the king. In 1628 Sir John Davies proudly declared that the common law surpassed "all other lawes in upholding a free Monarchie, which is the most excellent forme of government, exalting the prerogative Royall, and being very tender and watchfull to preserve it, and yet maintaining withall, the ingenuous liberty of the subject." [4] As late as 1640 an outstanding parliamentary writer, Henry Parker, maintained that "by the true fundamentall constitutions of England, the beame hangs even between the King and the Subject; the Kings power doth not tread under foot the peoples liberty, nor the peoples liberty the kings powers." [5] That is how matters were supposed to be, nor had anyone yet said anything very different from this. But in the presence of the sort of profound political disputes which occupied the years 1640–1642, it gradually became clear that the legalistic version of double majesty would not support the claims of either king or parliament.

In the meantime, however, thought and action continued to be grounded in the traditional framework, though its translation into a legal form gradually became more pronounced. Comparatively mild and narrowly framed criticism of the challenge of equity to the common law began to find expression in Elizabethan times. A good example of the character of this early protest is supplied by Edward Hake's work, *Epieikeia,* subtitled, "A Dialogue on Equity in Three Parts." The most interesting aspect of this work is that it is not preoccupied with the great constitutional questions which were soon to absorb the energies and wit of English lawyers, politicians, and theorists.[6] The principal points which Hake was concerned to make may be summarized thus. In the first part of the dialogue, he denies that there is a great disjunction between equity and law. The second part undertakes to show that, contrary to what many have assumed, the common law possesses its own proper equity; and this leads to an interesting discussion of the nature of

English government. The principal discussion in the third part is an effort to compare the Chancellor's equity with that of the common law.

Hake begins by setting forth what is meant by equity and goes on to deny that there is a hiatus between equity and law. The discussion starts on a note of resentment. The original intention of his work, Hake says, was to describe the equity practiced in the Chancery and thus to show that "the common lawe is not so severed from Equity as amongste many hath bine fondlye conceived," nor should it "be so often (as it hath bine) refused as helples . . ." Hence, "the Chauncery shoulde not be resorted unto but uppon some pointe of conscience byeng helpless and succorles at the Common lawe." [7] But, he says, he soon realized that this enterprise required him to discuss equity in general. He proceeds, therefore, to a rehearsal of opinion on the question.[8] It would appear, at first glance, as if equity were something outside the law, something imposed upon it. But this is not true. On the contrary, it is of the law itself. It is an exception, to be sure, drawn from the law of God or the law of reason, but "an exception secreatlie understoode in every generall rule of every posityve lawe." Equity exhibits the "secreat sense and hidden (but the righte and trewe) meaning of the lawe . . . not [to] chaunge the lawe, but . . . to sett the lawe in his right place, and rather to give life to the lawe which otherwise in the letter thereof would be dead." [9] In short, equity follows the intent of the law.[10] Equity, then, is to be found in the law itself and, Hake adds, if someone were to ask him who was to apply it, he "wolde saye — *per artificem,* that is to say, by the judge or expositor of the same law." In the event that even the equity of the law is defective, "then the only waie is to flye unto the supreame authority for the supplye of a newe lawe." [11]

At this point, one of the interlocutors in the dialogue, Eliott, raises another point, which was to be debated more hotly in the near future. Is it not dangerous, he asks, to leave judges with this much liberty? Hake's reply is that those who have remarked on this problem referred not to the equity of the law but to judicial decisions which are flatly contrary to law. Moreover, this sort of objection is not even germane, because their topic is the exposition of law, not its alteration; these are two entirely different things. The problem is not really difficult. All it requires, according to Hake, is a righteous and knowledgeable judge.[12] Actually, of course, Eliott's question raises one of the most intractable problems in legal theory. Pious repetition of the axiom that it is the office of the judge to interpret and apply law, not to make it, solves no problems.[13] But it was important for the partisans of the common law to show that this was the path of certainty, while equity, as Selden would have it, was "the same that the spirit is in religion, whatever one pleases to make it." "Equity is a roguish thing, for Law we have a measure, know what to trust too; Equity is according to the Conscience of him that is Chancellor, and as it is larger or narrower so is equity. 'Tis all one as if they should make the standards for the measure a Chancellor's foot; what an uncertain measure would this be? One Chancellor has a long foot, another a short foot; a third an indifferent foot; it is the same thing in the Chancellor's conscience." [14] In Hake's work one finds this view shadowed out, though it has not yet been infused with the bitterness of political strife which was to characterize it later.

The corollary of the doctrine of certainty in the common law is the idea of the artificial reason of the law. Once again, in Hake's treatise the idea is not set forth with the full ideological trappings that Sir Edward Coke later supplied. Hake says only that the equity which is intrinsic in legal rules should be construed by the judge in accordance with his craft. Coke's doctrine is the same, but it is expressed with an intensity and reverence appropriate to a period in which fundamental disagreement was coming to be recognized. According to Coke,

> reason is the life of the law, nay the common law itselfe is nothing else but reason; which is to be understood of an artificial perfection of reason, gotten by long study, observation, and experience, and not of every man's naturall reason . . . This legall reason *est summa ratio*. And therefore if all the reason, that is dispersed into so many severall heads, were united into one, yet could he not make such a law as the law of England is; because by many successions of ages it hath been fined and refined by an infinite number of grave and learned men, and by long experience grown to such a perfection, for the gouvernement of this realme, as the old rule may be justly verified of it, *neminen oportet esse sapientiorem legibus:* no man (out of his own private reason) ought to be wiser than the law, which is the perfection of reason.[15]

This was the doctrine which Coke set against the claims of King James I to legal knowledge based on natural reason, and against the jurisprudence of conscience practiced in the Court of Chancery. But the exponents of equity were not without an answer. Lord Chancellor Ellesmere accused the common law judges of engaging in the same sort of discretion: "the Judges themselves," he said, "do play the Chancellors Parts upon Statutes, making Construction of them according to Equity, varying from the Rules and Grounds of Law, and enlarging them *pro bono publico,* against the Letter and Intent of the Makers, whereof our Books have many Hundreds of Cases." [16] It is, in short, a variation on an ancient theme: theoretical positions lying poles apart are virtually indistinguishable on the level of fact. For, as Thorne has observed, "the substitution of the *ratio legis* for *epieikeia* did not in fact confine common law judges more closely than they had been or lead to results more limited than those reached earlier." [17]

The second part of Hake's dialogue undertakes to argue that, contrary to what many have assumed, the common law possesses its own proper equity. The equity of the common law, the author says, concerns either exposition or the giving of actions. Expository equity consists in abridging or enlarging the letter of the law. On the level of actions, equity means either giving "an action where none before was at the Common lawe, or else in equalling of actions . . ." Hake notes that the records of English law do not expressly mention equity. Nevertheless, he argues, there are plentiful examples of the practice; they only lack explicit avowal.[18] He then proceeds to expound a considerable number of cases.[19] It should be observed, once again following Thorne, that the cases he cites do not support his thesis. The contemporary idea is, instead, read back into the cases.[20] Hake assumed that medieval judges had been practicing equity when they undertook to extend or restrict rules, whereas theories of equity developed only much later. Hake was anxious to make out that the rules of the common law themselves were filled with equity, even if secretly. But the older practice of interpretation turned on no such theory. St. Germain's view was nearer the older practice. For him, it was a question of departing from the law in the name of the law of God or the law of reason. Medieval practice was cavalier in the extreme. Hake, on the other hand, insists that equity is in the law; to practice equity is to appeal to the intent of the law itself. In spite of the obvious difficulties, Hake persuades his companions. Lovelace says Hake's discussion has demonstrated that it is an error to think of the common law as "severe, sharpe and inflectible . . ." Rather, it is now clear that its exposition is guided by equity, which signifies "sweetnes, gentlenes, goodnes, myldnes, moderation and such like." He is persuaded "that the Common lawes of England are altogither guyded and ruled by Equity." A little later Eliot says the common laws "permitt themselves to be expounded by Equity and to be directed by Reason, the mother directrex of all humane lawes." [21]

Hake also develops an interesting discussion of English government in this part of his treatise. It is of particular interest because it stands between the medieval version of double majesty and the interpretation of the earlier half of the seventeenth century. The shift is made from a political to a legalist emphasis. England was passing from a *dominium politicum et regale* to a *dominium regale et legale;* the partners in double majesty were becoming the king and the law. Moreover, there had begun to emerge the ideology of legalism: the idea that all the institutions and jurisdictions of English government were controlled by the common law. Hake's brief and rather casual observations on government take their departure from a problem raised by the king's exercise of his prerogative. The imprisonment of persons, contrary to the Magna Carta, is "by the absolute power of the Prince, of which to dispute at this tyme or at any other tyme, for my part, I acknowledge myselfe a greate deale to weake . . . I will rather reverence and obaye it then in any the leaste degree seeme to drawe it into question or dowbte . . ." Is the prince above the law then? Not exactly. For Hake has several quite different things to say. First he advances an apology for prerogative power. There are in "this presuming age," he says, many grave offenses for which the ordinary punishments of the law are insufficient. Moreover, there are the "greate ones" — unruly magnates, in other words — who defy the processes of the law.[22] It should be recalled, on this point, that the king's Court of Star Chamber was a popular institution in Tudor days. For the disruptive effects of baronial disorder in the fifteenth century had produced a persistent legacy of apprehension, of anxiety for the keeping of the peace. The Tudor monarchs handled the problem very well indeed, and their instrument was precisely prerogative jurisdiction. It is thus understandable that a Tudor lawyer would be loath to attack the prerogative courts. Indeed, the common lawyers had to be driven into outright opposition by the full-scale attack on the jurisdiction of the ordinary common law courts which was part of the policy of James I. They were certainly a reluctant and cautious opposition. But in Hake's time matters had not come to this, and the result was that he only fumbled with the problem. Having pointed to the need for prerogative courts, he goes on merely to offer a presumption of royal rectitude. Referring to his statement on the prerogative, he says, "And yet I must tell yow that my meaning is not hereby so to affirme of the absolute power or royall estate of the King as that it will admitt of any wrong to be done by the Prince to the subiecte, for there are dyvers good cases in our bookes wherein the royall estate of the Kinge may be discerned to be of that sanctity as that it will in no wise doe wrong unto the subiect." This is a perfectly orthodox if not particularly helpful medieval doctrine. But then, as if to support it, Hake goes on to cite a case from the fifteenth century which he glosses in such a way as to advance an entirely different idea. According to his reading, the case shows "that the King by his graunt can neither alter a lawe nor chaunge a lawe, so in all cases where the King's acte or graunte is against the lawe, the subiect is not holden thereby or bownde to the performaunce thereof by the absolute power of the Prince." [23]

This is clearly an important departure from the traditional notion of a king who ought to rule with counsel and consent. In fact, Hake's view represents the beginning of the new legalistic current in English thought which has so often been read back into even the early medieval period. It is clear that this view is not justified by the evidence. Actually, the legalistic outlook expressed by Hake only makes sense in correlation with the emergence of professional lawyers, permanent courts, and the keeping of records. And there was no more than a beginning of professionalization in the twelfth and thirteenth centuries. At that stage of development, however, judges were direct instruments of the royal will: witness the loyalty of the bench to Richard II in 1387. The real solidity and sense of professional identity in bench and bar cannot be separated from the appearance and development of those unique schools of English law, the four Inns of Court. Unfortunately, the origins of this peculiar "university," perhaps as early as the fourteenth century, are not at all clear. Sir John Fortescue boasted about them, however, toward the end of the fifteenth century. But the main point is that they entered on a clear and influential career in the Tudor period.[24]

It is thus no accident that a legalistic approach to politics made its appearance then.

But to return to Hake's argument. At the point where he says the subject is not bound by an illegal act of the king, Lovelace introduces a reference to the discussion of absolute power in Sir Thomas Smith's *De Republica Anglorum*. According to Hake, this is an entirely different matter. His own discussion is designed to cover only particular acts, while Smith raises the general question whether English government is "legall and regulate, or absolute, or whether it be partly regulate & partly absolute." Smith has shown clearly, Hake says, that English government is partly limited and partly absolute, just as Sir John Fortescue had done before him.[25] Here is a statement, in so many words, of the modern legalistic interpretation of the Middle Ages. All that is missing is the addition of the idea of fundamental or constitutional laws, and that was added in late Tudor and early Stuart times. The only difficulty is that it is inappropriate before that time. It has been shown that this was not Fortescue's opinion, with due respect to Hake and all the others who followed him in the interested use of medieval writings in the constitutional quarrels of the seventeenth century. What is most striking about those appeals, however, is not that they were employed as an ideological buttress for parliamentary opposition to the king, but that, on the contrary, the same documents and writers were used on both sides of legal debate. The reason is clear enough. For not only is it natural to expect both parties to appeal to their shared tradition, but the tradition literally contained both positions. That is part of the reason for calling it double majesty.

The actual conception of the Middle Ages was that English government was primarily the affair of the king, but that important alterations required the counsel and consent of the magnates. The leading impulse of the parliamentary opposition under James I and Charles I, on the other hand, was to claim that all the institutions of government were controlled by law. Hake's work supplies an early statement of this legalistic ideal. The English people are the freest in the world, for "whereas the peoples of all other nations and kingdomes, for the most part, are ruled and governed by the absolute beck, will and power of their Prince, only the Englishe nation is ruled and governed by the lawes of their countrey, or rather by their kings and rulers whose rule & government is according to their lawe, and not otherwise." The rule of the English king, then, is "lymitted and directed by her lawes . . ." [26] Here is the idea that politics is somehow governed dispassionately by law. But in Hake, as in the controversialists of the pre-civil-war period, the independent power of the monarch survived. There was the rub, and it required civil war to settle the issues which collected around the contrast between prerogative and law.

"But nowe, if upon all this matter yow will saye unto mee, what if the King shall in any of the aforesaid cases doe contrary to his said lawes, is there any power in or by the same lawe whereby to restreyne him? Surely, no, neither weare it fitt, safe or reasonable that there shold be any such restrayning, much lesse that any subiect might dare therein to controll the Prince afterwards . . . if any such thing should happen, this must be our only comfort, that the lawes of the realme are against it. And for the rest wee must referre it to the divine ultion . . ." [27] This conception seems quite medieval, at first glance. Yet the difference is significant, for in medieval doctrine the wicked prince was somehow no prince at all; acts of tyranny were a falling away from reality, not legality. According to Fortescue, even Herod's decree that the children of his kingdom should be slaughtered was law. Hake is sure that arbitrary acts of regal will are against the positive law of England. Indeed, the so-called statute Prerogativa Regis, which contains a long list of feudal prerogatives, is but "an affirmance of the Common lawe, and was made to put the prerogatives in more certainty, for . . . at the Common lawe the king had his prerogative." [28] Here appears yet another element of the modern interpretation: that English law is a translation of custom. Once again, however, the interpretation is in fact a notable departure from medieval doctrine, produced by lawyerlike resentment of royal equity and prerogative jurisdiction. That it was tailored to suit the needs and interests of the legal fraternity trained in the Inns of Court is obvious, for it is a doctrine which places all the important questions of jurisdiction in the hands of bench and bar. Hake's statement of the idea refers to a particular statute and so lacks the generality attained in the Stuart period, but in tone it hardly falls short of Selden's comment on the prerogative in the midst of the quarrels which eventuated in civil war.

> Prerogative is something that can bee told what it is, not something that has no name. Just as you see the Arch Bishopp has his prerogative Court, but wee knowe what is done in that Court,

so the Kings prerogative [is] not his will, or what Divines make it, a power to doe what hee lists.

The Kings Prerogative, that is the Kings Law. For Example, if you aske, if a patron may present to a living after six monthes by Lawe, I answer no. If you aske whether the King may, I answer, the King may by his prerogative, that is by the Law, that concernes him in that Case.[29]

This biting comment was produced by an outlook alien to the Middle Ages. As the civil war approached, the climate of opinion which had made kings sacrosanct began to dry up. "A King," said Selden, "is a thing men have made for their owne sakes, for quietness sake." [30] To be sure, royalist authors advanced arguments that raised kingship to unaccustomed theoretical heights. But kings now had unaccustomed competition.

The third and last part of Hake's dialogue is anticlimactic. Its principal aim is to point out the difference between the jurisprudence of conscience and the equity of the common law and to urge, indirectly, that the former is too frequently employed. Civil lawyers, Hake says, appear to hold that when the law "in anything cometh shorte, there it oughte to be supplied by the *Equity* of the Chauncellor, who (saye they) is to gather owte of his owne brest, by comparing the lawe and circumstances of the present facte togither, what the same, if it had breathe and life in the present case, wolde have determined." It is true that the equity practiced in Chancery is derived solely "from the conscience of the Lord Chaunccellor," and that it takes account of circumstances. "But what of this? Doe not the Common lawes of England admitte circumstances also?" The difference is that the Chancellor's equity considers matters which are "owte of or beside the case." The circumstances considered in Common law are not "collaterall or owte of the case, much lesse contrary to the lawe, but . . . are circumstances which may stand with the case and which maie best declare the justice and righteousness of the lawe . . ." [31]

Hake tries to show that even though the Chancellor's equity helps where the common law does not, this does not mean that the law is defective. The "cause why the law helpeth not is indeed for that it will not helpe, neyther wolde it ever have bine the minde of the law maker to have holpen in such a case if the case had bine foreseene unto him." [32] The reason for this quaint argument is that consideration of individual cases would be a general inconvenience, and that would be dangerous to the commonwealth. This really undercuts the rationale for equity in favor of general rules, and so, if it proved anything, it would prove more than Hake appears to have intended. This is not a stricture against Hake. The difficulty is embedded in the problem of considering the merits of general rules as against decisions tailored to unique circumstances. The problem was raised and discussed by Plato and Aristotle, and it remains unsolved.[33] For Plato and Aristotle, the contrast lay between the unfettered operation of intelligence, in the form of the philosopher king or Aristotle's wise man (the *phronimos*), the man who knows how to hit the center of the moral target, and the application of general rules to particular cases. The Greek bias was for free intelligence, though Aristotle took account of the frailties of the position more soberly than Plato. Thus Plato's Athenian Stranger says that general rules of law are like the orders of "a self-willed, ignorant man . . ."[34] Generally speaking, until the close of the sixteenth century, political and legal theories inclined to the Greek view. Again and again, theorists raised the problem of whether it was better to be ruled by the best man or the best laws. Theoretically, the best man, the righteous prince, was the preferred alternative. Modern thought runs to the contrary opinion and is crystallized in the ideal of rule by laws rather than by men. As Judge Learned Hand has put it, "it would be most irksome to be ruled by a bevy of Platonic Guardians, even if I knew how to choose them, which I assuredly do not. If they were in charge, I should miss the stimulus of living in a society where I have, at least theoretically, some part in the direction of public affairs."[35]

This ancient dispute comprises one aspect of a celebrated debate in contemporary American constitutional law over what is now most often called judicial self-restraint as contrasted with judicial activism.[36] The fact that the contrast between discretion and general rules is the core of the current debate, however, should not be allowed to obscure its modernity. For the curious and peculiarly modern dress of the discussion is marked. The most recent contributions have centered on the merits or faults, as the case may be, of the position taken by Justice Frankfurter, on one side, and that of Justice Black on the other. Justice Frankfurter and those who support his views take the position that consideration of the merits of the case avoids foisting a rigid, mechanically applied general rule on the multifarious problems of American law. Justice Black and his partisans, replying that this increases the scope of judicial discretion rather than constricting it, support the principle of judgment by general rule. Thus both camps claim to occupy the side of the angels, or rather the modern angels, because both assert that their views vindicate the rule of law rather than men. The debate is bound to continue, but it is less important here to consider a solution to a problem which has involved reflective men in bafflement for centuries than to point out the deep contrast between the modern legalist posture and the contrary bias of antique and medieval thought.

Once again, Hake stood midway in the passage from medieval to modern patterns of thought. He was of two minds on the view that the commonwealth was better off ruled by the best man than by the best laws.[37] On balance, however, he came down on the side of law, while attempting to preserve a place for the Chancellor's equity. Within a very few years, however, common lawyers had seized one horn of the dilemma, and Hake's mediatory position was abandoned. In the context of Stuart policy, they elected government by the general rules of the common law. This is what accounts for Coke's assault on Chancery and, indeed, all the prerogative courts. This is the period in which the peculiar reverence for the rule of law crystallized into a meaningful and potent political theory, from which much modern opinion descends.

The medieval inheritance, then, had begun to undergo profound alteration, the heart of which was the assertion that the common law supplied the answers to all mooted points of jurisdiction. But this view, even at the pinnacle of its career in the work of Coke, failed to solve the political problems of the early seventeenth century, and the theoretical reason was that it did not reduce the monarchy to a mere administrative office. Not even Coke denied that such matters of supreme political importance as foreign affairs were subject to the royal prerogative. The difficulty was that the commons were no longer willing to entrust that function to the Stuarts. The dilemma was severe, and until the 1640's the labors of the opposition produced only legal deadlock. The platform of the common law was simply too narrow to support the widening claims of the commons. The kind of difficulty in which the leaders of the opposition found themselves is nicely illustrated in the views of Sir

John Eliot. Eliot was one of the principal leaders of the commons in the 1620's. Indeed, it was under his leadership that the House of Commons collided so bitterly with Charles I in 1629 that Charles set out on his course of eleven years of rule without parliament. Eliot was an outspoken, impetuous man — so much so, that the king had him, among others, confined to the Tower following the parliamentary wrangle of 1629. Eliot died in the Tower in 1632.[38] During his imprisonment he composed a treatise entitled *De Jure Maiestatis*. He there sponsors the view that in the last resort final authority rests with the king. As Hill has observed, even Eliot, "slowly being done to death in prison for acting on the principle that Parliament's authority must prevail over the King, was unable to express this idea in theoretical form. This remarkable stop in the mind was not peculiar to Eliot. It was shared by all the Parliamentarian leaders before 1640." [39] They had not yet shrugged off their medieval inheritance, and the chief reason lies in the peculiar nature of the opposition to the king. For it was led by common lawyers, who were stuck fast in the conservative sentiments natural to lawyers. As was mentioned earlier, they had to be driven into opposition by remarkably foolish royal policies.

According to Sir John, sovereignty consists in the supreme power and honor in any commonwealth. It is indivisible.[40] Indeed, if "wee doe suppose that Kings & people have both equall power against one another neither cann be called cheife . . ." To suppose that there are two powers in the state is to destroy the nature of order. The subject cannot even partake in sovereignty, for "partakers of sovereignty are equal to Majesty and Majesty perishes . . ." Again, "to have equall power destroyes the definition of Majesty." [41] In contrast to the body of traditional political thought, this is a startlingly clear and unambiguous position. It appears, in fact, to be an assimilation of the ideas of Jean Bodin, which were circulating in England by this time. However this may be, a new logical rigor in the discussion of *majestas* is evident. Indeed, Eliot has verbally abandoned the idea of double majesty and embraced a doctrine very close to the concepts of sovereignty formulated in and after the period of the civil wars. The main theoretical difference is that the later conception included the notion that sovereign power is by definition arbitrary power. More importantly, Eliot acted in terms of double majesty but wrote in terms of royal sovereignty. Ironically, this parliamentary leader chose the wrong horn of the dilemma, for the ambivalence of the tradition of double majesty was solved in both theory and practice by the idea of parliamentary sovereignty. Be that as it may, his new logical rigor was a remarkable achievement.

Eliot goes on to say that possession of full majesty entails the proposition that the ruler is free of law.[42] More properly, he is not subject to coercion by law but is nevertheless to govern according to law and reason. But the king's transgressions are not punishable by human law. Majesty "cann neither be judged, punished, brought into order, deposed, &c., of any, but of god alone, to whom only he is to make his accompt." At this point, Eliot draws a distinction between law and morals which is quite alien to medieval thought. The king is freed from law, for "the very vertue & generall force of all lawes is to compell & punish. And hear lies the very maine difference, between law & vertue . . . law drawes by fear & foule meanes; vertue persuades by fayr reasons." The very life of law is its execution by a superior power.[43] Law, therefore, is not what Cicero thought it was: "it is not soe much reason imbred in nature as Tully thinkes, that is the fountaine of lawes: as it is power to compell obedience, which they must have from Majesty. Otherwise lawes would be but like spiders webs, which greater flies would breake through. Every fearfull hare can say I prescribe equity to all, but lyons would but laugh at rules of rights, if superiour power doe not compell them to obey." [44] To be sure, kings are bound by the law of God and the law of nature, the latter being the golden rule. Moreover, it is fitting that kings should abide by law of their own accord, though they cannot be compelled to do so. All that differentiates a true king from a tyrant is that the true king will not do what he may do.[45] In "case of necessity there is noe doubt but that the Kinge may impose hard things upon his subjects, albeit it be against the positive and written lawes . . ." [46] Punishment, therefore, is left to God, but kings would do well to remember it.[47]

To reinforce his discussion on this point, Eliot turns aside to attack several of the leading books in the monarchomachic tradition, condemning their advocacy of resistance as "false doctrine, pernicious to princes, pestilent to comonweales." If the people were allowed such a right, the door would be opened "to all libertie, licence, rapine, spoile, rebellion, etc." A king is not even bound by his coronation oath, for "they are not Kings because they take an oath but because they are Kings therefore doe they swear." [48] More generally, this means that the idea of a contract embodied in the coronation oath is worthless as a principle justifying resistance. A king does not become king because he is crowned; he is crowned because he is a king. In short, regal rule is not contingent upon the acceptance of certain conditions. Even if there were a contract, the people would be bound to maintain their original submission.[49] John Selden entertained the same view. "If our fathers have lost their libertye — whether may wee not labour to regaine it. Ans[wer]: we must looke to the contract; if that be rightly made wee must stand to it. If once wee grant [we may recede] from contracts upon any inconvenyance, may afterwards happen wee shall have noe bargain keept." [50] Such was the opposition view before the 1640's. In 1647 it was the view of the conservative wing of the revolution. At the Putney Debates, Henry Ireton replied to Leveller demands with an argument precisely like Selden's. The notion that men are free to break engagements "is a principle that will take away all commonwealth[s] . . ." [51] "Covenants freely made, freely entered into, must be kept one with another. Take away that, I do not know what ground there is of anything you can call any man's right . . . we are under a contract . . . and that agreement is what a man has for matter of land that he hath received by a traduction from his ancestors." [52] Not only does Eliot subscribe to this view, he goes on to argue that the king is not even bound by his predecessors, nor can he bind himself. Kings have an obligation to observe laws, but only because that was the original compact with the people. This is partly a matter of mere prudence, for if the laws are too frequently undone, the commonwealth will dissolve. But it is also a matter of principle, for contracts made for the public good are binding. Here Eliot appeals to the laws of God and nature, as well as the public good.[53]

In the Second Book of *De Jure Maiestatis,* Eliot repeats his view that sovereignty is indivisible but says that its several rights, which are called prerogatives in England, may be distinguished. Even so they are inseparable from majesty; they "attend it as the shadow the body for they doe flow out of the nature of Majesty . . ." [54] Without them, no government can subsist. He divides these into greater and lesser rights, and the Second Book is given over to a discussion of the greater rights: the making of laws, the creation of magistrates, the making of peace and war, the establishment and maintenance of religion, and control of the coinage. These greater rights

of majesty "cleave to the bones and person of an absolute prince
. . . [and] cannot be separated from him without destruction of him
noe more then can the sun beames from the sunn . . ." [55]

Eliot's royalist view of majesty and its prerogatives is sustained
in his discussion of law. He tells us that law or right is threefold:
divine, natural, and positive or civil. Divine law contains the unchanging rules requisite to living a right and godly life; these are
partly revealed in Scripture and "partly engraven on the mindes
of men in their first creation . . ." [56] Natural law is right reason, the
light of divine truth left in men's minds since the fall. Consisting of
unchanging precepts which enable men to distinguish between virtue and vice, it is the foundation of all virtue. Since these precepts
are engrafted in the nature of man, they are the common possession
of all men, commanding what should be done and forbidding the
contrary.[57] Neither princes nor popes may do away with natural
law or divine law, although in cases of extreme necessity a prince
may dispense with them, provided that no sin is committed thereby.
More particularly, majesty may not revoke a man's last will and
testament or break its own contracts, for these are principles of the
jus gentium and the natural law. Even in the case of divine and
natural law, however, the prince "may declare them, and with due
weighing of the circumstances apply them to the diversity of facts
with equity . . ." [58] A king, therefore, is rightly called a living law,
the fountain of justice, and lawmaker (*lex animata, fons justitiae,*
and *conditor legum*). He is the "umpire and lord of his owne actions,
to alter them upon good occasion of state . . ." [59]

The Third Book is a discussion of the lesser rights of majesty,
which Eliot calls fiscal rights. These are not inherent in the nature
of majesty. The principal discussion concerns the right of property.[60]
Here the king's dominion is limited to jurisdiction, while each man
is "private lord over his owne goods and estate . . ." Still, all tenure
in England is held from the king, so that he is every man's lord,
while the individual is the owner.[61] The king's lordship means that
"if in some case supreme power be compelled to lay hands uppon
private goods: subiects must take it in as good part as things naturall
doe when we see them destroyed of the universal cause, lest the universe should want his order and perfection." [62] However, the prince
must have a just cause, namely the public good, for otherwise he
offends against justice.[63]

The editor of *De Jure Maiestatis,* Alexander Grosart, was clearly puzzled by Eliot's generous view of the royal prerogative. "One has a feeling," he says, "that even so clear-headed and strong-brained a man as Eliot had a superstitious idea of 'the King.' In his treatise he makes prodigious concessions of 'right' to 'kings,' even to passing obliviousness of the kingdom's rights." [64] But this is just the point. The "kingdom" did not have rights, for Englishmen had not yet hit upon that general idea. For that matter, individual men did not have rights — not in the modern sense, at least. Rather, they were only the holders of various kinds of royal concessions, and this idea is, at bottom, incompatible with the idea of an individual or collective right. What is conceded to one is not his right, it is the right of him who grants it. Even the "right" of private property was exposed to the dangerously vague doctrines of reason of state and national emergency, so often employed by Charles I in his financial distress. From a theoretical perspective, it does not matter that many of the king's assertions of national emergency were bogus. It was the doctrine of the courts that the interpretation of emergency was a royal prerogative. Practically, however, it made all the difference in the world, for eventually it meant that parliament would arrogate that royal function to itself. Even the common law, despite its "fundamentals," proved to contain no definitive reply to the royal prerogative. It conceded to the king vast powers associated with matters of war and peace, and Charles had only to manufacture rumors of danger in order to exert the full force of the prerogative in domestic politics. In Bate's case (1606), the king's judges found that the king might levy impositions on imported goods because it was a matter of international relations, and in this sphere the national law did not impose limits upon him. In the five knights' case (1627), it was held that for reason of state the king might arrest persons without showing any cause. And in Hampden's case (1638), it was decided that the king could levy taxes without the consent of parliament in cases of necessity.[65]

It is not to be inferred, however, that the parliamentary opposition and the common lawyers in particular had no reply to these claims. The theoretical difficulty was that their answer was inconclusive. The opposition recognized, as Holdsworth has said, "that both the king . . . and Parliament, had important functions in the state; and it aimed at delimiting their respective spheres of action." [66] Sir Edward Coke is often singled out, quite rightly, as the best possible representative in the early Stuart period of the ethos of legalistic resistance to the crown. His thought embodies both the affirmations and the uncertainties in the outlook of the prerevolutionary opposition. Coke was an outstanding figure. He reached the pinnacle of the legal profession in the reign of James I. In 1606 he was named Chief Justice of the Court of Common Pleas and in 1613 he became Chief Justice of the King's Bench. He employed both positions to launch an attack on the prerogative courts, the aim of which was to subordinate them to the courts of the common law. His was a commanding and vigorous personality which tended to dominate his brethren on the bench. The result of his leadership was a series of jurisdictional altercations between the common law and prerogative courts. In 1616 Coke managed to collide with his monarch head-on, and the result was his removal from the bench. It was said to be common knowledge that " 'Four P's have overthrown and put him down, that is pride, prohibitions, premunire, and prerogative.' " The king's faithful servant, Francis Bacon, held a view more politic in 1616. "The twelve Judges of the Realm," he said, "are as the twelve lions under Solomon's Throne. They must be lions, but yet lions under the throne, being circumspect that they do not check or oppose any points of sovereignty." [67] Coke was not deterred, for he promptly repaired to parliament and continued to ventilate his views on the proper functioning of the political order. For the rest of the pre-civil-war period, however, the bench was a supine instrument of the crown. Both James I and his son practiced removal of objectionable judges. In the end, this produced the doctrine of judicial tenure during good behavior rather than during the pleasure of majesty.

Coke's dismissal served only to sharpen the contrast between prerogative power and law. Bacon drew the moral of the collision of 1616, for "when James I decided the dispute between the common law courts and the court of chancery in favor of the latter, Bacon pointed out that the order made the Chancery the court of the King's 'absolute power.' " [68] Sir John Davies, addressing himself to Lord Chancellor Ellesmere, describes him as "the sole judge of that High Court which is *Sedes misericordiae,* and therefore exalted above al seats of Iustice: where he hath *Potestam absolutam,* as well as *regulatam,* in binding and loosing the proceedings of the law, and in deciding causes by the rules of his owne conscience." [69] That was the difficulty in a nutshell, for it will be recalled that Hake's mediatory position had turned on distinguishing between absolute and regulated powers rather than identifying both with the king's conscience. But to provide any remedy for this circumvention of double majesty involved a degree of resistance to the king that the common lawyers were clearly reluctant to initiate.

Strictly speaking, Coke was not a theorist. He left no sustained and orderly treatises on such a plane. Like that of his contemporaries, it was Coke's habit of mind to conceive of legal and governmental principles in the plural. The result of such an outlook was that no general theory of the constitution was developed in explicit terms. Men thought and spoke in terms of fundamental laws, rather than fundamental law. The whole body of the law was similarly plural. For Coke it was a cluster of discrete rules and privileges. He said much of rights and privileges, but his language shows that the generality and universality peculiar to the modern conception of rights were not to be found in his world. This is well illustrated by his explanation of the word "liberties." For Coke, the word meant three things.

> 1. First . . . it signifieth the Laws of the Realm . . . 2. It signifieth the freedomes, that the Subjects of England have; For example, the Company of the Merchant Tailors of England, having power by their charter to make ordinances, made an Ordinance, that every brother of the same Society should put the one half of his clothes to be dressed by some cloth-worker free of the same Company, upon pain of forfeit . . . and it was adjudged that this Ordinance was against Law, because it was against the liberty of the Subject, for every Subject hath freedome to put his clothes to be dressed by whom he will . . . 3. Liberties signifieth the franchises, and priviledges, which the Subjects have of the gift of the King, as the goods, and chattels of Felons, Out-Laws, and the like, or which the Subject claim by prescription, as wreck, waife, straie, and the like.[70]

Still, there is a legitimate sense in which one may say that, for Coke, the constitution of England was grounded in the common law. Coke himself said nothing so general as this. His own pronouncements were singular and normally addressed to particular jurisdictional questions. Hence any attempt to extract a general theory from his writings cannot help being a departure from his own perspective. In short, his views have to be pieced together. Yet what emerges from the welter of common law rules and privileges is the notion that somehow the law is controlling. All the institutions are founded on the common law. Some of these are coordinate, in the sense that they are not subject to control by some other organ, while others are merely derivative from the principal institutions. But the ultimate guarantor of each, in its appropriate sphere, is the common law. The determination of jurisdictional disputes is the office of the common law courts. In this way, the common law takes on the character of a fundamental law, or rather, a collection of fundamental laws. This persistent pluralism comes out well in Coke's discussion of Magna Carta. "This parliamentarie charter hath divers appellations in law. Here it is called Magna Charta, not for the length or largenesse of it . . . but it is called the great charter in respect of the great weightinesse and weightie greatness of the matter contained in it in a few words, being the fountain of all the fundamentall lawes of the realm . . . This statute of Magna Charta is but a confirmation or restitution of the common law . . ." [71]

Like Hake's work, Coke's announces the new legalist dogma that English statutes are merely a codification of the customary law of England. It is probably Coke's work that has supplied the inspiration for what was called in an earlier chapter the fundamental law perspective on medieval and early modern political thought. Certainly Coke was the leading exponent of what was in fact a comparatively new idea. Thus he divided the law of England into three parts. First there was "the common law, which is the most general and ancient law of the realme . . . 2. Statutes or acts of parliament; and 3. Particular customes . . . I say particular, for if it be the generall custome of the realme, it is part of the common law." [72] It is clearly the common law which occupies the place of honor. This is obvious in the famous exchange between Coke and James I, as it is reported by Coke. The king, he says, held that

> the law was founded upon reason and that he and others had reason as well as the judges. To which it was answered by me that true it was God had endowed his Majesty with excellent science and endowments of nature, but his Majesty was not learned in the laws of his realm of England, and causes which concern the life, or inheritance, or goods, or fortunes of his

subjects are not to be decided by natural reason but by the artificial reason and judgment of law, which law is an act which requires long study and experience before that a man can attain to the cognizance of it; and that law was the golden metwand to try the causes of the subjects, and which protected his Majesty in safety and peace; with which the King was greatly offended, and said that then he should be under the law, which was treason to affirm: to which I said that Bracton saith Quod rex non debet esse sub homine, sed sub Deo — et lege [that the king ought not to be under any man, but under God and the law].[73]

The chief recommendation of the common law was its antiquity. To be sure, Coke did not deny that innovation in the law by parliamentary statute was a legitimate enterprise. But it was certainly marginal. The great thing was that the common law reached back through time immemorial: "the time prescribed or defined by law is, time whereof there is no memorie of man to the contrary." Prescriptive right was grounded on this notion of outrunning any record which might prove the contrary. Any record, including an act of parliament, was enough to cut it off. But the time must really be immemorial: "For if there be any sufficiente proofe of record or writing to the contrary, albeit it exceed the memory, or proper knowledge of any man living, yet it is within the memory of man." [74] Taking the common law as a whole, it was Coke's opinion, extravagant though it might be, that there was little in it that did not antedate the Conquest. Far from being a reproach, Coke found this enormously gratifying. "And (to speak what we think) we would derive from the conqueror as little as we could." [75] He prosecuted his unhistorical attitude as far as any one man could. Thus, according to Coke, the principal institutions of England dated at least from the Anglo-Saxon period and, no doubt, would have been discovered among the ancient Britons had it not been for the calamitous fact that the records of the Britons had vanished.[76] Coke was confident that some portions of the common law derived from the legislation of King Arthur.[77] Parliament, the Courts of Common Pleas and King's Bench, the Chancery and Exchequer, the Courts Baron, the office of the Lord Admiral, the jurisdiction of the Cinque Ports, jury trial, feudal tenure, and the division of England into counties all dated from Anglo-Saxon times.[78]

Coke's admiration for ancient usages was far from being mere antiquarianism, for in his view both reason and right itself rested secure precisely because they reached back time out of mind. This outlook was well expressed in his report on Calvin's Case. Thus, "we are but of yesterday, (and therefore had need of the wisdom of those that were before us) and had been ignorant (if we had not received light and knowledge from our forefathers) and our past, wherein the laws have been by the wisdom of the most excellent men; in many successions of ages, by long and continual experience, (the trial of right and truth) fined and refined, which no one man, (being of so short a time) albeit he had in his head the wisdom of all the men in the world, in any one age could ever have effected or attained unto. And therefore . . . no man ought to take upon himself to be wiser than the laws." [79] This entails a profound conservatism, of course, and Coke did not shrink from the implication. Law is the perfection of reason itself and therefore ought not to be changed. Indeed, "the wisdome of the judges and sages of the law have always suppressed new and subtile inventions in derogation of the common law. And therefore the judges say in one booke, We will not change the law which alwayes hath been used. And another saith, It is better that it be turned to a default, than the law should be changed, or any innovation made." [80] The method of legal wisdom, then, is not a matter of abstract reason; it is more a matter of excavation or exploration.

> Our student shall observe, that the knowledge of the law is like a deepe well, out of which each man draweth according to the strength of his understanding. He that reachest deepest, he seeth the amiable and admirable secrets of the law, wherein, I assure you, the sages of the law in former times . . . had had the deepest reach. And as the bucket in the depth is easily drawn to the uppermost part of the water, (for *nullum elementum in suo proprio loco est grave*) but take it from the water, it cannot be drawne up but with great difficulties; so albeit beginnings of this study seem difficult, yet, when the professor of the law can dive into the depth, it is delightfull, easie, and without any heavy burthen, so long as he keep himselfe in his owne proper element.[81]

Thus, despite Coke's attempts at ordering the patchwork of the common law, despite his obvious pride in its antiquity and its great reasonableness, it was not to be discovered so much by the use of reason as by plumbing the depths of English legal antiquity. Nevertheless, logic had a role to play in legal method. Coke's estimate of this emerges in his discussion of Littleton. Littleton was the sublime master of the appropriate "artificial reason and judgment of law." "He was learned also in that art, which is so necessary to a compleat lawyer; I mean of logick, as you shall perceive by reading of these Institutes, wherein are observed his syllogisms, inductions, and other arguments; and his definitions, descriptions, divisions, etymologies, derivations, significations, and the like . . ." According to Coke, Littleton combined both the necessary requisites: that sort of knowledge of the law which is drawn up from the well of the past, and the mastery of logic. This resulted in Littleton's treatise on tenures, which Coke thought was "the most perfect and absolute work that ever was written in any human science." [82] Legal method is thus a painfully acquired art, which fashions the wisdom of the ages into a suitable instrument for solving contemporary problems. "And by reasoning and debating of grave learned men the darknesse of ignorance is expelled, and by the light of legall reason the right is discerned, and thereupon judgment given according to law, which is the perfection of reason. This is of *Littleton* here called *legitima ratio,* whereunto no man can attain but by long studie, often conference, long experience and continuall observation. Certaine it is, that in matters of difficultie the more seriously they are debated and argued, the more truely they are resolved, and thereby new inventions justly avoided." [83]

The common law, then, was not justified because it conformed to the demands of abstract logic. On the contrary, it was self-justificatory. It contained within itself a principle of ratification, the idea of prescription, the operation of which meant that the common law had secured its place as the fundamental law of the realm. Even so, it would be going too far to say that Coke held a theory of sovereignty, even the sovereignty of the law. In the debates on the Petition of Right, the lords had introduced the notion that the petition must be understood to leave the king's sovereignty entire. Coke exploded. "I know that prerogative is part of the law, but *sovereign power* is no Parliamentary word. Should we now add it, we shall weaken the foundation of law and then the building must needs fall. Take heed what we yield unto! Magna Charta is such a fellow that he will have no sovereign . . . If we grant this, by implication we give a sovereign power above all these laws . . . Let us hold our privileges according to the law." [84] It is clear enough that Coke did not regard the king as sovereign, but neither did he succeed in driving home the idea of a fundamental law. As Carl Friedrich has observed, "Coke was struggling to grasp clearly the concept of a basic law or constitution, but again and again got lost in medieval notions which were then still very much alive in English law." [85] Viewed from the perspective of the idea of sovereignty, Coke's opinions on all the major institutions were, to say the very least, ambiguous. To begin with, he was perfectly clear that the common law could be overturned by parliament. "The common law hath no controller in any part of it, but the high court of parliament; and if it be not abrogated or altered by parliament, it remaines still . . ." Again, the jurisdiction of parliament "is so transcendent, that it maketh, inlargeth, diminisheth, abrogateth, repealeth, and reviveth lawes, statutes, acts, and ordinances, concerning matters ecclesiasticall, capitall, criminall, common, civill, martiall, maritime, and the rest." [86] Echoing Fortescue, he says that "Parliament is so high and mighty in its Nature, that it may make Laws; and that, that is Law, it may make no Law." [87]

Such statements as these must be borne in mind when considering the famous language of Dr. Bonham's case. There Coke delivered the opinion that "it appears in our books, that in many cases, the common law will controul acts of Parliament, and sometimes adjudge them to be utterly void: for when an act of Parliament is against common right and reason, or repugnant, or impossible to be performed, the common law will controul it, and adjudge such act to be void." [88] Numerous commentators, in search of precedents for the idea of judicial review, have fastened on this language as its origin. Perhaps this particular ghost has been laid to rest by Thorne.[89] He has shown that this passage gives but one reason among five, is one portion of a line of reasoning in the case, and that what Coke was engaging in is more appropriately construed as the practice of statutory interpretation. In particular, Coke was pointing out that a statutory privilege of the College of Physicians, which Bonham challenged, manifestly violated a basic tenet of interpretation because it made the college both party and judge in its own cause. The college had been granted the privilege of imposing fines on persons who undertook to practice medicine without its certification. The difficulty was that the college judged these cases itself and then pocketed a share of the fine. Moreover, there are general considerations which make it implausible to suppose that Coke's opinion in Bonham's case was an assertion of judicial review, for judicial review supposes a separation between legislation and adjudication that was not yet recognized.[90] Again, Coke himself appears not to have attached this sort of significance to the Bonham opinion. No such view appears in his *Institutes,* to begin with; and, as Thorne has said, this absence is an acute embarrassment for those who have been inclined to inflate this single utterance, quite out of context, into one of the most important statements in legal history. Finally, Coke explicitly regarded as valid a statute which he said violated the "law of the land" clause of the Magna Carta.[91] Surely this would have been an odd view for the alleged author of judicial review to entertain, especially since he had said that Magna Carta was "the fountain of all the fundamentall lawes of the realm." [92]

On the other hand, Coke did believe that the common law had an independent, objective existence, and that it was the foundation of the constitution. Although he did not generalize his views, the overall impact of the doctrines scattered throughout his work is striking. Consider, for example, the statement that the "interpretation of all statutes concerning the clergy, being parcell of the lawes of the realme, doe belong to the judges of the common law." [93] Parliament itself is called "a part of the frame of the common laws." [94] But the chief institution was the kingship. For Coke, the king occupied an office to which were attached a variety of prerogatives. These were of two kinds: separable and inseparable. The separable prerogatives, such as the king's private holdings, could be alienated by him, but the inseparable prerogatives could not be disposed of by the king's personal action. Not even parliament could perform the sort of surgery required to cut the inseparable prerogatives from kingship. "No act can bind the King from any prerogative which is sole and inseparable to his person, but that he may dispense with it by a *Non obstante,* as a sovereign power to command any of his subjects to serve him for the public weal; and this solely and inseparably is annexed to his person; and this royal power cannot be restrained by any act of Parliament . . . but that the King by his royal prerogative may dispense with it; for upon commandment of the King, and obedience of the subject doth his government subsist." [95] In the case dealing with proclamations Coke insisted that "the king hath no prerogative but that which the law of the land allows him . . ." [96] Again, the "common law hath so admeasured the prerogative of the King, as he cannot take, nor prejudice the inheritance of any." [97] But even Coke could not resist the king's acknowledged power in foreign affairs. As late as 1621 Coke said: "I will not examine the Kinges Prerogative. There is a Prerogative disputable and Prerogative indisputable, as to make warre and Peace; the other concernes *meum et tuum* and are bounded by Lawe." [98] The law protects private property, then, while preserving an independent sphere for kingship in matters of international relations. But this was exactly the difficulty. For the Stuart monarchs learned how to use the doctrines of reason of state and national emergency in domestic affairs, and the effect was to deprive men of their property without the consent of parliament.

Though Coke did not invent a doctrine of judicial review nor frame a theory of the sovereignty of law, his legal and political ideas were both the reflection and the best expression of the legalistic ideology cast up against the Stuart monarchy. Despite the fact that the political issues of the day could not be solved within the assumptions of the common law, the monarchy appreciated the magnitude of the challenge. When Lord Chancellor Ellesmere installed Sir Henry Montagu as Coke's successor as Chief Justice of the King's Bench, he gave expression to the royalist alarm and annoyance which Coke's efforts had produced. Ellesmere delivered an address to Montague, but, as Lord Campbell said, it was directed "*at* Sir Edward Coke . . ." [99] "Remember your worthy grandfather, Sir Edward Montague," said the Lord Chancellor, pointing out that *he* had not strained statutes in order to reach the Court of Chancery, nor denied that judges were not to proceed without consulting the king if so commanded. "*He* challenged not powers from this court to correct all misdemeanors, as well extra-judicial as judicial, nor to have power to judge statutes void, if he considered them against common right and reason, but left the parliament and the King what was common right and reason." Sir Henry replied that he would "not be busy in stirring questions, especially of jurisdictions." [100]

For the moment, then, the king had had the better of the legal collision which characterized the prerevolutionary period. This is not surprising, for there were abundant precedents for Stuart actions. English political and legal thought had long rested on the assumption that fundamental conflict between king and community would not develop. Yet that tradition was an inadequate frame of reference when such a disjunction finally did emerge. Thus Hake's work gives expression to the impulse to transform personal kingship into a matter of law, but it also reveals his inability or unwillingness to recognize what such an operation would involve. To legalize the royal prerogative would be to deprive the king of his regality, to make him, in other words, an officer of state, answerable for his deeds. Coke's legalism was much more elaborate and extended to a great many more discrete topics, but even he was reluctant to generalize. His many-sided ambivalence on the subject of the king's prerogative is as eloquent testimony to the legal perplexity of the time as one could wish for. Eliot, to be sure, seems to solve the problem of double majesty. But in some ways his work is even more interesting than the legalized form of the traditional outlook. For his solution was only verbal. At the level of political behavior he acted on the principle he had disavowed.

However, neither legal deadlock nor political action deprived of intellectual support was any bar to the ambitions of the affluent gentry (bent upon achieving political power commensurate with their economic strength), nor to the religious enthusiasm which demanded far-reaching changes in the organization and doctrine of the Church of England. On the contrary, they meant that the traditional frame of government would be shattered. The end of the tether was reached in 1628, when the parliamentary opposition extorted the Petition of Right from Charles I. During the period 1629–1640, Charles summoned no parliament. It was a period of prerogative rule, but it proved only that the monarchy could not subsist without the support of the House of Commons. The king's financial distress drove him to summon parliament in 1640, and it was the second parliament called in that year — the Long Parliament — that broke with the past. Parliament moved uncertainly to the heart of the matter but finally took the decisive step of eliminating the independent authority of the monarchy, for the regal will was simply incorporated into the will of parliament. It is at this point that the medieval formula of double majesty collapsed, as if at a stroke, for the Long Parliament had given birth to the idea of sovereignty and the unitary state. Thus a solution was achieved, but it required a sharp departure from the assumptions of the past.

ten From Kingdom to Commonwealth

The attempt of Charles I to rule without parliament, to govern England solely on the basis of the royal prerogative, broke down in 1640. The immediate occasion of the king's summoning of parliament was the outbreak of rebellion in Scotland against the attempts of the king and Archbishop Laud to ensure the reception of Anglicanism. The king's financial needs were thus suddenly made acute, and only parliament could supply a remedy. But discontent with the crown's religious policy was also widespread in England itself. Nor was this the only source of disaffection. From 1629 to 1640 the king had had to raise revenue in devious ways. This had led to intimidation through arbitrary arrest and prosecution of the recalcitrant in the prerogative courts. As a mode of justification, the king had adopted two ideas originally designed for the conduct of foreign affairs and, to the increasing alarm of his subjects, had applied them to the issues of domestic politics. Both these ideas — the doctrine of emergency and the notion of reason of state — proved to be elastic enough to suit the monarch's purposes. But the result was that when Charles could no longer avoid summoning parliament, the members' interest centered on the redress of grievances rather than the satisfaction of the king's urgent financial needs. The exasperated king dismissed the first parliament of 1640, the Short Parliament. But this proved to be a serious political mistake, for in fact he had no choice but to deal with parliament. His second summons, which produced the Long Parliament, served to underline his desperate need of money. Indeed, Charles acceded to all the demands of parliament until it was insisted that he relinquish control of the army. It was over this issue that the civil war began.

The eruption of armed hostility between king and parliament in 1642 ruptured the English political order, and when the monarchy was restored in 1660, it was set on an entirely different foundation.

From the perspective of the medieval tradition, the essential point is that the revolutionary movement accomplished what the medieval *populus* had never been able to do: it destroyed the independent authority of the monarchy. The traditional assumption that kingship somehow carried with it its own legitimacy was so far undermined that it could be doubted whether it ought to exist at all. In the end, indeed, that profound rejection of the past came to be positively affirmed. Majesty, in short, was to be double no longer. But there is a broader and more important point. The opposition in parliament had overthrown the tradition, but this had been accomplished on the narrowest possible platform. Parliament solved the problem of double majesty on its own terms, carefully avoiding any lofty theoretical ground. But in doing so it got a great deal more than it anticipated. For the assumption of sovereignty by the Long Parliament released an avalanche of political debate and speculation. This great debate was the first full expression of articulate civic consciousness. For the first time since classical antiquity, men undertook a completely general discussion of the nature and purpose of society and government from a humanistic standpoint. This linkage of ancient and modern civic consciousness and loyalty was deliberate, for it was perceived at the time. Thus Milton reminded his readers that it was the absorption of the literary tradition of antiquity that made the difference between his own day and Europe's barbarian past. It was to that "polite wisdom and letters," he said, that "we owe that we are not yet Goths and Jutlanders . . ." [1] This discussion involved deliberate, self-conscious exploration of the fundamental questions of the relationship which ought to obtain among men as fellow citizens and, in turn, between the whole body of citizens and their rulers. It is the appearance of this consciousness of the public dimension of the issues that separates the modern from the traditional political order of the Middle Ages.

To be sure, the realization that the issue at stake was nothing less than the constitution of England was not achieved immediately. Initially the quarrel between king and parliament was perceived and discussed in traditional and legal terms. It was only in the process of political activity and debate in the years immediately after 1642 that men came to appreciate the fundamental nature of their differences. This was novel in itself, but the really critical stage was reached only when consciousness of the public character of those differences produced a pronounced shift of the focus of attention from law to society in general. Discussion moved away from the language of fundamental laws and constitutions toward concern with the ultimate source of any legal and political obligation whatever. From the point of view of the history of ideas, the great instrument of change was that much maligned theory of the social contract, for it was the outlook expressed in contract thinking which transformed all the questions that had been under debate. Step by step parliament pre-empted the king's traditional authority and thus, all unwittingly, opened the way to the debates that eventually produced widespread and self-conscious concern with the problem of a new constitutional arrangement.

The legal deadlock that had developed during the first four decades of the seventeenth century was overcome in 1642 by the assumption of omnicompetence by the Long Parliament. But if the political theories advanced later may be called the high road to the new settlement, the parliament itself took the low road, for it stuck fast to traditional modes of argument.[2] The parliament was essentially a conservative, reluctant opposition composed of the great men of the realm. They had no wish to exaggerate the differences between themselves and their king. James Harrington, certainly one of the keenest political thinkers of the seventeenth century, made the point this way: "a nobility strikes not at the throne without which they cannot subsist, but at some king they do not like . . ."[3] Another acute observer said, "Many of the nobility and gentry were contented to serve his [King Charles I] arbitrary designs, if they might have leave to insult over such as were of a lower order."[4] It was certainly not necessary to be an outsider to appreciate this; the great men of the kingdom were perfectly well aware of the dangers involved in defying kingship. Thus Lord Clarendon remarked of William Cavendish, successively earl, marquis, and duke of Newcastle, that he "loved monarchy, as it was the fountain and support of his own greatness."[5] Indeed, the outlook of the privileged men of parliament was expressed in an official statement as late as August 1642. It was "most improbable," they said, "that the nobility and chief gentry of this kingdom should conspire to take away the law, by which they enjoy their estates, are protected from any sort of violence and power, and differenced from the meaner sort of people . . ."[6] The privileged orders of English society were loath to oppose the king, and the majority of them eventually repaired to the royal standard in the civil wars. It would be quite wrong to infer that the only motive entertained by such men was fear for their personal fortunes. Some of them, in fact, spent huge sums of money in the cause of royalty, and of episcopacy in religion. Moreover, a sense of both familial and social tradition — expressed in a sharply graded system of rank and status — earnest attachment to the established church, and genuine belief in the idea of personal loyalty to a king regarded as a sacred figure are all credible motives. Thus Sir Edmund Verney is reported to have said: "I do not like the quarrel, and do heartily wish that the king would yield and consent to what they [the parliament] desire; so that my conscience is only concerned in honour and in gratitude to follow my master. I have eaten his bread and served him near thirty years, and will not do so base a thing as to forsake him . . ." [7] Here is the familiar sentiment of personal fealty, and, as an eminent historian of the period has said, such affection probably moved many royalists.[8] Nor is there any reason to doubt the sincerity of this plea from Sir Edmund to his brother: "I beseech you consider that majesty is sacred; God sayth 'Touch not mine anointed.' " [9]

But even so devoted a royal servant as Lord Clarendon could be found in the opposition before the outbreak of the war. The king's high-handedness had alienated some of his natural supporters, at least temporarily. Though the Long Parliament certainly began hesitantly, perhaps even reluctantly, it was not deterred. It did choose to frame its declarations cautiously and narrowly, and it pretended not to depart from the path of legality. Selden recognized the oddity of the procedure and commented that the "parliamentary party, if the law bee for them, they call for law, if it bee against them they will goe to a parliamentary way." [10] It is this "parliamentary way" that requires examination. For however far removed from the radical political theorizing that was to follow, it was the Long Parliament that accomplished the decisive alteration when it divorced the king's natural capacities from his political capacities and itself absorbed the latter. But it was exactly the notion that kingliness is a personal attribute that constituted regality. This is exemplified in a statement which Queen Elizabeth addressed to her ministers: "as I am but one body naturally considered, though by His [God's] permission a body politic to govern, so shall I desire you all, my Lords, chiefly you of the nobility, every one in his degree and power to be assistant to me; that I with my ruling and you with your service may make a good account to Almighty God, and leave some comfort to our posterity on earth . . ." [11] The opposition in the Long Parliament met and overturned the tradition within the same universe of discourse. The intellectual device employed in this operation was the familiar distinction between the king and the crown which had emerged during the reign of Edward II. In 1308 it was the rationale of the baronial opposition, but by 1321 it was said to be the doctrine of the traitorous Despensers. The Despensers, it was charged, held that "homage and oath of allegiance is more by reason of the crown than by reason of the king's person and is more bound to the crown than to the person . . . Wherefore if the king by chance be not guided by reason, in the right of the crown, his lieges are bound by oath made to the crown to guide the king and the estate of the crown back again by reason, and otherwise the oath would not be kept." [12]

It was precisely by adopting and tightening the treasonous doctrine attributed to the Despensers that the Long Parliament carried out the reduction of the kingship to a mere office of the state, controlled by parliament. The radical surgery by which the king's natural and political bodies were severed from each other was not accomplished in a single stroke. On the contrary, the parliament worked into the assertion of sovereignty by degrees.[13] This is understandable, because the idea of a distinction between the king and the crown had been the crux of a most important law suit decided in 1608 and conventionally known as Calvin's case. Before his accession to the English throne in 1603, James I had been James VI of Scotland, and it was one of his fondest hopes that his accession would be recognized as having united England and Scotland. Unfortunately for the king's ambition, parliament refused to enact legislation recognizing the union. Calvin's case is another approach to this problem, and it illustrates the complexities of the legalistic version of double majesty.

According to English law no alien could hold land in England, but since James's accession the question was whether a Scot was still an alien. Thus, after 1603 certain English lands were claimed by inheritance on behalf of a Scottish child by the name of Calvin. Counsel for Calvin argued that since the child had been born after James came to the English throne, the personal allegiance owed by every subject to his king meant that Calvin owed the same allegiance as an Englishman; therefore, he could inherit English lands. Opposing counsel argued that the allegiance of Englishmen and the allegiance of Scots were two entirely different things, it being only accidental that both were owed to the same man; one man possessed two distinct royal offices, but this had no legal consequences. The most interesting opinion in the case is that of Sir Edward Coke. His problem was this: how to give the king the case, thereby avoiding what Coke admitted was the "damnable and damned opinion" in the case of the Despensers, and yet avoid deciding that England and Scotland had been unified through King James. If it was treasonous to hold that allegiance was due to the crown rather than to the king's person, how could Calvin's argument be met? Coke's answer was that allegiance was indeed due to the king's person. So Calvin had the same relationship of allegiance as an Englishman and could, therefore, maintain his suit. But Coke also held that this relationship did not unite the two kingdoms because it was a moral relationship which, like kingship, antedated all legal systems. Although by that time a legal stage of history had been reached, the prelegal relationship of allegiance still obtained. The result was that England and Scotland were two kingdoms with two different legal orders.[14] The frailty and complexity of this dual system is apparent. The main thing, however, is to observe that Coke's opinion involved the common law opposition in the denunciation of the idea of allegiance to the crown. To be sure, his opinion also involves accepting the distinction between the king and crown; but loyalty is still owed to the natural person of the king. Even this was unsatisfactory from a royalist perspective. As befitted a faithful royal servant, Lord Chancellor Ellesmere was profoundly alarmed by the use of the distinction.

> But in this new learning, there is one part of it so strange, and of so dangerous consequent, as I may not let it pass, *viz.* that the king is as a king divided in himselfe; and so as two kinges of two several kingdomes; and that there be severall allegeances, and several subjections due unto him respectively in regarde of his severall kingdomes, the one not participating with the other.
>
> This is a dangerous distinction between the King and the Crowne, and between the King and the Kingdome: It reacheth too farre; I wish every good subject to beware of it. It was

never taught, but either by traitors, as in *Spencers* Bill in Ed. 2. time . . .

This bond of Allegiance whereof we dispute, is *Vinculum fidei;* it bindeth the soule and conscience of every subject, severally and respectively, to bee faithfull and obedient to the King: And as a Soule or Conscience cannot be framed by Policie; so Faith and Allegiance cannot be framed by policie, nor put into a politike body . . .

Now then, since there is but one king, and soveraigne to whom this faith and allegiance is due by al his loyal subjects of *England* and *Scotland,* can any humane policie divide this one King, and make him two kings? [15]

This peculiar tension between king and kingdom was also the intellectual atmosphere in which debate moved in the early months of the Long Parliament's session. During the period of prerogative rule after 1629, however, the problem of arbitrary rule had been sharpened. For Charles I had been forced to resort to a variety of questionable means to raise revenue, including the unpopular tax called ship-money. There was a well-established obligation upon coastal towns to supply ships for the royal navy, but Charles extended the levy inland and began issuing writs for ship money annually. Widespread resentment and resistance developed, and John Hampden's refusal to pay brought the issue to court in 1637. The importance of the case was well recognized. Indeed, one judge expressed the view that it was "one of the greatest cases that ever came in judgment . . ." [16] It was decided that the king had the right to raise such a tax under conditions of emergency and, moreover, that the king was the judge of the existence of the emergency.[17] Nor was this all. One of the judges, Sir Robert Berkeley, went so far as to argue that he had "never read nor heard, that lex was rex; but it is common and most true, that rex is lex, for he is 'lex loquens,' a living, a speaking, an acting law." [18] It was this sort of extreme royalist view that alienated some among even the greater nobility, for, as Lord Clarendon said, the decision rested on "a logic that left no man anything which he might call his own . . ." [19]

Out of this setting came the later declarations of the Long Parliament. The first step on what proved to be the road to parliamentary sovereignty was the claim that parliament alone might determine who should supply counsel to the king — a question that had lain at the heart of medieval politics. But this affirmation was purely negative. It did not provide any rationale for legislation without the king. Soon such a rationale was needed, and the next stage of the debate centered on parliament's claim to decide whether a given bill was for the common good.

> There must be a Judge of that Question wherein the safety of the Kingdom depends (for it must not lie undetermined). If then there be not an agreement between his Majestie and his Parliament, either his Majestie must be the Judge against his Parliament, or the Parliament without his Majestie . . . if his Majestie in this difference of opinions should be Judge, he should be Judge in his own Case, but the Parliament should be Judges between his Majestie and the Kingdom . . . And if his Majesty should be Judge he should be Judge out of his Courts and against his highest Court, which he never is, but the Parliament should onely judge without his Majesties personal consent . . . And if the Kingdom best knows what is for its own good and preservation; and the Parliament be the Representative Body of the Kingdom, it is easy to judge who in this case should be the Judge.[20]

The parliament, then, might decide what was in the public good, without the king if need be. This absorption of the king's authority culminated in the parliamentary claim to legislate by ordinance without the king, indeed against his express (but merely personal) will. The rationale was the doctrine of the Despensers.

> The High Court of Parliament is not only a court of judicature, enabled by the laws to adjudge and determine the rights and liberties of the kingdom, against such patents and grants of His Majesty as are prejudicial thereunto, although strengthened both by his personal command and by his proclamation under the Great Seal; but it is likewise a council, to provide for the necessities, prevent the imminent dangers, and preserve the public peace and safety, of the kingdom, and to declare the King's pleasure in those things as are requisite thereunto; and what they do herein hath the stamp of royal authority, although His Majesty, seduced by evil counsel, do, in his own person, oppose or interrupt the same; for the King's supreme and royal

pleasure is exercised and declared, in this High Court of Law and Council, after a more eminent and obligatory manner than it can be by any personal act or resolution of his own . . . And the High Court of Parliament and all other His Majesty's officers and ministers ought to be subservient to that power and authority which law hath placed in His Majesty to that purpose, though he himself in his own person should neglect the same.[21]

So the king's personal will was no longer a political will at all; politically, his will was what the parliament said it was. As it turned out, this series of collisions was definitive. It wrote the obituary of double majesty. In the result, it marked the end of the Middle Ages, for it formed a prelude to nearly two decades of rich and various intellectual and institutional experimentation, in which the basic assumptions of medieval thought came to be widely disputed and finally abandoned.

To this point, the novelty of the struggle between king and parliament had been cast in an extremely narrow framework. The idea of double majesty had been repudiated without really extending the terms of the debate. Once that had been accomplished, however, some men came to recognize the magnitude and generality of the issue. John Selden, for example, saw that the rules of the law, fundamental or otherwise, had been outrun. He certainly cannot be accused of any lack of affection for the common law, but he saw clearly enough that its ground rules were no longer relevant. "The King and Parliam[en]t now falling out, are just as when there is offered foule play betwixt Gamesters. One snatches the others stake, they seize what they cann of one anothers. 'Tis not now to be asked, whether it belongs not to the King to doe this or that; before when there was faire play it did, But now they will doe both, what is most convenient for their owne safety . . ."[22] If one bears in mind the ambiguities of the tradition of double majesty, the perception of Philip Hunton, in his *A Treatise of Monarchy* (1643), illustrates the alteration in perception extremely well: "To demand which Estate may challenge this power of finall determination of Fundamentall controversies arising betwixt them is to demand which of them shall be absolute." Even more revealing is the following statement of Hunton's. Recognizing that king and parliament were hopelessly deadlocked, he observed that "in this case, which is beyond the Government, the Appeal must be to the Community, as if there were no Government . . ." [23]

This was the key-note, as it were, for the great debate in which the entire perspective of the Middle Ages was overthrown and the concept of public consciousness emerged. The critical point was precisely the realization that the issues under debate were questions of public import. It was this that enabled men to transcend the original terms of the debate — a more or less limited contest between king and parliament, couched in traditional concepts — and to bring into issue the general question of the relation of all men to any government whatever. Once the perception was gained that the problem was fundamental and general, the social contract theory became the vehicle which carried really novel ideas into politics. For it was the libertarian and egalitarian premises involved in the contract theory that destroyed the hierarchical universe which was the object of medieval speculation. Contract thinking depicts men as essentially equal, discrete, and autonomous units of will, whose consent is the only legitimate source of obligation. This broad conception involves the repudiation not only of the basic assumption of a static and graded social order, but also the whole style of a traditional political order: ancestral piety and reverence for the past, the personal and familial nature of obligation and loyalty, and the fragmentary and local character of organization and interests. Sir Henry Maine suggested long ago that the deepest sort of social and legal transformation furnished by our experience was precisely of this sort. It is what he called the transition from status to contract.[24] In recent years, it has been suggested that the social alteration Maine intended to convey by his famous phrase has wide applicability in the study of contemporary underdeveloped societies.[25] Certainly many of these are presently involved in various stages of the transition to modernity from a traditional past. That is essentially the change that occurred in English history in the years after 1640.

It is important to note, however, that there was considerable hesitation and even flat resistance to the reorientation of standards implied in Maine's notion of the passage from status to contract. The privileged orders, who resented the erosion of social barriers, knew that many of the "meaner sort" now felt that the gentry had "been our masters a long time and now we may chance to master them . . ." [26] The social anxiety of the nobility and greater gentry led, of course, to a determined defense of the old order, which in substance meant cleaving to the legalistic version of double majesty. Thus neither the legalistic ethos nor attachment to order and hierarchy was by any means eliminated. Nor indeed have they ever been. But the revolutionary period did have the effect of shattering uniform attachment to the principles of the tradition. The result was the immensely important fact that an entirely different image of society and politics was available as the foundation for systematic prosecution of alternative public policies. It is not difficult to see that the existence of differing general views is essential to the creation and maintenance of constitutional government. For neither party politics nor principled opposition — that is, enduring and organized expression of policy alternatives — is possible otherwise. Moreover, the occurrence of the great debate in England during the revolutionary period meant that the traditional view itself was altered. For it would either have had to acquire a public focus or sink into irrelevance. The most general point, then, is not that the past was erased; on the contrary, it survived in a new setting, that of public consciousness.

Thus the sort of disagreement, within the accepted framework of legalistic double majesty, which had been the chief feature of the pre-civil-war period was broken in 1642. Those who clung to it in the following years were those sympathetic to the king's cause, and many of those who were not royalists in the early stages eventually migrated into the royalist camp. Thus Judge Jenkins maintained even in 1647 that the "law of this land hath three grounds: First, custom: secondly, judiciall records: thirdly, acts of parliament. The two latter are but declarations of the common law and custome of the realme touching royall government; and this law of royall government is a law fundamentall." [27] Sir Roger Twysden said it seemed to him that "there is no rule for either the liberty of the subject or the prerogative of the king but the law of the land, which in some sense may be said to be the genus, and they the two distinct species." [28] Here, certainly, is a fine expression of the view that the political order contains no political principle, no sovereign, but is governed by law. But at that juncture it was a view without a setting. The consensus on which an established legal system reposes had evaporated. Even Judge Jenkins recognized the extremity of the situation, though his legalist faith survived: "the King declares it treason to adhere to the Houses in this war, the Houses declare it treason to adhere to the king. What surer guide to action, therefore, has the subject but the law of the land?" [29] A sure guide was exactly what the law of the land was not. But it is interesting to observe that what had become a clearly royalist view by 1647 was not far removed from the earlier parliamentary outlook. This may be gathered from the opinion of so staunch an opponent of the king as James Whitelocke. During the debate over the king's impositions in 1610, Whitelocke allowed that "soveraigne power is agreed to be in the king: but in the king is a two-fold power; the one in parliament, as he is assisted with consent of the whole state; the other out of parliament, as he is sole, and singular, guided by his own will." Disputed questions ought to be resolved by resort to the law. The king's attempt to levy impositions without parliamentary consent, for example, "subverteth the fundamentall law of the realme, and induceth a new forme of state and government." [30]

It is not surprising to find royalists cleaving to the traditional outlook. What is much more interesting is that the radical opposition began its migration to a new political theory from the same platform. That is, the demand for liberty and equality was at first grounded on a purely traditional idea. This was the curious but widely received notion that the object of the revolution was to recover the Anglo-Saxon laws and liberties which had been destroyed by the Norman conquerors.[31] Thus, according to *A Remonstrance of Many Thousand Citizens* (1646), the expectation was deliverance from "Norman bondage . . . and from all unreasonable Lawes made ever since that unhappy conquest." [32] The great Leveller organizer and political pamphleteer, John Lilburne, began with the traditional idea. He says, for example, that he has "as true a right to all the priviledges that do belong to a free man as the greatest man in England whatsoever he be . . . and the foundation of my freedome I build upon the grand Charter of England . . ." In another tract, he admits that the House of Commons is the supreme power, since they "have residing in them that power that is inherent in the people . . ." Nevertheless, they are "not to act according to their own wils and pleasure, but according to the fundamentall constitutions and customes of the Land, which I conceive provides for the safety and preservation of the people . . ." [33] Employing the familiar diction of the common lawyers, Lilburne informs his readers that English law is "the perfection of reason, consisting of lawful and reasonable customs, received and approved of by the people, and of old constitutions and modern acts of Parliament . . ." [34]

The appeal, then, was at first expressed in terms of tradition and the task seen as a recovery of the distant past. But, as Hobbes said, a future was being fashioned from a conception of the past.[35] As the political debates went on, it became clear to the more radical parties that both the past and the existing legal systems were an inadequate foundation for their claims to equality and liberty. The levelling impulse, indeed, is already present in the statements just quoted from John Lilburne. But as yet Lilburne and those who thought like him had not moved beyond the level of replying to the tradition with a broader interpretation of the same tradition. But vigorous opposition to their desire to equalize men before the law and to extend the franchise drove the radicals on to high theoretical ground. In terms of the view just discussed, the crux of the matter was the radicals' repudiation of history as a source of validation. This was the really critical step. For whatever the substance of their proposals — whether radical or modest — the mode of validation was profoundly radical. By abandoning precedent they moved, as Christopher Hill has said, "from historical mythology to political philosophy." [36] This involved outright rejection of ancestral piety and opened the way to a total re-evaluation of authority and obligation. Thus Lilburne's friend William Walwyn argues with him that "Magna Charta hath been more precious in your esteem than it deserveth; for it may be made good to the people and yet in many particulars they may remain under intolerable oppression." Actually, he says, it is only "a part of the peoples rights and liberties, being no more but what with much striving and fighting was . . . wrestled out of the pawes of those Kings, who had by force conquered the Nation." Walwyn sees the opposition movements of the Middle Ages as unbelievably narrow, roused only "by accident or intollerable oppression," and aimed only as far as affirmation of the Magna Carta. But far from being the sheet anchor of English liberty, Magna Carta is merely a "messe of pottage." [37] Richard Overton was even more emphatic. Addressing himself to Parliament, he said: "Ye know the laws of this nation are unworthy a free people, and deserve from first to last to be considered and seriously debated and reduced to an agreement with common equity and right reason, which ought to be the form and life of every government. Magna Carta itself (being but a beggarly thing, containing many marks of intolerable bondage) and the laws that have been made since by Parliaments have in very many particulars made our government much more oppressive and intolerable." [38] Of course, criticism of Magna Carta and subsequent laws did not necessarily involve abandonment of the myth of Anglo-Saxon liberty. Certainly, however, there were those who were not prepared to rely even on pre-Conquest history. One of the participants in the Putney debates observed that "the Norman laws were not slavery introduced upon us, but an augmentation of our slavery before." [39] But whatever the view of the state of freedom before William the Conqueror, the abandonment of argument from precedent and the refusal to ground duty in history opened a deep gulf between past and present. Here is profound intellectual revolution in a nutshell: "whatever our forefathers were," said Richard Overton, "or whatever they did or suffered, or were forced to yield unto, we are the men of the present age, and ought to be absolutely free from all kinds of exorbitancies, molestations or arbitrary power." [40] For Overton, even the testimony of medieval historians was worthless: "whereas it's spoken much of chronicles, I conceive there is no credit to be given to any of them; and the reason is because those that were our lords, and made us their vassals, would suffer nothing else to be chronicled." [41]

So the past was irrelevant. What standards were to replace the old ones? The radical parties were driven to the criteria of utility, reason, and natural right, and it was the generality of these standards which gave radical argumentation the quality that so shocked the more conservative brethren, even within the revolutionary camp. This difference of view inside the revolution emerged sharply in the Putney debates of 1647. These were a series of discussions, extending over several days, in which various proposals for a constitutional settlement were argued within the revolutionary New Model Army. Together with a number of collateral documents from both the more conservative army leaders and the radical Leveller pamphleteers, the debates at Putney supply abundant illustrations of a number of important points. To begin with, they demonstrate that serious differences of opinion had appeared inside the revolutionary movement. In short, the critical question as to how far the revolution ought to go had arisen. They also provide an immensely instructive case of collision between fundamentally different judgments concerning what matters most in politics — probably the best confrontation of this kind since Greek antiquity. For in the last resort the numerous disagreements over specific issues come down to what may very well be irreducible differences of temperament. The conservative parties to the debate recur again and again to the same principles of justification: history, tradition, precedent, and law. Similarly, their radical opponents always return to the rationalism of the theory of natural rights. Moreover, it is not just the methods of justification that are important. On the contrary, both the general theories of politics — particularly the idea of a social contract — and the specific proposals based on them are extremely significant. For it is these which present a permanent alternative to the hierarchical system of the medieval past. Finally, the character of political behavior and ideas had been revolutionized by the appearance of public consciousness.

It is true, of course, that the Putney debates and the political radicalism which emerged there represent only a small portion of political argument in the period. Moreover, the radicals both in and out of the army, and more particularly the Levellers, did not possess or acquire any lasting political influence. Nonetheless, these debates and the literature produced by them supply perhaps the best single example of the intellectual revolution which occurred during the civil war. Furthermore, despite the ephemeral character of their part in high politics, it remains true that they possessed at least momentary leverage, for at this juncture Cromwell could not afford to dispense with their support. Once the radicals had introduced their ideas, the terms of the argument could not really ever be the same again. This is best illustrated by the obvious and simple fact that after the interregnum the prime political value of the radicals, liberty, came to be the accepted touchstone in discussing the nature and merits of the English political order. Unless the impact of the radicals' insistence on liberty as the principal test of the worth of institutions is recognized, it becomes impossible to understand the nearly universal agreement on the subject which emerged in the latter half of the seventeenth century and which came to be accepted in the eighteenth century as the center of what was so widely believed to be the political genius of the English people. It was precisely liberty that was supposed to be ensured by the institutional arrangements called mixed monarchy; and everyone agreed that that described the English constitution. But liberty was certainly not the cardinal value of the most influential political groups, if, indeed, it was a value at all. The political revolution was made by the largely Calvinist gentry, and they were unconcerned with the value of liberty. It was, instead, the relatively small and politically weak minority that introduced the modern idea of individual liberty into European history. The point is, however, that the idea came to be widely embraced and endured long after the radicals themselves had passed into obscurity.

On the surface, the debates center on two major questions: whether the army is bound by certain engagements relating to the constitutional settlement proposed to parliament by the leaders of the army, and the extent of the franchise to be established. In fact, these two issues serve as the occasion to raise many of the most important problems of political theory. The depth of disagreement is evident from the outset, for the radicals challenge the validity of the army's engagements in the name of justice. At this stage of the argument, however, it is not clear what content will be given to the idea of justice. What emerges most clearly is the radicals' disavowal of the ideas of self-validating contractual obligation and passive obedience. It is the argument over the extent of the franchise that brings out the substance of the radicals' conception of justice. It calls above all for liberty, by which they mean literal consent to government and laws and the marking off of certain areas from the scope of governmental authority. The principal matter to be made thus free is religious belief. Justice also means a broad equality before the law, that is, abolition of privileged treatment for the nobility.

The first major problem in the debates, then, is the nature of obligation. The radicals undertake to dispute their leaders' engagements on the ground that no contract is self-validating, for "if it were not just it doth not oblige the persons, if it be an oath itself." Thus, contractual obligation is to go the way of precedent; neither supplies any justification for an unjust agreement. The conservative reply to this view, presented by Ireton, is that a logical extension of the radicals' principle would involve anarchy, for all authority could be indicted in the same way: "this is a principle that will take away all commonwealth[s] . . ." [42] The charge of anarchy was indignantly denied,[43] and no doubt quite sincerely, but Ireton was perfectly right. At the level of fact, there is no doubt, the Levellers did not advocate anarchy, but they had no answer at the level of principle. Their doctrine of natural rights was radical, for in their view it involved a very far-reaching individualism. Thus John Wildman held that he "or any commoner" had a perfect right to advance his conception of "what is fit for the good of the kingdom." [44] It is true that no one really worked out all the implications, whether to extend or to restrict them, so that it is not at all clear what should be inferred from them. What the radicals did realize, however, was that from the position developed by Henry Ireton one could infer tyranny just as easily as anarchy could be attributed to their position. For Ireton's view was that the foundation of all right is in keeping covenants. "Covenants freely made, freely entered into, must be kept one with another. Take away that, I do not know what ground there is of anything you can call any man's right." But like the laissez-faire interpretation of contract in American constitutional history, this is a view which refuses to countenance the fact that not all men are free to refuse to enter into palpably unjust contracts. However, even this is not the end of the matter. For Ireton goes on to empty the idea of consent to government of all its real content, in precisely the same way as Hooker had done. English law and the existing distribution of property rest on a covenant "received by a traduction from [our] ancestors . . ." [45] The consequence of this view is that passive disobedience is as far as one can go; if it is felt that a covenant cannot be performed in good conscience, one must accept whatever penalties attach to abandoning it. At this point, of course, it is not easy to see how Ireton could justify his own participation in the revolution, for his view is that one may not act on unlawful principles unless the kingdom cannot survive without doing so. But as the Leveller John Wildman had already pointed out, submission to an unjust law is a dangerous principle. [46]

Thus far there has come to light only an obviously deep division over the question of how far the revolutionary movement is to proceed, and an abstract collision between appeals to history and law and those to justice. But the argument over the extent of the franchise gives a very good idea of the content of both views. The debate on this question was precipitated by a reading of the first article of the Levellers' Agreement of the People, according to which the elective power of the people should be proportioned according to population. The two major alternatives were well put by Ireton. The language of the Agreement, he says, "doth make me think that the meaning is, that every man that is an inhabitant [of England] is to be equally considered, and to have an equal voice in the election" of members of parliament. This he wants to object to. On the other hand, "if it be only that those people that by the civil constitution of this kingdom, which is original and fundamental" have such a right, then he has no objection.[47] Ireton's own position, reiterated throughout the debate, is that no one has a right to the franchise who has "not a permanent fixed interest in this kingdom . . ."[48] This means possession of a landed estate.[49] The radical reply was given by Colonel Rainborough. "I do hear nothing at all that can convince me, why any man that is born in England ought not to have his voice in election of burgesses. It is said that if a man have not a permanent interest, he can have no claim; and [that] we must be no freer than the laws will let us be . . . [But] I do not find anything in the Law of God, that a lord shall choose twenty burgesses, and a gentleman but two, or a poor man shall choose none; I find no such thing in the Law of Nature, nor in the Law of Nations."[50] The depth of the differences of principle, then, is perfectly clear. Rainborough's radicalism, indeed, runs almost as deep as Rousseau's, for he considers that the only free man in the kingdom is the elected knight of the shire.[51]

The radical appeal to natural right drove the debate to another level, in which the issue was whether any government or any property right was consistent with the doctrine of natural right. In the course of this argument there appeared the egalitarian and libertarian sentiments that mark this period off so sharply from the Middle Ages. Once again, Ireton carries the burden of the conservative side of the argument. He says he would have "an eye to property," for it is "the most fundamental part of the constitution of the kingdom . . ."[52] The result of giving the franchise to the poor might very well mean a law abolishing property.[53] Rainborough's reply consists of two points, which he insists on throughout the debate. The first is that he wants to know how it is that the franchise is only the property of some men.[54] His second point is a denial that the consequence of his views would be either anarchical or destructive of property. This contention turns on a distinction between two rights that had been confused in medieval political thought: private property — "estates and those kinds of things, and other things that belong to men" — and a political right. As far as the political right is concerned, Rainborough says flatly that "the law of the land in that thing is the most tyrannical law under heaven."[55] What else, he asks, have we fought for? What of all the common men who have fought for parliament in the war?[56] Edward

Sexby adds that since liberty was the object of the war, it is "a wonder we were so much deceived." Have we "fought all this time for nothing?" Addressing himself to Ireton and Cromwell, representing the conservatives, Sexby says that if what they maintain is true, it would have "been good in you to have advertised us of it, and I believe you would have [had] fewer under your command to have commanded." [57]

The gulf between great landed property and broad citizenship as alternative social foundations for government is by now abundantly clear. As Rainborough points out, there is a "great deal of difference between us . . . If a man hath all he doth desire, [he may wish to sit still]; but [if] I think I have nothing at all of what I fought for, I do not think the argument holds that I must desist as well as he." [58] In short, the parties to the debate have entirely different conceptions of the ultimate aims of the revolution. According to Ireton, what was sought was parliamentary rule, and that has been achieved. He considers that the well-being of the people is ensured by the establishment of parliamentary authority to override the king's will.[59] This was certainly the issue in 1642. The great trouble was that the breach thus opened in the established order had immense side-effects which had not been foreseen. The exigencies of waging war to ensure parliamentary supremacy meant that the gentry had to seek support outside their own circles. Thus they themselves brought great numbers of ordinary men into the affairs of state. What they could not foresee was that this would produce widespread expectation of much greater change. It was this great wave of extravagant expectation — including even anticipation of the establishment of the kingdom of heaven on earth — that gave rise to a tremendous outburst of novel political thinking which, in turn, led to still more enthusiasm. In the context of utopian and millennial hopes, the Levellers do not seem remarkably radical. But their views — revealed in the Putney debates — on the goals of the war and the constitutional settlement to be desired are nevertheless profoundly different from those of the conservative wing of the revolution.

Thus, to Ireton's contentment with the establishment of parliamentary authority, the radicals oppose the proposition that the end of the revolution is liberty.[60] Liberty, as Milton says, is their religion.[61] They deny that this involves any threat to property. Indeed, Maximilian Petty contends that the preservation of property is the reason for establishing government. The great trouble is that under the existing constitution there are too many "men of substance" without the franchise.[62] So the contrast is not really between those with and those without property; it is more nearly small property contending for political equality with great property. For the Levellers agree that alms-takers and servants should be excluded from the franchise. It was felt in their day that such people were not capable of displaying proper political independence. Moreover, their interests were thought to be so closely tied to the persons on whom they depended that the franchise of the latter would be enough to accomplish their representation.[63] All the same, the Levellers' reform proposals would have doubled the number of qualified electors. Moreover, it is not the exact content of their scheme that matters most. Rather, it is the fundamental revolution in the assumptions of political thought and the methods used to justify them that merits attention. Liberty was the ideological spring of their campaign, and this meant, as Wildman said, that "Every person in England hath as clear a right to elect his representative as the greatest person in England. I conceive that's the undeniable maxim of government: that all government is in the free consent of the people." [64] At a verbal level, the conservatives agreed with this. The difference lay in the definition of the people. Ireton, specifying that the "people" are those who have a permanent, local interest in the land, and holding that their political position is secure, admits quite candidly that he will maintain the existing constitution as long as he can.[65] The argument, therefore, is that everyone is obligated to obey parliament. The radicals' reply to this shows how deep a departure from medieval political thinking is involved in the enunciation of general principles. For them it is not a particular question at all, whether of parliaments, kings, lords, or whatever. On the contrary, it is the quite general problem of the proper relation between the generality of men and government, whether monarchical or otherwise. Thus Captain Clarke says, "I presume that all people, and all nations whatsoever, have a liberty and power to alter and change their constitutions if they find them to be weak and infirm. Now if the people of England shall find this weakness in their constitution, they may change it if they please." [66] Similarly, Colonel Rainborough maintains that there is no reason to deter anyone "from endeavouring by all means to gain anything that might be of more advantage to them [the people] than the government under which they live." [67]

To be sure, the language of the radicals was broader than their intentions, but this does not set aside the theoretical importance of their arguments. For here is a cluster of novel and profoundly significant assumptions. The very idea of self-conscious, deliberate change of government in accordance with human preferences had been in eclipse since classical antiquity. Moreover, not only did the radicals propose willful alteration of the foundation of the constitution, they were well aware that this involved them in principled disagreement with others. As one acute observer has pointed out, the radicals had abandoned "the fiction of a one-minded community." [68] Thus Rainborough assumes that there are bound to be differences of opinion, and there ought to be no mystery about this.[69] Petty observes that those who feel bound by the present arrangements ought to abide by that obligation, but those who do not feel so obliged should prosecute their efforts to bring about change.[70] Milton tells us that it is not possible to obtain complete agreement; "that let no man in this world expect; but when complaints are freely heard, deeply considered and speedily reformed, then is the utmost bound of civil liberty attained . . ." [71] It would be difficult to overestimate the importance of this view. For it amounts to the reception of the idea that plural interests and values have a legitimate place in the same political order. This entails the view that politics turn on human preferences rather than the articulation of a single body of divine and therefore changeless truth. It is precisely this extension of the idea of religious tolerance into political life that makes the practice of a politics of moderation possible. Clearly, just such a view is the foundation of party politics, which in turn is the organizational spring of constitutionalized politics. For it is in this way that permanent policy alternatives may be brought to bear, and without such sustained public purposes a constitutional system would be deprived of both its motive power — its purposes — and the sort of organized pressure that is the only guarantee of limited government.

It has been argued here that such fundamental presuppositions of constitutional government depend on an appreciation of the public dimension of political life. It was suggested at the beginning that the birth of civic consciousness and loyalty was the result of the constitutional quarrels of the seventeenth century. That considerable numbers of men had achieved a public focus is evident in the materials that have been discussed. Indeed, the whole drift of the

330

Putney debates is that the issue at stake is nothing less than a decision on the nature of a constitutional settlement. For this there is no parallel in the Middle Ages. Thus Cromwell opened the debates by announcing that "those that had anything to say concerning the public business . . . might have liberty to speak." [72] Of course, it is not merely the words that are important, for medieval men had learned to use such diction from the Roman law. It is rather the consciousness that what is at stake is the general character of government as such, and the effort that is made to gauge the effects of various proposals on the welfare of the generality of people in the kingdom. Again, it is not so much that something called the public interest is under discussion, for what is alleged to be the public good varies widely among the participants. The important thing is not what actually is the public good, but awareness that this is the topic being scrutinized.

Even the radicals' conception of the "people" was far too narrow to include everyone, but that is not really the point. The medieval notion of the *populus* had been a fiction. The revolutionary idea, despite the fact that it embraced only about half the adult male population, was an operational principle. This is most apparent in the Levellers' constitutional schemes. For they addressed their appeals directly to the people, and they took the idea of a contract of government literally. Thus neither representation nor consent was to be merely presumed. Anticipating Locke's famous view, Ireton argued, "A man ought to be subject to a law, that did not give his consent, but with this reservation, that if this man do think himself unsatisfied to be subject to this law he may go into another kingdom." [73] It was Ireton, too, who defended what Locke was to make famous as the doctrine of tacit consent: presumed approval of the ancestral contract.[74] For the radicals this view was totally inadequate: "every man that is to live under a government ought first by his own consent to put himself under that government; and I do think that the poorest man in England is not at all bound in a strict sense to that government that he hath not had a voice to put himself under . . ." [75] If representation and consent were not to be fictitious, however, there would be need not only for a theory but for constitutional machinery, and that is what the Levellers' Agreement of the People was designed to supply.

It is in relation to actual constitutional arrangements that the radicals' literal appeals to the people, the contract of government, and the idea that all government is held on trust by delegation from the sovereign people come into an operational setting. Thus Overton's address to the parliament is a conscious and profound break with the past. "It is confessed that our English histories and records of the actions and transactions of our predecessors, both of ancient and late times, so far as I can understand, do not afford me any example or precedent for any appeal from parliaments to people. Neither is there any such liberty provided in the letter of our law." But he points out that the people may take their political lessons from parliament, just as the barons and parliaments did from their kings: "I shall return even the late words of our now degenerate parliament: *that reason hath no precedent . . .*" [76] Overton then goes on to frame as good an expression of the trust theory of government as one is likely to find.

> For as formerly the Parliament averred, and as now this honourable Army assumeth . . . all authority is fundamentally seated in the office, and but ministerially in the persons. Therefore, the persons in their ministrations degenerating from safety to tyranny, their authority ceaseth, and is only to be found in the fundamental original rise and situation thereof, which is the people, the body represented. For though it ceaseth from the hands of the betrusted, yet it doth not, neither can it, cease from its being; for kings, parliament, &c., may fall from it, but it endureth for ever. For were not this admitted, there could be no lawful redress in extremity . . . It always is either in the hands of the betrusted or of the betrusters. While the betrusted are dischargers of their trust it remaineth in their hands, but no sooner the betrusted betray and forfeit their trust but (as all things else in dissolution) it returneth from whence it came, even to the hands of the trusters. For all just human powers are but betrusted, conferred, and conveyed by joint and common consent; for to every individual in nature is given an individual propriety by nature, not to be invaded or usurped by any . . . for every one as he is himself hath a self propriety — else he could not be himself — and on this no second may presume without consent; and by natural birth all men are equal, and alike born to like propriety and freedom . . .[77]

So the forfeiture of the people's trust by parliament means that the political order has dissolved, and the authority of establishing a new order has reverted to the people. They were expected to rise up at last to claim their right. Milton put this point with characteristic grandeur. "Methinks I see in my mind a noble and puissant nation rousing herself like a strong man after sleep, and shaking her invincible locks." [78]

Leveller concern for a constitutional settlement culminated in the several drafts of a proposed constitution called the Agreement of the People. The seriousness of the idea of a contract and of government as a trust comes out very clearly. The Levellers intended that Englishmen be asked to affix their signatures to the document, thus conveying their consent. The three Leveller Agreements differ somewhat, but their general tone is consistent enough. They embody the notion that parliament, like the king, has forfeited the trust conferred upon it and that this has dissolved the political order. England is to be reorganized on the basis of the proposed Agreement. For a start, the people are to be divided into single-member electoral constituencies based on population. With the exception of almstakers and servants, the franchise is to extend to all men. They will elect a unicameral Representative possessing full governmental authority, reaching whatever "is not expressly or impliedly reserved by the represented to themselves." Five such reservations are set forth in the first Agreement. Most importantly, "matters of religion, and the ways of God's worship, are not at all entrusted by us to any human power . . ." Again, no one is to be impressed for service in war, and everyone is to have indemnity for his actions during the civil wars, except those presently being considered in the parliament. Fourth, "in all laws made, or to be made, every person may be bound alike, and that no tenure, estate, charter, degree, birth, or place, do confer any exemption from the ordinary course of legal proceedings . . ." Finally, "as the laws ought to be equal, so they must be good, and not evidently destructive to the safety and well-being of the people." [79] The second Agreement of the People introduces the principle of the separation of powers. It provides for an executive Council of State, chosen by the Representative, and forbids any interference in the executive function by the legislature, except to call these officers to account. A third Agreement adds to the number of restrictions placed upon the power of the Representative.[80]

The general idea of a constitutional settlement, as well as many of the specific concerns expressed in the Levellers' agreements, produced two written constitutions for England in the 1650's — the Instrument of Government and the Humble Petition and Advice. Neither of these schemes was very successful, for England remained dangerously divided until the restoration of the kingship. Moreover, both constitutions were too clearly dependent upon Cromwell's military power. Following Cromwell's death, the problems of a constitutional settlement were debated again. From the perspective of constitutional theory, the most important point about these debates of 1659 is the recognition that there was required some institutional machinery to implement the limitations on government, and that these arrangements must not be revocable by any ordinary act of the legislature.[81] Here, of course, is the notion of a fundamental law, ultimately dependent only upon the constituent power of the people. Constitutionalism in England does not have such a basis; it survives despite the location of formal sovereignty in the king in parliament. But the idea has certainly found a home in American constitutional theory and practice.

Altogether, then, there appeared during the seventeenth century both the formal or mechanical ideas associated with constitutional government and the civic consciousness necessary to sustain them. Thus, according to Milton, the task was "to place every one his private welfare and happiness in the public peace, liberty, and safety." [82] It is important to appreciate what a dramatic departure in loyalties this involved. The medieval conception of loyalty had been familial and personal, rising to its summit in kingship. The revolutionary struggle produced loyalty to abstract principles of government, justified in the name of concern for the public good. The fact that men could not agree on what constituted the public interest was explicitly recognized, but the principle survived as the vital framework of discussion. This is evident on both sides of the Putney debates. At Putney, Cromwell makes the following observation: "I think we are not only to consider what the consequences are if there were nothing else but this paper [the Levellers' Agreement of the People], but we are to consider the probability of the ways and means to accomplish [the thing proposed]: that is to say, whether, according to reason and judgment, the spirits and temper of the people of this nation are prepared to receive it and to go along with it . . ." [83] Ireton states that he will be bound by decisions of parliament, for the good of the kingdom, even if it means abolition of king, lords, and property.[84] Similarly, on the radical side, Rainborough says that if he can be persuaded that his view is destructive of the kingdom, "I shall withdraw [from] it as soon as any." [85] To be sure, there may prove to be a great distance between this kind of assertion and actual political behavior. But that is a normal risk in any constitutional system; no verbal magic will cover that contingency. The important development is that men are capable of addressing the problem of balancing self-interest and the general good.

When this much has been said about the development of the perspectives and assumptions necessary to the achievement of constitutionalized politics, it must be pointed out that the actual constitutional schemes of the revolutionary period fell on barren soil. They were the first efforts to contrive a formal constitution for the English people, but the egalitarian and libertarian aims of the Levellers and the radical sects who succeeded them in the 1650's were too advanced for public reception. As Cromwell observed at Putney, it was "not enough for us to insist upon good things. That every one would do . . . but it behoves honest men and Christians . . . to see whether or no they be in a condition — whether, taking all things into consideration, they may honestly endeavour and attempt that that is fairly and plausibly proposed." [86] He also understood why this caution was necessary. Nine years later Edmund Ludlow reproached Cromwell for failing to base his government on consent. Cromwell's reply was that he was "as much for government by consent as any man; but where shall we find that consent? Amongst the prelatical, Presbyterian, Independent, Anabaptist, or Levelling parties?" [87] That was certainly the difficulty. American experience suggests that a much less involved history was required for the successful inauguration of a political order of the kind envisioned by the radicals of the civil war period. It was not and could not be just a question of principles, for these must always come to terms with history. In England it was discovered that a viable platform for settlement would have to include the restoration of monarchy. It is this that explains the great popularity and durability of the theory of mixed monarchy. For on that basis the ancient tradition of personal kingship could be knit to the present and future. It could be pretended that sovereignty in England was the joint affair of king, lords, and commons. In fact, the civil wars had introduced parliamentarism in the place of personal kingship. That the will of parliament should in the last resort prevail over the king's will was common ground for the vast majority of those who counted politically.

To be sure, not all the details had been hammered out. About half a century more of argument and refinement was required before parliamentary supremacy was riveted into place.[88] But none of this required warfare. Thus the king's prerogative to summon parliament had been set aside by the Triennial Act of the Long Parliament, which was repealed in 1664 but re-enacted in 1694. Similarly, the problem of dissolution was solved by acts of 1694 and 1716. There was, further, the problem of parliamentary impeachment of the government's servants. The question whether the king could grant a pardon in such a case was settled against the prerogative in 1701. All this leaves little enough of the substance of mixed monarchy. The crown still possesses a theoretical veto, but it has not been used since 1708. Again, the exclusive right of the commons to originate money bills was not settled until 1678. Evidently, then, the actual techniques of constitutional government were by no means established at the time of the civil wars. But the intellectual revolution that necessarily underlies that achievement was accomplished at that time. Above all, the great wave of speculation, experiment, and discussion which filled the years of the interregnum produced the recognition of the uniquely public character of political life. Without the appearance of this civic orientation, there would be no possibility of constitutional government.

Conclusion

Constitutional government made its first appearance on the stage of European history in seventeenth century England. The essential precondition of that achievement was the development of public consciousness and civic loyalty, as contrasted with the fragmented and local preoccupations and personal loyalties of the traditional political order of the Middle Ages. The formation of a civic focus in politics was accompanied by a drastic alteration in the fundamental assumptions of political thought. For the consciously nontraditional values of contract theory — individual liberty and equality — were employed to combat the ideas of status, hierarchy, and degree which had satisfied and justified the medieval social order, and thus they provided a systematic and permanent alternative to the static values of a landed aristocracy. It is this dramatic transformation of the premises of political thought which has attracted the attention of modern observers, and there is obviously good reason for this. On the other hand, it is less important to appreciate these doctrinal changes, significant as they are, than to recognize that both old and new ideas were revolutionized by the perception of the public scope of politics. This meant that the focus of both practice and idea came to be channeled to the public level rather than deflected to questions of proper local and personal apportionment of governmental rights and duties.

Thus even though elements of the traditional outlook survived — chiefly attachment to the hierarchical principle — they too were redirected and lifted to a general level. But this is not the only reason for emphasizing the appearance of a civic orientation, as contrasted with exclusive concentration on matters of doctrine. For fixation on doctrine ties consideration of the possibility of constitutional government too closely to a single body of political ideas. Yet there is no reason to believe that the ideologies generated in the revolution might not have been quite different and nevertheless have achieved a constitutional result. But had civic consciousness failed to appear, the collision of the 1640's would most likely have been just another modification or adjustment in the politics of double majesty. The point of casting the discussion in this way, then, is that the problem of constitutionalizing politics may be seen in general rather than historically specific terms. Moreover, if it is considered from this perspective, the record of English experience carries some interesting implications farther afield. Of course, it is a plausible foundation for reflection on general problems in constitutional theory, and this is in no way surprising. But, as was mentioned at the beginning of this inquiry, the intimate association of the emergence of constitutional rule with operative ideas and concrete politics suggests that some orthodox assumptions may be questioned. Secondly, it has been argued here that it is the emergence of civic consciousness that marks the transition from a traditional to a recognizably modern political order. The historical record, therefore, may be found useful in puzzling over the developmental problems of contemporary traditional societies. Further, it seems clear that wider inquiry, extended to the quite different paths to modernity followed by the several political orders of medieval Europe, would be rewarding.[1] For the record of our own past is long and rich, and there is every reason to believe that it could be profitably exploited in the effort to frame theories of development, as well as in the more general concerns of comparative politics. Perhaps an equally important service may be derived from reflection on our intellectual history. At the beginning of this essay it was suggested that some of the important ideas employed in the study of political development draw much of their content from the intellectual past, particularly from the political thought of seventeenth century England. Now that the examination of one important current in our intellectual and political history has been completed, it will be appropriate to recur to this suggestion. First the outstanding features of the historical record will be summarized, and some of the ways in which that record may be helpful in considering the theoretical problems of comparative politics will be indicated. Then, in conclusion, some problems at the level of constitutional theory and the political philosophy of liberalism will be considered.

The political style of double majesty appears to have been the result of broad conditions that are far from unique: the inheritance

338

of territories and political power by traditional tribal societies in a general context of primitive technology. Under these conditions, the foundation of durable political power lay in immediate control of the land, both as a source of revenue and a treasury from which followers could be rewarded. But, for the same reasons, essentially private competition for lands was intense and violent. In the absence of effective methods of communication and control at a distance, rulers had little choice but to rely on local concentrations of power to keep the peace. This meant that political life revolved almost exclusively around the interests of the ruler and a small number of great men, superimposed on a largely inert social mass. Their needs and interests were interdependent, and this was the real source of cohesion above the local level. For the fact that governmental authority was dependent upon local centers of military and economic strength reinforced the lack of centralization inherent in a society organized in terms of landholding. But this same fragmentation of the sources of power and authority meant also that opposition most often represented only segments of the aristocracy and was often poorly organized and ephemeral. Government, therefore, could work in the interstices of this porous social fabric, balancing clusters of personal alliances against each other. Moreover, despite the centrifugal tendency of such a system, it did contain elements of coherence, concentrated in the king's person. The ruler's sacred ritual position in society had an understandable basis in the anxieties natural to a violent social order, and support also derived from the need for a social rationale and the settlement of disputes.

The result of these factors was the strain of coexisting tendencies driving in contrary directions, a fact that was dutifully reflected in the politics of double majesty. Several interesting conclusions can be drawn from all this. Most importantly, what might be called the mechanics of the system invited the failure to perceive political issues as public problems, for both everyday security and plain self-interest depended on local military power. Government, therefore, was essentially aristocratic and military. In addition, it was bound to be arbitrary to a very considerable extent, since it operated in a context of recurrent emergency. At the level of the central government, there was often little alternative but to rule in a high-handed fashion. In considering the politics of contemporary traditional societies, it would be wise to acknowledge the difficulty of achieving civic consciousness and loyalty. In its absence, it is not only unrealistic to engage in evaluation and planning from the standpoint of mature public consciousness but probably futile to anticipate successful transplantation of the form and techniques of western constitutionalism, at least in the short run. For one of the principal inferences from the English evidence is surely this: the path to civic consciousness is not primarily a function of doctrine or techniques, but of the political process itself.

The course traversed to civic consciousness was anything but simple, even, and clear. From the vantage point afforded by hindsight, however, it is possible to discern some fairly definite stages, which may be helpful for comparative purposes. There were, in fact, five general phases in the history of the politics of double majesty. The first was nothing more than the bare operation of a system of straightforward domination of agrarian populations by war leaders and their lieutenants, organized primarily for military purposes, that is, for the pursuit of booty. This form, of course, was the initial result of the break-up of tribal society under the impact of Roman commerce, technology, and diplomacy. The result of Roman withdrawal, however, was the settlement of chieftains and men on extensive territories, but without any clear lines between the various successor kingdoms. At this stage rule was located spatially, if indefinitely, but there was a marked tendency to blur public and private lands, rights, and revenues. But settlement had the effect of putting a high premium on the inheritance of lands and privileges, and this tended to harden into an identifiable relationship between the king and the military aristocracy. At this point — the second stage — the relationship of double majesty had become durable, but it had no native ideological equipment. By the twelfth and thirteenth centuries, however, a third stage was reached, in which double majesty was assumed to be the standard of correct governance by those who counted politically, though there was room for wide differences of interpretation; but the opposition to the king's government was specific and temporary, with no real alternatives at hand. The remainder of the medieval period (up to the time of the Tudor monarchy) formed the fourth distinct stage, when the invention and elaboration of political trials by parliament represented a definite restraining technique, supported by the idea of a distinction between the king and the kingdom or crown. Lastly, the combined effects of prolonged and unsuccessful war, weak kingship, and competition among the great supplied a climate so favorable to the monarchy that it was finally able to curb disorder decisively. Moreover, it could do so with legal instruments and ideology, despite a distinct flavor of both the purely political and the grossly arbitrary. It would be difficult to overestimate the importance of the Tudor monarchy. For it was the Tudor bureaucracy, above all, that employed, trained, and domesticated the aristocracy and gentry to the habits of stable and vigorous central rule. From these segments of society the first decisively modern opposition to the traditional system emerged in the seventeenth century, and it was their action which provided the opportunity for a fundamental restructuring of political practices and ideas in the latter half of the century.

The fundamental weakness of the medieval political order, like traditional orders generally, was that political ties were excessively weak: they were only partly political, and the political unit was indistinct. Thus the central political institutions resembled meetings at the level of diplomacy almost as much as the practices of representation and government. Legitimate rights of government and the interests which grew up around them, as well as the military force to defend them, were parceled out in varying degrees, for different reasons and on different principles. As a result, cohesion was more nearly a function of kinship and simple proximity than of any national sentiment or consciousness. The effects are easily seen, and they serve to underline the fragility and volatility of the system. At the level of domestic politics, the fragmented collection of tenures, franchises, and powers was bound together formally only by the individual loyalty of the great men to the king. This produced a kind of mechanical unity under favorable circumstances, but one which could easily fall into disarray. Personal allegiance meant that there was a recurrent temptation to discredit others in the incessant competition for the king's favor. This was not a politics of party, much less of principles designed to guide state action, but of family competition, intrigue, and jockeying for position at court. At all levels of society there was always the possibility of withdrawal of allegiance, though the nature of the system encouraged shifts of alignment rather than independence, which would have required not only more self-conscious identity of interests but more diversity of opportunity. But shifting allegiances and ad hoc alliances, unlike party politics, do not produce alternative policies in any programmatic sense. The result was failure to solve or even to recognize general problems. In brief, the political order lacked any real motive power and purposeful direction.

In some ways, the effects of social fragmentation and personal loyalty can be seen more sharply in international relations. At a crucial turn of diplomacy or war, a ruler might discover that one of his chief men had shifted his allegiance to a rival, and a campaign might be shattered as a result. It was as if the governor of an American state were to forswear allegiance to the President and adopt, say, the cause of Mexico. What would be an absurdity in the integrated nation state was a not infrequent occurrence in the Middle Ages. So indefinite were national boundaries and jurisdictions, so complex and fragile were the lines of personal allegiance, that it was not even clear that such conduct was treasonous. The collapse and retreat of European imperial systems has left us a legacy of this sort, not entirely unlike the confusion in Europe when Roman political organization crumbled and was withdrawn from the western provinces of the Empire. For we are confronted today with multiple traditional political structures, without any very good idea where boundaries ought to lie or any certain tests of legitimacy or legality. Is it not likely that such a situation will breed agglomerations of political power based on kinship, locality, and personal superiority — power which lies somewhere between private and public? In European history, this condition involved a long period of political instability and violence. Territorial identity was a very long time in coming, for there were really only two ways of bringing it about: outright conquest, and fortunate results in alliances based on marriage. But this took place under the general form of the politics of double majesty, rather than in a context of self-conscious or sustained policies aimed at the achievement of stable frontiers or even aggrandizement of the territory of the kingdom as such.

A consideration of the subject of contemporary developing societies should begin with a negative but nonetheless important point. It is certainly not the case that early European experience is directly translatable into a kind of code for either domestic or foreign politics in premodern societies.[2] That is, it cannot be appealed to as a reservoir of examples of concrete behavior. To use history in this way would only be to repeat a familiar error.[3] It has been persuasively argued, moreover, that the tradition of liberal democracy in the West is the product of a unique constellation of historical factors — historical memories of classical antiquity, Roman legalism,

342

the Christian emphasis on the worth of the individual, the Protestant ethic, the rise of the middle classes, laissez-faire capitalism, and so on.[4] This view may well be correct. At a minimum, it is an argument that has been so skillfully developed that the utmost caution, if not skepticism, regarding the prospects of liberal democracy in the underdeveloped states seems well warranted. But it is worth observing, simply on logical grounds, that if the argument for western uniqueness is designed to show that liberal democracy cannot develop elsewhere, it is not conclusive. For while it may well be that the historical factors that account for western liberal democracy were indeed unique, it does not follow that constitutional government or liberal democracy can be achieved only in that way. Moreover, a major argument of this book has been that it is a mistake to associate constitutionalized politics exclusively with specific political theories and particular institutional arrangements and procedures. What is required, above all, is civic consciousness and loyalty, wedded to a politics of moderation and tolerance. On the other hand, a long and involved course was traveled in English history before the appearance of public consciousness. Western observers sometimes sound as if they expected the new states to accomplish virtually overnight the sort of change that required centuries in European history. But the development of civic loyalty is anything but simple. Moreover, it is extremely difficult to disengage seventeenth century ideas and practices from their medieval point of departure. For without a complex set of historical circumstances, both domestic and international, reaching very far into the medieval past — a long tradition of political instruction from medieval kings and their bureaucracies, and the benefits as well as the liabilities of vigorous if sometimes crude and ruthless kingly rule — without all this, it seems unlikely that there would have been any nonregal element in English society sufficiently coherent and sophisticated to achieve a genuine public perspective in the seventeenth century. In the preceding centuries, it was the absence of any coherent constituency aware of the public scope of politics that excluded deliberate formation of public policies — that is to say, purposeful direction of the political order. A comparable disability affects the political life of contemporary traditional and transitional societies.[5] Hence it may not be unreasonable to expect some analogous elements in political behavior. But it would also seem reasonable to anticipate a similarly involved and uncertain course of development.

It does not follow that the development of civic consciousness can only proceed in one way or that it must involve so long and complex a course. Indeed, there is reason to believe that some of the more serious liabilities of European history are avoidable, at least in principle. For the kingdoms of medieval Europe had no living models of civic order from which to work. On the contrary, they had only a half-understood literary recollection of classical antiquity. This cultural reminiscence was immensely important, but it could not provide the actual stimulus of competition which modern political systems do for contemporary traditional societies. Moreover, the modern polity not only supplies a model and the sting of competition, it has also helped to train some of the political leaders of the new states. There is, therefore, this very great difference: contemporary traditional societies have the advantage, at least potentially, of leadership equipped with a public orientation.[6] Further, the age of technology has produced a truly universal international system, one which contains permanent competition. Unfortunately, this is unlikely to be exclusively beneficial, for the advanced technology of the modern world is also a constant source of danger. Nor is that danger solely one of war. On the contrary, it may have quite other deleterious effects. It is likely to encourage the diversion of energies and resources into unproductive channels: armaments, the impulse to territorial aggrandizement, inconstancy in alliance relationships, and costly display, for example. Moreover, there is the danger that the international rivalry of the superpowers will continue to have the effect of excluding genuine solutions to many of the most important problems of the new states. European history suggests two broad sorts of lessons here. In the first place, it demonstrates that there is very little reason to suppose that developing areas will maintain even the nominal identity bestowed by ruling dynasties or geographical barriers. Secondly, it illustrates the tragic truth that political stability has most often been achieved by violence. But it is precisely the problem of attaining at least territorial identity that tends to be excluded by the mutual fear of great-power manipulation and escalating involvement. This has the result, as Stanley Hoffmann has said, of freezing a very large class of unsatisfactory situations.[7] Thus there is a great deal to be said for a less demanding international atmosphere. And yet, the pressures of international politics might still mean a much more rapid development of public consciousness in the underdeveloped world.

In sum, there appear to be good reasons for supposing, first, that western history cannot provide the student of political development and comparative politics with specific patterns, and, secondly, that there is little reason to anticipate that developing states must follow the path of European development in order to achieve constitutional government. The important analogies between the European past, particularly during the medieval period, and contemporary traditional societies lie in the fact that both the domestic and international situations — at the level especially of regional subsystems — turn in large measure on the persistence of traditional values and loyalties in a context of technological deprivation, political fragmentation, and the concomitant absence of broad civic consciousness. Both in medieval European history and in large parts of the contemporary world, therefore, politics approximates a fascinating hybrid model. For the two principal models employed in political studies are in many ways quite inadequate to the fragmented, local, and personal character of premodern politics. In such a context neither the model of the integrated community nor that of the international system of fully legitimate and independent states provides a characterization of the peculiar mixture of internal and foreign politics in the premodern political order.[8] If these two models are taken as the two ends of a continuum, traditional politics clearly falls between the poles. The point, then, is that comparison is to be made in the interest of theory formation rather than in any search for specific sequences of events.

More immediate advantages, however, may be derived from our past when it is considered in terms of the dominant assumptions and political perceptions we have inherited. The suggestion here is simply that the contemporary study of political development may be sharpened by increased self-consciousness of elements in our own political and intellectual history, elements which have contributed to our conceptions of ourselves, our past, and, more recently, to scholarly inclinations in developmental studies. In order to do this, it is unnecessary to argue that our intellectual history has in some mysterious way determined the categories and criteria employed in these studies. In short, it is not a question of a kind of intellectual determinism, of an inability to transcend a set of inherited assumptions. Certainly to transcend these assumptions would be a genuine task, but that is no reason for supposing that it could not be done nor for not trying to do it. Moreover, it should be emphasized that the suggestions to be made here do not decide the question of the scientific or the philosophical utility of any of the ideas that, nonetheless, will bear examination.

For the sake of convenience, the collection of assumptions, doctrines, and modes of argument to be examined may be referred to as elements of the liberal philosophy of politics. All of them were generated in seventeenth century England, and all of them have come to constitute an important part of our political and intellectual outlook. That outlook rests, above all, on the idea that there is and ought to be a sharp distinction between society and government. This contrast is at once elementary and fundamental. It is fundamental in the sense that so much else has been made to rest on it; it is elementary because it seems so natural to make it. Does it not come close to being self-evidently true? In a trivial sense, of course, it all depends on what is meant by the key terms. But a definitional solution is not normally very illuminating, nor does it, in this case, advance the inquiry into assumptions. To begin with, there are both factual and normative elements in the idea. Thus, to observe that there was no parallel to the distinction between government and society in the political thought of classical antiquity is enough to suggest that it is not simply a factual affair. But there is another aspect to the matter which is too frequently overlooked: that the distinction between society and government is also an ideologically conditioned perception. In short, it gives expression to certain emphases, purposes, and hopes. Moreover, if it is to be fully understood, it must be seen as an idea which carries manifold consequences for those who embrace it. For the original political point of the distinction was to assert that society is a meaningful reality quite apart from government. This, in turn, implied two other major assumptions. It was necessary to argue, in the first place, that there are forces of cohesion native to society without any governmental institutions. The second major point followed easily from this and had a much more marked normative thrust. It was the view that government is derivative and artificial, that it is merely an instrument of society or the people. Opinions about the importance of government diverge at this point, running from an anarchic view to the notion that some coercive institutions are necessary, at least in the attenuated sense that they are aids to an enhanced existence. What is rejected in all these versions, as Sheldon Wolin has rightly insisted,[9] is the notion, so well articulated by Hobbes, that the absence of government must mean not only anarchy in the technical sense but literally chaos, a condition of radical insecurity which must involve the terrors of a state of war, rather than spontaneous or natural organization. Early liberalism, then, assumed a kind of inherent social virtue in men which naturally gives rise to an ordered existence. Government can then be at least depreciated, perhaps emasculated, and at most dispensed with, once the necessity of coercion is removed by eliminating its source, the falsehood and ignorance inflicted upon society by monarchs and clerics. On this outlook government can be made to seem merely epiphenomenal, nothing more than the purely contingent and instrumental contrivance of society. The outcome of these assumptions was a new understanding of man's natural condition. The central point is that society could be conceived of as tending naturally to stability, a condition which suffered merely occasional interruptions. It is clear, too, that this idea depends in turn on an underlying notion of a uniform human nature. But it is not so much the specific content of the idea of human nature that matters, for that could and did vary considerably, as it still does.[10] Rather, the important assumption was the notion of some sort of uniformity underlying the obvious lack of agreement in politics. As Judith Shklar has pointed out, it is the stupefying denial of the obvious facts that makes this assumption one of the great myths of political thought, and which allowed social theorists to persist in the articulation of general theories of underlying peace and stability, precisely in the age of the wars of religion;[11] that is, in the time of the greatest ideological struggles in western history prior to those of the twentieth century.

The political outlook which emerged from the English civil wars rested on these general assumptions. But what most needs recognition is that they represent the ideology of the revolutionary opposition, which, in turn, was a set of generalized responses to a particular traditional system. In terms of ideologically motivated perceptions, the question is this: Why should the opposition to the ancient kingship have fastened so resolutely on the distinction between society and government and the secondary assumptions which gave it meaning? The specific answer to this question is to be found not so much in the general idea of the passage to political modernity as in the character of the political ideas confronted by the gentlemen of the opposition. It is to be found, in short, in the specific doctrines of royalist theoreticians. One expects royalists to find general modes of justifying monarchical rule, but the royalists of the first half of the seventeenth century did much more than that. In brief, their basic contention was that a people without a single head is simply not a people at all. A society — any society at all — without a government was regarded as a flat impossibility. The most they would grant was that any society without a monarch was inevitably inferior. The following passage from the royalist writer, Edward Forsett, is representative of the view that was so enthusiastically espoused during the reign of James I. If there is no sovereign, Forsett asserts, "no people can ever as subjects raunge themselves into the order, and communitie of humane societie, howsoever, as men, or rather as wild savages, they may perhaps breath a while upon the earth." [12] The king himself entertained the same view. According to James, there was simply no possibility of organization of any sort without a sovereign. Except for the organizing power of kingship, a people could be no more than a "headlesse multitude." [13] It is reasonable, then, to conclude that the peculiar general emphases and perceptions of the English liberal tradition were tailored to meet a particular body of thought. Moreover, it is possible to pursue this line of inquiry further. Royalist writers, like Hobbes later in the century, insisted on the idea that law is and can only be the expression of the sovereign's will. This was, of course, a natural enough accompaniment of the doctrine that there could be no social order without a sovereign. But it came to be articulated in such a way that it provoked an elaborate and specific counterideology, which turns on the idea that law is pre-existent and superior to government. This reply was provoked by the royalists' insistence that, in the last resort, the will of the sovereign was arbitrary. Sir Robert Filmer expressed this view as well as any, in this way: "We do but flatter our selves, if we hope ever to be governed without an arbitrary power . . . There never was, nor ever can be any people governed without a power of making laws, and every power of making laws must be arbitrary . . ." [14]

It was not only royalist doctrines but the kingly practices grounded on them, or at least justified by them, that gave rise to parliamentary resentment. The reply of the opposition was essentially twofold: theoretical, and institutional. At the level of theory, it was contended that an arbitrary, willful decision was not a "law" at all. On the contrary, a genuine rule of law must necessarily be both general and prospective; that is, it must preclude bills of attainder and *ex post facto* legislation. It is this view that leads directly to the notion of a fundamental or constitutional law, which contains, *inter alia,* the injunctions designed to exclude the element of arbitrariness. But there was a further difficulty, because royalists could point to tolerably good historical evidence that kingly rule had, in fact, preceded the creation of legal systems. It was the power of the royalist case from history that drove the opposition to the more general level of political theory in their controversy, and which was responsible for the specific reliance on an essentially non-historical notion of natural rights and contract theory. But there remained the troublesome fact that the executive decisions of a political order are inescapably singular rather than general, as well as the added complication that where the individual citizen is most likely to meet his government is in a court of law, whose judges were then appointed and removable by the king. It was this set of circumstances that produced the widespread and remarkable enthusiasm for the antique doctrine of mixed monarchy, and the specific division of executive, legislative, and judicial functions, along with the idea of checks and balances which it supports.

The main ideological thrust which lies behind all these theoretical ideas is the general normative notion that it is only in this way that the liberty of the individual can be secured. This, in turn, rests on two other presumptions of the liberal outlook. The idea of individual liberty presupposes that there is and ought to be a distinct sphere of private life, not only separable from public life but constitutionally insulated from the expansive and coercive grasp of government. But it is just here, at the ideological heart of liberalism, that the second presumption is invoked. The question is, how could the revolutionary opposition suppose that the primary goal of individual liberty could be achieved if, and only if, government were constituted in accordance with the doctrine of mixed monarchy and its corollaries? The answer, in a word, is that they assumed that all coercion was governmental. Because the general theory involved the supposition that men are naturally social creatures, the source of political evil must be located elsewhere. And where else but in the coercive institutions of government? What better way to minimize a necessary evil than to do one's best to paralyze it? It is this view that has been rightly called "the least defensible notion of classical liberalism: the identification of privacy, freedom, and choice with the non-governmental, while sanctions and force are entirely identified with governmental action." [15] It requires only a little reflection today to realize the startling inadequacy of such a view. For it is only too evident that a social order is shot through with coercive relationships, and that governmental power is sometimes the only recourse for the maintenance or increase of freedom. But once this article of the liberal political faith is undermined, it draws all the other elements of the outlook into question, or, rather, it ought to do so, because it raises serious problems of both normative and conceptual adequacy.

The conceptual problem will be considered first, to elucidate some genuine difficulties which are especially acute in relation to developmental studies. The ideas to be discussed are neither especially vulnerable nor comparatively unsatisfactory. On the contrary, they possess considerable merit. Moreover, they are among the principal intellectual instruments being used in the study of political development, and that alone is enough to justify the most careful scrutiny. But any conceptual apparatus is likely to contain some measure of implicit, unacknowledged, or unnoticed content, and it is best to make it as explicit as possible. At the most general level, our understanding of the modern, as contrasted with the traditional, appears to be historically specific. Indeed, as Reinhard Bendix has pointed out, the very notion that there *is* such a contrast turns on the reaction of nineteenth century intellectuals to the events of the French Revolution.[16] It is surely undeniable that the frustrated hopes, the imagined fears, the real anguish and desolation, and the contempt for the new social order — all these impulses severally contributed to the appearance and the content of some of the major categories of social reflection and, in time, of the social sciences.[17] It does not follow, of course, that having noticed the social and intellectual origins of an idea, one has thereby shown either its falsity or its lack of utility. But the implications of such historical specificity may well be considered. In connection with the idea of a general contrast between the traditional and the modern, it is possible to be quite specific. More particularly, it seems likely that continuing appraisal of analysis conducted in terms of the various formulations of Talcott Parsons' pattern variables will be especially rewarding.[18] For it is no exaggeration to observe, with Lucian Pye, that these "pattern-variables have been widely accepted by contemporary social scientists as illuminating the crucial differences" between traditional and modern societies.[19]

As was suggested at the beginning of this study, the Parsonian pattern variables are strikingly similar to the principal ideological and moral claims of the revolutionary opposition in the English civil wars, though they have been cast in much more abstract language. At any rate, it is possible to effect a direct translation of the particular normative demands and new perceptions[20] into the language of pattern variables, without any very significant loss of their ethical content. This is clearest in the case of the two contrasting pairs, ascription-achievement and particularism-universalism. Rejection of the ancient ascriptive and particularist tests is abundantly clear in the language of the Agreement of the People: "in all laws made, or to be made, every person may be bound alike, and that no tenure, estate, charter, degree, birth, or place do confer any exemption from the ordinary course of legal proceedings . . ."[21] Similarly, John Lilburne asserted that he had "as true a right to all the priviledges that do belong to a free man as the greatest man in England whatsoever he be . . ."[22] Moreover, another of the pattern variables, the contrast between affectivity and affective neutrality, seems to be implied by such views — implied, that is, by the normative demands of generality and legal equality. The old ties were explicitly repudiated in Overton's revolutionary leap into self-conscious modernity: "whatever our forefathers were," he said, "or whatever they did or suffered, or were forced to yield unto, we are the men of the present age, and ought to be absolutely free from all kinds of exorbitancies, molestations or arbitrary power."[23] But a fourth pair of concepts in pattern-variable analysis appears to present more difficulty for the argument here. This is the contrast between institutional and functional specificity, as opposed to the tendency in traditional societies to blur distinguishable functions and features of situations. But most of the major intellectual controversies of the 1640's eventuated in a set of institutional demands that, in substance, amount to the contention that, since governmental functions fall into the three broad classes of legislation, execution, and adjudication, they ought also to be discharged by distinct institutions. As far as institutional theory is concerned, widespread agreement was reached on the arrangements labelled "mixed monarchy." But the whole point of this institutional specificity was the contentious definition of "genuine law" in terms of generality and prospectivity. This was, precisely and self-consciously, the institutional defense of liberalism against coercion and arbitrariness, in the name of individual free-

dom and the concerns of private life. In contemporary functionalism, one important empirical presumption is substituted for another:
institutional specificity enhances societal "effectiveness," rather than
private life and personal freedom. Ideologically, both these presumptions are raised on hopes rather than facts, for there is surely
much doubt as to whether either one is empirically warranted. In
the developed — or perhaps it should be overdeveloped — world, the
assumption of specificity and effectiveness evades the critical question
that haunted Max Weber: what would be the effect of increasing
specialization and bureaucratization on the values and prospects of
liberal society? [24]

By themselves, however, these observations about pattern-variable
analysis do not necessarily constitute a reproach. For there are good
reasons for attaching high value to the ideals of generality, of criteria based upon achievement, of specified functions, and even of
impersonality. The important point, substantively, is to recognize
the historical particularity of these political and ethical preferences.
In a trivial sense, it may be held that an investigator may mean by
modernity whatever he chooses to mean. But in that case, more than
one possibility has to be recognized. Indeed, there are three: that
the content of the contrast between tradition and modernity is historically unique; that it is general despite its origins; or, most
likely perhaps, that the range of its utility is limited and therefore
can only be tested against other historical data. The first of these
views was the one maintained by Weber, from whose work so much
of this scheme derives. Indeed, it can fairly be said that the most
general effect of Weber's work was to show that these characteristics,
which he summed up under the label of rationality, were the distinguishing marks of western civilization.[25] The empirical adequacy
of this general view may be doubted, but Weber was perfectly clear
about the central point of substance: "rationality" was a compen-
dious way of referring to western uniqueness. There is no reason why
a social scientist ought not to employ these ideas in the effort to
construct ideal-types for purposes other than those embraced by
Weber, or at quite different social levels and at different points in
space and time.[26] But do social scientists want to mean that modernity, as such, is to be characterized in this way? This is bound to be
the result when modernity is adopted as part of the conceptual apparatus of a system that is represented as perfectly general. What is
really important, in other words, is not the mere fact that the

scheme happens to reflect a particular set of political preferences: the political ethic that Weber called ethical rationalism, as opposed to the ethical systems of the Orient. The error lies, rather, in supposing that that particular morality is a necessary part of a general conceptual scheme, for the claim of generality is also necessarily a claim to ethical exclusiveness. It is the moral exclusiveness that cannot be reconciled, even superficially, with the overwhelming evidence of moral diversity.[27]

To hold that modernity simply *is* the collection of characteristics subsumed by pattern-variable analysis, then, appears to involve a commitment to the specific political and ethical outlook of liberalism. It does so because it cannot really be disentangled from the obvious normative thrust of the idea of rationality. For rationality, in this context, does not refer merely to instrumental rationality, but to the overall standard of organization and behavior in accordance with explicitly articulated general rules. It is not the content of the rules that is in question here. Rather it is the point which has been made so well in Judith Shklar's study of legalism: that the idea of rule-following is itself a morality, one political choice among other possibilities.[28] To elucidate that choice, which he thought was the essence of western civilization, was perhaps Weber's chief reason for exploring the profoundly different moralities of India and China.[29] The morality of rule-following necessarily involves a certain generality, consistency, and even impartiality and impersonality. At the level of government, it means that the standard of value is at least the exclusion of arbitrariness. In fact, of course, it is often useful to characterize government as arbitrary, in the sense that while decisions are made they do not reflect the kind of settled and roughly predictable outcome that is precisely the fruit of legal rationalization. It is this stability of expectation that is the great strength of legalistic morality, of the rule of laws rather than men. But it is profoundly different from a legal order organized on the basis of equity, or on the sort of decision-making that Weber called khadi justice.[30] In short, the morality of rule-following is not the morality of primitive and traditional societies generally, nor is it the political morality of totalitarian rule.[31] On the assumptions of pattern variable analysis, it follows that contemporary totalitarian governments are necessarily not modern or that they are underdeveloped. It is one thing, therefore, to suppose, or rather, to hope that all nonwestern societies can be usefully characterized in one way (as essentially nonrational or perhaps prerational); or to undertake the task of investigating and describing societies accurately to find out the extent to which they resemble or differ from the ideal-type; or to advocate, as an explicit political preference, the cultivation of the morality of rule-following throughout the nonwestern world.[32] But it is quite another thing to build that morality into a general conceptual scheme, in such a way that the essential elements of classical liberalism are converted from political preferences into conceptual necessities, for that they cannot be.

A quite different kind of point can be made by considering some of the other assumptions of liberal ideology. Just as the normative and conceptual apparatus of liberalism rests on the fundamental contrast between society and government, and entails the sorts of ancillary assumptions outlined above, so too does analysis of tradition and modernity in terms of pattern variables, as this has come to be embedded in the concepts of systems theories, theories of political culture, and functionalism. For in these contemporary analytical schemes, government — the political system — tends to be treated as merely epiphenomenal, treated, that is, as it has been in liberalism. Certainly there is a marked tendency in contemporary social science to treat the political system as a kind of effluence of society or economy, as a mere function of the social order, conceptualized in terms of the idea of conversion functions. Leonard Binder has asked the crucial question here: is it always to be the case that the political system will be treated as a dependent variable? [33] Is it not the conceptual predisposition contained in liberalism which makes this theoretical tendency so plausible?

However that may be, the vital substantive point is that such a perspective can easily and naturally lead an observer to two closely related kinds of analytical shortcomings. The most obvious of these is the one already mentioned: the inclination to depreciate the role of government in traditional and transitional societies.[34] The second is a tendency to overconcentrate on purely internal processes of growth and development which, once launched, somehow pursue a natural course to modernity.[35] It has been a major argument of this book, however, that monarchical needs and initiatives not only were crucial in the course of English political development, but were the single most significant set of impulses in domestic politics, and that the ultimate source of many important royal initiatives was the urgency of affairs at the level of international politics. In the language of systems theory, the demand inputs of premodern England were, to a very considerable extent, governmental rather than social inputs. Indeed, even the problem of assessing the adequacy of governmental output was often largely governmental. For one of the chief features of a system lacking public consciousness is that response to governmental action is fitful, fragmentary, and highly selective. The intention here is not to argue against (or for) the scientific utility of any analytical scheme, but rather to indicate the ways in which our intellectual past appears to affect our conceptual vision. It is a question of emphasis and focus rather than general adequacy that is being raised. So, for instance, systems theory, as articulated by David Easton, includes a concept that serves to embrace inputs from inside the government, which he has called "withinputs." [36] Similarly, systems theory includes, in the concept of "extrasocietal environment," the capacity to emphasize the "stress" on a system that derives from war and diplomacy.[37] The point, then, is not that the effort to frame a set of concepts that will apply to all political systems is inherently impossible, nor that existing schemes are intrinsically inapplicable to the sort of political order represented by premodern England.[38] The point is, rather, that there will have to be *at least* shifts of emphasis and focus.

It is suggested, then, that an understanding of our own past may serve useful, if modest, theoretical purposes. It may also make a contribution to the business of reflecting on our own political system. The argument here has been that the development of civic consciousness in seventeenth century England was the indispensable precondition of the achievement of constitutional government. For it was this which made possible a politics of principle, a political life centered on diverse but enduring views and sustained purposes at the level of public policy. To be sure, this perception of the generality and importance of public issues did not by itself entail constitutional politics, much less the invention of any particular procedural techniques or any specific doctrines. Any variety of organized and enduring political processes requires civic consciousness, but something more is needed for constitutionalized politics. This additional element, I believe, is best summarized as the acceptance of plural interests and of the multitude of recognized values which spring from such diversity. The rest of this concluding chapter will be devoted to a discussion of this contention.

It should be emphasized that the concept of pluralism is used here to refer to the values of an explicit philosophy of politics, and not to the quite distinct set of questions raised by the specific approach in political science which undertakes analysis of American politics in terms of multiple and competing interest groups.[39] The debate on the accuracy, adequacy, and, indeed, the morality of the pluralistic approach continues, as it should.[40] The question here, however, is not whether the United States *is* a pluralist democracy, in Robert Dahl's phrase. Rather, the question is whether there are good reasons for adopting the value of tolerance of moral diversity. It is not suggested that the first question is any less important than the second. Clearly, the factual and conceptual issues raised by pluralist analysis are of great interest. One does want to know whether the American polity truly exhibits a meaningful distribution of power, and the extent to which that distribution embraces the general population. In Galbraith's phrase, do the "countervailing powers" really countervail?[41] Moreover, it is perfectly true that serious liabilities would be involved if the questions of political philosophy were always to be discussed in complete isolation from such critical questions. It does not follow, however, that the two types of questions are indistinguishable. Indeed, at present it is more than usually important to maintain this analytical distinction precisely because it has been increasingly obscured by the multiplication of literature which insists on confusing the quite different sorts of questions that are at issue — which insists, in short, on making the ideal of tolerance of diversity somehow responsible for what is considered, in most such literature, the deplorable condition of American politics. The point, however, is simply this. There is absolutely no philosophical reason why the advocate of freedom through tolerance of moral diversity could not agree completely with such critics, factually and conceptually, without abandoning his attachment to the values of the philosophy itself. To be sure, there is always the possibility that a polity may be so far removed from the philosophical ideal as to make it seem inordinately difficult, perhaps impossible, to attain. But even this is not by itself a conclusive reason for abandoning the ideal. Indeed, the function of a political standard is to gauge the discrepancy between fact and value. Presumably, even in utopia there would remain some use for standards with which to reproach actions and institutions. In short, a philosophy of politics is not isolable, but it is concerned with distinguishable questions.

Returning to the particular historical case presented by English politics during the civil war period, it is possible to consider that period as the critical turning point in the passage from a traditional to a modern political order, or, to recur to Maine's apt usage, from status to contract. The notion that contract is a suitable metaphor in characterizing the essence of political relationships was a perfect ideological instrument. For it rests on the assumption that all obligations, private and public, must be a matter of the express will of the parties involved. On this assumption none of the criteria of the past — birth, rank, or usage — was relevant. Contract was, in short, a levelling instrument, equipped with an inherent libertarian thrust. It was this which made possible the reappearance of views that had not been sponsored in politics since the days of the Sophists in Greek antiquity: the assumption not only of a radical individualism, but also that government is essentially a human affair rather than a part of a general plan ordained in advance by divine agency, and that political life is subject to willful manipulation in accordance with human purposes. To be sure, in the seventeenth century these ideas were not the point of departure. Nor is it suggested that everyone came to see it that way or, for that matter, that they ever have. There were — and still are — many who insisted that the standards of political life were given in some form which transcended merely human preference. The point, therefore, is not that such views were abandoned, but that they were no longer the only perceived alternative. Moreover, it is only fair to recognize that the religious tolerance which was the forerunner of political tolerance was more the product of exhaustion than of principle. The essential point can be made from the obviously disillusioned remark of Edmund Chillenden in 1656: "Let religion alone; give me my small liberty." [42]

The breakdown of the dominant political conceptions and values of the Middle Ages thus produced an alternative set of assumptions, new tests for the assessment of political behavior and institutions, and new modes of argument. Altogether these constitute the greatest alteration in political ideas since the Greeks first fashioned the elements of political theory out of the disruption of their own traditional past.[43] Just as then, the stress involved resulted in profoundly different reactions, ranging from despair to the most buoyant optimism.[44] Expectations were literally boundless. Enthusiasms were intense and various: some gentle and humane, like the limitless tolerance of the Leveller William Walwyn;[45] some ferocious, like the attempts of the Fifth Monarchy men to inaugurate the kingdom of heaven on earth forthwith, however high the cost;[46] some merely erratic or bizarre.[47] Thus it is perfectly clear that humanistic assumptions did not hold the field alone. But men did come to see the necessity of composing their differences on less lofty ground than that of a single, immutable criterion of ultimate truth. This was explicitly recognized by many of the participants in the Putney debates. Cromwell himself pointed out quite carefully that what they were discussing was of immense importance, but that it was a question of choice and feasibility nonetheless.[48]

In this original context, then, there appears what might be called the toleration of diversity from necessity. The contention here, however, is that plural interests and values ought not to be the subject of toleration but of affirmation. Given civic consciousness, this affirmation is the heart of a working constitutional system. It is not simply a matter of accommodating to diversity more or less reluctantly. Pluralism is not a condition to which the appropriate reaction is acquiescence in view of a regrettable absence of complete agreement. It is, on the contrary, both a vital support and the source of the motive power of constitutional government. It is possible to distinguish a variety of considerations related to this, though it is actually their interlocking character that sustains the system. In short, positive pluralism and tolerance are the cardinal virtues of the politics of moderation. This is clearest perhaps at the level of value. For it is the range of concrete choices supplied by a diverse society that makes individual freedom a genuinely operational matter. To be sure, this presupposes the political liberty of consent to government, implemented by the civil liberties. But this is by no means the end of the matter. It is worth recalling familiar considerations. The traditional lines of defense should not be neglected on the ground that they are not new, for they contain elements of permanent value. Thus it is correct to argue that pluralism dampens conflict, since multiple loyalties will result in contrary pressures on the individual citizen.[49] Resolute and singleminded opposition is much reduced in this way. Again, liberty and pluralism contribute to stability because they constitute a safety valve for the expression of frustration and opposition. Moreover, the most solid varieties of cohesion and loyalty are generated at the level of the small group, as Morton Grodzins pointed out.[50] It is also clear that constitutional safeguards are dependent upon some form of power dispersal. But it is

358

less often noticed that a plural structure supplies the drive of the constitutional system.[51] That is why one can afford to adopt the view that the essence of constitutional government is the framework and techniques through which divergent interests are negotiated and compromised.[52]

The essence of the system, then, is not substantive agreement, not consensus on all the most important matters of policy. For the drive to prosecute interests, as well as the content of policy proposals, derives from self-conscious diversity, so that it is this very diversity which is the engine of the system. Politics is both conflict and co-operation precisely because of the multiplicity of individual concerns. Both in terms of the value of individual liberty and the motive power of constitutionalism, the one thing the system cannot withstand is the institutionalization of truth. Here the example of Hooker's political thought is most instructive, for it gives us a rather neat demonstration of the fascination with uniformity and its fatal shortcoming. It will be recalled that Hooker's point was to preserve uniformity of opinion from Puritan dissent by showing that all the questions on which men differed were incapable of rigorous demonstration. Given this, he thought it followed that such differences could not concern essential matters. But matters of indifference were to be settled decisively by public authority — that is, by government. There are two main points that this ingenious and completely fallacious argument makes very clearly. Public purposes must be tied to the interests and values of the vital groups in which individuals find their highest satisfaction. The effect of ruling out their purposes in advance by a logical trick was a damaging self-deception, one which dammed up enough resentment in the end to produce a divorce between government and major segments of English society. This is, of course, an immensely important matter at the level of fact. Theoretically it is more interesting to note that Hooker's argument demonstrates the strictly logical frailty of arguments of this kind. It is intended to show how the preservation of a truth which transcends mere preference is to be attained. The argument must do one of two things: either the truth must be left with no connection with the world at all, in which case it is quite safe but useless, or some institutional arrangement has to be devised. But the effect of this is to drive a wedge between the eternal truth and the affairs of this world by absorbing and domesticating truth in the political process. What is supposed to have saved eternal truth thus has the result of politicizing it.

This is a general technique employed in a great many different ways. In substance it is an attempt to guarantee the validity of institutions, or, to put it another way, to assume that the institutions which are supposed to embody the values of the society cannot be wrong. The great trouble is that validity is inescapably factual: either men behave as if they accept it or they do not, and that is not a matter of logic. There are two other broad alternatives to this same problem of relating institutions to human purposes. A second and equally drastic technique is to set questions of value off to one side, restricting analysis to a nonevaluational framework. Fortunately there is a third alternative. It is simply not the case that we are impaled on the dilemma of resignation to value-relativism or of acceptance of an alleged body of substantive truth. For one can accept the possibility of a disjunction between values and the institutions which are supposed to give them expression. This is where the problems are real. The possibility of stress means that for some men, some of the time, there will exist the peculiarly tense but creative region between unquestioning loyalty and outright disavowal and disobedience, since it is here that the intermittent but continual effort to test institutions and policies in terms of principles goes on. This is the real source of the social energy necessary for the formation and alteration of public purposes. It is also the gray ground on which the most important and most difficult problems of dissent and agreement have to be considered. The other two kinds of answers are unsatisfactory: one because it tries to solve problems of fact and value with a logical instrument, and the other because it does not try to solve them at all. The framework in which the discussion must go on is the uniquely public dimension of the problem. But the motives and purposes derive from diversity. That is why plural interests should be applauded rather than merely tolerated more or less grudgingly. Government is not itself a purpose but an instrument, nor is politics just bargaining; it is the effectuation of purposes that fortunately do not and cannot coincide completely.

Now it will be fruitful to examine an entirely different view, one which is hostile to the perspective and values defended here. Ever since the nineteenth century reaction to the French Revolution, criticism of the political philosophy of liberalism has been frequent, voluminous, and sometimes cogent. Indeed, it has already been shown that some central assumptions of liberalism are open to damaging criticism, at the very least, and that these weaknesses appear to warrant a thorough reassessment. Although such a full-scale treatment cannot be undertaken here, some interesting considerations can be adduced by scrutinizing the radical criticism recently developed by Robert Paul Wolff and Herbert Marcuse in *A Critique of Pure Tolerance*.[53] The general burden of these essays is simple enough. The philosophy of tolerance must be rejected on the ground that in contemporary America it serves only to mask and support the reality of injustice, inequality, alienation, and suppression. Their effort is new in the rather limited sense that the self-identified philosophers of intolerance ground their arguments on a conscious paradox, or rather, a double paradox. There is, first, the contention that the philosophy of tolerance has somehow led to an intolerable society. But secondly, the creation of a genuinely tolerable society can be achieved only by abandoning tolerance. We are thus presented with the proposal that we ought to repudiate that tolerance of diversity which has been thought to be the chief support of individual freedom, but to repudiate it allegedly in the name of that same value. The philosophy of intolerance, then, differs from the usual lines of attack on the ideal of freedom. For it is neither a criticism clearly and explicitly grounded on alternative values, nor is it a refinement conducted from within the premises of the value system of liberalism.

The fundamental difficulty with the radical criticism of tolerance is that it rests rather precariously on a systematically sustained confusion of two quite different kinds of problems. Broadly, this is a confusion of history with a philosophy of politics. This procedure raises two closely related but distinct issues. The more general of these is the tacit assumption of a kind of intellectual determinism; the second is the notion that a political philosophy somehow involves approval of specific results and policies by its advocate. Neither one of these assumptions is proven, nor need they be accepted. On the contrary, there are good reasons for rejecting both of them. Apart from any questions of evidence, the idea of intellectual determinism — the notion that what the philosophers of intolerance regard as the lamentable condition of contemporary America has been brought about by the liberal philosophy of politics — is, quite simply, implausible.[54] For in order to condemn the political philosophy of individual freedom secured through tolerance, it becomes necessary tacitly to adopt the view that the vast numbers of men and activities that have shaped contemporary liberal society were moved by their attachment to the liberal philosophy of politics. Without entering into dispute about the extent to which men are motivated by their ideas, only two choices are available, both of which are implausible. For the argument, if it were to be made explicit, would have to be either that there is no difference between the liberalisms of the philosophers and nonphilosophical men in general, or that the men and movements which seem to have brought about a particular social order and specific policies did not really do so; instead, the philosophers have done it. In fact, of course, it is unnecessary to adopt either of these extreme views. It is perfectly obvious, to begin with, that there has always been a great deal of difference between the liberal philosophy and those commonly held views which are often characterized as liberalism.[55] In short, the ideal of individual freedom has no necessary relationship with the greed of great industrialists or petty capitalists, or with the crude and ruthless social Darwinism that so often accompanied it.

In any case, no evidence of any causal link between the philosophy of tolerance and social structure or public policy is offered. This is plainly crucial, but, instead of being based on evidence or even detailed argumentation, it is simply assumed. Even if evidence were offered, it is difficult to see how it could be held to demonstrate that the ideal ought to be abandoned. For there is an obvious alternative: to argue that to the extent the ideals of liberalism are involved in actual historical developments, what is to be lamented is that they have been so poorly defended and articulated. It is perfectly possible for a libertarian to agree that a given society contains social inconsistencies, that it is too easily self-congratulatory, that the legitimate interests of far too many people have been and, indeed, are being overlooked, that it exhibits injustices, that clarity and consistency are not necessarily virtues to be found in its public philosophers or policy makers — that, in sum, something called the common good may well be neglected.[56] It may be true that the philosophy of tolerance and pluralism is widely held in a society that is too conservative for its own good. But precisely the same thing could be said of any political philosophy whatever. In the absence of any showing that somehow all that is wrong is attributable to the ideals of the philosophy, it is surely going much too far to urge upon us the abandonment of principles whose inherent critical powers are in no way disproved. Certainly it is true that liberalism grew increasingly conservative in the course of the nineteenth century, until there is today hardly any remnant of the forward-looking confidence and optimism of the original article. But surely the disillusioning course of modern history has had something to do with this. And that accumulation of disappointed hopes is far too general to be blamed on liberalism. Moreover, it has had the same dulling effect on all political philosophies;[57] none is any more buoyant or any more hopeful than liberalism, including the "radical criticism" sponsored by the philosophers of intolerance. An acute critic of Marcuse has made the essential point here: "What paralyzes utopian thought and stifles dreams of a millennium in the West is not so much ignorance of the future as knowledge of the present."[58] None of this, however, goes a single step in the direction of showing that the values of liberty and tolerance and the techniques of constitutional politics ought to be abandoned. Why ought we not to go on caring and trying to cultivate the sort of citizen that Raymond Aron has called the "true Westerner"? For this is "the man who accepts nothing unreservedly in our civilisation except the liberty it allows him to criticize it and the chance it offers him to improve it." [59]

The less general assumption that a liberal must maintain certain quite specific positions is equally unwarranted. A political philosophy does not imply any particular social result or specific policy. On the contrary, its chief business is the articulation of goals, of final values, of standards with which to judge the worth of actions and institutions. It can also involve consideration of instrumental values, problems of relating means to ends, in the light of the facts — so far as these can be ascertained with some degree of confidence — and in terms of the probable outcomes of alternative courses of action. But it is perfectly obvious that even within a given system of value there is abundant room for disagreement both about the facts and appropriate means. The point that is involved here can be put another way. The advocate of liberty, of tolerance, and the politics of moderation is in no way obliged by his philosophy to accept or endure the "intolerable." On the contrary, he is free to condemn what he judges ought to be condemned. Indeed, one could agree that all that is deplored by the philosophers of intolerance is deplorable. Certainly this could be done without in any way violating the creed of liberty and tolerance. At this level, disagreement would most likely revolve around matters of fact and of tactics, of means rather than goals. Precisely which specific political conditions one judges to be both deplorable and remediable is much less likely to be a matter of philosophy than a matter of individual experience and temperament. In any case, the important point is that one's views on war and armaments, racial equality, or urban poverty simply are not prescribed for him by the philosophy of tolerance.

It is recognition of this simple but important point that raises the question of what general interpretation is to be put on the philosophy of intolerance. For it is just here — on the question of what the ground of the discussion is — that it is so unclear. Is it a question of discussing the intellectual inadequacies of liberalism and the political and social weaknesses of contemporary America, but in the name of enhanced freedom? If this is the case, then the philosophical frame of the discussion is the liberal conception of freedom. On the other hand, if the point is thought to be the wholesale repudiation of that tradition, then the stakes are so much higher that it would seem pitifully unintelligent not to inquire of such radical critics what they propose to erect in its stead. Needless to say, this is exactly where the outlook that Marcuse has named the "Great Refusal" is at its weakest. Indeed, it is a great deal worse than that. For here the charter of real self-development retreats to the disarming view that it is neither possible nor desirable to provide any idea of the sort of society that ought to replace the present one.[60] One is at least entitled to observe that this persistent refusal to say anything about the nature of utopia is hardly calculated to inspire a very high level of confidence in its architects.

In any case, if one refuses to accept the attribution to his philosophy of all the ills of modern history, he can quite properly indulge in criticism of our intellectual inheritance. The philosophers of intolerance certainly have no exclusive title to that. One need not accept the proven frailties of liberalism. It simply is not true that the political preference which embraces individual freedom as its highest value *must* be allied with a lack of regard for the public order; or that it need cling to an outmoded and simplistic model of political life, in which the essence of politics is depicted as the perpetually renewed struggle between the individual and the state. These features of liberalism can be and, indeed, have been criticized from the standpoint of the cardinal values of that tradition itself. That is exactly as it should be. It is, in

Judith Shklar's phrase, the "prospect of a tolerant society" that ought always to be kept in view. And, on the other hand, it is opposition to the politics of fanaticism that must always be maintained.[61] It is true that in such an outlook the value of individual freedom cannot be the sole element. It also involves a profound skepticism on the subject of total renovation of the human personality, the "re-education" of men which, after all, has so often been a euphemism for intellectual and political tyranny. Skepticism, it is true, can be made to yield narrow, perhaps even cynical, conclusions, but it need not. It is quite compatible with general humane concerns, as, for example, the political thought of David Hume demonstrates.[62] Nor is it incompatible with a capacious view of what ought to be attempted in the name of those humane concerns. The point is rather the one which Aron made so well at the conclusion of *The Opium of the Intellectuals*. "If tolerance is born of doubt, let us teach everyone to doubt all the models and utopias, to challenge all the prophets of redemption and the heralds of catastrophe. If they alone can abolish fanaticism, let us pray for the advent of the sceptics." [63] Such a view entails nothing in the way of accepting injustice. It does mean that one believes himself to have good reasons for rejecting the notion of politics as the relentless pursuit of some curious result which is at once completely vague and yet felt to be meaningful enough to inspire a willingness to impose it on those who do not want it. It does mean a refusal — admittedly based on a reading of history and an estimate of the probabilities — to believe it at all likely, again in Aron's words,[64] that "a single class, a single technique of action and a single ideological system" represent a master key to the endlessly renewed disappointments and aspirations of political man.

However, the philosophy of intolerance believes itself to be equipped with a sufficient answer to these considerations, particularly as it is represented by Marcuse. This reply is the Marxian notion of false consciousness. This idea is no doubt a useful rhetorical device, but it certainly does not represent a powerful argument. On the contrary, it is both an illusion and an evasion. It is an illusion because it fails to perform the intellectual task for which it is designed: to supply an explanation for the regrettable fact that men fail to understand their own real interests. The great difficulty, of course — whether in the hands of Marx or of Marcuse — is that its sponsors wish at the same time to exempt some men, normally themselves, from the operation of the vast historical forces which are supposed to account for false consciousness. The sort of argument to which this view gives rise is no more than a verbal trick: if one fails to see the "truth" of the matter — that is, fails to agree with the unmaskers of false consciousness — he is by definition suffering from a more or less advanced case of false consciousness. Obviously this relieves the critic of the much more difficult task of either meeting or marshaling argument and evidence. How is it, after all, that some few men have escaped the malady? Surely this is not unbelievable intrinsically. But how are we to know — apart from self-identification, as in the case of the Platonic philosopher-king? Historically there has never been any shortage of self-designated seers. But the results of their being power holders have scarcely been uniformly happy. One thinks easily of the Inquisition, the Barebones Parliament of Cromwellian England, the Jacobins, and the Bolsheviks. All one can say in Marcuse's case is that he has the courage of his convictions, for his elitism is open and straightforward, even if in practice one might encounter just a little difficulty in identifying his choice of an elite: those who are in the "maturity of their faculties." [65]

The doctrine of false consciousness is also an evasion, because it fails completely to grapple with the real substance and complexity of politics. Actually this is not surprising, for it is at bottom a survival of the deeply antipolitical views of nineteenth century Marxism, that curious combination of a myth of proximate catastrophe and ultimate harmony which is the content of Marxian utopianism. The abolition of politics by a private act of definition, however, is hardly a satisfactory approach to the world as it is. Indeed, the doctrine of false consciousness is something of an emergency measure, dredged up to defend the essentially romantic outburst against another of the intellectual inventions of the nineteenth century, the notion of a "mass society." At this level, the philosophers of intolerance offer us no more than the presumptuousness of the aristocrat or the Platonist, for the man in the maturity of his faculties does not differ intellectually from the Platonic wise man, or, for that matter, from John Stuart Mill's collapse into the notion that ordinary men ought to capitulate to the judgment of their betters.[66] Now Plato, at least, was consistently aristocratic; his disgust with Athenian democracy and his contempt for the Periclean ideal of freedom are well known. But the philosophers of intolerance purport to be involved in a libertarian campaign. It is just at this point that the several strands of the argument meet. For in the short run, at least, the general liberation, which is supposed to be the goal of radical criticism, yields to the elitism entailed by the distinction between the benighted and "those who know," a doctrine eked out only by reliance on the idea of false consciousness.

The blending of incompatible ideas — elitism at the level of political knowledge, and an allegedly libertarian aim — is no more acceptable in the case of the philosophers of intolerance than in any other case, including that of Wolff's central target, John Stuart Mill. An advocate of freedom through tolerance is no more obliged to embrace Mill's version of liberalism than any other. Indeed, it is a version which not only can be, but in part ought to be, abandoned. For Mill was quite mistaken, from the point of view of a philosophy of liberty, to have repudiated Bentham's insistence that it is nonsense to suppose that what is really good for a man is truly known only by some other man.[67] Bentham's great merit, from the point of view of a libertarian, was that he was inflexible precisely where he ought to have been inflexible, just at those crucial points at which Mill gave himself up to the literary excellence and political poverty of Anglo-German romanticism. Abandonment of the idea that we ought to consider that a man knows his own good, in the only sense in which that phrase has any ascertainable meaning, is to begin the descent into a doctrine of coercion for "one's own good." In short, the liberalism of John Stuart Mill is only partly true to the idea of liberty and is only one element of the tradition. Thus if Wolff supposes that he can dispose of the matter by indulging in a criticism of Mill, he is simply wrong. To be sure, Wolff's essay on pluralism and tolerance is in many ways both penetrating and fascinating, but it is certainly not conclusive. Indeed, it is downright surprising to find a philosopher whose expertise has been generated on the philosophy of Immanuel Kant[68] making the astonishing assertion that the tradition of tolerance involves treating men only as means.[69] What has happened to the categorical imperative? Was it not Kant who insisted that the foundation of morality was that every man must be treated as an end in himself? [70] Or has Kant simply been defined out of the liberal tradition, quite contrary to his own express intention?

The idea of false consciousness is an evasion, finally, because it refuses even to acknowledge the relevance of what any number of men plainly want. Like those whom Aron has called the churchmen and faithful of Marxism,[71] the philosophers of intolerance employ the idea of false consciousness as a convenient method of papering over the same difficulty: that so few people, in whose name the crusade is to be carried on, are willing to follow. Here again the temptation to resort to some more or less effectively camouflaged doctrine of virtuous coercion is liable to be found compelling.

What is it, after all, that we are urged to pursue with such passion? The answer, in a single word — and there is usually not much more than that — is "community." With the doctrine of community, we arrive at the ethically disappointing terminal of the argument. Like the idea of false consciousness, the refusal to say anything about utopia is both an illusion and an evasion. But more important, it is morally completely empty. This is an amazing result after so much ethical heat: no light whatever is provided. The ethical thrust of the philosophy of intolerance is, in fact, exclusively negative, completely antagonistic. Consider the treatment of the opposed outlooks as they are developed in Wolff's essay. On one side, we are presented with a carefully thought out and well-articulated critique of pluralism and tolerance. On the other side, we are treated to an account of the idea of community presented without the slightest attempt to subject it to the same searching criticism. It is difficult to view with much seriousness an ethical enterprise that is devoted only to destruction. Certainly it is the task of political theory to indulge in criticism, but it has never been an exclusive task. What has marked the great works of political philosophy is a combination of both criticism and construction, at least in the sense that an alternative set of standards is articulated. Sustained criticism presupposes some standards of value, but either they can be articulated as they ought to be, or they are unacknowledged, possibly even unexamined. It is precisely such examination that constitutes an exercise in political philosophy. For the crucial question is really this: are the alternatives acceptable? Can good reasons, or at least reasoned argument, be supplied for adopting them? But all that is offered to us, after an act of "wholesale reorganization" which is left totally unspecified, is a single phrase: we must go beyond tolerance to community.[72] In short, we discover what the philosophers of intolerance do not like, but nothing at all about what reasons there may be for preferring something, or indeed anything, else. This means that their utopia is not just vague, it is no utopia at all. It is simply a renewal of the ancient claim to some immensely important but incommunicable truth. Moreover, the entire enterprise founders on the contradictory characterizations of human capacities that are implied in the argument. For on the one hand, the attack on individual freedom relies on the assumption that men are so childlike, so fearful, so weak that they cannot really endure freedom.[73] And the doctrine of false consciousness implies that we are the helpless and none too bright or resourceful victims of men and forces beyond our understanding, to say nothing of control. But on the other hand, men are presumed to be capable enough to recognize and presumably accomplish the truly heroic feat of creating community. It seems clear that one cannot have it both ways.

The idea of community, since it was invented in the nineteenth century reaction against the French Revolution, has tended to reduce to one of two things. In one version, it has involved accepting a particular reading of the European past, from the point of view of the anguished reaction of aristocrats and intellectuals to what they considered was the catastrophic failure of the French Revolution. Of course, the judgment as to whether the revolution had failed, or whether the destruction of medieval "community," privilege, and aristocracy is something to be lamented or to be applauded, depended largely on one's real or imagined status in the *ancien régime*. What is not in dispute, however, is that the assault on the "warm" community life of a society organized on the basis of a landed aristocracy was carried on in the name of freedom. That idea is no more refuted by pointing to the record of the revolution than the ideal of a wise aristocracy is refuted by pointing to the facts of the *ancien régime*, or any more than the values of Christianity are refuted by the history of Christian Europe. To the extent that the ground of discussion is political theory, the appropriate method is the marshaling of reasoned arguments, not pointing to the inevitable gap between ideals and performance. To be sure, the facts are a relevant part of one's final judgment, of his choice of the set of values he prefers for society. Also, just as the facts are relevant, but not by themselves conclusive, so is the question of feasibility, the problem of weighing alternative probabilities. But how can this task be done in the complete absence of any indication of what the idea of community is supposed to mean?

Let it be assumed, however, that the radical critics of the philosophy of tolerance do not wish to associate themselves with the aristocratic past. This leaves the other version of the notion of community, the nineteenth century tradition of utopia-building in the manner of Owen, Fourier, Saint-Simon, and Karl Marx. Clearly there is nothing inherently base in the idea of community as such. But unless the philosophers of intolerance are truly serious about the problem of expunging the profound differences among men on the subject of what matters most, they will have to entertain the prospect of multiple communities, at the very least. The only other alternatives are either simple coercion, or, as in the case of real or imagined manipulative states, a program of enforced and massive reorganization of the human personality. It may be, of course, that the alternatives would be indistinguishable in practice. Of the philosophy — if not, indeed, the practice — of pluralism and tolerance, it may at least be said that there is theoretical room for as many "communities" as the critics can find men who will agree to inhabit them. Once again, it is scarcely conclusive to point out that the history of liberal society exhibits intolerance, indeed frequent failures, in this regard. This is undeniably true. But surely the remedy is not to be found in accentuating that failure by abandoning outright even the ideal. Whatever the road to community might be like, there appear to be only two general alternatives for seeking it: the path of an enhanced milieu of tolerance, or the path of manipulation and coercion, in short, of tyranny. It is at just this point that the moral emptiness of the idea of community doubles back to make the philosophy of intolerance dangerous even to itself. For the absence of any positive moral content means that anyone at all may adopt the title of "maturity," proceed with the abandonment or destruction of the rotten framework, and simply insert his own preferences into the morally vacuous categories of the philosophy of intolerance. What on earth is to prevent it?

It is just here, oddly, that the radical critics of right and left join hands. For they share the same apolitical impatience, the same indifference to what men say they prefer to do with their own lives, and the same contempt for the painfully won methods of constitutionalized politics. From both left and right, "constitutional government, the balance of power, legal guarantees, the whole edifice of political civilization slowly built up over the course of the ages and always incomplete, is calmly pushed aside." [74] And that with neither serious historical inquiry into the social or intellectual past from which their views derive, or the slightest indication of the sort of loaf we may reasonably expect once we have destroyed the bit of bread we have in hand. In short, both extremes have been characterized rightly as "those strange builders who always begin by destroying." [75] Both the extreme poles join that company of social theorists whom Morton Grodzins aptly called the "Gemeinschaft grouses," [76] that is, those who, finding the modern world uncomfortable, have supposed that the past was better. The great difficulty is that this view rests either on a refusal to recognize the realities of the European Middle Ages or on a clearly hopeless yearning for the supposed moral agreement and certainty of the polis of classical antiquity. But neither of these sources of inspiration has anything to recommend it to anyone interested in individual freedom. For the notion of community appears to rest in the last resort on an idea of complete agreement, on uniformity at the level of value. This, in turn, reflects the view that politics is not, after all, a matter of choice, of preferences, and therefore an affair of bargaining and negotiating the diverse interests that are an inevitable accompaniment of a complex society, but rather a matter of truth. No amount of intellectual gymnastics can succeed in evading the crucial point: if the idea of "discriminatory tolerance" [77] is to mean anything at all, it presupposes some more or less arcane knowledge and ultimately the supposition, not only that there is some truth, but *a* truth, and that somebody knows it. Logically there are only two alternatives. Societies may be grounded on the assumption that the pursuit of truth is at most tentative, piecemeal, and must necessarily remain open — necessarily, because we can hardly be said to know when and if we have uncovered truth, for otherwise we could, in principle, know it in advance, which is surely a contradiction. Or one may suppose that societies are or ought to be grounded on the truth. The trouble is that this is an idea usually accompanied by the assertion that there are some people who know what that truth is. Oddly, the truth is usually found to have existed in the past. But the essential point is simply that there is no objection to the quest for community as such; what is objectionable is the devotee's urge to carry everyone with him, whether willingly or not.

It is perfectly true, on the level of fact, that none of the ideals of the philosophy of tolerance can remove the possibility that the avenues of change will be closed, that what was once a libertarian polity may no longer be so. Nor can it solve the individual citizen's problem of deciding when it is both right and prudent to resist government. But neither can any general philosophy, for such a decision requires that a particular citizen decide that a given set of facts ought to be described as intolerable tyranny, and also that he resolve the necessarily individual problem of multiple and conflicting commitments and loyalties. His fellow citizens may not agree that the facts warrant such a designation and may, therefore, resist him. Or for that matter, many may agree that the facts do constitute tyranny, but they may not agree that the appropriate response is resistance. In short, there are a good many factors to be taken into account — matters of fact, of competing values and obligations, and of prudence. Circumstances may be such, for example, that resistance would be futile, in the sense that it would only worsen an already deplorable situation. That might be the case, for instance, when the power to be opposed is simply overwhelming, or when one's cause fails to elicit broad enough support to make it even superficially justifiable. Such dilemmas are surely the cruelest that the citizen can confront. It is entirely appropriate that political philosophy should undertake to address such problems, to consider the elements of the situation, the chances of success, the probable consequences of action — the reasons, in sum, which can be offered for choosing one or another course of action. But what political philosophy cannot do is produce automatic answers, nor can any system of principles — religious, philosophical, or political.[78] For, in the last resort, an individual must decide, must choose, and neither facts nor reasons nor principles compel a specific choice in a specific context. All that a thought process can do, and it is not a little, is to make the choice more or less well informed. To pretend that the situation is otherwise, that there exists some source that relieves one of his responsibility for choice, is to risk dulling men's critical capacities. In the last resort, it deprives them of the ultimate source of their dignity, the freedom to choose. Our age has no premium on the frailties of man in society — excessive preoccupation with one's own affairs, narrowness of vision and perhaps of spirit, fear of uncertainty and often merely of change — all the frailties that have always made it incredibly difficult for men to recognize that there are others in desperate straits. But verbal incantation is no substitute for reasoned argument, nor is repeated emphasis a substitute for logic, nor caricature for serious analysis. The plain fact is that many of us certainly do not want, and feel that we do not need, self-designated prophets, wardens, or psychic counsellors, and that is precisely the problem: we do not and are not likely to agree even on the issue of that supposed need.

At the level of philosophy, then, liberalism does not necessarily involve specific postures. It is certainly true that it can be used and, for that matter, abused in the business of justifying a specific choice. That, however, is true of any political outlook. All that liberalism needs to embrace is the view that individual liberty is the highest political value. The remaining components do not have the character of an ethical postulate but are, rather, broad empirical judgments. The view adopted here involves the assumption that politics, more particularly the use of power, is apt to be dangerous but is also inescapable. Rather than being a liability, this distrust of power is a decisive advantage as against the several forms of antipolitics, for it candidly confronts what appears to be the case: that men will continue to employ and to abuse power. Rightly understood, then, liberalism teaches skepticism in the face of pseudopolitical fanaticism, a certain reserve in reposing trust in men. It recognizes that politics ought properly to be a human enterprise, a matter of prudence, rather than one of inflated emotion and exalted goals, and it represents the conviction that men may differ legitimately, and hence that the virtue of tolerance is indispensable. It thus refuses to be either apolitical or totally political. Its meaning is at once to accept politics, but also to quarry out and hedge with protective devices some portion of private life. To be sure, the judgment on politics is not very flattering. As one of the most eloquent and incisive defenders of its political modesty has put it, politics has always been the choice of the least evil.[79] This does not prove, nor could it prove, that other views are less good. What liberalism does do, however, is to fit the range of historical experience in politics far better than the others. Its greatest achievement is constitutional government wedded to the still developing ideal of representative democracy. To be sure, that is not a reason to hold that change is undesirable. It is a reason for adopting a stance of reserve when one is urged to embrace some political fanaticism.

Constitutional government, then, is dependent in the first place upon civic consciousness and loyalty. But it also rests essentially and not merely accidentally on plural interests and values, which are at once the source of genuine alternatives, organized power, purposes, and social energy. The particular forms and techniques of constitutional rule do not constitute its essence, but rather are its expressions, and the values we cherish are the fluctuating measures of its successes and failures. Admittedly these are modest enough conclusions, for which I cannot claim originality. But it has seemed worthwhile to illustrate the dependency of constitutionalized politics on elements so fundamental that they have been too often simply assumed. This has meant that much discussion has been deflected to the wrong subjects in considering the likelihood of creating or maintaining such a system. Moreover, despite the modesty of these suggestions, the permanent value of pluralism and tolerance deserves emphasis, particularly since the value of uniformity has perhaps had the better of it in the classical tradition of political theory.[80] At all events, the theorist of a constitutional system ought not to be either the priest of any substantive orthodoxy or the prophet of some refurbished fanaticism, for neither enhances our understanding or appreciation of the real limits and possibilities of the politics of moderation and tolerance.

Notes, Bibliography and Index

Notes

Chapter One. Politics in Two Worlds

1. For an illuminating effort to obtain some clarity on these notoriously fuzzy concepts, see Stanley Hoffmann, "Obstinate or Obsolete? The Fate of the Nation-State and the Case of Western Europe," *Daedalus*, 95:862–915 (1966), esp. 867–869. National consciousness, Hoffmann argues, is "the sense of 'cohesion and distinctiveness' which sets one off from other groups." Nationalism, he suggests, we ought to confine to the doctrine "that gives to the nation in world affairs absolute value and top priority." The kind of political consciousness referred to in the text as "national consciousness" follows Hoffmann's usage. An analogous point has been made in a perceptive essay by Ali Mazrui, "Borrowed Theory and Original Practice in African Politics," in Herbert J. Spiro, ed., *Patterns of African Development* (Englewood Cliffs, N.J., 1967), p. 94. Fred R. von der Mehden, *Politics of the Developing Nations* (Englewood Cliffs, N.J., 1964), pp. 30–52, refers to the same range of phenomena as the problem of national identity. Rupert Emerson, *From Empire to Nation* (Boston, 1962), calls it nationalism.

2. Emerson, *Empire to Nation*, p. 213.

3. Karl W. Deutsch, *Nationalism and Social Communication* (Cambridge, Mass., 1966), p. 173.

4. Samuel P. Huntington, "Political Modernization: America vs. Europe," *World Politics*, 18:378–414 (1966).

5. Carl J. Friedrich, *The New Image of the Common Man* (Boston, 1950), pp. 43–80; Francis D. Wormuth, *The Royal Prerogative 1603–1649* (Ithaca, N.Y., 1939), pp. 74–77. Frederick Mundell Watkins, *The State as a Concept of Political Science* (New York, 1934), pp. 7–41, presents a broad historical discussion.

6. Watkins, *The State*, pp. 42–62. A more useful definition, of course, is supplied by the Weberian idea of a monopoly of the legitimate use of force. Max Weber, *The Theory of Social and Economic Organization*, trans. A. M. Henderson and Talcott Parsons, ed. Talcott Parsons (Glencoe, Ill., 1947), pp. 154–157. On this point, see Robert A. Dahl, *Modern Political Analysis* (Englewood Cliffs, N.J., 1963), pp. 4–6.

7. David Hume, "Of the First Principles of Government," in Frederick

378

Watkins, ed., *Hume: Theory of Politics* (Edinburgh, 1951), p. 148. It was this which Charles E. Merriam, *Political Power* (Chicago, 1934), pp. 159–183, referred to as the "poverty of power." See also, Carl J. Friedrich, *Constitutional Government and Democracy* (Boston, 1950), pp. 22–24.

8. See the acute discussion of Heinz Eulau, "The Depersonalization of the Concept of Sovereignty," *Journal of Politics*, 4:3–19 (1942), reprinted in Heinz Eulau, *Journeys in Politics* (New York, 1963), pp. 57–72.

9. Penry Williams has observed, in another connection, that "so much of English history has been written in terms of this concept — the creation of a sovereign state in the sixteenth century, the struggle for sovereignty within that state in the seventeenth — that doubts of its value may seem heretical. But many historians seem to take up their stand at the nineteenth-century finishing-post of Austinian sovereignty, and as they watch the progress of past ages toward them their binoculars impose serious distortions." Penry Williams, "The Tudor State," *Past & Present*, no. 25 (July 1963), p. 44.

10. Emerson, *Empire to Nation*, p. 370.

11. Hoffmann, "Obstinate or Obsolete?" p. 867.

12. A. L. Rowse, *The England of Elizabeth* (New York, 1961), pp. 31–65.

13. *Ibid.*, p. 532.

14. The problems raised by the introduction of the doctrine of reason of state into English domestic politics are brought out especially well in George L. Mosse, *The Struggle for Sovereignty in England* (East Lansing, Mich., 1950), 50–56, 67–68, 118–122, and in Wormuth, *The Royal Prerogative*, pp. 69–82. C. J. Friedrich, *Constitutional Reason of State* (Providence, R.I., 1957), discusses the general problems raised by this idea on a broader historical and theoretical plane.

15. Gabriel A. Almond and G. Bingham Powell, Jr., *Comparative Politics: A Developmental Approach* (Boston, 1966), p. 36.

16. Hoffmann, "Obstinate or Obsolete?" p. 915, n. 41.

17. Charles W. Anderson, *Politics and Economic Change in Latin America* (Princeton, N.J., 1967), pp. 3–46, has insisted on the vital role of the assumption of citizen competence and has emphasized the indispensable part played by the state in this process. It is just this that has so persistently been overlooked in the study of development in European history. For some suggestions as to why this is so, see my concluding chapter.

18. Huntington, "Political Modernization," p. 383.

19. Edward C. Banfield, *The Moral Basis of a Backward Society* (Glencoe, Ill., 1958), p. 7, makes a related point.

20. Samuel P. Huntington, "The Political Modernization of Traditional Monarchies," *Daedalus*, 95:763–788 (1966). Professor Huntington argues, indeed, that the very process of modernization enhances "group consciousness of all kinds: village, tribe, religion, caste." *Ibid.*, p. 769. He cites a most interesting statement by an Ibo leader, reporting on his efforts to create group consciousness, that Ibo villagers " 'couldn't even imagine all Ibos.' " Quoted *ibid.*, from David Abernethy, "Education and Politics in a Developing Society: The Southern Nigerian Experience" (unpub. diss. Harvard University, 1965), p. 307. The problems involved in the search

for the "nation" have been explored in Emerson, *Empire to Nation*; on the point here, see esp. pp. 105–131. The following statement is illuminating, coming as it did from a prominent Nigerian political figure: "Nigeria is not a nation. It is a mere political expression." Quoted *ibid.*, p. 129. Fascinating discussions on the problems of relations between primitive political organization and the new states, from an anthropological perspective, may be found in Lucy Mair, *Primitive Government* (Baltimore, 1964), pp. 251–279, and at length in her *New Nations* (London, 1963); and in Max Gluckman, *Custom and Conflict in Africa* (Glencoe, Ill., 1955), pp. 137–165. For a brief general treatment, see Fred G. Burke, *Africa's Quest for Order* (Englewood Cliffs, N.J., 1964), pp. 19–34, 46–48. For a very interesting effort to employ both primitive and medieval European materials for comparative theory, see Almond and Powell, *Comparative Politics*, esp. pp. 213–254.

21. For a brilliant and provocative treatment, see J. H. Plumb, *The Origins of Political Stability: England 1675–1725* (Boston, 1967).

22. Harry Eckstein, "Political Theory and the Study of Politics," *American Political Science Review*, 50:475–487 (1956).

23. Almond and Powell, *Comparative Politics*, p. 51.

24. This is most often and most obviously the case in the study of political ideas. For some purposes, especially when the object is philosophical adequacy as such, context, behavior, and so on may be rightly dispensed with. But this sort of inquiry certainly ought not to exhaust the study of the history of ideas. On the other hand, it is not infrequently the case that inquiry into behavior is prosecuted without benefit of the aids to insight that are provided by political ideas in the area under investigation. For a criticism along these lines, see the review by Aristide Zolberg, *American Political Science Review*, 60:119–121 (1966), of Lucian W. Pye and Sidney Verba, eds., *Political Culture and Political Development* (Princeton, N.J., 1965).

25. This curious feature of triumphant liberalism has been noted from a variety of perspectives. Michael Walzer, *The Revolution of the Saints* (Cambridge, Mass., 1965), pp. 302–303, stresses the bland assumption of men's capacity for political virtue as contrasted with the earlier Puritan emphasis on the need for discipline and organization. Sheldon Wolin, *Politics and Vision* (Boston, 1960), esp. pp. 286–294, 305–314, is concerned with the liberal view that society is organized spontaneously without coercion and therefore is the realm of freedom, as contrasted with the realm of the political. His argument is that this alteration of focus from government to society, along with the identification of government and the idea of coercion, is the beginning of the decline of a specifically political philosophy. In quite another vein, Hannah Arendt has undertaken analysis and criticism of Western European liberalism in terms of the debilitating impact of private ambition on the public realm in both domestic and foreign affairs. See for example, *The Origins of Totalitarianism* (New York, 1958), pp. 123–157, 305–339. It should be noted that Miss Arendt's emphasis on this theme rests on her exposition and apprecia-

tion of a distinction between private and public realms drawn from ancient Greek political theory. On this see *The Human Condition* (Garden City, N.Y., 1959), pp. 23–69. The distinction, alas, is relevant only to the polis; that is, a small and immensely sophisticated society. Miss Arendt is fully aware of the fact that the Greek idea is not adaptable to modern large-scale societies; indeed, her analysis turns on a sharp contrast between classical antiquity and the modern world. See her *Between Past and Future* (New York, 1961). A brief statement referring to the Middle Ages, however, is exactly apposite in the context under discussion here: "the secular realm under the rule of feudalism was indeed in its entirety what the private realm had been in antiquity. Its hallmark was the absorption of all activities into the household sphere, where they had only private significance, and consequently the very absence of a public realm." *The Human Condition*, p. 32.

In terms of the view being developed here, however, it is crucial to recognize that since political assumptions and reflection achieved a civic focus in the seventeenth century, thus becoming canalized on the political order as a whole, it has been possible, at least in principle, to recognize and appreciate the gap between civic consciousness and its absence, between a public frame of reference and subpolitical preoccupations. I think this is the vital background to the observations made by these acute critics of liberal political thought.

26. This is a point made especially well in Ernst H. Kantorowicz, *The King's Two Bodies* (Princeton, N.J., 1957).

27. The spiritual regeneration and the drive to distinguish the temporal and spiritual which goes under the name of Gregorian reform has been acutely treated in brief compass in R. W. Southern, *The Making of the Middle Ages* (New Haven, 1953), pp. 118–154. A fine detailed treatment is Gerd Tellenbach, *Church, State and Christian Society at the Time of the Investiture Contest*, trans. R. F. Bennett (Oxford, 1940).

28. From a governmental point of view, the most important feature of this period was the articulation of an efficient legal system. There is a lucid treatment of this complex subject in Brian Tierney, *Foundations of the Conciliar Theory* (Cambridge, Eng., 1955), parts I, II. As Tierney says, "to sketch in outline the growth of the *Corpus Iuris Canonici* from the appearance of Gratian's *Decretum* to the outbreak of the Great Schism is, in effect, to record the process by which the Church became a body politic, subject to one head and manifesting an external unity of organization." *Ibid.*, pp. 13–14. The whole subject of Church government has received characteristically stimulating treatment in Walter Ullmann, *The Growth of Papal Government in the Middle Ages* (London, 1955). For a criticism of Ullmann's thesis that the ideology of papal supremacy was not a late medieval development, but is to be found implicitly as early as the Patristic Age, see Alfons M. Stickler, "Concerning the Political Theories of the Medieval Canonists, *Traditio*, 7:450–463 (1949–51).

29. Walter Ullmann, *Medieval Papalism* (London, 1949), p. 2.

30. Michael Wilks, *The Problem of Sovereignty in the Later Middle Ages* (Cambridge, Eng., 1963), pp. 418–419; see also pp. 419–425.

31. Wilks notes, *ibid.*, p. 121, that the feudal world seldom entered into the range of vision of the theorists he discusses.

32. M. V. Clarke, *Medieval Representation and Consent* (London, 1936), p. 5.

33. In Samuel H. Beer and Adam B. Ulam, eds., *Patterns of Government* (New York, 1962), p. 35.

34. Eckstein, "Political Theory and the Study of Politics," p. 485.

35. Particularly helpful on the narrow gauge of medieval politics are J. E. A. Jolliffe, *Angevin Kingship* (London, 1955), and J. C. Holt, *Magna Carta* (Cambridge, Eng., 1965), esp. pp. 19–42.

36. In one view military necessities are held to be the origin of feudalism. A recent and vigorous restatement of this view may be found in Lynn White Jr., *Medieval Technology and Social Change* (Oxford, 1962), esp. pp. 2–14. White's views have been criticized by R. H. Hilton and P. H. Sawyer, "Technical Determinism: the Stirrup and the Plough," *Past & Present*, no. 24 (April 1963), pp. 90–100. The view, on the contrary, that feudalism was essentially a system of government has received notable statement by Joseph R. Strayer, "Feudalism in Western Europe," in Rushton Coulborn, ed., *Feudalism in History* (Princeton, 1956), pp. 15–25.

37. Marc Bloch, *Feudal Society*, trans. L. A. Manyon (Chicago, 1961), p. 443.

38. J. M. Wallace-Hadrill, *The Barbarian West* (New York, 1962), p. 144.

39. This is one of the central points in the masterly survey of English constitutional history by B. Wilkinson, *Constitutional History of Medieval England 1216–1399* (3 vols; London, 1948–1958).

40. G. Barraclough, *The Origins of Modern Germany* (New York, 1963), pp. 3–246, is particularly valuable in underlining the importance of complications arising from international relations in the faltering career of medieval Germany. Southern, *Making of the Middle Ages*, pp. 81–104, presents a lively sketch of the county of Anjou in the eleventh century.

41. Kantorowicz, *The King's Two Bodies*, pp. 233–234; Holt, *Magna Carta*, p. 27.

42. *Tractatus de legibus et consuetudinibus regni Anglie qui Glanvilla vocatur*, ed. and trans. G. D. G. Hall (London, 1965), IX, 4, p. 107.

43. Wilks, *The Problem of Sovereignty*, p. 59.

44. *Disquisitio theologico-iuridica*, V, 1357–58: "Ordo totius universi seu totius mundi . . . consistit in gradibus inferiorum et subditorum . . . sine quo ordine mundus stare non possit nec homines vivere." Quoted in Wilks, *The Problem of Sovereignty*, p. 58.

45. There is an excellent exposition of the hierarchical world view of the Middle Ages in Paul E. Sigmund, *Nicholas of Cusa and Medieval Political Thought* (Cambridge, Mass., 1963), pp. 39–66.

46. J. H. Hexter, *Reappraisals in History* (New York, 1963), pp. 80–81.

47. G. R. Elton, *England under the Tudors* (London, 1960), p. vi.

48. The chief point of G. R. Elton, *The Tudor Revolution in Govern-*

ment (Cambridge, Eng., 1953), as the title suggests, is to insist on a revolutionary change in the bureaucratic structure of English government. Elton emphasizes the influence of a single man, Thomas Cromwell. Elton's thesis as presented in this and other works is discussed critically by Penry Williams and G. L. Harriss, "A Revolution in Tudor History?" *Past & Present,* no. 25 (July 1963), pp. 3–58.

49. The classical expression of the view that feudalism was introduced at the time of the Conquest is J. H. Round, *Feudal England* (London, 1909), pp. 225–314. This view has received a powerful statement more recently by Sir Frank Stenton, *The First Century of English Feudalism* (Oxford, 1961). The thesis, on the other side, of essential continuity between Anglo-Saxon and Norman England was the view taken in the classic works of Freeman and Stubbs. More recently, the theme of continuity, at least in many important respects, has been advanced in two interesting works of C. Warren Hollister, *Anglo-Saxon Military Institutions* (Oxford, 1962), and *The Military Organization of Norman England* (Oxford, 1965), and in the important works of Eric John, *Land Tenure in Early England* (Leicester, 1960), and *Orbis Britanniae* (Leicester, 1966), esp. pp. 128–153. A review and some acute observations on the recent stages of the debate is provided by J. O. Prestwich, "Anglo-Norman Feudalism and the Problem of Continuity," *Past & Present,* no. 26 (November 1963), pp. 39–57.

50. H. G. Richardson and G. O. Sayles, *The Governance of Mediaeval England* (Edinburgh, 1953), pp. 22–118, present a vigorous statement of the view that the concept "feudalism" is not a serviceable intellectual tool and, even if it were, is peculiarly inappropriate in the English context. The second part of this judgment appears to rest primarily on the fact that the Norman and Angevin monarchy represented comparatively strong general government.

51. The literature on all these questions is extensive, and this note makes no pretense at completeness. The great historian of Tudor England, A. F. Pollard, *Factors in Modern History* (London, 1907), announced the main themes around which these controversies have swirled: that sixteenth century monarchies were "new" and essentially absolute and, therefore, that representative institutions fell into decline, and that this was also the period of the rise of the middle class. A sustained and acute criticism of all these themes is to be found in Hexter, *Reappraisals in History,* esp. pp. 26–44, 71–162. The view that absolutist new monarchies were characteristic of sixteenth century Europe has been defended more recently in Gerhardt Ritter, *Die Neugestaltung Europas in 16 Jahrhundert* (Berlin, 1950); Henri Hauser, *Les Débuts de l'age moderne* (Paris, 1956), and Roland Mousnier, *Histoire générale des civilisations: les XVIe et XVIIe siècles* (Paris, 1961). On the other hand, it has been argued that sixteenth century monarchy is more accurately described in terms of a heightened and refurbished medievalism. This is the view, for example, of Leon Cahen, *L'Évolution politique de l'Angleterre* (Paris, 1960). G. R. Elton, *England under the Tudors,* has provided a very convenient sum-

mary discussion of the arguments over the middle class: see esp. pp. 255–261.

52. Raymond Aron, "Evidence and Inference in History," *Daedalus*, 87: 11–39 (1958).

53. F. L. Ganshof, *Feudalism*, trans. Philip Grierson (New York, 1964), p. 168: "Feudal institutions lasted in western Europe to the end of the *Ancien Régime*, and in some countries elements of them survived into the nineteenth and even the twentieth centuries. But from the end of the thirteenth century they ceased in western Europe to be the most fundamental element in the structure of society . . ."

54. An admirable statement of the issues involved and the distinctions which I agree ought to be made in comparing the Tudor and Stuart periods from the perspective of parliamentary development is J. S. Roskell, "Perspectives in English Parliamentary History," *Bulletin of the John Rylands Library*, 46: 448–475 (1964).

55. See the fascinating study of E. M. W. Tillyard, *The Elizabethan World Picture* (New York, n.d.)

56. Samuel H. Beer, *British Politics in the Collectivist Age* (New York, 1965), pp. 5–8.

57. Garrett Mattingly, *Renaissance Diplomacy* (Baltimore, 1964), particularly pp. 140–147. With reference to the European situation in 1618, C. V. Wedgwood, *The Thirty Years War* (Garden City, N.Y., 1961), p. 18, writes: "the dynasty was, with few exceptions, more important in European diplomacy than the nation. Royal marriages were the rivets of international policy and the personal will of the sovereign or the interests of his family its motive forces. For all practical purposes France and Spain are misleading terms for the dynasties of Bourbon and Hapsburg."

58. See n. 1, above.

59. Roskell, "Perspectives in English Parliamentary History," pp. 448–475.

60. Bloch, *Feudal Society*, p. 421.

61. *Ibid.*, p. 422.

62. Owing principally to a series of careful studies by Gaines Post, students of medieval political thought have been made aware of the extensive and varied use of ideas drawn from Roman law. For the point here, see especially "The Theory of Public Law and the State in the Thirteenth Century," *Seminar*, 6: 42–59 (1948), and *Studies in Medieval Legal Thought* (Princeton, N.J., 1964), pp. 241–309, 333–367. Happily, this book incorporates many of the separate articles Mr. Post has contributed to our understanding.

63. The crucial role of overseas affairs in the construction of Angevin administration is rightly given great weight in Richardson and Sayles, *The Governance of Mediaeval England*, pp. 156–215. See also Holt, *Magna Carta*, pp. 20–25. Holt observes, for instance, "War was the compulsive urgency behind administrative experiment . . ." *Ibid.*, p. 20.

64. Richardson and Sayles, *The Governance of Mediaeval England*, p. 319.

384

65. *Ibid.*, pp. 265–284.

66. This is a point rightly emphasized in Norman F. Cantor, *Medieval History* (New York, 1963).

67. Jolliffe, *Angevin Kingship*, p. 344.

68. Christopher Hill, *The Century of Revolution, 1603–1714* (Edinburgh, 1961), p. 190.

69. A. S. P. Woodhouse, ed., *Puritanism and Liberty* (Chicago: University of Chicago Press, 1951), p. 53.

70. *Ibid.*, p. 80.

71. To be sure, the debates of the prewar period did center precisely on the ancient liberties, or rather, on the more general ground of immemorial custom. But prior to the civil wars, both parties to the constitutional debates shared the same assumptions. J. G. A. Pocock has observed in his acute study, *The Ancient Constitution and the Feudal Law* (Cambridge, Eng., 1957), pp. 54–55, that "the belief in an immemorial law was not a party argument put forward by some clever lawyer as a means of limiting the king's prerogative: it was the nearly universal belief of Englishmen. The case for the crown was not that the king ruled as a sovereign and that there was no fundamental law, but that there was a fundamental law and that the king's prerogative formed part of it . . . It is too easily forgotten that there was a common-law case for the crown as well as against it, and the former case was expressed in the same language and based on the same assumptions as the latter." I think this is exactly right. For an extended discussion of this common background before the civil wars and its breakup, see Margaret Atwood Judson, *The Crisis of the Constitution* (New Brunswick, N.J., 1949), esp. pp. 12–14, 44–67, 381–436. A quite different interpretation has been ably presented in G. L. Mosse, *The Struggle for Sovereignty in England* (East Lansing, Mich., 1950); he argues that the intellectual issues were settled by 1628–29.

72. C. B. Macpherson, *The Political Theory of Possessive Individualism* (Oxford, 1962), pp. 107–159; and see pp. 294–298 for references to the secondary literature which his argument seeks to correct.

73. Beer, *British Politics*, p. 9.

74. *Ibid.*, pp. 3–9. Immensely helpful in this regard is the definitive work of J. E. Neale, *Elizabeth I and Her Parliaments* (2 vols.; New York, 1958). For example, Neale writes (I, 16): "In the sixteenth century the system of government was personal monarchy. Questions of policy and the direction of the administration were the Crown's preserve, entrenched in its prerogative . . . Politically speaking, Parliament was little more than a convenient safety-valve."

75. Walter Bagehot, *The English Constitution* (London, 1872).

76. This definition of constitutionalism derives from Carl J. Friedrich, *Constitutional Government and Democracy* (Boston, 1950), pp. 121–131.

77. For a penetrating discussion of a considerable sampling of the modern literature of nostalgia, see Wolin, *Politics and Vision*, pp. 352–434.

78. See, e.g., Max Gluckman, *Politics, Law and Ritual in Tribal So-*

ciety (Oxford, 1965), p. 57: "Tribal society is as torn between the pressures of economic interest, and even survival, and the demands of cultural and moral values as society is everywhere else."

79. Friedrich Heer, *The Medieval World,* trans. Janet Sondheimer (New York, 1963), p. 28. J. M. Wallace-Hadrill, *The Long-Haired Kings* (London, 1962), p. 147, rightly observes that the "marvel of early medieval society is not war but peace."

80. Kenneth Pickthorn, *Early Tudor Government: Henry VIII* (Cambridge, Eng., 1951), p. 6. More generally, see Otto Kirchheimer, *Political Justice,* (Princeton, N.J., 1961), particularly pp. 25–172, and Judith N. Shklar, *Legalism* (Cambridge, Mass., 1964), pp. 111–221.

81. *The Federalist,* 51.

82. *Ibid.,* 78.

83. Edward Hallett Carr, *The Twenty Years' Crisis* (London, 1946).

84. Wormuth, *The Royal Prerogative 1603–1649,* p. 3.

85. Southern Pacific Co. v. Jensen, 244 U.S. 222.

86. Shklar, *Legalism,* esp. pp. 1–28.

87. The most explicit use of this contrast is to be found in Charles Howard McIlwain, *The High Court of Parliament and Its Supremacy* (New Haven, 1910), esp. pp. 257–328, and *The Growth of Political Thought in the West* (New York, 1932), pp. 364–394. It is implicit, however, in other works devoted to expounding the idea that law was always "found" in an adjudicative process, never (or hardly ever) "made" by conscious legislation. For example, Fritz Kern, *Kingship and Law in the Middle Ages,* trans. S. B. Chrimes (Oxford, 1948), pp. 154–155: the medieval conception is that "the law is sovereign, not the State, the community, the magistracy, the prince, or any other person or body which we should contrast with the law. The State cannot change the law." R. W. and A. J. Carlyle, *A History of Mediaeval Political Theory in the West* (Edinburgh, 1950), VI, 507, maintain "that the first principle of medieval political society was the supremacy, not of the prince but of the law . . . [the law] . . . was not properly something deliberately or consciously made." See also George H. Sabine, *A History of Political Theory* (New York, 1950), pp. 198–222.

88. Marc Bloch, *Les Rois thaumaturges* (Strasbourg, 1924), pp. 155–156.

89. Stanley Hoffmann, *The State of War* (New York, 1965), p. 276.

90. T. F. T. Plucknett, *Edward I and Criminal Law* (Cambridge, Eng., 1960), pp. 91–101.

91. This does not mean, of course, that there was no interest in England in these and other great controversies. But just as surely the investiture controversy was mainly an Italian and German affair, as Bloch, *Les Rois thaumaturges,* p. 190, has pointed out. Also, by comparison English activity in conciliarism was very modest. E. F. Jacob, *Essays in the Conciliar Epoch* (Manchester, 1943), pp. 57–84, has argued that the years 1408–1418 were a period of considerable English involvement. Yet this was followed by near withdrawal. *Ibid.,* pp. 44–56.

Chapter Two. Double Majesty

1. Frederic William Maitland, *Domesday Book and Beyond* (Cambridge, Eng., 1921), p. 9.

2. The ingenious expression, double majesty *(duplex majestas)*, was coined by Otto Gierke, *Natural Law and the Theory of Society*, trans. Ernest Barker (Cambridge, Eng., 1958), pp. 40–60. It is used here, however, in a quite different way. I am greatly indebted in this connection to a penetrating study by Francis D. Wormuth, *The Origins of Modern Constitutionalism* (New York, 1949), and still more to instruction received from its author. His is the only work I know that takes up Gierke's suggestion and turns it to illuminating analytical use.

3. Dorothy Whitelock, *The Beginnings of English Society* (Harmondsworth, Eng., 1952), pp. 12–13, points out that the Anglo-Saxons were fully conscious of their racial origins and continental relatives. Thus in a letter concerning his efforts to convert the Saxons, Boniface says: "Have pity on them, for even they themselves are wont to say; 'We are of one blood and one bone' . . ." See "Letter of Boniface to the Whole English Race, appealing for the conversion of the Saxons (738)," in Dorothy Whitelock, ed. (David C. Douglas general ed.), *English Historical Documents, c. 500–1042* (London: Eyre & Spottiswoode [Publishers] Ltd., 1955), p. 748. Hereafter this volume will be cited as *EHD*. For other striking examples, see Bede, *A History of the English Church and People*, trans. Leo Sherley-Price (Harmondsworth, Eng., 1965), I, 15, and V, 9.

4. Wallace-Hadrill, *The Barbarian West*, p. 146.

5. R. K. Gordon, ed. and trans., *Anglo-Saxon Poetry* (New York, n.d.), p. 346. The same image occurs in "The Wanderer," *ibid.*, p. 82, and "The Ruin," *ibid.*, p. 92.

6. McIlwain, *Growth*, pp. 168ff.

7. IV Edgar, 12. Translations of Anglo-Saxon law are available in F. L. Attenborough, ed. and trans., *The Laws of the Earliest English Kings* (Cambridge, Eng.: Cambridge University Press, 1922); A. J. Robertson, ed. and trans., *The Laws of the Kings of England from Edmund to Henry I*; and B. Thorpe, ed. and trans., *Ancient Laws and Institutes of England* (2 vols.; London, 1840). Extensive portions of all the codes are also to be found in *EHD*, pp. 357–439. The texts are printed in Felix Liebermann, *Die Gesetze der Angelsachsen* (Halle, 1898–1916), vol. I.

8. K. Sisam, "Anglo-Saxon Royal Genealogies," *Proceedings of the British Academy*, 39: 287–348 (1953). The most celebrated product of Anglo-Saxon literature, *Beowulf*, is full of this. Here is a single example from the *Anglo-Saxon Chronicle*, ed. and trans. G. N. Garmonsway (London, 1954), for the year 755, in which King Offa's ancestry is traced back to the god Woden: "and the same year Offa succeeded to the kingdom and ruled thirty-nine years . . . That Offa was the son of Thing-

frith, the son of Eanwulf, the son of Osmod, the son of Eawa, the son of Pybba, the son of Creoda, the son of Cynewald, the son of Cnebba, the son of Icel, the son of Eomer, the son of Angeltheow, the son of Offa, the son of Wermund, the son of Wihtlaeg, the son of Woden." Such genealogical enthusiasm begins with the preface of one version and may be found in many other entries, e.g., for 449, 547, 552, 560, 562, 626, and 853 (which goes all the way back to Adam). All quotations from the *Anglo-Saxon Chronicle*, translated and with an introduction by G. N. Garmonsway (Everyman's Library edition), are used by permission of J. M. Dent & Sons, Ltd., London, and E. P. Dutton & Co., Inc., New York.

9. IV Edgar, 2.1a.

10. III Ethelred, 1.

11. VIII Ethelred, 37.

12. VIII Ethelred, 43.

13. *Anglo-Saxon Chronicle*, for 937. See also *ibid.*, for 1067.

14. Aelfric, *Treatise on the Old and New Testament*, in *EHD*, pp. 853–854. The same description of the social order was used by King Alfred in his translation of Boethius, *De Consolatione Philosophiae*. See *EHD*, pp. 845–846. It was borrowed later by Archbishop Wulfstan, *Institutes of Polity*, in Thorpe, *Ancient Laws and Institutes*, II, 306.

15. Jordanes, *The Gothic History*, trans. with intro. by Charles Christopher Mierow (Princeton, N.J., 1915), XXXIX, 203–206.

16. *Beowulf*, trans. Lucien Dean Pearson, ed. with notes and intro. by Rowland L. Collins (Bloomington, Ind., 1965), p. 19. It is not proposed here to enter into the details of the vast literature devoted to *Beowulf*. As George K. Anderson, *The Literature of the Anglo-Saxons* (Princeton, N.J., 1966), p. 63, has said, it is "a happy hunting-ground for the linguist, the scholar, and the critic." In all fairness, however, it should be noted that interpretation tends to fall into two classes, the pagan Germanic and the Christian. An older view, with which I agree, stressed its pagan, heroic character. Perhaps the most influential statement of this view is H. Munro Chadwick, *The Heroic Age* (Cambridge, Eng., 1912), pp. 47ff. More recently, a good many commentators have emphasized the Christian elements of the poem. See, e.g., Dorothy Whitelock, *Changing Currents in Anglo-Saxon Studies* (Cambridge, Eng., 1958), pp. 9–10. Levin L. Schucking, "Das Königsideal im Beowulf," *Bulletin of the Modern Humanities Research Association*, 3: 143–154 (1929), argues that the essence of the poem is that it develops a specifically Christian code of conduct for kings; the curious thing about this discussion is that despite the author's efforts, the Germanic elements emerge more clearly than the Christian. The observation of W. T. H. Jackson, *Medieval Literature* (New York, 1966), p. 33, seems quite right: "There has been much discussion of the relation between the pagan and Christian elements of the poem. It should be stated at once that the culture and morality are thoroughly Germanic." In this vein also is Kenneth Sisam, *The Structure of Beowulf* (Oxford, 1965), pp. 78–79.

17. *Beowulf*, pp. 76, 80.

18. Eric John, *Orbis Britanniae* (Leicester, Eng., 1966), p. 119.

19. *Anglo-Saxon Chronicle,* for the year 975.

20. There have appeared recently two penetrating works on the Germanic peoples by E. A. Thompson, *The Early Germans* (Oxford, 1965), and *The Visigoths in the Time of Ulfila* (Oxford, 1966), to which my debt is very great.

21. There are accounts earlier than Tacitus from Greek authors, but Tacitus is incomparably the most valuable. For discussion of his sources, see Cornelii Taciti, *De Origine et situ Germanorum,* ed. J. G. C. Anderson (Oxford, 1938), pp. xix–xxvi. The standard full-length discussion is Eduard Norden, *Die germanische Urgeschichte in Tacitus' Germania* (Berlin, 1923).

22. Let there be no misunderstanding. The argument here is in no way an effort to revive the so-called Germanist interpretation of European history, which has consumed so much energy since the middle of the nineteenth century. Nor is it another futile attempt to weigh the relative impact of Germanic as against Roman sources of influence. Discussion of historical opinion may be found, for example, in Carl Stephenson, *Mediaeval Institutions,* ed. Bryce D. Lyon (Ithaca, 1954). For a very detailed investigation at the level of legal ideas, see Julius Goebel, Jr., *Felony and Misdemeanor* (New York, 1937); on the Anglo-Saxon witenagemot, H. Munro Chadwick, *Studies on Anglo-Saxon Institutions* (Cambridge, Eng., 1905), pp. 308–354, and now the full survey of Tryggvi J. Oleson, *The Witenagemot in the Reign of Edward the Confessor* (Toronto, 1955), esp. pp. 6–16 and appendix A, pp. 114–116, where Oleson has marshaled references to the views of the leading authorities, old and new; on the notion of the folk in arms, C. Warren Hollister, *Anglo-Saxon Military Institutions* (Oxford, 1962), and for a more complete rejection of the Germanist view, John, *Orbis Britanniae,* pp. 64–153. There is a general survey in Henry J. Ford, *Representative Government* (New York, 1924), pp. 3–111. That both Germanic and Roman traditions were involved is obvious, and in some cases it is clear enough what the source of an idea was. But in truth it hardly matters, for the result of the blend was just that: a compound and unmistakably new and different society, and it is this which should occupy our attention. This is a point made very forcefully by Wallace-Hadrill, *The Long-Haired Kings,* pp. 1–24. On the Anglo-Saxons, see John, *Orbis Britanniae,* pp. 1–63. In any case, it is not the Germanic quality of barbarian ideas that matters, but the fact that they were primitive.

23. On the point of classifying societies as "primitive" solely on the basis of technology, see Lucy Mair, *Primitive Government* (Baltimore, 1964), pp. 7–8.

24. Caesar, *The Gallic War,* trans. H. J. Edwards (London, 1930), IV, 1–2, VI, 24.

25. *Ibid.,* IV, 1, VI, 23.

26. *Ibid.,* VI, 22, 23.

27. *Ibid.,* IV, 19, VI, 23.

28. Mair, *Primitive Government*, pp. 61–77.

29. *Ibid.*, pp. 63–66. For a full-scale account see E. E. Evans-Pritchard, *The Nuer* (Oxford, 1941), and for a summary by the same author, see M. Fortes and E. E. Evans-Pritchard, eds., *African Political Systems* (Oxford, 1940), pp. 272–296.

30. Caesar, *The Gallic War*, VI, 23: "And when any of the chiefs [principes] has said in public assembly that he will be leader, 'Let those who will follow declare it,' then all who approve the cause and the man rise together to his service and promise their own assistance, and win the general praise of the people. Any of them who have not followed, after promise, are reckoned as deserters and traitors, and in all things afterwards trust is denied to them." Caesar also wrote about the comitatus among the Gauls, *ibid.*, III, 22, and VI, 15, where such relationships are said to be "the one form of influence and power known to them." Caesar, *ibid.*, VII, 40, says, "according to the custom of Gaul, it is a crime [nefas] in dependents to desert their patrons, even in desperate case."

31. On this see Heinrich Dannenbauer, *Grundlagen der Mittelalterlichen Welt* (Stuttgart, 1958), pp. 121–178, and Walter Schlesinger, *Beitrage zur deutschen Verfassungsgeschichte des Mittelalters* (Göttingen, 1963), I, 9–52.

32. Tacitus, *Germania*, trans. H. Mattingly (Baltimore, 1948), XIV: "Many noble youths, if the land of their birth is stagnating in a protracted peace, deliberately seek out other tribes, where some war is afoot." Bede, *History*, III, 14, says of King Oswin that he "soon won the affection of everyone by his regal qualities of mind and body, so that nobles came from every province to serve him." See Thompson, *The Early Germans*, p. 58 and n. 1.

33. Thompson, *The Early Germans*, pp. 48ff.

34. See, e.g., Tacitus, *The Histories*, trans. Kenneth Wellesley (Baltimore, 1964), IV, 15.

35. Tacitus, *Germania*, XIV, where he says that the liberality of the chiefs "must have war and plunder to feed it." For similar situations among contemporary primitives, see Mair, *Primitive Government*, pp. 107–122.

36. See Thompson, *The Early Germans*, pp. 17–28, and Robert Latouche, *The Birth of Western Economy*, trans. E. M. Wilkinson (New York, 1961), pp. 29–47.

37. Wallace-Hadrill, *The Long-Haired Kings*, pp. 159–163, and Whitelock, *Beginnings of English Society*, p. 36.

38. Latouche, *Birth of Western Economy*, p. 43.

39. Thompson, *The Early Germans*, pp. 72–108.

40. Walter Schlesinger, "Über germanisches Königtum," in *Das Königtum* (Lindau, 1956), pp. 105–141.

41. Tacitus, *Germania*, XIII.

42. *Anglo-Saxon Chronicle*, for the year 1009.

43. *Ibid.*, for 1015–1016, and 1012 (source of quotation).

44. On vassal loyalty, see Bloch, *Feudal Society*, pp. 219–238.

45. Quoted in Whitelock, *Beginnings of English Society*, p. 33.

46. III Edmund, 1.

47. *Anglo-Saxon Chronicle*, for 1085. The same principle appears in *The Ten Articles of William I*, 2, in Robertson, *Laws of the Kings of England*, p. 239, and in *Willelemi Articuli Retracti*, 2 and 9, in Robertson, pp. 245, 249.

48. This point about a system organized in terms of personal allegiance has been well made in Max Gluckman, *Custom and Conflict in Africa* (Glencoe, Ill., 1955), pp. 151–162.

49. See the "Letter of Bede to Egbert, archbishop of York (5 November 734)," in *EHD*, pp. 733–745, and the commentary on it by John, *Orbis Britanniae*, pp. 66–67.

50. *Anglo-Saxon Chronicle*, for 1040, is a good example of this outlook. It relates that when King Harold died, Harthacnut was sent for. He came but "imposed a severe tax . . . and all who had been zealous on his behalf now became disloyal to him." This outlook set in very early. See Gregory of Tours, *The History of the Franks*, trans. with intro. by O. M. Dalton (Oxford, 1927), vol. II, IX, 30, pp. 400–401, and other citations and discussion in Wallace–Hadrill, *The Long-Haired Kings*, pp. 66–68. Particularly good discussions of alienation of royal lands are given in *The Long-Haired Kings*, pp. 1–24, and in John, *Orbis Britanniae*. For the treatment of the problem in the political theory of the later Middle Ages, see Peter N. Reisenberg, *Inalienability of Sovereignty in Medieval Political Thought* (New York, 1956).

51. J. C. Holt, *Magna Carta* (Cambridge, Eng., 1965), esp. pp. 242–268.

52. *Anglo-Saxon Chronicle*, for 1047. There are a great many such painfully brief reports. See, e.g., for 868, 911, 992, 994, 995, 999, 1002, 1006, 1009, 1012, 1015, 1020, 1036, 1047, 1048, 1051, 1052, 1055, 1065. The majority of these concern decisions taken on military or diplomatic questions.

53. Bede, *History*, supplies numerous fine examples. See, e.g., III, 11–13, for an extended account of miracles associated with King Oswald.

54. Coulborn, *Feudalism in History*, p. 190.

55. Eric John, "English Feudalism and the Structure of Anglo-Saxon Society," *Bulletin of the John Rylands Library*, 46: 14–41 (1963), reprinted in *Orbis Britanniae*, pp. 128–153. For the passage quoted, see *Orbis Britanniae*, p. 146.

56. *The Wanderer*, in *EHD*, pp. 801–802.

57. *The Battle of Maldon*, in Gordon, *Anglo-Saxon Poetry*, pp. 366–367.

58. Tacitus, *Germania*, XIV; *Beowulf*, p. 119.

59. *Beowulf*, pp. 112–119.

60. H. St. L. B. Moss, *The Birth of the Middle Ages* (Oxford, 1957), p. 40.

61. The character of the Anglo-Saxon settlement is a much debated question. I follow John, *Orbis Britanniae*, pp. 123–127.

62. Eric John, *Land Tenure in Early England* (Leicester, Eng., 1960), pp. 1–23, 51–62.

63. This crucial point has been established by Ernst Levy, *The West Roman Vulgar Law* (Philadelphia, 1951). Levy's work has been integrated in the accounts of the successor kingdoms in Wallace–Hadrill, *The Long-Haired Kings,* and in John, *Land Tenure* and *Orbis Britanniae.*

64. Bloch, *Feudal Society,* pp. 190–210.

65. John, *Orbis Brittaniae,* pp. 117–127.

66. *Ibid.,* pp. 64–65.

67. Quoted in Donald W. Sutherland, *Quo Warranto Proceedings in the Reign of Edward I 1278–1294* (Oxford, 1963), p. 82, n. 2.

68. The Germanic expression "folk" has long been an object of controversy, because it has sometimes been argued that it refers to the equalitarian and even libertarian standing of an entire people. It is unnecessary to inquire into this mythology, since there is no evidence for it. It is, in fact, a problem relating to the sociology of history rather than of the Germanic peoples. For a penetrating discussion of the aristocratic and military meaning of the term, see John, *Orbis Britanniae,* pp. 121–127. Reference should also be made to the works cited in n. 22 above.

69. Bede, *History,* II, 5, 13.

70. Alfred, Introduction, 49.9–49.10. For other examples see Alfred and Guthrum, Prologue; II Edward, Preface; IV Athelstan, 1; V, Athelstan, 1. The evidence for the reign of Edward the Confessor has been collected in Oleson, *The Witenagemot,* esp. pp. 25–47. See further, II Edgar, Prologue; IV Edgar, 1; II Ethelred, Prologue; III Ethelred, Prologue; V Ethelred, Prologue; VIII Ethelred, Prologue; I Cnut, Prologue; II Cnut, Prologue.

71. Peter Hunter Blair, *An Introduction to Anglo-Saxon England* (Cambridge, Eng., 1962), p. 217. Blair says, *ibid.,* "For some five centuries the laws of kings were in fact normally approved and sanctioned by the king's councillors . . ."

72. *Ibid.,* p. 218.

73. For an interesting discussion of the various "supremacies" from which the single monarchy emerged, see John, *Orbis Britanniae,* pp. 1–63. John writes, *ibid.,* p. 62: "It was the Mercians and West Saxons who made 'England.' By 1066 the notion of 'England' made sense. It was not a racial entity, nor a cultural unity either. Its limits were determined politically. In 1066 'England' was where the English king's writ ran, it was articulated in a network of shires, hundreds, and dioceses roughly equivalent to what we call England now. This structure was still far from uniformly stable, and the subjugation of the North in particular was very far from complete. But what there was was solid enough." On the development of territorial administration, see Whitelock, *Beginnings of English Society,* pp. 77–82; Blair, *Introduction to Anglo-Saxon England,* pp. 222–244; H. R. Loyn, *Anglo-Saxon England and the Norman Conquest* (London, 1962), pp. 301–314.

74. Oleson, *The Witenagemot,* especially the conclusions on pp. 110–113.

75. I do not mean that either the spiritual or the administrative importance of the clergy should be ignored. Yet neither should it be overestimated in the context of early medieval society and politics. Blair, *Anglo-Saxon England,* pp. 210–211, writes: "Till at least the eighth century, the Anglo-Saxon royal household wears an almost wholly military aspect and there is little room for much beyond. The personality of the king himself created, or failed to create, a household to which fighting men were attracted. The main duties of such men were courage and loyalty, their rewards the simple ones of land, treasure, food and drink." It is no doubt true, as Blair goes on to say, that "the Church was the most important factor tending to direct the royal household away from the ideals governing the *comitatus* . . ." *Ibid.,* p. 211. But the ethos of the aristocratic warrior as the key element of the outlook of the lay magnate had still a very long future. For the more elevated spiritual nature of Christianity was not readily comprehensible to laymen, nor the gap to be completely overcome even in the great spiritual movement of the eleventh century. Moreover, one has to take account of the penetration of the Church by a society of warriors. Such was the power of that society that on a local basis the men filling clerical office were often relatives or vassals, quite indistinguishable from their kindred and lay lords. See, above all, Bloch, *Feudal Society,* pp. 345–352.

76. For a general discussion stressing the merits of the Anglo-Saxon conception of compensation for injuries, see T. F. T. Plucknett, *Edward I and Criminal Law* (Cambridge, Eng., 1960), pp. 1–50. The most helpful brief survey is Whitelock, *Beginnings of English Society,* esp. pp. 29–47, 50–52, 135–154. Two recent broadly gauged surveys of English legal history contain brief accounts of the Anglo-Saxon period: Alan Harding, *A Social History of English Law* (Baltimore, 1966), pp. 13–29, and George W. Keeton, *The Norman Conquest and the Common Law* (London, 1966). Keeton's book undertakes comparison of the Anglo-Saxon and post-Conquest outlooks on a topical basis, but it seems less sensitive of the alterations in perspective which recent study suggests than Harding's more chronologically organized survey. For full discussion, the older masterworks remain indispensable: above all, Frederick Pollock and Frederic William Maitland, *The History of English Law before the Time of Edward I* (Cambridge, Eng., 1923), I, 1–63.

77. Aethelbert, 43.

78. Aethelbert, 54, 1–5.

79. Aethelbert, 55.

80. Aethelbert, 1.

81. II Aethelstan, 4.

82. For observed theft, Ine, 12; II Aethelstan, 1; IV Aethelstan, 6; for arson, II Aethelstan, 6, 2; for death by sorcery, II Aethelstan, 6. II Cnut, 64, provides a summary: "House-breaking and arson and obvious

theft and manifest murder and betrayal of a lord are beyond compensation according to the secular law."

83. II Cnut, 30.5.

84. Dorothy Whitelock, "Wulfstan and the Laws of Cnut," *English Historical Review*, 63: 433–452 (1948), and "Wulfstan's Authorship of Cnut's Laws," *English Historical Review*, 70:72–85 (1955).

85. V Ethelred, 3–3.1. This kind of ferocity was certainly not rare. The *Anglo-Saxon Chronicle*, for the year 1036, relates that Earl Godwin and his men attacked prince Alfred, the son of king Ethelred, "dispersing his followers besides, slaying some in various ways; Some of them were sold for money, some cruelly murdered, Some of them were put in chains, and some of them were blinded, Some were mutilated, and some were scalped." On the Frankish parallel, with particular reference to scalping, see Wallace–Hadrill, *The Long-Haired Kings*, p. 59.

86. Wihtred, 16: "A bishop or a king's word, [even] though unsupported by an oath, shall be incontrovertible."

87. Wihtred, 18, 19, 21.

88. On the frequently accused man, III Ethelred, 3.4; on the man of suspicious character, II Cnut, 30; on the thief, Ine, 12, and 15,2; Wihtred, 26; on the perjurer, I Edward, 3; II Aethelstan, 26; I Cnut, 36–36.1.

89. The chief sources on the ordeal are II Aethelstan, 23, and III Ethelred, 6–7. See Whitelock, *Beginnings of English Society*, pp. 141–143. A large body of comparative material is assembled in Henry Charles Lea, *Superstition and Force* (Philadelphia, 1892).

90. II Aethelstan, 23. According to another text, *Exorcismus*, in Liebermann, *Die Gesetze*, I, 401, the accused was obliged to fast for three days before the ordeal.

91. Quoted in Whitelock, *Beginnings of English Society*, p. 142.

92. III Ethelred, 6, and "Of Incendiaries and Those Who Secretly Compass Death," appendix I, in Attenborough, *Laws*, p. 171.

93. "Decree Concerning Hot Iron and Water," appendix II, in Attenborough, *Laws*, pp. 171–173.

94. In cases regarded as more serious than usual, the ordeal was "threefold." This meant that the hot iron to be carried would weigh three times as much, or that the arm must be submerged to the elbow in the boiling water. See "Of Incendiaries," and II Aethelstan, 4–6; III Ethelred, 3.4.

95. Reputation was clearly critical. Thus II Cnut, 30: "And if any man is so regarded with suspicion by the hundred and so frequently accused, and three men together then accuse him, there is then to be nothing for it but that he is to go to the three-fold ordeal." See also III Edgar, 7.

96. The document from which our knowledge of this case derives is a letter, presumably from Ealdorman Ordlaf, to King Edward the Elder. It is to be found in *EHD*, pp. 501–503. The case is discussed in John, *Orbis Britanniae*, pp. 148–150, and in Whitelock, *Beginnings of English Society*, pp. 147–149.

97. John, *Orbis Britanniae,* p. 149.

98. See Bertha Surtees Phillpotts, *Kindred and Clan in the Middle Ages and After* (Cambridge, Eng., 1913).

99. Whitelock, *Beginnings of English Society,* p. 39.

100. Nearly all the standard authorities have discussions of the feud: F. M. Stenton, *Anglo-Saxon England* (Oxford, 1947), p. 384, n. 1; Pollock and Maitland, *History of English Law,* I, 46; Loyn, *Anglo-Saxon England,* pp. 294–298; especially helpful is Whitelock, *Beginnings of English Society,* pp. 37–47. There is a brilliant discussion of the blood feud in Merovingian Gaul in Wallace–Hadrill, *The Long-Haired Kings,* pp. 121–147. The following observation is, I think, particularly important: "To legal historians feud dies a slow, inevitable death, yielding to the superior equity of royal justice; chaos and bloodshed give place to good order because they must. But it is possible to see the matter otherwise. Royal justice and the local courts are still far too unsettled in function and fluid in procedure to offer a clear alternative to feud. They are more concerned with compromises than with principles." *Ibid.,* pp. 146–147. This fine essay is written from the perspective suggested by contemporary social anthropology; see particularly Max Gluckman, *Custom and Conflict in Africa,* pp. 1–26.

101. See the illuminating discussion in Mair, *Primitive Government,* pp. 40–46, 68–69, and passim, where the feud is associated with those peoples with a bare minimum of government. Max Gluckman, *Politics, Law and Ritual in Tribal Society* (Oxford, 1965), esp. pp. 109–116, discusses the role of feud in maintaining order in the context of what he calls "stateless societies." Gluckman explicitly draws attention to the European Middle Ages and suggests that the historians' emphasis on the violence and asocial character of the feud misses the point.

102. Bloch, *Feudal Society,* p. 125.

103. Tacitus, *Germania,* XXI.

104. Gluckman, *Custom and Conflict in Africa,* pp. 54–80.

105. Bloch, *Feudal Society,* pp. 190–210.

106. *Ibid.,* p. 234.

107. Alfred, 42, 6.

108. I Cnut, 20.1.

109. *Anglo-Saxon Chronicle,* for the year 755.

110. Alfred, 42.

111. II Edmund, esp. 1, and 7–7.2.

112. "The Thegns' Guild in Cambridge," in *EHD,* p. 557.

113. This story is related in Whitelock, *Beginnings of English Society,* pp. 44–45.

114. *Anglo-Saxon Chronicle,* for 979.

115. Wulfstan, *The Sermon of the Wolf to the English,* in *EHD,* p. 856.

116. *The Politics of Aristotle,* trans. Ernest Barker (Oxford, 1952), III, ix, 11.

Chapter Three. The Sanctity and Utility of Kings

1. Ewart Lewis, *Medieval Political Ideas* (London, 1954), I, 241.
2. *James Harrington's Oceana,* ed. S. B. Liljegren (Heidelberg, 1924), p. 48.
3. Gluckman, *Custom and Conflict,* pp. 27–53.
4. Bloch, *Les Rois thaumaturges,* p. 65.
5. I might refer here to a fine phrase in Bloch, *ibid.,* p. 185, in which he speaks of setting medieval belief "dans cette ambiance pleine de merveilleux dont les peuples . . . entourèrent leurs princes." This profound and rich book, far too little used in discussing medieval political ideas, virtually exhausts the subject of popular belief in sacred kingship. I can only acknowledge my indebtedness to it.
6. *The Register of John de Grandisson,* ed. F. C. Hingeston–Randolph (London, 1894–1899), II, 840: "A de primes, que la substance de la nature de la Corone est principaument en la persone le Roi come teste, et en les Piers de la Terre come membres . . . quiele chose est si annexe a la dite Corone qele ne poet pas estre sevree sans division du Roiaume . . ."
7. There is a vast literature on the subject of ancient kingship, though it has been largely neglected by historians of political ideas. Among the most helpful and suggestive general treatments are these. Ivan Engnell, *Studies in Divine Kingship in the Ancient Near East* (Uppsala, 1943); Henri Frankfort, *Kingship and the Gods* (Chicago, 1948); Henri Frankfort et al., *The Intellectual Adventure of Ancient Man* (Chicago, 1946); C. J. Gadd, *Ideas of Divine Rule in the Ancient East* (London, 1948); S. H. Hooke, ed., *Myth, Ritual and Kingship* (Oxford, 1958); E.O. James, *Myth and Ritual in the Ancient Near East* (London, 1958); Sigmund Mowinckel, *He That Cometh,* trans. G. W. Anderson (Oxford, 1956). For specific judgments bearing on the statement in the text, see Hooke, ed., *Myth, Ritual and Kingship,* pp. 71, 74, and S. H. Hooke, *The Origins of Early Semitic Ritual* (London, 1938), pp. 12–13.
8. Erwin R. Goodenough, "The Political Philosophy of Hellenistic Kingship," *Yale Classical Studies,* 1:55–102 (1928).
9. Sisam, "Anglo-Saxon Royal Genealogies," pp. 287–348; Bloch, *Les Rois,* pp. 54–55; Wallace–Hadrill, *The Long-Haired Kings,* pp. 220–221.
10. Sir John Fortescue, *De natura legis naturae,* II, viii, xv, xxiv-xl, in Thomas (Fortescue) Lord Clermont, ed., *The Works of Sir John Fortescue, Knight* (London, 1869), vol. I.
11. Bloch, *Les Rois,* p. 209.
12. *Ibid.,* pp. 246–256.
13. Schlesinger, "Über germanisches Königtum."
14. Tacitus, *Germania,* VII.
15. Thompson, *The Early Germans,* pp. 32–41.
16. *Ibid.,* pp. 150–152; Thompson, *The Visigoths,* esp. pp. 51–53; Wallace–Hadrill, *The Long-Haired Kings,* pp. 153–163. Wallace–Hadrill says on pp. 154–155: ". . . movements of big integrated tribes (*gentes*) were not

396

at all common after the first century A.D. In the face of Roman opposition, the *gentes* showed some disposition to break up into fighting bands. A group of such bands, perhaps from various *gentes,* might unite under one leader to seek its own fortune within the Empire, as mercenaries, as brigands in search of land and booty, or as both."

17. See P. Grierson, "Election and Inheritance in Early Germanic Kingship," *Cambridge Historical Journal,* 7:1–22 (1941).

18. Wallace–Hadrill, *The Long-Haired Kings,* p. 155.

19. Mair, *Primitive Government,* pp. 107–122.

20. John, *Orbis Britanniae,* pp. 117–127; Blair, *Anglo-Saxon England,* pp. 194–222; Loyn, *Anglo-Saxon England,* pp. 199–219; Stenton, *Anglo-Saxon England,* pp. 298–299; Wallace–Hadrill, *The Long-Haired Kings,* esp. pp. 1–24, 165–166, 190.

21. Bloch, *Les Rois,* pp. 32, 54–62; Fritz Kern, *Kingship and Law in the Middle Ages,* trans. S. B. Chrimes (Oxford, 1948), pp. 12–27.

22. Blair, *Anglo-Saxon England,* p. 196.

23. *Anglo-Saxon Chronicle,* Preface, and for the year 449, 547, 552, 560, 626.

24. Bede, *History,* I, 15; see also III, 1, 7, 14, 18, on royal blood.

25. *Anglo-Saxon Chronicle,* for 867A. See Blair, *Anglo-Saxon England,* pp. 195–197.

26. *Anglo-Saxon Chronicle,* for 604; Bede, *History,* III, 21; V, 23.

27. *Anglo-Saxon Chronicle,* for 611, 616, 617, 634, 640, 643.

28. *Ibid.,* for 757E (Oswulf), 774E (Ahlred), 894 (Ethelred), 755 (Sigeberht).

29. Bloch, *Les Rois,* p. 70, n. 3.

30. *Ibid.,* pp. 62–75; Wallace–Hadrill, *The Long-Haired Kings,* pp. 178–179, 220–226.

31. Bede, *History,* I, 27; II, 9, 12, 14; III, 6.

32. *Ibid.,* II, 5, 15; III, 1, 30.

33. *Ibid.,* II, 6; III, 7.

34. *Ibid.,* III, 22.

35. VIII Ethelred, 2.1.

36. Aelfric, *Catholic Homilies,* in *EHD,* p. 851.

37. See Bloch, *Feudal Society,* pp. 203–208.

38. See Mair, *Primitive Government,* pp. 214–233; Bloch, *Les Rois,* pp. 62–75, 79–86, 194–195, 258–260; Blair, *Anglo-Saxon England,* pp. 204–208.

39. *Anglo-Saxon Chronicle,* for 449E.

40. Bloch, *Les Rois,* pp. 51–76.

41. Richardson and Sayles, *Governance,* p. 138.

42. The classic work is Arnold van Gennep, *The Rites of Passage,* trans. Monika B. Vizedom and Gabrielle L. Caffee (Chicago, 1960). For a recent discussion centering on the social meaning of ritual behavior, see Max Gluckman, ed., *Essays on the Ritual of Social Relations* (New York, 1962).

43. *Promessio Regis,* in Robertson, *Laws of the Kings of England,* p. 43. Paragraph numbers have been omitted.

44. These hymns have been most thoroughly studied in Ernst H. Kantorowicz, *Laudes Regiae* (Berkeley, 1946).

45. William of Malmesbury, *De Gestis Regum Anglorum,* in *EHD,* p. 279.

46. Quoted by F. W. Maitland, "The Crown as Corporation," in *Maitland Selected Essays,* ed. H. D. Hazeltine, G. Lapsley, and P. H. Winfield (Cambridge, Eng., 1936), p. 104.

47. Mair, *Primitive Government,* p. 208.

48. See Richardson and Sayles, *Governance,* pp. 151ff.

49. For parallel practices in African kingdoms, see Mair, *Primitive Government,* pp. 205–211.

50. Bede, *History,* III, 18.

51. *Ibid.,* IV, 15.

52. See Loyn, *Anglo-Saxon England,* pp. 179ff.

53. See, for example, Simeon of Durham, *Historia Regum,* for the year 800, in *EHD,* p. 250, and *Anglo-Saxon Chronicle,* for 722A, and 725E, which states: "Ine [the king of Wessex] fought against the South Saxons, and there slew Ealdberht, the prince whom he had banished."

54. These matters are set out in great detail in Percy Ernest Schramm, *A History of the English Coronation,* trans. Leopold G. Wickham Legg (Oxford, 1937). Thus Mair, *Primitive Government,* p. 224: "In most royal rituals important parts are allotted to persons representing major divisions of country and people."

55. Bloch, *Les Rois,* p. 15, took this line from Montesquieu as the motto of his work: "Ce roi est un grand magicien . . ."

56. Today "scrofula" refers to a tubercular inflammation of the cervical lymph nodes, but in the Middle Ages it was a much looser term, serving as a name for most ganglionic inflammation and a good many unrelated afflictions of the face and eyes. See Bloch, *Les Rois,* pp. 27–28.

57. *Ibid.,* pp. 54, 60–62, 79–86, 156–157.

58. Bede, *History,* III, 11–13.

59. Gregory of Tours, *History of the Franks,* IX, 21, p. 395.

60. Bloch, *Les Rois,* pp. 120–145, 258–260.

61. *Ibid.,* pp. 65–75, 194–215.

62. Quoted, *ibid.,* p. 71, n. 1: "Et tanto est dignitas pontificum major quam regum, quia reges in culmen regium sacrantur a pontificibus, pontifices autem a regibus consecrari non possunt."

63. *Ibid.,* pp. 199, 200.

64. *Ibid.,* p. 209.

65. *Ibid.,* pp. 238–242.

66. *Ibid.,* pp. 74–75.

67. Letter of Gregory to Bishop Hermann of Metz, March 15, 1081, in *The Correspondence of Pope Gregory VII,* trans., with intro. Ephraim Emerton (New York, 1932), p. 169.

68. *Ibid.,* p. 171. See Bloch, *Les Rois,* pp. 201–202.

69. Bloch, *Les Rois,* p. 60, writes: "Ainsi s'explique peut-être que le rite du toucher, qui nous occupe ici, se soit développé plus facilement

398

dans les sociétés où la religion interdisait d'attribuer aux rois une influence sur les grands phénomènes cosmiques qui commandent la vie des nations."

70. Quoted in Raymond Crawfurd, *The King's Evil* (Oxford, 1911), pp. 19–20.

71. Quoted *ibid.*, p. 24. See also Bloch, *Les Rois,* pp. 41–42.

72. Bloch, *Les Rois,* pp. 89–157, 210–215.

73. *Ibid.,* pp. 97–105. Extracts from these records are printed in Crawfurd, *King's Evil,* pp. 33–34, 36, 40.

74. Bloch, *Les Rois,* p. 99.

75. Fortescue, *Defensio juris domus Lancastriae,* III, in *Works,* I, 498.

76. Bloch, *Les Rois,* pp. 111–112.

77. *A Complete Collection of State Trials,* ed. T. B. Howell (London, 1816), XI, 1035–1037. See also Bloch, *Les Rois,* p. 85.

78. Bloch, *Les Rois,* pp. 211–215.

79. *Ibid.,* pp. 92–94. Crawfurd, *King's Evil,* pp. 52–56, prints the service administered in Tudor times.

80. Quoted in Crawfurd, *King's Evil,* p. 51.

81. Quoted *ibid.,* p. 66.

82. *Macbeth,* IV, iii.

83. Crawfurd, *King's Evil,* pp. 82–85; Bloch, *Les Rois,* p. 242.

84. Crawfurd, *King's Evil,* p. 106.

85. *The Diary of John Evelyn,* ed. E. S. de Beer (Oxford, 1955), IV, 374.

86. James Boswell, *Life of Johnson* (London, 1953), pp. 31–32.

87. H. G. Richardson, "The English Coronation Oath," *Speculum,* 24:44–75 (1949).

88. Richardson and Sayles, *Governance,* p. 374.

89. Holt, *Magna Carta,* p. 86.

90. *Ibid.,* pp. 224–225; Richardson and Sayles, *Governance,* p. 387.

91. T. F. T. Plucknett, *Legislation of Edward I* (Oxford, 1949), p. 77.

92. *Ibid.,* pp. 102–108.

93. *Ibid.,* pp. 77–78.

94. *Ibid.,* pp. 79–83.

Chapter Four. Counsel and Consent

1. Henry de Bracton, *De legibus et consuetudinibus Angliae,* ed. George E. Woodbine (New Haven, Conn., 1915–1942), vol. II, fol. 34, p. 109. With occasional alterations, the translations of Bracton in the text are those presented in Ewart Lewis, *Medieval Political Ideas* (London: Routledge & Kegan Paul, Ltd., 1954), I, 39–41, 279–283, and are quoted by permission of Routledge & Kegan Paul, Ltd., and Alfred A. Knopf, Inc.

2. Bracton, *De legibus,* vol. II, fol. 6, p. 33.

3. *Ibid.,* fol. 107, p. 305.

4. *Ibid.,* fol. 5b, p. 33.

5. *Ibid.,* fol. 1b, p. 21.

6. Ewart Lewis, "King Above Law? 'Quod Principi Placuit' in Bracton," *Speculum,* 39:240–269 (1964), esp. 244, 247.

7. "The judicial function is that of interpretation; it does not include the power of amendment under the guise of interpretation. To miss the point of difference between the two is to miss all that the phrase 'supreme law of the land' stands for and to convert what was intended as inescapable and enduring mandates into mere moral reflections." West Coast Hotel Co. v. Parrish, 300 U.S. 404 (1937).

8. Lewis, "King Above Law?" pp. 240–269; Fritz Schulz, "Bracton on Kingship," *English Historical Review,* 60:136–176 (1945). Schulz says on p. 165: "In truth Bracton's opinion was indubitably that the king was legally bound by the law . . ." In fact, there is excellent reason for doubting the indubitable.

9. Brian Tierney, "Bracton on Government," *Speculum,* 38:295–317 (1963). Wiebke Fesefeldt, *Englische Staatstheorie des 13. Jahrhunderts* (Göttingen, 1962), pp. 42–77, suggests that Bracton's king is so well guarded from legal processes that we may see there the foreshadowing of a modern theory of reason of state. There is a brief consideration of Bracton in Marcel David, *La Souveraineté et les limites juridiques du pouvoir monarchique du IXe au XVe siècle* (Paris, 1954), pp. 245–251. M. David takes the view that Bracton drew no juridical implications from the language which asserts that the king is under the law.

10. Kantorowicz, *The King's Two Bodies,* pp. 143–192.

11. Charles Howard McIlwain, *Constitutionalism Ancient and Modern,* (Ithaca, 1958), pp. 67–92, and *Growth,* pp. 192–197, 371–382. S. J. T. Miller, "The Position of the King in Bracton and Beaumanoir," *Speculum,* 31:263–296 (1956), accepts McIlwain's distinction between *gubernaculum* and *jurisdictio.*

12. Ullmann, *Principles of Government and Politics in the Middle Ages,* pp. 176–178.

13. On this point see the astute remarks of Marc Bloch, *The Historian's Craft* (New York, 1953), pp. 29–35.

14. Bracton, *De legibus,* vol. II, fol. 107–107b, pp. 305–306.

15. The text does present problems of translation, some of which are quite independent of the impact of the translator's frame of reference. The translator's view, however, has played no small part. Disagreement abounds. The problems begin with the opening phrase. Kantorowicz, *The King's Two Bodies,* p. 150, reads: "The king has no other power, since he is the vicar of God and his minister on earth, save that alone which he has of right." This has been objected to by Lewis, "King Above Law?" p. 258, on the ground that it needlessly introduces discontinuity into Bracton's thought. However, this criticism, in turn, rests on the particular interpretation of this Bractonian passage (fol. 107) which Lewis tries to establish. See also Lewis, *ibid.,* p. 258, n. 60, where

400

a number of other variants are collected. Lewis' argument on this passage is considered in the text.

Much disagreement has centered on the *cum* clause which follows the words "for there follows at the end of 'law' . . ." McIlwain made it read in such a way that the prince's pleasure has the force of law, but only together with the *lex regia* which confers on him his authority. In this way McIlwain was able to reconcile Bracton's reference to an absolutist sentiment with his alleged constitutionalism. McIlwain, *Constitutionalism*, pp. 70–71. This view has been criticized and rejected by Lewis, "King Above Law?" pp. 240–242; Tierney, "Bracton on Government," pp. 306–310; Schulz, "Bracton on Kingship," pp. 154–155; and Fesefeldt, *Englische Staatstheorie*, p. 73, n. 84.

Finally, there has been disagreement as to whether the words just after the citation of the lex regia refer to what the king rashly presumes, or what is rashly presumed to be the king's will. See, e.g., McIlwain, *Constitutionalism*, p. 70; Lewis, "King Above Law?" p. 259, n. 62.

16. *Digest*, I, iv, 1: "Quod principi placuit, legis habet vigorem, utpote cum lege regia, quae de imperio eius lata est, populus ei et in eum omne suum imperium et potestatem conferat." See also *Institutes*, I, ii, 6.

17. McIlwain, *Constitutionalism*, p. 71.

18. *Ibid.*, p. 70.

19. *Ibid.*, p. 71.

20. McIlwain, *Growth*, pp. 195–196, and *Constitutionalism*, p. 158, n. 9.

21. McIlwain, *Constitutionalism*, pp. 71–72.

22. *Ibid.*, p. 71.

23. Lewis, "King Above Law?" p. 242.

24. Schulz, "Bracton on Kingship," p. 155, n. 2.

25. Bracton, *De legibus*, vol. II, fol. 107, p. 304.

26. See chap. iii at n. 43.

27. McIlwain, *Constitutionalism*, p. 72.

28. There has been much discussion of the oath, especially as taken by Edward II. See e.g., Robert S. Hoyt, "The Coronation Oath of 1308: The Background of 'Les leys and les custumes,'" *Traditio*, 11:235–257 (1955).

29. McIlwain, *Constitutionalism*, p. 74.

30. Bracton, *De legibus*, vol. II, fol. 55b, pp. 166–167.

31. McIlwain, *Constitutionalism*, p. 76.

32. *Ibid.*, p. 77.

33. This is well expressed in McIlwain, *Growth*, pp. 192–193: "The most interesting aspect politically of this general regime of custom was the view men took of the nature and consequence of its formal promulgation and of the respective parts taken in this by princes, the learned in the law, the magnates, and the people. *Consuetudo*, or law in its true sense, could not be made . . ."

34. McIlwain, *Constitutionalism*, pp. 82–83.

35. Tierney, "Bracton on Government," p. 309.
36. Bracton, *De legibus,* vol. II, fol. 1, p. 19.
37. McIlwain, *Constitutionalism,* p. 77.
38. Tierney, "Bracton on Government," pp. 307–308. If any more proof were needed of the fictitious character of this allegedly sharp distinction, it could be readily supplied from McIlwain's own text. When he turns to discuss the content of jurisdictio, he says that "in many places it is clearly used in distinction to *gubernatio* or *gubernaculum* . . ." McIlwain, *Constitutionalism,* p. 84. But the discussion which follows this announcement contains no reference to Bracton.
39. Tierney, "Bracton on Government," p. 301.
40. Lewis, "King Above Law?" pp. 258–259, 267–269.
41. Bracton, *De legibus,* vol. II, fol. 107–107b, pp. 305–306.
42. Tierney, "Bracton on Government," p. 305.
43. *Codex,* I, 14, 4: "Digna vox maiestate regnantis legibus alligatum se principem profiteri: adeo de auctoritate iuris nostra pendet auctoritas. Et re vera maius imperio est submittere legibus principatum."
44. Tierney, "Bracton on Government," pp. 302–303.
45. Lewis, "King Above Law?" p. 248, n. 28.
46. *Ibid.,* pp. 244, 247.
47. Tierney, "Bracton on Government," p. 298. See also p. 302.
48. Lewis, "King Above Law?" p. 243; p. 243, n. 14; pp. 258–259; p. 259.
49. *Ibid.,* p. 242.
50. *Ibid.,* p. 248, n. 28.
51. *Ibid.,* p. 268.
52. The political ideas of the *Song of Lewes* are considered in chap. v.
53. Bracton, *De legibus,* vol. II, fol. 55b, pp. 166–167.
54. Lewis, "King Above Law?" p. 267.
55. Bracton, *De legibus,* vol. II, fol. 5b–6, p. 33. Editor's brackets.
56. Kantorowicz, *The King's Two Bodies,* pp. 156–157; Schulz, "Bracton on Kingship," p. 173; Lewis, "King Above Law?" pp. 264–265 (my brackets).
57. Tierney, "Bracton on Government," p. 303. See also F. W. Maitland, ed., *Select Passages from the Works of Bracton and Azo* (London, 1895), p. 65.
58. Bracton, *De legibus,* vol. II, fols. 34–34b, pp. 109–110. Editor's brackets.
59. McIlwain, *Constitutionalism,* p. 69; Woodbine in Bracton, *De legibus,* I, 333. Lewis, "King Above Law?" p. 257, n. 58, says it is "obviously someone's interpolation . . ." Gaillard Lapsley, "Bracton and the Authorship of the 'addicio de cartis,'" *English Historical Review,* 62:1–19 (1947), rejects Bracton's authorship on the ground that it is too radical to have been entertained by a "serious, learned, and responsible judge . . ." *Ibid.,* p. 16. Lapsley also developed a more general reason, namely, that the doctrine of the addicio "is repugnant to the notions of the nature of kingship current in western Europe in the thirteenth century" (*ibid.,* p. 17). This view has been severely criticized

by Tierney, "Bracton on Government," pp. 311–313. Schulz, "Bracton on Kingship," p. 175, regards the addicio as highly suspect, primarily on grounds of literary style.

60. Hermann Kantorowicz, *Bractonian Problems* (Glasgow, 1941), p. 52: "no passage more genuinely Bractonian stands in the whole treatise . . ." This opinion and, for that matter, the thesis and supporting arguments of the entire book have met with a veritable barrage of scholarly criticism. The principal argument of the book is that the errors to be found in Bracton, especially those which appear to betray a considerable amount of misunderstanding of Roman law, should be ascribed not to Bracton but to his scribe. Kantorowicz also contended that Bracton's work was written before 1239, much earlier than the date accepted by most students, the 1250's. In addition to the articles of Lapsley and Schulz cited in the preceding note, H. G. Richardson has presented persuasive counter-argument in several articles, resting primarily on a comparison of Bracton's text with works from which he appears to have derived portions of his arguments. In his "Azo, Drogheda, and Bracton," *English Historical Review*, 59:22–47 (1944), Richardson sets out evidence which seems to show that Bracton borrowed from William of Drogheda's *Summa aurea*, and that this borrowing probably occurred while both were at Oxford, about 1239–1245. This would mean that Kantorowicz's view must be rejected, for otherwise Bracton would not have had the time to acquire the learning for which his book is the evidence. Richardson's textual argument is reinforced with a detailed investigation of a number of well-established facts which supply an independent control. An additional argument driving in the same direction is developed by H. G. Richardson in "Tancred, Raymond, and Bracton," *English Historical Review*, 59:376–384 (1944). He there argues that in certain passages dealing with marriage, legitimacy, and dower Bracton borrowed, not from Tancred, as had been thought, but from the *Summa de matrimonio* of Raymond de Penafort. Since Raymond wrote ca. 1235–1240, while Tancred seems to have composed the book which was Raymond's model ca. 1210–1214, Richardson concludes that Bracton's dependence upon Raymond "adds to the difficulties, which seem otherwise quite insuperable, of supposing that the *De legibus* was written at an early stage in Bracton's career." *Ibid.*, p. 384.

Kantorowicz also levelled an intemperate general criticism at Woodbine's editorship of the Bractonian texts. *Bractonian Problems*, pp. 127–131. To this there have been a number of replies, which seem decisive as against Kantorowicz. See George E. Woodbine, "Bractonian Problems," *Yale Law Journal*, 52:428–444 (1943). Fritz Schulz, "Critical Studies on Bracton's Treatise," *Law Quarterly Review*, 59:172–180 (1943), also comes to the defense of Woodbine's text and shows that Kantorowicz made some errors of his own. Charles Howard McIlwain, "The Present Status of the Problem of the Bracton Text," *Harvard Law Review*, 57:220–240 (1943), accepts Kantorowicz's view that Bracton was a better Romanist than Maitland thought. But he rejects the dating advanced by Kantorowicz, and the view that Bracton was the author of the addicio de cartis.

Richardson and Sayles, on the other hand, have lent the considerable weight of their opinion to the view that there is no good reason to reject Bracton's authorship of this addicio. The principal reason is that they believe Bracton expressed the same view, though more moderately, elsewhere, at fol. 171b. See H. G. Richardson, "The Commons and Medieval Politics," *Transactions of the Royal Historical Society*, 4th ser., 28:21–45 (1946); Richardson and Sayles, *Governance*, p. 145 and n. 1. Earlier, Ludwik Ehrlich, *Proceedings Against the Crown (1216–1377)*, in *Oxford Studies in Social and Legal History*, ed. Paul Vinogradoff (Oxford, 1921), VI, 44–51, 202–205, had argued that the addicio de cartis is a genuine Bractonian passage.

61. F. W. Maitland, ed., *Bracton's Note Book* (London, 1887), I, 31–32. He cites fols. 5b, 52, 107, 368b, and 412. But cf. Tierney, "Bracton on Government," pp. 314–317.

62. Tierney, "Bracton on Government," p. 314, p. 315, p. 315, p. 316, p. 317.

63. As Lewis has said, "King Above Law?" p. 268, Romanist influences are obvious, but what Bracton knew well was English law, and that was his primary concern.

64. In this connection, it is well to bear in mind an observation made by H. G. Richardson, "Studies in Bracton," *Traditio*, 6:61–104 (1948). He points out that Bracton sometimes failed to understand what he read, and that this should be borne in mind in considering "how far he understood or misunderstood Roman lawbooks and the technical terms of Roman law." *Ibid.*, p. 78.

65. Thus F. W. Maitland, ed., *Select Passages from the Works of Bracton and Azo* (London, 1895), p. xviii, entertained a low estimate of Bracton's proficiency as a Romanist. A modern editor of Bracton's work thought that Bracton's use of Roman legal maxims and ideas was quite untechnical and inexpert. See Woodbine in Bracton, *De legibus*, I, 51. On the other hand, Kantorowicz, *Bractonian Problems*, p. 77, argues that Bracton's skill as a Romanist was of a very high order. He admits, as anyone must, that there are manifold errors of interpretation in Bracton's treatment of Roman law, but he accounts for these by attributing them to a systematically clumsy and ignorant scribe. Carl Güterbock, *Bracton and His Relation to the Roman Law*, trans. Brinton Coxe (Philadelphia, 1866), pp. 56–62, took the view that Bracton effected a powerful synthesis of English and Roman law.

66. Richardson and Sayles, *Governance*, p. 145.

67. I can hardly do better than quote Richardson's summary: "The so-called Laws of Edward the Confessor have come down to us in three recensions. The original text was probably compiled about 1130–1135 and then was revised about the middle of the century. Although the other recensions continued to be copied, it was the third recension that was regarded as authoritative in official circles and consequently it was

the recension used by Bracton. A noteworthy feature of the third recension is the expanded section upon the kingly office." Richardson,
"Studies in Bracton," p. 75. Text in Felix Liebermann, *Die Gesetze
der Angelsachsen* (Halle, 1898), I, 627–672. The section on kingship may
be found *ibid.*, 635–637.

68. Richardson, "Studies in Bracton," pp. 76–77.

69. These selections are reproduced in translation in Wilkinson, *Constitutional History*, III, 100–101.

70. Both Richardson, "Studies in Bracton," p. 77, n. 11, and Tierney,
"Bracton on Government," p. 297, have suggested that in this commentary
on the coronation oath Bracton seems to have Glanvill's words in mind.

71. Glanvill, *De legibus*, prologue, p. 24.

72. Bracton, *De legibus*, vol. III, fol. 171b, pp. 42–43. My brackets.

73. Translated in B. Wilkinson, *Constitutional History of Medieval
England, 1216–1399* (London: Longmans, Green & Co., Ltd., 1948–1958),
III, 104. Wilkinson's brackets.

74. James Conway Davies, *The Baronial Opposition to Edward II*
(Cambridge, Eng., 1918), p. 16.

75. *Fleta*, ed. and trans. H. G. Richardson and G. O. Sayles (London:
Selden Society, 1955), vol. II, I, 17, pp. 35–37. Editors' brackets.

76. *Britton*, ed. and trans. Francis Morgan Nichols (Oxford, 1865),
vol. I, bk. I, prologue and chap. 1, pp. 1–2.

77. Davies, *Baronial Opposition*, p. 16.

78. F. M. Powicke, *King Henry III and the Lord Edward* (Oxford,
1947), I, 390, has suggested that Bracton's view may easily have been
affected by his cooperation with the barons in the years 1258–1260, but
that even the addicio de cartis need not be construed as antimonarchical.
Holdsworth, *A History of English Law*, II, 187, thought Bracton's sym-
pathies may have lain with the baronial party. Maitland considered that
the evidence of Bracton's text suggested that he wavered between adherence to the king and to the baronial party. Pollock and Maitland,
The History of English Law, I, 209.

79. Jolliffe, *Angevin Kingship*, p. 32.

80. Bracton, *De legibus*, vol. II, fol. 2, p. 22, and fol. 1, p. 19. See
on this the fine study of Frederic Cheyette, "Custom, Case Law, and
Medieval 'Constitutionalism': A Re-examination," *Political Science Quarterly*, 78:362–390 (1963); also Tierney, "Bracton on Government," p. 309;
and Lewis "King Above Law?" p. 241, n. 9, and p. 251.

81. Cheyette, "Re-examination," pp. 367–376.

82. Holt, *Magna Carta*, p. 202.

83. See the discussion of the *Song of Lewes* in chap. v.

84. Lewis, "King Above Law?" p. 260, n. 69, and p. 265, n. 89; Tierney,
"Bracton on Government," p. 304.

Chapter Five. King and Crown

1. I owe this point to Judith N. Shklar.

2. See Holt, *Magna Carta,* esp. pp. 19–42.

3. The impact of the king's involvement in affairs overseas on the emergence of bureaucratic rule is brought into focus sharply in Richardson and Sayles, *Governance,* pp. 157–166, 215. Robert S. Hoyt, *The Royal Demesne in English Constitutional History 1066–1272* (Ithaca, 1950), is especially helpful in drawing attention to the administrative needs deriving from the king's personal holdings in land.

4. Richardson and Sayles, *Governance,* pp. 17, 38, 147. The centrality of the king's council in governance is the theme of Richardson and Sayles, *Parliaments and Great Councils in Medieval England.*

5. Jolliffe, *Angevin Kingship,* pp. 334–335.

6. Richardson and Sayles, *Governance,* pp. 392–393.

7. Holt, *Magna Carta,* pp. 43–62.

8. William Sharp McKechnie, *Magna Carta* (Glasgow, 1914), pp. 232, 248.

9. *Ibid.,* p. 253.

10. *Ibid.,* pp. 233–234.

11. Holt, *Magna Carta,* pp. 269–292.

12. McKechnie, *Magna Carta,* p. 375.

13. Jolliffe, *Angevin Kingship,* pp. 334–335; see Barnaby C. Keeney, *Judgment by Peers* (Cambridge, Mass., 1949), for a full discussion.

14. Holt, *Magna Carta,* pp. 242–268.

15. Jolliffe, *Angevin Kingship,* pp. 335–336.

16. Hoyt, *The Royal Demesne,* pp. 149, 153, 233.

17. *Ibid.,* p. 9, p. 10.

18. *Ibid.,* pp. 10, 15, 20–24, 50–51, 74–75.

19. *Ibid.,* pp. 134–155.

20. The Articles of the Barons of 1215 attacked both scutages and tallage, as well as aids. Article 32 states that tallage and aids required of London and other cities which have liberties should, like scutage, be dependent on the common counsel of the realm. But chapter 12 of John's charter reads: "No scutage nor aid shall be imposed on our kingdom, unless by common counsel of our kingdom, except for ransoming our person, for making our eldest son a knight, and for once marrying our eldest daughter; and for these there shall not be levied more than a reasonable aid. In like manner it shall be done concerning aids from the city of London." McKechnie, *Magna Carta,* p. 232. Chapter 25 declares that "all counties, hundreds, wapentakes, and tithings (except our demesne manors) shall remain at the old rents, and without any additional payments." *Ibid.,* p. 317.

21. *Ibid.,* p. 320.

22. Hoyt, *The Royal Demesne,* pp. 117, 161–162, 147.

23. *Ibid.,* p. 150.

24. *Annales Monastici,* ed. Henry Richards Luard (London, 1864), I, 395; reproduced in translation in Wilkinson, *Constitutional History,* III, 141–142. Much of the space in the three volumes of this remarkable study by Wilkinson is devoted to the collection and translation of a vast number of documents from the thirteenth and fourteenth centuries. Many of the passages cited in this chapter may be found there, and I am greatly indebted to Wilkinson's extraordinarily valuable and skillful collection of these documents, as well as to his insightful arguments on general constitutional history.

25. The general contours of the reign of Henry III are discussed in Wilkinson, *Constitutional History,* I, 1–37, 69–88, 99–110, 117–126, 132–163.

26. Roger of Wendover, *Flores Historiarum,* ed. Henry G. Hewlett (London, 1886–1889), III, 47–48; reproduced in translation in Wilkinson, *Constitutional History,* I, 110–111.

27. Matthew Paris, *Chronica Majora,* ed. Henry Richards Luard (London, 1872–1883), V, 20; trans. in Wilkinson, *Constitutional History,* I, 164–165.

28. Wilkinson, *Constitutional History,* I, 34.

29. The relevant sections of the Provisions of Oxford are in Wilkinson, *Constitutional History,* I, 167–171.

30. *Ibid.,* I, 33.

31. *Statutes of the Realm,* I, 12–17; reproduced in Wilkinson, *Constitutional History,* I, 184–186. Wilkinson's brackets.

32. *The Song of Lewes,* ed. C. L. Kingsford (Oxford, 1890), pp. 43–44, pp. 44–45.

33. *Ibid.,* p. 46. Editor's brackets.

34. *Ibid.,* pp. 47–48.

35. *Ibid.,* p. 48.

36. *Ibid.,* pp. 51–52.

37. *Ibid.,* pp. 49–50.

38. *Ibid.,* p. 50, p. 53 (emphasis added), p. 54.

39. R. F. Treharne, "The Significance of the Baronial Reform Movement, 1258–1267," *Transactions of the Royal Historical Society,* 4th ser., 25:35–72 (1943).

40. *Ibid.,* p. 70.

41. *Ibid.,* p. 71.

42. The crisis of 1297 is treated in Wilkinson, *Constitutional History,* I, 187–210.

43. See Richardson, "The Commons and Medieval Politics," pp. 21–26; J. S. Roskell, "Perspectives in English Parliamentary History," pp. 448–475; J. G. Edwards, *Historians and the Medieval English Parliament* (Glasgow, 1960); J. G. Edwards, *The Commons in Medieval Parliaments* (London, 1958).

44. There is a detailed treatment in Michael Powicke, *Military Obligation in Medieval England* (Oxford, 1962), pp. 103–117.

45. Willelmi Rishanger, *Chronica et Annales,* ed. Henry Thomas Riley (London, 1865), pp. 175–176; trans. in Wilkinson, *Constitutional History,* I, 220–222.

46. Walter of Hemingburgh, *Chronicon,* ed. Hans Claude Hamilton (London, 1848–1849), II, 152–154; in Wilkinson, *Constitutional History,* I, 225–226.

47. *Statutes of the Realm,* I, 123; reproduced in Wilkinson, *Constitutional History,* I, 226–228.

48. Walter of Hemingburgh, *Chronicon,* II, 182–183; trans. in Wilkinson, *Constitutional History,* I, 229–230.

49. Quoted in Wilkinson, *Constitutional History,* I, 64.

50. *Ibid.*

51. See Wilkinson, *Constitutional History,* I, 230–232.

52. Davies, *Baronial Opposition,* pp. 78–86, 99–102.

53. Quoted in Wilkinson, *Constitutional History,* II, 100.

54. Quoted in translation in Richardson, "The English Coronation Oath," p. 67. The text and a slightly different translation of the Declaration of 1308 are now available in Richardson and Sayles, *Governance,* pp. 466–469.

55. *Statutes of the Realm,* I, 182.

56. Wilkinson, *Constitutional History,* II, 19 (esp. n. 22), 100–104, 134–147.

57. It ought to be noticed that this interpretation of the statute has been challenged by Richardson, "The English Coronation Oath," pp. 72–73; Richardson believes that the statute was designed only to repeal the Ordinances of 1311. Wilkinson, *Constitutional History,* II, 139–142, takes the broader view that it was an effort to repudiate the whole baronial outlook. There is an acute treatment of a wide range of problems, and a review of the literature on this much debated statute, in Gaillard T. Lapsley, *Crown, Community and Parliament in the Later Middle Ages,* ed. Helen M. Cam and Geoffrey Barraclough (Oxford, 1951), pp. 153–228.

58. *Vita Edwardi Secundi,* ed. and trans. N. Denholm-Young (London, 1957), p. 10.

59. *Gesta Edwardi di Carnarvan Auctore Canonico Bridlingtoniensi,* in *Chronicles of Edward I and Edward II,* ed. William Stubbs (London, 1882–1883), II, 36–37; trans. in Wilkinson, *Constitutional History,* II, 122–123.

60. *Annales Londoniensis,* in *Chronicles of Edward I and Edward II,* I, 167; trans. in Wilkinson, *Constitutional History,* II, 123–124. Emphasis added.

61. Quoted in Wilkinson, *Constitutional History,* II, 125, 126.

62. *Statutes of the Realm,* I, 157; reproduced in Wilkinson, *Constitutional History,* II, 127–132.

63. W. J. Whittaker, ed. and trans., *The Mirror of Justices* (London, 1895), pp. 155–156. Paragraph numbers omitted.

64. *Ibid.,* p. 7. Emphasis added. Editor's brackets.

65. Bracton, *De legibus,* vol. II, fol. 119b, p. 337: "Videtur sine praeiudicio melioris sententiae quod curia et pares iudicabunt, ne maleficia remaneant impunita . . ."

66. *Ibid.,* vol. IV, fols. 368b–369, pp. 157–159.

67. See n. 57, above.

68. *Statutes of the Realm,* I, 189; reproduced in Wilkinson, *Constitutional History,* II, 155–156. Wilkinson's brackets.

69. Wilkinson, *Constitutional History,* II, 170–171.

70. Quoted *ibid.,* II, 172.

71. Quoted *ibid.,* II, 174. See also B. Wilkinson, "The 'Political Revolution' of the Thirteenth and Fourteenth Centuries in England," *Speculum,* 24: 502–509 (1949).

72. There is a sustained treatment in H. L. Gray, *The Influence of the Commons on Early Legislation* (Cambridge, Mass., 1932). This should be considered in conjunction with the extended criticism and commentary in S. B. Chrimes, *English Constitutional Ideas in the Fifteenth Century* (Cambridge, Eng., 1936), pp. 226–249. Cf. also Richardson, "The Commons and Medieval Politics," pp. 21–45.

73. For example, *Statutes of the Realm,* I, 252, 255, 257, 261. The sanctioning clauses are collected in Wilkinson, *Constitutional History,* II, 172–173. See also Richardson, "The Commons and Medieval Politics," esp. pp. 26–32.

74. A reconsideration of this charge is developed in Wilkinson, *Constitutional History,* III, 339–349.

75. *Rotuli Parliamentorum,* II, 165; trans. in Wilkinson, *Constitutional History,* III, 209, n. 83. Emphasis added.

76. *Rotuli Parliamentorum,* III, 145ff.

77. Richardson, "The Commons and Medieval Politics," pp. 25–26 and p. 26, n. 1.

78. *The Register of John de Grandisson,* ed. Hingeston-Randolph, II, 840.

79. The quarrel of 1340–1341 is discussed in May McKisack, *The Fourteenth Century* (Oxford, 1959), pp. 159–181.

80. *Croniques de London,* ed. George James Aungier (London, 1844), p. 90; trans. in Wilkinson, *Constitutional History,* II, 193–194. Emphasis added.

81. A. W. Goodman, ed. and trans., *The Chartulary of Winchester Cathedral* (Winchester, Eng., 1927), pp. 131–133; reproduced in Wilkinson, *Constitutional History,* II, 194–197. Emphasis added.

82. *Rotuli Parliamentorum,* II, 126; trans. in Wilkinson, *Constitutional History,* II, 197. Emphasis added.

83. *Statutes of the Realm,* I, 395.

84. *Statutes of the Realm,* I, 297. Quoted in Wilkinson, *Constitutional History,* II, 203, n. 45. Emphasis added.

85. *Rotuli Parliamentorum,* II, 139; trans. in Wilkinson, *Constitutional History,* II, 203.

86. There has been considerable discussion on the question of the

origin of impeachment. T. F. T. Plucknett, "The Origin of Impeachment," *Transactions of the Royal Historical Society*, 4th ser., 24: 47–71 (1942), argues that the central idea was extracted from the common law principle of notoriety. M. V. Clarke, *Fourteenth Century Studies*, ed. L. S. Sutherland and M. McKisack (Oxford, 1937), pp. 242–271, emphasizes the procedure of indictment. Both of these views are discussed in Wilkinson, *Constitutional History*, II, 205–208, and the position is taken that the origin lies, rather, in the attempts of earlier years to achieve political aims by parliamentary trial.

87. Quoted in Wilkinson, *Constitutional History*, II, 215–216.

88. See the account of Thomas of Walsingham, *Chronicon Angliae*, ed. E. M. Thompson (London, 1874), pp. 68ff. A number of passages are collected in Wilkinson, *Constitutional History*, II, 214–221.

89. Quoted in Wilkinson, *Constitutional History*, II, 237, n. 33.

90. Quoted *ibid.*, II, 313.

91. *Rotuli Parliamentorum*, III, 415; trans. in Wilkinson, *Constitutional History*, II, 303.

92. Quoted in Wilkinson, *Constitutional History*, II, 243, 244. My brackets.

93. *Statutes of the Realm*, II, 95–98; reproduced in Wilkinson, *Constitutional History*, II, 248–249.

94. *Statutes of the Realm*, II, 102; reproduced in Wilkinson, *Constitutional History*, II, 249–251.

95. See Wilkinson, *Constitutional History*, II, 252–269.

96. Quoted *ibid.*, 280.

97. *Rotuli Parliamentorum*, III, 339; trans. in Wilkinson, *Constitutional History*, II, 306, 307. Wilkinson's brackets.

98. *Rotuli Parliamentorum*, III, 408; trans. in Wilkinson, *Constitutional History*, II, 307–308.

99. There is a discussion of the alternative views in Wilkinson, *Constitutional History*, II, 288–292.

100. Quoted in Wilkinson, *Constitutional History*, II, 316. My brackets.

101. Quoted *ibid.*, 313.

102. *Ibid.*, 312.

103. Jolliffe, *Angevin Kingship*, p. 329. My brackets.

104. The poverty of the Lancastrian monarchy is discussed in E. F. Jacob, *The Fifteenth Century* (Oxford, 1961), pp. 436–448. The policies and practices of the great families are treated *ibid.*, pp. 305–346.

105. J. E. A. Jolliffe, *The Constitutional History of Medieval England* (London, 1937), p. 426.

106. Jacob, *Fifteenth Century*, pp. 319, 336.

107. *Ibid.*, p. 406: "Constitutionally, after Henry IV had grasped the throne, there was no experiment. Everyone, save the avowed supporters of Richard II, was anxious to go on as before." Chrimes, *English Constitutional Ideas*, pp. 300–303, attributes the intellectual sterility of the century to England's curious but indomitable insularity in that day.

108. Holdsworth, *A History of English Law*, II, 416.

109. H. S. Bennett, *The Pastons and Their England* (Cambridge, Eng., 1922), p. xix.

110. *The Paston Letters,* ed. James Gairdner (London, 1904), nos. 217, 241. The numbers in these references to the Paston correspondence are those assigned to individual letters by the editor. The numbers so assigned vary considerably in different editions. All references here will be to the Gairdner edition.

111. *Ibid.,* nos. 617, 720, 722–724, 730–731. The Paston materials by no means stand alone in testifying to these conditions. See, e.g., *Rotuli Parliamentorum,* V, 367; VI, 8.

112. *The Paston Letters,* no. 406. This did not mean that men failed to take their contests to court. On the contrary, the volume of litigation in this period is nothing short of astounding. *Ibid.,* nos. 314, 414, 461. John Paston, for example, pursued no less than a dozen actions for his sister in a single legal term. See Bennett, *The Pastons,* p. 172, n. 3. On this point, J. R. Lander, *The Wars of the Roses* (London, 1965), p. 26, has remarked quite rightly, "Underdeveloped agrarian societies are always fiercely litigious."

113. *The Paston Letters,* no. 37.

114. On bribery and perjury in general, see *ibid.,* nos. 142, 164, 175, 185, 267–268, 278, 359, 396, 455, 565, 639, 690, 815; on bribery of juries, nos. 188, 586; of sheriffs, nos. 188–189, 193, 222, 330; of justices, no. 308.

115. *Ibid.,* nos. 179–180, 189, 192, 229, 599.

116. Chrimes, *English Constitutional Ideas,* pp. 76–80.

117. See the detailed treatment *ibid.,* pp. 80–125.

118. M. V. Clarke, *Medieval Representation and Consent* (London, 1936), presents a detailed consideration of the Modus Tenendi Parliamentum.

119. Chrimes, *English Constitutional Ideas,* pp. 126–130.

120. *Year Books, 39 Edward III* (Rolls Series), fol. 7: "Comment per proclamation ne soit mi fait en le conte chescun est tenu de le scaver maintenant quand il est fait en Parliament, car tantost ad conclude ascun chose, le ley entende qe chescun person ad conusance de ce; car le Parliament represent le corps de tout le Royalme . . ." Quoted in translation in S. B. Chrimes, *English Constitutional Ideas in the Fifteenth Century* (Cambridge, Eng.: Cambridge University Press, 1936), p. 76; the text is printed *ibid.,* appendix 8. pp. 351–352. See also Theodore F. T. Plucknett, *Statutes & Their Interpretation in the First Half of the Fourteenth Century* (Cambridge, Eng., 1922). p. 103. Needless to say, such a view does not attain to the level of a theory of representation. It is, rather, a convenient assumption, a legal fiction. The same observation applies to a similar statement in court in 1481: "Every man is bound by every act of parliament, for every man is privy and party to parliament, for the commons have one or two representatives for each community who can bind the whole." *Year Books, 21 Edward IV,* 45, pl. 6, as rendered in Helen Cam, *Law-Finders and Law-Makers* (London, 1962), p. 158, from the text supplied in S. E. Thorne, ed., *A Discourse upon the Exposicion*

& Understandinge of Statutes (San Marino, Calif., 1942), pp. 20–21, n. 37: "Catesby: . . . 'par chescun act de parlement chescun a que act extend serra lie, pur ceo que chescun home est priue & partie al parlement, car les Commons ont vn ou ij pur chescun commune pur lier ou deslier tout le commune . . .'"

121. See George P. Cuttino, "A Reconsideration of the 'Modus Tenendi Parliamentum,'" in Francis Lee Utley, ed., *The Forward Movement of the Fourteenth Century* (Columbus, Ohio, 1961), pp. 31–60.

122. The texts of Bishop Russell's drafts are printed in Chrimes, *English Constitutional Ideas*, pp. 167–191. The passage cited may be found *ibid.*, p. 174. Bracketed words added.

123. *Ibid.*, pp. 174, 178, 187.

124. *Rotuli Parliamentorum*, V, 487. Quoted in Chrimes, *English Constitutional Ideas*, p. 132. Other instances are collected in Chrimes, pp. 131–132, from *Rotuli Parliamentorum*, III, 581; IV, 22; V, 239–240, 284–285, 572, 622; VI, 8.

125. Chrimes, *English Constitutional Ideas*, p. 131.

126. *Ibid.*, pp. 168, 180.

127. Jolliffe, *Constitutional History*, pp. 433–437, 442–443. "Above all, as we approach the middle of the century, the decay of order begins to affect every aspect of life, and the progress which has been made towards parliamentary government becomes more and more a mere screen for dynastic and party intrigue." *Ibid.*, p. 433.

128. *Political Songs*, ed. Thomas Wright (London, 1859–1861), II, 252.

129. *Rotuli Parliamentorum*, V, 464.

130. To be sure, not all the blame for the decrepitude of the English polity in this period should be fastened on the great men. Their private armies were fundamentally a product of the Hundred Years' War. Still, family ambitions played no small part in the collapse of order. A leading English historian of the fifteenth century has assessed the matter thus: "It is easy to make too much of the family broils and dissensions of this unquiet time; it is equally simple to regard them as an irrelevance in the social and economic growth of England. Neither view is adequate, but the first comes nearest to the truth, however old-fashioned it may sound. Our history until the days of democracy, and perhaps even beyond, is the history of our families, of the local leadership that gave tone and life to the countryside and formed the opinion of our people." Jacob, *Essays in the Conciliar Epoch*, p. 106.

131. *Rotuli Parliamentorum*, V, 410; quoted in Chrimes, *English Constitutional Ideas*, p. 36; see also Chrimes, pp. 149–151.

132. *Rotuli Parliamentorum*, V, 242, 289–290.

133. Quoted in Richardson, "The Commons and Medieval Politics," p. 25. See also Richardson and Sayles, *Parliaments and Great Councils in Medieval England*, pp. 40, 44.

412

Chapter Six. Law, Custom, and Politics

1. Cam, *Law-Finders and Law-Makers in Medieval England*, p. 132.
2. Plucknett, *Legislation of Edward I*, p. 6, n. 1.
3. *Ibid.*, pp. 1–20. See also Charles Ogilvie, *The King's Government and the Common Law* (Oxford, 1958), pp. 10–12.
4. For example, McIlwain, *Growth*, p. 188: " 'Law,' the only law in the highest sense, is something that none can 'make,' not even a king. He should approve it, and man may find, and preserve or maintain it, but it comes solely from ancient custom. These *consuetudines* or ancient customs are maintained or preserved by usage of the people (*more utentium*) and the king approves them either tacitly or by making provisions to ensure their enforcement. The latter may be *assisae, provisiones, ordinationes, ordonnances, stabilimenta,* or *etablissements,* even *statuta;* they are *leges,* but they are not yet 'law.' " *Ibid.*, p. 367: "the medieval king was 'absolute' and irresponsible, but he was 'limited.' There were things beyond his legitimate power and if he overstepped that power his acts were *ultra vires.*" See also McIlwain, *The High Court of Parliament,* pp. vii–viii; *ibid.*, p. 271: "statutes are void entirely, because against reason or the fundamental law." For additional citations relating to the fundamental law thesis, see chap. i, n. 64, and chap. iv, n. 36, above.
5. Cheyette, "Re-examination," p. 363.
6. *Ibid.*, p. 369.
7. Shklar, *Legalism*, p. 17.
8. Cheyette, "Re-examination," p. 375.
9. *Ibid.*, p. 367.
10. See above, chap. iv.
11. Cheyette, "Re-examination," p. 378.
12. *Institutes,* I, ii, 9.
13. Bracton, *De legibus,* vol. II, fol. 1, p. 19.
14. *Britton,* I, 1.
15. Cheyette, "Re-examination," p. 382.
16. There are helpful discussions of "seizen" *ibid.*, pp. 382–385, and in Plucknett, *Legislation of Edward I,* pp. 51–66.
17. Cheyette, "Re-examination," p. 379.
18. Quoted *ibid.*, p. 380.
19. Bracton, *De legibus,* vol. II, fol. lb, p. 21.
20. Cheyette, "Re-examination," p. 390.
21. See Christopher Hill, *Puritanism and Revolution* (New York, 1964), pp. 50–122.
22. F. W. Maitland, *The Constitutional History of England* (Cambridge, Eng., 1911), p. 100.
23. *The Laws of William the Conqueror,* in David C. Douglas and George W. Greenaway, eds. (David C. Douglas, general ed.), *English Historical Documents, 1042–1189* (London: Eyre & Spottiswoode [Publishers] Ltd., 1953), II, 399–400. Cited hereafter as *EHD,* II.

24. *The Coronation Charter of Henry I*, in *EHD*, II, 400–402. The passages cited are numbered 1 and 13 respectively.

25. *Charter of Stephen* (1135), in *EHD*, II, 402.

26. *The Coronation Charter of Henry II* (1154), in *EHD*, II, 407.

27. McIlwain, *The High Court of Parliament*, p. 45.

28. *The Constitutions of Clarendon (January 1164)*, in *EHD*, II, 718.

29. *EHD*, II, 725.

30. *Ibid.*, pp. 725–726, n. 5.

31. *Ibid.*, p. 731. Emphasis added.

32. *Letter from Thomas Becket to Henry II (May 1166)*, in *EHD*, II, 743–744. Emphasis added.

33. *Letter from Gilbert Foliot to Thomas Becket (1166)*, in *EHD*, II, 748–749. Emphasis added.

34. Holt, *Magna Carta*, p. 18.

35. *Ibid.*, p. 285.

36. Powicke, *King Henry III and the Lord Edward*, pp. 148–155.

37. *Statutes of the Realm*, I, 4; reproduced in Wilkinson, *Constitutional History*, III, 258.

38. Cam, *Law-Finders and Law-Makers*, p. 137.

39. *Epistolae Roberti Grosseteste*, ed. Henry Richards Luard (London, 1861), p. 96; trans. in Wilkinson, *Constitutional History*, III, 257.

40. See Dionna Clementi, "That the Statute of York of 1322 is no longer ambiguous," in *Album Helen Maud Cam*, II (Louvain 1961), 96.

41. Matthew Paris, *Chronica Majora*, V, 369; cited in Wilkinson, *Constitutional History*, III, 242.

42. Bracton, *De legibus*, vol. II, fol. 1b, p. 21.

43. Plucknett, *Legislation of Edward I*, pp. 51–57.

44. Quoted *ibid.*, p. 58.

45. Trial by battle had been the traditional method of settling an action pursued upon a writ of right, though by the middle of the thirteenth century it was falling into disuse. Charles Johnson has described it as follows. "The form of procedure is that the parties produce their champions, who are deemed to be witnesses (though not necessarily eye-witnesses) of the facts asserted, but were in fact frequently professionals, battle is formally waged; the lists are set; and the champions cudgel each other till one or other gives in." Charles Johnson, "Notes on Thirteenth-century Judicial Procedure," *English Historical Review*, 62: 508–521 (1947). As for trial by grand assize, this "was an alternative to the judicial combat, and was only applicable in cases, such as writ of right, which involved that method of proof. Here the court nominated four knights, who elected the jury of twelve from the knights of the county." *Ibid.*, 515.

46. The foregoing account rests on the discussion in Plucknett, *Legislation of Edward I*, pp. 58–72.

47. *Ibid.*, pp. 72–73.

48. Plucknett, *Legislation of Edward I*, p. 74. Plucknett's brackets.

414

Bereford's remark occurs in *Year Books of Edward II* (Selden Society), IV, 161.

49. The following discussion relies on Plucknett, *Legislation of Edward I*, pp. 29–48, and Sutherland, *Quo Warranto Proceedings*.

50. Sutherland, *Quo Warranto Proceedings*, pp. 5–15.

51. *Ibid.,* pp. 71–81.

52. *Ibid.,* pp. 92–97.

53. *Ibid.,* p. 82.

54. Quoted *ibid.,* p. 82, n. 2.

55. *Year Books, 4 Edward II* (Selden Society): "car un canoun defet plussours leis, auxi le statut defet plussours choses qe sunt a la commun lei." Quoted in Plucknett, *Statutes & Their Interpretation,* p. 31.

56. The text is printed in Chrimes, *English Constitutional Ideas,* appendix 7, p. 351.

57. *Rotuli Parliamentorum,* III, 243.

58. *Ibid.,* V, 35.

59. *Ibid.,* 239.

60. Charles Johnson, ed. and trans., *Dialogus de Scaccario* (London, 1950), p. 1; see also pp. 101, 120.

61. *Select Cases in the Court of King's Bench under Edward I,* ed. and trans. G. O. Sayles (London, 1936), II, 68.

62. *Ibid.,* I, 54.

63. Wilkinson, *Studies in the Constitutional History of the Thirteenth and Fourteenth Centuries,* p. 223.

64. *Rotuli Parliamentorum,* I, 71.

65. *Year Books, 8 Edward II* (Selden Society), p. 74.

66. Quoted in Plucknett, *Statutes & Their Interpretation,* pp. 139–140.

67. Quoted *ibid.,* p. 140.

68. *Rotuli Parliamentorum,* V, 376.

69. Cited in Wilkinson, *Constitutional History,* I, 111.

70. Declaration of 1308, trans. in Richardson, "The English Coronation Oath," p. 67.

71. Quoted in Wilkinson, *Constitutional History,* II, 280. Wilkinson's brackets.

72. Quoted *ibid.,* 282.

73. Plucknett, *Legislation of Edward I,* p. 8.

74. For valuable criticisms see Cheyette, "Re-examination," pp. 362–366, 368–369, 384–385, 388–389; Plucknett, *Statutes & Their Interpretation,* pp. xxv, 26–34, 66–71. Chrimes, *English Constitutional Ideas,* pp. 291–292, has shown that there are no instances of judicial nullification in terms of general principles in the fourteenth and fifteenth centuries. See also *ibid.,* pp. 271–279. Another review of some crucial cases is set out in J. W. Gough, *Fundamental Law in English Constitutional History* (Oxford, 1955), pp. 7–47. In addition to the fundamental work of Plucknett, *Legislation of Edward I,* there is a rewarding discussion of Edwardian lawmaking in Maurice Powicke, *The Thirteenth Century* (Oxford, 1953), pp. 322–380.

Chapter Seven. Political and Regal Dominion

1. Chrimes, *English Constitutional Ideas in the Fifteenth Century,* p. 304, has observed that Fortescue is undoubtedly the outstanding political thinker of fifteenth century England.

2. *De Natura Legis Naturae,* I, xxxiv, xxxv. (All references to this work will be to the edition of Thomas [Fortescue] Lord Clermont, ed., *The Works of Sir John Fortescue, Knight* [London, 1869], vol. I.)

3. *Ibid.,* I, xxvi, xxviii.

4. *Ibid.,* I, xxxvii, xxxviii.

5. *Ibid.,* I, xlii, xliii.

6. *Ibid.,* I, iv, v.

7. *Ibid.,* I, x, xxix.

8. Chrimes, *English Constitutional Ideas,* p. 201. It is interesting to note that the quotation just given continues as follows: "and a statute could not enact any rule other than natural law or custom." "Statutes are thus purely declaratory of law which exists already either as customary or as natural law; they therefore do not create new law, even though they may convert natural into positive law." *Ibid.,* pp. 201–202.

9. McIlwain, *Growth,* p. 362.

10. *De Natura,* I, xxx.

11. Sir John Fortescue, *De Laudibus Legum Anglie,* trans. and ed. S. B. Chrimes (Cambridge, Eng.: Cambridge University Press, 1942), XV. All references to this work will be to this edition.

12. *De Natura,* I, v.

13. *Ibid.,* I, vii. My brackets.

14. *Ibid.,* I, ix.

15. *Ibid.,* I, xviii.

16. *Ibid.,* I, x.

17. *Ibid.,* I, xvi. My brackets. Fortescue gives a number of cases from history which he considers illustrative of dominium politicum et regale.

18. *De Laudibus,* IX.

19. Sir John Fortescue, *The Governance of England,* ed. with introduction, notes, and appendices by Charles Plummer (Oxford, 1885), I.

20. *De Natura,* I, xliv.

21. *Ibid.,* I, xxvii, xxviii.

22. *Ibid.,* I, xxix, vi, xxix, xxviii.

23. *Ibid.,* I, xxvii, xxix.

24. R. W. K. Hinton, "English Constitutional Theories from Sir John Fortescue to Sir John Eliot," *English Historical Review,* 75: 410–425 (1960). Quotation is from p. 415. My brackets.

25. *Governance,* III; *De Laudibus,* XXIV.

26. *De Natura,* I, xxi, xxii.

27. *Ibid.,* I, xxii.

28. Chrimes, *English Constitutional Ideas,* p. 337, n. 39.

416

29. *De Natura,* I, xxii.

30. Plummer, ed., Sir John Fortescue, *Governance,* p. 179. See *De Laudibus,* XI, XIV, XXXIV, XXXVII; *Governance,* VI.

31. *De Natura,* I, xxvi.

32. Fortescue derives the argument from Boethius, *The Consolation of Philosophy,* Book IV.

33. *De Laudibus,* X, XI (source of quotation), XII.

34. *Ibid.,* XIII.

35. Max Adams Shepard, "The Political and Constitutional Theory of Sir John Fortescue," in *Essays in History and Political Theory in Honor of Charles Howard McIlwain* (Cambridge, Mass., 1936), p. 306, n. 56, refers to this passage as expressing a typical formulation of Fortescue's idea of regal and political dominion. His general description of Fortescue is notable as an example of the sort of interpretation with which I cannot agree. Shepard says that Fortescue "distinguishes . . . the *dominium politicum et regale,* from the purely royal government, the *dominium regale* . . . In the former the king rules inside the law, in the latter above it and by his own arbitrary discretion and will." *Ibid.,* p. 305. Again, the "king in the royal and political government is most emphatically limited by law—not only by natural law, by which all kings are, or should be, limited, but also by the common, customary, or constitutional law of his own realm." *Ibid.,* p. 306. This reading of Fortescue's various descriptions of political and regal dominion is gratuitous. It supplies an emphasis on legal limitation which is not in the text. If one has not decided in advance that Fortescue must somehow mean this, these passages say something quite different, and they say it in a more subtle way than is allowed by this kind of reading. The passages uniformly suggest that the laws that are to obtain in England are the product of the joint authority and consent of the king and "people." Only after this political process has been accomplished is there a warrant for observing that everybody, including the king, should proceed according to these agreements. This is in no way incompatible with the idea that the king is obligated to uphold the law, or that, once the law is established, the king cannot instruct his judges to settle litigation in a way contrary to what has been established. But it is an idea quite different from that of limitation by fundamental, organic, or constitutional law. Fortescue says nothing so general as the views Shepard attributes to him. What he does say suggests only that the king and parliament (or three estates, or people, or the great men of the realm) can make, amend, and repeal laws. If any modern idea were to be read into Fortescue, that of parliamentary sovereignty would be most plausible. But even this is to make him hold an opinion on a subject which he did not confront.

36. *De Laudibus,* XVIII: "there is no gainsaying nor legitimate doubt but that the customs of the English are not only good but the best."

37. *Ibid.,* XVI.

38. A point made by Hinton, "English Constitutional Theories," p. 415.

39. *De Natura,* I, xix.

40. *De Laudibus,* LIII.

41. *Ibid.,* XVIII.

42. *Ibid.,* IV, XVI.

43. This is a phase of Fortescue's argument which did not find expression in his other works, as Plummer, ed., Sir John Fortescue, *Governance,* p. 83, has observed.

44. *De Natura,* I, xxv.

45. *Ibid.,* I, xxiv.

46. *Ibid.,* I, xxv, and xxiv.

47. *Ibid.,* I, xvi.

48. Chrimes, *English Constitutional Ideas,* p. 349.

49. Sir Frederick Pollock, for instance, in his *Essays in the Law* (London, 1922), pp. 53–54, describes *De Natura* as artificial and of "slight interest and no value." See also Caroline A. J. Skeel, "The Influence of the Writings of Sir John Fortescue," *Transactions of the Royal Historical Society,* 3d ser., 10: 77–114 (1916). Most recent judgment is less harsh.

50. E. F. Jacob, *Essays in the Conciliar Epoch* (Manchester, 1943), pp. 106–108.

51. Fortescue's refutation of his earlier works on behalf of the Lancastrian title goes under the name of *The Declaracion Made by John Fortescu, Knyght, upon Certayn Wrytinges Sent Oute Of Scotteland, Ayenst the Kinges Title to the Roialme of Englond;* it is printed in *Works,* I, 523–541.

52. This was a live question because the Yorkist title rested on the claim that succession could descend through females, the descendants of Lionel, Duke of Clarence. For a detailed account of the political complexities produced by the proliferation of royal blood, see S. B. Chrimes, *Lancastrians, Yorkists and Henry VII* (London, 1964).

53. *De Natura,* II, ii, xiii.

54. *Ibid.,* II, xvi. The grandson's arguments are not very persuasive. He says he inherits from his grandfather through his mother, who is a mere medium. He resorts to likening his mother to a rope, to the medium through which sound passes, and the like. *Ibid.* His great uncle rightly retorts that these similitudes are mere sophisms. *Ibid.,* II, xxxii. But it is difficult to see how his own analogies are any less sophistical. In any event, the grandson contends that his position is no different from the parallel case of inheritance through a father. He would have succeeded, he says, if his grandfather had had a son instead, who died while the king was still alive. Certainly—and here Fortescue shows himself the advocate—if there had been only a granddaughter, then the kingdom would descend to the king's brother, if he had one. He glides over the crucial question: why would the brother succeed in that case? *Ibid.,* II, xvi.

55. *Ibid.,* II, vii.

56. *Ibid.,* II, xxiii, xxv.

57. *Ibid.,* II, iv, xxviii.

58. *Ibid.*, II, 1.

59. *Ibid.*, II, iii.

60. *Ibid.*, II, xxv–xxvi, xliv.

61. *Ibid.*, II, xxiv.

62. *Ibid.*, II, viii, xv, xxiv–xl.

63. *Ibid.*, II, lii. In part, this appeal to Roman law is only a reply to one of the grandson's arguments, drawn from the Roman law of guardianship. He had argued that an analogy obtained between his case and the case of guardianship bestowed on the son of a maternal or paternal aunt, a law which bypassed the aunt explicitly in favor of the male. *Ibid.*, II, xlviii. The brother objects that this is merely a case of bestowing a private trust and so does not support a claim to the regal dignity, which is not a bestowal but an inheritance. *Ibid.*, II, 1.

64. *Ibid.*, II, xlvii, liv.

65. *Ibid.*, II, xxxiii.

66. *Ibid.*, II, xxxiv–xxxvi.

67. *Ibid.*, II, xxxv.

68. *Ibid.*, II, xxxvii.

69. *Ibid.*, II, x, xxxviii.

70. *Ibid.*, II, xxvi.

71. *Ibid.*, II, li, liv.

72. *Ibid.*, II, li.

73. *Ibid.*, II, xii.

74. *Ibid.*, II, lix–lxvi, lxvii, lxix (source of quotation).

75. *Ibid.*, II, xvi.

76. See, for example, Shepard, "Political and Constitutional Theory," pp. 294–296, 305–308, 312–319; Hinton, "Constitutional Theories," pp. 410–411.

77. McIlwain, *Growth,* pp. 358–359; Chrimes, *English Constitutional Ideas,* pp. 314–318; Chrimes, ed. and trans., Sir John Fortescue, *De Laudibus,* pp. xciv ff; Plummer, ed., Sir John Fortescue, *Governance,* pp. 171–177.

78. A point made, for differing reasons, by McIlwain, *Growth,* p. 359; Chrimes, ed., Sir John Fortescue, *De Laudibus,* p. xciv; and Felix Gilbert, "Sir John Forescue's 'Dominium Regale et Politicum,'" *Medievalia et Humanistica,* 2: 88–97 (1944).

79. Some authorities hold that St. Thomas considered monarchy the best form of government, whether or not it was hedged by any limitations. See Gerald B. Phelan, introduction to St. Thomas Aquinas, *On the Governance of Rulers,* ed. and trans. Gerald B. Phelan (Toronto, 1935). On the other hand, there are those who take the view that, while Aquinas preferred monarchy, this was true only if suitable restraints were framed which would prevent the monarchy from degenerating into tyranny. The result of this line of argument is that Aquinas really preferred a limited monarchy. This general view is taken, for example, by Etienne Gilson, *The Christian Philosophy of St. Thomas Aquinas* (New York, 1956), pp. 328–331; Alexander Passerin d'Entrèves, *The Medieval*

Contribution to Political Thought (New York, 1959), pp. 37–40; Dino Bigongiari, ed., *The Political Ideas of St. Thomas Aquinas* (New York, 1953), pp. xxix–xxx.

80. For a recent discussion, see Carl J. Friedrich, *Transcendent Justice* (Durham, N.C., 1964), pp. 23–39.

81. Commenting upon *Digest*, I, iii, 31—*Princeps legibus solutus est*—Aquinas says that the prince is freed from the coercive power of the law. Nevertheless, "with respect to the directive power of law, a ruler is voluntarily subject to it, in conformity with what is laid down [in the *Decretals*, I, ii, 6]: 'Whoever enacts a law for another should apply the same law to himself.' " *Summa Theologica*, I–II, Q. 96, art. 5, ad 3, quoted by permission of Basil Blackwell and Barnes & Noble, Inc., from *St. Thomas Aquinas: Selected Political Writings*, ed. A. P. d'Entrèves, trans. J. G. Dawson (Oxford: Basil Blackwell, 1948).

82. *Summa Theologica*, I–II, Q. 95, art. 2.

83. *Ibid.*, Q. 105, art. 1.

84. *Ibid.*, ad 2.

85. *De Regimine Principum*, I, xiii.

86. *Ibid.*, I, xii.

87. *Summa Theologica*, I–II, Q. 96, art. 5, ad 3.

88. *De Regimine Principum*, I, vi.

89. *Summa Theologica*, I–II, Q. 97, art. 3, ad 3.

90. *Ibid.*, Q. 90, art. 3.

91. In connection with the problem of what Aquinas preferred as the best form of government, it is interesting to note that two Thomist scholars who have made a careful study of Aquinas' views conclude that St. Thomas took all his statements concerning government seriously, and, therefore, that there is no way nor any reason to isolate one sort of statement to the exclusion of another. According to these authors, St. Thomas preferred what they call an intermediate regime. Both prince and people have independent sources of authority from which flow independent though related prerogatives. Mortimer J. Adler and Walter Farrell, "The Theory of Democracy," *The Thomist*, 4:724–743 (1942). See also the acute discussion in Wilks, *The Problem of Sovereignty in the Later Middle Ages*, pp. 118–148, 200–229, where Aquinas is described as occupying a via media.

92. This is a point made by Chrimes, ed. and trans., Sir John Fortescue, *De Laudibus*, p. xciv, and since developed in detail by Felix Gilbert, "Sir John Fortescue's 'Dominium Regale et Politicum,' " pp. 88–97. I think we may regard it as settled—as far as such matters are susceptible of resolution—as Gilbert argues, that Fortescue derived his famous expression from *De Regimine Principum*, III, 20, where the phrase actually used is *regimen politicum et regale*.

It should be noted that there is a second general point in Gilbert's skillful discussion, one with which I cannot agree and, indeed, which is upset by his own line of argument. If it were acceptable, however, it would be an important point in interpreting Fortescue and, therefore, deserves examination. Gilbert's argument is that Fortescue's conception of regal and political dominion is radically different in the earlier *De Natura,* as contrasted with the later *De Laudibus* and *Governance.* In the earlier book, Gilbert maintains, Fortescue's conception rests firmly on the account of imperial government in *De Regimine Principum,* III, 20, while in the later books the idea has become much more precise and departs widely from its alleged authority. According to Gilbert, the essence of the idea in both *De Natura* and *De Regimine Principum* is not that any particular features are combined but only that there is *some* combination. On the other hand, he argues that in the later works regal and political dominion means that "the right to give laws or to change them must belong to the people, not to the king, and taxes can be raised only if consented to by the people." This is simply not true, as a comparison of *De Natura,* I, xvi with *De Laudibus,* IX shows. In both cases Fortescue clearly says that in a regal and political dominion a king may neither make nor change laws, nor levy taxes without assent. Gilbert has allowed himself to be sidetracked by the examples, other than England, which Fortescue borrowed from *De Regimine Principum.* The fact that they are all quite dissimilar apparently led him to formulate the view that the essential point was combination as such. But this is to ignore, for the sake of the examples, the substance of what Fortescue says in defining dominium politicum et regale. Moreover, the idea of some combination is not abandoned in the later works. Thus if the criterion were merely combination, as Gilbert maintains, it would follow that there could not be any radical change between the earlier and later works, since there would be no standard from which to depart.

Gilbert observes justly that the point about derivation from *De Regimine Principum* was made long ago by A. Passerin d'Entrèves, "San Tommaso d'Aquino e la Costituzione Inglese nell'opera di Sir John Fortescue," *Atti della Reale Accademia delle Scienze di Torino,* 62:261–285 (1927). D'Entrèves argued, however, that "what constitutes the nature of the imperial government for Ptolemy does not quite correspond to the essence of the dominium regale et politicum according to Fortescue" (my translation). Gilbert chides d'Entrèves for this view, but it seems to me that d'Entrèves is undoubtedly correct; indeed, if anything, the view that it does not "quite correspond" (*non corrisponde affato*) is an understatement.

Gilbert's argument has a final leg: that in the later works Fortescue allows the distinct form of political lordship to fade — so much so, that it is hard to see how it is to be distinguished from regal and political lordship at all. Moreover, in *Governance* Fortescue speaks only of two kinds of kingdom and no longer of three forms of government. Gilbert thinks it will not do merely to say that Fortescue's concerns have shifted and that he is no longer interested in political dominion. I cannot see why, for regal government was the accepted ground of discourse on government outside the Italian cities. Gilbert thinks he can establish this point by saying that "the idea of a republic never came into his [Fortescue's] mind." This is assuming a great deal, particularly if we are to accept Gilbert's contention that Fortescue was a student of *De Regimine Principum*, for it contains (II, viii) a full discussion of nonregal government. Moreover, Fortescue himself refers generously (*De Laudibus,* XIII) to "any other body politic."

93. Plummer, ed., *Sir John Fortescue, Governance,* pp. 85 and *passim.*

94. McIlwain, *Growth,* p. 359.

95. *Ibid.,* pp. 354–363. This general view has been followed by a number of authors. Shepard, "Political and Constitutional Theory," pp. 289–319, has endorsed it, but with slightly more emphasis on the idea of institutional restraint in parliament. E. F. Jacob, *Essays in the Conciliar Epoch,* p. 112 and n. 2, has said that Fortescue's dominium politicum et regale is a political order "in which the king's power is supreme save in certain spheres delimited by law and custom . . ." Franklin le van Baumer, *The Early Tudor Theory of Kingship* (New Haven, 1940), p. 10, maintains that Fortescue "did not doubt, to borrow Chrimes' expression, that 'the king [is] absolute, even though limited . . .'" Fortescue's king, he says, "cannot alter the fundamental law of the land . . ." *Ibid.,* p. 11.

96. Chrimes, *English Constitutional Ideas,* p. 339, n. 68. This view is repeated in Chrimes, ed. and trans., *Sir John Fortescue, De Laudibus,* p. 156.

97. *Ibid.,* pp. 161 and 156.

98. Hinton, "Constitutional Theories," p. 411.

99. *Ibid.,* pp. 410 and 417.

100. *Laws,* III, 693 (source of quotation), and VI, 756.

101. *Politics,* II, vi, 1265b.

102. *Ibid.,* IV, viii-xi, 1294a–1296b.

103. *Ibid.,* IV, vii-ix, xi-xvi, 1293b–1301a.

104. *The Histories,* VI, 11.

105. *Ibid.,* VI, 7–13.

106. In Sidney J. Herrtage, ed., *England in the Reign of King Henry the Eighth* (London, 1878), II, ii, lines 95–103, p. 181.

107. Quoted in McIlwain, *Constitutionalism Ancient and Modern,* p. 104.

108. Corinne Comstock Weston, "Beginnings of the Classical Theory of the English Constitution," *Proceedings of the American Philosophical Society,* 100:133–144 (1956).

109. Stanley Pargellis, "The Theory of Balanced Government," in Read, ed., *The Constitution Reconsidered,* pp. 39–40, rightly observes that the theory of mixed monarchy, "first seriously entered English politics . . . during the heated, profound constitutional discussions that preceded the outbreak of the civil wars." Wormuth, *The Origins of Modern Constitutionalism,* pp. 31, 51, has observed that there were expressions of the classical doctrine in the Middle Ages and beyond, but he considers that these represent more a literary tradition than a serious theoretical enterprise. Corinne Comstock Weston, "The Theory of Mixed

Monarchy under Charles I and After," *English Historical Review*, 75:426–443 (1960), notes that even if one were to attribute a theory of mixed monarchy to Fortescue, it remains true that the literary source of the theory in the 1640's was not Fortescue but Polybius. Even Hinton has noted that the theory did not enter into the constitutional conroversies of the pre-civil-war period. See R. W. K. Hinton, "The Decline of Parliamentary Government under Elizabeth I and the Early Stuarts," *Cambridge Historical Journal*, 13:116–132 (1957). Fortescue, like Bracton, was quoted again and again in these early controversies, but his views were turned to the purposes of both kingly supremacy and the supremacy of law. See Holdsworth, *History of English Law*, II, 571. As chap. ix shows, this dualism was the peculiar form taken by double majesty in the pre-civil-war period. For a collection of quotations employing Fortescue on both sides of the constitutional quarrels, see Skeel, "The Influence of the Writings of Sir John Fortescue," pp. 77–114.

110. Wormuth, *Origins*, p. 52. The same view has been expressed by Weston, "The Theory of Mixed Monarchy," p. 427.

111. Quoted in Wormuth, *Origins*, pp. 52–53. The full text is given as an appendix to Weston, "Beginnings of the Classical Theory," pp. 143–144.

112. Wormuth, *Origins*, pp. 53–58; Weston, "The Theory of Mixed Monarchy," pp. 433–443.

113. Wormuth, *Origins*, p. 55.

114. Robert Filmer, *The Anarchy of a Limited or Mixed Monarchy*. Thomas Hobbes, *Leviathan*, II, 18.

115. William Blackstone, *Commentaries on the Laws of England* (Oxford, 1768), I, 2, pp. 154–155.

116. Jeremy Bentham, *A Fragment on Government with An Introduction to the Principles of Morals and Legislation*, ed. Wilfrid Harrison (Oxford, 1948), p. 81.

117. Weston, "The Theory of Mixed Monarchy," p. 430, says that it was written by Viscount Falkland and Sir John Colepepper.

118. Wormuth, *Origins*, p. 53.

119. Chrimes, *English Constitutional Ideas in the Fifteenth Century*, pp. 320–321.

120. Wormuth, *Origins*, p. 174.

121. *De Natura*, I, v.

122. *Ibid.*, x.

123. Chrimes, *English Constitutional Ideas*, p. 348.

124. Wilkinson, *Studies in the Constitutional History of the Thirteenth and Fourteenth Centuries*, p. 272.

Chapter Eight. The King's Conscience

1. This expression derives from an essay by Milton C. Abrams, "Kingship, Equity and Natural Law in Christopher St. Germain," in

Morris D. Forkosch, ed., *Essays in Legal History in Honor of Felix Frankfurter* (Indianapolis, 1966), pp. 467–480. I owe a great deal to this penetrating discussion, and to Mr. Abrams for the loan of his own copies of St. Germain's works.

2. Samuel E. Thorne, "Preface," Edward Hake, *Epieikeia. A Discourse on Equity in Three Parts*, ed. D. E. C. Yale (New Haven, 1953), p. 8, n. 11.

3. There is an extended discussion of the literature devoted to the theme of obedience in Baumer, *The Early Tudor Theory of Kingship*, pp. 85–119. See also J. W. Allen, *A History of Political Thought in the Sixteenth Century* (London, 1928), pp. 125–133.

4. Baumer, *The Early Tudor Theory of Kingship*, p. 21.

5. Elton, *England Under the Tudors*, pp. 160–175.

6. *Ibid.*, pp. 42–69 and *passim*.

7. Thorne, "Preface," Hake, *Epieikeia*, p. 6; Holdsworth, *History of English Law*, II, 270; Theodore F. T. Plucknett, *A Concise History of the Common Law* (London, 1948), p. 279.

8. Rainer Pineas, "Sir Thomas More's Controversy with Christopher St. Germain," *Studies in English Literature*, 1:50 (1961).

9. Allen, *History of Political Thought*, p. 165.

10. Baumer, *The Early Tudor Theory of Kingship*, pp. 35–84.

11. Christopher Morris, *Political Thought in England: Tyndale to Hooker* (London, 1953), pp. 50–51.

12. It ought to be observed that St. Germain's place in the history of political thought has been construed differently. McIlwain contends that he was an advocate of the supremacy of that fundamental law which provides legal limitations on the exercise of political power. See McIlwain, *The High Court of Parliament*, pp. 98–99, 105–108, and *Growth*, p. 365. This interpretation has been taken up and elaborated by Baumer, *The Early Tudor Theory of Kingship*, p. 140: "St. Germain was too much in favor of Henry VIII's ecclesiastical reforms ever to become involved in a discussion of the king and natural law. However, there can be no doubt that if he had been asked for a candid opinion, he would have had to answer, as Fortescue had done before him, that the *Jus Regis* can no more be compared to the law of nature than a fly to an eagle. Had St. Germain lived a hundred years later, he would have turned his law of reason protecting private rights and property to no little advantage against James and Charles Stuart. Here was unquestionably a potential Sir Edward Coke." But here is what St. Germain himself says on the sanctity of private property: "It is holden by them that be learned in the lawe of this realm, that the Parliament hath an absolute power as to the possession of all temporal things within this realm, in whose hands so ever they be, spiritual or temporal, to take them from one man, and give them to another *without any cause or consideration*. For if they do it it bindeth in the law." Christopher St. Germain, *A Treatise Concerning the Division between the Spiritualtie and the Temporaltie* (London, 1532), IX. Emphasis added.

13. See Morris, *Political Thought in England, passim.*

14. *The Doctor and Student or Dialogues Between A Doctor of Divinity and a Student in the Laws of England,* ed. William Muchall (Cincinnati, 1874), introduction. Because so many editions of this work are available, citations here will refer first to the dialogue, then to chapter, and, finally, to the page of the edition cited above when St. Germain is quoted.

15. *Ibid.,* I, i.

16. *Ibid.,* I, iii.

17. *Ibid.,* I, ii, p. 5.

18. *Ibid.,* I, iv, p. 10.

19. *Ibid.,* p. 11.

20. *Ibid.,* I, v, p. 12: "It is not used among them that be learned in the laws of England to reason what thing is commanded or prohibited by the law of nature, and what not, but all the reasoning in that behalf is under this manner. As when anything is grounded upon the law of nature, they say, that reason will that such a thing be done; and if it be prohibited by the law of nature, they say it is against reason, or that reason will not suffer that to be done."

21. *Ibid.,* p. 13.

22. *Ibid.,* I, vi.

23. *Ibid.,* I, vii, p. 25. Other statements of St. Germain's make it plain that he did not identify the law of reason and the common law. See *ibid.,* II, iii; II, x; II, xxviii, xliv.

24. *Ibid.,* I, vii, pp. 24–25: "All these [customs] and such other cannot be proved only by reason, that it should be so, and no otherwise, although they be reasonable; and that, with the custom therein used, sufficeth in the law, and a statute made against such general customs ought to be observed . . ." My brackets. See also *ibid.,* I, xxvi, and II, ii, where the common law is described as law which obtained before any statute had been made on a question.

25. *Ibid.,* I, viii, p. 26.

26. *Ibid.,* I, x, p. 34. Italics omitted.

27. *Ibid.,* I, xi, pp. 35–36.

28. *Ibid.,* I, xii, p. 38. My brackets.

29. *Ibid.,* I, xvi, pp. 44–45. My brackets. Muchall's text has "love," where the sense of the passage seems to require "leave."

30. *Ibid.,* I, xvii.

31. *Ibid.,* I, xix, p. 53.

32. *Ibid.,* I, xvii, p. 48. Italics omitted.

33. *Ibid.,* II, lv, p. 279.

34. *A Replication of a Serjeant at the Laws of England, to certain Points alledged by a Student of the said Laws of England, in a Dialogue in English between a Doctor of Divinity and the said Student.* This tract is included in the Muchall edition of *Doctor and Student* cited in n. 14 above. The words quoted in the text appear on pp. 347 and 349. It is possible that St. Germain himself was the author of this critique of the

arguments of *Doctor and Student,* and that it was designed as a foil with which to parry the predictable reaction of common lawyers.

35. *A Replication,* p. 353.

36. *A Little Treatise concerning Writs of Subpoena.* This tract is a reply to *A Replication,* cited in the two preceding notes. It is also included in Muchall's 1874 edition of *Doctor and Student.* It appears to have been written by St. Germain, though there is no conclusive evidence.

37. St. Germain's contributions to this extremely wordy debate were these: *A Treatise Concerning the Division between the Spiritualtie and the Temporaltie; A Dialogue Betwixt two Englysshe Men, Whereof one was Called Salem and the other Bizance* (London, 1533); and *The Addicions of Salem and Byzance* (London, 1534). More's side of the debate may be found in his *Debellacyon of Salem and Bizance* (London, 1533), and in *The Apologye of Sir Thomas More,* ed. Arthur I. Taft (London, 1930).

38. These writings include the following: *An Answere to a Letter* (London, 1534); *The Power of the Clergy and the Lawes of the Realm* (London, 1534); and *Constitucyons Provincial and Legatine* (London, 1534). All three of these works were published *cum privilegio Regali.*

39. *The Power of the Clergy,* IX. There is a good summary of St. Germain's views in *An Answere to a Letter,* I, pp. 3–12.

40. *The Power of the Clergy,* XVIII.

41. *An Answere to a Letter,* VII, p. 95.

42. *A Treatise Concernynge Division,* VII.

43. *An Answere to a Letter,* VII, pp. 95–97.

44. *Salem and Bizance,* XVIII, pp. 71–73. The pagination in the original is in Roman numerals.

45. *The Addicions of Salem and Byzance,* p. 30. Emphasis added.

46. Richard Hooker, *A Preface to Them that Seek (as They term it), The Reformation of the Laws and Orders Ecclesiastical in the Church of England,* I, 2. This portion of Hooker's book will be cited hereafter as *Preface.*

47. There is a detailed exposition of the parallels between Hooker's views and those of Aquinas in Peter Munz, *The Place of Hooker in the History of Thought* (London, 1952), pp. 49–59.

48. *Of the Laws of Ecclesiastical Polity,* I, ii, 1. Cited hereafter as *Ecclesiastical Polity.*

49. *Ibid.,* I, ii, 6.

50. *Ibid.,* I, ii, 3; I, iii, 4.

51. *Ibid.,* I, iii, 1. Emphasis omitted.

52. *Ibid.,* I, iii, 2.

53. *Ibid.,* I, vii, 4.

54. *Ibid.,* I, vii, 2.

55. *Ibid.,* I, viii, 2.

56. *Ibid.,* I, viii, 3.

57. *Ibid.*, I, viii, 5.
58. *Ibid.*
59. *Ibid.*, I, viii, 7, 10.
60. *Ibid.*, I, viii, 8.
61. *Ibid.*, I, viii, 9.
62. *Ibid.*, I, viii, 11.
63. *Ibid.*, I, vii, 2; I, viii, 11.
64. *Ibid.*, I, xii, 2.
65. *Ibid.*, I, ix, 1, and *Preface*, VI, 3.
66. *Ecclesiastical Polity*, I, x, 4.
67. *Preface*, VIII, 5.
68. *Ecclesiastical Polity*, I, x, 3.
69. *Ibid.*, I, x, 4.
70. *Ibid.*, I, x, 1.
71. *Ibid.*, I, x, 4.
72. *Ibid.*, I, x, 5.
73. *Ibid.*, I, x, 6.
74. *Ibid.*, I, x, 1.
75. *Ibid.*, I, x, 7.
76. *Ibid.*, I, x, 8.
77. *Ibid.*, I, xiv, 15. In the *Preface*, III, 2 and 10, Hooker says that the Scriptures are perfectly plain on the vital principles of Christian doctrine; what is necessary for salvation is plain and familiar.
78. *Preface*, IV, 1.
79. *Ibid.*, VI, 3.
80. *Ibid.*, VI, 6. The same doctrine is set out in *Ecclesiastical Polity*, I, xvi, 5.
81. *Preface*, II, 7. Addressing himself to English Calvinists, Hooker says there is no necessity in anything which either they or Calvin maintain.
82. *Ibid.*, VI, 5. Elsewhere he says that nature, Scripture, and experience all teach that men should submit to definitive judgment. *Ibid.*, VI, 1.
83. *Ibid.*, VI, 3.
84. *Ibid.*, V, 2.
85. *Ecclesiastical Polity*, VIII, ii, 2.
86. *Ibid.*, VIII, ii, 5.
87. *Ibid.*, V, lxxx, 11; VIII, vi, 1.
88. *Ibid.*, VIII, ii, 11.
89. *Ibid.*, VIII, ii, 12.
90. *Ibid.*, VIII, ii, 13.
91. *Ibid.*, VIII, viii, 9.
92. *Ibid.*, I, x, 8.
93. *Ibid.*, VIII, ii, 10.
94. *Ibid.*, VIII, ii, 11.
95. *Ibid.*, VIII, ii, 10.
96. *Ibid.*, VIII, ii, 3.

97. *Ibid.,* VIII, ii, 18.

98. *Ibid.,* VIII, ix, 2.

99. *Ibid.,* VIII, ii, 14.

100. *Ibid.,* VIII, ii, 16. See also *ibid.,* VIII, viii, 2.

101. *Ibid.,* VIII, i, 2: "We hold, that seeing there is not any man of the Church of England but the same man is also a member of the commonwealth; Nor any man a member of the commonwealth, which is not also of the Church of England; therefore as in a figure triangular the base doth differ from the sides thereof, and yet one and the selfsame line is both a base and also a side . . . so, albeit properties and actions of one kind do cause the name of a commonwealth, qualities and functions of another sort the name of a Church to be given unto a multitude, yet one and the selfsame multitude may in such sort be both, and is so with us, that no person appertaining to the one can be denied to be also of the other."

102. F. J. Shirley, *Richard Hooker and Contemporary Political Ideas* (London, 1949), p. 133.

103. *Ecclesiastical Polity,* VIII, vi, 11.

104. *Ibid.,* VIII, ii, 16.

105. *Ibid.,* VIII, viii, 4.

106. *Ibid.,* VIII, vi, 11.

107. *Ibid.,* VIII, vi, 12.

108. *Ibid.,* VIII, vii, 5.

109. *Ibid.,* VIII, viii, 4. My brackets.

110. *Ibid.,* V, ix, 2.

111. *Ibid.,* V, ix, 3.

112. *Ibid.,* V, ix, 4. It should be noted that in this discussion of equity Hooker is referring to spiritual causes, and in these the king does not have direct jurisdiction. He is, rather, the ultimate guarantor of all jurisdictonal arrangements. In the case of ecclesiastical courts, Hooker says that the equity practiced there is controlled by law and superior power.

113. *Ibid.,* VIII, vi, 5. F. J. Shirley seems quite correct in arguing that "Hooker was eminently an authoritarian; his philosophic position demanded above all things a submission to the higher powers, just because he regarded order as 'a gradual disposition', and the whole creation as hierarchical in form." Shirley, *Richard Hooker,* pp. 130–131. To be sure, in a theoretical structure as complex as Hooker's there is considerable ground for disagreement, and the secondary literature abounds with it. Munz, *The Place of Hooker,* pp. 77–78, 102–108, 205–208, considers that Hooker's work contains a strain of "deep constitutionalism." But Munz does not specify what one is to understand by constitutionalism. It seems to mean the rule of law, since at one point Munz does say that this is all that passed from Hooker into Locke, and hence into modern constitutionalism. *Ibid.,* pp. 104–105. But the rule of law, by itself, is surely not enough. A legal system may contain rules of any kind in the absence of a basic law. Moreover, the rule of law is not the only line of emphasis in Hooker's argument. Hooker deprives the idea of natural law of any

428

real meaning as a possible external standard when he argues that all matters of probable truth may be concluded upon by king and parliament. E. T. Davies, *The Political Ideas of Richard Hooker* (London, 1946), pp. 77ff, seems closer to the mark in arguing that the drift of Hooker's system is toward royal absolutism. It is certain, as Shirley, *Richard Hooker*, p. 104, has remarked, that "passive obedience is the maximum protest . . ." Hooker's "limitations on royal power are vague, procedure against him undefined. Indeed, on the question how far the King is 'legibus solutus' Hooker is very far from clear." Shirley concludes that his is "a practical position when examined, not so much unlike Bodin's or Hobbes's, for all we read of law, consent, compact and agreement." *Ibid.*, p. 125.

114. *Ecclesiastical Polity*, VIII, vi, 5.

115. *Ibid.*, VIII, vi, 11.

Chapter Nine. Law and Prerogative: Legal Deadlock

1. Thorne, "Preface," Hake, *Epieikeia*, p. vii.

2. *Ibid.*, p. viii.

3. Wormuth, *The Royal Prerogative*, pp. 5, 50–60, 60.

4. John Davies, *Le Primer Report des Cases et Matters en Ley* (London, 1628), "A Preface Dedicatory." The preface lacks pagination, save for the number 3 at the foot of the first page. Reckoning from that, the passage quoted appears on p. 7.

5. Quoted in Theodore Calvin Pease, *The Leveller Movement* (Washington, D.C., 1916), p. 11, n. 8.

6. Thorne, "Preface," Hake, *Epieikeia*, p. v.

7. *Epieikeia*, p. 2.

8. *Ibid.*, pp. 7–12.

9. *Ibid.*, pp. 13, 28

10. *Ibid.*, p. 16.

11. *Ibid.*, pp. 14, 23. When it becomes necessary to repair to the supreme authority for a new law, the fault is not to be ascribed to the lawmaker or to the law; rather, it is "to be imputed to the iniquity of tymes and to occasions of maners, as by the which ever and anon particularityes are mynistered for the necessity of newe lawes to be made." *Ibid.*, p. 23.

12. *Ibid.*, pp. 25–38.

13. On this subject Hazeltine has remarked that "all too often our historical vision has been obscured or blurred by the theories of lawyers. One particular dogma of the lawyers has concealed the actual working of the process of interpretation, the dogma which Bacon expresses in his essay *Of Judicature* when he declares that 'judges ought to remember, that their office is *ius dicere*, and not *ius dare*; to *interpret law*, and not to *make law*, or *give law*.' . . . The more one examines the historical processes by which the judicature interprets the written and the unwritten

laws . . . the more clearly one sees that the office *ius dicere,* to interpret law, involves also the office *ius dare,* to make law." H. D. Hazeltine, "General Preface," Plucknett, *Statutes & Their Interpretation,* p. vii.

14. John Selden, *Table Talk of John Selden,* ed. Frederick Pollock (London: Selden Society, 1927), p. 43.

15. Edward Coke, *The First Part of the Institutes of the Laws of England; or, A Commentary Upon Littleton,* revised and corrected by Francis Hargrave and Charles Butler (Philadelphia, 1853), 97b. Cited hereafter as *Coke on Littleton.*

16. Quoted from Thorne, ed., *A Discourse upon the Exposicion & Understandinge of Statutes,* pp. 80–81, n. 169.

17. Thorne, "Preface," Hake, *Epieikeia,* p. x.

18. *Epieikeia,* pp. 49, 49–50.

19. *Ibid.,* pp. 50–76, 85–116.

20. Thorne, "Preface," Hake, *Epieikeia,* p. ix.

21. *Epieikeia,* pp. 103–104, 104, 117.

22. *Ibid.,* p. 75.

23. *Ibid.,* pp. 75–76, 76.

24. Harding, *A Social History of English Law,* pp. 167–193.

25. *Epieikeia,* p. 78. The most interesting statements in Sir Thomas Smith's *De Republica Anglorum* are those which express the characteristic ambiguity of the times. He says: "To be short the prince is the life, the head, and the authoritie of all thinges that be doone in the realme of England." Sir Thomas Smith, *De Republica Anglorum,* ed. L. Alston (Cambridge, Eng., 1906), p. 62. Again: "The most high and absolute power of the realme of Englande consisteth in the Parliament." What is done there is "the Princes and whole realmes deede: whereupon justlie no man can complaine, but must accomodate himselfe to finde it good and obey it." *Ibid.,* p. 48. ". . . the parliament of Englande . . . representeth and hath the power of the whole realme both the head and the bodie. For everye Englishman is entended to be there present." *Ibid.,* p. 49. But another statement of Smith's is best borne in mind: "What can a commonwealth desire more than peace, liberty, quietness, little taking of base money, *few parliaments* . . ." Quoted in Roskell, "Perspectives in English Parliamentary History," p. 456. Emphasis added.

26. *Epieikeia,* pp. 78–79, 80.

27. *Ibid.,* p. 84. "Ultion" means "vengeance" or "revenge." See *ibid.,* n. 159.

28. *Ibid.,* p. 95.

29. Selden, *Table Talk,* p. 112.

30. *Ibid.,* p. 61.

31. *Epieikeia,* pp. 121, 122, 122, 123.

32. *Ibid.,* p. 126.

33. For a penetrating discussion, see Francis D. Wormuth, "Aristotle on Law," in Milton R. Konvitz and Arthur E. Murphy, eds., *Essays in Political Theory* (Ithaca, 1948), pp. 45–61.

34. Plato, *Statesman,* trans. J. B. Skemp, in *The Collected Dialogues of*

Plato, ed. Edith Hamilton and Huntington Cairns (New York, 1963), p. 1063 (S. 294c).

35. Learned Hand, *The Bill of Rights* (Cambridge, Mass., 1958), p. 73.

36. Among the recent contributions to this discussion are Hand, *Bill of Rights,* pp. 1–30 and *passim;* Herbert Wechsler, *Principles, Politics, and Fundamental Law* (Cambridge, Eng., 1961), pp. 3–48; George D. Braden, "The Search for Objectivity in Constitutional Law," in Walter F. Murphy and C. Herman Pritchett, eds., *Courts, Judges, and Politics* (New York, 1961), pp. 653–660; Wallace Mendelson, *Justices Black and Frankfurter: Conflict in the Court* (Chicago, 1961), which develops an extended defense of Justice Frankfurter.

37. Thorne, "Preface," Hake, *Epieikeia,* p. xi.

38. Godfrey Davies, *The Early Stuarts 1603–1660* (Oxford, 1959), pp. 41–45.

39. Hill, *The Century of Revolution, 1603–1714,* p. 63.

40. John Eliot, *De Jure Maiestatis,* ed. Alexander B. Grosart (Printed for private circulation by Earl St. Germans, 1882), pp. 3, 9.

41. *Ibid.,* pp. 9–10, 99, 100.

42. *Ibid.,* p. 10.

43. *Ibid.,* pp. 15, 16.

44. *Ibid.,* pp. 107–108.

45. *Ibid.,* p. 92.

46. *Ibid.,* p. 94.

47. *Ibid.,* pp. 17–21.

48. *Ibid.,* pp. 60, 67.

49. *Ibid.,* pp. 67–69.

50. Selden, *Table Talk,* pp. 36–37. Editor's brackets.

51. A. S. P. Woodhouse, ed., *Puritanism and Liberty* (Chicago: University of Chicago Press, 1951), p. 11.

52. *Ibid.,* p. 26.

53. Eliot, *De Jure,* pp. 76–85.

54. *Ibid.,* p. 87.

55. *Ibid.,* p. 99.

56. *Ibid.,* p. 109.

57. *Ibid.,* pp. 109–110, 114–115.

58. *Ibid.,* p. 116.

59. *Ibid.,* pp. 117, 118.

60. *Ibid.,* pp. 158–160.

61. *Ibid.,* pp. 162, 163. Selden, *Table Talk,* p. 67, remarks similarly that it is "a true proposition, all the Land in England is held either immediately or mediately of the King."

62. Eliot, *De Jure,* p. 165.

63. *Ibid.,* pp. 170–171.

64. Grosart, ed., Eliot, *De Jure,* p. xvii.

65. Howell, *State Trials,* II, 331; III, 1, 825.

66. Holdsworth, *History of English Law,* VI, 103.

67. Quoted in Catherine Drinker Bowen, *The Lion and the Throne* (Boston, 1957), pp. 388, 294.

68. Huntington Cairns, *Legal Philosophy from Plato to Hegel* (Baltimore, 1949), p. 234.

69. Davies, *Le Primer Report,* "A Preface Dedicatory," p. 28.

70. Edward Coke, *The Second Part of the Institutes of the Laws of England* (London, 1671), 47. Cited hereafter as *Second Institute.*

71. *Coke on Littleton,* 81a.

72. *Ibid.,* 115b.

73. Edward Coke, *The Reports of Sir Edward Coke, Knight,* ed. J. H. Thomas and J. F. Fraser (London, 1826). The passage cited is from Prohibition del Roy, 12 Coke's *Reports,* 63 (1608). My brackets. Cited hereafter as *Reports.*

74. *Coke on Littleton,* 114b, 115a.

75. Edward Coke, *The Third Part of the Institutes of the Laws of England* (London, 1797), Proeme, iii.

76. *Second Institute,* Proeme: "Some fragments of the Statutes in the raigns of the abovesaid [Saxon] Kings do yet remain, but not only many of the Statutes, and Acts of Parliament, but also the Books and Treatises of the Common Laws both in these and other Kings times, and specially in the times of the ancient Brittons (an inestimable loss) are not to be found."

77. *Coke on Littleton,* 68b; *Second Institute,* 70.

78. *Coke on Littleton,* 110a (Parliament); *ibid.,* 71b (Court of Common Pleas and King's Bench); *Second Institute,* 23 (Chancery and Exchequer); *Coke on Littleton,* 58a (Courts Baron); *ibid.,* 260b (Office of the Lord Admiral); *Second Institute,* 557 (jurisdiction of the Cinque Ports); *Coke on Littleton,* 155b (jury trial); *ibid.,* 76b (feudal tenure); *Second Institute,* 71 (division into counties).

79. 7 Coke's *Reports,* 4a.

80. *Coke on Littleton,* 282b.

81. *Ibid.,* 71a.

82. *Ibid.,* preface, pp. xxxv-xxxvi, xxxvi.

83. *Ibid.,* 232b.

84. Quoted in Bowen, *The Lion and the Throne,* p. 496.

85. Carl J. Friedrich, *The Philosophy of Law in Historical Perspective* (Chicago, 1958), p. 83.

86. *Coke on Littleton,* 115b, 110a.

87. 13 Coke's *Reports,* 64. Elsewhere Coke says: "The power and jurisdiction of the parliament for making of laws in proceeding by bill, is so transcendent and absolute, as it cannot be confined either for causes or persons within any bounds." *The Fourth Part of the Institutes of the Laws of England* (London, 1669), 36.

88. 8 Coke's *Reports,* 107, 118.

89. Thorne, "The Constitution and the Courts" pp. 15-24.

90. Gough, *Fundamental Law,* p. 46.

432

91. *Second Institute,* 51.
92. *Coke on Littleton,* 81a.
93. *Second Institute,* 617a.
94. 9 Coke's *Reports,* Preface.
95. 12 Coke's *Reports,* 18.
96. 12 Coke's *Reports,* 74.
97. *Second Institute,* chap. 21.
98. *Commons Debates, 1621,* ed. Wallace Notestein, Frances H. Relf, and Hartley Simpson (New Haven, 1935), IV, 79.
99. John Campbell, *The Lives of the Chief Justices of England* (Philadelphia, 1851), I, 291.
100. Quoted *ibid.,* 292, 293.

Chapter Ten. From Kingdom to Commonwealth

1. Milton, *Areopagitica,* in *Milton's Prose Writings,* ed. K. M. Burton (London, 1958), p. 148.
2. Pease, *The Leveller Movement,* pp. 7–49.
3. Harrington, *Oceana,* p. 48.
4. *The Memoirs of Edmund Ludlow,* ed. C. H. Firth (Oxford, 1894), I, 96.
5. Quoted in Davies, *The Early Stuarts,* p. 127, n. 3.
6. *Lords Journal,* V, 258.
7. Quoted in Davies, *The Early Stuarts,* p. 126.
8. *Ibid.*
9. *Memoirs of the Verney Family during the Civil War,* ed. Frances Parthenope Verney (London, 1892), II, 136.
10. Selden, *Table Talk,* p. 91.
11. Quoted in Edith Sitwell, *The Queens and the Hive* (Harmondsworth, Eng., 1966), p. 58. I owe this reference to Francis D. Wormuth.
12. *Statutes of the Realm,* I, 182.
13. Wormuth, *The Royal Prerogative,* p. 109.
14. Howell, *State Trials,* II, 607–658.
15. *Ibid.,* 690–691.
16. *Ibid.,* III, 1078.
17. *Ibid.,* 1105, 1243.
18. *Ibid.,* 1098.
19. Quoted in Hill, *Puritanism and Revolution,* pp. 203–204.
20. Quoted in Wormuth, *The Royal Prerogative,* p. 112.
21. *Lords Journal,* V, 112.
22. Selden, *Table Talk,* p. 66.
23. Philip Hunton, *A Treatise of Monarchie* (London, 1643), pp. 69, 28–29.
24. Henry Maine, *Ancient Law* (London, 1917), esp. pp. 99–100.
25. Gluckman, ed., *Essays on the Ritual of Social Relations;* Mair, *Primitive Government,* p. 234.

26. *Memoirs of the Verney Family,* II, 69.

27. David Jenkins, *Lex Terrae,* in Walter Scott, ed., *Somers Tracts* (London, 1809–1815), V, 98.

28. Roger Twysden, *The Government of England* (London, 1849), p. 83.

29. William H. Terry, ed., *Judge Jenkins* (London, 1929), p. 48.

30. Howell, *State Trials,* II, 481–482. Whitelocke's speech is wrongly attributed to Yelverton. See Joseph R. Tanner, *Constitutional Documents of the Reign of James I* (Cambridge, Eng., 1930), p. 259.

31. See Hill, *Puritanism and Revolution,* pp. 50–122.

32. *A Remonstrance of Many Thousand Citizens,* in William Haller, ed., *Tracts on Liberty in the Puritan Revolution* (New York, 1934), III, 369.

33. Quoted in Joseph Frank, *The Levellers* (Cambridge, Mass., 1955), p. 57.

34. Quoted in A. S. P. Woodhouse, ed., *Puritanism and Liberty* (Chicago: University of Chicago Press, 1951), p. 5n.

35. Thomas Hobbes, *English Works,* ed. Sir William Molesworth (London, 1839–1845), VI, 259.

36. Hill, *Puritanism and Revolution,* p. 75.

37. William Walwyn, *Englands Lamentable Slaverie,* in Haller, *Tracts on Liberty,* III, 315, 313–314.

38. *A Remonstrance of Many Thousand Citizens,* in Haller, *Tracts on Liberty,* III, 365.

39. Woodhouse, *Puritanism and Liberty,* p. 96.

40. *A Remonstrance of Many Thousand Citizens,* in Haller, *Tracts on Liberty,* III, 354–355.

41. Woodhouse, *Puritanism and Liberty,* p. 66.

42. *Ibid.,* pp. 10, 11.

43. *Ibid.,* pp. 59, 61.

44. *Ibid.,* p. 90.

45. *Ibid.,* p. 26.

46. *Ibid.,* pp. 11, 52, 24.

47. *Ibid.,* p. 52.

48. *Ibid.,* p. 54; and see pp. 57, 62.

49. *Ibid.,* pp. 67, 70–71.

50. *Ibid.,* pp. 55–56. Editor's brackets.

51. *Ibid.,* p. 56: "Truly I know nothing free but only the knight of the shire, nor do I know anything in a parliamentary way that is clear from the height and fulness of tyranny, but only [that]."

52. *Ibid.,* p. 57.

53. *Ibid.,* p. 63, and the parallel views of Colonel Rich on pp. 63–64.

54. *Ibid.,* pp. 60, 63, 64.

55. *Ibid.,* p. 61.

56. *Ibid.,* pp. 61, 71, 67.

57. *Ibid.,* pp. 69, 74.

58. *Ibid.,* p. 78.

434

59. *Ibid.,* p. 72.

60. *Ibid.,* pp. 33, 66, 69.

61. Milton, *The Ready and Easy Way to Establish a Free Commonwealth,* in *Milton's Prose Writings,* ed. Burton, p. 223.

62. Woodhouse, *Puritanism and Liberty,* pp. 62, 64.

63. *Ibid.,* pp. 82–83.

64. *Ibid.,* p. 66.

65. *Ibid.,* pp. 70–71, 88.

66. *Ibid.,* p. 80.

67. *Ibid.,* p. 14.

68. Hill, *Puritanism and Revolution,* p. 175.

69. Woodhouse, *Puritanism and Liberty,* p. 87.

70. *Ibid.,* p. 48.

71. Milton, *Areopagitica,* in *Milton's Prose Writings,* ed. Burton, p. 147.

72. Woodhouse, *Puritanism and Liberty,* p. 1.

73. *Ibid.,* p. 67.

74. *Ibid.,* pp. 26, 67.

75. *Ibid.,* p. 53.

76. Richard Overton, *An Appeal from the Commons to the Free People,* in Woodhouse, ed., *Puritanism and Liberty,* p. 323.

77. *Ibid.,* pp. 326–327.

78. Milton, *Areopagitica,* in *Milton's Prose Writings,* ed. Burton, p. 179.

79. *An Agreement of the People,* in Woodhouse, ed., *Puritanism and Liberty,* pp. 443–445.

80. *The Second Agreement of the People,* ibid., pp. 355–367. The changes made in this agreement by the third version are printed in notes accompanying the second.

81. Wormuth, *Origin of Modern Constitutionalism,* pp. 98–127, 140–159.

82. Milton, *The Ready and Easy Way,* in *Milton's Prose Writings,* ed. Burton, p. 233.

83. Woodhouse, *Puritanism and Liberty,* p. 8.

84. *Ibid.,* pp. 50, 70.

85. *Ibid.,* p. 74.

86. *Ibid.,* pp. 8–9.

87. Quoted in Wormuth, *Origins of Modern Constitutionalism,* p. 85.

88. See Roskell, "Perspectives in English Parliamentary History," pp. 448–475.

Conclusion

1. Some interesting and important work has been done: S. N. Eisenstadt, *The Political Systems of Empires* (New York, 1962); Seymour Martin Lipset, *The First New Nation* (New York, 1963); Reinhard Bendix, *Nation-Building and Citizenship* (New York, 1964); Barrington Moore, Jr.,

Social Origins of Dictatorship and Democracy (Boston, 1966). Samuel P. Huntington has illustrated in several essays the stimulus that can be derived from broadly gauged historical inquiry: "Political Development and Political Decay," *World Politics,* 17:386–430 (1965); "Political Modernization: America vs. Europe," *World Politics,* 18:378–414 (1966); "The Political Modernization of Traditional Monarchies," *Daedalus,* 95: 763–788 (1966).

2. For a fully warranted cautionary note, see Carl J. Friedrich, "Some Reflections on Constitutionalism for Emergent Political Orders," in Herbert J. Spiro, ed., *Patterns of African Development* (Englewood Cliffs, N.J., 1967), pp. 9–33, esp. p. 25.

3. For an effective criticism, see Barrington Moore, Jr., *Political Power and Social Theory* (Cambridge, Mass., 1958), pp. 111–159, esp. 131–159.

4. The *locus classicus,* of course, is Max Weber, *The Protestant Ethic and the Spirit of Capitalism,* trans. Talcott Parson (London, 1948). More recently, this view has been translated into an inquiry into the prerequisites for democracy, in which the classic is undoubtedly Seymour Martin Lipset, *Political Man* (Garden City, N.Y., 1960), part I. But Lipset observes *(ibid.,* p. 71), "Men may question whether any aspect of this interrelated cluster of economic development, Protestantism, monarchy, gradual political change, legitimacy, and democracy is primary, but the fact remains that the cluster does hang together." See also Karl de Schweinitz, *Industrialization and Democracy* (New York, 1964); James S. Coleman, "The Political Systems of the Developing Areas," in Gabriel A. Almond and James S. Coleman, eds., *The Politics of the Developing Areas* (Princeton, N.J., 1960), pp. 538–544; Phillips Cutright, "National Political Development: Measurement and Analysis," *American Sociological Review,* 28:253–264 (1963).

5. There is, as Huntington says in "Political Development and Political Decay," p. 387, widespread agreement that the problems of group consciousness which have been distinguished here as national and civic consciousness are probably the most critical ones in the developing areas. See, for instance, Lucian W. Pye, *Aspects of Political Development* (Boston, 1966), p. 63; and in Lucian W. Pye, *Politics, Personality, and Nation Building* (New Haven, 1962), p. 287: "Fundamentally, the hope for transitional peoples resides in their quests for new collective as well as individual identities." See also Von der Mehden, *Politics of the Developing Nations,* pp. 30–52; Charles W. Anderson, Fred R. von der Mehden, and Crawford Young, *Issues of Political Development* (Englewood Cliffs, N.J., 1967), part one; Almond and Powell, *Comparative Politics,* p. 52.

6. Indeed, Huntington, "Political Modernization," p. 768, has argued that for "modernizing innovation" to occur "the only minimum requirement is the exposure of at least some groups in the society to the earlier experience of the West."

7. Hoffmann, *The State of War,* p. 220.

436

8. The suggestion that the model of contemporary international politics would be more nearly adequate has been made by Fred W. Riggs, "The Theory of Political Development," in James C. Charlesworth, ed., *Contemporary Political Analysis* (New York, 1967), pp. 325-326. The great difficulty with this, however, is that it would fail to reach the heart of the phenomena: the fact that individual men of social importance construe their relationships in subnational and sometimes transnational terms. The idea that international politics provides a good analogy appears to rest on the misleading assumption that it is a primitive political system. But it is not, in too many important ways — chiefly the fact that the separate states of the system are not primitive, nor are the leading ones either traditional or transitional. The great difference, then, is that in a traditional society we are confronted with "traditional" units of analysis, whatever units we choose to set at the center of analysis. The point is that domestic and foreign politics are blurred, without clear lines of division, in a primitive or traditional milieu, and that is fundamentally because the idea of loyalty remains personal.

9. Wolin, *Politics and Vision*, pp. 239-351.

10. For example, the eminent ethologist, Konrad Lorenz, *On Aggression*, trans. Marjorie Kerr Wilson (New York, 1967), takes the view that natural man is pacific; while, from a psychoanalytic perspective, Anthony Storr, *Human Aggression* (London, 1968), argues for natural aggressiveness.

11. Judith N. Shklar, "Facing Up to Intellectual Pluralism," in David Spitz, ed., *Political Theory and Social Change* (New York, 1967), pp. 283-284.

12. Edward Forsett, *A Comparative Discourse of the Bodies Natural and Politique* (London, 1606), quoted in Wormuth, *The Royal Prerogative*, p. 7. This book contains a penetrating discussion of both royalist and parliamentary political theories.

13. *Trew Law of Free Monarchies*, in *The Political Works of James I*, ed. C. H. McIlwain (Cambridge, Mass., 1918), p. 68.

14. Robert Filmer, *The Anarchy of a Limited or Mixed Monarchy*, Preface, in *Patriarcha and Other Political Works of Sir Robert Filmer*, ed. Peter Laslett (Oxford, 1949), p. 277.

15. Shklar, *Legalism*, p. 56.

16. Reinhard Bendix, "Tradition and Modernity Reconsidered," *Comparative Studies in Society and History*, 9:292-346 (1967).

17. On this general point, see the fascinating discussion in Leon Bramson, *The Political Context of Sociology* (Princeton, N.J., 1961), and, in a more general setting, Robert A. Nisbet, *Community and Power* (Oxford, 1962), *passim*, esp. chaps. 2 and 3, and pp. 80-84.

18. See Talcott Parsons, *The Social System* (Glencoe, Ill., 1951); Talcott Parsons and Edward A. Shils, eds., *Toward A General Theory of Action* (Cambridge, Mass., 1951); Talcott Parsons, "Pattern Variables Revisited: A Response to Robert Dubin," *American Sociological Review*, 25:467-483 (1960). The number, characterization, and use of pattern variables by Parsons himself has varied. For a recent critical discussion, see Eugene J.

Meehan, *Contemporary Political Thought* (Homewood, Ill., 1967), esp. pp. 134–139, 152–156. Moreover, I am aware that speaking of pattern-variable analysis in general terms involves the risk of injustice to Parsons. This is especially true because some uses of the pattern variables by others have resulted in a considerable alteration in their meaning. Nonetheless, I do not think these points affect the general argument in the text. For some widely different uses, see, for example, F. X. Sutton, "Social Theory and Comparative Politics," in David E. Apter and Harry Eckstein, eds., *Comparative Politics* (New York, 1962), pp. 67–81; Almond and Powell, *Comparative Politics*, esp. pp. 42–72; Seymour Martin Lipset, *The First New Nation*, esp. chaps. 6, 7.

19. Pye, *Aspects of Political Development*, p. 62.

20. See above, chap. x.

21. *An Agreement of the People*, in A. S. P. Woodhouse, ed., *Puritanism and Liberty* (Chicago: University of Chicago Press, 1951), pp. 443–445.

22. Quoted in Frank, *The Levellers*, p. 57.

23. *A Remonstrance of Many Thousand Citizens*, in Haller, ed., *Tracts on Liberty*, III, 354–355.

24. For one such statement of Weber's, see J. P. Mayer, *Max Weber and German Politics* (London, 1943), pp. 125–131. See also Karl Loewenstein, *Max Weber's Political Ideas in the Perspective of Our Time* (Amherst, 1966), pp. 23–27, 30–40.

25. For example, see Weber, *The Protestant Ethic*, pp. 13–28, 76–78, 182–183; and Reinhard Bendix, *Max Weber: An Intellectual Portrait* (Garden City, N.Y., 1962), pp. 49, 69, 278–279, 327–328.

26. As I understand it, this is one of the chief points in much of Seymour Martin Lipset's work. See, in particular, *Political Man*, pp. 72–75; *The First New Nation*, chaps. 6, 7.

27. These crucial points have been brilliantly made, in a different connection, in Shklar, *Legalism, passim*.

28. *Ibid.*, esp. part I, pp. 29–110.

29. Bendix, *Max Weber*, pp. 49, 98–199; Max Weber, *The Religion of China*, trans. and ed. H. H. Gerth (Glencoe, Ill., 1951), pp. 100–104, 147ff, 226–249.

30. See Max Weber, *Law in Economy and Society*, trans. Edward Shils, ed. Max Rheinstein (Cambridge, Mass., 1954), pp. 234–250, 304–305; Bendix, *Max Weber*, pp. 385–416.

31. It is unnecessary to enter into the controversy over the nature of "totalitarianism." On the point in the text, see, for example, Ernest Fraenkel, *The Dual State* (New York, 1941); Franz Neumann, *Behemoth* (New York, 1966), esp. pp. 440–467; Carl J. Friedrich and Zbigniew K. Brzezinski, *Totalitarian Dictatorship and Autocracy* (New York, 1961), esp. pp. 118–149; Hannah Arendt, *The Origins of Totalitarianism* (New York, 1958), esp. pp. 447–451, 460–468; Alan Bullock, *Hitler: A Study in Tyranny* (London, 1955), esp. pp. 366–373, 735–738.

32. Some students of political development have simply equated it with western liberal democracy. For an astute criticism of this tendency,

438

at least when it is unacknowledged, see Joseph A. LaPalombara, ed., *Bureacracy and Political Development* (Princeton, N.J., 1963), pp. 35–38. It is one of the great merits of David E. Apter, *The Politics of Modernization* (Chicago, 1965), that the fundamental moral differences are explicitly recognized and the choice made. For a reasoned defense of the view that pluralism may yet supply the foundations for what Apter calls a "reconciliation system," if not yet democracy, see *ibid.*, pp. 422–463.

On the other hand, see Karl von Vorys, "Use and Misuse of Development Theory," in Charlesworth, ed., *Contemporary Political Analysis*, pp. 350–363, for a gloomy prognosis. Von Vorys may well be right after all. His view at least has the great strength of recognizing that the kind of political development that has occurred in the West required centuries. He concludes as follows: "It would be unfortunate indeed if advance in political science would hand the decision-maker the most effective strategy of total mastery. It would be outright tragic if the fruits of development theory would present the Asian and African masses with a choice between continued frustration and chaos on one hand and total submission on the other." *Ibid.*, p. 363. Certainly it ought to be recognized that this deep pessimism may be warranted. But the point is that we do not, at this stage, *know* that it is. Development theory is nowhere near the stage of sophistication that would be required to be confident about any particular outcome. If a modern democrat could have surveyed the West in, say, the year 1300, he would have been appalled at the level of poverty, superstition, disease, lack of political consciousness, and so on. For a fine example of acute medieval historiography devoted to such questions among whole populations, rather than to recounting the deeds of heroes and saints, see Georges Duby and Robert Mandrou, *A History of French Civilization: From the Year 1000 to the Present,* trans. James Blakely Atkinson (New York, 1964).

Rather different but similarly pessimistic analyses appear, for example, in Edward Feit, "Military Coups and Political Development," *World Politics,* 20:179–193 (1968), which argues that the likely outcome in Ghana and Nigeria is a return to traditional tribal rule; and Guenther Roth, "Personal Rulership, Patrimonialism, and Empire-Building in the New States," *World Politics,* 20:194–206 (1968), which argues that development is likely to be the casualty of a kind of invincible heterogeneity.

33. See Leonard Binder, *Iran: Political Development in a Changing Society* (Berkeley, Calif., 1962).

34. This criticism of many developmental studies has been well made, for example, by Manfred Halpern, "Toward Further Modernization of the Study of the New Nations," *World Politics,* 17:157–181 (1964), esp. 163–165. It is a theme also often adverted to by Fred W. Riggs: "The Theory of Developing Polities," *World Politics,* 16:147–171 (1963), esp. 153; and "Theory of Political Development," esp. pp. 324–326.

35. This a point rightly insisted upon by Riggs, "Theory of Developing Polities," esp. pp. 167–171, and "Theory of Political Development," esp. pp. 325–326.

36. David Easton, *A Framework for Political Analysis* (Englewood Cliffs, N.J., 1965), chap. 7.

37. For a brief synoptic account of these and the other primary concepts of his systems theory, see David Easton, *A Systems Analysis of Political Life* (New York, 1965), chap. 2. Similarly, Almond and Powell, *Comparative Politics,* p. 27, have insisted that their use of the idea of inputs does not mean that they "necessarily come only from the society of which the political system is a part. It is typical of political systems that inputs are generated internally by political elites . . . Similarly, inputs may come from the international system . . ."

38. Riggs, "Theory of Political Development," has argued that the input-output model *is* instrinsically inapplicable. However, this may be doubted, at least in terms of the reasons he offers. For the chief theoretical point is that the Almondian model is that of a formal organization. But it is not clear to me that Almond is obliged to accept Riggs's interpretation and redefinition of his general scheme.

39. Some of the leading statements of the pluralist approach include David Truman, *The Governmental Process* (New York, 1953); Robert A. Dahl, *A Preface to Democratic Theory* (Chicago, 1963), esp. chap. 5, and *Who Governs?* (New Haven, 1961), esp. pp. 311–325; Daniel Bell, *The End of Ideology* (Glencoe, Ill., 1960), esp. pp. 43–67; Nelson Polsby, *Community Power and Political Theory* (New Haven, 1963); and Arnold Rose, *The Power Structure* (New York, 1967).

40. Sustained criticism of the pluralist approach is to be found, for example, in Peter Bachrach, *The Theory of Democratic Elitism* (Boston, 1967); Henry S. Kariel, *The Promise of Politics* (Englewood Cliffs, N.J., 1966), esp. pp. 103–113; Peter Bachrach and Morton S. Baratz, "Two Faces of Power," *American Political Science Review,* 56:947–952 (1962); Theodore Lowi, "The Public Philosophy: Interest-Group Liberalism," *American Political Science Review,* 61:5–24 (1967).

41. John Kenneth Galbraith, *American Capitalism* (Boston, 1952).

42. Quoted in Davies, *The Early Stuarts,* p. 314.

43. Just as in the case of early European history, the history of classical antiquity provides some fascinating comparative material on the shattering of a traditional social order. Especially enlightening on Greek history in this connection is M. I. Finley, *The World of Odysseus* (New York, 1964). For a detailed account of the moral confusion produced by the awakening of civic consciousness, see Arthur W. H. Adkins, *Merit and Responsibility: A Study in Greek Values* (Oxford, 1960).

44. For a fine study of some differing reactions, see Irene Coltman, *Private Men and Public Causes* (London, 1962).

45. William Walwyn, *The Power of Love,* in Haller, ed., *Tracts on Liberty,* II, 273–304.

46. Louise Fargo Brown, *The Political Activities of the Baptists and Fifth Monarchy Men in England During the Interregnum* (Washington, D.C., 1912).

440

47. See Gertrude Huehns, *Antinomianism in English History* (London, 1951), for some of the more extreme positions.

48. Woodhouse, ed., *Puritanism and Liberty*, pp. 44–45.

49. See Lewis Coser, *The Functions of Social Conflict* (Glencoe, Ill., 1964), and from an anthropological perspective, Gluckman, *Custom and Conflict in Africa*, and *Politics, Law and Ritual in Tribal Society*.

50. Morton Grodzins, *The Loyal and the Disloyal* (New York, 1966); and see Nisbet, *Community and Power*, pp. 248–279.

51. On this point, see Robert A. Dahl and Charles E. Lindblom, *Politics, Economics and Welfare* (New York, 1953), pp. 78ff; and Charles E. Lindblom, "The Science of Muddling Through," *Public Administration Review*, 19:79–88 (1959).

52. Bernard Crick, *In Defence of Politics* (Baltimore, 1964).

53. Robert Paul Wolff, Barrington Moore, Jr., and Herbert Marcuse, *A Critique of Pure Tolerance* (Boston, 1965). Moore's contribution is not considered here because it raises an entirely different set of questions.

54. The philosophy of intolerance, in this respect, is simply a reversal of the intellectual determinism of contemporary conservative liberalism; that is, the simplistic devotion to the ideal of laissez-faire, which turns on the argument that the decay of the West is the result of the meddlesome rationalism of intellectuals. On this equally implausible rendition of modern history, see the treatment in Judith N. Shklar, *After Utopia* (Princeton, N.J., 1957), pp. 235–239.

55. For an account which recognizes the difference between these two things in the context of nineteenth century England, see Adam B. Ulam, *The Unfinished Revolution* (New York, 1960), pp. 90–107.

56. These are some of the points stressed by Wolff, *Critique of Pure Tolerance*, pp. 40–51.

57. For a general account of this crucial loss of political faith, see Shklar, *After Utopia, passim,* but esp. pp. 218–273.

58. Raymond Aron, *The Industrial Society* (New York, 1968), p. 179. For the same point, on a much more general level, see Shklar, "Facing Up to Intellectual Pluralism."

59. Raymond Aron, *The Opium of the Intellectuals,* trans. Terence Kilmartin (New York, 1962), p. 57.

60. Herbert Marcuse, *One-Dimensional Man* (Boston, 1966), pp. 254–257.

61. Shklar, *Legalism*, pp. 151, 206.

62. For an excellent discussion of Hume's political thought, see Shirley Robin Letwin, *The Pursuit of Certainty* (Cambridge, 1965), part I.

63. Aron, *Opium of the Intellectuals*, p. 324.

64. *Ibid.*, p. 323.

65. *Critique of Pure Tolerance*, p. 106.

66. See Shklar, *After Utopia*, p. 228.

67. On this crucial point, the best discussion is Isaiah Berlin, *Two Concepts of Liberty* (Oxford, 1958).

68. Robert Paul Wolff, *Kant's Theory of Mental Activity* (Cambridge, Mass., 1963).

69. *Critique of Pure Tolerance*, p. 28.

70. See, for example, Immanuel Kant, *Foundations of the Metaphysics of Morals*, trans. Lewis W. Beck (New York, 1959), pp. 47, 53, 66; *The Metaphysical Elements of Justice*, trans. John Ladd (New York, 1965), pp. 13–14, 35, 43–44, 78–80. See also Carl Joachim Friedrich, *Inevitable Peace* (Cambridge, Mass., 1948), esp. pp. 157–187; and M. J. Gregor, *Laws of Freedom* (Oxford, 1963).

71. Aron, *Opium of the Intellectuals*, pp. 105–134.

72. *Critique of Pure Tolerance*, p. 52.

73. *Ibid.*, pp. 30–35.

74. Aron, *Opium of the Intellectuals*, p. 156.

75. Aron, *Industrial Society*, p. 158.

76. Grodzins, *The Loyal and the Disloyal*, pp. 238–242.

77. *Critique of Pure Tolerance*, p. 106.

78. On this crucial point, see the excellent discussions in Guenther Lewy, "Resistance to Tyranny: Treason, Right or Duty," *Western Political Quarterly*, 13:581–596 (1960); and Franz Neumann, *The Democratic and the Authoritarian State* (Glencoe, Ill., 1957), pp. 149–159.

79. Aron, *Opium of the Intellectuals*, p. 158. Sir Karl R. Popper has expressed a view close to this in *Conjectures and Refutations* (New York, 1963), p. 351: "We are democrats, not because the majority is always right, but because democratic traditions are the least evil of which we know."

80. Nisbet, *Community and Power*, p. 172, rightly notes: "Despite the manifest pluralism of the universe and the diversity of society, only rarely have philosophers and statesmen made this pluralism and diversity the perspectives of their thought and policy."

Bibliography

Abrams, Milton C. "Equity and Natural Law in Christopher St. German," in *Essays in Legal History in Honor of Felix Frankfurter*, ed. Morris D. Forkosch. Indianapolis: Bobbs-Merrill Co., 1966.

Adkins, Arthur W. H. *Merit and Responsibility: A Study in Greek Values.* Oxford: Clarendon Press, 1960.

Adler, Mortimer J., and Walter Farrell. "The Theory of Democracy," *The Thomist*, 4:724–743 (1942).

Allen, J. W. *A History of Political Thought in the Sixteenth Century.* London: Methuen & Co., 1928.

Almond, Gabriel, and G. Bingham Powell, Jr. *Comparative Politics: A Developmental Approach.* Boston: Little, Brown and Company, 1966.

—— and James S. Coleman, eds. *The Politics of the Developing Areas.* Princeton: Princeton University Press, 1960.

Anderson, Charles W. *Politics and Economic Change in Latin America.* Princeton: D. Van Nostrand Co., 1967.

——, Fred R. von der Mehden, and Crawford Young. *Issues of Political Development.* Englewood Cliffs, N.J.: Prentice-Hall, Inc., 1967.

Anderson, George K. *The Literature of the Anglo-Saxons.* Princeton: Princeton University Press, 1966.

Anglo-Saxon Chronicle. Ed. and trans. G. N. Garmonsway. London: J. M. Dent & Sons, 1953.

Annales Monastici. Ed. Henry Richards Luard. London: Rolls Series, 1864.

Apter, David E. *The Politics of Modernization.* Chicago: University of Chicago Press, 1965.

Aquinas, Thomas. *On the Governance of Rulers*, ed. and trans. Gerald B. Phelan. Toronto: The Pontifical Institute of Mediaeval Studies, 1935.

—— *The Political Ideas of St. Thomas Aquinas*, ed. Dino Bigongiari. New York: Hafner Publishing Co., 1953.

—— *St. Thomas Aquinas: Selected Political Writings*, ed. A. P. d'Entrèves, trans. J. G. Dawson. Oxford: Basil Blackwell, 1948.

Arendt, Hannah. *Between Past and Future.* New York: Meridian Books, 1963.

442

———— *The Human Condition.* Garden City, N.Y.: Doubleday Anchor
Books, 1959.

———— *The Origins of Totalitarianism.* New York: Meridian Books, 1958.

Aristotle. *The Politics of Aristotle,* ed. and trans. Ernest Barker. Oxford:
Clarendon Press, 1952.

Aron, Raymond. "Evidence and Inference in History," *Daedalus,* 87:11–39
(1958).

———— *The Industrial Society.* New York: Simon and Schuster, 1968.

———— *The Opium of the Intellectuals,* trans. Terence Kilmartin. New
York: W. W. Norton & Company, 1962.

Attenborough, F. L., ed. and trans. *The Laws of the Earliest English
Kings.* Cambridge, Eng.: Cambridge University Press, 1922.

Aungier, George James, ed. *Croniques de London.* London: Camden
Society, 1844.

Bachrach, Peter. *The Theory of Democratic Elitism.* Boston: Little, Brown
and Company, 1967.

———— and Morton S. Baratz. "Two Faces of Power," *American Political
Science Review,* 56:947–952 (1962).

Bagehot, Walter. *The English Constitution.* Garden City, N.Y.: Doubleday, 1965.

Banfield, Edward C., with the assistance of Laura F. Banfield. *The Moral
Basis of a Backward Society.* Glencoe: Free Press of Glencoe, Ill., 1958.

Barraclough, Geoffrey. *The Origins of Modern Germany.* New York:
Capricorn Books, 1963.

Baumer, Franklin le van. *The Early Tudor Theory of Kingship.* New
Haven: Yale University Press, 1940.

Bede. *A History of the English Church and People,* trans. Leo Sherley-
Price. Harmondsworth, Eng.: Penguin Books, 1965.

Beer, Samuel H. *British Politics in the Collectivist Age.* New York: Alfred
A. Knopf, 1965.

———— and Adam B. Ulam, eds. *Patterns of Government.* New York:
Random House, 1962.

Bell, Daniel. *The End of Ideology.* Glencoe: Free Press of Glencoe, Ill.,
1960.

Bendix, Reinhard. *Max Weber: An Intellectual Portrait.* Garden City,
N.Y.: Doubleday Anchor Books, 1962.

———— *Nation-Building and Citizenship.* New York: Wiley & Sons, 1964.

———— "Tradition and Modernity Reconsidered," *Comparative Studies
in Society and History,* 9:292–346 (1967).

Bennett, H. S. *The Pastons and Their England.* Cambridge, Eng.: Cambridge University Press, 1922.

Bentham, Jeremy. *A Fragment on Government with An Introduction to
the Principles of Morals and Legislation,* ed. Wilfrid Harrison. Oxford: Basil Blackwell, 1948.

Beowulf. Ed. with notes and intro. Rowland L. Collins, trans. Lucien
Dean Pearson. Bloomington: Indiana University Press, 1965.

Berlin, Isaiah. *Two Concepts of Liberty.* Oxford: Clarendon Press, 1958.

444

Binder, Leonard. *Iran: Political Development in a Changing Society.* Berkeley: University of California Press, 1962.

Blackstone, William. *Commentaries on the Laws of England.* Vol. I, 3d ed. Oxford: Oxford University Press, 1768.

Blair, Peter Hunter. *An Introduction to Anglo-Saxon England.* Cambridge, Eng.: Cambridge University Press, 1956.

Bloch, Marc. *Feudal Society,* trans. L. A. Manyon. Chicago: University of Chicago Press, 1961.

—— *The Historian's Craft,* trans. Peter Putnam. New York: Vintage Books, n. d.

—— *Les Rois thaumaturges.* Strasbourg: Librairie Istra, 1924.

Boswell, James. *Life of Johnson.* London: Oxford University Press, 1953.

Bowen, Catherine Drinker. *The Lion and the Throne.* Boston: Little, Brown and Company, 1957.

Bracton, Henry de. *De legibus et consuetudinibus Angliae,* ed. George E. Woodbine. 4 vols. New Haven: Yale University Press, 1915–1942.

Braden, George D. "The Search for Objectivity in Constitutional Law," in *Courts, Judges, and Politics,* ed. Walter F. Murphy and C. Herman Pritchett. New York: Random House, 1961.

Bramson, Leon. *The Political Context of Sociology.* Princeton: Princeton University Press, 1961.

Britton. Ed. and trans. Francis Morgan Nichols. 2 vols. Oxford: Oxford University Press, 1865.

Brown, Louise Fargo. *The Political Activities of the Baptists and Fifth Monarchy Men in England During the Interregnum.* Washington, D.C.: American Historical Association, 1912.

Bullock, Alan. *Hitler: A Study in Tyranny.* London: Odhams Press Limited, 1955.

Burke, Fred G. *Africa's Quest for Order.* Englewood Cliffs, N.J.: Prentice-Hall, Inc., 1964.

Caesar, Julius. *The Gallic War,* trans. H. J. Edwards. Loeb Classical Library. Cambridge, Mass.: Harvard University Press, 1917.

Cairns, Huntington. *Legal Philosophy from Plato to Hegel.* Baltimore: Johns Hopkins Press, 1949.

Cam, Helen. *Law-Finders and Law-Makers in Medieval England.* London: Merlin Press, 1962.

Campbell, John. *The Lives of the Chief Justices of England.* 2 vols. Philadelphia: Blanchard & Lea, 1851.

Cantor, Norman F. *Medieval History.* New York: The Macmillan Company, 1963.

Carlyle, R. W., and A. J. Carlyle. *A History of Mediaeval Political Theory in the West.* 6 vols. Edinburgh: William Blackwood and Sons, 1950.

Carr, Edward Hallett. *The Twenty Years' Crisis,* 2nd ed. London: Macmillan & Co., 1946.

Chadwick, H. Munro. *The Heroic Age.* Cambridge, Eng.: Cambridge University Press, 1912.

—— *Studies on Anglo-Saxon Institutions.* Cambridge, Eng.: Cambridge University Press, 1905.

Cheyette, Frederic. "Custom, Case Law, and Medieval 'Constitutionalism': A Re-examination," *Political Science Quarterly,* 78:362–390 (1963).

Chrimes, S. B. *English Constitutional Ideas in the Fifteenth Century.* Cambridge, Eng.: Cambridge University Press, 1936.

—— *Lancastrians, Yorkists and Henry VII.* London: Macmillan & Co., 1964.

Clarke, M. V. *Fourteenth Century Studies,* ed. L. S. Sutherland and M. McKisack. Oxford: Oxford University Press, 1937.

—— *Medieval Representation and Consent.* London: Longmans, Green & Co., 1936.

Clementi, Dionna. "That the Statute of York of 1322 is no longer ambiguous," in *Album Helen Maud Cam,* vol. II. Louvain: Presses universitaires de Louvain, 1961.

Coke, Edward. *The First Part of the Institutes of the Laws of England; or, A Commentary Upon Littleton,* revised and corrected by Francis Hargrave and Charles Butler. 2 vols. Philadelphia: Robert H. Small, 1853.

—— *The Second Part of the Institutes of the Laws of England.* London: J. Streater *et al.,* 1671.

—— *The Third Part of the Institutes of the Laws of England.* London: E. and R. Brooke, 1797.

—— *The Reports of Sir Edward Coke, Knight.* In Thirteen Parts. Ed. J. H. Thomas and J. F. Fraser. London: Butterworth & Co., 1826.

Coltman, Irene. *Private Men and Public Causes: Philosophy and Politics in the English Civil War.* London: Faber and Faber, 1962.

Coser, Lewis. *The Functions of Social Conflict.* New York: The Free Press of Glencoe, 1964.

Coulborn, Rushton, ed. *Feudalism in History.* Princeton: Princeton University Press, 1956.

Crawfurd, Raymond. *The King's Evil.* Oxford: Clarendon Press, 1911.

Crick, Bernard. *In Defence of Politics.* Baltimore: Penguin Books, 1964.

Cutright, Phillips. "National Political Development: Measurement and Analysis," *American Sociological Review,* 28:253–264 (1963).

Cuttino, George P. "A Reconsideration of the 'Modus Tenendi Parliamentum,'" in *The Forward Movement of the Fourteenth Century,* ed. Francis Lee Utley. Columbus: Ohio State University Press, 1961.

Dahl, Robert A. *Modern Political Analysis.* Englewood Cliffs, N.J.: Prentice-Hall, Inc., 1963.

—— *A Preface to Democratic Theory.* Chicago: University of Chicago Press, 1963.

—— *Who Governs?* New Haven: Yale University Press, 1961.

—— and Charles E. Lindblom. *Politics, Economics and Welfare.* New York: Harper & Row, 1953.

Dannenbauer, Heinrich. *Grundlagen der Mittelalterlichen Welt.* Stuttgart: W. Kohlhammer, 1958.

David, Marcel. *La Souveraineté et les limites juridiques du pouvoir monarchique du IXe au XVe siècle.* Paris: Librairie Dalloz, 1954.

Davies, E. T. *The Political Ideas of Richard Hooker.* London: Society for Promoting Christian Knowledge, 1946.

Davies, Godfrey. *The Early Stuarts, 1603–1660,* 2nd ed. Oxford: Clarendon Press, 1959.

Davies, James Conway. *The Baronial Opposition to Edward II.* Cambridge, Eng.: Cambridge University Press, 1918.

Davies, John. *Le Primer Report des Cases et Matters en Ley resolues & adiudges en les Courts del Roy en Ireland.* London: Printed for the Company of Stationers, 1628.

de Beer, E. S., ed. *The Diary of John Evelyn.* 6 vols. Oxford: Clarendon Press, 1955.

Denholm-Young, N., ed. and trans. *Vita Edwardi Secundi.* London: Thomas Nelson and Sons, 1957.

d'Entrèves, Alexander Passerin. *The Medieval Contribution to Political Thought.* New York: The Humanities Press, 1959.

———— "San Tommaso d'Aquino e la Costituzione Inglese nell'opera di Sir John Fortescue," *Atti della Reale Accademia delle Scienze di Torino,* 62:261–285 (1927).

de Schweinitz, Karl. *Industrialization and Democracy.* New York: The Free Press of Glencoe, 1964.

Deutsch, Karl W. *Nationalism and Social Communication.* Cambridge, Mass.: M.I.T. Press, 1966.

Douglas, David C., and George W. Greenaway, eds. *English Historical Documents, 1042–1189.* London: Eyre & Spottiswoode, 1953.

Duby, Georges, and Robert Mandrou. *A History of French Civilization: From the Year 1000 to the Present,* trans. James Blakely Atkinson. New York: Random House, 1964.

Easton, David. *A Framework for Political Analysis.* Englewood Cliffs, N.J.: Prentice-Hall, Inc., 1965.

———— *A Systems Analysis of Political Life.* New York: John Wiley & Sons, 1965.

Eckstein, Harry. "Political Theory and the Study of Politics," *American Political Science Review,* 50:475–487 (1956).

———— and David E. Apter, eds. *Comparative Politics.* New York: The Free Press of Glencoe, 1963.

Edwards, J. G. *The Commons in Medieval English Parliaments.* London: Athlone Press, 1958.

———— *Historians and the Medieval English Parliament.* Glasgow: Jackson, Son & Co., 1960.

Ehrlich, Ludwik. *Proceedings Against the Crown (1216–1377).* Vol. VI of *Oxford Studies in Social and Legal History,* ed. Paul Vinogradoff. Oxford: Clarendon Press, 1921.

Eisenstadt, S. N. *The Political Systems of Empires.* New York: The Free Press of Glencoe, 1963.

Eliot, John. *De Jure Maiestatis,* ed. Alexander B. Grosart. Printed for Private Circulation only by Earl St. Germans, 1882.

Elton, G. R. *England under the Tudors.* London: Methuen & Co., 1955.

—— *The Tudor Revolution in Government.* Cambridge, Eng.: Cambridge University Press, 1953.

Emerson, Rupert. *From Empire to Nation.* Boston: Beacon Press, 1962.

Emerton, Ephraim, trans. *The Correspondence of Pope Gregory VII.* New York: Columbia University Press, 1932.

Eulau, Heinz. "The Depersonalization of the Concept of Sovereignty," *Journal of Politics,* 4:3–19 (1942).

Evans-Pritchard, E. E. *The Nuer.* Oxford: Clarendon Press, 1940.

Feit, Edward. "Military Coups and Political Development," *World Politics,* 20:179–193 (1968).

Fesefeldt, Wiebke. *Englische Staatstheorie des 13. Jahrhunderts: Henry de Bracton und sein Werk.* Göttingen: Musterschmidt, 1962.

Filmer, Robert. *Patriarcha and Other Political Works of Sir Robert Filmer,* ed. with intro. Peter Laslett. Oxford: Basil Blackwell, 1949.

Finley, M. I. *The World of Odysseus,* rev. ed. New York: The Viking Press, 1965.

Firth, C. H., ed. *The Memoirs of Edmund Ludlow.* Oxford: Clarendon Press, 1894.

Fleta. Ed. and trans. H. G. Richardson and G. O. Sayles. Vol. II. London: Selden Society, 1955.

Fortes, M. and E. E. Evans-Pritchard, eds. *African Political Systems.* London: Oxford University Press, 1940.

Fortescue, John. *The Governance of England,* ed. Charles Plummer. Oxford: Clarendon Press, 1885.

—— *De Laudibus Legum Anglie,* ed. and trans. S. B. Chrimes. Cambridge, Eng.: Cambridge University Press, 1942.

—— *The Works of Sir John Fortescue, Knight,* ed. Thomas (Fortescue) Lord Clermont. London: Privately Printed, 1869.

Fraenkel, Ernst. *The Dual State,* trans. E. A. Shils. New York: Oxford University Press, 1941.

Frank, Joseph. *The Levellers.* Cambridge, Mass.: Harvard University Press, 1955.

Friedrich, Carl J. *Constitutional Government and Democracy,* rev. ed. Boston: Ginn and Company, 1950.

—— *Constitutional Reason of State.* Providence: Brown University Press, 1957.

—— *Inevitable Peace.* Cambridge, Mass.: Harvard University Press, 1948.

—— *The New Image of the Common Man.* Boston: Beacon Press, 1950.

—— *The Philosophy of Law in Historical Perspective.* Chicago: University of Chicago Press, 1958.

—— "Some Reflections on Constitutionalism for Emergent Political Orders," in *Patterns of African Development,* ed. Herbert J. Spiro. Englewood Cliffs, N.J.: Prentice-Hall, Inc., 1967.

448

—— *Transcendent Justice: The Religious Dimension of Constitutionalism*. Durham, N.C.: Duke University Press, 1964.
—— and Zbigniew K. Brzezinski. *Totalitarian Dictatorship and Autocracy*. New York: Frederick A. Praeger, 1961.
Gairdner, James, ed. *The Paston Letters*. 6 vols. London: Chatto & Windus, 1904.
Galbraith, John Kenneth. *American Capitalism*. Boston: Houghton Mifflin, 1952.
Ganshof, F. L. *Feudalism*, trans. Philip Grierson, 3d ed. New York: Harper & Row, 1964.
Gennep, Arnold van. *The Rites of Passage*, trans. Monika B. Vizedom and Gabrielle L. Caffee. Chicago: University of Chicago Press, 1960.
Gierke, Otto. *Natural Law and the Theory of Society*, trans. Ernest Barker. Cambridge, Eng.: Cambridge University Press, 1958.
Gilbert, Felix. "Sir John Fortescue's 'Dominium Regale et Politicum,'" *Medievalia et Humanistica*, 2:88–97 (1944).
Glanville, Ranulf de. *Tractatus de legibus et consuetudinibus regni Anglie qui Glanvilla vocatur*, ed. and trans. G. D. G. Hall. London: Thomas Nelson and Sons, 1965.
Gluckman, Max. *Custom and Conflict in Africa*. Glencoe: Free Press of Glencoe, Ill., 1955.
—— *Politics, Law and Ritual in Tribal Society*. Oxford: Basil Blackwell, 1965.
——, ed. *Essays on the Ritual of Social Relations*. Manchester: Manchester University Press, 1963.
Goebel, Julius, Jr. *Felony and Misdemeanor*. London: Oxford University Press, 1937.
Goodenough, Erwin R. "The Political Philosophy of Hellenistic Kingship," *Yale Classical Studies*, 1:55–102 (1928).
Goodman, A. W., ed. and trans. *The Chartulary of Winchester Cathedral*. Winchester: Warren & Son, 1927.
Gordon, R. K., ed. and trans. *Anglo-Saxon Poetry*. London: J. M. Dent & Sons, 1954.
Gough, J. W. *Fundamental Law in English Constitutional History*. Oxford: Clarendon Press, 1955.
Gray, H. L. *The Influence of the Commons on Early Legislation*. Cambridge, Mass.: Harvard University Press, 1932.
Gregor, Mary J. *Laws of Freedom*. Oxford: Basil Blackwell, 1963.
Gregory of Tours. *The History of the Franks*, trans. with intro. O. M. Dalton. 2 vols. Oxford: Clarendon Press, 1927.
Grierson, P. "Election and Inheritance in Early Germanic Kingship," *Cambridge Historical Journal*, 7:1–22 (1941).
Grodzins, Morton. *The Loyal and the Disloyal*. New York: Meridian Books, 1966.
Güterbock, Carl. *Bracton and His Relation to the Roman Law*, trans. Brinton Coxe. Philadelphia: J. B. Lippincott Co., 1866.
Hake, Edward. *Epieikeia. A Dialogue on Equity in Three Parts*, ed.

D. E. C. Yale, preface by Samuel E. Thorne. New Haven: Yale University Press, 1953.

Haller, William, ed. *Tracts on Liberty in the Puritan Revolution.* 3 vols. New York: Columbia University Press, 1934.

Halpern, Manfred. "Toward Further Modernization of the Study of the New Nations," *World Politics,* 17:157–181 (1964).

Hand, Learned. *The Bill of Rights.* Cambridge, Mass.: Harvard University Press, 1958.

Harding, Alan. *A Social History of English Law.* Baltimore: Penguin Books, 1966.

Harrington, James. *Oceana,* ed. S. B. Liljegren. Heidelberg: Carl Winters, 1924.

Hauser, Henri, and Augustin Renaudet. *Les Débuts de l'âge moderne,* 4th ed. Paris: Presses universitaires de France, 1956.

Heer, Friedrich. *The Medieval World,* trans. Janet Sondheimer. New York: New American Library, 1963.

Herrtage, Sidney J., ed. *England in the Reign of King Henry the Eighth.* London: Early English Text Society, 1878.

Hexter, J. H. *Reappraisals in History.* New York: Harper & Row, 1963.

Hill, Christopher. *The Century of Revolution, 1603–1714.* Edinburgh: Thomas Nelson and Sons, 1961.

—— *Puritanism and Revolution.* New York: Schocken Books, 1964.

Hilton, R. H., and P. H. Sawyer, "Technical Determinism: The Stirrup and the Plow," *Past & Present,* no. 24 (April 1963), pp. 90–100.

Hinton, R. W. K. "The Decline of Parliamentary Government under Elizabeth I and the Early Stuarts," *Cambridge Historical Journal,* 13:116–132 (1957).

—— "English Constitutional Theories from Sir John Fortescue to Sir John Eliot," *English Historical Review,* 75:410–425 (1960).

Hobbes, Thomas. *The English Works of Thomas Hobbes,* ed. William Molesworth. Vol. VI. London: Bohn, 1839–1845.

Hoffmann, Stanley. "Obstinate or Obsolete? The Fate of the Nation-State and the Case of Western Europe," *Daedalus,* 95:862–915 (1966).

—— *The State of War.* New York: Frederick A. Praeger, 1965.

Holdsworth, William. *A History of English Law.* 13 vols. London: Methuen & Co., 1903–1952.

Hollister, C. Warren. *Anglo-Saxon Military Institutions on the Eve of the Norman Conquest.* Oxford: Clarendon Press, 1962.

—— *The Military Organization of Norman England.* Oxford: Clarendon Press, 1965.

Holt, J. C. *Magna Carta.* Cambridge, Eng.: Cambridge University Press, 1965.

Hooker, Richard. *Works.* 3 vols, arranged by John Keble; 7th ed. revised by R. W. Church and F. Paget. Oxford: Oxford University Press, 1888.

Howell, T. B., ed. *A Complete Collection of State Trials.* 21 vols. London: Longman, Hurst, 1816.

Hoyt, Robert S. "The Coronation Oath of 1308: The Background of 'Les Leys and les custumes,' " *Traditio,* 11:235–257 (1955).

—— *The Royal Demesne in English Constitutional History, 1066–1272.* Ithaca: Cornell University Press, 1950.

Huehns, Gertrude. *Antinomianism in English History.* London: Cresset Press, 1951.

Huntington, Samuel P. "Political Development and Political Decay," *World Politics,* 17:386–430 (1965).

—— "Political Modernization: America vs. Europe," *World Politics,* 18:378–414 (1966).

—— "The Political Modernization of Traditional Monarchies," *Daedalus,* 95:763–788 (1966).

Hunton, Philip. *A Treatise of Monarchie.* London, 1643.

Jackson, W. T. H. *Medieval Literature.* New York: Collier Books, 1966.

Jacob, E. F. *Essays in the Conciliar Epoch.* Manchester: Manchester University Press, 1943.

—— *The Fifteenth Century, 1399–1485.* Oxford: Clarendon Press, 1961.

Jenkins, David. *Lex Terrae,* in *Somers Tracts,* vol. V, 2d ed., ed. Walter Scott. London: T. Cadell, 1809–1815.

John, Eric. *Land Tenure in Early England.* Leicester: Leicester University Press, 1960.

—— *Orbis Britanniae.* Leicester: Leicester University Press, 1966.

Johnson, Charles. "Notes on Thirteenth-century Judicial Procedure," *English Historical Review,* 62:508–521 (1947).

Jolliffe, J. E. A. *Angevin Kingship.* London: Adam and Charles Black, 1955.

—— *The Constitutional History of Medieval England.* London: Adam and Charles Black, 1937.

Jordanes. *The Gothic History,* trans. Charles Christopher Mierow. Princeton: Princeton University Press, 1915.

Judson, Margaret Atwood. *The Crisis of the Constitution: An Essay in Constitutional and Political Thought in England, 1603–1645.* New Brunswick, N.J.: Rutgers University Press, 1949.

Kant, Immanuel. *Foundations of the Metaphysics of Morals,* trans. Lewis W. Beck. New York: Liberal Arts Press, 1959.

—— *The Metaphysical Elements of Justice,* trans. John Ladd. New York: Liberal Arts Press, 1965.

Kantorowicz, Ernst H. *The King's Two Bodies.* Princeton: Princeton University Press, 1957.

—— *Laudes Regiae.* Berkeley: University of California Press, 1946.

Kantorowicz, Hermann. *Bractonian Problems.* Glasgow: Jackson, Son & Co., 1941.

Kariel, Henry S. *The Promise of Politics.* Englewood Cliffs, N.J.: Prentice-Hall, Inc., 1966.

Keeney, Barnaby C. *Judgment by Peers.* Cambridge, Mass.: Harvard University Press, 1949.

Keeton, George W. *The Norman Conquest and the Common Law.* London: Ernest Benn, 1966.

Kern, Fritz. *Kingship and Law in the Middle Ages,* trans. S. B. Chrimes. Oxford: Basil Blackwell, 1948.

Kirchheimer, Otto. *Political Justice.* Princeton: Princeton University Press, 1961.

Lander, J. R. *The Wars of the Roses.* London: Secker & Warburg, 1965.

LaPalombara, Joseph A., ed. *Bureaucracy and Political Development.* Princeton: Princeton University Press, 1963.

Lapsley, Gaillard. "Bracton and the Authorship of the 'addicio de cartis,' " *English Historical Review,* 62:1–19 (1947).

―――― *Crown, Community and Parliament in the Later Middle Ages,* ed. Helen M. Cam and Geoffrey Barraclough. Oxford: Basil Blackwell, 1951.

Latouche, Robert. *The Birth of Western Economy,* trans. E. M. Wilkinson. New York: Harper & Row, 1966.

Letwin, Shirley Robin. *The Pursuit of Certainty.* Cambridge, Eng.: Cambridge University Press, 1965.

Levy, Ernst. *The West Roman Vulgar Law.* Philadelphia: American Philosophical Society, 1951.

Lewis, Ewart. "King Above Law? 'Quod Principi Placuit' in Bracton," *Speculum,* 39:240–269 (1964).

―――― *Medieval Political Ideas.* 2 vols. London: Routledge & Kegan Paul, 1954.

Lewy, Guenther. "Resistance to Tyranny: Treason, Right or Duty," *Western Political Quarterly,* 13:581–596 (1960).

Liebermann, Felix. *Die Gesetze der Angelsachsen.* 3 vols. Halle: Max Niemeyer, 1898–1916.

Lindblom, Charles E. "The Science of Muddling Through," *Public Administration Review,* 19:79–88 (1959).

Lipset, Seymour Martin. *The First New Nation.* New York: Basic Books, 1963.

―――― *Political Man.* Garden City, N.Y.: Doubleday & Company, 1960.

Loewenstein, Karl. *Max Weber's Political Ideas in the Perspective of Our Time.* Amherst: University of Massachusetts Press, 1966.

Lorenz, Konrad. *On Aggression,* trans. Marjorie Kerr Wilson. New York: Harcourt, Brace & World, 1966.

Lowi, Theodore. "The Public Philosophy: Interest-Group Liberalism," *American Political Science Review,* 61:5–24 (1967).

Loyn, H. R. *Anglo-Saxon England and the Norman Conquest.* London: Longmans, Green & Co., 1962.

McIlwain, Charles Howard. *Constitutionalism: Ancient and Modern,* rev. ed. Ithaca: Great Seal Books, 1958.

―――― *The Growth of Political Thought in the West.* New York: The Macmillan Company, 1932.

―――― *The High Court of Parliament and Its Supremacy.* New Haven: Yale University Press, 1910.

452

────── "The Present Status of the Problem of the Bracton Text," *Harvard Law Review*, 57: 220–240 (1943).

──────, ed. *The Political Works of James I.* Cambridge, Mass.: Harvard University Press, 1918.

McKechnie, William Sharp. *Magna Carta*, 2d ed. Glasgow: James Maclehose and Sons, 1914.

McKisack, May. *The Fourteenth Century, 1307–1399.* Oxford: Clarendon Press, 1959.

Macpherson, C. B. *The Political Theory of Possessive Individualism.* Oxford: Clarendon Press, 1962.

Maine, Henry. *Ancient Law.* London: J. M. Dent & Sons, 1954.

Mair, Lucy. *The New Nations.* London: Weidenfeld and Nicolson, 1963.

────── *Primitive Government.* Baltimore: Penguin Books, 1964.

Maitland, F. W. *The Constitutional History of England.* Cambridge, Eng.: Cambridge University Press, 1911.

────── "The Crown as Corporation," in *Maitland Selected Essays*, ed. H. D. Hazeltine, G. Lapsley, and P. H. Winfield. Cambridge, Eng.: Cambridge University Press, 1936.

────── *Domesday Book and Beyond.* Cambridge, Eng.: Cambridge University Press, 1897.

──────, ed. *Bracton's Note Book.* London: C. J. Clay & Sons, 1887.

──────, ed. *Select Passages from the Works of Bracton and Azo.* London: Selden Society, 1895.

Marcuse, Herbert. *One-Dimensional Man.* Boston: Beacon Press, 1966.

Mattingly, Garrett. *Renaissance Diplomacy.* Baltimore: Penguin Books, 1964.

Mayer, J. P. *Max Weber and German Politics.* London: Faber & Faber, 1943.

Mazrui, Ali. "Borrowed Theory and Original Practice in African Politics," in *Patterns of African Development*, ed. Herbert J. Spiro. Englewood Cliffs, N.J.: Prentice-Hall, Inc., 1967.

Meehan, Eugene J. *Contemporary Political Thought.* Homewood, Ill.: Dorsey Press, 1967.

Mendelson, Wallace. *Justices Black and Frankfurter: Conflict in the Court.* Chicago: University of Chicago Press, 1961.

Merriam, Charles E. *Political Power.* Chicago: University of Chicago Press, 1934.

Miller, S. J. T. "The Position of the King in Bracton and Beaumanoir," *Speculum*, 31:263–296 (1956).

Milton, John. *Milton's Prose Writings*, ed. K. M. Burton. London: J. M. Dent & Sons, 1958.

Moore, Barrington, Jr. *Political Power and Social Theory.* Cambridge, Mass.: Harvard University Press, 1958.

────── *Social Origins of Dictatorship and Democracy.* Boston: Beacon Press, 1966.

Morris, Christopher, *Political Thought in England: Tyndale to Hooker.* London: Oxford University Press, 1953.

Moss, H. St. L. B. *The Birth of the Middle Ages.* London: Oxford University Press, 1957.

Mosse, George L. *The Struggle for Sovereignty in England: From the Reign of Queen Elizabeth to the Petition of Right.* East Lansing: Michigan State College Press, 1950.

Mousnier, Roland. *Histoire générale des civilisations: les XIVe et XVIIe siècles.* Paris: Presses universitaires de France, 1954.

Munz, Peter. *The Place of Hooker in the History of Thought.* London: Routledge & Kegan Paul, 1952.

Neale, J. E. *Elizabeth I and Her Parliaments.* 2 vols. New York: St. Martin's Press, 1958.

Neumann, Franz. *Behemoth.* New York: Harper & Row, 1966.

———— *The Democratic and the Authoritarian State,* ed. Herbert Marcuse. New York: The Free Press of Glencoe, 1964.

Nisbet, Robert A. *Community and Power.* New York: Oxford University Press, 1962.

Norden, Eduard. *Die germanische Urgeschichte in Tacitus' Germania.* Leipzig: B. G. Teubner, 1923.

Notestein, Wallace, and Frances H. Relf, eds. *Commons Debates for 1629.* Minneapolis: University of Minnesota Press, 1921.

————, Frances H. Relf, and Hartley Simpson, eds. *Commons Debates,* *1621.* 7 vols. New Haven: Yale University Press, 1935.

Ogilvie, Charles. *The King's Government and the Common Law, 1471–1641.* Oxford: Basil Blackwell, 1958.

Oleson, Tryggvi J. *The Witenagemot in the Reign of Edward the Confessor.* Toronto: University of Toronto Press, 1955.

Pargellis, Stanley. "The Theory of Balanced Government," in *The Constitution Reconsidered,* ed. Conyers Read. New York: Columbia University Press, 1938.

Paris, Matthew. *Chronica Majora,* ed. Henry Richards Luard. London: Rolls Series, 1872–1883.

Parsons, Talcott. "Pattern Variables Revisited: A Response to Robert Dubin," *American Sociological Review,* 25:467–483 (1960).

————*The Social System.* Glencoe: Free Press of Glencoe, Ill., 1951.

———— and Edward A. Shils, eds. *Toward A General Theory of Action.* Cambridge, Mass.: Harvard University Press, 1951.

Pease, Theodore Calvin. *The Leveller Movement.* Washington, D.C.: American Historical Association, 1916.

Phillpotts, Bertha Surtees. *Kindred and Clan in the Middle Ages and After.* Cambridge, Eng.: Cambridge University Press, 1913.

Pickthorn, Kenneth. *Early Tudor Government: Henry VIII.* Cambridge, Eng.: Cambridge University Press, 1951.

Plato. *The Collected Dialogues,* ed. Edith Hamilton and Huntington Cairns. New York: Bollingen Foundation, 1963.

Plucknett, Theodore F. T. *A Concise History of Common Law,* 4th ed. London: Butterworth & Co., 1948.

———— *Edward I and Criminal Law.* Cambridge, Eng.: Cambridge University Press, 1960.

———— *Legislation of Edward I.* Oxford: Clarendon Press, 1949.

———— "The Origin of Impeachment," *Transactions of the Royal Historical Society,* 4th ser., 24:47–71 (1942).

———— *Statutes & Their Interpretation in the First Half of the Fourteenth Century.* Cambridge, Eng.: Cambridge University Press, 1922.

Plumb, J. H. *The Origins of Political Stability: England 1675–1725.* Boston: Houghton Mifflin, 1967.

Pocock, J. G. A. *The Ancient Constitution and the Feudal Law.* Cambridge, Eng.: Cambridge University Press, 1957.

Pollard, A. F. *Factors in Modern History.* London: A. Constable & Co., 1907.

Pollock, Frederick. *Essays in the Law.* London: Macmillan & Co., 1922.

———— and F. W. Maitland. *The History of English Law before the Time of Edward I.* 2 vols. Cambridge, Eng.: Cambridge University Press, 1899.

Polsby, Nelson. *Community Power and Political Theory.* New Haven: Yale University Press, 1963.

Polybius. *The Histories,* trans. W. R. Paton. 6 vols. Loeb Classical Library. Cambridge, Mass.: Harvard University Press, 1960.

Popper, Karl R. *Conjectures and Refutations.* New York: Basic Books, 1963.

Post, Gaines. *Studies in Medieval Legal Thought.* Princeton: Princeton University Press, 1964.

———— "The Theory of Public Law and the State in the Thirteenth Century," *Seminar,* 6:42–59 (1948).

Powicke, F. M. *King Henry III and the Lord Edward.* 2 vols. Oxford: Clarendon Press, 1947.

———— *The Thirteenth Century, 1216–1307.* Oxford: Clarendon Press, 1953.

Powicke, Michael. *Military Obligation in Medieval England.* Oxford: Clarendon Press, 1962.

Prestwich, J. O. "Ango-Norman Feudalism and the Problem of Continuity," *Past & Present,* no. 26 (November 1963), pp. 39–57.

Pye, Lucian W. *Aspects of Political Development.* Boston: Little, Brown and Company, 1966.

———— *Politics, Personality, and Nation Building.* New Haven: Yale University Press, 1963.

The Register of John de Grandisson. Ed. F. C. Hingeston-Randolph. 2 vols. London: G. Bell & Sons, 1894–1899.

Reisenberg, Peter N. *Inalienability of Sovereignty in Medieval Political Thought.* New York: Columbia University Press, 1956.

Richardson, H. G. "Azo, Drogheda, and Bracton," *English Historical Review,* 59:22–47 (1944).

———— "The Commons and Medieval Politics," *Transactions of the Royal Historical Society,* 4th ser., 28:21–45 (1946).

———— "The English Coronation Oath," *Speculum,* 24:44–75 (1949).

———— "Studies in Bracton," *Traditio,* 6:61–104 (1948).

———— "Tancred, Raymond, and Bracton," *English Historical Review,* 59:376–384 (1944).

———— and G. O. Sayles. *The Governance of Mediaeval England from the Conquest to Magna Carta.* Edinburgh: Edinburgh University Press, 1963.

———— and G. O. Sayles. *Parliaments and Great Councils in Medieval England.* London: Stevens & Sons, 1961.

Riggs, Fred W. "The Theory of Developing Polities," *World Politics,* 16:147–171 (1963).

———— "The Theory of Political Development," in *Contemporary Political Analysis,* ed. James C. Charlesworth. New York: The Free Press of Glencoe, 1967.

Rishanger, Willelmi. *Chronica et Annales,* ed. Henry Thomas Riley. London: Rolls Series, 1865.

Ritter, Gerhard. *Die Neugestaltung Europas im 16. Jahrhundert.* Berlin: Verlag des Druckhauses Tempelhof, 1950.

Robertson, A. J., ed. *The Laws of the Kings of England from Edmund to Henry I.* Cambridge, Eng.: Cambridge University Press, 1925.

Roger of Wendover. *Flores Historiarum,* ed. Henry G. Hewlett. London: Rolls Series, 1886–1889.

Rose, Arnold. *The Power Structure.* New York: Oxford University Press, 1967.

Roskell, J. S. "Perspectives in English Parliamentary History," *Bulletin of the John Rylands Library,* 46:448–475 (1964).

Roth, Guenther. "Personal Rulership, Patrimonialism, and Empire-Building in the New States," *World Politics,* 20: 194–206 (1968).

Rowse, A. L., *The England of Elizabeth.* New York: The Macmillan Company, 1961.

Sabine, George H. *A History of Political Theory,* rev. ed. New York: Henry Holt and Co., 1950.

St. Germain, Christopher. *The Addicions of Salem and Byzance.* London: Thomas Berthelet, 1534.

———— *An Answere to a Letter.* London: Thomas Godfray, 1934.

———— *Constitucyons Provincial and Legatine.* London: Thomas Godfray, 1534.

———— *A Dialogue Betwixt two Englysshe Men, Whereof one was Called Salem and the other Bizance.* London: Thomas Berthelet, 1533.

———— *The Doctor and Student or Dialogues Between A Doctor of Divinity and a Student in the Laws of England,* ed. William Muchall. Cincinnati: Robert Clarke and Co., 1874.

———— *The Power of the Clergy and the Lawes of the Realm.* London: Thomas Godfray, 1534.

———— *A Treatise Concerning the Division between the Spiritualtie and the Temporaltie.* London: Robert Redman, 1532.

Schlesinger, Walter. *Beitrage zur deutschen Verfassungsgeschichte des Mittelalters.* 2 vols. Gottingen: Vandenhoeck & Ruprecht, 1963.

—— "Über germanisches Königtum," in *Das Königtum, seine geistigen und rechtlichen Grundlagen.* Lindau: Jan Thorbecke, 1963. Institut für Geschichtliche Landesforschung des Bodenseegebietes, Constance. *Vorträge und Forschungen,* bd. 3, pp. 105–141.

Schramm, Percy Ernest. *A History of the English Coronation,* trans. Leopold G. Wickham Legg. Oxford: Clarendon Press, 1937.

Schucking, Levin. "Das Königsideal im Beowulf," *Bulletin of the Modern Humanities Research Association,* 3:143–154 (1929).

Schulz, Fritz. "Bracton on Kingship," *English Historical Review,* 60:136–176 (1945).

—— "Critical Studies on Bracton's Treatise," *Law Quarterly Review,* 59:172–180 (1943).

Selden, John. *Table Talk of John Selden,* ed. Frederick Pollock. London: Selden Society, 1927.

Shepard, Max Adams. "The Political and Constitutional Theory of Sir John Fortescue," in *Essays in History and Political Theory in Honor of Charles Howard McIlwain.* Cambridge, Mass.: Harvard University Press, 1936.

Shirley, F. J. *Richard Hooker and Contemporary Political Ideas.* London: Society for Promoting Christian Knowledge, 1949.

Shklar, Judith N. *After Utopia.* Princeton: Princeton University Press, 1957.

—— "Facing Up to Intellectual Pluralism," in *Political Theory and Social Change,* ed. David Spitz. New York: Atherton Press, 1967.

—— *Legalism.* Cambridge, Mass.: Harvard University Press, 1964.

Sigmund, Paul E. *Nicholas of Cusa and Medieval Political Thought.* Cambridge, Mass.: Harvard University Press, 1963.

Sisam, K. "Anglo-Saxon Royal Genealogies," *Proceedings of the British Academy,* 39:287–348 (1953).

—— *The Structure of Beowulf.* Oxford: Clarendon Press, 1965.

Sitwell, Edith. *The Queens and the Hive.* Harmondsworth, Eng.: Penguin Books, 1966.

Skeel, Caroline A. J. "The Influence of the Writings of Sir John Fortescue," *Transactions of the Royal Historical Society,* 3d ser., 10:77–144 (1916).

Smith, Thomas. *De Republica Anglorum,* ed. L. Alston. Cambridge, Eng.: Cambridge University Press, 1906.

The Song of Lewes. Ed. C. L. Kingsford. Oxford: Clarendon Press, 1890.

Southern, R. W. *The Making of the Middle Ages.* New Haven: Yale University Press, 1953.

Stenton, Frank. *Anglo-Saxon England.* Oxford: Clarendon Press, 1947.

—— *The First Century of English Feudalism, 1066–1166,* 2d ed. Oxford: Clarendon Press, 1961.

Stephenson, Carl. *Mediaeval Feudalism.* Ithaca: Cornell University Press, 1942.

Stickler, Alfons M. "Concerning the Political Theories of the Medieval Canonists," *Traditio,* 7:450–463 (1949–1951).

Storr, Anthony. *Human Aggression.* London: Penguin Press, 1968.

Stubbs, William, ed. *Chronicles of Edward I and Edward II.* London: Rolls Series, 1882–1883.

Sutherland, Donald W. *Quo Warranto Proceedings in the Reign of Edward I, 1278–1294.* Oxford: Clarendon Press, 1963.

Sutton, F. X. "Social Theory and Comparative Politics," in *Comparative Politics,* ed. Harry Eckstein and David E. Apter. New York: The Free Press of Glencoe, 1963.

Tacitus. *On Britain and Germany,* trans. H. Mattingly. Baltimore: Penguin Books, 1948.

—— *The Histories,* trans. Kenneth Wellesley. Baltimore: Penguin Books, 1964.

—— *De Origine et situ Germanorum,* ed. J. G. C. Anderson. Oxford: Clarendon Press, 1938.

Tanner, Joseph R., ed. *Tudor Constitutional Documents, A. D. 1485–1603,* 2d ed. Cambridge, Eng.: Cambridge University Press, 1930.

Tellenbach, Gerd. *Church, State and Christian Society at the Time of the Investiture Contest,* trans. R. F. Bennett. Oxford: Basil Blackwell, 1940.

Terry, William H., ed. *Judge Jenkins.* London: G. Richards and H. Toulmin, 1929.

Thomas of Walsingham. *Chronicon Angliae,* ed. E. M. Thompson. London: Rolls Series, 1874.

Thompson, E. A. *The Early Germans.* Oxford: Clarendon Press, 1965.

—— *The Visigoths in the Time of Ulfila.* Oxford: Clarendon Press, 1966.

Thorne, Samuel E. "The Constitution and the Courts: A Reexamination of the Famous Case of Dr. Bonham," in *The Constitution Reconsidered,* ed. Conyers Read. New York: Columbia University Press, 1938.

——, ed. *A Discourse upon the Exposicion & Understandinge of Statutes.* San Marino, Calif.: Huntington Library, 1942.

Thorpe, B., ed. and trans. *Ancient Laws and Institutes of England.* 2 vols. London: G. E. Ayre and A. Spottiswoode, 1840.

Tierney, Brian. "Bracton on Government," *Speculum,* 38:295–317 (1963).

—— *Foundations of the Conciliar Theory.* Cambridge, Eng.: Cambridge University Press, 1955.

Tillyard, E. M. W. *The Elizabethan World Picture.* New York: Vintage Books, n.d.

Treharne, R. F. "The Significance of the Baronial Reform Movement, 1258–1267," *Transactions of the Royal Historical Society,* 4th ser., 25:35–72 (1943).

Truman, David. *The Governmental Process.* New York: Alfred A. Knopf, 1951.

458

Twysden, Roger. *The Government of England.* London: Camden Society, 1849.

Ulam, Adam B. *The Unfinished Revolution.* New York: Random House, 1960.

Ullmann, Walter. *The Growth of Papal Government in the Midde Ages.* London: Methuen & Co., 1956.

—— *Medieval Papalism.* London: Methuen & Co., 1949.

—— *Principles of Government and Politics in the Middle Ages.* New York: Barnes & Noble, 1961.

Verney, Frances Parthenope, ed. *Memoirs of the Verney Family during the Civil War.* 4 vols. London: Longmans, Green & Co., 1892–1899.

von der Mehden, Fred R. *Politics of the Developing Nations.* Englewood Cliffs, N.J.: Prentice-Hall, Inc., 1964.

von Vorys, Karl. "Use and Misuse of Development Theory," in *Comtemporary Political Analysis,* ed. James C. Charlesworth. New York: The Free Press of Glencoe, 1967.

Wallace-Hadrill, J. M. *The Barbarian West.* New York: Harper & Row, 1962.

—— *The Long-Haired Kings.* London: Methuen & co., 1962.

Walter of Hemingburgh. *Chronicon,* ed. Hans Claude Hamilton. 2 vols. London: English Historical Society, 1848–1849.

Walzer, Michael. *The Revolution of the Saints.* Cambridge, Mass.: Harvard University Press, 1965.

Watkins, Frederick Mundell. *The State as a Concept of Political Science.* New York: Harper & Brothers, 1934.

——, ed. *Hume: Theory of Politics.* Edinburgh: Thomas Nelson and Sons, 1951.

Weber, Max. *Law in Economy and Society,,* trans. Edward Shils and Max Rheinstein, ed. Max Rheinstein. Cambridge, Mass.: Harvard University Press, 1954.

——*The Protestant Ethic and the Spirit of Capitalism,* trans. Talcott Parsons. New York: Charles Scribner's Sons, 1958.

—— *The Religion of China,* trans. and ed. H. H. Gerth. Glencoe, Ill.: Free Press, 1951.

—— *The Theory of Social and Economic Organization,* trans. A. M. Henderson and Talcott Parsons, ed. Talcott Parsons. Glencoe, Ill.: Free Press, 1947.

Wechsler, Herbert. *Principles, Politics, and Fundamental Law.* Cambridge, Mass.: Harvard University Press, 1961.

Wedgwood, C. V. *The Thirty Years War.* Garden City, N.Y.: Doubleday Anchor Books, 1961.

Weston, Corinne Comstock. "Beginnings of the Classical Theory of the English Constitution," *Proceedings of the American Philosophical Society,* 100: 133–144 (1956).

—— "The Theory of Mixed Monarchy under Charles I and After," *English Historical Review,* 75:426–443 (1960).

White, Lynn, Jr. *Medieval Technology and Social Change.* Oxford: Oxford University Press, 1962.

Whitelock, Dorothy. *The Beginnings of English Society.* Harmondsworth, Eng.: Penguin Books, 1954.

—— *Changing Currents in Anglo-Saxon Studies.* Cambridge, Eng.: Cambridge University Press, 1958.

—— "Wulfstan and the Laws of Cnut," *English Historical Review,* 63:433–452 (1948).

—— "Wulfstan's Authorship of Cnut's Laws," *English Historical Review,* 70:72–85 (1955).

——, ed. *English Historical Documents, c. 500–1042.* London: Eyre & Spottiswoode, 1955.

Whittaker, W. J., ed. and trans. *The Mirror of Justices.* London: Selden Society, 1895.

Wilkinson, B. *The Constitutional History of Medieval England, 1216–1399.* 3 vols. London: Longmans, Green & Co., 1948–1958.

—— "The 'Political Revolution' of the Thirteenth and Fourteenth Centuries in England," *Speculum,* 24:502–509 (1949).

—— *Studies in the Constitutional History of the Thirteenth and Fourteenth Centuries,* 2d ed. Manchester: Manchester University Press, 1952.

Wilks, Michael. *The Problem of Sovereignty in the Later Middle Ages.* Cambridge, Eng.: Cambridge University Press, 1963.

Williams, Penry. "The Tudor State," *Past & Present,* no. 25 (July 1963), pp. 39–58.

—— and G. L. Harriss. "A Revolution in Tudor History?" *Past & Present,* no. 25 (July 1963), pp. 3–58.

Wolff, Robert Paul, Barrington Moore, Jr., and Herbert Marcuse. *A Critique of Pure Tolerance.* Boston: Beacon Press, 1965.

Wolin, Sheldon S. *Politics and Vision.* Boston: Little, Brown and Company, 1960.

Woodbine, George E. "Bractonian Problems," *Yale Law Journal,* 52:428–444 (1943).

Woodhouse, A. S. P., ed. *Puritanism and Liberty.* Chicago: University of Chicago Press, 1951.

Wormuth, Francis D. "Aristotle on Law," in *Essays in Political Theory Presented to George H. Sabine,* ed. Milton R. Konvitz and Arthur E. Murphy. Ithaca: Cornell University Press, 1948.

—— *The Origins of Modern Constitutionalism.* New York: Harper & Brothers, 1949.

—— *The Royal Prerogative, 1603–1649.* Ithaca: Cornell University Press, 1939.

Wright, Thomas, ed. *Political Songs.* 2 vols. London: Rolls Series, 1859–1861.

Index

Accession rites, 79–80, 83
Act in Restraint of Appeals, 255
Addicio de cartis, doctrine of the, 116–127, 164–165
Aelfric (abbot of Eynsham), 46
Aethelbert (king), 58
Agreement of the People, 325, 326, 332, 350
Alfred (king), 68
Alienation of land, 51–52, 143–146
Allegiance, 53–56, 162, 312. *See also* Loyalty
Allen, J. W., 256
Almond, Gabriel A., 6, 10
Ammianus Marcellinus, 75
Anglo-Saxon Chronicle, 51, 67, 68, 76, 77
Anglo-Saxon England: and the comitatus, 56, 58–59; and land tenure, 56–58; and rule with counsel, 58–59; and feud, 59, 61, 68; and compensation, 59–60; and wergeld, 59–60; criminal justice in, 59–62; trial procedure in, 60–63; and kinship and lordship, 63–69; and book right, 65
Aquinas, Saint Thomas, 226, 229, 240, 241–244
Aristotle: and civic consciousness, 69–70; and one-man rule, 73, 226, 229; and logic, 115; and natural inferiority, 235; and mixed monarchy, 241, 246; and pluralism, 273; and general rules of law, 292
Aron, Raymond, 362, 364, 367
Artificial reason of the law, 284–286, 301–302
Attila, 46
Augustine, Saint, 226, 227
Avowry, 205

Bacon, Francis, 299
Bagehot, Walter, 29, 249
Baronage, the: as political opposition, 22–23; and relation to kingship, 23–24, 52; political power and book right, 65; claims of, 135, 139–140, 146; and relations with knights, 153, 154; stages of opposition, 175, 191
Baronial ideology: and alienation of royal land, 51–52, 143–146; and bureaucratic rationalization, 129–130; and counsel and consent, 132–133, 136, 150–151, 152–153; as a crisis ideology, 133, 135, 163; and judgment by peers, 141–142; in the *Song of Lewes,* 149–153; and distinction between king and kingdom, 150; and Bracton, 151–152; as opposition to arbitrary rule, 152; development of, 154; and distinction between king and crown, 158–161, 162, 163; and loyalty to the crown, 163; and use of regal ideas, 163–164, 179; and the king's judges, 176; and the king's council, 185–186
Barons' War, 147–148, 153, 204
Bate's case (1606), 298
Baumer, Franklin le van, 256
Becket, Thomas (archbishop of Canterbury), 86, 198, 199–200
Bede, Venerable, 77, 78, 84
Beer, Samuel H., 13, 14, 29
Bendix, Reinhard, 349
Bentham, Jeremy, 250, 366
Beowulf, 46, 47
Bereford, William de, 211, 212
Berkeley, Sir Robert, 315
Binder, Leonard, 353
Black, Hugo, 292–293
Blackstone, Sir William, 249–250
Blair, Peter Hunter, 58
Bloch, Marc, 57, 77; on European political development, 19; on private vengeance, 63–64; on thaumaturgic kingship, 84–91

Bodin, Jean, 294
Bonham's case, 305–306
Book right, 65
Bracton, Henry de, 14, 24, 192, 193, 194,
210, 245, 251; ambiguity of views
on kingship and law, 97–98; and
double majesty, 98–99, 121–122,
126–127; commentaries on, 99–101;
and the problem of the prince's
pleasure (the *lex regia*), 102–104,
108, 110–113; and the interpretation of McIlwain, 103–109; and
gubernaculum and *jurisdictio*, 103,
105–109, 113; and the coronation
oath, 104–105; and the problem of
absolutism and constitutionalism,
105–108; and the interpretation of
Lewis, 109–116; and the interpretation of Tierney, 110–111, 117–118;
and *digna vox*, 110–111; and the
problem and doctrine of the *addicio de cartis*, 116–127, 164–165;
and Roman law, 118–119; and inherited ideas, 119–121; and distinction between judgment and
will, 119, 128; and contemporary
parallels, 122–126; and contemporary politics, 126–127, 129–131; and
Christian ethics, 127; anachronistic
interpretations of, 130–131; and
operative political thought, 132;
and baronial ideology, 151–152;
and the problem of ministerial responsibility, 165; and the problem
of custom, 196; and changes in the
law, 203
Bradley, F. H., 54
Bradwardine, Thomas, 88
Bribery, 182–183
Britton, 125–126, 194
Bureaucracy, royal: and political development, 19–20; and relation to
the baronage, 129–130, 132–133,
136–137; and development of operative political thought, 136–137;
and distinction between king and
kingdom, 137–138; and parliament,
167, 169–172; of Tudor England,
340

Caesar, Julius, 47–48, 63
Calvinism, 265
Calvin's case, 303, 313–315
Cam, Helen, 202
Carr, E. H., 34
Centralization, 20–23, 92–93
Chadwick, H. Munro, 47

Charlemagne (emperor), 75
Charles I (king), 248–249, 294, 298, 308,
309, 315
Charles II (king), 91
Chartulary of Winchester Cathedral,
170–171
Checks and balances, 31–32
Cheyette, Frederic, 192, 193, 196
Chillenden, Edmund, 356
Chrimes, S. B., 226, 232, 245–246, 250,
252
Cicero, Marcus Tullius, 268, 295
Civic consciousness: and political modernity, 1, 336–337; and constitutional politics, 1–2, 30–40, 342, 372–
373; and national consciousness,
2–4, 6; and international politics,
2–4, 343–344; and constitutional
crisis, 5; and medieval localism, 8;
and modern political thought, 9–
10; and the medieval Church, 12;
and the baronage, 22–23; and the
English civil wars, 25–26, 310, 329–
330, 333–334, 335; and *The Federalist*, 33; and Aristotle, 69–70;
and double majesty, 134–138; and
problems of public policy, 186
Clarendon, Edward Hyde, Earl of,
311, 312
Clarke, Captain, 28, 328
Clement V (pope), 157, 158
Coke, Sir Edward, 277, 280; and legalism, 282, 301, 305, 307; and the
artificial reason of the law, 285–
286, 301–302; his leadership, 298–
299; and equitable jurisdiction, 293,
299–300; on custom and statute,
301; dispute with James I, 301–302;
on the antiquity of the common
law, 302–304; his conservatism, 303;
on legal method, 304; and sovereignty, 304; and judicial review,
305–306; on Bonham's case, 305–
306; on kingship and prerogative,
306–307; on Calvin's case, 304
Comitatus, the: and personal loyalty,
44, 49; account of by Caesar, 48–49;
and reciprocity, 48–49; Roman influence on, 49; and the successor
kingdoms, 49–50, 52, 76; and
double majesty, 53; and the idea of
rule with counsel, 53–54; character
of, 53–54; in Anglo-Saxon politics,
58–59, 76–77; and the Heroic Age,
63, 75–76; impact on kinship, 64;
in the age of barbarian migration,
75–76; and the establishment of
kingship, 75–77

Index

Common law, the: as the king's law, 189; and baronial ideology, 190; of seizin and distress, 204–207; and relation to king, 211–213; and relation to baronial opposition, 213–215; and the doctrine of certainty, 254, 285; and the royal prerogative, 254, 281; and equity, 277–278, 281, 283–287, 293, 299–300; and the artificial reason of the law, 284–286, 301–302; and controversy in the civil wars, 319–320. *See also* Custom, Fundamental law, Law, Natural law

Commons, the: and parliament, 154–155, 167; and alliance with lords, 168, 190; and money bills, 335

Community, idea of, 367–369

Confirmatio Cartarum, 157

Constitutionalism: and civic consciousness, 1–2, 30–40, 336–337, 342, 372–373; and liberalism, 11–12, 30–34; medieval influence on, 39–40; and the medieval baronage, 180; and the Levellers, 330–333; American, 333; and tolerance, 370–373

Constitutions of Clarendon, 198

Contra formam feoffamenti, 205–207

Coronation Charters, 198

Counsel and consent: idea of rule with, 53; in Anglo-Saxon England, 58–59; and baronial ideology, 136, 150–151, 152–153; and personal monarchy, 140; in Magna Carta, 141–142; as criterion of cooperation, 153; and parliament, 158; and the Statute of York, 166; and fundamental law, 201

Court of Star Chamber, 287

Critique of Pure Tolerance, A, 360

Cromwell, Oliver, 333, 334, 357

Crown, the, 138. *See also* King and crown, King and kingdom

Custom: in Bracton, 106–108; as procedural law, 127–129, 192–193; as a mode of argument, 127, 201; as fundamental law, 191–193; uses of, 193–202; in Fortescue, 220–222, 252; in St. Germain, 254, 264; in Hake, 290; in Coke, 301. *See also* Common law, Fundamental law, Law

Dahl, Robert, 355

Davies, Sir John, 299

De Laudibus Legum Anglie, 224, 226–227

De Natura Legis Naturae, 219, 227, 232

De Regimine Principum, 240

De Tallagio non Concedendo, 156–157

Deposition: of Edward II, 161, 166–167; of Richard II, 178–179

Despencer, Hugh, 160

Deutsch, Karl, 2

Development, political: and international politics, 19–20, 343; and centralization, 20–23; in contemporary societies, 341–344; and civic consciousness, 343; English, and international politics, 353–354; in the English civil wars, 356–357

Development, theory of political: and English history, 7–8; and intellectual history, 344–354; and the idea of modernity, 349–352; and pattern-variable analysis, 349–353

Dictum of Kenilworth, 148–149

Digna vox, 110–111

Doctor and Student, The, 256–262

Double majesty: and operative political thought, 24–26; in Fortescue, 24–25, 218, 223, 224, 239; and Tudor England, 25, 187, 252; and role of kingship, 42; and role of baronage, 43; uses of, 43–44; and the comitatus, 53; and social fragmentation, 54; social base of, 57; and cooperation of king and baronage, 58–59, 134–135; and political narrowness, 59; and primogeniture, 78–79; and civic consciousness, 134–138; evolution of, 135, 179–180, 186–188, 339–340; as symbolized by the crown, 138; as a style of argument, 149; and Barons' War, 153; and legalism, 191, 254, 264, 280, 283, 287, 313, 319–320; and counsel and consent, 201; contrasted with theory of mixed monarchy, 217, 250–251; in St. Germain, 259, 261, 280; in Hooker, 275, 280; and law and prerogative, 281; and Eliot, 294–295; and parliamentary solution, 308, 310, 317; social setting of, 337–339

Easton, David, 354

Eckstein, Harry, 10, 14

Edgar (king), 45

Edmund (king), 51, 68

Edward the Confessor (king), 58, 88, 197; laws of, 128

Edward I (king), 57, 93, 154–157, 203, 207

Edward II (king), 86, 158–159, 161, 162

Edward III (king), 88, 167, 168–169, 171–172
Edward IV (king), 184, 185
Edward VI (king), 265
Eliot, Sir John: as opposition leader, 282, 293–294; on sovereignty, 294–296; and double majesty, 294–295; on kingship, 295–296; on prerogative, 296–298; on law, 297
Elizabeth I (queen), 312
Ellesmere, Sir Thomas Egerton, Lord Chancellor, 286, 299, 307, 314–315
Emergency doctrine, 309, 315. See also Reason of state
Emerson, Rupert, 2, 4
English Constitution, The, 249
Equitable jurisdiction. See Equity
Equity: and Fortescue, 231; and Tudor England, 253–254; and St. Germain, 256, 259–262, 264, 277, 278, 280, 286; and Hooker, 277–278; and the common law, 277–278, 281, 283–287, 293, 299–300; and Hake, 283–287, 291–292
Estates of the realm, the, 184
Ethelred (king), 45; laws of, 60

Federalist, The, 33
Feud, 59, 61, 63–68
Fifth Monarchy, 356–357
Filmer, Sir Robert, 249, 347
Fitz Stephen, William, 199
Five knights' case, 298
Fleta, 123–126
Foliot, Gilbert (bishop of London), 200
Forsett, Edward, 347
Fortescue, Sir John, 14, 181, 257, 261, 264; and double majesty, 24–25, 218, 224, 239, 240; on kingship, 74–75, 88–89, 227, 233; on parliament, 210–211, 225, 229; and dominium politicum et regale, 218, 223–227, 244–245; on natural law, 219–222, 224–225, 227–228, 234–237; on the origin of government, 220, 222–223, 227; and custom, 220–222, 252; on statute law, 221–222; on tyranny, 222, 244; on equity, 231; on regal dominion, 231; on succession, 233–237; style of argument, 233, 251; as Lancastrian advocate, 233–234; and divine law, 235; on property, 236–237; and the chain of being, 236–237; weaknesses of his argument, 237–240; and operative political thought, 252
Frankfurter, Felix, 292

Friedrich, Carl J., 305
Fundamental law, 189–190, 191–193, 215–216, 333

Galbraith, John Kenneth, 355
Gaveston, Peter, 158
Genealogy, 45, 76–77
Gennep, Arnold van, 81
Germanic peoples, the: and admiration of Rome, 44–45; legal ideas of, 44–45; and veneration of the past, 44–47; and the heroic ethic, 45–47; as primitive, 47; and the comitatus, 48–50, 52–53; and the absence of public policy, 50–52; conception of obligation, 54–56; and land tenure, 56–58; and double majesty, 53, 54, 57, 58–59; and leadership, 75–76; and kingship, 75
Glanvill, Ranulf de, 121, 123, 130, 193
Governance of England, The, 224
Gregory VII (pope), 85, 87
Gregory of Tours, 74, 84
Grodzins, Morton, 357, 370
Grosart, Alexander, 297–298
Grosseteste, Robert (bishop of Lincoln), 202–203

Hake, Edward: and common lawyers' resentment of equitable jurisdiction, 281–283; on equity, 283–287; and the artificial reason of the law, 284–285; on English government, 287–290, 299–300; and double majesty, 287, 300; on the prerogative, 287, 290; and legalism, 289–290, 293; and custom, 290; equity and general rules of law, 291–292
Hamilton, Alexander, 33
Hampden, John, 315
Hampden's case, 298
Hand, Learned, 292
Harrington, James, 71, 311
Heer, Friedrich, 32
Heerkönige, 75
Helmstan's case, 62–63
Hengham, Ralph (chief justice), 206
Henry I (king), 92, 198
Henry II (king), 86, 88, 92, 198
Henry III (king), 113, 130, 137, 140, 145, 157, 202, 203
Henry IV (king), 86, 174, 180, 181
Henry VI (king), 185
Henry VIII (king), 4, 254, 265
Hermann (bishop of Metz), 87
Heroioc age, the, 47
Heroic ethic, 45–47
Hexter, J. H., 17

High court of parliament, the, 173, 177, 191
Hill, Christopher, 27, 294, 321
Hincmar (archbishop of Rheims), 85
Hinton, R. W. K., 225, 246
Hobbes, Thomas, 249, 269, 321, 345, 346
Hoffmann, Stanley, 4, 6, 343
Holdsworth, William, 182, 298
Holinshed, Ralph, 98
Holmes, Oliver Wendell, 35
Holt, J. C., 128, 141
Hooker, Richard: and sovereignty, 255–256, 276; on necessary and probable proofs, 266, 270–272, 278–279; on types of law, 266–267; on natural law, 267–268; on knowledge, 267–268; and dissent, 268–269; on government, 269–270, 272–274; and Aristotelianism, 269; and contract theory, 269; on English government, 274; on consent, 275; and double majesty, 275, 280; on kingship, 276–277; on equity, 277–278; and papal jurisdiction, 278; and legalism, 280; and institutionalization of values, 358–359
Humble Petition and Advice, 333
Hume, David, 3, 228, 364
Hundred Years' War, 168, 181
Huntington, Samuel P., 2, 7
Hunton, Philip, 317–318

Impeachment, 173, 175, 191
Inalienability, 145
Innocent III (pope), 85
Instrument of Government, 333
Ireton, Henry, 296, 324, 325, 326, 327, 333

James I (king), 86, 91, 282, 286, 288, 299, 313, 347
Jenkins, David (judge), 319
John (king), 144
John, Eric, 54, 63
Johnson, Samuel, 91
Jolliffe, J. E. A., 128, 143, 179
Jordanes, 46
Judgment by peers, 141, 142, 171
Judicial activism, 292
Judicial review, 190, 305–307
Judicial self-restraint, 292
Judicial tenure, 299
Jurisprudence of conscience, 282

Kant, Immanuel, 366
Kantorowicz, Ernst, 99, 114, 115
Kemp, John, 185

King and crown: and barons' distinction between kingdom and king, 138; and loyalty to the crown, 138, 158–161, 162, 163; and the royal demesne, 143, 145; and political trials, 173. See also King and kingdom
King and kingdom: distinction between, and growth of bureaucracy, 138; and stimulus to political thought, 138–139; and loyalty to the office of kingship, 139; and baronial ideology, 146, 150; and operative political thought, 187; and parliamentary opposition, 312–317. See also King and crown
King's chancellor, the, 253, 260
King's conscience, the, 253, 260
King's council, the, 136–137, 147–148, 184, 185–186, 202
King's demesne, the, 137, 141, 143–146
King's evil, the, 84, 87–91
King's peace, the, 82–83
Kingship: as agency of change, 19–20; and constitutional crisis, 26–29; and parliamentarism, 27–29; and relation to Church, 44–45, 77–78; and the idea of ancestry, 45, 74–75; and the claim to direct allegiance, 51, 155, 312; and alienation of land, 51–52; and the baronage, 52–54; general character of, 71–73; and Plato and Aristotle, 73; in antiquity, 73–74; and Christianity, 73–74, 80–81; ideals of, 74–75, 81–82; and the idea of royal blood, 74, 75, 76–77; beginning of Germanic, 74; and role of the comitatus, 75–77; in the Anglo-Saxon Chronicle, 76–77; and consecration, 79–87; and political role of accession rites, 79–80, 83; and the idea of "mixed persons," 80–81; and political myths, 82; and the king's peace, 82–83; and magical powers, 84–91; coronation ritual, 84–86; and controversy over priestly powers, 84–87; and the king's evil, 84, 87–91; and unction, 85–87; and adjudication, 91–95; and centralization, 92–93; and uses of statute law, 93–95; and bureaucracy, 136–137; and relation to law, 211–213; exaltation of in Tudor England, 253; and civil war argument, 309–310; and distinction between natural and political capacities, 312–317; and veto power, 335. See also Personal monarchy

466

Kinship, 63–64, 66–69

Lancastrian dynasty, the, 181, 233, 234

Land tenure, 56–57, 64–65

Laud, William (archbishop of Canterbury), 309

Law: idea of sovereignty of, 37; and relation to medieval politics, 189–191; and lawmaking, 189, 202–211. *See also* Common law, Custom, Fundamental law, Natural law

Lawyers, professional, 288–289

Legalism: and liberalism, 34–38; and Bracton, 99–100, 126–132; and double majesty, 191, 254, 264, 280, 283, 287, 313, 319–320; and Hooker, 280; and Coke, 282, 301, 305, 307; and the artificial reason of the law, 284–286, 301–302; and the professional lawyer, 288–289; and Hake, 289–290, 293

Levellers, 320, 330–333

Lewis, Ewart, 99, 104, 110, 111–113, 131

Lex regia, 102–104, 108, 110–113

Liberal democracy, 341–342

Liberalism: and social science, 11; and constitutionalism, 11–12, 30–34; and legalism, 34–38; and Whig ideology, 34–35; and law and politics, 36; in the seventeenth century, 345–349; as response to traditionalism, 345–349; and pattern-variable analysis, 350–354; and historical criticism, 359–360; and contemporary criticism, 359–372. *See also* Libertarianism

Libertarianism: and traditionalism, 320–321; and mixed monarchy, 323–324; in the Putney debates, 324; as seventeenth century radicals' goal, 327; meaning in seventeenth century radical thought, 328. *See also* Liberalism, Social contract theory

Lilburne, John, 320, 350

Livery and maintenance, 64

Locke, John, 330

Longueville, John de, 122, 123

Lordship, 63–64, 66–69

Loyalty: in traditional societies, 5–7; and medieval politics, 15–16; personal, 8, 15–17, 44, 49, 50–56, 60–61, 69, 333; and the claims of kingship, 51, 155, 312; types of, 69–70; to the crown, 138, 158–161, 162, 163

Ludlow, Edmund, 334

McIlwain, Charles Howard, 100, 103 109, 245

Magna Carta, 52, 140, 141–142, 152–153, 158, 179, 201

Maine, Henry, 193, 218

Mair, Lucy, 48, 83

Maitland, Frederic W., 41–42, 117, 197

Marcuse, Herbert, 360, 362, 363, 364

Mare, Sir Peter de la, 174

Marlborough, statute of, 95, 205–206

Marsilius of Padua, 263

Martial prowess, 48, 73

Marx, Karl, 364, 369

Marxism, 367

Merciless Parliament, the, 176

Merton, king's council at, 202

Mill, John Stuart, 365, 366

Milton, John, 310, 327, 329, 332, 333

Ministerial responsibility, 165, 173

Mirror of Justices, The, 164–165

Mixed monarchy: and the restoration, 29, 334; and double majesty, 240, 246, 250–251; and Aquinas, 241–244; and tyranny, 241–242; in classical antiquity, 246–247; in Tudor England, 247–248; in seventeenth century England, 248–250; and Charles I, 248–249; Blackstone on, 249–250; Bentham on, 250; and liberty, 323–324

Mixed state, the. *See* Mixed monarchy

Modus Tenendi Parliamentum, 183

Monstraunces, the, 156

Montagu, Sir Henry, 307

Montfort, Simon de, 148, 149, 152, 153, 205

National consciousness, 2–4, 343

Natural law: in Fortescue, 219–222, 224–225, 227–228, 234–237; in Hooker, 267–268

Norman yoke, the, 197

Nuer, the, 48

Obligation, 54–56, 324, 325–326

Opium of the Intellectuals, The, 364

Ordeal, trial by, 61–62

Ordinances of 1311, 161, 165–166

Overton, Richard, 321, 322, 331–332

Papal jurisdiction, 255, 278

Paris, Matthew, 203

Parliament: origins, 154; and summoning of commons, 154–155, 167; and counsel and consent, 158; and aristocracy, 164; and baronial-regal rivalry, 167; and the royal bureaucracy, 167, 169–172; and ministerial responsibility, 168; and political trials, 172, 173–174, 175–176; as

high court, 177; and deposition of Richard II, 178–179; as a subsidiary institution, 180; conceptions of, 183–184; and representation, 183–184, 187; privileges and rights of, 189; and traditional political ideas, 311; assumption of sovereignty by, 315–317
Parliamentarism, 27–29
Parsons, Talcott, 349
Partible inheritance, 64–65
Paston correspondence, the, 182
Paston, William, 182
Pattern-variable analysis, 349–354
Peers of the realm, 169
Percy family, 181
Periodization, 17–18
Personal monarchy: and direct loyalty, 139, 155–156; and the prerogative, 139; and counsel and consent, 140; and Magna Carta, 140; and naming of counsellors, 147; and Barons' War, 148; and rights of the crown, 158; and defense of the king's servants, 165, 177
Personality of the law, 45
Peter of Blois, 88
Petty, Maximilian, 327, 329
Philip Augustus (king), 75, 86
Plato, 73, 226, 273, 292, 365
Platonism, 365
Plucknett, T. F. T., 93, 189, 204, 206, 207, 212, 215
Plummer, Charles, 226, 245
Pluralism: in the Middle Ages, 7–9; and constitutional politics, 32, 354–355, 356–359; in contemporary political science, 354–355; of values and tolerance, 357–359, 370–373
Pole, Michael de la, 175
Political development. See Development
Political modernity: and civic consciousness, 1, 9–10, 336–337; and sovereignty, 2; and citizen loyalty, 5–6; and citizen competence, 7; and tolerance, 7; in England, 25–26; and the interregnum, 27, 28; and parliamentarism, 27–29; and relation to the medieval tradition, 29; and development theory, 351–353
Political thought
operative thought in the Middle Ages: and systematic political theory, 12–14, 37–39; and double majesty, 24–26, 42–43; character of, 41–42; conception of authority in, 41–43; persistence of first principles, 44–47; retrospective standards of, 44–47; and conception of explanation, 46; basic ideas among the Germanic peoples, 47–49; and counsel and consent, 132; and baronial-regal rivalry, 135; and the royal bureaucracy, 136–137; and political context, 140, 187–188; and Fortescue, 252
radical thought in the civil wars: and appeal to the legalist tradition, 320–321; and new sources of validation, 321–322; and liberty, 323, 327, 328; and the franchise, 324, 325–328; and obligation, 324, 325–326; and acceptance of principled differences, 329; and consent, 330; and contract theory, 330, 331, 332; and the trust theory of government, 331–332
Political trials, 172, 173–176, 178, 191
Politics of moderation, 31–32, 329, 342, 373
Pollock, Sir Frederick, 82
Powell, G. Bingham, Jr., 6, 10
Prerogative, royal: and baronial claims, 57, 139, 158, 176; and equity, 231, 282–283; and the common law, 254, 281; and St. Germain, 263–264; and double majesty, 281; and Hake, 287, 290; and the civil wars, 290–291; and Eliot, 296–298; in domestic politics, 298; and Coke, 306–307; and summoning of parliament, 335
Primogeniture, 65, 78
Private warfare, 64, 182
Property, 56–57, 233, 236–237; and public jurisdiction, 15, 144, 145, 147
Provisions of Oxford, 148
Public policy, 49–52, 134–135, 186
Putney debates, 27, 296; conservative principles in, 323; and radicals' rationalism, 323; and natural rights, 323, 326; and the franchise, 324, 325–326; and obligation, 324–325; and revolutionary aims, 325, 327; and distinction between property and political rights, 326; and property, 327, 328; and liberty, 328; and tolerance, 329, 357; and civic consciousness, 329–330; and limitations of radical proposals, 334
Pye, Lucian W., 349

Quia Emptores, statute of, 93–94
Quo warranto proceedings, 207–209

Rainborough, Colonel Thomas, 27, 326, 327, 328, 329, 333–334
Reason of state, 2–5, 309. *See also* Emergency doctrine, Sovereignty
Remonstrance of Many Thousand Citizens, A, 320
Representation, 154–155, 183–184, 187
Richard II (king), 172, 174–179
Rights, 194–195
Roman law, 118–119, 193–194
Rousseau, Jean-Jacques, 269, 326
Rowse, A. L., 4
Royal clan, 75
Royal demesne. *See* King's demesne
Royalist political thought, 346–348
Russell, John (bishop of Lincoln), 183–184

St. Germain, Christopher, 230; and sovereignty, 255; as political pamphleteer, 256; controversy with More, 256, 263; on types of law, 257–258; and natural law, 257; on sources of English law, 258; and equity, 259–262, 264, 277, 278, 280, 286; and double majesty, 259, 261, 264; and parliament, 261–262; and common lawyers' opposition to equity, 262; and royal supremacy, 262–263; and lay-cleric disputes, 263; and prerogative and common law, 263–264; and legalism, 264
Schulz, Fritz, 115
Scoland v. Grandison, case of, 212–213
Seizin, law of, 195–196, 204–207
Selden, John, 285, 290–291, 296, 312, 317
Sexby, Edward, 326, 327
Shakespeare, William, 90–91
Ship-money, 315
Shklar, Judith N., 35, 36, 346, 352, 364
Shrewsbury Parliament, 178–179
Smith, Sir Thomas, 289
Social contract theory, 28, 269, 310–311, 317–319, 330, 331, 332, 336, 356
Song of Lewes, 149–153
Sophists, 7, 356
Sovereignty: internal and external, 2–4; in England, 4–5; legal, 191; and Tudor England, 232, 254–255; assumption of by parliament, 308, 315–317; and St. Germain, 255; and Hooker, 255–256, 276; and Eliot, 294–296; and Coke, 304
Star Chamber, Court of, 287
Statute law, 93–95
Statutes: Marlborough, 95, 205–206; Quia Emptores, 93–94; Quo Warranto, 208, 209; Westminster I, 94; Westminster II, 206; York, 160, 166
Stirps regia, 75, 76
Successor kingdoms: politics in, 52–54; and the comitatus, 52; and lordship, 56, 59; and feud, 63–69; and kinship, 56, 63, 64, 66–68
Summa Theologica, 240

Tacitus, 48, 55, 63, 64, 75
Thaumaturgic kings, 84–91
Thompson, E. A., 75
Thorne, Samuel E., 281, 286, 305
Thorpe, Robert (chief justice), 183
Tierney, Brian, 107, 109, 111, 115, 117–118, 131
Tolerance: and civic consciousness, 5, 7–8; in the Putney debates, 329, 357; and liberalism, 360–361, 363–364, 369, 370–373
Traditional societies, 2, 9–10, 343–344
Treason, 53–54, 55, 159–160, 176–177, 184–185
Treatise of Monarchy, A, 317
Treharne, R. F., 153
Trial by combat, 205
Trial by ordeal, 61–62
Trust theory of government, 28, 330–332
Tudor England: and national consciousness, 4; as a traditional society, 4; and modern political thought, 18–19; and double majesty, 25, 187, 252; and mixed monarchy, 247–278; and exaltation of kingship, 253; and equity, 253–254; and sovereignty, 254–255; and bureaucracy, 340
Twysden, Sir Roger, 319

Ullmann, Walter, 12–13, 100
Unction, 85–87

Vendetta. *See* Feud
Vengeance, 63–64. *See also* Feud, Private warfare
Vergil, Polydore, 90
Verney, Sir Edmund, 312

Wallace-Hadrill, J. M., 15, 44, 76
Walwyn, William, 321, 356
Warwick, house of, 181
Weber, Max, 351–352
Wergeld, 59–60
Westminster I, statute of, 94
Westminster II, statute of, 206
Whig view of constitutional crisis, 34–35

Index

Whitelock, Dorothy, 63
Whitelocke, James, 320
Wildman, John, 324, 325, 328
Wilkinson, B., 148, 252
Wilks, Michael, 13
William the Conqueror (king), 51, 197, 198

Wolff, Robert Paul, 360, 366, 367
Wolin, Sheldon, 345–346
Writ of replevin, 205–206
Writs, royal, 92, 194
Wulfstan (archbishop of York), 60, 68

York: house of, 181; statute of, 160, 166

Harvard Political Studies

*Out of print

*John Fairfield Sly. *Town Government in Massachusetts (1620–1930)*. 1930.
*Hugh Langdon Elsbree. *Interstate Transmission of Electric Power: A Study in the Conflict of State and Federal Jurisdictions.* 1931.
*Benjamin Fletcher Wright, Jr. *American Interpretations of Natural Law.* 1931.
*Payson S. Wild, Jr. *Sanctions and Treaty Enforcement.* 1934.
*William P. Maddox. *Foreign Relations in British Labour Politics.* 1934.
*George C. S. Benson. *Administration of the Civil Service in Massachusetts, with Special Reference to State Control of City Civil Service.* 1935.
*Merle Fainsod. *International Socialism and the World War.* 1935.
John Day Larkin. *The President's Control of the Tariff.* 1936.
*E. Pendleton Herring. *Federal Commissioners: A Study of Their Careers and Qualifications.* 1936.
*John Thurston. *Government Proprietary Corporations in the English-Speaking Countries.* 1937.
Mario Einaudi. *The Physiocratic Doctrine of Judicial Control.* 1938.
*Frederick Mundell Watkins. *The Failure of Constitutional Emergency Powers under the German Republic.* 1939.
*G. Griffith Johnson, Jr. *The Treasury and Monetary Policy, 1933–1938.* 1939.
*Arnold Brecht and Comstock Glaser. *The Art and Technique of Administration in German Ministries.* 1940.
*Oliver Garceau. *The Political Life of the American Medical Association.* 1941.
*Ralph F. Bischoff. *Nazi Conquest through German Culture.* 1942.
*Charles R. Cherington. *The Regulation of Railroad Abandonments.* 1948.
*Samuel H. Beer. *The City of Reason.* 1949.
*Herman Miles Somers. *Presidential Agency: The Office of War Mobilization and Reconversion.* 1950.
*Adam B. Ulam. *Philosophical Foundations of English Socialism.* 1951.
*Morton Robert Godine. *The Labor Problem in the Public Service: A Study in Political Pluralism.* 1951.
*Arthur Maass. *Muddy Waters: The Army Engineers and the Nation's Rivers.* 1951.
*Robert Green McCloskey. *American Conservatism in the Age of Enterprise: A Study of William Graham Sumner, Stephen J. Field, and Andrew Carnegie.* 1951.
*Inis L. Claude, Jr. *National Minorities: An International Problem.* 1955.
*Joseph Cornwall Palamountain, Jr. *The Politics of Distribution.* 1955.
*Herbert J. Spiro. *The Politics of German Codetermination.* 1958.
Harry Eckstein. *The English Health Service: Its Origins, Structure, and Achievements.* 1958.
Richard F. Fenno, Jr. *The President's Cabinet: An Analysis in the Period from Wilson to Eisenhower.* 1959.
Nadav Safran. *Egypt in Search of Political Community: An Analysis of the Intellectual and Political Evolution of Egypt, 1804–1952.* 1961.
Paul E. Sigmund. *Nicholas of Cusa and Medieval Political Thought.* 1963.

Sanford A. Lakoff. *Equality in Political Philosophy.* 1964.

Charles T. Goodsell. *Administration of a Revolution: Executive Reform in Puerto Rico under Governor Tugwell, 1941–1946.* 1965.

Martha Derthick. *The National Guard in Politics.* 1965.

Bruce L. R. Smith. *The RAND Corporation: Case Study of a Nonprofit Advisory Corporation.* 1966.

David R. Mayhew. *Party Loyalty among Congressmen: The Difference between Democrats and Republicans, 1947–1962.* 1966.

Isaac Kramnick. *Bolingbroke and His Circle: The Politics of Nostalgia in the Age of Walpole.* 1968.

Donald W. Hanson. *From Kingdom to Commonwealth: The Development of Civic Consciousness in English Political Thought.* 1970.